PRABHAT VIDYARTHI
HINDI-ENGLISH DICTIONARY

~~·~~

प्रभात विद्यार्थी
हिंदी-अंग्रेजी कोश

PRABHAT VIDYARTHI
HINDI-ENGLISH DICTIONARY

प्रभात विद्यार्थी
हिंदी-अंग्रेजी कोश

बदरीनाथ कपूर

प्र

प्रभात
प्रकाशन

PRABHAT VIDYARTHI HINDI-ENGLISH DICTIONARY
Ed. Badri Nath Kapoor
Published by • **PRABHAT PRAKASHAN PVT. LTD.**
4/19 Asaf Ali Road, New Delhi-110002
Edition • 2025

Price • ₹ 400.00 (Rupees Four Hundred only)
ISBN • 978-93-5266-955-4
E-mail • prabhatbooks@gmail.com

❖

प्रकाशक • **प्रभात प्रकाशन प्रा. लि.**
4/19 आसफ अली रोड,
नई दिल्ली–110002

संस्करण • 2025
मूल्य • चार सौ रुपए
मुद्रक • आर–टेक ऑफसेट प्रिंटर्स, दिल्ली

विद्यार्थियों से

कुछ वर्ष पहले 'प्रभात व्यावहारिक हिंदी-अंग्रेजी कोश' प्रकाशित हुआ था, जिसका पाठकों ने अद्‌भुत स्वागत किया और अपनी जो प्रतिक्रियाएँ व्यक्त कीं वे संपादक और प्रकाशक दोनों के लिए उत्साहवर्धक रहीं। मुझे इस बात की विशेष प्रसन्नता हुई कि हिंदी में कोशों के प्रबुद्ध पाठकों की अभिवृद्धि हो रही है।

कुछ मित्रों का आग्रह था कि विद्यार्थियों के लिए इतना ही उपयोगी छोटा कोश भी तैयार हो, जिससे विद्यार्थियों में भाषा-ज्ञान बढ़े और भाषा-प्रेम भी। विद्यार्थियों के लिए कोश बनाना अधिक कठिन कार्य है। पहले तो प्रविष्टियों के रूप में उन्हीं शब्दों को ग्रहण किया जाना चाहिए जो उनकी पाठ्य-पुस्तकों में प्रयुक्त हों और दूसरे, उनके वही या उतने ही अर्थ लिये जाने चाहिए जिनका उनसे प्रयोजन हो। तीसरे, अर्थ-विवेचन में ऐसे सरल शब्दों का प्रयोग हो जिनका ज्ञान सामान्यत: विद्यार्थियों को रहता है। प्रस्तुत कोश का निर्माण करते समय इन बातों का ध्यान रखा गया है।

भाषिक-सामर्थ्य सफल जीवन-निर्वाह का मूल्य उपकरण है। इस उपकरण की प्राप्ति शब्दों के उपयुक्त अर्थों और प्रयोगों की सिद्धि से ही संभव है।

आशा है, व्यावहारिक संस्करण की तरह यह कोश भी उपयोगी तथा संतोषप्रद सिद्ध होगा।

—बदरीनाथ कपूर

ABBREVIATIONS

abbr.	=	abbreviation	*lit.*	=	literal meaning
adj.	=	adjective	*log.*	=	logic
abv.	=	adverb	*m.*	=	masculine noun
agri.	=	agriculture	*math.*	=	mathematics
anat.	=	anatomy	*mech.*	=	mechanics
anthrop.	=	anthropology	*meteor.*	=	meteorology
arch.	=	archaeology	*m.c.*	=	more current
astrol.	=	astrology	*mus.*	=	music
astron.	=	astronomy	*myth.*	=	mythology
aux. v.	=	auxiliary verb	*opp.*	=	opposite
biol.	=	biology	*pej.*	=	pejorative
bot.	=	botany	*phil.*	=	philosophy
buil.	=	building science	*phon.*	=	phonetics
chem.	=	chemistry	*phot.*	=	photography
comm.	=	commerce	*phys.*	=	physics
dim.	=	diminutive form	*physiol.*	=	physiology
econ.	=	economics	*pl.*	=	plural form
e.g.	=	for example	*pol.*	=	political science
Eng.	=	English	*post.*	=	postposition
eng.	=	engineering	*pp.*	=	past participle
f.	=	feminine noun	*pref.*	=	prefix
fem.	=	feminine form	*prob.*	=	probably
fig.	=	figurative meaning	*pron.*	=	pronoun
geog.	=	geography	*psych.*	=	psychology
geol.	=	geology	*sply.*	=	specially
geom.	=	geometry	*stat.*	=	statistics
gram.	=	grammar	*suff.*	=	suffix
H.E.	=	Hindi Equivalent	*v.*	=	verb
hist.	=	history	*vi.*	=	verb intransitive
ind.	=	indeclinable	*vt.*	=	verb transitive
interj.	=	interjection	*zool.*	=	zoology

अ

अ The first vowel of the Nagari alphabet.
Prefix. 1. un, not; अनिश्चित uncertain, अनियमित not regular. 2. bad, evil; अकाल bad times. 3. opposite of; अन्याय injustice.

अंक m. 1. figure or number. 2. digit. 3. mark or marks obtained in a test. 4. number or issue of a journal. 5. act of a drama. 6. lap; ~ भरना to embrace.

अंकगणित m. arithmetic.

अँकटा m. pebble.

अंक-तालिका f. marks-sheet.

अंकन m. 1. act or state of marking, writing, drawing etc. 2. vivid description.

अँकवार lap; ~ भरना to embrace.

अंकसूची f. marks-sheet.

अंकित adj. written, painted, drawn, marked or described; ~ करना to write, paint, mark, draw or describe, to portray, depict; ~ मूल्य face value.

अँकुड़ा m. hook.

अंकुर m. shoot, sprout; ~ जमना germination of a seed; ~ फूटना to sprout.

अंकुरण m. act of sprouting/germinating.

अंकुरना vi. to sprout/germinate.

अंकुरित 1. sprouted. 2. germinated.

अंकुश m. 1. iron hook or goad for driving an elephant. 2. restraint, control; (किसी पर) ~ लगाना to put (someone) under control.

अंकुश-कृमि m. hookworm.

अँखुआ m. sprout.

अँखुआना vi. to sprout.

अंग m. 1. body. 2. part of the body, limb; फूले ~ न समाना to be at the height of joy. 3. side, aspect, facet. 4. department. 5. part; जीवन का ~ part of life.

अंगचारी m. companion.

अंगज m. 1. son. 2. hair or sweat.

अंगजा f. daughter.

अंगजात adj. born or produced from the body.

अंगड़-खंगड़ m. junk.

अँगड़ाई f. stretching of limbs (for relaxation); ~ लेना to stretch limbs (for relaxation).

अँगड़ाना vi. to stretch limbs (for relaxation).

अंगत्राण m. armour.

अंगद m. 1. armlet. 2. son of Bali (Ramayan).

अँगना m. = आँगन (courtyard).

अंगना f. belle.

अंग-प्रत्यंग m. each and every part of the body.

अंग-प्रदर्शन m. displaying of one's sexual organs in public.

अंगभंग m. injury to a limb.

अंगभंगिमा f. = अंगभंगी।

अंगभंगी f. posture or stance, calculated to fascinate.

अ

अंगमर्दन m. massage.

अंगमारी f. paralysis.

अंगरक्षक m. bodyguard.

अँगरखा m. an old type of loose longish male garment.

अंगराग m. cosmetic.

अंगवस्त्र m. a shawl given as a mark of respect to a person for some work or achievement.

अंगहीन adj. without a body or its limb.

अंगा m. = अँगरखा।

अंगार m. = अंगारा।

अंगारा m. live coal; ~ हो जाना to be wild with rage; अंगारे उगलना to spit fire; अंगारे बरसना intense heat raining like fire; अंगारों पर लोटना to get savage with anger.

अँगिया f. a kind of bodice.

अंगी adj. having a body.

अंगीकरण m. act of accepting (as one's own).

अंगीकार adj. accepted; ~ करना to accept, to own. m. = अंगीकरण।

अँगीठा m. a furnace.

अँगीठी f. a kind of Indian stove, grate, firepot.

अंगुल f. = उँगली।

अंगुलछाप f. finger-print.

अंगुश्त m. finger.

अंगुश्ताना m. thimble.

अँगूठा m. 1. thumb; ~ दिखाना/दिखा देना to turn down (a request) with derision. 2. great toe.

अँगूठी f. finger-ring; ~ का नगीना a gem among jewels.

अंगूर m. (usu. plu.) grapes; ~ खट्टे होना—अंगूर खट्टे हैं The grapes are sour.

अंगूरी adj. 1. made of grapes, vinous. 2. having the colour of grapes.

अंगोच्छेदन m. surgery, amputation.

अंग्रेज़ m. an Englishman.

अंग्रेज़ियत f. Anglicism.

अंग्रेज़ी adj. 1. of Englishman. 2. of England. f. English language.

अंचल m. 1. the part of the saree which covers the front portion of the woman's body, border. 2. region.

अंजन m. collyrium.

अंजर-पंजर m. joints or parts of a body, machine or structure; ~ ढीले हो जाना to become very tired.

अंजलि f. hollow of the curved palm; ~ भर handful.

अंजलिबद्ध adj. having hands folded, with the palms joined together.

अंजाम m. result, consequence.

अंजीर m. fig (tree and its fruit).

अंजुमन m. 1. association. 2. society.

अंटशंट adj. incoherent, irrelevant; ~ बकना to indulge in irrelevant talk.

अंटा m. spool of thread.

अंटाचित adj. sprawling; ~ हो जाना to lie sprawling/flat, chest upward.

अंटी f. 1. a gesture with one finger over the other; ~ मारना to hide something deceitfully. 2. spool of cotton-thread etc. 3. knot.

अंड m. 1. egg. 2. testicles. 3. universe.

अंडकोश m. scrotum.

अंडज adj. born from an egg. m. a bird, fish or snake.

अंडबंड adj. 1. incoherent. 2. meaningless. 3. miscellaneous. m. 1. meaningless talk. 2. improper language.

अंडा m. egg; अंडे की ज़र्दी yolk of an egg; अंडे की सफ़ेदी white of an egg; अंडे देना to lay eggs; अंडे सेना (i) to hatch/ incubate (eggs), (ii) to sit idle.

अंडाकार adj. egg-shaped, oval.

अंडाशय m. ovary.

अंडी f. 1. castor oil-seed; ~ का तेल castor oil. 2. a kind of rough silken cloth.

अंत:करण m. 1. heart. 2. inner-self.

अंत:कालीन adj. interim.

अंत:पुर m. seraglio, harem.

अंत:प्रेरणा f. inner urge.

अंत:स्राव m. internal secretion.

अंत m. 1. end, the last part; ~ में in the end, eventually, at last; ~ बनना to have a good end. 2. end, termination; प्रथा का ~ end of a custom; ~ करना या कर देना (i) to put to an end, (ii) to kill or destroy completely. 3. secret; ~ पाना; to be able to know someone's secret; ~ लेना to gauge the secret, to probe into the secret.

अँतड़ी f. intestine.

अंतत: adv. ultimately.

अंततोगत्वा adv. ultimately.

अंतर् prefix. inner, inter.

अंतरंग adj. 1. inner; ~ परिषद inner council. 2. intimate, fast; ~ मित्र fast friend.

अंतर[1] m. 1. difference; ~ करना to discriminate or differentiate, उन्नीस बीस का ~ a nominal difference. 2. distinction. 3. interval of time or space.

अंतर[2] prefix. inter.

अंतरजातीय adj. intercaste; ~ विवाह intercaste marriage.

अंतरण m. 1. spacing. 2. transference.

अंतरप्रांतीय adj. inter-provincial.

अंतरप्रादेशिक adj. inter-state.

अंतरमहाविद्यालयीन adj. inter-college.

अंतरराष्ट्रीय adj. international.

अंतरराष्ट्रीयता f. internationalism.

अंतरस्थ adj. lying within.

अंतरात्मा f. conscience.

अंतराल m. 1. interval 2. space.

अंतरिक्ष m. outer space, inter-planetary space.

अंतरिक्ष-किरण f. cosmic ray.

अंतरिक्ष-यात्रा f. space-travel.

अंतरिक्ष-यात्री m. astronaut.

अंतरिक्ष-यान m. spaceship.

अंतरिक्ष-युग m. space age.

अंतरिक्ष विज्ञान m. meteorology.

अंतरिम adj. interim.

अंतरीप m. headland.

अंतर्कथा f. episode.

अंतर्गत adj. included in; सूची के ~ included in the list.

अंतर्ग्रस्त adj. involved.

अ

अंतर्चक्र m. inner circle.

अंतर्जगत m. the world within, inner world.

अंतर्ज्ञान m. 1. intuition, 2. enlightenment.

अंतर्ज्योति f. inner light.

अंतर्दर्शन m. introspection.

अंतर्दाह m. heart-burning.

अंतर्दृष्टि f. insight, inner sight.

अंतर्देशीय adj. inland; ~ पत्र inland letter.

अंतर्द्वंद्व m. conflict.

अंतर्धान adj. disappeared, vanished; ~ होना/हो जाना to disappear.

अंतर्धारा f. undercurrent.

अंतर्ध्वंस m. sabotage.

अंतर्निहित adj. inherent.

अंतर्बोध m. = अंतर्ज्ञान।

अंतर्भूत adj. included in, permeated.

अंतर्मुखी adj. inward, introver-tive.

अंतर्यामी adj. immanent.

अंतर्लीन adj. self-engrossed.

अंतर्वर्ती adj. intermediate.

अंतर्वस्तु m. contents.

अंतर्हित adj. contained.

अंतस्थ adj. intermediary. m. semi-vowels—य, र, ल and व।

अंतहीन adj. endless.

अंतिम adj. last, final.

अंत्यज adj. & m. untouchable.

अंत्याक्षरी f. a kind of competition in verse recitation.

अंत्येष्टि f. the last rites, obsequies.

अंत्र m. intestine.

अंत्रशूल m. colic pain.

अंदर adv. within (something), inside.

अंदर, के postposition. 1. inside; घर के ~ inside the house. 2. within; एक घंटे के ~ within an hour.

अंदरवाला m. inner being.

अंदरूनी adj. internal.

अंदाज़ m. 1. guess, 2. surmise.

अदाज़न adv. conjecturally.

अंदाज़ा m. guess, surmise.

अंदेशा m. misapprehension.

अंध adj. 1. blind. 2. dark.

अंधकार m. 1. darkness. 2. gloom.

अंधकार-युग m. Dark Ages.

अंधकूप m. 1. dark well.2. blac-kout.

अंधखोपड़ी adj. block-headed.

अंधड़ m. windstorm.

अंधपरंपरा f. blind tradition.

अंधभक्त m. blind devotee.

अंधभक्ति f. blind devotion.

अंधविश्वास m. 1. blind faith. 2. superstition.

अंधविश्वासी adj. & m. superstitious (person).

अंधा adj. 1. blind; 2. dark, full of darkness. 3. without opening; अंधी घाटी blind valley. m. a blind person.

अंधाधुंध adv. blindly, indiscriminately.

अंधानुकरण m. blind following.

अंधापन m. blindness.

अँधियारा m. = अँधेरा।

अंधी घाटी f. blind valley.

अंधेर m. = अंधेर-खाता।

अंधेर-खाता m. 1. grave irregularity. 2. lawlessness, anarchy.

अंधेर नगरी n. lawless city.

अँधेरा m. dark, poor light; ~ हो रहा है It is getting dark.

अँधेरा घुप्प m. pitch dark.

अँधेरी f. blinkers.

अँधेरी कोठरी f. dark cell.

अंबर m. sky.

अंबा f. mother.

अंबार m. heap, pile, stockpile.

अँबिया f. small unripe mango.

अंबु m. water.

अंबुज m. lotus.

अंबुधि m. ocean.

अंभ m. water.

अंश m. 1. part, portion. 2. share (in property etc.) 3. degree (of an angle). 4. fraction. 5. numerator (of a fraction).

अंशकालिक adj. part-time.

अंशतः adv. in part, partly.

अंशदान m. contribution.

अंशदानी m. contributor.

अंशावतार m. partial incarnation.

अंशी adj. & m. having/consisting of a number of parts.

अंशु m. ray, beam.

अंशुमाली m. sun.

अकंटक adj. thornless; ~ राज्य unobstructed reign.

अकंप adj. = अकंपित।

अकंपित adj. unwavering, not vibrating.

अकच adj. without hair, bald.

अकड़ f. 1. proudness, conceit; ~ दिखाना to show impudence. 2. strut.

अकड़न f. stiffness.

अकड़ना vi. 1. to become stiff; मरकर अकड़ जाना to become stiff on death. 2. to behave conceitedly, to strut; अकड़कर चलना to walk affectedly, to strut.

अकड़फूँ f. airs, arrogance.

अकड़बाज़ m. one who talks affectedly, swaggerer.

अकथनीय adj. 1. unsayable, unutterable. 2. unworthy of being spoken. 3. too great to be described in words, ineffable.

अकथित adj. unsaid, untold.

अकथ्य adj. = अकथनीय।

अकबरी adj. pertaining to King Akbar.

अकरणीय adj. undoable, wrong, improper.

अकर्ता m. non-doer, not an agent.

अकर्म m. 1. absence of work, inaction. 2. misdeed.

अकर्मक adj. intransitive; ~ क्रिया intransitive verb.

अकर्मण्य adj. indolent, idle, inactive.

अकलंक adj. spotless, blotless.

अकलंकित adj. = अकलंक।

अकल f. = अक़्ल।

अकलुष adj. blotless.

अकलुषित adj. = अकलुष।

अकल्पनीय adj. unthinkable.

अकल्पित adj. unthought of.

अकस्मात् adv. suddenly.

अकाज m. 1. (lit.) absence of work. 2. loss, harm; इससे तुम्हारा कौन-सा ~ होगा What do you lose thereby?

अकाजी adj. (person) having no work to do.

अ

अकाट्य adj. impossible to disprove, irrefutable.

अकादमिक adj. academic.

अकादमी f. academy.

अकाम adj. 1. free from desire. 2. uninfluenced by love or passion.

अकारण adv. without cause, without any rhyme or reason.

अकारथ adj. futile, ineffectual. adv. in vain.

अकाल m. 1. famine. 2. acute shortage of anything; कोयले का ~ coal famine.

अकालकुसुम m. untimely thing.

अकालपीड़ित adj. famine stricken.

अकालप्रौढ़ adj. precocious.

अकालमृत्यु f. untimely death, premature death.

अकाली m. 1. a sect among the Sikhs. 2. a follower of this sect. adj. of Akalees'.

अकिंचन adj. & m. destitute, poor, pauper.

अकिंचनता f. destitution, poverty, pauperism.

अकिंचित adj. trifling, unimportant.

अकिंचित्कर adj. immaterial.

अकीर्ति f. disgrace, ill-repute, infamy.

अकीर्तिकर adj. disgraceful, inglorious.

अकुंठित adj. not blunted i.e. sharp.

अकुलाना vi. to feel restless/uneasy.

अकुलाहट f. restlessness, uneasiness.

अकुलीन adj. not of noble descent, of low birth.

अकुशल adj. unskilled.

अकूत adj. inestimable.

अकृतघ्न adj. not ungrateful, grateful.

अकृतज्ञ adj. ungrateful.

अकृतज्ञता f. ungratefulness.

अकृत्रिम adj. not artificial, natural.

अकृत्रिमता f. 1. naturalness. 2. unaffectedness.

अकृषिक adj. non-agricultural.

अकृषित adj. uncultivated.

अकेतन adj. homeless.

अकेला adj. 1. alone. 2. unique. 3. sole; ~ स्वामी sole proprietor.

अकेलापन m. loneliness, solitariness.

अकेली जान f. lonely person; तुम तो ~ हो You are all alone.

अकेले adv. alone, without companion.

अक्खड़ adj. recalcitrant.

अक्खड़पन m. recalcitrance.

अक्तूबर m. October (month).

अक्रिय adj. inactive.

अक्रियता f. inactivity.

अक़्ल f. wisdom; ~ आना to attain the age of wisdom; ~ का अंधा (person) devoid of common sense; ~ का दुश्मन duffer; ~ का पुतला wisdom personified; ~ के घोड़े दौड़ाना to indulge in mental gymnastics; ~ के पीछे लट्ठ लिए फिरना to be pursuing a course of folly; ~ गुम होना या हो जाना to be at (one's) wit's end; ~ घास चरने जाना to be bereft of all sense; ~ दौड़ाना to exercise (one's) brains;

~ पर पत्थर पड़ना to be bereft of all brains; ~ पर परदा पड़ना to be out of one's wits; ~ मारी जाना to be out of (one's) wits; ~ लड़ाना to exercise (one's) brains; ~ सठिया जाना to be in (one's) dotage.

अक़्लमंद adj. wise.

अक़्लमंदी f. wisdom.

अक्ष m. axis, axle.

अक्षत adj. 1. uninjured, unhurt. 2. whole, entire. m. whole grains of rice used in religious ceremonies.

अक्षत योनि f. maiden, virgin.

अक्षम adj. 1. unable, powerless. 2. incompetent, incapable.

अक्षमता f. 1. inability, disability. 2. incompetence, incapability.

अक्षम्य adj. inexcusable, unforgivable.

अक्षय adj. 1. undecaying, imperishable. 2. inexhaustible.

अक्षर adj. undecaying, indestructible. m. 1. character (of the alphabet). 2. syllable. 3. letter (of the alphabet).

अक्षरशः adv. to the letter, verbatim, literally; बात ~ सत्य थी It was literally true.

अक्षांश m. latitude.

अक्षि f. eye.

अक्षिगोलक m. eye-ball.

अक्षिसाक्षी m. eye-witness.

अक्षीय adj. axial.

अक्षुण्ण adj. 1. intact, unbroken. 2. uncurtailed.

अक्षुण्णता f. intactness, unbrokenness.

अक्षुब्ध adj. undisturbed, unagitated, unperturbed.

अक्षौहिणी f. a brigade consisting of 21870 chariots, 21870 elephants, 65610 horses and 109350 foot-soldiers.

अक्स m. reflection.

अक्सर adv. often, usually.

अक्सरियत f. majority.

अक्सीर adj. efficacious.

अखंड adj. 1. unbroken; ~ धारा unbroken current. 2. non-stop; ~ पाठ non-stop recitation. 3. undivided; ~ भारत undivided India; तुम्हारा सौभाग्य ~ रहे May you have a never-ending marital life.

अखंडता f. unbrokenness, indivisibility, integrity.

अख़बार m. newspaper.

अख़बारवाला m. 1. owner of a newspaper. 2. one who sells newspapers, paper boy.

अखरना vi. to be sore/hurtful; तुम्हारी बात मुझे अखर गई What you have said was sore enough for me.

अख़रोट m. walnut.

अखाड़ा m. 1. arena, rendezvous. 2. muster, assemblage, school, congregation or the like.

अखाड़िया m. = अखाड़ेबाज़।

अखाड़ेबाज़ m. 1. master wrestler (lit.). 2. strategist, man-oeuvrer.

अखाड़ेबाज़ी f. bellicosity.

अखाद्य adj. uneatable, inedible.

अखिल adj. all; ~ भारतीय सम्मेलन All India Conference.

अगड़ा m. person belonging to upper caste. adj. of upper class;

अगड़ी जाति upper class.

अगणनीय adj. countless, innumerable.

अगणित adj. countless.

अगण्य adj. = अगणित।

अगम्य adj. 1. impassable. 2. beyond reach.

अगम्या f. female, not to be cohabited with.

अगम्यागमन m. incest; ~ संबंधी incestuous.

अगर conj. if, in case. m. aloe-wood.

अगरचे conj. = अगर।

अगरबत्ती f. incense stick used sply on religious or ceremonial occasions.

अगर-मगर f. ifs and buts; ~ करना to dilly-dally.

अग़ल-बग़ल adv. 1. on either side, to the right and left. 2. side by side; वे दोनों ~ ही रहते हैं They both live side by side.

अगला adj. 1. next, following; 2. frontal, fore; ~ पहिया front wheel, fore wheel. m. the other person (concerned); अगले की भी तो कुछ सुनो Give your ears to the other (one) as well.

अगला-पिछला adj. fore and aft.

अगवानी f. reception; ~ करना to receive ceremoniously.

अगस्त m. August (month).

अगहन m. ninth month of the Hindu calendar.

अगहनी adj. pertaining to the month of अगहन।

अगाऊ adj = अग्रिम।

अगाड़ी-पिछाड़ी f. ropes used for tying the horse by the neck and the two hind legs.

अगाध adj. 1. unfathomable; ~ पानी unfathomable water. 2. profound; ~ पांडित्य profound scholarship. 3. immense; ~ धन immense wealth.

अगाह्य adj. unfathomable.

अगुआ m. 1. leader, 2. initiator.

अगोचर adj. imperceptible.

अगोरना vt. to keep watch (over).

अग्नि f. 1. fire. 2. the fire of the stomach, power of digestion; ~ मंद होना to lose appetite.

अग्निकांड m. conflagration.

अग्निकुंड m. fire-pot.

अग्निक्रीड़ा f. a firework display.

अग्नि-परीक्षा f. acid test.

अग्निपिंड m. fire-ball.

अग्निपूजक m. a fire-worshipper.

अग्निपूजा f. fire-worship.

अग्निबाण m. rocket.

अग्निभीति f. pyrophobia.

अग्निवर्धक adj. that stimulates appetite, digestive.

अग्निवर्षा f. shower of fire.

अग्निशामक m. fire-extinguisher.

अग्निसंस्कार m. cremation (of a dead body).

अग्निसह adj. fire-proof.

अग्न्यस्त्र m. fire-arm.

अग्न्याशय m. pancreas.

अग्र adj. 1. foremost. 2. pre-eminent, best, topmost.

अग्रगण्य adj. first and foremost.

अग्रगति f. advancement, furtherance.

अग्रगामी adj. pioneering, for-ward. m. pioneer.

अग्रज m. elder brother.

अग्रजा f. elder sister.

अग्रणी adj. foremost.

अग्रता f. priority; ~ सूची priority list.

अग्रदूत m. herald.

अग्रलेख m. leading article.

अग्रसर adj. ~ करना to forward; ~ होना to advance forward.

अग्रसारण m. forwarding.

अग्रसारित adj. forwarded; ~ करना to forward.

अग्राह्य adj. unacceptable.

अग्रिम adj. 1. (price or subscription) paid in advance. 2. advance; ~ प्रति advance copy; ~ भुगतान advance payment.
m. money given in advance.

अघ m. guilt, sin.

अघटित adj. unoccurred, unhappened.

अघातक adj. not fatal, harmless.

अघाना vi. to be satiated.

अघोर adj. not dreadful.

अघोरी m. one for whom nothing is unacceptable or filthy.

अघोष adj. 1. voiceless. 2. unvoiced; ~ व्यंजन unvoiced consonant.

अचंभा m. amazement, astonishment.

अचकचाना vi. 1. to be confounded. 2. to hesitate.

अचकन f. an old Indian attire worn as a long coat.

अचर adj. 1. immovable. 2. constant, invariable.

अचरज m. surprise, astonishment.

अचल adj. 1. immovable; ~ संपत्ति immovable property. 2. firm; ~ रहना to remain firm, stagnant.

अचला f. earth.

अचानक adv. suddenly, unexpectedly. adj. happening unexpectedly.

अचार m. pickles; ~ डालना (i) to prepare pickles, pickling; (ii) to pick up in large quantity.

अचालक adj. non-conductor.

अचिंतनीय adj. inconceivable.

अचिंतित adj. not thought of, not conceived of.

अचिंत्य adj. inconceivable.

अचिकित्स्य adj. incurable.

अचिर adj. 1. not lasting. 2. recent, new.

अचूक adj. unfailing, infallible.

अचेत adj. senseless, unconscious.

अचेतन adj. unconscious; ~ मन unconscious mind.

अचेतनता f. unconsciousness.

अचेष्ट adj. inactive, passive.

अच्छा adj. 1. good, nice; देखने में ~ good-looking; अच्छे दिन good/better days. 2. right; अच्छे काम के लिए for a right cause. 3. kind, helpful. adv. well; अच्छे आना to reach (unexpectedly) at a right moment. interj. 1. Is it! 2. Oh, I see! 3.well, well then.

अच्छाई f. goodness, virtue, merit, excellence.

अ

अच्छाई-बुराई f. merit and demerit.

अच्छा-ख़ासा adj. 1. quite big. 2. fairly good.

अच्छापन m. = अच्छाई।

अच्युत adj. 1. not fallen, not deviating. 2. infallible. m. Lord Krishna.

अछूत adj. & m. outcast, untouchable (person).

अछूता adj. untouched.

अछूतोद्धार m. uplift of the untouchables.

अजगर m. python.

अजगव m. bow of Lord Shiva.

अज़दहा m. python, dragon.

अजनतांत्रिक adj. undemocratic.

अजनबी adj. & m. stranger.

अजन्मा adj. unborn.

अजब adj. 1. surprising. 2. strange, peculiar.

अजय adj. unconquerable.

अजर adj. undecaying.

अजर-अमर adj. 1. neither subject to old age nor to death. 2. that remains for ever.

अजल adj. anhydrous.

अजवायन f. Trachyspermum ammi.

अजस्त्र adj. perpetual, constant; ~ धारा perpetual stream.

अजात adj. unborn; ~ शत्रु having no enemy.

अजान adj. 1. ignorant; ~ में unknowingly. 2. innocent.

अज़ान f. prayer-call, given from the mosque.

अजाने adv. unknowingly.

अजायब घर m. museum.

अजित adj. unconquered.

अजिल्द adj. unbound; ~ पुस्त[क] unbound book.

अजी interj. an expression fo[r] calling attention like the Englis[h] 'Hallo'.

अज़ीज़ adj. dear; वह मेरा ~ दोस्त थ[ा] He was my dear friend.

अजीब adj. 1. strange, peculia[r] 2. odd.

अजीबोग़रीब adj. 1. peculia[r] 2. baffling.

अजीर्ण m. indigestion (esp. due t[o] over-eating).

अजूबा m. wonder, curio.

अजेंडा m. agenda.

अजेय adj. unconquerable, in vincible.

अजैव adj. inorganic.

अज्ञ adj. ignorant.

अज्ञता f. ignorance.

अज्ञात adj. unknown.

अज्ञात यौवना f. a girl yet unawar[e] of her youth.

अज्ञातवास m. dwelling in a[n] unknown place.

अज्ञान m. 1. absence of knowledge 2. ignorance.

अज्ञानवश adv. due to igno-rance, unknowingly.

अज्ञानी adj. ignorant.

अज्ञेय adj. unknowable.

अटक f. 1. hindrance, obstruction. 2. hitch.

अटकना vi. 1. to get held up. 2. to get stuck up; अटक-अटककर बोलना to speak with unnecessary pauses; मन ~ clinging of the heart.

अटकल f. guess, conjecture.

अटकल-पच्चू adj. based on conjecture.

अटकलबाज़ी f. conjecturing.

अटकाना vt. 1. to prevent or hinder. 2. to detain.

अटना vi. 1. to be accommodated, to be able to hold; बरतन में कितना पानी अटेगा How much water will the vessel hold? 2. to be the right size; क्या यह कोट तुम्हें अट जाएगा Does the coat fit you?

अटपटा adj. 1. absurd, odd, 2. unpleasant.

अटल adj. 1. immovable. 2. unalterable, inevitable.

अटारी f. a high imposing building sply. with several stories.

अटाला m. heap, dump.

अटूट adj. 1. unbroken, continuous. 2. unbreakable.

अटेरन f. a gadget for winding up thread.

अटेरना vt. 1. to wind up thread. 2. to grab (money); रकम ~ to grab money.

अट्टहास m. boisterous laugh, guffaw; ~ करना to guffaw.

अट्टा m. = अटा (अटारी)।

अट्टालिका f. = अटारी।

अट्टी f. hank; सूत की ~ hank of cotton.

अट्ठाईस adj. & m. twenty-eight.

अट्ठाईसवाँ adj. twenty-eighth.

अट्ठानबे adj. & m. ninety-eight.

अट्ठावन adj. & m. fifty-eight.

अट्ठासी adj. & m. eighty-eight.

अठ abbreviation of आठ used as prefix meaning (i) eight, (ii) eighth.

अठखेली f. frolic, frolicsome movement.

अठगुना adj. eight-times.

अठन्नी f. half-rupee coin, 50 paise coin.

अठपहला adj. eight-faced.

अठपहिया adj. eight-wheeled.

अठपेजी adj. octavo.

अठमासा adj. (child) prematurely born in the eighth month of pregnancy.

अठवारा m. week (consisting of eight days).

अठहत्तर adj. & m. seventy-eight.

अठारह adj. & m. eighteen.

अड़ंगा m. obstacle, obstruction; ~ लगाना to put an obstacle.

अड़ंगी f. a leg trick in wrestling.

अड़ंगेबाज़ m. filibuster, obstructionist.

अड़ंगेबाज़ी f. filibustering, obstructing tactics.

अड़ f. obstinacy, stubbornness.

अड़चन f. impediment, hindrance, obstacle; ~ लगना—एक न एक अड़चन लगी ही रहती है Some obstacle or the other is always there.

अड़तालीस adj. & m. forty-eight.

अड़तीस adj. & m. thirty-eight.

अड़दार adj. stubborn.

अड़ना vi. to be obstinate.

अड़सठ adj. & m. sixty-eight.

अड़हुल m. a plant of china rose and its red flower.

अड़ाना vt. to put or place im-

अ

pediment in the way to cause obstruction; टाँग ~ to butt in.

अडिग adj. absolutely firm.

अड़ियल adj. restive, mulish; ~ **टट्टू** stubborn fellow.

अड़ोस-पड़ोस m. neighbour-hood.

अड़ोसी-पड़ोसी m. (plu.) persons who live near or next to another, neighbours.

अड्डा m. 1. halting place, resting place. 2. perch (of birds). 3. stand (of vehicles). 4. base; सैनिक ~ military base. 5. rendezvous, den; जुए का ~ gambling den; 6. loom.

अढ़तिया m. commission agent.

अढ़ाई adj. two and a half.

अणी f. point of needle, instrument.

अणु m. atom.

अणुजीव m. a very small living being.

अणुबम m. atom bomb.

अणुयुद्ध m. atomic war.

अणुवीक्षण यंत्र m. microscope.

अणुशक्ति f. atomic power/ energy.

अतः conj. hence, therefore, so.

अतएव conj. hence, therefore.

अतरसों adv. 1. day previous to day before yesterday. 2. day next to day after tomorrow.

अतर्कित adj. 1. not argued. 2. not thought of.

अतर्क्य adj. 1. incontrovertible. 2. indisputable.

अतल adj. bottomless.

अतलस्पर्शी adj. deep and profound.

अतलांतिक m. Atlantic.

अता-पता m. whereabouts.

अति prefix. 1. over, too. 2. supe f. excess; ~ कर देना to act or g beyond the normal or accepte limits.

अतिकाय adj. gigantic, huge.

अतिक्रमण m. 1. transgressio 2. encroachment. 3. an ur authorised construction.

अतिचार m. 1. trespass. 2. violatio

अतिथि m. 1. unannounced visito 2. guest; ~ कलाकार m. gues artist.

अतिथि-गृह m. guest-house.

अतिथिशाला f. = अतिथि-गृह।

अतिथि-सत्कार m. generou reception of guests, hospitality

अतिथि-सेवा f. service (s) rendere to a guest.

अतिमानव m. superman.

अतिमानस m. supermind.

अतिरंजन m. exaggeration.

अतिरंजना f. = अतिरंजन।

अतिरंजित adj. exaggerated; ~ कर to exaggerate.

अतिराष्ट्रीय adj. chauvinistic.

अतिराष्ट्रीयता f. chauvinism.

अतिरिक्त adj. 1. extr 2. additional. 3. surplus.

अतिरेक m. excess, exuberance.

अतिवर्षण m. = अतिवृष्टि।

अतिवात m. tempest.

अतिवाद m. extremism.

अतिवादिता f. extremeness.

अतिवादी adj. & m. extremist.

अतिवृष्टि f. excessive rain, pletho of rain.

अ

अतिशय adj. exceeding, excessive. adv. exceedingly, excessively.

अतिशयोक्ति f. 1. hyperbole, 2. exaggeration.

अतिशयोक्तिपूर्ण adj. 1. hype-rbolic, 2. exaggerated.

अतिसार m. diarrhoea, dysentery.

अतिस्वन adj. supersonic.

अतींद्रिय adj. beyond the reach of the senses, transcendental; ~ दृष्टि clairvoyance; ~ श्रवण clairaudience.

अतीत adj. passed away, gone by or over. m. the time long gone by, past.

अतीव adj. exceeding. adv. exceedingly.

अतुकांत adj. unrhymed; ~ कविता blank verse.

अतुल adj. immeasurable, immence.

अतुलनीय adj. = अतुल।

अतुल्य adj. = अतुल।

अतृप्त adj. unsatiated, unsatisfied.

अतृप्ति f. unsatiation, want of satisfaction.

अत्तार m. perfumer.

अत्तारी f. avocation of an अत्तार।

अत्यंत adj. very, very much. adv. extremely.

अत्यधिक adj. very much, too much, ~ बहुमत से by an overwhelming majority. adv. exorbitantly.

अत्यल्प adj. too little, infin- itesimal.

अत्याचार m. tyranny.

अत्याचारी adj. tyrannical; ~ शासक tyrant. m. tyrant.

अत्याज्य adj. not to be given up/ forsaken.

अत्यानंद m. ecstasy.

अत्यावश्यक adj. very necessary, pressing.

अत्युक्ति f. exaggeration.

अत्युक्तिपूर्ण adj. exaggerated.

अत्युत्तम adj. most excellent, very best.

अथक adj. indefatigable, untiring, unceasing; ~ परिश्रम unceasing labour; ~ रूप से indefatigably, tirelessly.

अथवा conj. or.

अथाह adj. unfathomable, very deep; ~ ज्ञान profound knowledge.

अदंडनीय adj. unpunishable.

अदक्ष adj. inefficient.

अदक्षता f. inefficiency.

अदत्त adj. 1. not given. 2. unpaid.

अदद m. 1. piece; एक ~ one piece. 2. number.

अदना adj. 1. puny, very small. 2. insignificant.

अदब m. 1. regard, respect; ~ करना to pay due respect. 2. literature.

अदम्य adj. irrepressible.

अदरक m. ginger (in the green state).

अदला-बदली f. 1. interchange. 2. barter, exchange.

अदह्य adj. incombustible.

अदा f. an expressive gesture or pleasing movement, carriage, posture. adj. paid; ~ करना to pay.

अदाकार m. 1. actor. 2. performer.

अ

अदाकारी f. 1. acting. 2. performance.

अदायगी f. payment, defrayal; कर्ज की ~ repayment of debt.

अदालत f. court.

अदालती adj. concerning/pertaining to a court of justice; ~ कार्रवाई legal proceedings; ~ जाँच judicial enquiry; ~ भाषा court language.

अदावत f. enmity.

अदावती adj. inimical.

अदाह्य adj. non-combustible.

अदूरदर्शिता f. absence of far-sightedness, shortsighted-ness.

अदूरदर्शी adj. not farsighted, shortsighted (person).

अदृश्य adj. invisible.

अदृष्ट m. destiny, fate, luck.

अदेय adj. 1. that cannot be given. 2. non-transferable.

अद्धा adj. half.
m. 1. a pint, half a bottle. 2. half brick. 3. counterfoil.

अद्धी f. a kind of fine muslin like cloth.

अद्भुत adj. amazing, wonderful, marvellous.

अद्य adv. today.

अद्यतन adj. up-to-date.

अद्यावधिक adj. = अद्यतन।

अद्वितीय adj. unique.

अद्वैत adj. not dual. m. absence of duality, oneness.

अद्वैतवाद m. monism, Adwai-tism.

अद्वैतवादी adj. monistic, Adwai-tist. m. monist, Adwaitist.

अधः prefix. under, beneath.

अधःपतन m. downfall.

अधःपतित adj. downfallen.

अधकचरा adj. 1. half-ripe 2. immature, unassimilated.

अधकहा adj. half-said.

अधखिला adj. half-bloomed.

अधखुला adj. half-open.

अधजल adj. half-full of water.

अधनंगा adj. half-naked.

अधपका adj. 1. half-ripe. 2. half-cooked.

अधपन्ना m. counterfoil.

अधपेट adv. with half-filled belly.

अधबिच adv. in the midway.

अधम adj. mean, low.

अधमता f. meanness, lowliness.

अधमरा adj. half-dead.

अधमर्ण m. debtor.

अधर m. 1. lower lip. 2. space between heaven and earth; ~ में झूलना/लटकना (i) to hang without a support, (ii) to hang fire i.e. to be delayed.

अधरपान m. sucking/kissing of the (beloved's) lips.

अधराधर m. plu. lower and upper lips.

अधर्म m. 1. unrighteousness. 2. sin, sinful act.

अधर्मी adj. impious, irreligious, sinful.

अधातु f. non-metal.

अधात्विक adj. non-metallic.

अधार्मिक adj. irreligious, pro- fane.

अधिक adj. 1. more; ~ से अधिक to the utmost; दस से ~ more than ten. 2. additional; ~ मास additional month.

अधिकतम adj. maximum.

अधिकतर adv. 1. mostly. 2. more often.

अधिकता f. 1. plenty, 2. excess.

अधिकर m. supertax.

अधिकरण m. tribunal.

अधिकांश m. major part; ~ में (i) mostly, (ii) generally.
adj. most; ~ लोग most people. [अधिक+अंश]

अधिकांशतः adv. 1. mostly. 2. generally.

अधिकाधिक adj. maximum; ~ संख्या में in maximum numbers.

अधिकार m. 1. right; जन्मसिद्ध ~ birth right. 2. claim. 3. possession. 4. official power, authority. 5. command.

अधिकार-क्षेत्र m. jurisdiction.

अधिकारपूर्वक adv. authoritatively.

अधिकारातीत adj. beyond one's (legal) power, ultra vires.

अधिकारी m. 1. officer, official; उच्च ~ high official/officer. 2. authority. [Fem. अधिकारिणी]

अधिकारी-तंत्र m. bureaucracy.

अधिकृत adj. authorised; ~ विक्रेता authorised dealer.

अधिगत adj. attained.

अधिगम m. 1. access. 2. attainment.

अधिग्रहण m. acquisition.

अधित्यका f. tableland, plateau.

अधिदेश m. mandate.

अधिनायक m. dictator.

अधिनायक-तंत्र m. dictatorship.

अधिनायकता f. dictatorship.

अधिनियम m. act (of legislature); ~ बनाना to enact/legislate.

अधिनियमन m. enactment.

अधिनियमित adj. enacted.

अधिपति m. 1. proprietor, 2. lord, king.

अधिपत्र m. warrant.

अधिपद m. article (of asso-ciation).

अधिपुरुष m. boss.

अधिप्रभार m. = अधिभार।

अधिभार m. surcharge.

अधिमास m. additional month, leap month.

अधिमिलन m. accession.

अधिमिलित adj. acceded.

अधिया m. half portion; अधिए पर at fifty-fifty.

अधिरूढ़ adj. ascended.

अधिरोहण m. ascension.

अधिलाभ m. bonus.

अधिवक्ता m. advocate.

अधिवर्ष m. leap year.

अधिवेशन m. 1. session; खुला ~ open session. 2. sitting; ~ चल रहा था The sitting was on.

अधिशासी adj. executive; ~ अभियंता executive engineer.

अधिसंख्य adj. exceeding a regular or fixed number, supernumerary.

अधिसूचन m. act of notifying, notification.

अधिसूचना f. formal notice, notification.

अधीक्षक m. superintendent. [Fem. अधीक्षिका]

अधीक्षण m. superintendence.

अधीत adj. read, studied.

अधीति f. reading, study.

अ

अधीन adj. dependent, subservient; ~ करना to subjugate.

अधीन, के postposition. under; खेती वर्षा के ~ है Agriculture is dependent on rains.

अधीनता f. 1. subordination, subjection; (की) ~ स्वीकार करना to accept the authority. 2. dependence.

अधीनस्थ adj. subordinate.

अधीर adj. impatient, restless.

अधीरता f. impatience.

अधीश m. lord, master.

अधीश्वर m. lord, master. [Fem. अधीश्वरी]

अधुना adv. now.

अधुनातन adj. 1. up-to-date. 2. modern.

अधूरा adj. 1. incomplete. 2. imperfect.

अधूरापन m. 1. incompleteness. 2. imperfection.

अधेड़ adj. middle-aged.

अधेला m. an old Indian half-pice coin.

अधेली f. half-rupee coin. [M.C. अठन्नी]

अधैर्य m. = अधीरता।

अधोगति f. debasement, decadence.

अधोगमन m. degradation, decline, fall.

अधोगामी adj. going downwards, descending.

अधोबिंदु m. nadir.

अधोभूमि f. subsoil.

अधोमुख adj. = अधोमुखी।

अधोमुखी adj. descending from a higher to lower place o condition, downward.

अधोलोक m. 1. underworld 2. Hades.

अध्यक्ष m. 1. head. 2. chairman 3. speaker 4. president.

अध्यक्षता f. 1. headship. 2. chair manship. 3. speakership 4. presidentship.

अध्यक्षीय adj. presidential.

अध्ययन m. study, reading, perusal ~ करना to study.

अध्ययन-कक्ष m. study-room.

अध्ययनशील adj. studious, given to study.

अध्यर्थन m. claim..

अध्यवसाय m. assiduity, diligence perseverance.

अध्यवसायी adj. assiduous, diligent persevering.

अध्यात्म m. 1. the science o knowing the self. 2. relation between the Supreme and the (individual) Soul.

अध्यात्मवाद m. spiritualism.

अध्यात्मवादी adj. spiritual m. spiritualist.

अध्यादेश m. ordinance.

अध्यापक m. teacher.

अध्यापकी f. teaching profession.

अध्यापन m. teaching.

अध्यापन-कला f. art of teaching.

अध्यापिका f. lady teacher.

अध्याय m. 1. a main division of a book, chapter.

अध्यास m. 1. illusion. 2. illusory knowledge.

अध्याहरण m. inference.

अध्याहार m. 1. ellipsis. 2. inference.

अध्याहृत adj. 1. inferred. 2. understood.

अध्येता m. one who studies, reader, student.

अनंग adj. bodiless, incorporeal. m. Cupid.

अनंत adj. eternal, infinite.

अनंतर, के postposition. after, following something in time.

अनंतिम adj. provisional, not final.

अनख f. 1. resentment. 2. envy.

अनखाना vi. 1. to show resentment. 2. to envy.

अनगढ़ adj. unchiselled.

अनगिनत adj. innumerable.

अनघ adj. sinless, innocent.

अनचाहा adj. undesired.

अनचीता adj. unthought of.

अनछपा adj. not printed.

अनछुआ adj. untouched.

अनजान adj. ignorant; ~ में (i) unknowingly, (ii) involuntarily.

अनजाना adj. unknown; अनजानी राहें unknown tracks.

अनजाने adv.; ~ में / ही (i) unknowingly, (ii) involuntarily.

अनदेखा adj. unseen; अनदेखे चेहरे unseen faces.

अनदेखी f; ~ करना to ignore / overlook.

अनद्यतन adj. out-of-date.

अनधिकार adj. unauthorised.

अनधिकारिक adj. 1. non-official; ~ टेस्ट शृंखला non-official test series. 2. unauthorised; ~ निर्माण unauthorised construction.

अनधिकारी adj. 1. not entitled, not having a title. 2. not fit.

अनधिकृत adj. unauthorised.

अनध्याय m. off day(s) from studies; ~ काल vacation.

अनन्नास m. pineapple plant and its fruit.

अनन्य adj. 1. exclusive. 2. complete; 3. close, intimate.

अनन्वय m. a figure of speech.

अनपच m. = अपच।

अनपचा adj. undigested.

अनपढ़ adj. uneducated, illite-rate.

अनपराध adj. not guilty.

अनपेक्षित adj. 1. not requird. 2. not expected.

अनबन f. rift, tiff.

अनबूझ adj. unintelligible.

अनभिज्ञ adj. ignorant.

अनभिज्ञता f. ignorance.

अनभिप्रेत adj. undesired.

अनभीष्ट adj. not desired.

अनभ्यस्त adj. unaccustomed.

अनमना adj. 1. inattentive. 2. absent-minded; 3. indisposed.

अनमेल adj. 1. not matching. 2. dissimilar. 3. discordant.

अनमोल adj. invaluable.

अनम्य adj. inflexible.

अनम्यता f. inflexibility.

अनम्र adj. immodest.

अनर्गल adj. incoherent, absurd.

अनर्जित adj. unearned.

अनर्थ m. calamity, disaster.

अनर्थकारी adj. disastrous.

अ

अनलंकृत adj. 1. unornamented. 2. undecorated.

अनल m. 1. fire. 2. digestive power.

अनलशिखा f. flame.

अनवकाश m. absence of leisure.

अनवधान adj. inattentive, careless.

अनवरत adj. without pause, continuously.

अनवरोध m. absence of obstruction. adv. without any obstruction.

अनवसर m. inopportune time.

अनशन m. 1. fasting. 2. hunger strike; ~ करना to go on a hunger strike; ~ तोड़ना to terminate a hunger strike.

अनशनकारी m. 1. one who fasts. 2. hunger striker.

अनश्वर adj. 1. imperishable. 2. immortal.

अनसुना adj. unheard; अनसुनी करना to pay no heed to.

अनस्तित्व m. non-existence.

अनहद नाद m. divine melody produced from within.

अनहोनी f. seemingly impossi-ble event; ~ होना happening of a seemingly impossible event.

अनाक्रमण m. non-aggression; ~ संधि non-aggression pact.

अनागत adj. not came or arrived, yet to come.

अनाचार m. immorality.

अनाचारी adj. immoral, corrupt.

अनाज m. corn, grain; ~ का दुश्मन glutton, voracious eater.

अनाज-बखरी f. barn.

अनाजी adj. made of corn; ~ मिठाई corn sweet.

अनाज्ञाकारिता f. disobedience.

अनाज्ञाकारी adj. disobedient, not obedient.

अनाड़ी adj. unversed, unskilled.

अनाथ m. orphan.

अनाथालय m. orphanage.

अनादर m. disregard, disrespect; ~ करना to show disrespect or neglect.

अनादरण m. dishonouring; चेक का ~ dishonouring of a cheque.

अनादि adj. having no beginning, eternal.

अनादृत adj. 1. disrespected. 2. dishonoured.

अनाप-शनाप m. incoherent and meaningless talk, nonsense; ~ बकना to talk loose.

अनाम adj. anonymous.

अनामय adj. healthy.

अनामिक adj. anonymous.

अनामिका f. ring finger.

अनामिष adj. & m. vegetarian.

अनायास adv. 1. without effort. 2. spontaneously, involuntarily.

अनार m. pomegranate.

अनारदाना m. dried seeds of pomegranate.

अनारी adj. tartan gold (colour).

अनार्जव m. dishonesty.

अनार्य adj. 1. non-Aryan. 2. not noble.

अनावरण m. unveiling; ~ उत्सव unveiling ceremony.

अनावर्ती adj. non-recurring.

अनावर्षण m. want of rain, drought.

अनावश्यक m. non-essential.

अनावृत adj. 1. uncovered. 2. unveiled.

अनावृष्टि f. want of rain, drought.

अनासक्त adj. detached.

अनासक्ति f. detachment.

अनासीन adj. unseated.

अनास्था f. want of faith.

अनाहत adj. not wounded /hurt.

अनाहत नाद m. = अनहद नाद।

अनाहूत adj. uninvited.

अनिंदनीय adj. 1. beyond all reproach. 2. flawless.

अनिंदित adj. uncensured, unreproached.

अनिंद्य adj. = अनिंदनीय।

अनिच्छा f. unwillingness.

अनिच्छापूर्वक adv. unwillingly, reluctantly.

अनिच्छित adj. undesired.

अनिच्छुक adj. unwilling, disinterested.

अनित्य adj. transient.

अनित्यता f. transience.

अनिद्र adj. sleepless.

अनिद्रा f. sleeplessness.

अनिपुण adj. unskilled.

अनिमेष adj. not winking, without a wink (said of eyes).

अनियंत्रित adj. uncontrolled, unrestricted.

अनियत adj. 1. not fixed, indefinite. 2. irregular.

अनियमित adj. 1. irregular. 2. unruly.

अनियमितता f. irregularity.

अनिर्णीत adj. 1. undecided. 2. draw.

अनिर्दिष्ट adj. unspecified.

अनिर्वचनीय adj. inexpressible, ineffable.

अनिल m. wind, air.

अनिलसुत m. Hanuman.

अनिवार्य adj. 1. compulsory. 2. inevitable.

अनिवार्यता f. inevitability.

अनिवास्य adj. non-residential.

अनिश्चय m. 1. indecision. 2. doubt.

अनिश्चित adj. 1. undecided. 2. uncertain.

अनिश्चितता f. uncertainty.

अनिष्ट m. ill, evil; ~ की संभावना है Evil is apprehended; किसी का ~ चाहना to wish ill of someone.

अनिष्टकर adj. = अनिष्टकारी।

अनिष्टकारी adj. 1. disastrous, 2. ominous.

अनिष्ठा f. lack of faith, want of loyalty.

अनी f. sharp point.

अनीदार adj. sharp pointed.

अनीक f. army.

अनीति f. 1. injustice, high-handedness, impropriety. 2. immorality.

अनीश्वरवाद m. atheism.

अनीश्वरवादी adj. atheistic. m. atheist.

अनुकंपा f. 1. compassion. 2. kindness, clemency.

अनुकरण m. imitation, copying.

अनुकरणीय adj. 1. imitable. 2. ideal, exemplary; ~ प्रयास exemplary effort.

अनुकर्ता m. imitator.

अनुकूल adj. 1. favourable. 2. suitable.

अनुकूलता f. 1. favourableness. 2. suitability.

अनुक्रम m. order, succession, sequence.

अनुक्रमणिका f. 1. sequence. 2. index.

अनुगमन m. 1. act of following (on the heels). 2. induction.

अनुगामी adj. following, obedient. m. follower.

अनुगृहीत adj. obliged.

अनुग्रह m. favour, grace.

अनुचर m. 1. attendant. 2. follower.

अनुचिंतन m. recalling.

अनुचित adj. 1. improper. 2. unreasonable.

अनुच्छेद m. paragraph.

अनुज m. younger brother.

अनुजा f. younger sister.

अनुज्ञा f. 1. permission. 2. licence.

अनुज्ञेय adj. permissible.

अनुतान m. intonation.

अनुताप m. 1. penitence. 2. repentance, remorse.

अनुतोष m. 1. gratification. 2. relief.

अनुत्तरदायी adj. irresponsible.

अनुत्तीर्ण adj. not passed, failed, plucked,

अनुत्पादक adj. unproductive.

अनुदात्त adj. not sublime.

अनुदान m. grant.

अनुदार adj. 1. not liberal, not generous. 2. conservative.

अनुदारता f. conservatism.

अनुदिन adv. daily.

अनुनय m. entreaty; ~ करना to entreat, to implore, to beseech.

अनुनय-विनय m. earnest entreaty, humble supplication.

अनुनाद m. resonance.

अनुनादित adj. resounded.

अनुनासिक adj. nasal; ~ ध्वनि nasal sound.

अनुपजाऊ adj. unfertile.

अनुपम adj. 1. matchless. 2. excellent.

अनुपयुक्त adj. 1. unfit, unsuitable. 2. improper.

अनुपयोगी adj. useless, of no use.

अनुपस्थित adj. absent.

अनुपस्थिति f. absence; ~ में in absence/absentia.

अनुपात m. 1. ratio. 2. proportion.

अनुपाती adj. proportional (Math).

अनुपादेय adj. useless.

अनुपादेयता f. uselessness.

अनुपान m. fluid vehicle in medicine, a drink taken with or after the medicine.

अनुपार्जित adj. unearned.

अनुपालन m. compliance, observance.

अनुपूरक adj. supplementary.

अनुप्रयुक्त adj. applied.

अनुप्रयोग m. application, use.

अनुप्राणित adj. influenced or imbued with life; ~ करना to imbue with life.

अनुप्रास m. alliteration.

अनुबंध m. 1. contract; ~ करना to make a contract. 2. condition. 3. appendage.

अनुबंध-पत्र m. document of contract, deed.

अनुबद्ध adj. tied up.

अनुभव m. experience; ~ करना to feel, to experience.

अनुभवसिद्ध adj. established by experience, empirical.

अनुभवहीन adj. inexperienced.

अनुभवहीनता f. inexperience.

अनुभवी adj. experienced.

अनुभाग m. section.

अनुभागीय adj. sectional.

अनुभाजन m. apportionment.

अनुभाव m. ensuent response.

अनुभूत adj. felt; ~ करना to experience.

अनुभूति f. 1. feeling, perception. 2. emotional experience.

अनुमत adj. permitted.

अनुमति f. permission.

अनुमान m. guess, conjecture; मेरा ~ ग़लत निकला I guessed wrong.

अनुमानित adj. estimated.

अनुमेय adj. estimable.

अनुमोदक m. seconder.

अनुमोदन m. seconding; ~ करना to second, to support.

अनुयान adj. trailer.

अनुयायी m. 1. follower. 2. supporter or disciple.

अनुरक्त adj. attached, fond (of), devoted (to).

अनुरक्ति f. attachment, fond-ness, devotion, affection.

अनुराग m. attachment, fondness, devotion.

अनुरागमय adj. 1. attached, fond of, devoted. 2. devotional.

अनुरागी adj. loving, devoted.

अनुराधा f. the seventeenth of the twenty-seven constellations.

अनुरूप adj. similar.

अनुरूप, के postposition. conformable to, conforming to; आशा के ~ as per expectation; निर्णय के ~ conformable to the judgement.

अनुरूपता f. 1. resemblance, similarity. 2. conformity.

अनुरोध m. (pressing) request; ~ करना to request earnestly; ~ स्वीकार करना to accept a pressing request.

अनुर्वर adj. unfertile, unproductive.

अनुलग्न adj. annexed.

अनुलेप m. ointment.

अनुलोम adj. 1. in due order. 2. agreeable, favourable; ~ विवाह marriage between a man of high caste and a woman of lower caste.

अनुवर्ती adj. 1. following. 2. succeeding.

अनुवाद m. translation.

अनुवादक m. translator.

अनुवादित adj. = अनूदित।

अनुवाद्य adj. translatable, worthy to be translated.

अनुवेदन m. commiseration.

अनुवेश m. entry.

अनुशंसा f. recommendation.

अनुशंसित adj. recommended.

अनुशासक m. disciplinarian.

अनुशासन m. 1. submission to authority. 2. discipline.

अनुशासनबद्ध adj. disciplined.

अनुशासन-भंग m. breach of discipline.

अ

अनुशासनहीन adj. indisciplined.

अनुशासनहीनता f. indiscipline.

अनुशासनात्मक adj. disciplinary.

अनुशासनिक adj. disciplinary.

अनुशासित adj. disciplined; ~ करना to discipline.

अनुशीलन m. repeated or careful study.

अनुश्रुत adj. legendary.

अनुश्रुति f. legend.

अनुषंग m. 1. association. 2. incidence.

अनुष्ठान m. any activity one has undertaken for religions purpose, undertaking.

अनुसंधान m. investigation, research; ~ केंद्र research centre.

अनुसंधायक m. investigator.

अनुसरण m. act of following; ~ करना to follow.

अनुसार, के postpositon. (i) according to; गीता के ~ according to Geeta, (ii) in conformity with; क्या उसका आचरण क़ानून के ~ ठीक था? Was his conduct in conformity with the law?

अनुसूचित adj. scheduled; ~ जातियाँ scheduled castes.

अनुसूची f. schedule.

अनुसूया f. jealousy.

अनुस्मरण m. 1. action of re-collecting. 2. something remembered.

अनुस्यूत adj. 1. sewn. 2. plaited, braided, intertwined.

अनुस्वार m. a nasal character of the Nāgari alphabet; it always follows a vowel; its sign is a dot on the headline of a letter (–)

अनुहार m. likeness.

अनूठा adj. unique.

अनूठापन m. uniqueness, rareness, curiousness.

अनूढ़ adj. unmarried.

अनूढ़ा f. unmarried woman, esp. in love with someone.

अनूदित adj. translated; अंग्रेज़ी से ~ translated from English.

अनूप adj. unequalled, unique.

अनृत adj. false, untrue.

अनेक adj. many, several; ~ बार many times.
pron. a large number of people or things.

अनेकता f. 1. numerousness. 2. diversity; ~ में एकता unity in diversity.

अनेकपदी adj. polypod.

अनेकरूप adj. multiform.

अनेकरूपता f. multiformity.

अनेकविध adj. varied, multifarious.

अनेकार्थक adj. having several meanings.

अनेकेश्वरवाद m. polytheism.

अनेकेश्वरवादी adj. polytheistic.
m. polytheist.

अनैक्य m. 1. discord, disunity. 2. disagreement.

अनैच्छिक adj. 1. unintended. 2. involuntary.

अनैतिक adj. immoral.

अनैतिकता f. 1. immoral act, immorality. 2. immoral behaviour.

अनैतिहासिक adj. unhistorical.

अनैसर्गिक adj. unnatural.

अनोखा adj. peculiar, queer.

अनोखापन m. peculiarity, queerness.

अनौचित्य m. 1. impropriety. 2. improper act.

अनौचित्यपूर्ण adj. improper.

अनौपचारिक adj. 1. informal; ~ बात-चीत informal talk. 2. un-official; ~ टेस्ट मैच unofficial test match.

अनौपचारिकता f. informal act, informality.

अन्न m. 1. food. 2. corn, grain.

अन्न-जल m. means of sustenance; उसका ~ यहाँ से उठ गया है The venue of his sustenance has shifted from here. ~ छोड़ना या ग्रहण न करना to give up taking food and water.

अन्नदाता m. sustainer, supporter, benefactor.

अन्नप्राशन m. ceremony of administering (non-liquid) food to an infant for the first time.

अन्नमय adj. made of grains; ~ शरीर the gross material body.

अन्न-वस्त्र m. food and clothing.

अन्नसंकट m. food famine, food crisis.

अन्य adj. other, different; ~ देशीय alien; ~ पुरुष third person. (Gram.)

अन्यतम adj. best.

अन्यतर adj. another.

अन्यत्र adv. somewhere else, elsewhere.

अन्यत्र-स्थिति f. alibi.

अन्यथा conj. otherwise.

अन्यमनस्क adj. absent-minded, indifferent.

अन्यमनस्कता f. absent-minded-ness.

अन्यान्य adj. many others.

अन्याय m. 1. injustice; ~ करना to do injustice/tyranny. 2. an unjust act, wrong.

अन्यायपूर्ण adj. 1. unjust, unjustifiable. 2. inequitable.

अन्यायपूर्वक adv. unjustly.

अन्यायमूलक adj. 1. unjust. 2. inequitable.

अन्यायी adj. unjust, oppressive, tyrannous.
n. unjust person, tyrant.

अन्योक्ति f. allegory.

अन्योन्य adj. one another, each other, mutual, reciprocal; ~ प्रजनन cross-breeding.

अन्योन्याश्रय m. interdependence.

अन्योन्याश्रित adj. interdependent.

अन्वय m. 1. logical connection of cause and effect. 2. connection, relation. 3. prose order (gram.)

अन्वित adj. related, connected.

अन्विति f. relation, connection.

अन्वेषक m. explorer.

अन्वेषण m. exploration.

अन्वेषित adj. explored.

अन्वेषी m. = अन्वेषक।

अन्वेष्य adj. explorable.

अपंग adj. crippled, disabled.

अपकर्म m. wrong act.

अपकर्ष m. downfall.

अपकर्षक adj. derogatory.

अपकर्षण m. deterioration, degradation.

अ

अपकार m. wrong act, harm or disservice, injury; ~ करना—तुमने मेरा ~ किया है You have done me a wrong.

अपकारी adj. & m. wrong-doer.

अपकीर्ति f. infamy, disrepute, ignominy.

अपक्व adj. 1. unripe. 2. imm-ature.

अपक्वता f. immaturity.

अपगति f. 1. plight. 2. downfall.

अपघटित adj. decomposed.

अपघर्षण m. abrasion.

अपघात m. violent death.

अपच m. indigestion, dyspepsia.

अपचार m. delinquency, aberration.

अपटु adj. inexpert, unskilled.

अपठनीय adj. not worth reading.

अपठित adj. unread, unseen.

अपढ़ adj. unlettered, uneducated.

अपतुष्टि f. appeasement.

अपत्य m. offspring.

अपथ्य m. unwholesome food.

अपदस्थ adj. deposed; ~ करना to depose.

अपनत्व m. = अपनापन।

अपनयन m. 1. kidnapping. 2. abduction.

अपना adj. & pron. 1. one's own, 2. personal; 3. self; उसने अपनी हजामत बनाई He shaved himself; ~ किया पाना to reap what one sows; ~ क्या जाता है What do we lose? ~ बनाना—मुझे अपना बना लो Regard me as thine own. ~ वक्त भूल जाना—अपना वक्त भूल गए Have you forgotten your own case? ~ समझना—मुझे अपना समझो Treat me as thine own; ~ -सा मुँह लेकर लौट आना—वह अपना-सा मुँह लेकर लौट आया He returned with his hopes shattered.

अपनाना vt. to adopt as one's own; मैं तुम्हारा ढंग अपनाऊँगा I shall adopt your method. अपना लेना to own.

अपनापन m. feeling of oneness with others.

अपना-पराया adj. (distinction between) one's own and other's.

अपनापा m = अपनापन।

अपनाम m. bad name, ill-fame.

अपभाषण m. vituperation, scurrility.

अपभ्रंश m. an old Indo-Aryan language.

अपमान m. insult, disgrace; ~ करना to insult.

अपमानजनक adj. insulting.

अपमानित adj. insulted, disgraced, ~ करना to insult.

अपमृत्यु f. unnatural death.

अपयश m. disgrace, ill-fame.

अपयशकर adj. disgraceful.

अपरंपार adj. boundless, infinite, limitless.

अपर adj. 1. additional. 2. other, different.

अपरदन m. corrosion.

अपरनिषेचन m. cross-fertilization.

अपराजित adj. unconquered, undefeated.

अपराजेय adj. unconquerable; unbeatable.

अपराध m. 1. offence. 2. crime, guilt.

अपराधशील adj. criminal; ~ जातियाँ criminal tribes.

अपराधिक adj. criminal.
अपराधी adj. & m. offender, criminal; ~ ठहराना to hold (someone) guilty.
अपराह्न m. afternoon.
अपरिग्रह m. habit or tendency not to accumulate anything for one's personal use, renunciation.
अपरिचय m. lack of acquaintance.
अपरिचित adj. unacquainted, unfamiliar. m. stranger.
अपरिपक्व adj. 1. unripe. 2. immature.
अपरिपक्वता f. immaturity.
अपरिमित adj. immense.
अपरिमितता f. immensity.
अपरिवर्तनीय adj. unchangeable.
अपरिवर्तित adj. unchanged.
अपरिष्कृत adj. not refined, unrefined, crude, impure.
अपरिहार्य adj. unavoidable.
अपरिहार्यता f. unavoidability.
अपरीक्षित adj. untested, untried.
अपरोक्ष adj. direct.
अपर्याप्त adj. inadequate.
अपर्याप्तता f. inadequacy.
अपलक adv. without a blink, unblinkingly.
अपलेख m. libel.
अपवचन m. slander.
अपवर्त्य m. multiple (math).
अपवाद m. exception; ~ के रूप में as an exception.
अपवादस्वरूप adv. as an excep-tion, यह बात ~ है This is an exception.
अपवादिक adj. exceptional.
अपवादी adj. exceptional.
अपवाह m. catchment, drainage; ~ क्षेत्र catchment area.
अपवित्र adj. impious, unholy.
अपवित्रीकरण m. desecration.
अपव्यय m. extravagance.
अपव्ययी adj. extravagant.
अपशकुन m. ill-omen, jinx.
अपशकुनकारक adj. ill-omened.
अपशब्द m. 1. dirty word, abuse. 2. abusive language.
अपसंचय m. hoarding.
अपसंचयी adj. hoarder.
अपस्फीति f. deflation.
अपस्मार m. epilepsy.
अपहरण m. kidnapping, abduction.
अपहर्ता m. kidnapper, abductor.
अपहृत adj. kidnapped, abducted.
अपाक adj. unholy, impure.
अपाठ्य adj. illegible.
अपात्र adj. unworthy or unfit.
अपात्रता f. 1. ineligibility. 2. unworthiness.
अपादान m. gram. ablative (case).
अपार adj. boundless.
अपारदर्शिता f. opacity.
अपारदर्शी adj. opaque.
अपारिभाषिक adj. nontechnical.
अपार्थिव adj. unearthly.
अपालन m. non-observance, non-execution.
अपाहिज adj. crippled, disabled.
अपि adv. & conj. 1. also, too. 2. though. 3. but, however.
अपितु conj. 1. but, however. 2. yet, even then.
अपील f. appeal; ~ करना to appeal.
अपुत्र adj. childless.

अ

अपुष्ट adj. 1. not nourished. 2. unconfirmed; ~ समाचार unconfirmed news.

अपूर्ण adj. 1. imperfect; ~ भूत past imperfect. 2. incomplete; ~ वाक्य incomplete sentence.

अपूर्णता f. 1. imperfection. 2. incompleteness.

अपूर्व adj. 1. quite new, novel. 2. extraordinary, unprece-dented.

अपेक्षया adv. relatively, comparatively.

अपेक्षा f. expectation, require-ment.

अपेक्षा, की postposition. in comparison to, com-paratively.

अपेक्षाकृत adv. relatively, comparatively; हिंदी ~ सरल है Hindi is relatively easy.

अपेक्षित adj. 1. required, desired. 2. due.

अपौरुषेय adj. nonhuman i. e. of divine origin; शास्त्र ~ हैं Shastras are divine.

अपौष्टिक adj. unnutritive.

अप्रकट adj. not apparent, unmanifested, hidden.

अप्रकाशित adj. 1. unlighted. 2. unpublished.

अप्रकृत adj. unnatural, artificial.

अप्रगतिशील adj. unprogressive.

अप्रगतिशीलता f. unprogressive-ness.

अप्रचलन m. non-currency, obsoleteness.

अप्रचलित adj. out of use, not current.

अप्रतिम adj. unequalled, un-surpassed.

अप्रतिष्ठा f. disgrace, ill-repute, infamy.

अप्रतिष्ठित adj. disgraced, ill-reputed; ~ करना to disgrace or disrespect.

अप्रत्यक्ष adj. 1. latent, not evident. 2. indirect.

अप्रत्याशित adj. unexpected.

अप्रभावी adj. ineffective.

अप्रयुक्त adj. unused.

अप्रशिक्षित adj. untrained.

अप्रसन्न adj. unhappy.

अप्रसन्नता f. displeasure, unhappiness.

अप्रसम adj. abnormal.

अप्रसिद्ध adj. not famous.

अप्रस्तुत adj. 1. not ready. 2. indirect.

अप्राकृतिक adj. unnatural.

अप्राप्य adj. 1. not available. 2. rare. 3. unattainable.

अप्रामाणिक adj. not authentic, unauthentic.

अप्रायिक adj. unusual.

अप्रासंगिक adj. irrelevant.

अप्रिय adj. 1. undesirable, disa-greeable. 2. unpleasant.

अप्रैल m. April.

अप्रौढ़ adj. immature.

अप्सरा f. nymph, fairy.

अफरना vi. to inflate (with gas).

अफरा m. accumulation of wind in the stomach.

अफरा-तफरी f. hurry-scurry, haste; उसने ~ में भोजन किया He took a hurried meal.

अफ़वाह f. rumour.

अफ़सर m. officer.

अफ़सरी f. 1. official authority, officialdom. 2. official duty.

अफ़साना m. story, tale.

अफ़सोस m. regret, sorrow. inter. alas!

अफ़ीम f. opium.

अफ़ीमची m. opium-addict.

अफ़ीमी adj. related to opium.

अफ़्रीकी adj. African.

अफ़्रेशियाई adj. Afro-Asian.

अब adv. now, just now; ~ से from now on, henceforth.

अबद्ध adj. untied, loose.

अबरक m. mica.

अबला f. weaker sex (woman).

अबवाब m. cess, tax, rate.

अबाध adj. 1. unobstructed, unrestricted. 2. absolute.

अबाधित adj. = अबाध।

अबीर m. mica-powder.

अबे interj. hey! ~ तबे करना to use discourteous or disparaging words or expressions.

अबोध adj. 1. innocent. 2. unintelligent.

अबोधगम्य adj. unintelligible.

अबोध्य adj. incomprehensible.

अबोला m. absence of speaking terms.

अब्द m. year; ~ कोश year-book.

अब्धि m. ocean.

अब्बा m. father.

अब्बा जान m. respectful form of addressing (one's) father.

अब्बासी adj. smoke-blue.

अब्राह्मण m. non-Brahmin.

अभंग adj. unbroken.

अभंगुर adj. infrangible.

अभक्ष्य adj. 1. uneatable, inedible. 2. forbidden (food).

अभद्र adj. indecent, impolite.

अभद्रता f. 1. indecency, impoliteness. 2. indecent act.

अभय adj. fearless. m. fearlessness.

अभागा adj. unfortunate, accursed, ill-fated. [Fem. अभागिन, अभागिनी, अभागी]

अभाज्य adj. indivisible.

अभारतीय adj. non-Indian.

अभाव m. 1. absence, lack, want. 2. scarcity.

अभावग्रस्त adj. scarcity-stricken.

अभावुक adj. unemotional.

अभिकरण m. agency.

अभिकर्ता m. agent.

अभिक्रिया f. reaction.

अभिगम m. access.

अभिगृहीत adj. 1. acquired. 2. postulate (maths.).

अभिग्रहण m. acquisition.

अभिचार m. black magic, exorcism.

अभिचारी m. exorcist, conjurer.

अभिजागर m. invigilator.

अभिजात adj. of or belonging to nobility.
m. a noble, aristocrat; ~ तंत्र aristocracy; ~ वर्ग nobility.

अभिज्ञ adj. (one) who knows, cognisant, well-versed.

अभिज्ञता f. knowledge, cognisance, conversance.

अ

अभिज्ञान m. 1. recognition. 2. token of recognition.
अभिदेश m. reference.
अभिधा f. 1. name. 2. denotation.
अभिधान m. 1. name, designation. 2. dictionary, lexicon.
अभिनंदन m. ceremonious offering of felicitations; ~ -ग्रंथ felicitation volume; ~ -पत्र welcome address.
अभिनंदनीय adj. praiseworthy, laudable.
अभिनय m. acting in a drama; ~ करना to act or perform.
अभिनव adj. novel, quite new.
अभिनिर्णय m. judgment.
अभिनिर्णायक m. umpire.
अभिनिवेश m. close attention.
अभिनीत adj. staged, enacted.
अभिनेता m. actor.
अभिनेत्री f. actress.
अभिनेय adj. actable, stageable.
अभिनेयता f. stageability.
अभिन्न adj. 1. non-different. 2. inseparable. 3. integral; कश्मीर भारत का ~ अंग है Kashmir is an integral part of India. 4. close, intimate; ~ मित्र close or fast friend.
अभिन्नता f. oneness, identity.
अभिप्राय m. 1. intention. 2. purpose. 3. meaning.
अभिप्रेत adj. intended; उसे यही अभिप्रेत था This is what he intended.
अभिभव m. decline, fall.
अभिभावक m. guardian.
अभिभाषण m. formal address.
अभिभूत adj. overwhelmed.
अभिमंत्रित adj. consecrated.
अभिमत m. (formal) opinion.
अभिमान m. 1. pride. 2. vanity.
अभिमानी adj. 1. proud. 2. vain, arrogant. [Fem. अभिमानिनी]
अभियंता m. engineer.
अभियांत्रिकी f. engineering.
अभियान m. 1. campaign; चुनाव ~ election campaign. 2. expedition; ~ दल expedition party.
अभियुक्त adj. & m. accused.
अभियोक्ता m. accuser.
अभियोग m. accusation, charge; ~ लगाना to accuse.
अभियोग-पत्र m. charge sheet.
अभियोजक m. accuser.
अभियोजन m. prosecution.
अभियोज्य adj. prosecutable.
अभिराम adj. charming.
अभिरुचि f. interest.
अभिरोपण m. supplanting.
अभिलषित adj. aspired, desired.
अभिलाषा f. aspiration, desire; ~ करना to aspire/desire.
अभिलाषी adj. aspirant, desirous.
अभिलेख m. record; ~ अधिकरण court of records; ~ पाल record-keeper.
अभिलेखक m. recorder.
अभिलेखन m. recording.
अभिलेखागार m. archives.
अभिलेखालय m. record-room.
अभिवादन m. 1. salutation, adoration. 2. salute; ~ करना to salute; परस्पर ~ करना to exchange greetings.
अभिवृत्ति f. attitude.
अभिवृद्धि f. 1. increase. 2. growth.

अभिव्यंजक adj. expressive.

अभिव्यंजना f. expression; ~ वाद expressionism; ~ शक्ति power of expression.

अभिव्यंजित adj. expressed.

अभिव्यक्त adj. expressed; ~ करना to express/reveal.

अभिव्यक्ति f. 1. expression. 2. manifestation.

अभिशप्त adj. cursed.

अभिशाप m. curse, calumny.

अभिषेक m. 1. coronation; राज्याभिषेक coronation of a king. 2. consecration.

अभिसंधि f. conspiracy, plot.

अभिसमय m. convention (esp. written one).

अभिसार m. 1. meeting, union. 2. rendezvous, tryst.

अभिसारिका f. woman, who goes to meat her lover clandestinely.

अभिसारी adj. convergent. (Maths.)

अभिहित adj. called, addressed.

अभी adv. 1. just now. 2. still; अभी समय है There is still time. 3. yet.

अभीप्सक adj. aspirant.

अभीप्सा f. aspiration.

अभीप्सित adj. aspired.

अभीष्ट adj. cherished. m. cherished thing or object, goal.

अभुक्त adj. unused, unutilised.

अभूत adj. non-existent.

अभूतपूर्व adj. unprecedented.

अभेद्य adj. impenetrable, impregnable; ~ दुर्ग impregnable fort.

अभौतिक adj. non-physical, non-material.

अभ्यंतर adj. inner, internal. m. interior, onside.

अभ्यर्थन m. 1. begging, solicitation, entreaty, prayer. 2. asking for a vote.

अभ्यर्थना f. entreaty, prayer, petition.

अभ्यर्थी m. candidate.

अभ्यस्त adj. 1. accustomed. 2. skilled and experienced.

अभ्यागत m. visitor, guest.

अभ्यास m. 1. practice. 2. ex-ercise. 3. habit.

अभ्युदय m. 1. rise (esp. of a luminary). 2. progress, prosperity.

अभ्रंकष m. sky-scraper.

अभ्र m. 1. cloud. 2. sky.

अमंगल adj. inauspicious. m. inauspiciousness.

अमंगलकारी adj. inauspicious.

अमचूर m. dried parings of raw mango; ~ की कली piece of dried mango fruit.

अमन m. peace.

अमन-चैन m. peace and tranquillity.

अमनस्क adj. 1. indifferent. 2. gloomy.

अमर adj. immortal.

अमरता f. immortality.

अमरबेल f. parasite creeper.

अमराई f. mango-grove.

अमरीकन m. American.

अमरीकी adj. American.

अमरूद m. guava.

अमर्त्य adj. immortal.

अ

अमर्यादित adj. 1. unlimited. 2. unrestrained.

अमर्ष m. anger, resentment.

अमल m. 1. acting upon; ~ करना to act upon; ~ में लाना to implement; 2. addiction. 3. clean, stainless.

अमला m. member of the staff.

अमली adj. practical.

अमांगलिक adj. inauspicious.

अमात्य m. minister.

अमानक adj. nonstandard.

अमानत f. anything given in trust; ~ में ख़यानत करना to commit a breach of trust (by misappropriation).

अमानतदार m. trustee.

अमानती adj. that which is entrusted.

अमानवीय adj. inhuman.

अमानी f. system of work in which payment is made on daily wages basis irrespective of amount of work done.

अमानुषिक adj. inhuman, beastly, barbarous.

अमानुषिकता f. inhumanity, inhuman behaviour.

अमान्य adj. 1. unacceptable. 2. invalid; ~ करना to invalidate.

अमान्यकरण m. invalidation.

अमापनीय adj. immeasurable.

अमापित adj. unmeasured.

अमाप्य adj. immeasurable.

अमालनामा m. character roll (esp. in the form of a book).

अमावट f. solidified mango juice made out into cakes.

अमावस f. = अमावस्या।

अमावस्या f. last day of the dark half of a month.

अमिट adj. indelible.

अमित adj. immense, immeasurable, enormous.

अमितव्ययी adj. unthrifty, unfrugal, one who squanders.

अमिताभ adj. having immeasurable brilliance. m. Lord Buddha.

अमिश्रित adj. unmixed, unadulterated.

अमीन m. bailiff.

अमीर adj. wealthy, rich. m. 1. nobleman. 2. chieftain.

अमीर-उमरा m. (plu.) the nobility.

अमीर-ग़रीब m. (plu.) the rich and the poor, haves and have-nots.

अमीरज़ादा m. 1. son of a richman. 2. an aristocrat.

अमीराना adj. rich-like, aristocratic; ~ ठाठ aristocratic splendour.

अमीरी f. 1. wealthiness, richness. 2. nobility.

अमुक adj. such and such.

अमूर्त adj. abstract, intangible.

अमूल्य adj. invaluable, very precious.

अमृत m. nectar, ambrosia.

अमृतबान m. jar (esp. of china clay).

अमोघ adj. infallible, unfailing.

अमोल adj. priceless.

अम्माँ f. mother.

अम्ल adj. sour, acid. m. 1. sourness. 2. acid. 3. acidity.

अम्लता f. acidity.

अम्लीकरण m. acidification.

अम्लीय adj. acidic.

अम्हौरी f. prickly heat.

अयशस्कर adj. disgraceful, ignominious.

अयाचित adj. unasked for, unsolicited.

अयाना adj. not mature or responsible, childish.

अयाल m. the hair on the neck of a horse, lion etc., mane.

अयुक्तियुक्त adj. unreasonable.

अयोग्य adj. 1. unfit, unworthy. 2. ineligible, unqualified. 3. disqualified; ~ ठहराना to disqualify.

अयोग्यता f. 1. unfitness, unworthiness. 2. inability. 3. disqualification.

अयोनिज adj. non-placental.

अरंडी f. castor oil plant.

अरक़ m. distilled extract/essence of a substance; ~ उतारना / खींचना to extract by distillation.

अरक्षित adj. 1. insecure. 2. unreserved.

अरगनी f. clothes-line.

अरज़ f. = अर्ज़।

अरज़ी f. = अर्ज़ी।

अरण्य m. jungle, forest.

अरण्यरोदन m. cry in the wilderness.

अरथाना vt. to explain the meaning.

अरथी f. bier.

अरदली m. orderly, peon.

अरदास f. prayer.

अरना m. wild buffalo.

अरब m. Arab. adj. & m. billion.

अरबपति m. billionaire.

अरबी f. Arabic language. adj. belonging to the Arabs, Arabian.

अरमान m. cherished desire.

अरविंद m. lotus flower.

अरवी f. a kind of taro (plant).

अरसा m. a long period of time.

अरसिक adj. (one) incapable of relishing things, dry and prosaic.

अरस्तू m. Aristotle.

अरहट m. water drawing wheel.

अरहर f. a kind of corn used mostly as a pulse, red gram.

अराजक adj. anarchical, anarchistic.

अराजकता f. anarchy.

अराजकतावाद m. anarchism.

अराजकतावादी adj. & m. anarchist.

अराजनीतिक adj. non-political.

अराजपत्रित adj. non-gazetted.

अराष्ट्रीय adj. anti-national.

अरि m. enemy, foe.

अरिष्ट m. 1. a distilled mixture. 2. enemy.

अरी interj. form of informal address like 'Hullo, Hei, Hi' (sply. for females).

अरुचि f. 1. lack of interest. 2. aversion, dislike.

अरुचिकर adj. 1. disagreeable, unpleasant, unpalatable. 2. uninteresting.

अरुण adj. reddish, scarlet; ~ ज्वर scarlet fever.

अरुणशिखा m. cock.

अरुणाभ adj. ruddy, reddish.

अरुणिमा f. reddish glow (of the dawn)

अ

अरुणोदय m. 1. rising of the sun. 2. dawn.

अरे interj. 1. a form of informal address like 'Hullo, Hei, Hi'. (sply. for males). 2. an exclamation of surprise; ~ भई! a form of informal address.

अरोचक adj. uninteresting.

अर्क m. the sun.

अर्गला f. clog, draw bar, bolt.

अर्घ m. 1. price, worth. 2. libation; ~ देना to offer libation.

अर्चन m. propitiation.

अर्चना f. propitiation.

अर्ज़ f. 1. request, prayer; ~ करना to request. 2. width.

अर्जन m. (act of) earning.

अर्जित adj. earned.

अर्ज़ी f. application.

अर्ज़ीदावा m. plaint.

अर्ज़ीनवीस m. petition writer.

अर्णव m. ocean.

अर्थ m. 1. meaning, import.

अर्थगर्भित adj. pithy, full of meaning.

अर्थदंड m. fine, monetary punishment.

अर्थनीति f. economic policy.

अर्थपिशाच m. heartless miser.

अर्थमंत्री m. Finance Minister.

अर्थलिप्सा f. greed, cupidity.

अर्थवान adj. meaningful.

अर्थविकार m. semantic change.

अर्थविज्ञान m. semantics.

अर्थविज्ञानी m. semanticist.

अर्थ-विधेयक m. money bill.

अर्थ-व्यवस्था f. economy.

अर्थशास्त्र m. economics.

अर्थशास्त्री m. economist.

अर्थशास्त्रीय adj. pertaining to economics, economic.

अर्थसंकट m. economic crisis.

अर्थसिद्धि f. fulfilment of a desire (esp. monetary).

अर्थहीन adj. meaningless.

अर्थांतर m. different meaning.

अर्थागम m. proceeds.

अर्थात् conj. namely, that is to say.

अर्थापत्ति f. logical result, corollary.

अर्थालंकार m. figure of speech depending on meaning.

अर्ध adj. used as prefix, half, semi, bi; ~ नग्न half-naked.

अर्धकुशल adj. semi-skilled.

अर्धचंद्र m. half moon, crescent; ~ देना to give the right about.

अर्धनारीश्वर m. Lord Shiva represented as half himself and half his spouse, Parvati.

अर्धवृत्त adj. semi-circle.

अर्धवृत्ताकार adj. semi-circular.

अर्धव्यास m. semi-diameter, radius.

अर्ध-शिक्षित semi-educated.

अर्ध-साप्ताहिक adj. bi-weekly.

अर्धांगिनी f. better half, wife.

अर्धाली f. half part of a चौपाई।

अर्पण m. 1. act of offering. 2. surrendering.

अर्पित adj. 1. offered. 2. surrendered.

अर्बुद m. 1. tumour. 2. one thousand million, a billion.

अर्राना vi. to crash down with a loud noise.

अर्वाचीन adj. modern, recent.

अर्श m. piles (disease).

अर्सा m. = अरसा।

अर्हंत m. Lord Buddha.

अर्ह adj. qualified.

अर्हता f. qualification.

अलंकरण m. ornamentation.

अलंकार m. 1. ornament. 2. figure of speech.

अलंकारशास्त्र m. tropology, rhetorics.

अलंकारशास्त्री m. rhetorician.

अलंकृत adj. 1. ornamented. 2. decorated, adorned.

अलंघ्य adj. impassable, insurmountable.

अलक f. lock of hair, curl.

अलकतरा m. coal-tar, tar.

अलकली m. alkali.

अलका f. 1. lass (between 8 and 10 years of age). 2. domicile of Kuber (God of wealth).

अलक्षित adj. unobserved, unmarked; ~ करना to put out of sight.

अलक्ष्य adj. 1. invisible. 2. unobserved, unmarked, unnoticed.

अलख adj. invisible, imperceptible; ~ जगाना (i) to invoke God by constantly repeating the word अलख; (ii) to beg, in the name of God.

अलग adj. 1. different. 2. apart, separated.

अलगनी f. clothes-line.

अलग़रज़ adj. careless.

अलग़रज़ी f. carelessness.

अलगाना vt. to disjoin/separate.

अलगाव m. 1. separation.

अलगाववादी adj. separatist; ~ आंदोलन a separatist movement. m. one who advocates secession, separatist.

अलतई adj. deep carmine.

अलता m. red dye.

अलबत्ता conj. nevertheless, of course.

अलबम m. album.

अलबेला adj. peculiarly attractive, frivolous.

अलभ्य adj. 1. not obtainable. 2. rare, scarce.

अलम adj. enough, sufficient.

अलमस्त adj. carefree, free from anxieties.

अलमारी f. almirah.

अलल-टप्पू adj. haphazard.

अलस adj. lazy, idle, sluggish.

अलसाना vi. to feel dull and sleepy, to feel drowsy; अलसाई आँखें drowsy eyes.

अलसी f. linseed.

अलहदगी f. separateness, separation.

अलहदा adj. of different type, separate.

अलाप m. augmentation (Music).

अलाभकर adj. unprofitable.

अलार्म m. alarm; ~ घड़ी alarm clock/time-piece.

अलाव m. camp-fire.

अलावा, के postpositon. in addition to, besides, apart from; इसके अलावा (i) besides this, (ii) further more.

अलि f. female friend. m. black-bee.

अलिखित adj. unwritten.

अलिजिह्वा f. uvula.

अलीक adj. false, incorrect.

अलील adj. indisposed, ailing.

अलोकप्रिय adj. unpopular.

अलोना adj. unsalted.

अलोप adj. disappeared.
m. disappearance.

अलौकिक adj. supernatural.

अलौह adj. non-ferrous.

अलौहिक adj. = अलौह।

अल्टिमेटम m. ultimatum.

अल्प adj. small, short; ~ मात्रा small quantity.

अल्पक adj. 1. diminutive. 2. minimum.

अल्पकालिक adj. short-lived, temporary, provisional.

अल्पजीवी adj. short-lived.

अल्पज्ञ adj. & m. knowing little, having a superficial knowledge.

अल्पतम adj. minimum, minimal.

अल्पता f. 1. smallness, shortness. 2. shortage.

अल्पप्राण adj. unaspirate (consonant).

अल्पबुद्धि adj. imbecile, silly.

अल्पमत m. minority.

अल्पवय adj. under-age

अल्पवयस्क m. minor.

अल्पवयस्कता f. (age of) minority.

अल्पविराम m. comma.

अल्पसंख्यक adj. in a minority; ~ वर्ग a minority community.
m. a person belonging to a smaller faction.

अल्पायु adj. short-lived.
f. short (span of) life.

अल्पार्थक adj. diminutive.

अल्पावधिक adj. short-term.

अल्पावस्था f. young age.

अल्पाहार m. short meal, refreshment.

अल्पाहारी adj. abstemious, moderate in food and drink.

अल्युमीनियम m. aluminium.

अल्ल m. family name.

अल्ला m. Almighty, God (Muslim mythology); ~ को प्यारा हो जाना to be a darling of the Almighty, as it were; to leave this world for the hereafter; अल्ला हो अकबर God is Great.

अल्लाताला m. God, the Great.

अल्हड़ adj. behaving like a child, childishly simple.

अवकाश m. 1. leisure; ~ मिलना to get leisure. 2. recess. 3. scope. 4. space, gap.

अवकाश-ग्रहण m. retirement; ~ करना to retire.

अवकाश-प्राप्त adj. retired.

अवकाश-प्राप्ति f. retirement.

अवकीर्ण adj. scattered.

अवगत adj. aware, apprised; ~ कराना to put (someone) wise.

अवगति f. 1. awareness. 2. comprehension.

अवगाहन m. immersion, plunging.

अवगुंठन m. veil, mask.

अवगुंठित adj. masked, veiled.

अवगुण m. demerit, defect.

अवचेतन m. subconscious; ~ मन subconscious mind.

अवज्ञा f. disobedience, defiance.

अवज्ञाकारी adj. disobedient.

अवतरण m. 1. descent. 2. lan-ding.

अवतरित adj. descended; ~ होना to appear as God incarnate.

अवतल adj. concave.

अवतार m. incarnation; ~ लेना to appear as God incarnate.

अवतारवाद m. theory of incarnation.

अवतीर्ण adj. 1. descended. 2. incarnated.

अवदान n. 1. contribution. 2. gift.

अवध m. region round Ayodhya, birth-place of God Ram.
adj. that cannot be killed or slaughtered.

अवधान m. attention.

अवधारणा f. 1. concept. 2. ascertainment, deter-mination.

अवधि f. 1. limit. 2. period, term.

अवधी f. a dialect of Hindi, spoken in अवध; the language in which the Ram-Charit-Manas of Tulsi Das is written.

अवधूत m. one who has re-nounced worldly connections.

अवनत adj. bowed down.

अवनति f. 1. downfall. 2. degradation, decadence, decline.

अवनि f. earth.

अवमान m. 1. contempt. 2. humiliation.

अवमानव m. subman.

अवमानित adj. 1. disregarded. 2. humiliated.

अवमान्य adj. fit for being disregarded.

अवमूल्यन m. devaluation.

अवयव m. limb, component, part.

अवयस्क adj. underage, minor.

अवयस्कता f. the state of being under the age of full legal responsibility, minority.

अवर adj. 1. inferior. 2. deputy.

अवरुद्ध adj. 1. blocked, ob-structed. 2. confined.

अवरोधक adj. causing obstruction/ hindrance/obstacle.

अवरोधी m. obstructionist.

अवरोह m. descent.

अवरोहण m. act of descending.

अवरोही adj. descending.

अवर्ण adj. colourless.

अवर्णनीय adj. indescribable.

अवलंब m. support, mainstay.

अवलंबन m. dependence.

अवलंबित adj. dependent.

अवलि, अवली f. 1. line, row. 2. range. 3. series.

अवलेह m. jelly.

अवलोकन beholding.

अवलोकना vt. to behold.

अवलोकनार्थ adv. for being seen.

अवशिष्ट adj. remaining, residual. m. residue.

अवशेष m. 1. remainder, residue. 2. remains.

अवश्यंभावी adj. inevitable.

अवश्य adv. necessarily, certainly, definitely.

अवश्यमेव adv. by all means, certainly, surely.

अवसन्न adj. 1. benumbed. 2. dispirited, dejected.

अवसन्नता f. 1. benumbedness.

2. dispiritedness, dejection.

अवसर m. 1. occasion, 2. opportunity, 3. chance.

अवसरवादी m. opportunist. adj. opportunistic.

अवसाद m. 1. gloom. 2. depression.

अवसादजनक adj. 1. causing gloom. 2. depressive.

अवसान m. expiry, end, termination; दिवस के ~ पर When the day is gone.

अवस्था f. 1. condition, situation. 2. position. 3. phase, state.

अवस्थान m. 1. situation. 2. station. 3. stage.

अवस्थित adj. 1. situated. 2. existing.

अवहार m. armistice, truce.

अवहेलना f. intentional disregard, ~ करना to disregard.

अवांछनीय adj. undesirable, unwelcome.

अवांछित adj. undesired, unwelcome.

अवांतर adj. 1. intermediary. 2. extraneous.

अवाक्, अवाक adj. 1. speechless, mute. 2. won-derstruck.

अवास्तविक adj. 1. unreal. 2. imaginary.

अविकल adj. 1. exactly the same, identical; ~ प्रतिलिपि exact/true copy. 2. whole, entire.

अविकसित adj. undeveloped.

अविकारी adj. not subject to variation/change.

अविकृत adj. unimpaired, not deformed.

अविगत adj. not gone off; present.

अविचल adj. 1. motionless. 2. firm, resolute.

अविचलित adj. 1. unperturbed, 2. firm, steadfast.

अविचारित adj. not well-considered.

अविचारी adj. indiscreet.

अविचार्य adj. unthinkable.

अविच्छिन्न adj. uninterrupted, unbroken; ~ रूप से constantly.

अविच्छेद्य adj. that cannot be separated, unbreakable.

अविजित adj. unconquered.

अविदित adj. unknown, hidden.

अविद्यमान adj. 1. not present, 2. not existing.

अविद्या f. ignorance.

अविधिक adj. illegal, unlawful.

अविनय m. immodesty, impoliteness.

अविनयी adj. immodest, impolite, rude.

अविनश्वर adj. = अविनाशी।

अविनाशी adj. 1. imperishable. 2. eternal, immortal.

अविनीत adj. 1. immodest, impolite. 2. rude, unruly.

अविन्यस्त adj. 1. unarranged. 2. deranged.

अविभक्त adj. undivided.

अविभाजित adj. undivided.

अविभाज्य adj. indivisible.

अविरत adj. unceasing, perpetual.

अविरल adj. 1. uninterrupted. 2. continuous.

अविराम adj. non-stop, incessant.

अविलंब adv. without delay.

अविलेय adj. insoluble.

अविवाद्य adj. indisputable.
अविवाहित adj. unmarried. [Fem. अविवाहिता]
अविवेक m. want of discrimination, indiscretion.
अविवेकी adj. indiscreet.
अविश्वसनीय adj. unreliable.
अविश्वस्त adj. untrustworthy.
अविश्वास m. lack of confidence, distrust; ~ प्रस्ताव no confidence motion.
अविश्वासी n. infidel.
अविस्मरणीय adj. unforgettable.
अवृष्टि f. drought.
अवैज्ञानिक adj. unscientific.
अवैतनिक adj. honorary; ~ पद honorary post.
अवैध adj. 1. illegal, unlawful. 2. illegitimate, illicit.
अवैधता f. 1. illegality, unlawfulness. 2. illegitimacy.
अवैधाचरण m. illegal practice.
अवैधानिक adj. unconstitutional.
अव्यक्त adj. 1. not expressed. 2. obscure.
अव्यक्तिक adj. impersonal.
अव्यय adj. indeclinable. m. an indeclinable word.
अव्ययीभाव m. compound word of which the first member is indeclinable, e.g. यथासाध्य।
अव्यवस्था f. 1. disorder, lawlessness. 2. confusion.
अव्यवस्थित adj. 1. disordered, chaotic. 2. fickle. 3. unmethodical.
अव्यवहार्य adj. impracticable.
अव्याख्येय adj. inexplicable.
अव्यावहारिक adj. 1. not practical, impracticable. 2. unrealistic.
अव्वल adj. first; ~ आना to come out first.
अशंक adj. fearless, bold.
अशंकनीय adj. unquestionable.
अशकुन m. ill/bad omen.
अशक्त adj. weak.
अशक्य adj. improbable.
अशरफ़ी f. a gold coin, sovereign.
अशरीरी adj. without body, incorporeal.
अशस्त्रीकरण m. disarmament.
अशांत adj. agitated, disturbed.
अशांति f. unrest, disturbance.
अशास्त्रीय adj. nonclassical.
अशिक्षा f. illiteracy.
अशिक्षित adj. illiterate.
अशिव adj. inauspicious.
अशिष्ट adj. immodest, rude.
अशिष्टता f. 1. immodesty, impoliteness. 2. a rude act.
अशुचि adj. impure.
अशुचिता f. impurity.
अशुद्ध adj. 1. impure. 2. incorrect, wrong; ~ प्रयोग wrong use/usage.
अशुद्धता f. 1. impurity. 2. inaccuracy.
अशुद्धि f. mistake, error.
अशुभ adj. inauspicious, ominous, sinister.
अशुभचिंतक adj. & m. (one) who wishes ill.
अशेष adj. 1. without a remainder. 2. complete, finished.
अशोक adj. without sorrow, merry-go-lucky. m. a tree, the

अ

leaves of which are used on religious occasions.

अशोचनीय adj. deplorable, distressing.

अशोभन adj. unbefitting, bad.

अश्मरी f. calculus (stone).

अश्रद्धा f. lack of faith.

अश्रांत adj. 1. tireless. 2. incessant, continuous.

अश्रु m. tear.

अश्रुगैस f. tear gas

अश्रुत adj. unheard.

अश्रुधारा f. stream of tears.

अश्रुपात m. flow of tears.

अश्रुपूर्ण adj. tearful.

अश्रुपूरित adj. tearful; ~ स्वागत tearful welcome.

अश्लिष्ट adj. disconnected.

अश्लील adj. obscene; ~ चित्र obscene picture.

अश्लीलता f. obscenity.

अश्व m. horse; ~ पालन horse-breeding; ~ मेध horse sacrifice; ~ शक्ति horse-power; ~ शाला stable.

अश्वगंधा f. a medicinal plant.

अश्वत्थामा m. son of Dron, a warrior of the Mahabharat.

अश्वारोही m. rider, horseman.

अश्वेत adj. nonwhite, black skinned.

अष्ट adj. & m. eight.

अष्टपाद m. octopod.

अष्टबाहु m. octopus.

अष्टभुज m. octagon.

अष्टमी f. eighth day of the dark or bright fortnight (lunar).

अष्टांग m. the eight branches of योग।

असंख्य adj. numberless, innumerable, countless.

असंगत adj. 1. irrelevant. 2. inconsistent.

असंगति f. 1. irrelevance. 2. inconsistency.

असंघटित adj. unorganised, disorganised.

असंतुलन m. disequilibrium.

असंतुलित adj. unbalanced.

असंतुष्ट adj. dissatisfied, discontented, disgruntled.

असंतोष m. 1. dissatisfaction, discontent. 2. unrest.

असंतोषजनक adj. unsatisfactory.

अंसतोषप्रद adj. unsatisfactory.

असंतोषी adj. 1. malcontent, discontented. 2. insatiable.

असंदिग्ध adj. unambiguous.

असंबद्ध adj. unconnected, irrelevant; ~ प्रलाप irrelevant prattle.

असंबद्धता f. irrelevancy.

असंभव adj. (utterly) impos-sible.

असंभावना f. improbability, impossibility.

असंभावित adj. unlikely, unexpected.

असंभाव्य adj. improbable.

असंयत adj. unrestrained.

असंयम m. lack of self-control, intemperance.

असंयमित adj. unrestrained, immoderate.

असंयमी adj. intemperate.

असंस्कृत adj. unrefined, uncultured.

असगंध f. a medicinal plant.

असत adj. 1. non-existing. 2. untrue.

असतत adj. discontinuous.
असत्य adj. untrue.
m. untruth.
असत्यवादी adj. & m. untruthful (person).
असफल adj. unsuccessful.
असफलता f. unsuccessfulness, failure.
असबाब m. traveller's baggage, luggage.
असभ्य adj. uncivilized, savage; ~ बनाना to decivilize.
असभ्यता f. incivility, savageness.
असमंजस m. suspense; ~ में पड़ना या पड़ जाना to be in suspense.
असम adj. 1. disparate. 2. unequal. 3. uneven. m. an Indian state.
असमता f. 1. disparity. 2. inequality.
असमय adv. 1. untimely. 2. before time.
असमयोचित adj. untimely, inopportune.
असमर्थ adj. 1. unable. 2. helpless.
असमर्थता f. 1. inability. 2. helplessness.
असमान adj. unequal, dissimilar.
असमानता f. inequality, dissimilarity.
असर m. 1. effect.
असल adj. 1. real, true. 2. genuine. m. the principal amount.
असलियत f. reality, truth.
असली adj. 1. real, true. 2. genuine, 3. pure.
असहनशील adj. unforbearing, intolerant.
असहनीय adj. unbearable, intolerable.
असहमत adj. disagreeing.
असहमति f. lack of approval, disagreement.
असहयोग m. non-cooperation; ~ आंदोलन non-cooperation movement.
असहाय m. helpless.
असहिष्णु f. intolerant.
असहिष्णुता f. intolerance.
असह्य adj. unbearable, intolerable.
असांसदीय adj. unparliamentary.
असाढ़ m. fourth month of the Hindu calendar.
असाधारण adj. 1. uncommon, unusual. 2. remarkable.
असाधु adj. 1. (person) not good, wicked. 2. (word or use) improper, not happy.
असाध्य adj. incurable, irremediable.
असामंजस्य m. incompatibility.
असामयिक adj. untimely; ~ मृत्यु untimely death.
असामान्य adj. uncommon, unusual, extraordinary.
असामी m. 1. tenant. 2. client.
असार adj. unsubstantial, unreal. m. sign, symptom.
असारता f. insignificance, unsubstantiality, futility.
असावधान adj. 1. careless, inattentive. 2. negligent.
असावधानी f. 1. carelessness, inattentiveness. 2. negligence.
असिद्ध adj. not proved, wrong.
असीम adj. limitless, boundless.
असीमित adj. unlimited, limitless, boundless.
असीस f. blessing, benediction;

अ

~ देना to bless; ~ लेना to receive benedicition.

असुंदर adj. ugly, dull.

असुर m. demon.

असुरक्षा f. insecurity.

असुरक्षित adj. insecure, unsafe.

असुविधा f. 1. inconvenience; ~ जनक inconvenient. 2. difficulty.

असूया f. spite, envy, malice.

अस्त adj. sunk; सूर्य का ~ होना setting of the sun; भाग्य का ~ होना sinking of the star (of fortune).

अस्तबल m. stable.

अस्तर m. lining (clothes).

अस्त-व्यस्त adj. 1. scattered here and there. 2. in great disorder.

अस्ताचल m. the mythological hill behind which the sun is supposed to set.

अस्ति f. existence, being.

अस्तित्व m. existence.

अस्तु adv. well, let it be so, now.

अस्तुति f. ill-speaking, slander.

अस्तेय m. abstention from theft.

अस्त्र m. weapon; ~ शस्त्र arms, armament; ~ शाला arsenal.

अस्त्रागार m. arsenal, armoury.

अस्त्रीकरण m. militarisation.

अस्थायी adj. 1. temporary. 2. provisional. 3. unstable.

अस्थि f. bone.

अस्थिपंजर m. skeleton.

अस्थिभंग m. fracture of a bone.

अस्थिर adj. not firm, unstable.

अस्थिरता f. 1. instability. 2. restlessness.

अस्थिशेष adj. reduced to a skeleton.

अस्पताल m. hospital; ~ गाड़ी ambulance.

अस्पष्ट adj. 1. not clear, indistinct. 2. illegible.

अस्पष्टता f. 1. lack of clarity, indistinctness. 2. illegibility.

अस्पृश्य adj. untouchable.

अस्पृश्यता f. untouchability.

अस्पृह adj. innocent.

अस्फुट adj. 1. inarticulate. 2. (flower) unblossomed; ~ विचार indistinct thought.

अस्मत f. chastity.

अस्मिता f. self-esteem, ego.

अस्वस्थ adj. unhealthy, indisposed.

अस्वस्थता f. indisposition, illness.

अस्वाभाविक adj. 1. unnatural. 2. artificial.

अस्वाभाविकता f. 1. unnatural behaviour. 2. artificiality.

अस्वीकार adj. not accepted.

अस्वीकृत adj. not accepted, rejected or refused.

अस्वीकृति f. denial, non-acceptance, refusal.

अस्सी adj. & m. eighty.

अहं m. ego.

अहंकार m. self- conceit.

अहंभाव m. ego.

अहंमन्य adj. egotistic.

अहंमन्यता f. egotism.

अहदी adj. lazy, slothful.

अहम adj. significant, important.

अहमक़ adj. stupid, foolish.

अहमियत f. importance.

अहलकार m. member of the staff, official (of a law-court).

अहस्तांतरणीय adj. not transferable.

अहा inter. good! Oh! alas!

अहाता m. compound, enclosure.

अहिंसक adj. non-violent.

अहिंसा f. non-violence.

अहिंसात्मक adj. non-violent.

अहिंसावादी adj. non-violent. m. believer in non-violence.

अहिंस्र adj. 1. non-carnivorous. 2. not fierce, harmless.

अहि m. serpent, snake.

अहित m. harm. damage, injury; ~ चाहना to mean ill.

अहितकर adj. harmful.

अहिवात m. woman's state when her husband is alive (suhag).

अहीर m. a Hindu subcaste, whose usual occupation is milk selling.

अहेतुक adj. 1. without any motive, gratuitous, 2. performed freely.

अहेर m. hunting.

अहेरी m. hunter.

आ

आ The second vowel of the Nagri alphabet; its sound resembles that of a in 'father'.

आँकड़ा m. data, statistics; कच्चे आँकड़े rough data; पक्के आँकड़े exact figures/data.

आँकना vi. to estimate/assess.

आँख f. 1. eye. 2. eyesight, vision. 3. inner eye; उसे ~ नहीं है He has no inner eye. 4. eye of a needle. 5. joint (in a plant) shaped like a human eye; ~ आना ophthalmia; उसकी आँख आ गई है He is suffering from ophthalmia. ~ उठाकर देखना to cast a glance; ~ ऊँची न कर सकना to have no courage to raise one's eyes; ~ का अंधा blind despite having eyes. ~ का डेला eye-ball; ~ का तारा (i) apple of the eye. (ii) darling, pet; ~ कान खुले रखना keeping eyes and ears open, being on the alert; ~ का परदा उठ जाना (i) being lost to all sense of shame; (ii) being disillusioned; ~ का पानी उतर/ढल/मर जाना being lost to all sense of shame; ~ न लगना not to get a wink of sleep; ~ पड़ना—मेरी ~ उस पर पड़ी My eye fell on her. ~फड़कना pulsation in the eye; ~ मारना (i) to wink; (ii) to give the glad eye, to wink amorously; ~ मिचना—उसकी ~ मिच गई He died. ~ मिलाना—वह मुझ से ~ नहीं मिला सकता He connot look me in the eye. ~ मीचना to close one's eye.

आँख-मिचौनी f. hide and seek; ~ खेलना to play hide and seek.

आँगन m. courtyard.

आँच f. 1. heat. 2. flame. 3. fire.

आँचल m. 1. border. 2. one end of the sari which usually covers a woman's breast; उसने ~ से छाती ढक ली She covered her breast with the sari.

आंचलिक adj. regional, pro-vincial.

आँजना vt. to apply collyrium (to the eyes).

आँट f. 1. knot. 2. misunderstanding.

आंटी f. 1. reel of thread. 2. fold of dhoti round the waist. 3. (Eng.) aunt.

आँड़ू adj. uncastrated.

आँत f. intestine.

आंतरिक adj. inner, internal.

आंदोलन m. 1. agitation;

आंदोलनकारी m. 1. agitator. 2. one who participates in a movement.

आँधी f. windstorm; ~ ख़त्म हो गई है The windstorm is over. ~ आना—आँधी आई है Windstorm has set in.

आंध्र m. Andhra, an Indian State.

आंध्रवासी m. an inhabitant of आंध्र।

आंध्रीय adj. of or pertaining to आंध्र।

आँव m. mucus

आँय-बाँय-शाँय f. nonsence; वह ~

करके रह गया He talked nothing but nonsence.

आँवल m. placenta.

आँवलनाल f. navel-string.

आँवला m. emblic myrobalan tree and its fruit.

आँवाँ m. kiln.

आंशिक adj. partial.

आँसू m. tear; ~ आना—आँखों में आँसू आ गए Tears came to the eyes. ~ गिरना falling of tears; ~ छलकना—आँसू छलक पड़े Tears welled up.

आइंदा adv. in future.

आइस्क्रीम f. ice-cream.

आईना m. looking glass, mirror.

आकंठ adv. 1. up to the throat. 2. up to the brim.

आक m. a kind of plant.

आकर-ग्रंथ m. source book.

आकर-भाषा f. source lan-guage.

आकर्ण adj. & adv. upto the ears.

आकर्षक adj. attractive.

आकर्षण m. attraction.

आकर्षण-केंद्र m. centre of attraction, cynosure (of all eyes).

आकर्षित adj. = आकृष्ट।

आकलन m. estimation.

आकलित adj. estimated.

आकस्मिक adj. accidental, sudden.

आकांक्षा f. aspiration, ambi-tion; ~ करना to aspire.

आकांक्षित adj. aspired.

आकांक्षी adj. aspirant.

आक़ा m. master, lord.

आकार m. size.

आकार-प्रकार m. size and shape.

आकाश m. 1. space. 2. sky.

आकाशकुसुम m. non-existent object, an object which exists in imagination (illusion) only.

आकाशगंगा f. the Milky Way.

आकाशदीप m. high hanging lamp.

आकाशमंडल m. celestial sphere.

आकाशवाणी f. 1. voice from heaven. 2. All India Radio.

आकाशवृत्ति f. haphazard livelihood.

आकीर्ण adj. 1. scattered all around. 2. filled; कंटकाकीर्ण filled with thorns, thorny.

आकुंचन m. contraction.

आकुंचनशील adj. contractile.

आकुल adj. eager, anxious; ~ हो जाना to become anxious.

आकुलता f. eagerness, anxiety.

आकृति f. figure, form, shape.

आकृष्ट adj. attracted.

आक्रंदन m. weeping, crying.

आक्रमण m. attack, invasion.

आक्रमणकारी m. attacker, invader.

आक्रांत adj. 1. attacked. 2. afflicted.

आक्रामक adj. aggressive.

आक्रोश m. resentment, wrath.

आक्षिप्त adj. projected.

आक्षेप m. allegation, charge.

आक्सीकरण m. oxidation.

आक्सीजन m. oxygen.

आखात m. gulf.

आख़िर adv. & conj. 1. after all. 2. at last.

आख़िरकार adv. & conj. after all, eventually.

आख़िरी adj. last.

आख़ीर m. end, termination.

आखेट m. the act of hunting.

आखेट-यात्रा f. hunting expedi-tion.

आखेटक m. hunter.

आख्या f. 1. name. 2. report.

आख्यान m. legend, fable.

आख्यायिका f. tale, story.

आगंतुक m. new-comer, visitor, guest.

आग f. fire; ~ उगलना to spit fire; ~ जलना (of fire) to burn; ~ जलाना to light/ignite fire; ~देना to light the funeral pyre.

आगज़नी f. arson.

आगम m. 1. coming, arrival. 2. income.

आगमन m. 1. arrival. 2. advent. 3. induction (logic).

आगा m. front, frontage.

आग़ा m. 1. chieftain, chief. 2. inhabitant of Afganistan.

आग़ाज़ m. beginning, start.

आगा-पीछा m. hesitation, hesitance; ~ करना to waver/hesitate.

आगामी adj. forthcoming, next.

आगार m. store.

आगाह adj. apprised, warned; ~ करना to apprise/warn.

आगे adv. 1. ahead, onward. 2. afterwards.

आगे, के postposition. 1. in front of. 2. before.

आगे-पीछे adv. 1. sooner or later. 2. in rapid succession.

आगे-पीछे, के postposition. accompanied by; उसके ~ बराबर दस-पाँच आदमी रहते हैं He is always accompanied by a few followers.

आग्नेयास्त्र m. fire-arm.

आग्रह m. earnest insistence; वह काम मैंने तुम्हारे ही ~ पर किया I did it but only at your insistence.

आग्रहपूर्वक adv. with due insistence.

आघात m. 1. blow. 2. shock. 3. attack (of a disease).

आचमन m. sipping (water from the palm of the hand with some religious object in view).

आचमनीय adj. worth sipping.

आचरण m. 1. conduct; उसका ~ प्रशंसनीय था His conduct was praiseworthy. 2. character; ~ पंजी character roll.

आचार m. 1. conduct; दुराचार bad conduct; सदाचार good conduct. 2. custom, customary law.

आचारभ्रष्ट adj. debased.

आचारवान्, आचारवान adj. virtuous.

आचार-विचार m. conduct and temperament.

आचार-संहिता moral code, code of conduct.

आचारशास्त्र m. ethics.

आचार्य m. professor.

आचार्यत्व m. professorship.

आच्छन्न adj. covered.

आच्छादन m. a covering.

आच्छादित adj. covered; मेघाच्छादित overcast with clouds.

आज adv. &. m. today.

आज-कल adv. &.m. now-a-days.

आजन्म adv. 1. since birth. 2. till life persists.

आज़माइश f. trial, test.

आज़माना vt. to try/test.

आजा m. paternal grandfather.

आज़ाद adj. independent, free.

आज़ादी f. independence, freedom.

आजानुबाहु adj. having very long arms (esp. extending to the knees.)

आजीवन adj. lifelong. adv. throughout one's life.

आजीविका f. means of subsistence, livelihood; पत्रकारिता ही उसकी ~ है Journalism is his livelihood.

आज्ञा f. 1. order. 2. permission.

आज्ञाकारी adj. obedient.

आज्ञानुवर्ती adj. obedient.

आज्ञानुसार, के postposition. as per order, as ordered.

आज्ञापालक adj. obedient.

आज्ञापालन m. obedience.

आज्ञाभंग m. 1. violation of an order. 2. disobedience.

आज्ञार्थक adj. imperative.

आज्ञावर्ती adj. obedient.

आटा m. flour, wheat-flour.

आटा-चक्की f. flour-mill.

आटोप m. pomp, ostentation.

आठ adj &. m. eight; ~ आठ आँसू रोना to shed profuse tears; आठों पहर all the twenty four hours, round the clock.

आठवाँ adj. eighth.

आडंबर m. ostentation.

आडंबरपूर्ण adj. ostentatious, showy.

आड़ f. 1. screen. 2. cover, shelter.

आड़ा adj. 1. horizontal. 2. oblique.

आडिटर m. auditor.

आड़ू m. peach.

आढ़त f. 1. agency, brokerage. 2. commission earned in an agency or brokerage.

आढ़तिया m. commission agent.

आणविक adj. molecular; ~ शस्त्रास्त्र molecular weapons.

आतंक m. 1. terror. 2. panic.

आतंकवाद m. terrorism.

आतंकवादी adj. & m. terrorist.

आतंकित adj. terror-stricken.

आतंकी adj. & m. terrorist.

आततायी m. tyrant, oppressor.

आतप m. heat.

आतपस्नान m. sun-bath.

आतिथ्य m. hospitality.

आतिथ्य-सत्कार m. respectful hospitality.

आतिश f. fire.

आतिशबाज़ m. manufacturer or dealer of fireworks.

आतिशबाज़ी f. fireworks; ~ छोड़ना to set off fireworks.

आतिशी शीशा m. a piece of glass which focusses the rays of the sun for producing fire.

आतुर adj. eager.

आतुरता f. eagerness.

आत्म adj. 1. pertaining to the soul. 2. of oneself. m. soul.

आत्मकथा f. autobiography.

आत्मकल्याण m. good of the self.

आत्मकेंद्रित adj. self-centered.

आत्मगत adj. subjective.

आत्मगौरव m. self-respect.

आत्मग्लानि f. remorse, compunction.

आत्मघात m. suicide.

आत्मघाती adj. suicidal.

आत्मचरित m. autobiography.
आत्मचिंतन m. self-contemplation.
आत्मचेतन adj. self-conscious.
आत्मचेतना f. self-consciousness.
आत्मज m. son.
आत्मजा f. daughter.
आत्मज्ञान m. self-knowledge, self-realisation.
आत्मतुष्ट adj. self-satisfied.
आत्मतुष्टि f. self-satisfaction.
आत्मत्याग m. 1. self-denial. 2. self-sacrifice.
आत्मदमन m. self-repression.
आत्मदर्शन m. knowledge of one's self.
आत्मनिग्रह m. self- control.
आत्मनिरीक्षण m. introspection.
आत्मनिर्भर adj. 1. self-sufficient. 2. self-reliant.
आत्मनिर्भरता f. 1. self-sufficiency, independence. 2. self-reliance.
आत्मनिष्ठ adj. subjective.
आत्मपीड़क m. masochist.
आत्मप्रदर्शन m. self-display, exhibitionism.
आत्मप्रवंचना f. self-deception.
आत्मप्रशंसा f. self-praise.
आत्मबल m. spiritual power.
आत्मबलिदान m. self-sacrifice.
आत्मबलिदानी m. one who is ready to sacrifice oneself for a good cause.
आत्मबोध m. enlightenment (of the self).
आत्मरक्षा f. self-defence.
आत्मवंचना f. self-deception.
आत्मविश्वास m. self-confidence.
आत्मविश्वासी adj. self-confident.
आत्मविस्मृत adj. self-forgetful, oblivious of self.
आत्मशक्ति f. willpower.
आत्मशुद्धि f. self-purification.
आत्मश्लाघा f. self-praise.
आत्मसंतोष m. self-satisfaction.
आत्मसंयम m. ability to control one's behaviour, self-control.
आत्मसंयमी adj. exercising self-control, self-controlled.
आत्मसमर्पण m. surrender.
आत्मसमीक्षा f. introspection.
आत्मसम्मान m. self-esteem.
आत्मसात् adj. assimilated; ~ करना to assimilate.
आत्मसुधार m. self-improve-ment.
आत्मसेवी adj. & m. self-seeker.
आत्मस्तुति f. self-praise.
आत्मस्वीकृति f. confession.
आत्महत्या f. suicide.
आत्मा f. 1. soul, spirit. 2. ghost. 3. conscience.
आत्मीय adj. intimate, very close.
आत्मीयता f. feeling of oneness, close affinity, fellow-feeling.
आत्मोत्कर्ष m. self-elevation.
आत्मोत्सर्ग m. self-sacrifice.
आदत f. habit.
आदतन adv. habitually.
आदम m. 1. the first man. 2. man. 3. Adam; बाबा ~ के ज़माने का of old times, of prehistoric times.
आदमक़द adj. of human size.
आदमख़ोर adj. & m. man-eater, cannibal.
आदमी m. 1. person, man. 2. servant. 3. worker. 4. husband.

आदमीयत f. the quality of being human, humanity.

आदर m. respect, regard.

आदरणीय adj. respected.

आदर-भाव m. high regard.

आदर-सत्कार m. hospitality.

आदर-सम्मान m. due respect.

आदर्श adj. & m. ideal.

आदर्शवाद m. idealism.

आदर्शवादी adj. idealistic. m. idealist.

आदाता m. receiver.

आदान m. act of receiving.

आदान-प्रदान m. receiving and giving, give and take.

आदाब m. salutation, compliments.

आदि m. beginning; ~ से अंत तक from beginning to the end. adv. et cetera.

आदिकल्प m. archaeozoic era.

आदिकवि m. the first poet, Valmiki.

आदित्य m. the sun.

आदिम adj. primitive.

आदिवासी adj. aboriginal; ~ जनजातियाँ aborigines. m. aborigine.

आदिष्ट adj. ordered.

आदी adj. accustomed, habituated. f. = अदरक।

आदृत adj. respected, honoured.

आदेश m. command, order; ~ देना (i) to order, (ii) to place an order.

आदेशानुसार, के postposition. as per order, as directed.

आद्यंत adv. from beginning to end.

आद्योपांत adv. from beginning to end, from start to finish; वह पुस्तक मैंने एक ही बैठक में ~ पढ़ डाली I read the book from beginning to end in one sitting.

आधा adj. half; ~ - आधा fifty-fifty; आधी टिकट child ticket; आधी रात को at midnight.

आधार m. 1. base. 2. basis, ground; किस ~ पर on what basis. 3. support.

आधारभूत adj. basic, funda-mental.

आधारभूमि f. base.

आधारशिला f. foundation stone.

आधारस्तंभ m. 1. main stay. 2. backbone.

आधारहीन adj. baseless, groundless, unfounded.

आधासीसी adj. hemicrania.

आधि f. mental agony; ~ दैविक supernatural; ~ भौतिक physical.

आधिकारिक adj. 1. official. 2. authoritative.

आधिक्य m. excess.

आधिपत्य m. 1. possession. 2. sway; ~ जमाना to hold (one's) sway.

आधुनिक adj. 1. of the present times, modern. 2. of a recent style.

आधुनिकता f. modernity.

आध्यात्मिक adj. spiritual.

आध्यात्मिकता f. spirituality.

आध्यात्मिकी f. spiritualism.

आनंद m. 1. happiness, joy, delight. 2. bliss, ecstasy.

आनंदकंद m. root of bliss.

आनंददायक adj. delightful, pleasant.

आनंदपूर्वक adv. happily.

आ

आनंदप्रद adj. delightful, pleasant.

आनंद-मंगल m. happiness and welfare.

आनंदमग्न adj. immersed in joy.

आनंदमय adj. blissful, full of joy, jubilant.

आनंद-मेला m. fete.

आनंदातिरेक m. boundless joy.

आनंदाश्रु m. (plu.) tears of joy.

आनंदित adj. delighted, glad.

आनंदोत्सव m. festivity.

आन f. honour, prestige.

आनन m. face.

आनन-फ़ानन adv. instanta-neously, without delay.

आन-बान f. elegance, pomp and show.

आनरेरी adj. & f. honorary. [H. E. अवैतनिक]

आनवाला adj. (one) who keeps his word of honour.

आना vi. 1. to come. 2. to fit; यह जूता मेरे पैर में नहीं आता This shoe does not fit me. 3. to know; उसे अंग्रेज़ी नहीं आती He does not know English. 4. to occur; ऐसा नहीं कि उसके दिमाग़ में यह बात न आई हो Not that it did not occur to him. 5. to feel; मुझे नींद आ रही है I feel like sleeping.

m. an act of coming; कैसे ~ हुआ? How did you happen to come?

आनाकानी f. putting off through pretexts.

आना-जाना m. 1. coming and going. 2. arrival and departure. 3. the act of visiting each other regularly.

आनी-जानी adj. transient, temporary; यह दुनिया ~ है This world is transient.

आनुतोषिक m. gift, present.

आनुपातिक adj. proportional.

आनुपूर्वी adj. successive; शब्दानुपूर्वी literal.

आनुवंशिक adj. hereditary.

आनुवंशिकता f. heredity.

आनुषंगिक adj. incidental, contingent.

आप (AP) pron. you.

आपकाजी adj. selfish.

आपत् f. = आपात।

आपत्ति f. objection.

आपत्तिकर्ता m. a person who objects, objector.

आपत्तिजनक adj. objectionable.

आपदा f. calamity, misfortune.

आपद्ग्रस्त adj. beset by diffi-culties.

आप-बीती f. 1. one's own life story.

आपरेशन m. surgical operation.

आपस adv.; ~ का between two or more persons (usu. intimate); ~ में mutually.

आपसदारी f. mutual relationship/dealings; ~ की बातें mutual affairs.

आपसवाला adj. & m. one's own (person).

आपसी adj. mutual.

आपा m. ego.

आपात m. 1. serious happening. 2. emergency.

आपातकाल m. period of emergency.

आपात-स्थिति f. emergency.

आपादमस्तक adv. cap-a-pie, from head to foot.

आपाधापी f. state of confusion or disorder in which everyone is seeking his own interest; सब लोग ~ में लगे थे Everyone was intent upon his own interest.

आपूरित adj. supplied.

आपूर्ण adj. full to the brim.

आपूर्ति f. supply.

आपेक्षिक adj. relative; ~ घनत्व relative density.

आप्त adj. 1. got. 2. reliable.

आप्तकाम adj. gratified.

आप्रवास m. immigration.

आप्रवासी m. an immigrant.

आप्लावन m. inundation.

आप्लावित adj. inundated.

आप्सरिक adj. nymphal.

आफ़त f. trouble, calamity.

आफ़िस m. office.

आफ़िसर m. officer.

आब m. 1. water. 2. lustre, brilliance; उसके चेहरे पर ~ है There is lustre on his face.

आबकारी f. excise; ~ महकमा excise department.

आबदस्त m. water used for cleaning oneself after defectation; ~ लेना to use water as a wash (in place of toilet paper).

आबदार adj. lustrous.

आबद्ध adj. 1. tied up. 2. joined, linked.

आबनूस m. ebony.

आबनूसी adj. jet-black.

आबपाशी f. irrigation.

आबरू f. 1. honour, dignity. 2. modesty, chastity.

आबाद adj. inhabited, populated.

आबादी f. population.

आबालवृद्ध m. (plu.) children and elders all.

आबेहयात m. nectar.

आबोदाना m. livelihood; उसका ~ यहाँ से उठ चला है He has to go somewhere else for his livelihood.

आबोहवा f. climate; यहाँ की ~ मेरे लिए उपयुक्त नहीं Here the elimate is unsuitable to me.

आभरण m. ornament.

आभा f. splendour, lustre.

आभामंडल m. halo.

आभार m. obligation.

आभार-प्रदर्शन m. expression of gratitude/indebtedness.

आभारी adj. obliged, grateful; ~ होना to feel obliged/grateful.

आभास m. inkling, hunch, hint, vague idea.

आभूषण m. ornament.

आभूषित adj. richly ornamen-ted; ~ करना to ornament.

आभ्यंतरिक adj. inner, internal.

आमंत्रण m. invitation, calling.

आमंत्रित adj. invited, called; ~ करना to invite.

आम m. mango. adj. 1. general; ~ चुनाव general election. 2. common; ~ आदमी common man. 3. public. खुले ~ publicly, in public.

आमद f. 1. income. 2. arrival.

आमदनी f. income; ~ और ख़र्च income and expenditure.

आमदरफ़्त f. traffic.
आमना-सामना m. 1. face to face meeting. 2. encounter.
आमने-सामने adv. facing each other, face to face.
आम-फ़हम adj. common.
आमरण adv. & adj. till death; ~ अनशन fast unto death.
आमरस m. mango juice.
आमर्ष m. 1. resentment. 2. wrath, rage.
आमवात m. a disease characterized by inflammation and pain of the joints, rheumatism and the like.
आमात्य m. counsellor, minister.
आमाशय m. a large sack like organ in the belly, stomach.
आमिष m. flesh, meat.
आमिषभोजी adj. 1. non-vegeta-rian, meat-eater. 2. carnivorous.
आमीन interj. amen!
आमुख m. preamble.
आमूल adj. drastic, radical.
आमोद m. amusement, pleasure.
आमोदकारी adj. amusing, pleasing.
आमोद-प्रमोद m. merriment, gaiety.
आम्र m. mango.
आय f. income.
आयकर, m. income tax.
आयकरदाता m. income tax payer.
आयत m. rectangle.
आयतन m. volume.
आयताकार adj. rectangular.
आयन m. ion.
आय-व्यय m. income and ex-penditure.
आय-व्ययक m. budget.
आय-स्रोत m. source of income.
आया f. nurse, female attendant. adj. of आना; आए दिन often.
आया-गया m. visitor; हमारे यहाँ ~ लगा ही रहता है One or other visitor is always at our door.
आयात m. 1. import. 2. importation.
आयातकर्ता m. importer.
आयात-निर्यात m. import and export.
आयात-शुल्क m. import duty.
आयातित adj. imported.
आयाम m. dimension.
आयास m. exertion, effort; बिना ~ के effortlessly.
आयु f. span of life, age.
आयुक्त m. commissioner.
आयुध m. arms, weapon.
आयुर्वेद m. Ayurved, ancient Indian Medical Science.
आयुर्वेदिक adj. pertaining to Ayurved.
आयुष्मती adj. fem. of आयुष्मान।
आयुष्मान्, आयुष्मान adj. having a long span of life.
आयुष्य m. 1. age. 2. life-force.
आयोग m. commission; विधिक ~ legal commission.
आयोजक m. 1. organiser. 2. planner. 3. convener.
आयोजन m. meeting, conference.
आयोजना f. 1. = आयोजन। 2. plan.
आयोजित adj. 1. convened. 2. organised. 3. planned.
आरंभ m. 1. beginning. 2. origin.
आरंभिक adj. 1. elementary, initial. 2. preparatory.

आरक्त adj. red.

आरक्षण m. reservation.

आरक्षित adj. reserved; ~ करना to reserve.

आरज़ू f. longing.

आरण्यक adj. pertaining to a jungle/ forest.

आरती f. 1. ceremonial adoration with kindled lamp(s); ~ उतारना to offer homage (with a view to please). 2. a pot in which a wick is kindled.

आर-पार adj. 1. across; देश के ~ across the country. 2. final, decisive; ~ की लड़ाई decisive war. adv. from one side to another; ~ करना to go cross.

आरब्ध adj. begun, commenced.

आरसी f. 1. mirror. 2. a ring-like thumb ornament fitted with a mirror.

आरा m. saw; आरे से चीरना to saw.

आराकश m. sawyer.

आराज़ी f. land.

आराधना f. 1. worship. 2. adoration.

आराधनीय adj. adorable.

आराध्य adj. adorable.

आराम m. 1. rest; मैं ज़रा ~ कर रहा हूँ I am just resting a bit. ~ हराम है Rest is taboo. 2. comfort. 3. relief. 4. peace[illegible] दिन ~ से कट रहे हैं I am passin[illegible]y days in peace. 5. leisure; ~ से leisurely.

आराम-कुर्सी f. easy chair.

आरामतलब adj. & m. comfort-seeking, easy-going.

आरामदेह adj. comfortable, easeful.

आरामपसंद adj. easy-going.

आरी f. hand-saw; कलेजे पर ~ चलना to feel pangs of jealousy; गर्दन पर ~ चलाना to do immense harm.

आरूढ़ adj. ascended; ~ होना to ascend.

आरेख m. diagram; ~ बनाना to draw a diagram.

आरेखन m. act of drawing.

आरोग्य m. perfectness of health.

आरोग्य-केंद्र m. health-centre.

आरोग्यता f. see आरोग्य।

आरोग्यप्रद adj. conducive to health, health-giving.

आरोप m. accusation, charge, allegation; ~ लगाना to blame /accuse; झूठा~ false accusation/ charge.

आरोपण m. attribution; दोषारोपण attribution of blame.

आरोप-प्रत्यारोप m. recrim- ination.

आरोपित adj. attributed, ascribed; ~ करना to attribute/ascribe.

आरोह m. ascent.

आरोह-अवरोह m. 1. ascent and descent, 2. modulation, cadence.

आरोहण m. the act of mounting on, ascent.

आरोही adj. ascending. m. rider; अश्वारोही (अश्व+ आरोही) rider on a horse, horseman.

आर्जव m. straight-forwardness.

आर्डर m. 1. order. 2. a request to supply things.

आर्त adj. grieved, distressed, afflicted.

आर्तनाद m. a loud sound expressing sorrow, grief or fear.

आर्तस्वर m. note of distress.

आर्थिक adj. 1. economic; ~ समस्या economic problem. 2. monetary; ~ सहायता monetary help. 3. financial; ~ हानि financial loss.

आर्द्र adj. 1. humid. 2. wet.

आर्द्रता f. 1. humidity. 2. wetness.

आर्द्रतामापी m. hygrometer.

आर्य m. Aryan.

आर्यपुत्र m. form of address used for respectable persons esp. the husband.

आर्यभाषा f. language of Aryans.

आर्यसमाज m. a reformist school of thought founded by Swami Dayanand Saraswati.

आर्यसमाजी adj. pertaining to आर्यसमाज। m. one who believes in the doctrine of आर्यसमाज।

आर्यावर्त m. abode of Aryans, northern India.

आर्ष adj. pertaining to the ancient sages; ~ प्रयोग ancient (sacred) usage.

आलंकारिक adj. 1. ornamental. 2. rhetorical, figurative.

आलंब m. 1. prop, stay, support. 2. perpendicular.

आलंबन m. 1. support, dependence. 2. generating source of emotion. 3. a person or object serving as the stimulus of a particular रस.

आलंबित adj. supported.

आल–औलाद m. off-spring.

आलकस m. = आलस।

आलकसी adj. = आलसी

आलपिन m. pin.

आलम m. 1. world. 2. the people.

आलमगीर m. conqueror of the world.

आलमपनाह m. protector of the world.

आलमारी f. = अलमारी।

आलय m. abode, house.

आलस m. laziness, sloth; ~ आना to feel lazy.

आलसी adj. lazy, lethargic.

आलस्य m. laziness, sloth.

आला adj. first-rate, excellent. m. niche.

आलाप m. modulation of voice preparatory to singing.

आलापना vi. to practise आलाप; अपना राग अलापते जाना to harp on the same tune.

आलिंगन m. embrace.

आलिंगित adj. embraced.

आलिम adj. scholarly, learned.

आली f. 1. young female friend (of a girl or woman). 2. line.

आलीशान adj. grand, stately, majestic.

आलू m. potato; ~ चिप्स potato chips; ~ दम a vegetable dish prepared of uncut potatoes.

आलूचा m. [illegible]

आलूबुख़ारा [illegible]ried plum.

आलेख m. 1. graph. 2. literary essay or sketch.

आलोक m. light.

आलोकित adj. lighted, lit.

आलोचक m. critic.
आलोचना f. criticism.
आलोचनात्मक adj. critical.
आलोच्य adj. fit to be criticized.
आलोड़न m. act of shaking/stirring.
आलोड़ित adj. stirred.
आल्हा m. A metre in Hindi poetry eulogising the chivalrous deeds of the warriors Alha and Udal.
आवक adj. incoming. m. incoming goods.
आवधिक adj. periodic.
आव-भगत f. hospitality.
आवरण m. cover, covering, धुएँ का ~ smoke-pall.
आवरण-पृष्ठ m. cover page.
आवर्ती adj. occurring again and again, recurring; ~ खाता recurring account.
आवर्धन m. magnification, augmentation.
आवश्यक adj. important, necessary, essential.
आवश्यकता f. 1. necessity. 2. need.
आवागमन m. 1. coming and going; यात्रियों का ~ coming and going of passangers. 2. transmigration.
आवाज़ f. 1. voice. 2. sound.
आवाज़ा m. an ironical remark, sarcasm; ~ कसना to have a fling (at).
आवारगी f. vagabondage, loa-fing.
आवारा m. vagabond, vagrant, loafer. adj. wandering from place to place; ~ पशु an animal roaming at large.
आवारागर्द adj. & m. = आवारा।
आवारागर्दी f. = आवारगी।
आवास m. abode, residence; स्थायी~ permanent residence, domicile.
आवासी adj. residing, resident.
आवासीय adj. residential; ~ विश्वविद्यालय residential university.
आवाहन m. 1. invocation (of gods, etc.). 2. call; नवयुवकों का ~ a call to youth.
आविर्भाव m. appearance, ad-vent, emergence.
आविर्भूत adj. 1. appeared, manifested, 2. emerged.
आविष्कर्ता m. inventor.
आविष्कार m. 1. invention. 2. a thing that has been invented.
आविष्कारक m. inventor.
आविष्कृत adj. invented.
आविष्ट adj. 1. possessed of; भूत से ~ possessed of an evil spirit. 2. charged with; विद्युत् से ~ charged with electricity.
आवृत adj. encircled.
आवृत्त adj. 1. repeated. 2. recurred.
आवृत्ति f. repetition.
आवेग m. 1. force. 2. momentum. (Math.)
आवेदक m. one who applies for something, applicant.
आवेदन m. act of applying; ~ करना to apply.
आवेदन-पत्र m. written application.
आवेदन-प्रपत्र m. application form.
आवेदित adj. applied.
आवेश m. flurry of excitement; ~ में आकर in the state of extreme excitementl/frenzy.

आशंका f. 1. apprehension. 2. misgiving.

आशंकित adj. apprehensive, suspicious.

आशंसा f. blessing.

आशय m. sense, purport.

आशा f. hope, ambition, aspiration.

आशाजनक adj. causing hope, full of promise, promising.

आशातीत adj. beyond hope/expectation; ~ सफलता success beyond expectation.

आशान्वित adj. hopeful, optimistic.

आशापूर्वक adv. hopefully.

आशाप्रद adj. 1. promising. 2. hope-inspiring.

आशावाद m. optimism.

आशावादी adj. optimistic. m. optimist.

आशावान्, आशावान adj. hopeful; हम भविष्य के प्रति ~ हैं We are hopeful about future.

आशिक़ m. lover; ~ मिज़ाज given to love making.

आशिक़-माशूक़ m. lover and beloved.

आशिक़ाना adj. amorous.

आशियाना m. nest.

आशिष f. benediction, blessing.

आशीर्वचन m. words of blessing.

आशीर्वाद m. blessing, benediction; माता-पिता ने इस नई जोड़ी को ~ दिया Parents gave blessings to this new couple. उनके ~ से मैं सफल हुआ I became successful with their blessings.

आशु adj. quick, speedy; ~ कवि extempore poet; ~लिपि shorthand; ~लिपिक stenographer.

आशुगामी adj. fast, express.

आशुतोष m. one who is easily pleased, Lord Shiva.

आश्चर्य m. astonishment, wonder, surprise.

आश्चर्यकारक adj. causing surprise, amazing, surprising.

आश्चर्यचकित adj. wonder-struck, bewildered.

आश्चर्यजनक adj. wonderful, surprising, astonishing.

आश्रम m. 1. hermitage. 2. one of the four stages in the life of a Hindu.

आश्रमवासी m. one who lives in a hermitage, inmate of an आश्रम।

आश्रय m. 1. shelter. 2. support.

आश्रयदाता m. one who provides shelter/support.

आश्रित adj. dependent.

आश्वस्त adj. assured; ~ करना to assure.

आश्वासन m. assurance; ~ देना to give assurance.

आश्विन m. seventh month of the Hindu calendar.

आषाढ़ m. fourth month of the Hindu calendar.

आस f. hope.

आसकत f. laziness, idleness.

आसकती adj. lazy, idle.

आसक्त adj. attached, infatuated, charmed.

आसक्ति f. strong or deep attachment, infatuation,

fascination; परिवार के प्रति उसमें गहरी ~ थी He was deeply attached to his family.

आसन m. 1. seat. 2. act of sitting. 3. posture of sitting.

आसन्न adj. 1. adjacent; ~ कोण adjacent angle. 2. imminent; ~ भय imminent danger.

आस-पास adv. near about; क्या ~ कोई होटल है Is there a hotel near here?

आस-पास, के postposition. 1. near; घर के ~ near the house. 2. near in number or time, about; दस के ~ about ten.

आसमान m. sky.

आसमानी adj. azure, sky-blue.

आसरा m. 1. support. 2. means of livelihood. 3. shelter.

आसव m. wine, liquor.

आसवन m. distillation.

आसवनी f. distillery.

आसान adj. simple, easy.

आसानी f. easiness; ~ से with ease.

आसीन adj. seated; गद्दी पर ~ seated on the throne.

आसुत adj. distilled.

आसुरी adj. devilish, demonic; ~ संपत्ति demonic attainments.

आस्तिक adj. theistic. m. theist.

आस्तिकता f. belief in the existence of god, theism.

आस्तीन f. sleeve; ~ का साँप a treacherous associate.

आस्थगन m. deferment, postponement.

आस्थगित adj. deferred, postponed.

आस्था f. faith.

आस्थावान्, आस्थावान adj. loyal, faithful.

आस्वाद m. relish.

आस्वादन m. act of relishing, enyoyment of something eaten or drunk.

आह f. sigh; ~ भरना to heave a sigh; आहें भरना to utter or express with sighing.
interj. used to express grief.

आहट f. light sound (as of a foot-step); ~ मिलना to draw inferences (of somebody's presence) from such a sound; ~ लेना to try to get a clue or hint (of somebody's presence).

आहत adj. hurt, injured, woun-ded.

आहरण m. 1. act of drawing (amount) from an account, bank etc. 2. amount drawn.

आहरित adj. (amount) drawn.

आहा interj. used to express joy, triumph etc. aha!

आहार m. food, meal, diet.

आहार-विहार m. daily routine like eating, sleeping, merry-making etc.

आहार्य adj. eatable, edible.

आहिस्ता adv. slowly, leisurely; ~ - आहिस्ता slowly and leisurely.

आहिस्ते adv. = आहिस्ता।

आहुति f. oblation offered to fire (god); ~ डालना to offer oblation; ~देना (i) to offer oblation, (ii) to sacrifice.

आहू m. deer.

आहूत adj. called, summoned, invited; ~ करना to call or summon.

आह्लाद m. delight, gladness, joy, mirth, exultation; ~ जनक delightful, gladdening.

आह्लादकारी adj. delightful, gladdening, jolly.

आह्वान m. 1. call, summon. 2. invocation.

इ

इ f. the third vowel of the Nagri alphabet; its sound corresponds to that of i in sin. Its sign is ि।

इंगला f. see इड़ा।

इंगलिश adj. of England. f. English.

इंगलिस्तान m. England.

इंगलिस्तानी adj. of England, English. m. Englishman.

इंगित m. hint, indication.

इंच m. 1. measure of length equal to 2.54 c.m. 2. a small distance; ~ -इंच करके inch by inch.

इंचार्ज m. in-charge.

इंजन m. engine.

इंजन-ड्राइवर m. engine-driver.

इंजीनियर m. engineer. [H.E. अभियंता]

इंजीनियरिंग m. engineering.

इंजीनियरी f. engineering.

इंजील m. the New Testament.

इंजेक्शन m. injection; ~ देना to inject.

इंटर m. an intermediate college. adj. having passed in termediate examination.

इंट्रैंस m. entrance.

इंतक़ाल m. death; ~ हो जाना to pass away, to expire.

इंतख़ाब m. selection.

इंतज़ाम m. 1. arrangement. 2. management.

इंतज़ार f. wait, waiting; ~ करना to wait.

इंतहा f. 1. limit. 2. extremity.

इंदराज m. 1. an act of recording in a register. 2. entry.

इंदिरा f. Lakshmi, Goddess of Wealth.

इंदीवर m. blue lotus.

इंदु m. 1. moon. 2. camphor.

इंद्र m. Lord Indra, God of Rains.

इंद्रजाल m. 1. magic. 2. witchcraft. 3. illusion.

इंद्रजाली adj. deceptive, illusive. m. magician.

इंद्रधनुष m. rainbow, iris.

इंद्रधनुषी adj. of rainbow colour.

इंद्रपुरी f. abode of Indra, hea-ven.

इंद्रवधू f. lady-fly.

इंद्राणी f. wife of Indra.

इंद्रासन m. throne of Lord Indra.

इंद्रिय f. (physical) organ; कर्म- ~ organ of action; ज्ञान- ~ organ of sense.

इंद्रियग्राह्य adj. that can be observed or noticed, perceptible.

इंद्रियजित adj. having full control over the senses and sexual desires.

इंद्रियज्ञान m. perception.

इंद्रियदमन m. = इंद्रियनिग्रह।

इंद्रियनिग्रह m. temperance.

इंद्रियबोध m. perception.

इंद्रियलिप्सा f. sensuality.

इंद्रियलिप्सु adj. sensual.

इंद्रियलोलुप adj. & m. running after sensual pleasures.

इंद्रियसुख m. sensual pleasure.

इंद्रियातीत adj. that cannot be obtained through senses, trans-sensual.

इंसान m. human being.
इंसानियत f. humanity.
इंसानी adj. humane.
इंसाफ़ m. justice.
इंसाफ़पसंद adj. justice-loving.
इंस्पेक्टर m. inspector. [H. E. निरीक्षक]
इक adj. & m. एक।
इकट्ठा adj. collected, gathered; ~ करना to accumulate/collect/gather.
इकतरफ़ा adj. one-sided.
इकतान adj. monotonic.
इकतारा m. one-stringed musical instrument.
इकतालीस adj. & m. forty-one.
इकतीस adj. & m. thirty-one.
इकन्नी f. an old one-anna coin.
इक़बाल m. confession; इकबालिया बयान confessional statement.
इक़बाली गवाह m. approver.
इक़रार m. 1. promise. 2. agreement.
इक़रारनामा m. contract.
इक़रारी adj. contractual.
इकलौता adj. only, single. m. an only son.
इकसठ adj. & m. sixty-one.
इकसार adj. 1. uniform. 2. even.
इकहत्तर adj. & m. seventy-one.
इकहरा adj. single-folded; इकहरे शरीरवाला slim.
इकाई f. unit.
इकार m. the vowel इ or its sound.
इकारांत adj. (word) ending in इ.
इक्का m. 1. an Indian horse-carriage; ~ हाँकना to drive an इक्का। 2. ace (in cards).
इक्का-दुक्का adj. & m. one or two; इक्के-दुक्के से मैं निपट लूँगा I will deal with one or two.
इक्की f. = इक्का ace (in cards).
इक्कीस adj. & m. twenty-one.
इक्के-दुक्के adv. in ones and twos.
इक्केवाला m. 1. driver of इक्का। 2. owner of इक्का।
इक्यानबे adj. & m. ninety-one.
इक्यावन adj. & m. fifty-one.
इक्यासी adj. & m. eighty-one.
इख़्तिलाफ़ m. 1. discord. 2. opposition.
इच्छा f. 1. wish, will. 2. desire or longing.
इच्छानुसार, के postposition. according to one's desire or wish.
इच्छापत्र m. written will.
इच्छाशक्ति f. will-power.
इच्छित adj. desired, wished for.
इच्छुक adj. willing, desirous.
इजलास m. court.
इज़हार m. 1. expression. 2. demonstration.
इजाज़त f. permission; ~ लेना to take/get permission.
इज़ाफ़ा m. increase.
इज़ारबंद m. string or lace of a पाजामा।
इज़्ज़त f. respect, honour, esteem.
इज़्ज़तदार adj. respectable.
इज़्ज़तवाला adj. & m. respectable (man).
इटालियन adj. Italian.
इटैलिक adj. Italic. m. Italic letters.
इठलाना vi. to strut.

इठलाहट f. strut.
इतना adj. this much, so.
इतमीनान m. satisfaction.
इतर adj. other, different.
इतराना vi. to put on airs.
इतवार m. Sunday.
इतस्ततः adv. hither and thither.
इति f. end, conclusion, finish.
इतिवृत्त m. historical record, chronicle.
इतिश्री f. finish.
इतिहास m. history.
इतिहासकार m. historian.
इतिहासज्ञ m. = इतिहासकार।
इत्तफ़ाक़ m. chance.
इत्तफ़ाक़न adv. by chance.
इत्तला f. information, notice; ~ देना to inform.
इत्तहाद m. 1. unity. 2. union.
इत्तहादी adj. & m. 1. (of) protagonist of a movement. 2. unionist.
इत्यादि adv. et cetera.
इत्र m. scent, essence.
इत्रदान m. a vase of perfume, scent case.
इधर adv. 1. here. 2. recently.
इधर-उधर adv. here and there.
इन adj. these; ~ दिनों these days. pron. these people.
इनकम m. income. [H.E. आय]
इनक़लाब m. revolution; ~ ज़िंदाबाद Long live the revolution.
इनकार m. refusal, denial; ~ करना to refuse/deny.
इनचार्ज m. in-charge.
इनफ़्लुएंजा m. influenza.
इनसान m. = इंसान।
इना-गिना adj. counted; सामान ~ था The luggage was very few in number.
इनाम m. prize, reward.
इनायत f. favour, grace.
इने-गिने adj. (pl.) a few, very few, a limited few.
इन्हें pron. them, these; ~ अंदर ले जाओ Take these/them inside.
इफ़रात f. plenty, abundance.
इबरानी adj. Jewish.
इबादत f. worship; ~ करना to worship.
इबादतख़ाना m. place of worship, temple.
इबादतगाह f. = इबादतख़ाना।
इबारत f. written passage.
इब्तिदा f. beginning.
इमदाद f. help, aid.
इमरती f. an Indian sweet made of paste of a variety of pulse.
इमला m. dictation; ~ बोलना to dictate (for writing).
इमली f. tamarind.
इमाम m. Muslim high priest.
इमामदस्ता m. mortar and pestle.
इमारत f. building.
इमारती adj. of or pertaining to a building; ~ लकड़ी timber.
इम्तहान m. 1. examination. 2. test; ईश्वर तुम्हारा ~ ले रहा है God is putting you to the test.
इरादतन adv. deliberately.
इरादा 1. intention, intent. 2. purpose. 3. determination.
इर्दगिर्द adv. around.
इर्दगिर्द, के postposition. around;

लोग थाने के इर्दगिर्द इकट्ठे होने लगे People began to gather around the police station.

इलज़ाम m. accusation, charge.

इलाक़ा m. area, region.

इलाज m. 1. treatment, cure. 2. remedy.

इलायची f. cardamom.

इलायचीदाना m. 1. seeds of cardamom. 2. small sugar ball with cardamom seed inside.

इलाही m. God, Allah.

इल्तिजा f. request, entreaty; ~ करना to request/entreat.

इल्म m. 1. learning, knowledge. 2. skill. 3. wisdom.

इल्मी adj. 1. educational. 2. academic.

इल्लत f. ailment, malady.

इल्ली f. caterpillar.

इशारा m. hint, indication.

इश्क़ m. 1. love. 2. love-play.

इश्क़बाज़ m. philanderer.

इश्क़बाज़ी f. philandering.

इश्तहार m. 1. poster. 2. advertisement.

इश्तहारबाज़ी f. propaganda through advertisement.

इष्ट adj. desired, wished. m. goal.

इष्टदेव m. (one's) deity.

इष्ट-मित्र m. close friends and relations.

इस pron. & adj. (form of यह with a postposition attached) this.

इसरार m. insistence.

इसलाम m. Islam, the religion of the Mohammedans.

इसलामी adj. Islamic.

इसलिए adv. 1. for that reason, therefore. 2. for this purpose.

इसी pron. & adj. this very; ~ से for this very reason; ~ तरह similarly.

इसीलिए adv. for this very pur-pose.

इसे pron. him, her, it.

इस्तीफ़ा m. resignation.

इस्तेमाल m. use, application; ~ करना to use/apply.

इस्त्री f. an iron; ~ करना to iron.

इस्पंज m. sponge.

इस्पंजी adj. spongy.

इस्पात m. steel.

इस्म m. noun, name.

इस्लाम m. = इसलाम।

इस्लामी adj. = इसलामी।

इहलीला f. earthly existence.

इहलोक m. this world.

इहलौकिक adj. worldly, mun- dane.

ई f. the fourth vowel of the Nagari alphabet. Its sound corresponds to that of ee in meet. Its sign is ी।

ईंगुर m. vermilion.

ईंट f. brick.

ईंधन m. fuel.

ईकार m. the letter ई or its sound.

ईकारांत adj. (word) having ई at its end.

ईक्षण m. act of seeing/obser-ving.

ईख f. sugarcane.

ईजाद f. invention.

ईथर m. ether.

ईद f. a Mohammedan festival; ~ का चाँद (i) the moon seen on the eve of Id, (ii) one who is seen once in a blue moon, appearing once in a long while.

ईदगाह f. place where congre-gational Id-prayers are offered.

ईप्सा f. wish, desire.

ईप्सित adj. wished, desired.

ईमान m. uprightness, honesty, fairness.

ईमानदार adj. upright, honest, just.

ईमानदारी f. honesty. integrity.

ईरानी adj. of or pertaining to Iran. m. inhabitant of Iran.

ईर्ष्या f. envy, jealousy; वह सचमुच मुझसे ~ करता था He really envied me.

ईर्ष्यालु adj. envious.

ईश m. God; ~ निंदा blasphemy.

ईशान m. north-east; ~ कोण north-east corner.

ईश्वर m. God.

ईश्वरत्व m. godhood, godliness.

ईश्वरप्रदत्त adj. god-given, god-gifted.

ईश्वरीय adj. divine; godly; ~ देन divine gift.

ईषत् adj. very little, partly.

ईसवी adj. of or belonging to Jesus Christ; ~ सन् A.D. (Anno Domini).

ईसा m. Jesus, Jesus Christ.

ईसाइन f. 1. a Christian lady. 2. wife of a Christian.

ईसाई adj. 1. pertaining to Christ. 2. Christian; ~ धर्म Christianity. m. a Christian. [Fem. ईसाइन]

ईसा-पूर्व adj. before christ, B.C.

ईसामसीह m. Christ.

ईहा f. wish, desire.

उ

उ m. the fifth vowel of the Nagari alphabet; its sound corresponds to that of u in full; its sign is ु ।

उंगल f. 1. finger. 2. the measure equal to the width of a finger.

उँगली f. finger; ~ उठाना to choose (someone) for blame, to pick on; ~ दिखाना to point with a finger.

उँगली-छाप f. finger-print.

उँघाई f. see ऊँघ ।

उंचन f. the string at the foot of a bedstead.

उँडेलना vt. to pour.

उऋण adj. free from debt.

उकठना vi. to become dry like wood.

उकड़ूँ m. the posture of sitting on hands with heels on the ground.

उकताना vi. to be tired of/fed up/ bored.

उकताहट f. state of being bored, boredom.

उकसाना vt. 1. to raise. 2. to incite or instigate.

उकसावा m. excitement, instigation.

उकार m. the letter उ or its sound.

उकेरना vt. to engrave.

उक्त adj. aforesaid, above-mentioned.

उक्ति f. 1. utterance, remark. 2. saying.

उखड़ना vi. 1. to be uprooted. 2. to be dislocated (of bones).

उखड़वाना vt. to cause to be uprooted.

उखली f. a household device for pounding rice, etc.

उखाड़ना vt.1. to uproot. 2. to eradicate.

उगना vi. 1. to germinate. 2. to grow. 3. to rise; सूरज उग आया The sun appeared on the horizon.

उगलना vt. to vomit out.

उगलवाना vt. to extort a confession.

उगाना vt. to cause to ger-minate/ grow.

उगाल m. the fluid secreted in the mouth, spittle.

उगालदान m. a receptacle for spit, spittoon.

उगाहना vt. to collect/realize.

उगाही f. recovery.

उग्र adj. 1. violent. 2. aggressive.

उग्रता f. aggressiveness.

उग्रपंथी adj. & m. = उग्रवादी ।

उग्रवाद m. extremism.

उग्रवादी adj. & m. extremist.

उग्रह m. cessation of an eclipse.

उघड़ना vi. to be exposed; उघड़कर नाचना to behave shamelessly.

उघाड़ना vt. to expose, to disclose.

उघाड़ा m. unmasking, exposure.

उचंत खाता m. suspense account.

उचकना vi. to stand on tip-toe.

उचक्का m. swindler, thief.

उचक्कापन m. swindling.

उचटना vi. 1. to become de-tached or separated from something, to come off. 2. to get weary of.

उचाट adj. mentally wearied.

उचित adj. 1. right, equitable. 2. justified, proper. 3. reasonable, fitting.

उच्च adj. 1. high, tall, 2. lofty. 3. loud; ~ स्वर में loudly. 4. upper.

उच्चतम adj. 1. highest. 2. maximum.

उच्चतर adj. higher; ~ माध्यमिक विद्यालय higher secondary school.

उच्चता f. 1. height. 2. loftiness.

उच्च न्यायालय m. high court.

उच्चरित adj. 1. uttered. 2. pronounced.

उच्च वर्ग m. upper class.

उच्च शिक्षा f. high education.

उच्च सदन m. upper house.

उच्चस्तरीय adj. high-level.

उच्चाकांक्षा f. ambition.

उच्चाकांक्षी adj. ambitious.

उच्चाटन m. magical incantation causing to root out (someone's) erstwhile inclination.

उच्चाधिकारी m. high officer.

उच्चायुक्त m. High Commis-sioner.

उच्चायोग m. High Commission.

उच्चारण m. pronunciation.

उच्चारना vt. to utter.

उच्चित्र adj. carved out in relief.

उच्छिन्न adj. dilapidated.

उच्छिष्ट adj. residual (leav- ings).

उच्छृंखल adj. undisciplined, unruly, boistrous; वह सचमुच ~ लड़की है She is a really cheeky girl.

उच्छृंखलता f. 1. indiscipline, unrestrained behaviour, cheekiness. 2. unruly act.

उच्छृंग m. cliff.

उच्छेदन m. 1. uprooting. 2. extraction.

उच्छ्वास m. a sigh.

उछल-कूद f. gambol, romping.

उछलना vi. 1. to jump, leap, or hop.

उछलना-कूदना vi. to run and jump in a playful way, to hop and jump.

उछाल f. leap, jump, hop.

उछालना vt. to toss; पैसा ~ to toss a pice; कीचड़ ~ to fling mud, to calumnise; पगड़ी ~ to insult publicly.

उछाह m. = उत्साह।

उजड़ना vi. to be ruined.

उजड़वाना vt. to cause to be ruined or destroyed,

उजड्ड adj. boor; rude.

उजड्डपन m. boorishness, rudeness.

उजबक adj. stupid, idiotic.

उजरत f. labour charges, remuneration.

उजरती adj. ~ काम job work, piece work.

उजला adj. 1. white. 2. bright.

उजलापन m. 1. whiteness. 2. brightness.

उजागर adj. ~ करना to demons-trate publicly.

उजाड़ m. a deserted place, wilderness.

उजाड़ना vt. to ruin.

उजाड़ू adj. spendthrift, prod- igal.

उजाला m. light, brightness; अँधेरे घर का ~ (i) shining star in a dark sky, (ii) only son in a family.

उज्ज्वल adj. bright, shining.

उ

उज्ज्वलता f. brightness, shine.

उज़्र m. objection.

उझकना vi. to be on tip-toe, to have a peep.

उटंगा adj. (clothing) a little too short to cover the nether portion of the body.

उठती जवानी f. budding youth.

उठते-बैठते adv. all the time, all too often; वह उसे ~ याद करती है She remembers her all the time.

उठना vi. 1. to get to one's feet, to rise. 2. to get out of bed, to get up, to wake up. 3. to start or to get ready; दर्द ~ the starting of pain. 4. to come to (one's) mind; तब यह ख़्याल मेरे मन में उठा Then this idea occurrred to me. 5. to be erected; दीवार उठ रही है The wall is being erected.

उठना-बैठना m. close association; हमारा उनका ~ है We are very close.

उठवाना vt. to cause to elevate, raise, lift, etc.

उठाईगीर m. petty thief, pilferer, swindler.

उठाईगीरी f. pilferage.

उठाऊ adj. portable; ~ चूल्हा portable oven, (fig.) rolling stone.

उठान f. height; लड़की की ~ अच्छी है The girl is of good height.

उठाना vt. 1. to lift; भार ~ to lift a load. 2. to raise, erect; हाथ ~ to raise hand. 3. to erect; दीवार ~ to erect a wall. 4. to hold; अपना सिर उठाए रखो Hold your head up. 5. to begin/ broach/take up/raise; बात ~ to broach a topic; प्रश्न ~ to raise or put a question. 6. to awaken; मुझे पाँच बजे ~ Awaken me up at five. 7. to take off; मुझे लड़के को स्कूल से ~ पड़ा I had to remove the boy off the school.

उठाव m. 1. height. 2. protuberance.

उड़ती ख़बर f. rumour afloat; ~ है कि उसकी हत्या कर दी गई है Rumour has it that he was murdered.

उड़ती चिड़िया f. a person difficult to understand; मैं उड़ती चिड़िया पहचानता हूँ I can read through people at a glance.

उड़द m. = उरद।

उड़न-क़िला m. flying fortress.

उड़न-खटोला m. flying cot (legendary).

उड़न-छू adj. disappeared, vanished; ~ हो जाना to vanish away.

उड़न-झाँई f. trickery or false allurement.

उड़न-तश्तरी f. flying saucer/disc.

उड़न-दस्ता m. flying squad.

उड़ना vi. 1. to fly. 2. to run fast; घोड़ा तो मानो उड़ने लगा The horse began to run fast as if flying. कहाँ उड़े जा रहे हो Where are you speeding off? 3. to fade; रंग उड़ गया The colour has faded away. 4. to disappear; घड़ी तो उड़ (ही) गई The watch has disappeared. 5. to scatter; काग़ज़-पत्रों का ~ scattering of papers by the wind.

उड़ाऊ adj. extravagant.

उड़ाऊ-खाऊ adj. & m. squan-derer.

उड़ाका m. a pilot of an aero-plane, aviator, flyer.

उड़ाका दल m. flying squad.

उड़ाकू m. aviator.

उड़ान f. 1. a journey made by air, flight; यह दिमाग़ी ~ नहीं This is not a brain-wave. 2. a journey made in an aircraft, flight; कोहरे के कारण सभी उड़ानें रदद् कर दी गई हैं All the flights have been cancelled due to fog.

उड़ाना vt. 1. to cause to move through air, to fly; गुड्डी ~ to fly a kite; जहाज़ ~ to fly an aeroplane. 2. to steal or kidnap. 3. to blow up; उसने पुल उड़ा दिया He blew up the bridge. अफ़वाह ~ to spread a rumour; खिल्ली ~ to ridicule; चुटकियों में ~ to trifle away; मज़ाक़ ~ to make fun of, to ridicule; हँसी में ~ to laugh away.

उड़िया f. the language of the state of Orissa. m. inhabitant of Orissa.

उड़ीसा m. an Indian state, Orissa.

उड्डयन m. aviation; ~ विभाग aviation department.

उढ़री f. kept woman, concubine.

उढ़ाना vt. to cover (with some cloth); चादर ~ to cover with a sheet.

उतना adj. & m. that much, so much, as much; हमारे लिए ~ यथेष्ट है That much is enough for us.

उतरन f. cast-off clothes.

उतरना vi. 1. to get down/off, come down (steps etc.), land. 2. to alight, to dismount; गाड़ी से ~ to alight from a carriage. 3. to fall or diminish; चित्त/निगाह से ~ to fall in one's eyes. 4. to subside; बुख़ार ~ subsiding of fever; बुख़ार धीरे-धीरे उतर गया The fever gradually subsided. 5. to be dislocated; उसका कंधा उतर गया He dislocated his shoulder. 6. to lodge or stay (in someone's house), to put up; कहाँ उतरे हो Where are you putting up? 7. to fade; धूप में गाड़ी का रंग उतर गया The colour of the car has faded in the sun. 8. (of wrath, etc.) to abate or quieten; उसका क्रोध उतर गया His wrath abated. 9. to come off; मेरे कोट का बटन उतर गया A button has come off my coat. उसका नाम इस क्षण मेरे दिमाग़ से उतर गया है His name has slipped my mind for the moment.

उतरवाना vt. 1. to cause to come down, alight, descend etc. 2. (of photo); फ़ोटो ~ to get (oneself) photographed. 3. (of clothes) to strip off. 4. (of hide); खाल ~ to get (some animal) skinned.

उतराई f. 1. slope. 2. ferry-toll (for crossing a river); पार~ ferry toll.

उतराना vi. to float, to be afloat.

उतराव m. decline.

उतार m. 1. descent; पहाड़ का ~ descent of the mountain. 2. decline; लोकप्रियता में ~ decline in popularity. 3. last part, fag-end; जाड़े का ~ fag-end of winter. 4. antidote; शराब का ~ antidote of wine.

उ

उतार-चढ़ाव m. 1. rise and fall, ups and downs. 2. fluctuation.

उतारना vt. 1. to take off, to remove; कपड़े उतारना to remove/take off clothes. 2. to unload goods (from wagon, ship etc.). 3. to bring down. 4. to copy (passage etc., from a book); (किसी की) नक़ल उतारना (i) to imitate, (ii) to copy (somebody), (iii) to mimic. 5. to cause to lodge or stay, to accomodate (as a marriage party in a garden, bungalow etc.). 6. to draw; तस्वीर ~ to draw a picture?

उतारा m. offerings made to ward off an evil spirit.

उतारू adj. bent upon, fully determined, dead set.

उतावला adj. very impatient.

उतावलापन m. impatience.

उतावली f. excessive impatience.

उत्कंठा f. 1. eagerness. 2. curiosity.

उत्कंठित adj. 1. eager. 2. curious.

उत्कट adj. ardent, strong, fervent, intense; ~ प्रेम intense love.

उत्कटता f. state or quality of being उत्कट, intensity.

उत्कर्ष m. eminence.

उत्कीर्ण adj. engraved, inscribed.

उत्कृष्ट adj. excellent, outstanding.

उत्कृष्टता f. excellence.

उत्कोच m. bribe.

उत्कोच-ग्रहण m. acceptance of bribe.

उत्क्षिप्त adj. ejected.

उत्खनन m. excavation.

उत्तप्त adj. 1. hot. 2. heated.

उत्तम adj. 1. best. 2. fine, excellent.

उत्तमता f. fineness, excellence.

उत्तम पुरुष m. first person (gram).

उत्तमावस्था f. superlative degree. (gram.)

उत्तमोत्तम adj. topping, choicest.

उत्तर m. 1. north. 2. answer, reply.

उत्तरजीवन m. survival.

उत्तरजीवी adj. surviving. m. survivor.

उत्तरण m. landing.

उत्तरदाता m. answerable, responsible.

उत्तरदान m. bequest, legacy.

उत्तरदायित्व m. responsibility.

उत्तरदायित्वहीन adj. irresponsible.

उत्तरदायी adj. responsible.

उत्तरपक्ष m. respondent.

उत्तरपद m. 1. last term of a proportion. (maths) 2. last part of a compound word, as रत in कार्यरत।

उत्तर-पश्चिम adj. north-west.

उत्तर-प्रत्युत्तर m. 1. question and answer. 2. argument and counter-argument.

उत्तर-प्रभाव m. after-effect.

उत्तरवर्ती adj. next to, subsequent.

उत्तराधिकार m. 1. succession. 2. inheritence.

उत्तराधिकारी m. 1. successor. 2. inheritor. [Fem. उत्तराधिकारिणी]

उत्तरायण m. heading (of sun) towards the tropic of cancer.

उत्तरार्ध m. 1. latter half part. 2. northern hemisphere.

उत्तरी adj. northern; ~ ध्रुव north pole.

उत्तरीय m. an upper outer garment.

उत्तरोत्तर adj. 1. successive. 2. gradual. adv. 1. successively. 2. gradually.

उत्तल adj. convex.

उत्तान adj. lying on the back.

उत्ताप m. intense heat.

उत्ताल adj. (rising) very high.

उत्तीर्ण adj. passed, successful; वह प्रतियोगिता में ~ हुआ He was successful in the competition.

उत्तुंग adj. high, lofty.

उत्तेजक adj. 1. provocative. 2. stimulating.

उत्तेजन m. 1. provocation. 2. stimulation.

उत्तेजना f. excitement, agita-tion; ~ फैलाना to spread excitement.

उत्तेजनापूर्ण adj. provocative, inflammatory.

उत्तेजित adj. provoked, excited.

उत्तोलक m. 1. lift. 2. lever. 3. crane.

उत्थान m. rise, upliftment; मुग़ल साम्राज्य का ~ और पतन rise and fall of the Moghal empire; ~ करना to uplift.

उत्पत्ति f. 1. production. 2. creation. 3. produce.

उत्पन्न adj. 1. born. 2. produced.

उत्पाटन m. extirpation.

उत्पाटित adj. extirpated.

उत्पात m. 1. mischief. 2. disturbance, nuisance. 3. riot, violence.

उत्पाती adj. trouble-maker, mischievous.

उत्पाद m. 1. produce, yield. 2. product.

उत्पादक adj. 1. producing. 2. productive, creating. m. producer.

उत्पादकता f. productivity.

उत्पादन m. 1. production. 2. produce; output.

उत्पादित adj. produced; ~ करना to produce.

उत्पीड़क adj. oppressive.

उत्पीड़न m. oppression.

उत्पीड़ित adj. oppressed, persecuted; ~ करना to persecute, victimize.

उत्प्रेक्षा f. a kind of simile (a figure of speech).

उत्प्रेरक adj. stimulating.

उत्प्रेरित adj. activated, ~ करना to activate.

उत्फुल्ल adj. 1. blossomed. 2. full of good cheers, merry.

उत्स m. 1. fountain. 2. source.

उत्सर्ग m. sacrifice.

उत्सर्जन m. 1. act of abandoning. 2. sacrifice.

उत्सव m. festival, festive event; ~ मनाना to celebrate a festival.

उत्साह m. enthusiasm, zeal.

उत्साहपूर्वक adv. enthu-siastically, zealously.

उत्साहवर्धक adj. enthusiastic, encouraging.

उत्साहवर्धन m. encouragement.

उत्साहित adj. encouraged; ~ करना to encourage.

उत्साही adj. enthusiastic.

उ

उत्सुक adj. 1. eager. 2. curious.

उत्सुकता f. 1. eagerness. 2. curiosity.

उत्सुकतापूर्वक adv. eagerly.

उत्सेध m. elevation.

उथल-पुथल f. upheaval, turmoil; ~ मचाना to create a turmoil, to cause an upheaval; ~ हो जाना the state of things being topsy-turvy.

उथला adj. shallow.

उथलापन m. shallowness.

उदग्र adj. vertical.

उदजन m. hydrogen; ~ बम hydrogen bomb.

उदधि m. sea, ocean.

उदय m. rise; सूर्योदय sunrise; भाग्योदय rise in fortune.

उदयास्त m. rising and setting (as of sun).

उदर m. abdomen, belly, stomach.

उदरपिशाच m. a person who eats too much, glutton.

उदरपूर्ति f. sustenance; ~ करना to make both ends meet, manage to live.

उदरशूल m. colic pain.

उदरस्थ adj. swallowed; ~ करना to stomach, to swallow.

उदात्त adj. lofty, sublime.

उदार adj. liberal, generous.

उदारचेता adj. broadminded, magnanimous.

उदारता f. liberality, generosity.

उदारीकरण m. liberalization; ~ के सुफल अभी तक गरीबों तक नहीं पहुँचे The fruits of liberalization have not yet reached the poor.

उदास adj. sad, gloomy.

उदासी f. sadness, gloom.

उदासीन adj. indifferent, apathetic.

उदासीनता f. indifference, apathy.

उदाहरण m. example.

उदाहरणस्वरूप adv. as an ex-ample.

उदाहरणात्मक adj. exemplary.

उदाहरणार्थ adv. as for example.

उदित adj. risen, ascended.

उदीची f. north direction.

उदीच्य adj. northern.

उदीयमान 1. rising. 2. promising.

उद्गम m. source, origin.

उद्गमस्थल m. place or point of origin.

उद्गार m. expression of one's emotions/feelings; उसने अपने उद्गारों को सौम्यता से प्रकट किया He expressed his feelings humbly.

उद्घाटन m. 1. inauguration; ~ भाषण inaugural speech. 2. revealing; रहस्य का ~ revealing of a secret.

उद्घाटनोत्सव m. inauguration ceremony.

उद्घाटित adj. 1. inaugurated; ~ करना to inaugurate. 2. revealed; ~ करना to reveal.

उद्घोष m. 1. loud call. 2. announcement, proclamation.

उद्घोषक m. an announcer.

उद्घोषणा f. proclamation; राजकीय ~ official proclamation.

उद्घोषित adj. announced, proclaimed.

उद्दंड adj. 1. (one) who holds a raised club to strike. 2. rude and impertinent, arrogant.

उद्दंडता f. any rude action or behaviour, brazen act.

उद्दाम adj. powerful.

उद्दिष्ट adj. set aside for parti-cular purpose, earmarked.

उद्दीपक adj. stimulating.

उद्दीपन m. stimulation.

उद्दीप्त adj. stimulated.

उद्देश्य m. 1. aim, motive, object. 2. purpose. 3. subject with its enlargements. (Grammar)

उद्धत adj. overbearing, haughty.

उद्धरण m. 1. quotation, excerpt; ~ देना to quote. 2. citation.

उद्धरणी f. recital.

उद्धार m. rescue, deliverance.

उद्धार-गृह m. rescue-home.

उद्धारक m. rescuer, redeemer.

उद्धृत adj. 1. quoted. 2. cited.

उद्बुद्ध adj. enlightened.

उद्भट adj. great, ~ विद्वान great scholar.

उद्भव m. 1. coming into exis-tence, birth. 2. origin; ~ और विकास origin and development.

उद्भावना f. fancy.

उद्भासित adj. 1. illuminated, radiant, lustrous. 2. appeared.

उद्भिज m. vegetation.

उद्भूत adj. produced, appeared, emerged.

उद्भेदन m. coming out after breaking through.

उद्भ्रांत adj. 1. bewildered, dis-tracted. 2. confused.

उद्यत adj. ready, bent upon.

उद्यम m. 1. effort, exertion. 2. enterprise. 3. business, pursuit.

उद्यमशील adj. = उद्यमी।

उद्यमी adj. 1. energetic, diligent, 2. enterprising, industrious. m. entrepreneur.

उद्यान m. garden, park.

उद्यानगृह m. garden house.

उद्यान-गोष्ठी f. garden party.

उद्योग m. 1. endeavour; ~ करना to endeavour. 2. industry.

उद्योग-धंधा m. industry.

उद्योगपति m. industrialist.

उद्योगशील adj. industrious.

उद्योगी adj. 1. industrious, 2. diligent. m. industrialist.

उद्योत m. light, lustre.

उद्रेक m. exuberance, excess.

उद्वासन m. displacement.

उद्वासित adj. displaced.

उद्विग्न adj. perturbed, agitated.

उद्विग्नता f. perturbation, agitation.

उद्वेग m. impulse, क्रोध के ~ में under the impulse of anger.

उद्वेगकारी adj. impulsive.

उद्वेलन m. agitation, perturbation, stir.

उद्वेलित adj. agitated, perturbed.

उधड़ना vi. to be unsewn; चमड़ी ~ —उसकी चमड़ी उधड़ गई His skin was torn off.

उधर adv. 1. towards that place, thither. 2. on that side.

उधार m. debt, loan, credit; ~ खाए बैठना to be bent upon; ~ देना to lend, to give on credit.

उ

उधारी f. loan.

उधेड़ना vi. to unweave/unroll/unsew.

उधेड़-बुन f. state of indecisiveness; ~ में पड़ना to be in a fix.

उन pron. & adj. p1u. of उस; those; ~ दिनों in those days, ~ का their, theirs; ~ को them.

उनचास adj. &. m. forty-nine, 49.

उनतालीस adj. & m. thirty-nine, 39.

उनतीस adj. & m. twenty-nine, 29.

उनसठ adj. & m. fifty-nine, 59.

उनहत्तर adj. & m. sixty-nine, 69.

उनासी adj. & m. seventy-nine, 79.

उनींदा adj. sleepy, drowsy.

उन्नत adj. 1. elevated, high. 2. lofty. 3. advanced, developed.

उन्नति f. 1. advancement, progress. 2. rise, increase. 3. development, improvement.

उन्नतिशील adj. developing, progressive.

उन्नयन m. lifting up, uplifting.

उन्नाबी adj. light maroon.

उन्नायक m. uplifter.

उन्नासी adj. & m. seventy-nine, 79.

उन्निद्र adj. insomniac, sleepless.

उन्निद्र रोग m. (med.) habitual inability to sleep, insomnia.

उन्नीस adj. & m. 1. nineteen, 19. 2. low or lower in importance, inferior; उसका काम मेरे काम से ~ है His work is inferior to mine. ~ -बीस का अंतर slight difference.

उन्मत्त adj. 1. intoxicated, drunk. 2. frantic, wild; क्रोध से ~ wild with rage.

उन्मत्तता f. 1. quality or state of being intoxicated or wild. 2. any wild act.

उन्माद m. 1. wild excitement. 2. insanity. 3. mania, craziness.

उन्मीलन m. opening; नयनोन्मीलन opening of eyes.

उन्मीलित adj. 1. opened. 2. blossomed.

उन्मुक्त adj. free; ~ करना (i) to set free; (ii) to discharge.

उन्मुक्ति f. freedom.

उन्मुख adj. 1. looking towards, facing; ~ होना to turn towards. 2. inclined.

उन्मुखता f. inclination.

उन्मूलन m. 1. uprooting. 2. rooting out, eradication.

उन्मूलित adj. 1. uprooted. 2. abolished.

उन्मेष m. 1. opening (of the eyes). 2. manifestation, appearance.

उन्मोचन m. setting free, liberation.

उन्मोचित adj. redeemed, rescued, liberated, set free.

उन्हीं pron. (used with postpositions except ने) they, themselves; आप ~ से क्यों नहीं पूछते Why don't you ask them only?

उन्हें pron. p1u. of उसे, to them; मैं ~ मिला था I met them. मैं यह पुस्तक ~ नहीं दूँगा I will not give this book to them.

उप prefix. 1. deputy; ~ मुख्य मंत्री deputy Chief Minister. 2. by (e); ~ चुनाव by-election. 3. sub; ~

खंड sub-section; ~ नगर suburb. 4. assistant; ~ संपादक sub-editor. 5. vice; ~ प्रधानाचार्य vice-principal.

उपकथा f. an incident that forms part of a narrative, episode.

उपकर m. cess.

उपकरण m. apparatus, accessories.

उपकार m. kindness, obligation, beneficence, the good; ~ करना to do good (to another); ~ मानना to feel grateful/obliged.

उपकारक adj. beneficial, beneficent. m. benefactor.

उपकारी adj. benevolent.

उप-कुलपति m. vice-chancellor.

उपकृत adj. obliged, grateful; आपने मेरा सम्मान किया है ~ हुआ You (have) obliged me by giving me respect.

उपकेंद्र m. a sub-station.

उपक्रम m. 1. preparation; यात्रा का ~ preparation for the journey. 2. initiative. 3. undertaking; भारत सरकार का ~ Government of India's undertaking.

उपक्रमणिका f. table of contents.

उपक्षार m. alkaloid.

उपखंड m. 1. sub-clause. 2. block.

उपचय m. 1. act of culling. 2. heap. 3. growth, increase.

उपचर्या f. nursing.

उपचर्या-गृह m. nursing home.

उपचार m. 1. treatment, remedy. 2. nursing.

उपचारक m. male nurse.

उपचारिका f. nurse.

उपचारी adj. remedial; ~ प्रशिक्षण remedial training.

उपचित adj. culled, gathered.

उपचुनाव m. by-election.

उपच्छाया f. penumbra.

उपज f. 1. yield. 2. new idea.

उपजना vi. 1. to sprout/spring up. 2. to grow.

उपजाऊ adj. fertile, productive.

उपजाऊपन m. fertility, productivity.

उपजाति f. sub-caste.

उपजाना vt. to produce, to cause to yield, to bring forth.

उपजीविका f. subsidiary occupation.

उपजीवी adj. & m. dependent, subsisting on others.

उपजेता m. runner-up.

उपज्ञा f. discovery.

उपज्ञात adj. discovered.

उपटन m. a cleansing cosmetic for annointing over the skin to soften it, unction.

उपड़ना vi. to be uprooted/dislocated/dislodged.

उपत्यका f. valley (at the foot of a mountain).

उपदंश m. syphilis.

उपदान m. subsidy, gratuity.

उपदेश m. 1. sermon. 2. precept, advice, preaching.

उपदेशक m. preacher, serm-oniser, instructor.

उपदेशात्मक adj. morally instructive, didactic.

उपद्रव m. 1. disturbance, tro-uble. 2. riot.

उपद्रवग्रस्त adj. trouble-hit, riot-ridden, disturbed.

उपद्रवी adj. riotous, rowdy. m.

rioter, rowdy fellow.

उपद्वीप m. island, isle.

उपधारा f. sub-clause.

उपनगर m. suburb.

उपनगरीय adj. suburban; ~ रेल suburban railway.

उपनयन m. sacred thread ceremony.

उपनाम m. 1. pen-name. 2. nick-name. 3. alias.

उपनायक m. side-hero, second hero.

उपनायिका f. side-heroine.

उपनिदेशक m. deputy director.

उपनियम m. sub-rule.

उपनिरीक्षक m. sub-inspector.

उपनिर्वाचन m. by-election.

उपनिवेश m. 1. a colony. 2. settlement. 3. dominion.

उपनिवेशक m. a colonizer.

उपनिवेशवाद m. colonialism.

उपनिवेशवादी adj. colonial. m. colonist.

उपनिवेश-विरोधी adj. anti-colonial.

उपनिवेशिक adj. colonial.

उपनिषद, उपनिषद् m. any of the sacred ancient books of Hindu philosophy.

उपनीत adj. brought near.

उपनेता m. deputy leader.

उपन्यास m. novel.

उपन्यासकार m. novelist.

उपपति m. paramour.

उपपत्ति f. proof.

उपपत्नी f. concubine, keep.

उपप्रमेय m. corollary.

उपबंध m. proviso, provision.

उपभाषा f. dialect.

उपभुक्त adj. consumed.

उपभेद m. sub-classification, sub-division.

उपभोक्ता m. consumer.

उपभोक्तावाद m. protcetion of consumer's interests, consumerism.

उपभोक्तावादी adj. consumerist; ~ दृष्टिकोण consumerist attitude.

उपभोग m. 1. consumption. 2. enjoyment. ~ करना to use.

उपभोगी adj. consuming.

उपभोग्य adj. that can be consumed, consumable.

उपमंत्री m. deputy minister.

उपमहाद्वीप m. sub-continent.

उपमा f. simile; उपमाओं से भरा rich in similes.

उपमाता f. 1. stepmother. 2. wet nurse.

उपमान m. that with witch one is compared.

उपमार्ग m. bypass.

उपमेय adj. & m. that which is compared.

उपयुक्त adj. 1. fit, suitable. 2. proper, appropriate.

उपयुक्तता f. 1. suitability, fitness. 2. propriety, appropriateness.

उपयोग m. use, utilization; ~ करना to use/utilize.

उपयोगिता f. utility, usefulness.

उपयोगितावाद m. utilitarianism.

उपयोगितावादी adj. & m. utilita- rian.

उपयोगी adj. 1. useful, helpful. 2. serviceable. 3. profitable.

उपयोजन m. use, appropriation.

उपयोज्य adj. usable.

उपरना m. outer covering/sheet.

उपरफट्टू adj. 1. superfluous. 2. additional.

उपरांत, के postposition. after, afterwards.

उपरा-चढ़ी f. vying, rivalry, competition between the rivals.

उपराजदूत m. charge d'affairs.

उपराज्यपाल m. lieutenant-governer.

उपराष्ट्रपति m. vice-president.

उपरोक्त adj. = उपर्युक्त।

उपर्युक्त adj. aforesaid, above-mentioned.

उपल m. hail (stone).

उपलक्ष्य m. object, purpose; के ~ में on the occasion of.

उपलब्ध adj. 1. available. 2. obtained, got. 3. attained.

उपलब्धि f. achievement, attainment.

उपलभ्य adj. available.

उपलभ्यता f. availability.

उपलवृष्टि f. hailstorm.

उपला m. dried cowdung cake used as fuel.

उपलेपन m. act of smearing/anointing.

उपवन m. 1. grove. 2. small wood.

उपवर्ग m. 1. a separate group within a larger body of people, things etc., section. 2. a separate part.

उपवास m. fast; ~ करना to fast.

उपविजेता m. runner-up.

उपविधि f. bye-law.

उपविभाग m. 1. sub-department. 2. sub-division.

उपविष्ट adj. sitting; ~ होना to be seated.

उपवृत्ति f. avocation.

उपवेष्टन m. enveloping.

उपव्यवसाय m. side-business.

उपशमन m. 1. pacifying, abatement. 2. extinguishment.

उपशमित adj. pacified, abated.

उपशाखा f. 1. sub-branch. 2. distributary.

उपशामक adj. pacifying, assuaging.

उपशीर्षक m. sub-title.

उपसंचालक m. deputy director.

उपसंपादक m. sub-editor.

उपसंहार m. 1. conclusion. 2. summary.

उपसचिव m. deputy secretary.

उपसभापति m. vice-chairman.

उपसमिति f. sub-committee.

उपसमूह m. sub-group.

उपसर्ग m. prefix.

उपसागर m. bay.

उपसिद्धांत m. corollary.

उपस्कर m. equipment.

उपस्थापन m. presentation.

उपस्थापित adj. presented; ~ करना to present, put forward.

उपस्थित adj. present; ~ करना to present; ~ होना to attend or appear.

उपस्थिति f. 1. presence. 2. attendance.

उपहत adj. 1. methylated. 2. injured. 3. distressed.

उपहार m. gift, present; ~ देना to make a gift/present.

उ

उपहार-गृह m. a gift-shop.

उपहास m. ridicule, derision; ~ करना to ridicule; ~ के योग्य ridiculous.

उपहासास्पद adj. ridiculous, laughable, ludicrous.

उपांग m. limb or minor limb.

उपांत m. margin.

उपांतिक adj. marginal.

उपांतिम adj. coming before the last one, last but one, penulti-mate.

उपांत्य adj. penultimate.

उपाख्यान m. episode, anecdote.

उपाटना vt. = उपाड़ना।

उपाड़ना vt. to uproot.

उपादान m. 1. (raw) material of which something is made, component. 2. ingredient.

उपादेय adj. useful, beneficial.

उपादेयता f. 1. useful quality. 2. usefulness, utility.

उपाधि f. 1. title. 2. degree.

उपाधिधारी adj. & m. title-holder.

उपाधिपत्र m. certificate of degree.

उपाध्यक्ष m. 1. vice chairman. 2.vice-president. 3. deputy speaker.

उपाध्याय m. 1. oriental or Sanskrit scholar. 2. a class of Brahmins.

उपानह m. boot, shoe.

उपाय m. 1. a way, manner or course of action of doing something, method. 2. remedy.

उपायुक्त m. deputy commis-sioner.

उपार्जन m. act of a earning.

उपार्जित adj. earned.

उपालंभ m. complaint.

उपासक m. worshipper, devotee. [Fem. उपासिका]

उपासना f. 1. worship. 2. religious meditation, prayer.

उपासित adj. worshippped.

उपास्थि f. cartilage.

उपास्य adj. worthy of worship.

उपाहार m. refreshment.

उपाहार-गृह m. a restaurant.

उपेक्षणीय adj. worthy of neglect, negligible.

उपेक्षा f. neglect, indifference.

उपेक्षापूर्वक adv. without paying any attention, negligibly.

उपेक्षित adj. 1. neglected. 2. ignored, discarded.

उपेक्ष्य adj. 1. (something) negligible. 2. neglected.

उपोत्पाद m. bye-product.

उपोद्घात m. introduction, foreword.

उफ़ interj. ah! f. a cry of pain, etc; ~ (तक) न करना not to utter (even) a sigh.

उफनना vi. to boil over.

उफान m. ebullience, ebullition; ~ आना (i) to reach boiling point, (ii) to move forward like waves, surge.

उबकना vi. to feel a vomiting urge or sensation, to feel nausea.

उबकाई f. nausea, feeling of vomiting.

उबटन m. a paste applied to the skin (used as a cosmetic).

उबरना vi. to be redeemed.

उबलना vi. to boil/simmer.

उबाऊ adj. boring.

उबाक m. 1. vomit. 2. vomiting tendency.

उबाना vt. to bore.

उबार m. deliverance, rescue.

उबारना vt. to redeem/liberate.

उबाल m. ebullition.

उबालना vt. 1. to cause water or other liquid to boil. 2. to cook by boiling.

उभड़ना vi. = उभरना।

उभय adj. both; ~ पक्ष both parties.

उभयतः adv. 1. both ways. 2. on both sides, in both the cases.

उभयनिष्ठ adj. 1. common to both. 2. loyal to both.

उभयपक्षीय adj. bilateral.

उभयमुखी adj. ambivalent.

उभयलिंग m. common gender.

उभयलिंगी adj. 1. having both male and female sexual organs, hermaphrodite. 2. (grammar) common to both genders.

उभयसंकट m. dilemma, quan-dary.

उभयार्थक adj. 1. having two possible meanings or inter-pretations. 2. ambiguous, having two or both meanings.

उभरना vi. 1. to come out, to protrude, to sprout forth. 2. to swell up, to upheave.

उभाड़ m. = उभार।

उभाड़ना vt. 1. to bring out. 2. to excite/instigate.

उभार m. protuberance, bulge.

उभारना f. = उभाड़ना।

उमंग f. a sudden fanciful desire, enthusiasm, zeal, gusto; ~ में आकर enthusiastically; ~ में आना / भरना to be filled with gusto; बड़ी ~ से with gusto.

उमड़ना vi. to swell; उमड़ पड़ना -आँसू उमड़ पड़े Tears swelled out. उसका मन उमड़ पड़ा He was visibly moved. घटाएँ उमड़ पड़ीं Clouds gathered up. नदी उमड़ पड़ी The river overflowed. भीड़ उमड़ पड़ी The crowd swelled.

उमड़ना-घुमड़ना vi. to move quickly up and down, bob; आकाश में बादल उमड़ने-घुमड़ने लगे The clouds were bobbing up and down in the sky.

उमर f. = उम्र।

उमरा m. (p1. of अमीर) aristocrats, aristocracy.

उमराव m. (p1.) = उमरा।

उमस f. sultriness.

उमसदार adj. humid, muggy, sultry.

उमा f. wife of Lord Shiva.

उमेठना vt. to twist; कान ~ to twist the ears. 2. to wind.

उम्दगी f. excellence.

उम्दा adj. nice, excellent, fine.

उम्मीद f. hope.

उम्मीदवार m. candidate; ~ होना to stand as a candidate.

उम्मीदवारी f. 1. candidature. 2. expectancy.

उम्र f. age.

उर m. heart.

उरद m. black gram.

उरु m. thigh.

उरूज m. advancement, rise, ascendancy.

उरेहना vt. to draw/paint.

उरोज m. breast (of a woman).

उर्द f. = उरद।

उर्दू m. Urdu (language).

उर्फ़ m. alias.

उर्मि f. ripple.

उर्मिला f. wife of Lakshman. (Ramayan)

उर्वर adj. fertile.

उर्वरक m. fertilizer.

उर्वरता f. fertility.

उर्वरा adj. (fem.) fertile; ~शक्ति fertility.

उर्वरीकरण m. fertilization.

उर्वशी f. a damsel of the celestial court of Lord Indra.

उर्वी f. earth.

उर्स m. day of a Muslim Saint's demise.

उलझट्टा m. complication, complexity.

उलझन f. 1. complication, predicament. 2. complexity. 3. intricacy; ~ खड़ी करना to create a complication; ~ में डालना to put (somebody) in a predicament; ~ सुलझाना to solve a problem. 4. fix. 5. problem.

उलझना vi. 1. to be entangled; किसी से ~ to be entangled with someone. 2. to be involved; किसी मामले में ~ to be involved in an affair.

उलझाना vt. 1. to make entangled or complicated. 2.to get someone involved.

उलझाव m. 1. entanglement, snarl. 2. involvement.

उलटना vi. to be turned over completely. vt. to cause to overturn, to reverse.

उलटना-पलटना vi. to turn or overturn, shuffle; वह दिन भर कागज़ों को उलटता-पलटता रहता है He shuffles the papers whole day.

उलट-पलट f. 1. shuffle. 2. reversal. 3. upset.

उलट-पुलट adj. = उलट-पलट।

उलट-फेर m. flip-flop, changes; ज़माने का ~ vicissitude.

उलटा adj. 1. inverse. 2. opposing, contrary, adverse. 3. wrong.

उलटाना vt. 1. to invert. 2. to reverse.

उलटा-पुलटा adj. irrelevent, topsy-turvy.

उलटाव m. reversal.

उलटा-सीधा adj. 1. obverse and reverse. 2. (fig.) inappropriate, improper.

उलटी f. vomiting; ~ करना to vomit.

उलटी-सीधी f. inappropriate phrase or improper statement; (किसी को) उलटी-सीधी सुनाना to tell off, to give a bit of one's mind.

उलटे adv. 1. in the opposite direction. 2. on the contrary, on the other hand.

उलफ़त f. sensual love.

उलरना vi. to lean, tilt.

उलार m. bending or bowing movement, tilt.

उलाहना f. gentle complaint; ~ देना to say you have done wrong to me.

उलीचना vt. to drain off (liquid), to draw out.

उलूक m. owl.

उल्का f. meteor.

उल्कापात m. meteoric fall.

उल्कापिंड m. meteorite.

उल्काश्म m. meteorite.

उल्टा adj. = उलटा।

उल्था m. translation.

उल्लंघन m. 1. violation. 2. transgression; 3. overstepping.

उल्लसित adj. jubilant, exhila-rated.

उल्लास m. jubilation, exultation, exhilaration.

उल्लासजनक adj. mirthful, exh-ilarating.

उल्लासपूर्ण adj. mirthful.

उल्लिखित adj. above menti-oned, (lit.) above written.

उल्लू m. 1. owl. 2. a foolish person. adj. foolish.

उल्लेख m. mention; ~ करना to mention.

उल्लेखनीय adj. 1. worth mentioning. 2. remarkable.

उषा m. dawn.

उषाकाल m. dawn, day-break.

उष्ण adj. hot.

उष्ण कटिबंध m. torrid zone.

उष्णता f. heat.

उष्म adj. hot.

उष्मा f. heat.

उस pron. inflexional base of वह; उस दिन that day; ~ समय (at) that time.

उसकाना vt. = उकसाना।

उसी adj. that very.

उसूल m. principle; उसूलों से जकड़ा tied with rules.

उसूली adj. (man) of principles.

उसे pron. 1. him; ~ दे दो Please give him. 2. he; ~ जाना है He has to go. 3. that one; हमने ~ चुना We chose that one.

उस्तरा m. razor.

उस्ताद m. 1. teacher. 2. master.

उस्तादी f. 1. profession or status of a teacher. 2. cleverness, tactics.

उस्तादी हाथ m. very skilful act, master-stroke.

उस्तानी f. 1. wife of a teacher. 2. lady teacher.

उस्तुरा m. = उस्तरा।

ऊ

ऊ m. sixth vowel of the Nagari alphabet; its sign is ू; its pronunciation is like that of oo in tool.

ऊँघ f. a brief light sleep, snooze, doze.

ऊँघना vi. to snooze, to doze; वह बैठे-बैठे ऊँघ रहा था He was snoozing/dozing while sitting.

ऊँघाई f. = ऊँघ,

ऊँच-नीच m. 1. the high and the low; 2. gain and loss.

ऊँचा adj. 1. high, tall; 2. ranking above others in caste, importance etc. 3. great, lofty, elevated; ~ विचार lofty idea. 4. loud; ऊँची आवाज़ loud voice.

ऊँचाई f. 1. height. 2. altitude. 3. summit. 4. high level, high.

ऊँचान f. = ऊँचाई।

ऊँचा-नीचा adj. uneven; पैर ~ पड़ जाना to go out of right or expected path.

ऊँट m. camel.

ऊँटनी f. she-camel.

ऊँहूँ interj. denoting refusal or denial; no, not, never!

ऊकार m. the letter ऊ or its sound.

ऊकारांत adj. (word) ending in ऊ।

ऊख m. sugarcane.

ऊखल m. mortar; ~ में सिर देना to invite trouble wilfully.

ऊखली f. small mortar.

ऊटक-नाटक m. 1. haphazard work. 2. work without any utility.

ऊटपटाँग adj. absurd.

ऊत adj. 1. issueless. 2. stupid.

ऊतक m. tissue.

ऊतक विज्ञान m. histology.

ऊद m. a tree named 'agar' or its wood.

ऊदबिलाव m. beaver, otter.

ऊदा adj. violet.

ऊधम m. turmoil, uproar. row, clamour; ~ मचाना create a row.

ऊधमी adj. uproarious.

ऊन adj. wanting, less, trifling. m. wool.

ऊनता f. want, deficiency.

ऊना adj. lacking something.

ऊनी adj. woollen; ~ कपड़ा woo- llen cloth.

ऊपर adv. on, upon, above.

ऊपर, के postposition. 1. above. 2. of greater importance.

ऊपरवाला m. 1. one who lives upstairs. 2. God (on high).

ऊपरी adj. 1. upper; ~ मंज़िल पर upstairs. 2. overhead; ~ व्यय overhead expenses. 3. additional, extra; ~ आमदनी extra income. 4. showy; ~ देशप्रेम showy patriotism. 5. superficial; ~ तौर से superficially; ~ हवा (i) superficial prestige, (ii) influence of evil spirit.

ऊब f. disgust, boredom, tedium; ~ जाना to feel disgust.

ऊबड़-खाबड़ adj. rough and rugged,

uneven; ~ कच्चा रास्ता bumpy mud track.

ऊबना vi. to feel bored; ऊबा हुआ bored.

ऊर्जस्विता f. energy, vigour, strength.

ऊर्जस्वी adj. energetic, vigorous, strong.

ऊर्जा f. 1. energy. 2. electricity.

ऊर्ध्व adj. vertical, upward; ~ गति vertical movement; ~ श्वास last breaths.

ऊर्ध्वगामी adj. moving upwards.

ऊर्ध्व विंदु m. zenith.

ऊल-जलूल adj. incongruous and irrelevant, desultory, baseless.

ऊषा f. = उषा।

ऊष्म adj. hot, warm.

ऊष्मा f. 1. heat. 2. warmth.

ऊसर adj. barren; m. unfertile soil.

ऊह interj. denoting pain, Oh!

ऊहापोह m. indecisiveness, shilly-shallying.

ऋ

ऋ m. seventh vowel of the Nagari alphabhet; its sign is ृ ; and pronunciation resembling that of ri in rich.

ऋक्थ m. legacy.

ऋक्थदान m. bequest.

ऋग्वेद m. Rig Veda, the first of the four Vedas.

ऋचा f. Vedic hymn.

ऋजु adj. 1. simple. 2. straight-forward, honest, sincere.

ऋजुता f. 1. simplicity. 2. strai-ght-forwardness, honesty, sincerity.

ऋण m. 1. loan, debt; ~ चुकाना to pay off debt. 2. debt of gratitude, obligation. मुझपर उनका ~ है I am under their obligation.

adj. negative, minus; ~ चिह्न minus sign (math).

ऋणग्रस्त adj. owing money, in-debted.

ऋणदाता m. creditor.

ऋणदायी adj. lending; ~ संस्थाएँ lending institutions.

ऋणपक्ष m. debit side.

ऋणपत्र m. a certificate of debit, bond.

ऋणभार m. a load of debt, encumbrance.

ऋणमुक्त adj. free from debt / obligation.

ऋणमुक्ति f. acquittance.

ऋणमोचन m. paying off.

ऋणशोधन m. paying off.

ऋणात्मक adj. negative.

ऋणी adj. grateful.

m. debtor.

ऋणेतर adj. not-credit; ~ नीति non-credit policy.

ऋत m. eternal truth.

ऋतु f. season; आम की ~ season of mangoes; ~ आना advent of a season; ~ जाना end of a season.

ऋतुकाल m. mating season.

ऋतुमती f. a woman in her menses.

ऋतुराज m. spring (season).

ऋतुवर्णन m. description of a season.

ऋतु विज्ञान m. meteorology.

ऋद्धि f. prosperity.

ऋद्धि-सिद्धि f. prosperity and success.

ऋषभ m. bull, ox.

ऋषि m. sage, saint, hermit; ~ का आश्रम hermitage.

ए

ए m. eighth vowel of the Nagari alphabet; its sign is ` and its sound is like that of a in gate.

एकंगा adj. 1. pertaining to one side or aspect. 2. unilateral.

एक adj. & m. 1. The number or figure1, one. 2. a single thing or a person. 3. united.

एक-आध adj. one or two, a few.

एकक m. unit.

एककालिक adj. happening at the same time, synchronic.

एकचित्त adj. concentrated, engrossed; ~ होना to be concentrated.

एकछत्र adj. absolute; ~ राज्य monarchy.

एकज़बान adj. true to one's promise.

एकजान adj. blended together.

एकजुट adj. united; ~ होकर unitedly.

एक-जैसा adj. resembling; बहुत कुछ एक-जैसे closely resembling.

एकटक adv. unblinkingly; ~ देखना to see unblinkingly.

एकड़ m. acre.

एकतंत्र m. monarchy.

एकतंत्रीय adj. monarchical.

एकतरफ़ा adj. 1. one-sided. 2. unilateral, ex parte. 3. one-way; ~ यातायात one-way traffic.

एकता f. 1. unity. 2. solidarity.

एकतार adv. continuously.

एकतावादी adj. unionistic. m. unionist.

एकत्र adv. at one place, together.

एकत्रित adj. collected together.

एकत्रीकरण m. act of gathering or collecting.

एकदम adv. forthwith, immediately.

एकदा adv. once upon a time, once.

एकदिल adj. 1. of the same mind. 2. blended together.

एकदेववाद m. monotheism.

एकदेशीय adj. regional.

एकनिष्ठ adj. devoted and loyal to one only.

एकनिष्ठा f. loyalty to one.

एकपक्षीय adj. 1. one-sided, unilateral; ~ अनुबंध unilateral agreement. 2. ex parte.

एकपत्नीत्व m. monogamy.

एक बार adv. once; ~ और once more.

एकबारगी adv. all at once.

एकभाषी adj. monolingual.

एकमंज़िला adj. one-storeyed.

एकमत adj. unanimous.

एकमहला adj. = एकमंज़िला।

एकमात्र adj. sole; ~ वितरक sole distributor.

एकमुश्त adv. all in a single instalment.

एकरंग adj. uniform.

एकरंगा adj. of one colour.

एकरस adj. monotonous.

एकरसता f. monotony.

एकरूप adj. uniform.

ए

एकरूपता f. uniformity, similarity.

एकल adj. 1. sole, single. 2. alone, solitary. m. a match played with one player on each side, singles.

एकलिंगी adj. unisexual.

एकवचन m. & adj. singular.

एकवर्षीय adj. one year old, yearling.

एकविवाह m. monogamy.

एकसदनी adj. unicameral.

एकसम adj. = एकसमान।

एकसमान adj. 1. same. 2. uni-form (math).

एक साथ adv. 1. en block. 2. at the same time. adj. simultaneous.

एकसार adj. 1. uniform. 2. even.

एकसुरा adj. monotonous.

एकसूत्र adj. ~ में बँधना to be in unison, to be well-knit, to be integrated.

एकस्व m. patent.

एकहरा adj. 1. single. 2. single-folded; ~ बदन thin/slim body.

एकांकी adj. oneact (play). m. one-act play.

एकांगी adj. one-sided; ~ निर्णय one-sided judgement.

एकांत m. 1. solitude; ~ में in solitude. 2. seclusion, isolation; ~ कारावास solitary confinement.

एकांतता f. 1. solitude, solitariness. 2. seclusion.

एकांतप्रिय adj. lover of solitude.

एकांतर adj. alternate.

एकांतरिक adj. alternate.

एकांतवास m. living in solitude or loneliness.

एकांतवासी m. one who lives alone, recluse.

एका m. oneness, unity; एके का अभाव lack of unity.

एकाएक adv. 1. suddenly, all at once. 2. unexpectedly, abrup-tly.

एकाकार adj. completely inter-mingled/unified; ~ हो जाना to become intermingled.

एकाकी adj. lonely, solitary.

एकाकीपन m. (feeling of) lone-liness.

एकाक्ष adj. one-eyed.

एकाक्षर adj. monosyllabic.

एकाग्र adj. concentrated, one-pointed.

एकाग्रचित्त adj. closely attentive.

एकाग्रता f. concentration (of mind), one-pointedness.

एकाग्रदृष्टि adj. having the eye focussed on one point.

एकात्म adj. integrated (into one), unitary.

एकात्मक adj. unitary; ~ राज्य unitary state.

एकात्मकता f. solidarity.

एकात्म्य m. identity. (maths)

एकादशी f. eleventh day of either half of a lunar month.

एकाध adj. = एक-आध।

एकाधिक adj. more than one, many.

एकाधिकार m. monopoly; ~जमाना to monopolize.

एकाधिकारी adj. having exclusive right. m. monopolist.

एकाधिकृत adj. monopolised.

एकाधिपत्य m. 1. absolute or exclusive right. 2. autocracy.

एकार्थक adj. 1. having the same meaning. 2. having one meaning, univocal.

एकालाप m. monologue.

एकीकरण m. 1. unification, integration. 2. amalgamation, consolidaton.

एकीकृत adj. 1. unified, integ- rated. 2.amalgamated, consolidated.

एकीभूत adj. 1. collected together. 2. unified, united.

एकेश्वरवाद m. monotheism.

एकेश्वरवादी m. a supporter of monotheism, monotheist.

एक्का m. 1. an Indian horse carriage. 2. ace (cards).

एक्की f. = एक्का (ace).

एक्केवान m. driver of an एक्का।

एक्सप्रेस adj. going or sent quic-kly, express.

एजेंट m. agent.

एजेंसी f. agency.

एटलस m. atlas.

एडवोकेट m. advocate.

एड़ f. = एड़ी ; ~ देना/मारना/लगाना to strike with the heel. (Horse-riding).

एड़ी f. the back part of the human foot, heel.

एतदर्थ adv. for this purpose, on this account.

एतद् द्वारा adv. hereby.

एतबार m. 1. trust, confidence. 2. credit.

एतबारी adj. trustworthy, credible.

एतराज़ m. objection; ~ करना to object.

एतवार m. = इतवार Sunday.

एरंड m. castor.

एलची m. emissary, envoy.

एलबम m. album.

एलान m. declaration, announ-cement; ~ करना to announce.

एलानिया adv. publicly.

एलार्म m. alarm.

एलार्म घड़ी f. alarm clock.

एल्यूमिनियम m. aluminium.

एवं adv. and, as well as, as also.

एव conj. अतएव (i) hence, (ii) therefore.

एवज़ में, के postposition. in place of, instead of.

एवमस्तु interj. Be it so!

एषणा f. strong desire.

एशिया m. Asia.

एशियाई adj. Asian, Asiatic. m. an inhabilant of Asia, Asian.

एहतियात f. precaution; ~ बरतना to take precaution.

एहतियातन adv. by way of precaution.

एहतियाती adj. precautionary.

एहसान m. obligation.

एहसानफ़रामोश adj. ungrateful.

एहसानमंद adj. grateful.

एहसास m. 1. feeling. 2. awareness, consciousness.

ए

ऐ m. 1. the ninth vowel of the Nagari alphabet; its sign is ै ; its sound resembles that of a in bat, rat etc. inter. O! ~ लड़के O boy!

ऐं interj. 1. indicating 'what did you say', 'what's that', 'what was it'. 2. eh!

ऐंचाताना adj. squint-eyed.

ऐंठ f. conceit, vanity; ~ दिखाना to show off conceit.

ऐंठन f. twist, contortion.

ऐंठना vt. 1. to twist. 2. to extort.

ऐंठू adj. 1. conceited. 2. ob-stinate.

ऐंद्रजालिक adj. magical. m. magician.

ऐंद्रिय adj. 1. sensuous. 2. sensual; ~ सुख sensual pleasure.

ऐकमत्य m. an agreement of opinion, concurrence, complete accord.

ऐकांतिक adj. pertaining to solitude.

ऐकात्म्य m. identity.

ऐकिक adj. unitary.

ऐक्य m. oneness, unity; ~ स्थापित करना to establish unity.

ऐच्छिक adj. 1. optional; ~ विषय optional subject(s). 2. voluntary; ~ अंशदान voluntary contribution.

ऐडवोकेट m. advocate.

ऐतिहासिक adj. historical.

ऐन adj. right; ~ मौक़े पर in the nick of time; ~ वक़्त पर just in time.

ऐनक f. spectacles, eye-glasses.

ऐब m. 1. defect, shortcoming. 2. flaw, fault.

ऐबदार adj. defective, faulty.

ऐबी adj. = ऐबदार।

ऐयार m. a spy who practises magic, wizard.

ऐयारी f. the profession and skills of a wizard, wizardry. adj. of a spy or wizard; ~ उपन्यास detective novel.

ऐयाश adj. & m. lewd, vol-uptuous, bohemian.

ऐयाशी f. lewdness, voluptu-ousness.

ऐरा-ग़ैरा adj. unknown or unfamiliar (person).

ऐरावत m. Lord Indra's elephant.

ऐलोपैथी f. allopathy.

ऐश f. merry- making; ~ करना to make merry, to luxuriate.

ऐशपरस्त adj. merry-minded, enjoying luxurious life.

ऐशपरस्ती f. merry-mindedness, luxury.

ऐश्वर्य m. 1. grandeur, glory. 2. riches, wealth.

ऐश्वर्यशाली adj. prosperous, affluent.

ऐसा adj. 1. like this, so, such; 2. of this type. pron. so; मेरे पिताजी ~ कहा करते थे My father used to say so. ~ है क्या? Is this so? Really? ~ ही है! So it is!

ऐसा-वैसा adj. 1. insignificant. 2. irrelevant. 3. undesirable.

ऐसे adv. in this manner/wise/way, thus. ~ में in the mean time.

ऐसे-वैसे adv. in haphazard or indecorous way.

ऐहिक adj. mundane, worldly.

ओ

ओ m. the tenth vowel of the Nagari alphabet; its sign is ो; its sound is like that of o in mole.

ओंकार m. om, the symbol, invocation etc., of Godhood, ॐ.

ओंठ m. = होंठ।

ओखली f. mortar; ~ में सिर देना deliberately to expose oneself to risks.

ओछा adj. shallow, lacking depth; ~ व्यक्ति shallow minded.

ओछापन m. shallowness, meanness.

ओज m. 1. verve, vigour. 2. lustre. 3. vitality, energy.

ओजपूर्ण adj. 1.vigorous. 2. lustrous.

ओजस्विता f. verve, vigour.

ओजस्वी adj. vigorous, lively, powerful; ~ भाषण vigorous speech.

ओझल adj. hidden, out of sight; ~ हो जाना to get out of sight.

ओझा m. wizard, exorcist, black magician.

ओझाई f. the skill or vocation of an ओझा, exorcism.

ओट f. 1. a partition serving to shelter or conceal, screen. 2. cover, veil.

ओटना vt. to free cotton of seeds with a gin.

ओटनी f. a gin that frees cotton of seeds.

ओटाई f. 1. act of ginning. 2. charges for ginning.

ओठ m. = होंठ।

ओढ़ना vt. 1. to cover or wrap (the body). 2. to take up (blame, responsibility etc.) on one's self. m. a shawl, sheet, blanket or quilt used to cover the body.

ओढ़ना-बिछौना m. 1. bedding and covering. 2. essential part of something, part and parcel of something.

ओढ़नी f. (woman's) shawl; ~ बदलना to establish friendship by exchanging shawls.

ओढ़ाना vt. to cover with cloth.

ओतप्रोत adj. imbued, soaked. देशभक्ति से ~ imbued with patriotism.

ओदा adj. wet, moist.

ओप f. 1. polish. 2. brightness, shine.

ओफ़ interj. exclamation of wonderment, plethora, joy, sadness, pain etc.

ओम m. = ओंकार

ओर f. side; सभी ~ से from all sides; चारों ~ all around, on all sides.

ओर, की postposition. towards.

ओर-छोर m. beginning and end.

ओलंपिक adj. Olympic; ~ खेल Olympic Games.

ओल m. hostage.

ओलती f. eaves of a thatching.

ओला m. hail.

ओवरकोट m. overcoat.

ओषधि f. medicine.

ओष्ठ m. = होंठ।

ओष्ठ्य adj. labial, ~ व्यंजन labial consonant.

ओस f. dew; ~ पड़ना dew-fall; ~ से भरा dewy; ~ से भीगना to become wet with dew.

ओसांक m. dewpoint.

ओसाना vi. to winnow.

ओसारा m. shed, verandah, portico.

ओसीला adj. wet with dew, dewy.

ओह interj. (of surprise or pain) eh!

ओहदा m. 1. post. 2. rank. 3. designation.

ओहदेदार m. office-bearer, office-holder.

ओहो interj. an exclamation of wonderment; oh!

औ

औ m. the eleventh vowel of the Nagari alphabet; its sign is ौ ; its sound resembles that of o in hot.

औंधा adj. having the upper part underneath, lying prostrate. adv. upside down; औंधे मुँह गिरना to fall face downward, to prostrate.

औंधी खोपड़ी m. stupid fellow, blockhead.

औंस m. ounce.

औक़ात f. 1. status. 2. capacity.

औगुन m. = अवगुण।

औघड़ m. an ascetic with strangely awkward ways.

औचक adv. ; ~ में suddenly, unexpectedly, abruptly.

औचट m. fix, predicament, quandary. adv. suddenly, unexpectedly.

औचित्य m. 1. propriety, appropriateness. 2. justification; ~ सिद्ध करना to justify.

औचित्यपूर्ण adj. 1. proper, appropriate. 2. justified.

औज़ार m. tool, implement.

औझड़ adj. whimsical.

औटना vi. to be thickened by boiling.

औटाना vt. to thicken by boiling.

औत्कर्ष्य m. = उत्कर्ष।

औत्सुक्य m. = उत्सुकता।

औदार्य m. liberality.

औद्धत्य m. = उद्धतता।

औद्योगिक adj. industrial.

औद्योगिकी f. the art or science of industrializing, techno-logy.

औद्योगीकरण m. industrialization; ~ करना to industrialize.

औद्योगीकृत adj. industrialized.

औना-पौना adj. a little less; औने-पौने दामों पर निकालना to dispose of (something) below par.

औपचारिक adj. formal; ~ कार्रवाई formal procedure.

औपचारिकता f. formality.

औपनिवेशिक adj. colonial.

औपनिवेशीकरण m. colonization.

औपन्यासिक adj. fictional. m. novelist.

और adj. other, different. conj. 1. and. 2. plus. 3. more. adv. (a little) more. pron. other.

औरत f. 1. woman, lady. 2. someone's wife. 3. maidservant.

औरस adj. legitimate; ~ संतान legitimate child.

औलाद m. progeny, issue.

औलिया m. an ascetic of a high order.

औषध m. medicine.

औषध विज्ञान m. pharmacology.

औषधालय m. 1. pharmacy, medical store. 2. dispensary.

औषधि f. = ओषधि।

औषधीय adj. 1. medicinal,

medical. 2. pharmacological.

औसत adj. average, mean; ~ दर्जे का mediocre. m. average; ~ से अधिक above average; ~ से कम below average.

औसतन adv. on an average.

औसाना vt. to winnow.

क

क m. the first consonant of the Nagari alphabet, the first of the soft palatal pentad of consonants; its sound is like that of k in kite.

कंकड़ m. pebble.

कंकड़ी f. 1. small pebble. 2. (plu.) small stones used to make roads, gravel.

कँकड़ीला adj. strewn with uneven pieces of stone; ~ रास्ता pathway strewn with uneven pieces of stone.

कंकण m. bracelet.

कंकरीट m. concrete.

कंकाल m. skeleton.

कंगन m. bracelet.

कंगला adj. = कंगाल।

कंगलापन m. = कंगाली।

कंगारू m. kangaroo.

कंगाल adj. & m. pauper, penniless.

कंगालपन m. = कंगाली।

कंगाली f. pauperism. penury.

कँगूरा m. turret, parapet, battle-ment.

कंघा m. comb.

कंघी f. small comb; ~ करना to comb.

कंघी-चोटी f. hair-do; ~ करना (i) act of tidying the hair with a comb, (ii) to do the hair.

कंचन m. gold; ~ बरसना raining of wealth, as it were.

कंचनकाया f. comely figure.

कंचुक m. 1. an old fashioned overcoat. 2. slough of a snake. f. bodice.

कंचुकी m. an attendant, door-keeper. f. bodice.

कंजर m. nomad.

कंजा adj. & m. 1. one having greyish blue eyes. 2. croo-ked.

कंजूस adj. miserly, niggardly. m. miser.

कंजूसी f. miserliness, niggard-liness.

कंटक m. 1. thorn. 2. nuisance. 3. difficulty.

कंटकमय adj. thorny.

कंटकाकीर्ण adj. 1. thorny, prickly. 2. full of trouble and difficulty.

कंटर m. decanter.

कँटिया f. 1. nail. 2. fish hook.

कँटीला adj. 1. thorny. 2. barbed.

कंट्रैक्ट m. contract.

कंट्रैक्टर m. contractor.

कंट्रोल m. control.

कंठ m. throat, ~ करना to commit to memory.

कंठगत adj. committed to memory.

कंठमाला f. scrofula, goitre, mumps.

कंठसंगीत m. vocal music.

कंठस्थ adj. committed to memory, memorized; ~ करना to learn by heart, to commit to memory.

कंठहार m. necklace.

कंठा m. necklace of big beads.

कंठाग्र adj. committed to mem- ory.

कंठी f. necklace or string of small beads.

कंठ्य adj. 1. guttural; 2. vocal.

कंडक्टर m. conductor.

कंडरा m. tendon.

कंडा m. dried cow-dung cake.

कंडाल m. a trough for preserving water.

कंडी f. 1. diminutive of कंडा 2. small basket. पेट में ~ पड़ जाना solidification of faecal matter in the intestines.

कंडील f. 1. candle-stick. 2. candle-lamp. 3. lantern.

कंडु m. itches, ringworm.

कंडौरा m. 1. heap of cow-dung cakes. 2. place where such cakes are kept.

कंत m. one's husband or lover.

कंथा f. a wrapper sewn out of worn-out garments.

कंद m. a thick root used as food, rhizome.

कंद-मूल m. edible root or the like.

कंदरा f. cave, cavern.

कंदील f.= कंडील।

कंदुक m. ball; ~ खेलना to play with a ball.

कंधा m. 1. the part between arm and neck, shoulder. 2. the part of the garment that covers the shoulder; मेरी क़मीज़ कंधे से फट गई My shirt split across the shoulder.

कँपकँपी f. tremor, shivering: ~ छूट जाना—उसकी कँपकँपी छूट गई A shiver ran through him.

कंपन m. 1. vibration. 2. the shiver, quiver.

कंपनी f. company.

कंपाउंडर m. compounder.

कंपायमान adj. quivering, trembling.

कंपास m. compass.

कंपित adj. trembling.

कंबख़्त adj. unfortunate, damned.

कंबख़्ती f. misfortune, ill-luck.

कंबल m. blanket.

कई adj. many, several; ~ एक several, many a; ~ कई बार repeatedly; ~ रोज़ several days.

ककड़ी f. cucumber; किसी को ~ -खीरा समझना to consider somebody as a weakling.

ककहरा m. alphabet.

कक्ष m. 1. orbit. 2. class. 3. room. 4. armpit.

कक्षा f. 1. orbit. 2. class. 3. classroom.

क ख ग m. A B C (elements of a subject).

कखौरी f. 1. a boil in the armpit.

कगार m. 1. very steep slope, precipice. 2. high and steep bank. 3. verge, brink.

कच adj. abbreviation of कच्चा used in compound words. m. hair.

कचकच f.= किचकिच।

कचकचाना vt. to grind the teeth in anger.

कचड़ा m. refuse.

कचदिला adj. weak-hearted.

कचनार m. a kind of tree which yields beans and flowers.

कचर-कचर f. sound produced while eating raw fruit.

कचरा m. 1. sweepings, rubbish. 2. worthless matter.

कचरी f. a slice of potato (or any other vegetable) dried and fried, chip.

कचहरी f. court; दीवानी ~ civil court; फौजदारी ~ session court.

कचाई f. = कच्चापन।

कचायँध f. smell of rawness.

कचालू m. 1. a variety of edible root. 2. Indian dish of vegetables or fruit with a dash of lemon/tamarind.

कचूमर m. 1. pickles prepared from crushed fruit. 2. anything crushed or reduced to pulp; ~ निकालना/निकाल देना (i) to crush/pound well, (ii) to defeat or humiliate completely.

कचूर m. medicinal plant (Curcuma zedoaria).

कचोट f. smarting sensation.

कचोटना vi. to smart.

कचौड़ी f. a variety of an Indian loaf fried and puffed.

कचौरी f. = कचौड़ी।

कच्चा adj. 1. unripe, green. 2. immature, weak. 3. not well-made, solid or strong; कच्ची सड़क unmetalled road; ~ घर a mud house; कच्ची ईंट a mud brick. 4. not fast; ~रंग colour likely to fade. 5. lacking skill; ~ कारीगर unskilled labour. 6. lacking in firmness. 7. raw; ~ माल raw material. 8. inexperienced; ~ हाथ an unskilled workman. 9. unrefined; कच्ची चीनी unrefined sugar. 10. rough; ~ चिट्ठा rough account; कच्ची नक़ल a rough copy; कच्ची बही a rough ledger. 11. provisional, not final; कच्ची रसीद a provisional receipt. 12. improper or unreliable; ~ असामी unreliable person.

कच्चा-पक्का adj. half-cooked.

कच्चापन m. the quality or state of being raw, rawness.

कच्चे-बच्चे m. children.

कच्छप m. tortoise.

कच्छप-गति f. snail's pace.

कछनी f. 1. lower garment. 2. small loin-cloth.

कछार m. alluvial land.

कछारी adj. alluvial.

कछुआ m. tortoise, turtle.

कछौटा m. cloth worn between the legs; ~ कसना/बाँधना to put on such a cloth.

कज adj. crooked, curved. m. defect, flaw.

कजरा adj. of jet black colour. m.= काजल।

कजरारा adj. jet-black.

कजरी f. a typical folk song usually sung in rainy season.

कजरौटा m. = कजलौटा।

कजलाना vi. 1. to become black. 2. to apply collyrium to the eyes.

कजली f. = कजरी।

कजलौटा m. a characteristic container for keeping collyrium.

कज्जल m. = काजल।

कटक f. army.

कटकट f. 1. sound of clicking teeth. 2. wordy warfare.

कटकटाना vi. = किटकिटाना।

कटकीना m. artifice, stratagem; कटकीने का आदमी man of tact.

कटखना adj. given to biting.

कटघरा m. witness box.

कटड़ा m. = कटरा।

कटन f. 1. incision. 2. erasion.

कटना vi. 1. to be cut; बाल कट गए हैं The hair has been cut. 2. to be cancelled, to be struck off. 3. to be deducted. 4. to be non-plussed. 5. to stand refuted. 6. to be divi-ded leaving no remainder; 35 पाँच (5) से कटता है 35 is divisible by 5.

कटनी f. 1. harvest. 2. harvest time.

कटपीस m. a piece of cloth (sold at a reduced price).

कटर m. a small boat.

कटरा m. 1. mart, small market. 2. male calf of a buffalo.

कटवाँ adj. wavy (border).

कटवाँ ब्याज m. simple interest.

कटवाना vt. 1. to cause to be cut or bitten. 2. to get (something) cut; बाल ~ to have hair cut.

कटहल m. jack tree or its fruit.

कटहा adj. prone to bite.

कटाई f. 1. act of cutting, reaping etc. 2. wages paid for cutting. 3. harvesting, reaping.

कटाई-छँटाई f. act of cutting and pruning.

कटाकटी f. bitter enmity.

कटाक्ष m. taunt, sarcasm; ~ करना to make a sarcastic remark or fling.

कटाक्षपूर्ण adj. sarcastic.

कटा-छँटा adj. well-pruned.

कटान m. 1. state or act of cutting. 2. manner/style of cutting.

कटाना vi. to get (someone or something) cut.

कटा-फटा adj. torn and mutilated.

कटामरी f. carnage, bloodshed.

कटार f. cutlass, dagger.

कटारी f. small dagger, hatchet.

कटाव m. shape (of land) resulting from erosion, notch.

कटावदार adj. (a variety of embroidery) involving the process of cutting with a pair of scissors.

कटि f. waist.

कटिबंध m. 1. zone. 2. girdle, belt.

कटिबद्ध adj. determined, gird up.

कटिबद्धता f. resolve, resolution.

कटिया f. 1. female calf of a buffalo. 2. fishing-hook.

कटीला adj. sharp-edged.

कटु adj. bitter, pungent.

कटुता f. bitterness, acrimony.

कटुभाषी adj. (one) who speaks bitterly.

कटूक्ति f. bitter remark.

कटोरदान m. metal bowl with a lid.

कटोरा m. metal bowl.

कटोरी f. small metal bowl.

कटौती f. 1. deduction, cut.

कट्टर adj. 1. staunch, orthodox. 2. fanatic.

कट्टरता f. 1. orthodoxy, big-otry. 2. fanaticism.

कट्टरपंथी adj. hardliner, ort-hodox.

क

कठघरा m. 1. large wooden cage. 2. witness box.

कठड़ा m. large wooden tub.

कठपुतली f. 1. a small doll moved by strings, puppet. 2. a person whose actions are controlled by another, puppet.

कठफोड़ा m. wood-pecker.

कठबहन f. uterine sister.

कठबाप m. step-father.

कठभाई m. uterine brother.

कठमुल्ला m. bigoted/staunch Muslim priest. (pej.)

कठवैद्य m. quack.

कठिन adj. 1. difficult. 2. hard, severe.

कठिनता f. difficulty.

कठिनाई f. difficulty, hardship.

कठुआना vi. to become dry and hard like wood.

कठोर adj. 1. hard. 2. strict, rigid. 3. cruel, hard. 4. rigorous; ~ कारावास rigorous imprisonment. 5. severe, drastic.6. stern; ~ चेहरा stern face, wry face.

कठोरता f. 1. hardness. 2. rigidity. 3. cruelty. 4. rigorousness. 5. severity, rigour.

कठौता f. wooden tub.

कड़क f. clap, thunder, crack.

कड़कड़ f. sound like cracking.

कड़कड़ाना vi. to crackle (as of oil boiling), to thunder.

कड़कड़ाहट f. clap.

कड़कना vi. to clap, to thunder; कड़ककर बोलना to speak loudly as thunder, to thunder forth.

कड़वा adj. bitter; कड़वी-मीठी यादें bitter-sweet memories.

कड़वा-कसैला adj. bitter and astringent; ~ मुँह bitter and astringent taste in the mouth.

कड़वा तेल m. mustard oil.

कड़वापन m. bitterness.

कड़वाहट f. bitterness, bitter taste.

कड़ा adj. 1. hard, stiff. 2. difficult. 3. strong, rigid, stringent. 4. strict. 5. rigorous, severe. 6. stern.

कड़ाई f. 1. strictness. 2. sternness.

कड़ाका m. loud crash.

कड़ापन m. = कड़ाई।

कड़ाबीन f. a short light rifle, carbine.

कड़ाहा m. huge frying pan, cauldron.

कड़ाही f. a kind of deep frying pan, wok.

कड़ी f. 1. link. 2. beam, rafter.

कड़ुआ adj. = कड़वा।

कढ़ना vi. 1. (a liquid) to thiken by boiling. 2. to come out or fly away; कढ़ जाना (a woman) to elope. 3. to be embroidered.

कढ़वाना vt. 1. to cause to thicken by boiling (a liquid). 2. to have (something) embroidered.

कढ़ाई f. 1. embroidery. 2. remuneration paid for embroidery.

कढ़ाना vt. to get (something) embroidered.

कढ़ी f. an Indian preparation akin to curry.

कण m. 1. particle. 2. drop.

कणिका f. particle.

क़तई adv. absolutely; ~ नहीं absolutely not.

कतना vi. to be spun.

कतरन f. paring, cutting.

कतरना vi. to clip/trim.

कतरनी f. scissors.

कतर-ब्योंत f. cutting to measurement. 2. manipulation.

क़तरा m. drop.

कतराना vi. to avoid meeting, shirk; कतराकर निकल जाना to avoid the sight and walk away.

कतला m. rectangular piece sply. of a sweet dish.

कतली f. small and thin rectangular piece of a sweet dish.

क़तलेआम m. = क़त्लेआम।

कतवाना vt. to have (something) spun.

कतवार m. 1. sweepings, refuse. 2. trash, rubbish.

कताई f. 1. spininig. 2. remuneration paid for spinning.

कताई-घर m. spinning house.

कताई-बुनाई f. spinning and weaving.

क़तार f. line, row; ~ बाँधना/लगाना to form a queue/beeline.

कतिपय adj. a few, some.

कत्थई adj. 1. of the colour of catechu. 2. of dark red colour.

कत्थक m. a variety of classical Indian dance.

कत्था m. catechu tree and its resin.

क़त्ल m. murder.

क़त्लेआम m. general massacre.

कथक m. teller of old stories, professional story-teller,

कथक्कड़ m. story-teller.

कथन m. 1. something said or stated, narration, statement. 2. assertion, view-point.

कथनानुसार, के postposition. as per (one's) statement or assertion, in accordance with (one's) statement.

कथनी f. anything said.

कथनीय adj. worth saying.

कथरी f. poorman's bedding made of rags.

कथांतर m. 1. digression. 2. side-story.

कथा f. 1. mythological story. 2. tale, story, narrative.

कथाकार m. story-writer.

कथानक m. plot of a drama, novel, story etc.

कथापुरुष m. legendary or fabulous person.

कथामुख m. introductory part of a story.

कथावस्तु f. contents of a story, drama etc.

कथावार्ता f. religious discourse, discourse on a mythological topic.

कथासार m. synopsis (of a story).

कथासूत्र m. clue of a story, drama etc.

कथित adj. 1. stated, said, narrated. 2. alleged; ~ व्यक्ति alleged person.

कथोपकथन m. conversation, dialogue.

कथ्य adj. = कथनीय।

कदंब m. Anthocephalus cadamba.

क़द m. size, stature, height.

कदन्न m. coarse grain, vile meal.

क़दम m. footstep, step, pace.

कदली m. plantain tree. (see केला)

कदाचार m. bad conduct, misbehaviour, misdeed.

कदाचित् adv. perhaps, probably.

कदापि adv. seldom; ~ नहीं never.

क़द्दावर adj. large-sized, full-grown.

कद्दू m. pumpkin, gourd.

कद्दूकस m. gadget for turning a pumpkin, gourd, coconut etc. into parings.

क़द्र f. 1. worth. 2. regard, appreciation.

क़द्रदान adj. & m. one who appreciates, admirer.

क़द्रदानी f. appreciation of merit, admiration.

कन m. 1. particle, grain. 2. abbreviation of कान।

कनक m. 1. gold. 2. thorn-apple. 3. wheat.

कनकटा adj. having an ear chopped/cut off.

कनकी f. fragment of a grain, esp. of rice.

कनकैया f. kite.

कनकौआ m. big kite.

कनखजूरा m. centipede.

कनखियाना vt. 1. to cast a side-glance. 2. to give a signal with the eye.

कनखी f. side-glance, wink; ~ मारना to give a wink.

कनछेदन m. (ceremony of) piercing a child's ear-lobe.

कनटोप m. large cap covering the ears, ear-cap.

कनपटी f. temple.

कनपेड़ा m. mumps.

कनफटा adj. having ears cut off.

कनफूल m. ear-ring of the shape like a flower.

कनमनाना vi. to move a little this side or that during sleep.

कनसुई f. act of secretly listening to other people's conversation; ~ लेना to eavesdrop.

कनस्टर m. = कनस्तर।

कनस्तर m. canister.

कनागत m. the dark fortnight of the month of Ashwin.

कनात f. side screen usually of a thick cloth.

कनियाना vi. 1. to avoid the sight of someone. 2. to incline one side (said of a kite).

कनिष्ठ adj. junior.

कनिष्ठिका f. little finger.

कनी f. small particle (of diamond, rice etc.).

कनीज़ f. woman attendant, maidservant.

कनीनिका f. 1. pupil of the eye. 2. unmarried girl, maiden.

कनेठी f. twisting of the ear (as a form of punishment).

कनौड़ा m. one-eyed person.

कन्नड़ m. 1. a region of South India. 2. an inhabitant of the above region.
f. the language of the above region.

कन्ना m. 1. string tied to a kite;

~ बाँधना to tie string to a kite; ~ साधना to tie the string to a kite properly for keeping its balance even. 2. small bits of rice.

कन्नी f. 1. edge of a kite; ~ काटना to avoid meeting someone; ~ खाना (of kite) to incline in some direction due to some defect or being imblanced.

कन्यका f. maiden.

कन्या f. 1. maiden, virgin, lass. 2. girl. 3. daughter.

कन्यादान m. offering a daughter in marriage.

कन्याधन m. property belonging to a girl before marriage.

कन्याराशि f. Virgo (sign of Zodiac).

कन्यारासी adj. unfortunate, unlucky, unpropitious.

कन्हैया m. Lord Krishna.

कपट m. deception, deceit, fraud.

कपटजाल m. stratagem to ensnare someone.

कपटपुरुष m. scare-crow, camouflage, impostor.

कपटपूर्ण adj. deceitful, fraudulent, cunning.

कपटपूर्वक adv. deceitfully.

कपट-योजना f. conspiracy, fraudulent plan.

कपटवेश m. disguise.

कपट-व्यवहार m. foul play.

कपटसंधि m. collusion.

कपटी adj. deceitful, insincere.

कपड़कीड़ा m. clothes-moth.

कपड़छन m. straining through cloth.

कपड़छान adj. which has been strained through cloth.

कपड़ा m. 1. cloth. 2. dress, clothes.

कपड़ा-लत्ता m. clothings, clothes, outfit.

कपड़े m. (plu.) clothes, garments, apparels.

कपाट m. 1. door. 2. valve.

कपाटिका f. valve.

कपार m. = कपाल।

कपाल m. skull, cranium.

कपालक्रिया f. Hindu rite of beating the skull of a burning corpse.

कपालिका f. Goddess Kali.

कपास f. 1. cotton plant. 2. cotton flower.

कपि m. monkey.

कपिल adj. reddish brown, of the colour of copper.

कपिलधारा f. the Ganga.

कपिश adj. darkish brown.

कपूत m. 1. a son given to bad or wicked ways. 2. undutiful son.

कपूर m. camphor; ~ खाना to take poison.

कपूरी adj. 1. made of camphor. 2. of the colour of camphor, of a yellowish hue.

कपोत m. 1. pigeon. 2. dove.

कपोतवृत्ति f. disposition of spending all that one earns.

कपोतव्रत m. tendency to suffer quietly and silently.

कपोती f. 1. female pigeon or dove. 2. virgin.

कपोल m. cheek.

कपोल-कल्पना f. fanciful or mere imagination.

कपोल-कल्पित adj. imagined.

कप्तान m. captain.

कफ़ m. 1. phlegm, mucus. 2. cuff of a shirt.

कफ़न m. funeral outfit, shroud.

क़फ़स f. 1. cage. 2. prison, gaol.

कबंध m. 1. headless trunk. 2. tube.

कब adv. at what time? when?

कबड्डी f. kabaddi, an Indian outdoor game.

कबरी f. braid.

कबाड़ m. lumber, junk.

कबाड़ख़ाना m. place where useless things are stored.

कबाड़ा m. mess, imbroglio.

कबाड़िया m. = कबाड़ी।

क़बाड़ी m. one who deals in old and broken articles, junk dealer.

कबाब m. roasted meat.

क़बाला m. title deed relating to ownership of some property.

क़बीला m. 1. tribe. 2. wife.

कबूतर m. pigeon.

कबूतरख़ाना m. pigeon house.

कबूतरबाज़ m. pigeon fancier.

कबूतरी f. female pigeon.

क़बूल m. 1. confession, admission. 2. agreement.

क़बूलना vi. to confess/admit; हार क़बूल करना to admit defeat.

क़ब्ज़ f. constipation.

क़ब्ज़ा m. 1. possession 2. occupation, 3. hinge.

क़ब्ज़ियत f. constipation.

क़ब्ज़ेदार adj. provided with a hinge; ~ पल्ला hinged door.

क़ब्र f. grave.

क़ब्रगाह f. = क़ब्रिस्तान।

क़ब्रिस्तान m. graveyard, cemetery.

कभी adv. 1. at some time. 2. at any time; ~ तो once a while; ~ न कभी sometime or the other; ~ नहीं never.

कमंडल m. a pot of a special kind, characteristic of a mendicant.

कमंद f. lasso.

कम adj. 1. less. 2. short. 3. (too) little.

कमअक़्ल adj. foolish.

कमउम्र adj. juvenile.

कमख़र्च adj. thrifty, miserly.

कमख़ाब m. brocade.

कमज़ोर adj. weak.

कमज़ोरी f. 1. weakness. 2. a weak point in a person's character.

कमती adj. = कम।

कमती-बढ़ती f. increase or decrease.

कमनसीब adj. unlucky, unfortunate.

कमनीय adj. comely, beautiful.

कमनीयता f. comeliness, beauty.

कमबख़्त adj. 1. unlucky, unfortunate, 2. darned.

कमबख़्ती f. ill-luck, misfortune.

कमर f. waist; ~ कसना to gird up

(one's) loins ~ सीधी करना to relax for a while.

कमरख f. a very sour and rather pungent fruit.

कमरतोड़ adj. back-breaking, very strenuous.

कमरबंद m. girdle, waistband.

कमरा m. room.

कमल m. 1. lotus. 2. jaundice.

कमल-ककड़ी f. root of lotus, used as a vegetable.

कमलगट्टा m. seed of lotus used as a vegetable.

कमलनयनी f. a woman having eyes like lotus.

कमलनाल m. the stalk of lotus.

कमला f. Lakshmi, goddess of wealth.

कमलिनी f. 1. small lotus. 2. pond full of lotuses.

कमली f. smallish blanket.

कमवाना vt. to cause to earn.

कमसिन adj. fairly young, youngish, sply. said of a girl.

कमांडर m. commander.

कमाई f. earnings, income.

कमाऊ adj. earning a livelihood, money earner.

कमाऊ-खाऊ adj. (one) who earns (well) and spends (well).

कमाची f. twig.

कमान f. 1. bow. 2. order.

कमाना vi. 1. to earn. 2. to tan (skin or hide). 3. to scavenge; पाख़ाना ~ to scavenge latrines.

कमाना-धमाना vt. = कमाना।

कमानी f. spring.

कमानीदार adj. fitted with a spring, springed.

कमाल m. 1. feat. 2. miracle. ~ का extremely remarkable.

कमासुत adj. (a person) who earns well.

कमिश्नर m. commissioner. [H.E. आयुक्त]

कमी f. 1. shortage; 2. reduction. 3. deficiency, shortcoming.

क़मीज़ f. shirt.

कमीना adj. mean, wretched.

कमीनापन m. meanness, wretchedness.

कमीशन m. 1. commisson. [H.E. आयोग] 2. discount. [H.E. छूट]

कमेटी f. committee. [H.E. समिति]

कमेरा m. workman, labourer.

कमोड m. commode.

कमोरा m. a large earthen pot (primarily used for keeping water).

कम्युनिज़्म m. communism. [H.E. साम्यवाद]

कम्युनिस्ट adj. & m. communist. [H.E. साम्यवादी]

क़याम m. stay for a time, sojourn; ~ करना to make a stay.

क़यामत f. disaster, catastrophe; ~ का दिन the last day of the world, doomsday, day of judgment.

क़यास m. 1. guess. 2. concep-tion.

कर m. 1. hand. 2. tax. suffix. 1. after; खाकर after eating. 2. on the plea of.

करखा m. lamp-black.

करघा m. loom; हथ-~ hand-loom.

कर-चोरी f. tax-evasion.

करछी f. ladle.

करछुल f. ladle.

करण m. 1. instrument, implement. 2. also करण कारक; instrumental case (gram.)

करणीय adj. worthy to be performed.

करतब m. feat.

करतबी m. 1. one who performs feats. 2. juggler.

करतल m. palm of a hand.

करतलध्वनि f. hand clapping, applause, cheers.

करतार m. the Creator.

करताल m. small cymbal.

करतूत f. misdeed, evil deed.

करदाता m. tax-payer.

करदेय adj. taxable.

करधनी f. girdle.

करनफूल m. ornamental ear-ring.

करना vi. 1. to do. 2. to perform/ execute. 3. to exercise.

करनी f. 1. doing, action, deed. 2. mason's trowel.

करपृष्ठ m. back part of the palm of the hand.

कर-भार m. burden of taxes.

करम m. = कर्म.

करमकल्ला m. cabbage.

कर-मुक्त adj. tax-free.

करवट f. side on which the body rests while lying.

करवा m. a small earthen pot with a spout.

करवाना vt. 1. to cause to be done, to get done/performed. 2. to make (someone) do (something).

करवैया m. doer, performer.

कराई f. the husk of pulses.

कराधान m. taxation.

कराना vt. to get done.

करामात f. feat, miracle.

करामाती adj. miraculous.

क़रार m. agreement.

क़रारनामा m. written agreement.

करारा adj. 1. crisp. 2. hard, stiff.

कराल adj. dreadful.

कराह f. moan, bemoaning sound, groan, whine.

कराहना vi. to moan/whine.

करिश्मा m. miracle.

क़रीना m. system, method,

क़रीब, के 1. near. 2. about, approximately.

क़रीबी adj. close.

करुण adj. pathetic.

करुणा f. compassion.

करुणाजनक adj. pathetic.

करुणानिधान m. the All-Merci-ful.

करुणानिधि m. the All-Merciful.

करुणामय adj. full of compassion, compassionate.

करेंट f. current. [H.E. विद्युत्-धारा] adj. current. [H.E. चालू]

करेंसी f. currency. [H.E. मुद्रा]

करेला m. bitter gourd.

करेली f. small करेला।

करैत m. a highly venomous type of Indian snake.

करोड़ adj. & m. crore, ten million.

करोड़पति m. multi-millionaire.

करौंदा m. gooseberry.

करौंदिया adj. blackish deep red.

करौली f. small dagger, poniard.

कर्क m. crab.

कर्कट m. crab.

कर्क राशि, Cancer (sign of zodiac).

कर्कश adj. harsh, strident.

कर्कशता f. harshness.

कर्कशा adj. & f. quarrelsome (woman).

क़र्ज़ m. loan, debt.

क़र्ज़दार m. debtor.

क़र्ज़दारी f. indebtedness.

क़र्ज़ा m. = क़र्ज़।

कर्ण m. 1. ear. 2. hypotenuse. (Geom.)

कर्णकटु adj. harsh (sound), jarring to the ears.

कर्णगोचर adj. audible.

कर्णधार m. 1. helmsman, steersman. 2. (fig.) leader.

कर्णप्रिय adj. melodious, pleasing to the ears.

कर्णफूल m. ear-top.

कर्णवेध m. (rite of) piercing of the ear.

कर्णेंद्रिय m. sense organ of hearing.

कर्तनी f. pair of scissors.

कर्तव्य m. duty.

कर्तव्यच्युत adj. fallen from duty.

कर्तव्यच्युति f. negligence, delinquency.

कर्तव्यनिष्ठ adj. dutiful.

कर्तव्यनिष्ठा f. dutifulness.

कर्तव्यपरायण adj. dutiful.

कर्तव्यपरायणता f. dutifulness.

कर्तव्यपालन m. fulfilment of duty/obligation.

कर्तव्यभावना f. sense of duty.

कर्तव्यविमुख adj. negligent of duty.

कर्तव्यविमूढ़ adj. on the horns of a dilemma.

कर्तव्यशील adj. dutiful.

कर्ता m. 1. Creator. 2. doer, performer. 3. Head of a joint Hindu family. 4. also कर्ता कारक; subject (grammar).

कर्तार m. Creator.

कर्तृत्व m. creative power.

कर्तृत्व-शक्ति f. executive cap-acity/power, creativity.

कर्तृवाच्य m. active voice. (Gram.)

कर्पूर m. camphor.

कर्फ़्यू m. curfew.

कर्म m. 1. deed, act, action. 2. object. (Gram.)

कर्मकांड m. the body of Hindu rituals.

कर्मकांडी m. 1. Hindu ritualist. 2. such a priest.

कर्म कारक m. (Gram.) accusative case.

कर्मक्षेत्र m. field of action.

कर्मचारी m. employee, worker.

कर्मजली adj. (woman) ill-favoured by Dame Fortune, extremely unlucky.

क

कर्मठ adj. working hard, energetic, diligent.

कर्मणा adv. by deed/action.

कर्मण्य adj. hardworking, energetic.

कर्मनिष्ठ adj. dutiful.

कर्मफल m. result of one's deeds.

कर्मबंधन m. bondage of (one's) deeds.

कर्मभूमि f. area of activity, field of action.

कर्मभोग m. undergoing the consequences of one's deeds.

कर्मयुग m. age of action.

कर्मयोग m. philosophy of action (adumbrated in the Gita).

कर्मयोगी m. man of action.

कर्मरेखा f. line of fate/destiny.

कर्मवाचक adj. passive.

कर्मवाच्य m. passive voice. (Gram.)

कर्मवीर m. man of action/dexterity.

कर्मशाला f. workshop.

कर्मशील adj. having a disposition to do (one's) duties.

कलंक m. stigma, blot.

कलंकित adj. stigmatised.

क़लंदर m. a Muslim mendicant.

कल adv. & m. 1. tomorrow. 2. yesterday. f. machine.

क़लई f. 1. plating, coating. 2. lime for whitewashing.

क़लईदार adj. plated/coated (said of utensils).

कलकंठ adj. having a sweet voice.

कलकंठी f. cuckoo.

कलकल f. (sweet) rippling sound. f. tiff; ~ मचाना to start a tiff.

कलक्टर m. collector. [H.E. समाहर्ता]

कलक्टरी f. 1. collectorate. 2. office or regime of a collector.

कल-कारख़ाना m. mill, factory.

कलग़ी f. 1. red fleshy crest of fowl. 2. tuft of feathers, hair and the like worn on head-dress.

कलछी f. ladle.

कलजिब्भा f. evil-tongued.

कलधौत adj. 1. golden. 2. silvery. m. 1. gold. 2. silver.

कलन m. calculus (Maths).

कलपना vi. to lament grumblingly; रोना- ~ to cry and bewail.

कलपाना vt. to tease (someone) to tears.

कल-पुर्ज़ा m. part of a machine.

कलफ़ m. starch.

कलफ़दार adj. starched.

कलबूत m. the mould on which a shoemaker shapes the shoes.

क़लम f. 1. pen. 2. graft. 3. the growth of hair on man's temple(s); ~ बनाना to trim the hair on the temple.

क़लमदान m. inkstand, pen-stand.

क़लमबंद adj. reduced to writing; ~ करना to reduce to writing.

कलमलाना vi. to change postures due to restlessness.

कलमा m. a fundamental formula of the Quran.

क़लमी adj. grafted; ~ आम grafted mango.

क़लमी शोरा m. saltpetre.

कलमुँहाँ adj. black faced.

कलरव m. sweet chirpings.

कलवरिया f. tavern, wine-shop.

कलवार m. a Hindu caste which formerly dealt in liquor.

कलश m. 1. a large roundish water-pot. 2. metallic pinnacle of a Hindu temple.

कलह m. internecine quarrel, conflict.

कलहप्रिय adj. given to कलह, quarrelsome.

कला f. 1. art. 2. phase of the moon. 3. degree (angle). 4. membrane. 5. minute. 6. skill, knack.

कलाई f. wrist.

कलाई-घड़ी f. wrist-watch.

कलाक़ंद m. a variety of Indian sweet.

कलाकार m. artist.

कलाकृति f. work of art, workmanship.

कला-कौशल m. art and craft.

कलात्मक adj. artistic.

कलापूर्ण adj. artful, artistic.

कलाप्रेमी m. lover of art.

कलाबत्तू m. silk thread covered with gilded silver.

कलाबाज़ adj. & m. acrobat.

कलाबाज़ी f. somersault.

कलाभवन m. art gallery.

कलाल m. = कलवार।

कलावंत adj. well-versed in some art.

कलावा m. a piece of thread, tied round the wrist on (Hindu) auspicious occasions.

कलाविद् m. connoisseur of (some) art.

कलि m. = कलियुग।

कलिका f. bud.

कलिकाल m. = कलियुग।

कलिया m. meat-curry.

कलियुग m. the fourth and last eon of creation according to Hindu mythology, the present eon.

कलियुगी adj. 1. of or pertaining to कलियुग। 2. having the qualities of the present eon.

कली f. 1. bud, blossom.

कलीसिया f. church.

कलुष m. 1. black spot. 2. sin. 3. impurity. 4. filth.

कलुषित adj. tarnished.

कलेंडर m. calendar.

कलेक्टर m. collector.

कलेजी f. liver of a goat or sheep.

कलेवर m. body; ~ बदलना to pass from one body into another.

कलेवा m. breakfast.

कलैया f. somersault.

कलोल m. frolic, play, sport.

कलौंजी f. stuffed and spiced preparation of brinjal, lady's finger etc.

कल्प m. eon/aeon.

कल्पक m. barber.

कल्पना f. imagination.

कल्पनातीत adj. unimaginable.

कल्पनाप्रसूत adj. born of imagination.

कल्पनामय adj. imaginative.

क

कल्पनालोक m. world of imagination.

कल्पनाशक्ति f. power of imagination.

कल्पनीय adj. imaginable.

कल्पवृक्ष m. a tree supposed to be in heaven which grants all desires of one who sits underneath it.

कल्पांत m. end of an era.

कल्पित adj. 1. supposed, assumed. 2. imaginary, imagined.

कल्मष m. 1. sin. 2. filth, impurity.

कल्याण m. welfare.

कल्याणकारी adj. beneficial; ~ राज्य welfare state.

कल्याणी f. harbinger of all good luck.

कल्ला m. sprout.

कल्लोल m. 1. wave. 2. mirth.

कल्लोलिनी f. river.

कवच m. 1. shell. 2. armour, shield. 3. amulet.

कवच-कोठरी f. pill-box.

कवचधारी adj. & m. armoured.

कवचित adj. armoured; ~ यान armoured car.

कवयित्री f. poetess.

कवर m. cover.

कवर्ग m. class of soft palatal consonants of the Nagari alphabet, letters क्, ख्, ग्, घ्, ङ् ।

कवर्गीय adj. pertaining to कवर्ग।

कवल m. morsel, mouthful.

कवलित adj. 1. eaten or swallowed. 2. devoured; काल-~ devoured by time.

क़वाम m. substance reduced to a paste by boiling.

क़वायद f. drill.

कवि m. poet. [Fem. कवयित्री]

कविता f. 1. poem. 2. poetry, verse.

कवितापाठ m. recitation of poetry.

कवित्त m. a type of meter in classical Hindi poetry.

कवित्व m. 1. poetic spirit. 2. poetry, versification.

कवित्वपूर्ण adj. poetic.

कविराज m. 1. prince among poets. 2. a title conferred on top class physicians.

कविवर m. very good poet, poet par excellence.

कवि-सम्राट m. a poet-laureat.

कवि-सुलभ adj. having the characteristics of a poet, poetic.

कवींद्र m. king among poets, best poet.

क़व्वाली f. a form of group recitation/song in Urdu poetry.

कश m. puff; ~ खींचना/लगाना/लेना to take a puff.

कशमकश f. struggle, pulling.

कशा f. 1. rope. 2. whip, lash.

कशिश f. attraction, fascination.

कशेरुका f. backbone.

कश्ती f. boat.

कषाय adj. dark red.

कष्ट m. trouble, suffering.

कष्टकर adj. troublesome, painful.

कष्टदाता m. trouble-maker.

कष्टदायक adj. troublesome, oppressive.

कष्ट-निवारण m. removal/redressal of trouble.

कष्टप्रद adj. troublesome, painful, trying.

कष्टमय adj. full of troubles, trying, vexatious.

कष्टसाध्य adj. onerous.

कस m. 1. test, trial. 2. touchstone.

कसक f. 1. throbbing heartache. 2. throbbing pain, sting.

कसकना vi. to have a lingering pain.

कसकुट m. bronze.

कसना vt. 1. to tighten. 2. to test. 3. to reduce to shreds by rubbing on a gadget.

कसब m. prostitution; ~ कमाना to earn money by prostitution.

क़सबा m. small town; क़सबे का आदमी townsman.

क़सबी f. prostitute.

क़सबीख़ाना m. brothel.

क़सम f. oath; ~ खाना to take an oath, to swear.

कसमसाना vi. to feel a constant desire to free oneself.

कसर f. deficiency, shortcoming.

कसरत f. exercise; ~ करना to take or undergo physical exercise.

कसरती adj. athletic; ~ शरीर body built-up by physical exercises.

कसवाना vt. to get tightened.

क़साई m. butcher.

क़साईख़ाना m. slaughter-house.

कसार m. flour roasted in ghee and mixed with sugar.

कसावट f. 1. tightness. 2. estrangement, tension.

क़सीदा m. embroidery.

क़सूर m. offence, guilt.

क़सूरवार adj. guilty.

कसेरा m. brazier. [Fem. कसेरिन]

कसैला adj. astringent.

कसैलापन m. astringency.

कसैली f. betel-nut.

कसोरा m. earthen bowl.

कसौटी f. 1. touchstone. 2. criterion.

कस्तूरी f. musk.

कस्तूरी मृग m. musk deer.

क़हक़हा m. loud laugh, peal of laughter, guffaw; क़हक़हे लगाना to indulge in peals of laughter.

कहना vt. 1. to say or tell. 2. to call. m. 1. advice, instruction. 2. saying, telling.

क़हर m. calamity, disaster.

कहरवा m. a style/melody of Indian folk music.

कहलवाना vt. = कहलाना।

कहलाना vt. to inform (through somebody).

क़हवा m. coffee.

कहाँ adv. where, at which place?

कहानी f. story, tale.

कहानीकार m. story-writer.

कहार m. a Hindu caste usually employed in doing domestic chores.

कहावत f. proverb, maxim.

कहा-सुना m. मेरा ~ माफ़ करना Forgive my unpleasant remarks.

कहा-सुनी f. wordy altercation, mild quarrel.

कहीं adv. 1. somewhere, 2.

क

if, if at all; ~तुम गए तो झगड़ा हो जाएगा If you go it will lead to a quarrel. 3. lest; ~ मेरा हाथ न उठ जाए Lest I should beat you. adj. very much; उससे ~ अच्छा very much better than that; ~ अधिक very much more.

काँइयाँ adj. cunning, crafty.

कांक्षा f. desire, longing.

कांक्षित adj. desired, longed for.

काँख f. armpit.

काँखना vi. to groan while discharging bodily waste matter.

काँग्रेस m. 1. congress. 2. Indian National Congress.

काँग्रेसी adj. of or belonging to the Congress. m. Congressman.

काँच m. glass.

कांचन adj. 1. of gold. 2. gol-den. m. gold.

काँजी f. a fermented sour drink of salt and mustard.

काँजीहौद m. cattle-pound, kine-house.

काँटा m. 1. thorn. 2. nail. 3. bone of fish. 4. balance, scale.

काँटी f. small nail.

काँटेदार adj. 1. thorny. 2. bar-bed.

कांड m. 1. division, section. 2. untoward incident.

कांत adj. lovely. m. 1. lover. 2. husband.

कांता f. 1. beloved, sweetheart. 2. wife.

कांति f. lustre, splendour.

कांतिमान adj. lustrous.

कांतिहीन adj. lustreless.

कांती लोहा m. a coarse type of iron.

काँदला adj. 1. muddy. 2. dirty.

काँपना vi. to shiver/tremble.

काँव-काँव f. 1. crowing; ~ करना to crow. 2. prattle.

काँस m. a certain type of grass.

काँसा m. bronze, bell-metal.

कांस्य adj. made of bronze.

कांस्य युग m. Bronze Age.

का postposition, of.

काई f. moss.

काउंटर m. counter (of a shop).

काक m. 1. crow. 2. cork.

काकपक्ष m. lock of hair along the temple.

काकपद m. the sign (^) in writing which indicates that something has been left out.

काकरेज m. purple colour.

काकरेजी adj. purple coloured.

काकल m. glottis; ~ ध्वनि glottal sound.

काका m. 1. paternal uncle. (East) 2. small child. (West)

काकी f. 1. paternal aunt. (East) 2. small girl. (West)

काकु m. pitch (of voice).

काकुल m. curling lock, lock of hair.

काग m. 1. crow. 2. cork.

काग़ज़ m. paper.

काग़ज़-पत्र m. (plu.) papers, documents.

काग़ज़ात m. (plu.) papers, documents.

काग़ज़ी adj. made of paper. ~ बादाम a variety of almond having a thin rind.

काग़ज़ी कार्रवाई f. paperwork.

काग़ज़ी सबूत m. written/documentary proof.

काछना vt. 1. to skim (cream, scum etc.) from milk, liquid or watery substance. 2. to tie lower garment up to the waist.

काज m. 1. business, profession. 2. buttonhole.

काजल m. 1. lampblack, soot. 2. collyrium.

क़ाज़ी m. Moslem judge.

काजू m. cashew nut.

काट f. 1. the way or style of cutting. 2. rebuttal. 3. antidote.

काट-कूट f. cancellations and overwritings.

काट-छाँट f. pruning, trimm- ing.

काटना vt. 1. to cut/chop. 2. to cancel or cross. 3. to disconnect.

काटू adj. biting (beast).

काट्य adj. capable of being cut down.

काठ m. 1. timber. 2. wood.

काठ-कबाड़ m. lumber.

काठा बादाम m. a variety of almond with a hard shell.

काठी f. 1. saddle. 2. constitution of the body.

काढ़ना vt. 1. to sift, to draw out; घूँघट ~ to cover the face with a veil; to veil the face. 2. to embroider. 3. to boil; दूध ~ to condense milk by boiling.

काढ़ा m. medicinal decoction.

कातना vt. to spin.

कातर adj. moved by despair, desperate.

काता m. spun thread.

कातिक m. = कार्तिक।

क़ातिब m. writer.

क़ातिल m. murderer, assassin.

क़ातिलाना adj. murderous.

कादंबरी f. 1. cuckoo. 2. parrot. 3. wine, liquor. 4. goddess of learning.

कादंबिनी f. row or band of clouds.

कान m. 1. the ear. 2. the organ of hearing. f. slight obliquity (as in cloth).

कानन m. 1. forest. 2. house.

काना adj. having only one eye; ~ फल fruit partly eaten away by insects.

कानाफूसी f. whispering, whis-per, gossip.

कानाबाती f. whispering.

कानी कौड़ी f. 1. mutilated kauri. (cowry). 2. something of too small a value; पल्ले ~ न होना to be almost penniless.

कानीहाउस m. = काँजीहौद।

क़ानून m. law.

क़ानूनगो m. an officer of the revenue department having charge of land records of a district (परगना)।

क़ानूनदाँ m. a person well-versed in law.

क़ानूनन adv. lawfully, legally.

क़ानूनी adj. lawful, legal.

कान्ह m. Lord Krishna.

कापाली m. Lord Shiva.

कापी f. 1. copy book. [H.E. अभ्यास पुस्तिका] 2. copy. [H.E. प्रतिलिपि]

3. manuscript. [H.E. पांडुलिपि]
कापीराइट m. copyright. [H. E. प्रकाशनाधिकार]
कापुरुष m. timid person.
क़ाफ़िया m. rhyme.
काफ़िर m. infidel.
क़ाफ़िला m. caravan.
काफ़ी adj. enough. f. coffee.
काफ़ी घर m. coffee house.
काफ़ूर m. camphor; ~ होना to disappear/vanish/run away.
काबा m. a sacred place of Muslims at Mecca.
क़ाबिज़ adj. 1. in possession; ~ होना to be in possession (of). 2. constipative.
क़ाबिल adj. able, qualified.
क़ाबिलीयत f. ability, qualification.
काबुली adj. of Kabul. m. an inhabitant of Kabul.
क़ाबू m. 1. possession. 2. control.
काम m. 1. work. 2. duty. 3. business. 4. sexual desire.
कामकाज m. 1. business. 2. work.
कामकाजी adj. working; ~ महिलाएँ working women.
कामचलाऊ adj. tentative.
कामचलाऊ सरकार f. caretaker government.
कामचोर adj. & m. work-shy, inactive.
कामदार adj. embroidered.
कामदेव m. God Cupid of Hindu mythology.
कामधंधा m. business.
कामधाम m. business.
कामधेनु f. celestial cow, which bestows anything asked for.
कामना f. longing, earnest desire.
कामपीड़ित adj. sex-starved.
कामयाब adj. successful.
कामयाबी f. success.
कामरेड m. comrade.
काम-वासना f. sexual desire, libido.
कामशास्त्र m. sexology.
कामांध adj. libidinous.
कामा m. comma. [H.E. अल्पविराम]
कामातुर adj. love-sick.
कामार्त adj. love-sick.
कामासक्त adj. lustful.
कामासक्ति f. lustfulness.
कामिनी f. charming woman.
कामिल adj. accomplished, expert.
कामी adj. = कामुक।
कामुक adj. lustful.
कामुकता f. lustfulness.
कामोत्तेजक adj. lascivious.
काय-चिकित्सा f. treatment of bodily ailments.
क़ायदा m. rule; ~ क़ानून rules and regulations.
क़ायम adj. 1. established. 2. firm, fixed.
कायर adj. timid, cowardly.
कायरता f. cowardice, timidity.
क़ायल adj. fully convinced.
कायस्थ m. a caste among the Hindus.
काया f. body.
कायाकल्प m. rejuvenation.
कायापलट m. overhaul.
कायिक adj. physical, bodily.
कार f. motor car; ~ चलाना to drive a car.

कारक m. 1. case. (Gram.) 2. agent, factor.

कारक-चिह्न m. case ending.

कारकुन m. = कारिंदा।

कारख़ाना m. factory, mill.

कारख़ानेदार m. mill-owner.

कारगर adj. effective, effectual.

कारचोब m. embroiderer.

कारचोबी f. embroidery.

कारज m. = काज (work).

कारटून m. cartoon. [H.E. व्यंग्यचित्र]

कारण m. 1. cause, reason, means. 2. motive, purpose.

कारण, के postposition. because of, on account of; वह पीड़ा के ~ बैठ गया He sat down because of pain.

कारणवश adv. due to (a certain) cause.

कारतूस m. cartridge.

कारनामा m. feat.

कारनिस f. cornice.

कारवाँ m. caravan.

कारसाज़ adj. skilful.

कारसाज़ी f. skilfulness.

कारस्तानी f. misdeed.

कारा f. prison, jail.

कारागार m. = कारागृह।

कारागृह m. prison, cell.

कारापाल m. jailor.

कारावास m. 1. imprisonment. 2. prison, jail.

कारिंदा m. work-agent.

कारीगर m. 1. artisan, craftsman. 2. mason.

कारीगरी f. workmanship, craftsmanship.

कारुणिक adj. pathetic.

क़ारूँ m. 1. Croesus, a fabulously rich king of Asia Minor of 6th century B.C. 2. a very rich man.

क़ारूँ का ख़जाना m. immense riches.

कारोबार m. business, trade, calling.

कारोबारी m. businessman.

कार्ड m. card. [H.E. पत्रक]

कार्तिक m. eighth month of Hindu calendar.

कार्तिकेय m. elder brother of Lord Ganesh.

कार्बन m. carbon.

कार्य m. 1. work, task, affair. 2. deed, act. 3. function; सर्वनाम संज्ञा का ही ~ करता है A pronoun does the work/function of a noun.

कार्यकर्ता m. 1. worker, agent. 2. staff.

कार्य-कारण m. cause and effect.

कार्यकारी adj. acting.

कार्यकाल m. term, tenure.

कार्यकुशल adj. efficient.

कार्यकुशलता f. efficiency.

कार्यक्रम m. 1. programme. 2. plan.

कार्यक्षम adj. competent.

कार्यक्षमता f. competence.

कार्यक्षेत्र m. field, scope.

कार्यदिवस m. workday.

कार्यनीति f. course of action.

कार्यपालिका f. the executive, executive body.

कार्य-प्रणाली f. working procedure, method.

कार्यभार m. charge.

कार्यभारी m. in-charge;~ संपादक

editor in-charge.
कार्य-योजना f. working plan.
कार्यरत adj. engaged in work, busy.
कार्यवाहक adj. acting, offciat-ing.
कार्यविधि f. procedure, methodology, method.
कार्य-विवरण m. proceedings.
कार्यशाला f. workshop.
कार्य-समिति f. working committee.
कार्यसिद्धि f. fulfilment, acc-omplishment of object/work.
कार्यसूची f. agenda.
कार्यस्थगन m. adjournment; ~ प्रस्ताव adjournment motion.
कार्यस्थल m. work-place.
कार्यान्वयन m. implementation.
कार्यान्वित adj. implemented; ~ करना to implement.
कार्यालय m. office.
कार्यावली f. agenda.
कार्रवाई f. 1. action, proceedings. 2. operation; सैनिक ~ military operation.
काल m. 1. time, 2. era, epoch. 3. tense (gram.). 4. = अकाल।
काल-कवलित adj. devoured up by time.
काल-कोठरी f. solitary cell of a prison.
कालक्रम m. chronology.
कालक्रमिक adj. chronological.
कालजयी adj. immortal.
कालदोष m. anachronism.
कालम m. column. [H.E. स्तंभ]
कालयापन m. 1. spending of time. 2. procrastination.
कालर m. collar.
कालरात्रि f. 1. night of annihila-tion, 2. aweful dark night.
काल-विभाजन m. 1. periodiza-tion. 2. forms of a verb that show time.
कालांतर m. interval (of time); ~ में in course of time, after some time.
काला adj. 1. black. 2. dark. 3. evil.
काला-कलूटा adj. dark skinned (connoting ugliness).
काला कौआ m. raven.
काला चोर m. 1. vilest of thieves. 2. vilest of men.
काला जीरा m. black tiny cumin seeds used as flavourings.
कालातीत adj. time-barred, lapsed.
काला धन m. black money.
काला नमक m. black salt.
काला नाग m. 1. blackish cobra. 2. venomous villain.
काला पानी m. transportation for life.
काला बाज़ार m. black market.
कालावधि f. period, duration.
काला-सफ़ेद adj. black and white.
कालिका f. = काली, चंडी।
कालिख f. stain, spot, slur, blackness; मुँह पर ~ पोतना/लगाना (i) to blacken (someone's) face, (ii) to tarnish (some-one's) image/face.
कालिमा f. blackness.
काली f. 1. goddess Durga. 2. black ink.
काली खाँसी f. whooping cough.
क़ालीन m. carpet.
काली मिर्च f. black pepper.
काली सूची f. black list.

कालेज m. college. [H.E. महाविद्यालय]
कालोचित adj. timely.
कालौंछ, कालौंस f. blackness.
काल्पनिक adj. 1. imaginary. 2. fictitious.
कावा m. lounging of a horse; ~ काटना (i) to move round and round; (ii) to bypass.
काव्य m. poetry.
काव्यपाठ m. recitation of poetic compositions.
काव्यमय adj. poetical.
काव्यशास्त्र m. poetics.
काव्यात्मक adj. poetical.
काश interj. oh, alas!
काशीफल m. squash gourd.
काश्त f. farming.
काश्तकार m. farmer, peasant.
काश्तकारी f. farming.
काषाय adj. brownish red.
काष्ठ m. 1. wood. 2. timber.
काष्ठ-कला f. woodcraft.
कासनी adj. violet.
कासमिक adj. cosmic. [H.E. ब्रह्मांडीय]
काहिल adj. sluggish, lethargic.
काहिली f. sluggishness.
काही adj. blackish green.
काहू pron. anyone, whosoever.
काहे adv. see क्यों (why); ~ को what for?
किंकर m. servant, lackey.
किंकर्तव्यविमूढ़ adj. not knowing what to do or say, at one's wits' end.
किंकिणी f. small bell.
किंगिरी f. a small stringed instrument.
किंचित adj. a little, some.
किंतु conj. but, however.
किंवदंती f. hearsay, rumour.
किंवा conj. or, otherwise.
कि conj. 1. that. 2. or; तुम पूरब जाओगे ~ पश्चिम Will you go East or West?
किचकिच f. squabble, quarrel.
किटकिटाना vi. to gnash teeth (in rage).
कितना adj. 1. how? 2. how much? 3. how many?
m. how much money?
क़िता m. unit (usu. immovable property); कै ~ मकान How many units of houses?
किताब f. book.
किताब-घर m. book-house, bookshop.
किताबी adj. bookish.
किताबी कीड़ा m. bookworm.
किधर adv. in what direction.
किन pron. (plu. of किस); ~ को to whom, to which persons?
किनारा m. 1. bank, shore. 2. border, brim. 3. edge.
किनाराकशी f. keeping aloof.
किनारी f. hem, border.
किनारीदार adj. bordered.
किन्नर m. eunuch.
किन्हें pron. whom (pl.)?
किफ़ायत f. thrift; ~ करना to observe thrift.
किफ़ायतशार adj. thrifty.
किफ़ायतशारी f. thriftiness.
किफ़ायती adj. economical.
क़िबला m. 1. Mecca, the holy city of

क

Muslims. 2. object of veneration.

किम् adv. what, which?

किमख़ाब m. brocade.

क़िमाम m. a semi-juicy savoury perparation of pulverised tobacco leaves.

किया m. deed, work done.

किया-कराया m. 1. the work done. 2. achievement(s).

किरंटा m. Christian. (pej.)

किरकिरा adj. sandy, gritty; मज़ा ~ हो जाना spoiling of fun/pleasure.

किरकिराना vi. to grate.

किरकिराहट f. grating sound.

किरकिरी f. 1. particle of dust. 2. disrespect, dishonour; ~ होना/हो जाना to feel ashamed.

किरक़िला m. kingfisher.

किरण f. ray, beam; ~ फूटना break of dawn.

किरन f. = किरण।

किरमिच m. canvas; ~ का जूता canvas shoe.

किरमिज़ी adj. crimson.

किराएदार m. tenant.

किराएदारी f. tenancy.

किराएनामा m. rent deed.

किराना m. grocery.

किरानी m. clerk.

किराया m. 1. rent, rental. 2. fare, hire.

किरासन m. kerosene oil.

किरिच f. bayonet.

किरीट m. crest, diadem, coronet; ~ धारी king.

किलकारना vi. to screech with joy.

किलकारी f. joyous screech.

किलकिला m. kingfisher.

किलनी f. tick.

क़िला m. fort.

क़िलेदार m. commander of a fort.

क़िलेबंदी f. fortification; ~ करना to fortify.

किलो m. kilogram.

किलोमीटर m. kilometer.

किलोल f. frolicking; किलोलें करना to frolic for joy.

किलोवाट m. kilowatt.

क़िल्लत f. scarcity, shortage.

किल्ली f. peg.

किवाड़ m. door.

किशमिश f. raisin, dried grape.

किशोर adj. adolescent, juvenile. m. teenager.

किशोरी f. 1. young girl, teen-ager. 2. belle, beautiful damsel.

किश्त f. check; ~ देना to check.

किश्ती f. boat.

किस pron & adj. 1. who? 2. which?

किसलय m. sprout, tender shoot.

किसान m. peasant, farmer.

किसानी f. husbandry.

किसी pron. inflectional form of कोई, anyone.

किसे pron. whom, to whom?

क़िस्त f. instalment.

क़िस्तबंदी f. fixation of instal-ments.

क़िस्तवार adv. by or in instal-ments.

क़िस्म f. kind, sort, variety, type.

क़िस्मत f. luck, fortune.

क़िस्मतवर adj. = क़िस्मतवाला।

क़िस्मतवाला adj. lucky, fortunate.

क़िस्सा m. story.

क़िस्सा-कोताह adv. in short.

की postposition. fem. form of का। vt. fem. form of किया (past tense of vi. करना)।
कीकर m. acacia tree.
कीच m. see कीचड़।
कीचड़ m. mud, mire.
कीट m. insect, worm.
कीटनाशक adj. insecticidal. m. insecticide.
कीट-पतंग m. (plu.) insects and moths.
कीटभक्षी adj. insectivorous.
कीटभोजी adj. insectivorous.
कीटविज्ञान m. entomology.
कीटाणु m. germ, bacillus.
कीटाणुनाशक adj. germicide.
कीड़ा m. worm.
कीड़े-मकोड़े m. (plu.) insects.
कीनना vt. to buy/purchase.
कीना m. envy, malice.
कीप f. funnel.
क़ीमत f. 1. price, cost. 2. value, worth.
क़ीमती adj. 1. expensive. 2. valuable.
क़ीमा m. hash.
कीमिया m. alchemy, chemistry.
कीर m. parrot.
कीर्तन m. congregational singing (in praise of the Lord).
कीर्ति f. 1.fame, renown. 2. glory.
कीर्तिगान m. glorification.
कीर्तिमान m. record.
कीर्ति-स्तंभ m. monument.
कील m. 1. nail. 2. a nail-like ornament worn by women in the nose, nose-pin. 3. core of a boil.
कीलक m. pivot.
कीलना vt. 1. to drive a nail (into). 2. to shut up (the mouth of a cannon).
कीली f. pivot, axis.
कुँअर m. 1. son, boy. 2. prince.
कुँआँ m. = कुआँ।
कुँआरा adj. unmarried. [Fem. कुँआरी] m. bachelor.
कुंचित adj. curled.
कुंज m. grove; आम्र ~ mango-grove.
कुंजगली f. grove lane.
कुँजड़ा m. green-grocer. [Fem. कुँजड़िन]
कुंजर m. elephant.
कुंजी f. 1. key. 2. notes on a book.
कुंठा f. frustration.
कुंठाग्रस्त adj. frustration-ridden.
कुंठित adj. 1. blunt, obtuse. 2. frustrated.
कुंड m. water-hole, pond.
कुंडल m. 1. ear-ring. 2. coil.
कुंडलाकार adj. circular, round.
कुंडलिनी f. serpent power (Hath Yoga).
कुंडली f. 1. coil; (said of a serpent). 2. horoscope.
कुंडा m. 1. large earthen bowl. 2. hasp. [Fem. कुंडी]
कुंतल m. 1. hair of the head. 2. = क्विंटल।
कुंद adj. 1. blunt, obtuse. 2. dull-headed.
कुंदन m. very fine and pure gold.
कुंदरू m. an Indian plant and its sour fruit.

कुंदा m. 1. block of wood, log. 2. butt of a gun.
कुंदी f. the act of calendering cloth.
कुंभ m. 1. pitcher. 2. religious congregation of the Hindus (usu. on the banks of some holy river).
कुंभकार m. potter.
कुँवर m. prince.
कुँवरी f. princess.
कुँवारा adj. unmarried, bachelor.
कुँवारापन m. bachelorhood, virginity.
कुँवारी adj. unmarried (woman).
कुआँ m. well.
कुआर m. seventh month of the Hindu calendar.
कुआरा adj. = कुँआरा।
कुईं water-lily.
कुकर्म m. evil/wicked deed.
कुकर्मी adj. nefarious.
कुकुर m. dog.
कुकुरखाँसी f. whooping cough.
कुकुरमुत्ता m. fungus, mushroom.
कुकृत्य m. evil/wicked deed.
कुक्कुट m. cock.
कुक्कुटपालन m. poultry farming.
कुक्षि f. 1. womb. 2. lap.
कुख्यात adj. notorious.
कुख्याति f. infamy.
कुच m. female breast.
कुचक्र m. plot, conspiracy.
कुचक्री m. conspirator, plotter.
कुचलना vt. 1. to trample (over). 2. to crush.
कुचला m. nux vomica.
कुचाल f. evil move.
कुचालक m. bad conductor.
कुचाली adj. wicked.
कुचेष्टा f. 1. misdeed. 2. evil intention.
कुछ adj. & pron. some, any.
कुजाति f. low caste.
कुटकी f. dog-fly or cattle-fly.
कुटनी f. procuress, bawd.
कुटाई f. pounding or charges paid therefor.
कुटिया f. hutment.
कुटिल adj. 1. crooked, 2. malicious.
कुटिलता f. 1. crookedness. 2. malice.
कुटी f. hut.
कुटीर f. 1. hut. 2. cottage.
कुटीर उद्योग m. cottage industry.
कुटुंब m. kinsfolk, spl. family including near relatives.
कुटुंबी m. kinsman, relative.
कुटू n. buckwheat.
कुटेव f. evil habit, addiction.
कुट्टी f. chopped fodder.
कुठला m. large earthen pot for storing grain/corn.
कुठाँव m. wrong spot.
कुठार m. hatchet, axe.
कुठाराघात m. a hard hit given with an axe.
कुठौर m. = कुठाँव।
कुड़क f. मुर्गी कुड़क गई है The hen has ceased to lay eggs.
कुड़बुड़ाना vi. to murmur.
कुढंग m. wrong method.
कुढंगा adj. unmannerly.
कुढ़न f. 1. envy, jealousy. 2. fretting, animosity.
कुढ़ना vi. 1. to be envious/jeal- ous.

2. to fret (usu. due to envy or jealousy).

कुतरन f. bits gnawed by birds, mice and the like.

कुतरना vt. to gnaw/nibble.

कुतर्क m. illogical argument.

कुतर्की m. one given to wrong mode of reasoning.

कुतिया f. bitch.

क़ुतुब m. pole star.

क़ुतुबनुमा m. compass.

कुतूहल m. curiosity.

कुतूहलपूर्ण adj. curious, inquisitive, astonishing.

कुतूहलवश adv. out of curiosity.

कुतूहली adj. inquisitive.

कुत्ता m. dog.

कुत्सित adj. despicable, contemptible.

कुदकना vi. to hop.

क़ुदरत f. nature.

क़ुदरती adj. 1. natural. 2. divine. 3. inborn.

कुदाँव m. deceitful move.

कुदान f. a jump.

कुदाना vt. to cause to jump or leap.

कुदाल f. a hoe/pick.

कुदाली f. a small hoe.

कुदिन m. 1. evil day. 2. bad time.

कुदृष्टि f. 1. malicious look. 2. leering look.

कुधातु f. bad metal.

कुनकुना adj. lukewarm.

कुनबा m. kinsfolk.

कुनबापरस्त m. nepotist.

कुनबापरस्ती f. nepotism.

कुनबी m. a peasant caste.

कुनाई f. saw-dust.

कुनैन f. quinine.

कुपथ m. wrong way, evil course.

कुपथगामी adj. deviated from certain moral standards.

कुपथ्य m. unwholesome diet.

कुपरिणाम m. evil result.

कुपात्र m. undeserving fellow.

कुपित adj. enraged.

कुपुत्र m. unworthy/unfaithful son.

कुपूत m. = कुपुत्र।

कुपूती f. mother of an un-worthy son.

कुपोषण m. malnutrition.

कुप्पा m. big leathern container.

कुप्पी f. small flask.

कुप्रथा f. evil/ bad custom.

कुप्रबंध m. mismanagement.

कुप्रभाव m. evil effect.

कुप्रवृत्ति f. bad tendency.

कुप्रशासन m. maladministration.

कुफल m. bad/evil result.

कुबड़ा adj. & m. hunch-backed. [Fem. कुबड़ी]

कुबेर m. Mammon.

कुमंत्रित adj. ill-advised.

कुमक f. reinforcement.

कुमकुम m. 1. = केसर। 2. = रोली।

कुमार adj. bachelor. m. 1. bachelor. 2. boy. 3. prince.

कुमारी adj. & f. maiden, virgin.

कुमार्ग m. bad way.

कुमार्गी adj. & m. (one) given to evil ways.

कुमुद m. lily (flower).

कुमुदिनी f. water-lily.

कुमेरु m. South Pole.

कुम्हड़ा m. sweet pumpkin.

कुम्हलाना vi. to fade/wither.
कुम्हार m. potter.
कुरकुरा adj. crisp.
क़ुरान f. Quran, the sacred book of Muslims.
कुरीति f. bad custom, evil practice.
कुरुक्षेत्र m. the field of war where महाभारत was fought.
कुरुचि f. bad taste.
कुरूप adj. ugly.
कुरूपता f. ugliness.
कुरेदना vt. 1. to scratch. 2. to probe (into).
क़ुर्क़ adj. confiscated.
क़ुर्क़-अमीन m. bailiff.
क़ुर्क़ी f. attachment (of property).
कुर्ता m. a loose outer garment with sleeves, kurta.
कुर्ती f. 1. blouse. 2. bodice.
क़ुर्बान adj. sacrificed.
क़ुर्बानी f. sacrifice.
कुर्सी f. 1. chair. 2. plinth.
कुल adj. total, gross. m. family.
कुलक m. set.
कुल-कलंक m. a shameful person, disgrace to one's family.
कुलकुलाना vi. to show restlessness.
कुलक्षण m. inauspicious or bad characteristic.
कुलटा f. unchaste woman.
कुलतंत्र m. oligarchy.
कुलदेवता m. family deity.
कुलधर्म m. family tradition.
कुलपति m. 1. chancellor. 2. vice-chancellor (of a university).
कुल-परंपरा f. family tradition.
कुलफ़ी f. ice-cream frozen in a conical container.
कुलबुलाना vi. to wriggle/ squirm.
कुलबुलाहट f. wriggling, squir-ming.
कुल-मर्यादा f. family tradition (time-honoured).
कुल-वधू f. lady (daughter-in-law) of the house.
कुल-वैर m. family feud.
कुलांगना f. = कुलवधू।
कुलाँच f. somersault.
कुलाचार m. family custom/tradition.
कुलाधिपति m. chancellor (of a university).
क़ुलाबा m. hinge.
कुलिया f. a minor canal.
कुली m. porter, coolie.
कुलीन adj. highborn, blue-blooded. m. a person of noble birth.
कुलीनतंत्र m. aristocracy.
कुलीनता f. 1. the state of being noble. 2. characteristics of a noble gentry.
क़ुल्ला m. cleansing the mouth with water.
क़ुल्ली f. = क़ुल्ला।
कुल्हड़ m. small earthen bowl.
कुल्हाड़ा m. axe.
कुल्हाड़ी f. hatchet.
कुल्हिया f. smallish earthen pot.
कुविचारी adj. indiscreet, imprudent.
कुश m. a kind of grass.
कुशल adj. skilful, skilled. m. well-being, welfare.
कुशल-क्षेम m. welfare.
कुशलता f. 1. skill. 2. efficiency. 3. well-being.
कुशलतापूर्वक adv. 1. skilfully. 2. well, in a right way.

कुशल-मंगल m. welfare.
कुशल-समाचार m. welfare tidings.
कुशा f. = कुश।
कुशाग्रबुद्धि adj. having a keen intellect.
कुशासन m. maladministration.
कुश्ती f. wrestling.
कुष्ट m. leprosy.
कुष्टी m. leper.
कुसंगति f. bad company.
कुसंस्कार m. evil tradition.
कुसगुन m. ill-omen.
कुसमय m. bad times. adv. untimely.
कुसुम m. flower.
कुहक f. cooing of a cuckoo.
कुहकना vi. to coo/warble/chirp.
कुहराम m. furore in time of distress.
कूँडा m. large earthen bowl.
कूँडी f. small earthen trough, bowl of stone.
कूक f. cooing of a cuckoo.
कूकना vi. to coo.
कूच m. 1. departure. 2. march.
कूचा m. 1. narrow street. 2. a variety of broom.
कूची f. a small brush for painting.
कूजना vt. to coo.
कूट adj. counterfeit. m. 1. mountain peak. 2. heap (of corn) as in अन्नकूट।
कूटना vt. to pound/pestle.
कूटनीति f. diplomacy.
कूटनीतिज्ञ m. diplomat.
कूटभाषा f. code-language.
कूटयोजना f. intrigue, plot.
कूटलिपि f. code-script.
कूटू m. a plant the seeds of which are powdered and used as flour.
कूड़ा m. refuse.
कूड़ा-करकट m. 1. rubbish. 2. worthless material.
कूड़ाख़ाना m. (public) place for dumping refuse.
कूड़ेदान m. a container for household rubbish, dust-bin.
कूढ़मग़ज़ adj. dullard.
कूत f. estimate.
कूतना vt. to estimate/appraise.
कूद m. jump, leap.
कूदना vi. 1. to jump/leap. 2. to hop/ spring.
कूद-फाँद f. gambol, frisking about.
कूप m. 1. well. 2. hole.
कूपन m. coupon.
कूपमंडूक m. 1. frog of the well. 2. person whose knowledge is confined to the narrow limits of his neighbourhood.
कूबड़ m. hump, hunch.
कूर्म m. tortoise.
कूल m. bank.
कूल्हा m. hip.
क़ूवत 1. physical strength 2. capability.
कृत adj. done, performed.
कृतकृत्य adj. gratified and happy.
कृतघ्न adj. ungrateful.
कृतघ्नता f. ungratefulness.
कृतज्ञ adj. grateful, thankful.
कृतज्ञता f. gratitude.
कृतज्ञतापूर्वक adv. gratefully.
कृतयुग m. = सतयुग।
कृतसंकल्प adj. determined, having a fixed purpose.
कृतार्थ adj. obliged.

क

कृति f. an artistic or literary work.
कृतिकार m. author.
कृतित्व m. achievements or works of a person.
कृत्य m. function.
कृत्रिम adj. 1. artificial. 2. unnatural; 3. affected.
कृत्रिमता f. 1. artificiality. 2. unnaturalness. 3. affectation.
कृदंत m. participle (Gram.); भूत ~ past participle.
कृपण adj. miserly, stingy.
कृपणता f. miserliness, stinginess.
कृपया adv. kindly.
कृपा f. kindness.
कृपाण f. dagger.
कृपादृष्टि f. sympathetic outlook.
कृपानिधान m. abode of kindness.
कृपापात्र m. favoured one.
कृपापूर्ण adj. kind, friendly.
कृपापूर्वक adj. kindly.
कृपालु adj. kind-hearted.
कृमि m. 1. worm. 2. insect. 3. maggot.
कृश adj. thin, emaciated.
कृशकाय adj. lean and thin.
कृषक m. peasant, cultivator.
कृषि f. agriculture.
कृषिक adj. agricultural.
कृषित adj. cultivated.
कृषि-भवन m. farmhouse.
कृषियोग्य adj. cultivable.
कृष्ट adj. cultivated.
कृष्ण adj. dark, black. m. Lord Krishna.
कृष्णपक्ष m. dark half of a lunar month.
कृष्णसागर m. Black Sea.
कृष्णाष्टमी f. eighth day of the dark half of Bhado ~ (sixth month of the Hindu calendar); birthday of Lord Krishna.
कृष्य adj. arable, cultivable.
केंचुआ m. 1. earthworm. 2. long worm nurtured in the intestines.
केंचुली f. slough (of a snake).
केंद्र m. 1. centre. 2. central government. 3. capital.
केंद्रित adj. centred.
केंद्रीकरण m. centralization.
केंद्रीकृत adj. centralized.
केंद्रीय adj. 1. central. 2. most inportant.
के postposition. 1. plural inflected form of case-ending का which shows relationship and ownership. 2. (also used independently or in combination); उसके मकान है He has a house.
केकड़ा m. crab.
केकी m. peacock.
केतकी f. an Indian flower of fragrant smell, screw-pine.
केतली f. tea kettle.
केतु m. mythological demon.
केबल m. cable.
केयूर m. an ornament for the arm.
केरल m. Kerala, a state in South India.
केला m. banana.
केलास m. crystal.
केलासन m. crystallization.

केलि f. frolic.
के लिए postposition. 1. for. 2. for the sake of. 3. to.
केवट m. oarsman, boatman.
केवड़ा m. 1. fragrant flower, pandanus. 2. extract of the flower.
केवल adv. 1. only. 2. exclusively, mainly.
केश m. hair.
केशर m. = केसर।
केशव m. Lord Krishna.
केशविन्यास m. hairdo, hair dressing.
केशिका f. capillary.
केसर m. saffron.
केसरिया adj. saffron-coloured.
केसरी m. lion.
केसरीनंदन m. Hanuman.
केंचा m. longish pair of scissors, shears.
कैंची f. pair of scissors.
कैंटीन f. canteen.
कैंडा m. tact.
कैंप m. camp.
कैंसर m. cancer.
कैंसिल adj. cancelled.
कै adj. how many?
क़ै f. vomit.
कैतव adj. cunning, dishonest.
कैथ m. wood-apple.
क़ैद f. imprisonment.
क़ैदख़ाना m. jail, prison.
क़ैदी m. 1. prisoner. 2. captive.
कैधौं conj. or, otherwise.
कैफ़ीयत f. 1. explanation. 2. remark.
कैमरा m. camera.
कैरट m. carat.
कैलाश m. = कैलास।
कैलास m. a lofty peak of the Himalayas, the abode of Lord Shiv.
कैलासनाथ m. Lord Shiv.
कैवल्य m. salvation.
कैश m. cash. [H.E. नगद]
कैसा adj. 1. how? 2. of what sort/kind/type? adv. how? वहाँ ~ रहा How had things gone there?
कैसे adv. 1. how? 2. for what purpose?
कोंचना vt. to pierce with a pointed gadget.
कोंपल f. sprout, tender offshoot.
को postposition. 1. to. 2. for.
कोई pron. someone, anyone. adj. 1. any. 2. some. adv. about, approximately.
कोकशास्त्र m. an ancient Indian treatise on sexology.
कोकिल m. = कोयल; koil, the Indian cuckoo (caculus).
कोकिला f. = कोयल।
कोकीन f. cocaine.
कोको m. 1. voice of a crow, caw-caw. 2. cocoa, cacao.
कोख f. abdomen, womb.
कोखजली adj. & f. (woman) whose children do not survive.
कोच f. coach.
कोचवान m. coachman, driver (of a horse-carriage).
कोट m. 1. coat. 2. fort, stronghold.
कोटपीस f. a game of cards.
कोटर m. hollow of a tree.

क

कोटा m. quota.

कोटि f. 1. category. 2. ten million.

कोटिशः adj. very many; ~ धन्यवाद many, many thanks.

कोटू m. buckwheat.

कोठरी f. small room, cell; अँधेरी ~ dark room/cell.

कोठा m. 1. brothel. 2. stomach.

कोठार m. storehouse.

कोठी f. 1. mansion. 2. typically Indian business house.

कोठेवाली f. prostitute.

कोड़ा m. whip.

कोड़ी f. score, set of twenty.

कोढ़ m. leprosy.

कोढ़ी m. 1. leper. 2. idler, out and out.

कोण m. angle.

कोणीय adj. angular.

कोतल m. horse decorated with all paraphernalia (usually for purposes of procession).

कोतवाल m. chief police officer of a town.

कोतवाली f. chief police station of a town.

कोताह adj. short, brief.

कोताही f. negligence.

कोदंड m. bow.

कोदों f. a variety of coarse grain.

कोना m. corner. adj. (in compounds) cornered; तिकोना three-cornered.

कोनिया m. set-square.

कोप m. anger, wrath.

कोपभवन m. an apartment in a mansion where the spouse shut herself up to express her resentment.

कोपभाजन m. victim of wrath.

कोफ़्त f. disgust.

कोफ़्ता m. a dish prepared of pounded and fried meat or vegetable, usu. oval shaped.

कोमल adj. soft, tender.

कोमलता f. softness, tenderness.

कोमलांग adj. of tender limbs.

कोमलास्थि f. cartilage.

कोयल f. Indian cuckoo.

कोयला m. coal.

कोयली adj. jet-black.

कोया m. 1. eye-ball. 2. pulpy seed of a jack-fruit.

कोर f. edge.

कोर-कसर f. deficiency, flaw.

कोरम m. quorum.

कोरमा m. dish of fried or roasted meat.

कोरस m. chorus.

कोरा adj. 1. unbleached (cloth). 2. unwashed or unused. 3. blank. 4. not very friendly. m. borderless dhoti of coarse silk.

कोरी m. a weaver class among the Hindus.

कोर्ट m. court.

कोर्स m. course.

कोल m. a jungle tribe.

कोलतार m. coal tar.

कोलाहल m. noise, uproar.

कोलाहलपूर्ण adj. noisy, uprorious.

कोलाहली adj. (person) noisy, rowdy.

कोल्हू m. crusher; ~ का बैल dru-dge.

कोश m. 1. dictionary. 2. she-ath. 3. shell.
कोशकला f. lexicography,
कोशकार m. lexicographer.
कोशवृद्धि f. hydrocele.
कोशिका f. cell.
कोशिश f. effort, endeavour.
कोशीय adj. lexical
कोष m. treasure.
कोषागार m. treasury.
कोषाध्यक्ष m. treasurer.
कोष्ठ m. 1. cell. 2. booth.
कोष्ठक m. parenthesis.
कोष्ठबद्धता f. constipation.
कोस m. a distance of two miles.
कोसना vt. to invoke a curse.
कोह m. mountain.
कोहनी f. elbow.
कोहरा m. mist, fog.
कोहराम m. tumult.
कौंध f. flash.
कौंधना vi. to flash.
कौंसिल f. council.
कौंसिलर m. councillor.
कौआ m. 1. crow. 2. uvula.
कौटुंबिक adj. familial.
कौड़ी f. cowrie, a small shell used as a coin in ancient India.
कौतुक m. 1. curious phenomenon, novelty. 2. trick (meant for entertainment).
कौतुकी m. skilful performer of wondrous tricks.
कौतूहल m. curiosity.
कौन pron. who?
कौन-सा adj. what, which?
कौपीन m. strip of cloth meant to cover the private male parts.
क़ौम f. nation, community.
कौमार्य m. virginity.
कौमार्य-भंग m. the act of deflowering or the state of being deflowered.
क़ौमियत f. nationality.
क़ौमी adj. national.
कौर m. morsel, mouthful.
क़ौल m. promise, word.
कौवा m. = कौआ।
कौशल m. skill, finesse.
कौशेय adj. silken.
क्या pron. what? interj. What! adv. used to make a sentence interrogative.
क्यारी f. bed (of flowers, vegetables etc.)
क्यों adv. why?
क्रंदन m. lamentation, bewailing.
क्रम m. order.
क्रमबद्ध adj. 1. orderly. 2. gra-ded.
क्रमशः adv. respectively.
क्रम-संख्या m. serial number.
क्रमांक m. serial number.
क्रमागत adj. consecutive.
क्रमात् adv. in due order.
क्रमानुसार adv. in due order, serially.
क्रमिक adj. 1. gradual. 2. successive.
क्रय m. purchase, buying.
क्रय-विक्रय f. 1. buying and selling. 2. purchase and sale.
क्रय-शक्ति f. buying capacity.
क्रांति f. revolution.
क्रांतिकारी adj. & m. revolu-tionary.
क्रांतिदूत m. herald of a revolution.
क्रिया f. 1. action. 2. verb.

क

क्रियाकर्म m. funeral rites.
क्रियाकलाप m. activity.
क्रियात्मक adj. practical.
क्रियान्वयन m. implementation.
क्रियान्वित adj. implemented,
क्रियापद m. verbal phrase.
क्रियाविधि f. procedure, methodology.
क्रिया-विशेषण m. adverb.
क्रियार्थक adj. verbal.
क्रियाशील adj. active.
क्रिश्चियन adj. & m. christian.
क्रीड़ा f. frolic, play.
क्रीड़ा-स्थल m. play-ground.
क्रीत adj. bought, purchased.
क्रीतदास m. slave.
क्रुद्ध adj. angry, enraged.
क्रूर adj. cruel.
क्रूरता f. cruelty.
क्रूरतापूर्ण adj. cruel.
क्रूरतापूर्वक adv. cruelly.
क्रूस m. cross.
क्रेता m. buyer, purchaser.
क्रेय adj. worth purchasing.
क्रोड़ m. lap, bosom.
क्रोड़पत्र m. supplement, appendix.
क्रोध m. anger, rage.
क्रोधाग्नि f. rage, wrath.
क्रोधित adj. see क्रुद्ध।
क्रोधी adj. hot-tempered.
क्लब m. club.
क्लर्क m. clerk.
क्लर्की f. 1. clerical job. 2. clerkship.
क्लांत adj. fatigued, tired.
क्लांति f. weariness, lassitude.
क्लास m. class.
क्लिष्ट adj. tough, hard to understand/comprehend.
क्लिष्टता f. toughness.
क्लीव adj. impotent.
क्लेश m. distress.
क्लोरोफ़ॉर्म m. chloroform.
क्वचित adv. seldom, scarcely.
क्वथन m. boiling.
क्वथनांक m. boiling point.
क्वाथ m. decoction.
क्वार m. seventh month of the Hindu calendar.
क्वारा adj. unmarried.
क्वारापन m. bachelorhood, virginity.
क्वार्टर m. quarter.
क्वालिटी f. quality.
क्षण m. moment, instant.
क्षणभंगुर adj. transient, fleeting.
क्षणिक adj. momentary.
क्षत m. wound, injury.
क्षत-विक्षत adj. wounded and dismembered.
क्षति f. 1. loss. 2. damage.
क्षतिग्रस्त adj. 1. damaged.
क्षतिपूरक adj. compensatory.
क्षतिपूर्ति f. compensation.
क्षत्राणी f. woman of the Kshatriya class.
क्षत्रिय adj. & m. (one) belonging to the Kshatriya class.
क्षत्रियत्व m. state or quality of being a क्षत्रिय।
क्षत्री adj. & m. = क्षत्रिय।
क्षमता f. capacity, capability.
क्षमा f. pardon, forgiveness.
क्षमादान m. clemency.
क्षमाप्रार्थी adj. & m. (one) who seeks forgiveness.

क्षमायोग्य adj. pardonable.
क्षमावान् adj. forgiving.
क्षमाशील adj. inclined to forgive.
क्षमाशीलता f. disposition to forgive.
क्षम्य adj. forgivable.
क्षय m. decay.
क्षय रोग m. tuberculosis.
क्षयी adj. decaying, waning.
क्षर adj. perishable.
क्षरण m. oozing.
क्षात्र adj. pertaining to a क्षत्रिय।
क्षात्रधर्म m. duty of a क्षत्रिय।
क्षार m. alkali.
क्षारक adj. caustic, salty.
क्षारता f. alkalinity.
क्षारीय adj. alkaline.
क्षारोद m. alkaloid.
क्षालन m. washing, cleaning.
क्षितिज m. horizon.
क्षितीश m. king.
क्षिप्त adj. thrown.
क्षिप्र adj. fast, quick.
क्षिप्रगामी adj. fast-moving, fast.
क्षिप्रता f. quickness.
क्षीण adj. 1. lean and thin. 2. feeble and weak.
क्षीणकाय adj. having a lean and thin body.
क्षीर m. milk.
क्षीरसागर m. ocean of milk.
क्षुद्र adj. 1. low, base, mean. 2. very small, insignificant.
क्षुद्रग्रह m. planetoid, asteroid.
क्षुद्रता f. 1. meanness, pettiness. 2. insignificance.
क्षुद्रहृदय adj. mean-minded.
क्षुधा f. hunger, appetite.
क्षुधापीड़ित adj. famished.
क्षुधावर्धक adj. appetising.
क्षुधित adj. hungry.
क्षुप m. shrub.
क्षुब्ध adj. agitated, perplexed.
क्षुर m. 1. razor. 2. hoof.
क्षेत्र m. 1. field. 2. area, region.
क्षेत्रफल m. area.
क्षेत्ररक्षक m. (in cricket) fielder.
क्षेत्ररक्षण m. (in cricket) act of fielding.
क्षेत्राधिकार m. jurisdiction.
क्षेत्राधिकारी m. area officer.
क्षेत्रीय adj. regional.
क्षेपक m. addition by way of interpolation, interpolation.
क्षेपण m. act of throwing.
क्षेप्यास्त्र m. missile.
क्षैतिज adj. horizontal.
क्षोभ m. agitation.
क्षौरकर्म m. act of shaving.

ख

ख m. second of the softpalatal pentad of consonants of the Nagari alphabet; its sound resembles that of kh in Gymkhana.

खँगालना vt. 1. to wash with water. 2. to ransack/probe.

खँजड़ी f. timbrel.

खंजन m. a wagtail.

ख़ंजर m. dagger.

खंड m. 1. bit, piece. 2. part, portion. 3. storey (of a building). 4. volume (of a book).

खंडन m. 1. repudiation, contradiction. 2. refutation.

खंडन-मंडन m. refutation and commendation.

खंडनात्मक adj. repudiative.

खंडनीय adj. refutable.

खंडशः adv. in parts.

खँडसारी f. sugar unprocessed.

खँडहर m. ruins.

खंडित adj. split, broken into fragments.

ख़ंदक़ f. ditch, trench.

खंभा m. pillar, post.

खकार m. letter ख or its sound.

खखार m. phlegm.

खखारना vi. to spit out phlegm forcefully and violently.

खग m. bird.

खगोल m. celestial sphere.

खगोलज्ञ m. Spherical Astronomer.

खगोल विज्ञान m. Spherical Astronomy.

खगोलवेत्ता m. Spherical Astronomer.

खगोलिकी f. = खगोल विज्ञान।

खगोलीय adj. pertaining to the Celestial Sphere.

खग्रास m. total eclipse.

खचना vi. to be embedded.

खचाखच adv. fully, completely; ~ भरा (i) packed to capacity; (ii) overcrowded.

खचित adj. embedded.

खच्चर m. mule.

खच्चरी f. she-mule.

खज़ांची m. treasurer.

खज़ाना m. 1. treasure. 2. treasury.

खजूर m. 1. date. 2. date-palm. 3. a variety of Indian sweetmeat.

खट से adv. at once.

खटक f. 1. something that mars the placidity. 2. misapprehension.

खटकना vi. 1. to rattle/strike. 2. to rankle. 3. to be estranged.

खटका m. 1. rap, rattling sound. 2. apprehension. 3. any contrivance which operates with a clicking sound as a switch or bolt.

खटखट f. knocking/tapping sound.

खटखटाना vt. to knock, rap.

खटना vt. to earn toilsomely.

खटपट f. tiff, quarrel.

खटमल m. bed bug.

खटमीठा adj. bitter-sweet.

खटाई f. 1. sourness. 2. anything

sour, e.g., tamarind.

खटास f. sourness.

खटिक m. a Hindu caste whose occupation is growing and selling of vegetables, fruits etc.

खटोला m. a child's bed, cot.

खटोली f. smallish cot.

खट्टा adj. sour.

खट्टाचूक adj. too sour.

खट्टा-मीठा adj. bitter-sweet.

खड़कना vi. to rattle.

खड़ा adj. 1. standing. 2. upright, vertical.

खड़ाऊँ f. plu. wooden sandal.

खड़िया f. chalk, piece of chalk.

खड़ी चढ़ाई f. steep ascent.

खड़ी पाई f. vertical line i.e. a full stop in Hindi.

खड़ी फ़सल f. standing crop.

खड़ी बोली f. 1. language spoken in Western U.P. 2. Modern Hindi.

खड्ग f. sword.

खड्गहस्त adj. ever ready to strike with a sword.

खड्ड m. ditch.

ख़त m. 1. letter. 2. handwriting. 3. postcard.

खतना vt. to be entered in req-uisite account books.

ख़तना m. circumcision.

ख़तरनाक adj. 1. dangerous. 2. risky.

ख़तरा m. danger.

ख़ता f. error, mistake.

खतियाना vt. to enter in the proper register.

खतौनी f. (Patwari's) detailed account book.

खत्ता m. covered pit used for storing grain.

खत्ती f. underground grain store.

ख़त्म adj. finished, ended.

खत्रानी f. woman of the Khatri caste.

खत्री m. caste among the Hindus.

खदबदाना vi. to bubble.

खदान f. mine.

खदिर m. catechu.

खदेड़ना vt. to drive away.

खद्दर m. hand-woven cloth.

खद्योत m. glow-worm, firefly.

खनकना vi. to jingle.

खनना vi. 1. to dig. 2. to dig out.

खनिज m. mineral.

खनिज विज्ञान m. mineralogy.

खपची f. a splint.

खपड़ा m. earthen roofing tile.

खपड़ैल f. roof made of earthen tiles.

खपत f. 1. consumption (of goods). 2. sales, demand.

खपना vi. 1. to be consumed. 2. to be sold. 3. to be engaged in toilsome work. 4. to be killed.

खपाना vt. 1. to use up, to consume. 2. to finish.

खप्पर m. 1. beggar's bowl. 2. human skull (used as a bowl).

ख़फ़ा adj. angry.

ख़बर f. news.

ख़बरदार adj. watchful, cautious.

ख़बरनवीस m. press reporter.

ख़बीस adj. uncultured.

ख़ब्त m. craze, whim.

ख़ब्ती adj. crazy.

ख़मियाज़ा m. unpleasant or evil result, loss.
ख़मीर m. leaven, yeast.
ख़यानत f. breach of trust.
ख़याल m. 1. thought. 2. idea.
ख़याली adj. imaginary.
खर m. straw.
ख़र m. ass, donkey.
खरका m. tooth-pick.
खरगोश m. rabbit, hare.
ख़रचना vt. to spend.
खरतल adj. frank.
खरब adj. & m. hundred billion.
खरबूज़ा m. musk melon.
खरमास m. month regarded by Hindus as inauspicious.
खरल m. mortar.
खरहरा m. curry comb.
खरहा m. see ख़रगोश।
खरा adj. 1. pure or genuine (object). 2. upright, honest (person).
खराद f. lathe.
खरादना vt. to turn on a lathe.
खरापन m. purity, genuineness.
ख़राब adj. 1. bad. 2. wicked. 3. inferior, defective.
ख़राबी f. defect, flaw.
ख़राश f. irritation.
ख़रीता m. 1. bag. 2. pocket. 3. scroll.
ख़रीद f. purchase.
ख़रीदना vt. to purchase/buy.
ख़रीद-फ़रोख़्त f. buying and selling.
ख़रीदार m. buyer.
ख़रीदारी f. 1. act of buying. 2. purchase.
ख़रीफ़ की फ़सल f. autumnal crop.
खरोंच f. scratch.
खरोंचना vt. to scratch.
खरोष्ठी f. an ancient script of India from which several modern scripts are evolved.
खर्च m. expense, expenditure.
खर्चना vt. = खरचना।
खर्चा m. = खर्च।
खर्चीला adj. extravagant.
ख़र्रा m. roll, a long paper.
खर्राटा m. the act of snoring.
खल adj. wicked, base.
खलना vt. to hurt/offend.
खलबली f. commotion.
ख़लल m. 1. obstruction, disturbance. 2. interference.
ख़लासी m. a mechanical labour.
खलियान m. = खलिहान।
खलिहान m. open place where the harvested crop is stored for processing.
खली f. oil-cake.
ख़लीफ़ा m. 1. Khalif.
खल्वाट adj. bald. m. baldness.
ख़वास m. personal attendant/ bodyguard who waits on kings and the like.
ख़स f. a variety of grass that exhales a pleasant odour.
ख़सख़स f. poppy seed.
ख़सम m. husband.
ख़सरा m. 1. measles. 2. Pat-wari's survey book.
ख़सीस adj. miserly.
खसोटना vt. to grab.
ख़स्ता adj. 1. crisp. 2. worn out, miserable.

ख़स्सी m. castrated he-goat.
ख़ाँ m. = ख़ान।
खाँग m. 1. thorn. 2. spike.
खाँचना vt. to scratch a groove, line etc.
खाँचा m. 1. groove, furrow. 2. bucket, rather biggish.
खाँड f. unrefined sugar.
खाँड़ा m. dagger, small sword.
खाँसना vi. to cough.
खाँसी f. cough.
खाई f. trench, ditch.
खाऊ adj. gluttonous.
खाऊ-उड़ाऊ adj. prodigal.
ख़ाक f. dust.
ख़ाकसार m. a title for one's own-self, expressing humility.
ख़ाका m. 1. sketch. 2. draft, outline.
ख़ाकी adj. Khaki, resembling the colour of dust.
खाज f. scabies, itch.
खाजा m. a variety of Indian sweet.
खाट f. cot.
खाड़ी f. bay, gulf.
खात m. pit.
खाता m. 1. account. 2. account book.
खाता-पीता adj. well off.
खाता-बही f. ledger.
ख़ातिर f. hospitality.
ख़ातिर, की postposition. for the sake of (someone).
ख़ातिरदारी f. hospitality.
ख़ातून f. lady.
खातेदार m. account holder.
ख़ात्मा m. 1. end. 2. liquidation.
खाद f. manure.
खादर m. alluvial tract.
खादी f. hand-spun and hand-woven cloth.
खाद्य adj. eatable, edible.
खाद्यान्न m. foodgrains.
खान f. mine.
ख़ान m. a title used for Pathans (sply. Muslim) as a mark of respect.
ख़ानगी adj. domestic. f. concubine, kept.
ख़ानदान m. family.
ख़ानदानी adj. belonging to well-to-do family.
खान-पान m. way of living with particular reference to eating and drinking.
खान मज़दूर m. miner.
ख़ानसामा m. Khansama, steward whose main duty is looking after the kitchen.
खाना vt. 1. to eat. 2. to consume or use. m. food, meal.
ख़ाना m. 1. house. 2. compartment. 3. case. 4. column.
खाना-पीना vt. to enjoy life.
ख़ानापुरी f. observance of formalities.
ख़ानाबदोश m. nomad.
ख़ानाबदोशी f. nomadic life.
ख़ानाबरबादी f. ruination of a family.
ख़ामख़ाह adv. without any rhyme or reason.
ख़ामी f. drawback, flaw.
ख़ामोश adj. quiet, silent.
ख़ामोशी f. quietude, silence.
ख़ार m. thorn. f. grudge.

खारा adj. saline.
खारापन m. salinity.
ख़ारिज adj. dismissed.
ख़ारिश f. itch.
खाल f. skin.
ख़ालसा m. a sect among Sikhs.
ख़ाला f. mother's sister.
ख़ालिस adj. pure.
ख़ाली adj. 1. empty. 2. vacant.
ख़ाविंद m. husband.
ख़ास adj. special.
ख़ासियत f. 1. speciality. 2. characteristic.
खिंचना vi. 1. to be drawn/pulled; मन ~ to be attracted. 2. to be expanded.
खिंचाव m. attraction.
खिचड़ी f. 1. a dish of rice and pulse mixed together. 2. hotch-potch.
खिजलाना vi. to fret.
खिजलाहट f. fretting.
ख़िज़ाँ f. season of defoliation.
ख़िज़ाब m. hair-dye.
खिझाना vt. to tease, irritate.
खिड़की f. 1. window. 2. counter.
खिड़की-बंद adj. (house) all entire, without any other occupant.
ख़िताब m. title.
ख़ित्ता m. tract of land.
ख़िदमत f. service.
ख़िदमतगार m. servant.
खिन्न adj. distressed.
खिन्नता f. suffering caused by someone's odd behaviour.
खिलखिलाना vi. to laugh in a happy cheerful way.
खिलखिलाहट f. guffaw, peel of laughter.
खिलना vi. to blossom.
खिलवाड़ m. child's play.
खिलवाड़ी adj. playful.
खिलाई f. 1. act of feeding. 2. act of eating.
खिलाड़ी m. player, sportsman.
खिलाड़ीपन m. sportsmanship.
खिलाना vt. 1. to cause to play. 2. to feed.
ख़िलाफ़, के postposition. against.
खिलौना m. toy.
खिल्ली f. derision, ridicule.
खिवैया m. oarsman.
खिसकना vi. to move away slowly.
खिसकाना vt. 1. to move/shift a little. 2. to pinch/purloin.
खिसियाना vi. to be piqued.
खींचतान f. rift.
खींचना vt. 1. to pull. 2. to draw.
खींचातानी f. = खींचतान।
खीज f. irritation.
खीजना vi. to chagrin.
खीर f. a sweet dish of milk, rice, dry fruit etc.
खीरा m. cucumber.
खीस m. teeth.
खुखड़ी f. curved dagger.
खुचर f. minor mistake or flaw.
खुजलाना vt. to scratch.
खुजलाहट f. itching sensation.
खुजली f. 1. itch. 2. scabies.
खुड्डी f. 1. pit for evacuation. 2. foot-rest in an Indian lavatory.
ख़ुद pron. & adv. self, oneself.
ख़ुदकाश्त f. land cultivated by owner.
ख़ुदकुशी f. suicide.

ख़ुदग़रज़ adj. selfish.
ख़ुदग़रज़ी f. selfishness.
खुदना vi. to be dug out.
ख़ुदमुख़्तार adj. master of one's own affairs.
ख़ुदमुख़्तारी f. state of being ख़ुदमुख़्तार.
ख़ुदरा adj. retail.
m. (small) change.
खुदवाई f. act of digging or charges paid therefor.
खुदवाना vt. to cause to dig.
ख़ुदा m. God.
खुदाई f. act of digging.
ख़ुदाई f. 1. godliness. 2. world. 3. creation.
ख़ुदावंद m. God, Almighty.
ख़ुदी f. 1. self. 2. egoism.
ख़ुनकी f. (light) cold.
ख़ुनस f. anger, wrath.
ख़ुफ़िया adj. secret.
ख़ुमारी f. drowsiness.
ख़ुमी f. fungus, mushroom.
खुरंड m. dry crust over a wound, scale.
खुर m. cloven hoof.
खुरक f. itch.
खुरचन f. 1. scrape, scraping. 2. a kind of sweet prepared of milk cream.
खुरचना vt. to scrape/scratch.
खुरचनी f. scraper.
खुरचाल f. mischief.
खुरचाली m. mischief-maker.
खुरदरा adj. rough, uneven.
खुरपका m. foot-disease of hoofed animals.
खुरपी f. small weeding hook.
खुरमा m. a sweet prepared of wheat-flour.
ख़ुराक f. 1. diet. 2. dose.
ख़ुराकी f. 1. (quantity of) food material (for a specified period). 2. daily allowance in lieu thereof.
ख़ुराफ़ात f. mischief.
ख़ुराफ़ाती adj. mischievous.
ख़ुर्राट adj. crafty, cunning.
खुलना vi. 1. to become open. 2. to be cleared. 3. to be set up. 4. to disclose.
खुलवाना vt. to cause to be opened.
खुला adj. 1. open. 2. uncovered. 3. wide, spacious. 4. untied.
ख़ुलासा m. summary, abstract.
खुल्लमखुल्ला adv. openly.
ख़ुश adj. 1. happy, 2. delighted, 3. pleased.
ख़ुशक़िस्मत adj. lucky.
ख़ुशख़बरी f. good news.
ख़ुशदिल adj. of joyous temperament.
ख़ुशनसीब adj. very lucky.
ख़ुशनुमा adj. beautiful, good-looking.
ख़ुशबू f. sweet smell, fragrance.
ख़ुशबूदार adj. sweet-smelling, fragrant.
ख़ुशमिज़ाज adj. gay tempered.
ख़ुशहाल adj. well-off, prosperous.
ख़ुशहाली f. state of being well-off, prosperity.
ख़ुशामद f. flattery.
ख़ुशामदी m. flatterer.
ख़ुशामदी टट्टू m. sycophant.
ख़ुशी f. 1. happiness, 2. merriment, 3. joy, pleasure.

ख़ुशी-ख़ुशी adv. gladly.

ख़ुश्क adj. dry, arid.

खुसुर-फुसुर f. whispering.

ख़ूँख़ार adj. ferocious.

खूँटा m. stake.

खूँटी f. peg.

खूँदना vt. to trample.

ख़ून m. 1. blood. 2. murder.

ख़ून-ख़राबा m. bloodshed, bloodbath.

ख़ूनी adj. 1. pertaining to blood. 2. blood-red. 3. bloody. 4. cruel.

ख़ूब interj. 1. Well done! Bravo! 2. Excellent. adv. very much.

ख़ूबसूरत adj. beautiful.

ख़ूबसूरती f. beauty.

ख़ूबानी f. apricot.

ख़ूबी f. 1. excellence. 2. speciality.

खूसट adj. insensitive to beau-ties of life. m. 1. owl. 2. old fogey.

खेड़ा m. small village.

खेड़ी f. placenta.

खेत m. 1. field, farm. 2. battle-field.

खेत-खलिहान m. field and its granary.

खेतिहर m. peasant.

खेती f. cultivation, farming.

खेती-बारी f. cultivation, agri-culture.

खेद m. regret, sorrow.

खेदजनक adj. regrettable.

खेदपूर्वक adv. regretfully.

खेद-प्रकाश m. regret.

खेना vt. to row or pull.

खेनेवाला m. oarsman.

खेप m. instalment.

ख़ेमा m. 1. tent. 2. faction, clique.

ख़ेमेबाज़ी f. factionalism.

खेल m. 1. play. 2. game, sport.

खेल-कूद f. sports.

खेलना vi. & vt. to play.

खेलना-खाना vt. to eat, drink and be merry, to enjoy.

खेल-प्रतियोगिता f. tournament.

खेलाना vt. to cause to play.

खेवैया m. 1. oarsman. 2. steersman.

खेस m. a kind of bedspread.

खेह f. dust, earth.

खैर m. catechu.

ख़ैर interj. well, let it be. f. welfare.

ख़ैरख़ाह m. well-wisher.

खैरा adj. of the colour of cate-chu.

ख़ैरात f. alms, charity.

ख़ैराती adj. charitable.

ख़ैरियत f. welfare.

खोंच f. rent (in a cloth).

खोंचा m. device for catching birds with a bamboo.

खोंचा m. = खोमचा।

खोंसना vt. 1. to tuck (in) 2. to thrust/pierce (into).

खोआ m. a thickened milk-product.

खोई f. dehydrated sugarcane.

खोखला adj. hollow.

खोखलापन m. hollowness.

खोखा m. 1. boy. 2. stall.

खोज f. 1. search, quest. 2. discovery.

खोजना vt. to search.

खोजबत्ती f. searchlight.

खोजवाना vt. to cause to search.

खोजा m. eunuch, usu. a servant in a harem.

खोजी m. one who looks thoroughly in order to find someone or something.

खोट m. 1. substance which adulterates a genuine commodity. 2. malice

खोटा adj. 1. counterfeit. 2. wicked, crooked.

खोटाई f. = खोटापन।

खोटापन m. wickedness, crookedness.

खोदना vt. to dig, to dig out.

खोना vt. to lose.

खोपड़ा m. 1. skull. 2. dried coconut.

खोपड़ी f. 1. skull. 2. head.

खोपा m. kernel of a coconut.

खोमचा m. a large plate in which pedlars display their goods for sale.

खोया m. = खोआ।

खोल m. cover, covering.

खोलना vt. 1. to open. 2. to unfasten, to untie.

खोली f. 1. covering. 2. a small room (for hire).

खोह f. cave, cavern.

ख़ौफ़ m. terror, dread.

ख़ौफ़नाक adj. dreadful.

खौलना vi. to boil.

खौलाना vt. cause to boil.

ख्यात adj. reputed.

ख्याति f. repute.

ख़्याल m. 1. = ख़याल। 2. a kind of tune in Indian music.

ख्रीष्ट m. Jesus Christ.

ख़्वाब m. dream.

ख़्वार adj. embarrassed beyond measure.

ख़्वारी f. state of being ख़्वार।

ख़्वाहमख़्वाह adv. for no rhyme or reason.

ग

ग m. third of the soft palatal pentad of consonants of the Nagari alphabet; sounds like g in gull.

गंगा-जमुनी adj. mixed.

गंगाजल m. the water of the Ganga which is considered sacred.

गंगाजली f. small brass vessel for carrying Ganga water.

गंगाराम m. parrot.

गंगावतरण m. descent of Ganga (from Heaven down below to the earth).

गंज m. baldness.

गँजना vi. to pile (things) up.

गंजा adj. bald.

गँजाना vt. to cause to heap/pile.

गंजी f. 1. pile, heap. 2. man's undervest.

गंजीफ़ा m. 1. an old game played with a pack of 96 cards. 2. a pack of such cards.

गँजेड़ी m. one who is given to smoking hemp-leaf.

गँठबंधन m. alliance.

गँड़ासा m. 1. axe. 2. chopper for cutting fodder.

गँडेरी f. small piece cut off from a sugarcane.

गंतव्य m. destination.

गंद m. rubbish, refuse.

गंदगी f. 1. filth. 2. obscenity.

गँदला adj. muddy (water).

गंदा adj. 1. dirty. 2. filthy. 3. obscene.

गंदी बस्ती f. slum.

गंदुम m. wheat.

गंदुमी adj. wheaten.

गंध f. smell, odour.

गंधक f. sulphur.

गंधबिलाव m. civet.

गंधर्व m. a class of celestial singers and musicians.

गंधर्व विवाह m. (in Hindu Law) marriage by agreement of both parties but without parents' consent.

गंधी m. perfumer.

गँधीला adj. emitting (foul) smell.

गंधेंद्रिय f. nose.

गंभीर adj. 1. deep. 2. serious. 3. sober.

गंभीरता f. 1. depth. 2. seriousness. 3. sobriety.

गंभीरतापूर्वक adv. profoundly.

गँवई f. small village.

गँवाना vt. to lose.

गँवार m. bumpkin, villager.

गँवारपन m. rusticity, boorishness.

गँवारू adj. 1. rustic. 2. uncivilized or unrefined.

गँसीला adj. piercing.

गऊ f. cow. adj. meek (as cow).

गगन m. sky.

गगनचुंबी adj. sky-high.

गगनभेदी adj. thundering.

गगरा m. biggish pitcher.

गगरी f. earthen pitcher.

गच f. 1. sound produced when a hard thing falls on a soft surface.

2. house-building mortar.

गच्चा m. hoodwinking.

गज m. elephant.

गज़ m. yardstick, measuring yard.

ग़ज़क f. sweet prepared with sesame and sugar/jaggery.

गजगामिनी f. (woman) having a graceful gait.

गज़ट m. gazette.

ग़ज़ब m. 1. wrath. 2. wonder.

गजमुख m. God Ganesh.

गजरा m. garland (usu. of flowers).

गजराज m. king of elephants.

ग़ज़ल f. a kind of amatory poem, profusely used in Urdu.

गजवदन m. God Ganesh.

गजेंद्र m. = गजराज।

गज़ेटियर m. gazetteer.

गटकना vt. to gulp down, swallow quickly.

गट्टा m. 1. wrist. 2. an Indian variety of hard toffee.

गट्ठर m. bundle, bale.

गठजोड़ m. alliance, nexus.

गठजोड़ा m. conjugal tie, bridal knot.

गठन f. constitution of a body, build. m. formation, composition.

गठबंधन m. alliance.

गठरी f. 1. bundle, package. 2. riches, wealth.

गठिया m. gout.

गठियाना vt. to tie up.

गठीला adj. well-built.

गड़गड़ा m. hookah/hubble-bubble.

गड़गड़ाना vt. to make a gurgling sound as in smoking a hookah.

गड़गड़ाहट f. rumbling/rolling sound.

गड़ना vi. 1. to be pitched. 2. to be buried. 3. to prick or give a pricking sensation.

गड़पना vt. to swallow.

गड़बड़ f. 1. untoward, 2. something wrong.

गड़बड़-घोटाला m. wholesale mess, big muddle.

गड़बड़-झाला m. hotchpotch.

गड़बड़ाना vi. 1. to get confused/perplexed. 2. to falter.

गड़बड़ी f. = गड़बड़।

गड़रिया m. shepherd.

गड़हा m. pit.

गड़ारी f. pulley.

गड़ेरिया m. = गड़रिया।

गड्ड-मड्ड adj. muddled, jumbled.

गड्डी f. pack, small pile.

गड्ढा m. 1. pit. 2. dent.

गढ़ m. 1. citadel, fort. 2. stronghold.

गढ़न m. state or quality of गढ़ना।

गढ़ना vt. 1. to chisel (wood etc.). 2. to carve (stone etc.). 3. to manufacture by hand. 4. to concoct (story etc.).

गढ़पति m. the chief executive of a fort.

गढ़ा m. = गड्ढा।

गण m. 1. group, class. 2. fawning follower, satellite.

गणक m. calculator (machine).

गणतंत्र m. republic.

गणतांत्रिक adj. republican.

गणन m. counting.

गणना f. counting.

गणनीय adj. countable.

ग

गणपति m. God Ganesh.
गणपूर्ति f. quorum.
गणराज्य m. republic.
गणिका f. prostitute.
गणित m. Mathematics.
गणितज्ञ m. Mathematician.
गणितज्योतिष m. Astronomy.
गणितीय adj. mathematical.
गणेश m. Lord Ganesh.
गण्य adj. countable.
गण्यमान्य adj. distinguished.
गत adj. past.
गतका m. an Indian type of mace.
गतप्राय adj. almost past.
गतांक m. the previous or last issue of a periodical etc.
गतात्मा m. departed soul.
गतावधि adj. time-barred.
गति f. 1. motion, movement. 2. velocity, speed. 3. state, position.
गतिमान adj. in motion, moving.
गतिरोध m. 1. speed-breaker. 2. stalemate, deadlock.
गतिविज्ञान m. dynamics.
गतिविधि f. 1. movement, activity. 2. state of affairs.
गतिशील adj. 1. dynamic. 2. mobile.
गतिशीलता f. 1. dynamism. 2. mobility.
गतिहीन adj. motionless, stagnant.
गत्ता m. strawboard, coarse card-board.
गत्ताल-खाता m. bad debt account.
गत्यवरोध m. = गतिरोध।
गत्यात्मक adj. dynamical.
ग़दर m. mutiny.
गदराना vi. to be on the verge of ripening.
गदहा m. = गधा।
गदा m. mace.
गदाधर m. Lord Vishnu.
गद्गद adj. over-whelmed with joyful emotion.
गद्दा m. mattress.
ग़द्दार m. traitor.
ग़द्दारी f. traitorous conduct/act.
गद्दी f. 1. cushion. 2. seat. 3. throne.
गद्दीनशीन adj. enthroned.
गद्य m. prose.
गद्यकाव्य m. poetic prose.
गद्यात्मक adj. in the form of prose.
गधा m. 1. donkey, ass. 2. stupid fellow.
गधा-पचीसी f. an age, round about twenty-five, chara-cterised by childish beha-viour.
गधापन m. stupidity.
गधेरा m. owner of a donkey.
ग़नीमत f. consoling factor.
गन्ना m. sugarcane.
गप f. gossip.
गपकना vt. to gulp down.
गपशप f. gossip.
गपोड़िया m. = गप्पी।
गप्प f. = गप।
गप्पी m. gossipmonger.
गफ़ adj. densely woven (texture)
ग़फ़लत f. semi-conscious state.
ग़बन m. embezzlement.
गबरू adj. youthful. m. husband.
ग़म m. 1. grief. 2. sorrow.
गमक f. fragrance.

गमकना vi. to give out fragrance.

ग़मख़ोर adj. given to suffer patiently without any ado.

ग़मख़ोरी f. habit of suffering patiently.

ग़मगीन adj. 1. grief-stricken. 2. gloomy.

गमछा m. thin towel of an Indian type.

गमन m. departure.

गमनागमन m. departure and arrival.

गमला m. flower-pot.

ग़मी f. bereavement, mourning.

गम्य adj. 1. passable. 2. accessible.

गयंद m. big elephant, tusker.

गया-गुज़रा adj. = गया-बीता।

गया-बीता adj. 1. good for nothing. 2. tattered and worn out.

गर conj. if.

ग़रक़ adj. sunk.

गरचे conj. although.

गरज f. roar, thundering sound.

ग़रज़ f. need.

गरजन m. roar, thundering sound.

गरजना vi. 1. to roar, thunder. 2. to shout.

ग़रज़मंद adj. needy.

ग़रज़ू adj. needy.

गरदन f. neck.

गरदनतोड़ बुख़ार m. meningitis.

गरदा m. dust.

गरम adj. 1. hot, warm. 2. heated. 3. live (wire). 4. extremist.

गरम मसाला m. powdered mix- ture of spices.

गरमाई f. warmth, heat.

गरमागरम adj. 1. hot from the oven. 2. exciting. 3. heated.

गरमागरमी f. heated discussion.

गरमाना vt. to heat.

गरमाहट f. warmth.

गरमी f. 1. heat. 2. hotness. 3. summer.

गरल m. poison, venom.

गराँव f. rope tied round an animal's neck.

गराज m. garrage.

गराड़ी f. pulley.

गरारा m. 1. gargle. 2. loose pyjama worn by ladies.

गरिमा f. 1. grace, sublimity. 2. dignity.

गरिमापूर्ण adj. 1. graceful, sub-lime. 2. dignified.

गरियाना vt. to abuse.

गरिष्ठ adj. not easily digestible.

गरी f. coconut kernel.

ग़रीब adj. poor. m. a poor person.

ग़रीबख़ाना m. one's humble abode (language of modesty).

ग़रीबनिवाज़ adj. kind, merciful to the poor.

ग़रीबपरवर adj. who supports the poor.

ग़रीबी f. poverty.

गरुड़ m. eagle.

गरुड़ध्वज m. Lord Vishnu.

ग़रूर m. vanity.

गरेबान m. part of a garment worn round the neck.

गरोह m. = गिरोह।

गर्जन m. roar, thunder.

गर्डर m. = गाटर।

गर्त m. pit.

ग

गर्द f. dust.
गर्द़ख़ोर adj. dust-absorbing.
गर्द-ग़ुबार m. cloud of dust.
गर्दन f. neck.
गर्दभ m. donkey, ass.
गर्दिश f. 1. revolution. 2. distress, trouble.
गर्भ m. 1. womb. 2. conception.
गर्भकेसर m. carpel.
गर्भपात m. abortion.
गर्भवती adj. pregnant.
गर्भस्थ adj. situated in the womb.
गर्भस्राव m. miscarriage.
गर्भाधान m. impregnation.
गर्भावस्था f. pregnancy.
गर्भाशय m. uterus.
गर्भिणी f. pregnant woman.
गर्म adj. 1. hot. 2. warm. 3. heated. 4. live (wire).
गर्मी f. 1. heat. 2. summer.
ग़र्रा m. vainglory.
गर्व m. pride.
गर्वित adj. proud.
गर्वीला adj. proudy, haughty.
गर्वोक्ति f. boast, brag.
गर्हणा f. 1. detestation. 2. condemnation.
गर्हणीय adj. detestable.
गर्हित adj. detestable or detested.
गलकंबल m. hanging part of a cow's neck, dewlap.
गलका m. whitlow,
ग़लत adj. wrong, improper.
गलतकिया m. side-pillow.
ग़लतफ़हमी f. misunderstan- ding.
ग़लतबयानी f. misstatement, misstating.
ग़लती f. 1. mistake, error, folly. 2. wrong.
गलन f. bitter cold.
गलना vi. 1. to melt/liquefy. 2. to soften by being boiled, as pulse, potatoes. 3. to thaw, as it were, due to frost bite.
गलफड़ा m. gill (of fish).
गलफाँसी f. 1. noose. 2. circumstance of extreme distress.
ग़लबा m. overwhelming preponderance.
गलबाहीं f. putting one's arm round another's neck.
गलमुच्छा m. whiskers.
गलसुआ m. mumps.
गला m. 1. throat. 2. voice. 3. something like a neck in shape or position.
गलाकाटू adj. cutthroat, fierce.
गलाना vt. 1. to melt/smelt. 2. to dissolve.
गलित adj. decayed, decaying.
गलित कुष्ठ m. wasting leprosy.
गलियारा m. corridor.
गली f. lane, street.
गलीचा m. carpet.
गल्प f. (fictitious) story.
गल्ला m. 1. herd, flock. 2. cash-box.
ग़ल्ला m. grain, corn.
गवर्नर m. Governor.
गवर्नर जनरल m. Governor General.
गवर्नरी f. 1. Governorship. 2. Governor's administration.
गवर्मेंट f. government.
गवाक्ष m. ventilator.
गवारा adj. tolerable.

गवाह m. witness.
गवाही f. 1. evidence, 2. witness.
गवेषणा f. 1. investigation. 2. research.
गवैया m. singer.
गव्य adj. produced from a cow.
ग़श m. fainting, fit.
गश्त f. act of patrolling, round.
गश्ती चिट्ठी f. circular letter.
गस्सा m. morsel.
गहन adj. 1. deep. 2. dense, thick.
गहना m. ornament. vt. to catch hold of.
गहमागहमी f. hustle-bustle.
गहरा adj. 1. deep. 2. sound.
गहराई f. deepness, depth.
गह्वर m. 1. hole. 2. cave.
गाँजना vt. to pile/heap up.
गाँजा m. 1. hemp plant. 2. leaves of the hemp plant having narcotic properties and used as smoking substance for intoxication.
गाँठ f. 1. knot. 2. joint. 3. a knob, splicing. 4. bale, bundle. 5. gland. 6. bulb.
गाँठगोभी f. kohlrabi, cabbage.
गाँठदार adj. full of knots.
गाँठना vt. 1. to stitch. 2. to repair.
गाँडर f. sweet-smelling grass.
गांडीव m. bow of Arjun.
गांधर्व adj. of or pertaining to गंधर्व।
गाँधी टोपी f. Gandhian cap.
गाँधीवाद m. Gandhism.
गांभीर्य m. 1. depth. 2. gravity.
गाँव m. 1. village. 2. the inhabitants of the village collectively.
गाँस f. malice, enmity.
गाउन m. gown.
गागर f. earthen pitcher for keeping water cool.
गाज f. 1. thunderbolt, 2. froth.
गाजर f. carrot.
गाजर-मूली f. (sing.) petty thing.
ग़ाज़ी m. a Muslim crusader.
गाटर m. a large beam made of steel, girder.
गाड़ना vt. 1. to bury. 2. to drive in. 3. to pitch (a tent).
गाड़ी f. any conveyance, such as cart, car, train etc.
गाड़ीवान m. 1. coachman. 2. cartman.
गाढ़ा adj. 1. thick, 2. thickly woven. 3. strong deep (colour). 4. intense, intimate.
गात m. body.
गात्र m. body.
गाथा f. 1. tale, story. 2. ballad.
गाद m. sediment.
गाधि m. father of Vishwamitra.
गान m. 1. act of singing. 2. song.
गाना vt. & vi. 1. to sing. 2. to praise. m. song; दुगाना duet.
गाना-बजाना m. (festivity in the form of) musical merrymaking.
ग़ाफ़िल adj. m. negligent, careless.
गाभ m. shoot, sprout.
गाभिन adj. pregnant (animal).
गाय f. 1. cow. 2. foolish fellow.
गायक m. singer, vocalist.
गायकी f. style of singing.
गायन m. act or art of the singer.
ग़ायब adj. disappeared, vanished.
ग़ारत adj. ruined.

ग

गारद f. batch of soldiers.
गारना vt. to squeeze.
गारा m. mortar.
गार्ड m. guard.
गार्हपत्य adj. 1. pertaining to a householder. 2. domestic.
गार्हस्थ्य m. household.
गाल m. cheek.
गाला m. a lump of something soft.
गाली f. vituperation, abuse.
गाली-गलौज m. invectives.
गालू adj. bragging.
गावतकिया m. long, roundish pillow.
गावदी adj. foolish.
गावदुम adj. conical.
गाहक m. = ग्राहक;
गाहकी f. clients collectively, clientele.
गाही f. unit of five.
गाहेबगाहे adv. sometimes.
गिंजना vi. to get spoiled by wrong handling.
गिंडुरी f. round cushion on the head for carrying a pitcher etc.
गिचपिच f. scribbled writing. adj. scribbled.
गिजगिजा adj. 1. viscous. 2. fleshy.
ग़िज़ा f. diet, sply. nutritive diet.
गिटकिरी f. (music) tremels.
गिटपिट f. unfamiliar language, sply. English.
गिटार f. guitar.
गिट्टी f. grit.
गिड़गिड़ाना vt. to beseech/implore.
गिड़गिड़ाहट f. beseeching, imploring.
गिद f. mucus (in the eyes).
गिद्ध m. vulture.
गिद्ध-दृष्टि f. long sight.
गिनतारा m. abacus.
गिनती f. counting, count.
गिनना vt. to count/enumerate.
गिनवाना vt. to cause to count.
गिना-गिनाया adj. already counted.
गिनी f. = गिन्नी।
गिने-चुने adj. (plu.)1. selected few. 2. in a limited number.
गिन्नी f. guinea.
गिरगिट m. chamelion.
गिरजा m. church, cathedral.
गिरधारी m. Lord Krishna.
गिरना vi. 1. to fall/drop. 2. to decrease. 3. deteriorate or decline.
गिरनार m. a hill in Gujarat, sacred to the Jains.
गिरफ़्त f. 1. catch, hold. 2. han-dle (of a weapon).
गिरफ़्तार adj. arrested.
गिरफ़्तारी f. arrest.
गिरमिट m. gimlet.
गिरमिटिया m. Indian labourer of eighteenth century on contract (in a colony).
गिरवाना vt. to cause to fall down.
गिरवी adj. mortgaged, pledged, hypothecated.
गिरह f. 1. knot. 2. pocket. 3. 1/16 of a yard, a unit of measurement.
गिरहकट m. pick-pocket.
गिराना vt. 1. to cause to fall. 2. to drop. 3. to demolish.
गिरावट f. fall, decline.
गिरि m. mountain, hill.
गिरिजा f. Goddess Parvati.

गिरिधर m. Lord Krishna.

गिरिधारी m. = गिरिधर।

गिरिपथ m. path between two mountains, pass.

गिरिराज m. Himalaya.

गिरिसुता f. Goddess Parvati.

गिरींद्र m. 1. Himalaya. 2. Lord Shiv.

गिरी f. kernel.

गिरीश m. Himalaya.

गिरोह m. gang, band.

गिलट m. nickel.

गिलहरी f. squirrel.

गिला m. complaint.

ग़िलाफ़ m. 1. pillow case. 2. covering.

गिलास m. a container for drin-king, glass, tumbler.

गिलोय f. see. गुरुच।

गिलौरी f. betel-leaf, stuffed and folded, fit to be offered and chewed.

गिल्टी f. swollen gland.

गिल्ली-डंडा m. = गुल्ली-डंडा।

गींजना vt. to spoil and crumple by handling roughly.

गीत m. song, lyric.

गीतकार m. composer of songs, lyricist.

गीति काव्य m. lyrical poem.

गीदड़ m. jackal.

गीदड़-भभकी f. hollow threat.

गीध m. vulture.

गीला adj. wet, damp.

गुंगी f. a snake having two mouths, one at each end.

ग़ुंचा m. bud.

गुंजन m. humming/buzzing sound.

गुंजाइश f. 1. space, room. 2. capacity.

गुंजारना vi. to make a humming sound.

गुंडई f. hooliganism, ruffianism.

गुंडा m. hooligan, ruffian.

गुंडागर्दी f. hooliganism.

गुँधना vi. to be kneaded.

गुँधवाना vt. to cause to be kneaded.

गुंफना vt. 1. to wreathe. 2. to make a sweet arrangement of words.

गुंफित adj. 1. wreathed. 2. well-arranged; intertwined.

गुंबज m. = गुंबद।

गुंबद m. dome.

गुइयाँ m. & f. chum.

गुच्छ m. = गुच्छा।

गुच्छा m. bunch.

गुज़रना vi. 1. to pass 2. to pass by. 3. to befall.

गुज़र-बसर m. subsistence, maintenance.

गुज़ारना vt. to pass time.

गुज़ारा m. maintenance allowance.

गुज़ारिश f. request, prayer.

गुज्झा m. pin of wood used in joinery, dowel.

गुट m. faction, clique.

गुटका m. 1. manual, handbook. 2. block.

गुटनिरपेक्ष adj. non-aligned.

गुटबंदी f. groupism, faction-alism.

गुटबाज़ m. factionalist.

गुटबाज़ी f. = गुटबंदी।

गुटरगूँ f. cooing of a pigeon.

गुठली f. stone (of a fruit).

ग

गुड़ m. jaggery.

गुड़गुड़ f. rumbling or bubbling sound.

गुड़गुड़ाना vt. 1. to smoke a hubble-bubble. 2. to make such a sound.

गुड़गुड़ाहट f. the sound like that of a hubble-bubble.

गुड़गुड़ी f. mini hubble-bubble.

गुड़िया f. doll.

गुड्डी f. paper kite.

गुण m. virtue, merit.

गुणक m. 1. multiplier. 2. coefficient.

गुणकारक adj. = गुणकारी।

गुणकारी adj. 1. beneficial. 2. curative, effective.

गुणगान m. praise, eulogy.

गुणग्राहक m. one who expresses appreciation, appreciative.

गुणग्राहकता f. appriciativeness.

गुणज m. multiple.

गुणज्ञ m. connoisseur.

गुण-दोष m. merits and dem- erits.

गुणधर्म m. property.

गुणन m. multiplication.

गुणनफल m. product (of multiplication).

गुणवंत adj. proficient.

गुणवत्ता f. quality.

गुणवाचक adj. qualitative.

गुणवान, गुणवान् adj. meritorious.

गुणसूत्र m. chromosome.

गुणहीन adj. void of merits, non-proficient.

गुणांक m. coefficient.

गुणा m. multiplication.

गुणात्मक adj. qualitative.

गुणानुवाद m. eulogy.

गुणी m. connoisseur.

गुण्य m. multiplicand.

गुत्थम-गुत्था m. close combat, scuffle.

गुत्थी f. 1. knot. 2. puzzle, riddle. 3. problem.

गुथना vi. to be interwoven/intertwined/interlaced.

गुदगुदा adj. soft and smooth.

गुदगुदाना vt. 1. to tickle. 2. to provoke.

गुदगुदी f. 1. tickling sensation. 2. an act of tickling.

गुदड़ी f. beggar's bedding.

गुदड़ी बाज़ार m. lumber market.

गुदना vi. to be tattooed on the skin. m. tattoo on the skin.

गुदवाना vt. causative of गोदना।

गुदा f. anus, rectum.

गुनगुना adj. slightly warm.

गुनगुनाना vi. 1. to hum (said of black bee). 2. to sing with close lips, to hum.

गुनना vt. to assimilate.

गुनहगार m. sinner.

गुना suffix. denoting 'manifoldness'; दु ~ double; दस ~ ten times, ten-fold. m. a fried sweet dish made of wheat flour.

गुनाह m. sin.

गुपचुप adv. secretly.

गुप्त adj. hidden, secret.

गुप्तचर m. spy, detective.

गुप्तदान m. anonymous donation.

गुप्ती f. swordstick.

गुफ़ा f. cave.

गुफ़्तगू f. conversation.

गुबरैला m. dung-beetle.

ग़ुबारा m. = ग़ुब्बारा।

ग़ुब्बारा m. balloon.

गुम adj. lost. m. suffocation.

गुमटा m. swelling or tumour caused by a blow.

गुमटी f. 1. watchman's cabin. 2. stall.

गुमराह adv. having gone astray.

गुमसुम adj. quiet and still, almost mute and motionless.

गुमान m. pride, vanity.

गुमानी adj. vain, proud.

गुमाश्ता m. agent (of a landlord, money-lender etc.)

गुर m. short formula.

गुरगा m. henchman, hoodlum.

गुरदा m. kidney.

गुरमुखी f. the script of the Punjabi language, initiated by Guru Arjun Dev.

गुरिल्ला m. guerilla.

गुरु adj. 1. heavy. 2. (a sign) denoting a long unit in prosody. m. 1. teacher. 2. preceptor.

गुरुकुल m. seminary.

गुरुजन m. elders.

गुरुजल m. heavy water.

गुरुता f. heaviness.

गुरुत्व m. 1. preceptorship. 2. gravity. 3. importance.

गुरुत्वाकर्षण m. gravitation, attraction of earth.

गुरुभाई m. fellow disciple/stu-dent.

गुरुमंत्र m. compendious formula.

गुरुवार m. Thursday.

गुरूघंटाल m. crafty fellow.

गुरेरना vt. to stare/frown.

गुर्जर m. an inhabitant of Gujarat.

गुर्दा m. kidney.

गुर्राना vi. to growl/snarl.

गुर्राहट f. growl.

गुल m. 1. rose. 2. flower. 3. burnt (upper) portion of a wick.

गुलक़ंद m. conserve prepared of rose petals (used as a medicine).

गुलगपाड़ा m. uproar.

गुलगुला m. a sweet of small round shape. adj. soft.

गुलछर्रा m. gay abandon, gaiety.

गुलज़ार adj. gay.

गुलदस्ता m. bouquet.

गुलदान m. flower-vase.

गुलदार adj. flowery. m. panther.

गुलबकावली f. a plant of the species of turmeric.

गुलबदन adj. having body like a flower, i.e. beautiful, cheerful.

गुलमा m. round protuberance.

गुलशन m. flower-garden.

गुलाब m. rose.

गुलाब-जल m. rose-water.

गुलाबजामुन m. a variety of Indian sweetmeat.

गुलाबपाश m. rose-water sprinkler.

गुलाबी adj. 1. rosy. 2. mild.

ग़ुलाम m. slave.

ग़ुलामी f. slavery.

गुलाल m. a red powder which the Hindus apply or throw at each other during the Holi festival.

गुलूबंद m. scarf.

गुलेल f. catapult.

गुलेला m. a shot of a pellet bow (गुलेल).

गुल्म m. cluster of plants.

ग

गुल्लक m. money-box.

गुल्ली-डंडा m. game of tipcat, children's game played with a stick and a smaller piece of wood.

ग़ुसलख़ाना m. bathroom.

गुस्ताख़ adj. impudent.

गुस्ताख़ी f. impudence.

ग़ुस्सा m. anger, wrath.

ग़ुस्सैल adj. hot-tempered.

गुह m. see गू।

गुहा f. cave.

गुहार f. call.

गुह्य adj. secret.

गूँगा adj. mute, dumb.

गूँगापन m. muteness, dumbness.

गूँज f. echo.

गूँजना vi. 1. to echo. 2. to buzz.

गूँथना vt. to wreathe/thread.

गूँधना vt. to knead.

गू m. faeces.

गूजर m. an agricultural community of Northern India.

गूजरी f. fem. of गूजर।

गूढ़ adj. abstruse, difficult.

गूदड़ m. lumber (spl. discarded clothes).

गूदड़साँईं m. mendicant who wears discarded clothes.

गूदा m. pith, pulp.

गूदेदार adj. pulpy.

गूमड़ा m. see गुमटा।

गू-मूत m. (human) excreta.

गूलर m. sycamore.

गूह m. = गू।

गृध्र m. vulture.

गृह m. home, house.

गृह-उद्योग m. cottage industry.

गृहकार्य m. homework.

गृहणी f. housewife.

गृह-मंत्री m. Home Minister.

गृह-युद्ध m. civil war.

गृह-सचिव m. Home Secretary.

गृहस्थ m. householder.

गृहस्थाश्रम m. the life of a householder.

गृहस्थी f. household.

गृहस्वामी m. owner of a house.

गृहासक्त adj. 1. unduly attached to the family. 2. homesick.

गृहीत adj. 1. taken, received. 2. accepted.

गेंडुली f. 1. coil of a snake. 2. coil of rope on the head.

गेंद m. ball.

गेंद-बल्ला m. ball and bat.

गेंदबाज़ m. bowler.

गेंदबाज़ी f. act of bowling.

गेंदा m. marigold (plant and its flower).

गेड़ी f. a stilt.

गेरुआ adj. ochrous.

गेरू m. red ochre.

गेली f. galley.

गेसू m. curl of the hair.

गेह m. house, home.

गेहुँअन m. venomous snake of wheatish colour.

गेहुँआँ adj. wheatish.

गेहूँ m. wheat.

गैंडा m. rhinoceros.

गैंती f. mattock.

ग़ैबी adj. divine.

ग़ैर adj. other than.
m. an outsider.

ग़ैर-इंसाफ़ी f. injustice.
ग़ैर-क़ानूनी adj. illegal.
ग़ैर-ज़िम्मेदार adj. irresponsible.
ग़ैर-ज़िम्मेदारी f. irresponsibility.
ग़ैरत f. sense of one's position, prestige etc.
ग़ैरतमंद adj. self-respecting.
ग़ैर-मुनासिब adj. improper.
ग़ैर-मुमकिन adj. impossible.
ग़ैर-मौजूदगी f. absence.
ग़ैर-वाजिब adj. improper.
ग़ैर-सरकारी adj. non-official.
ग़ैर-हाज़िर adj. absent.
ग़ैर-हाज़िरी f. absence.
गैरिज m. garage.
गैल f. 1. way, path. 2. lane.
गैलन m. gallon.
गैलरी f. gallery.
गैस f. gas.
गैसीय adj. gaseous.
गोंद m. gum.
गोंददानी f. gum-pot.
गोंदीला adj. gummy, sticky.
गोकुल m. region in the vicinity of Vrindavan, where Lord Krishna spent his childhood.
गोकुशी f. cow-slaughter.
गोघाती adj. cow-killer.
गोचर adj. perceptible.
गोचरभूमि f. pasture for cows.
गोचर्म m. leather of the cow.
गोजई f. mixture of wheat and barley.
गोजर m. centipede.
गोट f. border, hem.
गोटा m. gold or silver lace used for hemming.
गोटी f. piece or block with which several games are played, counter.
गोठ m. picnic.
गोड़ m. foot.
ग़ोता m. dive.
ग़ोताख़ोर m. diver.
गोती adj. see. गोत्रज।
गोत्र m. lineage, ascendancy.
गोत्रज adj. & m. (one) born in the same lineage, a relative.
गोद f. lap.
गोदना m. tattoo. vt. to tattoo.
गोदाम m. godown.
गोदी f. 1. harbour, dock; ~ मज़दूर docker. 2. = गोद।
गोधूलि f. dusk; ~ बेला dusk time.
गोप m. cowherd.
गोपन m. act of hiding.
गोपनीय adj. confidential.
गोपनीयता f. confidentiality.
गोपांगना f. a woman of the cowherd tribe.
गोपाल m. cow-owner.
गोपिका f. see गोपी।
गोपी f. a woman of the cow-herd tribe.
गोप्य adj. secret, confidential.
गोबर m. dung, cow-dung.
गोबरगणेश m. stupid person.
गोबरी f. dung-cake.
गोबरैला m. dung-beetle.
गोभी f. cauliflower.
गोमांस m. beef.
गोमुख adj. having face like that of a cow.
गोमुखी adj. a bag in which one

carries a rosary while the hand goes on telling the beads.

गोमूत्र m. urine of a cow.

गोमेद m. chaeledonyx.

गोया conj. as if.

गोरक्षा f. cow-protection.

गोरखधंधा m. 1. labyrinth. 2. complicated/intricate affair.

गोरखा m. 1. a tribe of Nepal. 2. a person belonging to this tribe.

गोरस m. milk of cow.

गोरा adj. fair-complexioned.

गोरा पत्थर m. soap-stone.

गोरापन m. fairness of the colour.

गोरिल्ला m. gorilla.

गोरी f. white-complexioned damsel.

गोरू m. cattle.

गोलंदाज़ m. gunner.

गोलंदाज़ी f. gunnery.

गोलंबर m. cupola, arch.

गोल adj. 1. spherical. 2. circular. m. 1. (in football or hockey) a successful attempt at scoring, goal (games). 2. flock.

गोलकी m. goalkeeper.

गोलगप्पा m. 1. small, Indian cake of a plumpy type. 2. anything with a puffed up, plumpy body.

गोल-मटोल adj. plump, almost round.

गोलमाल m. bungling.

गोलमिर्च f. black pepper.

गोलमेज़ f. round table.

गोला m. 1. round object. 2. globe. 3. bomb.

गोलाई f. roundness.

गोलाकार adj. spherical, globular, round.

गोलाबारी f. firing of explosive shells, bombing.

गोला-बारूद m. ammunition.

गोलार्ध adj. & m. hemisphere, hemispherical.

गोलियाना vt. to round (something).

गोली f. 1. tablet, pill. 2. bullet. m. goal-keeper.

गोलीकांड m. episode involving firing.

गोलोकवासी adj. & m. resident in Heaven.

गोविंद m. Lord Krishna.

गोशाला f. stable for cows.

गोष्ठी f. 1. meeting. 2. sym- posium.

गोसाईं m. 1. saint. 2. God.

गोस्वामी m. 1. owner of cows. 2. one who has controlled the senses. 3. ascetic.

गोह f. iguana (species of lizard).

गोहरा m. dung-fuel.

गोहराना vi. to call out loudly.

गोहार f. cry for help.

गौं f. imperative/compelling need.

गौण adj. secondary, subsidiary.

गौनहारिन f. woman whose profession is singing.

गौना m. ceremony in which the bride goes to the brideg-room's house (second time after marriage).

गौर adj. white-skinned, fair coloured.

ग़ौर m. close consideration/ attention.

ग

गौरव m. 1. glory. 2. prestige, dignity, honour.

गौरवशाली adj. 1. glorious. 2. dignified. 3. triumphant.

गौरी f. 1. fair damsel. 2. Parvati, wife of Lord Shiv.

गौरीशंकर m. 1. Parvati and Lord Shiv. 2. One of the famous and prestigious Himalayan peaks.

गौरैया f. sparrow.

ग्यारह adj. & m. eleven.

ग्रंथ m. 1. book, spl. voluminous book. 2. treatise.

ग्रंथकार m. writer of a book, author.

ग्रंथमाला f. 1. book series. 2. complete works (of a writer).

ग्रंथालय m. 1. library. 2. book-shop.

ग्रंथि f. 1. knot. 2. complex. (Psycho.) 3. gland.

ग्रंथिल adj. 1. knotty. 2. complicated.

ग्रसन m. 1. seizing. 2. swallowing.

ग्रसना vt. to sieze, to catch hold of.

ग्रस्त adj. siezed, caught.

ग्रह m. any of the planets that revolve around the sun.

ग्रहण m. 1. act of receiving. 2. assumption, taking. 3. eclipse.

ग्रहणीय adj. acceptable, admissible, eligible.

ग्रहदशा f. period of ill-luck/ misfortune.

ग्राम m. 1. village. 2. heap. 3. (music) gamut. 4. gramme (unit of weight).

ग्रामवासी m. villager.

ग्रामीण adj. rural, pertaining to a village. m. villager.

ग्रामोत्थान m. rural uplift.

ग्रामोद्योग m. village industry.

ग्रामोफ़ोन m. gramophone.

ग्राम्य adj. rural.

ग्रास m. 1. morsel, mouthful. 2. a bite-sized piece. 3. eclipse.

ग्राह m. alligator, crocodile.

ग्राहक m. 1. customer. 2. client.

ग्राही suffix. denoting accepter.

ग्राह्य adj. admissible, acceptable.

ग्रीवा f. neck.

ग्रीष्म m. the hot season, summer.

ग्रीष्मकाल m. summer-time, summer.

ग्रीष्मावकाश m. summer vacation.

ग्लानि f. shame for one's wrong action, compunction, lassitude, remorse.

ग्वाल m. = ग्वाला।

ग्वाल-गीत m. pastoral song.

ग्वाला m. 1. cowherd. 2. milkman.

ग्वालिन f. 1. female cowherd. 2. milkwoman, milkmaid.

घ

घ m. fourth consonant of the soft palatal pentad of the Nagari alphabet; aspirated form of ग.

घँघोलना vt. to make turbid by stirring, to rinse.

घंट m. gong.

घंटा m. 1. gong. 2. hour. 3. period, duration of time.

घंटाघर m. clock-tower.

घंटी f. 1. bell. 2. tinkling.

घघरा m. = घाघरा।

घट m. 1. earthen pot for storing water, pitcher. 2. heart.

घटक m. 1. (Math.) component. 2. constituent, factor.

घटता-बढ़ता adj. fluctuating, varying.

घटती f. 1. deficit. 2. decrease.

घटना f. event, occurrence, incident. vt. 1. to lessen/diminish/decrease. 2. to subside. 3. to be reduced. 4. to be subtracted. 5. to occur/happen.

घटना-बढ़ना vi. to fluctuate, to rise and fall.

घटनावली f. succession of events, series of incidents.

घटनास्थल m. 1. place of occurrence. 2. site of an accident.

घट-बढ़ f. fluctuation.

घटा f. a gathering of dark and dense clouds.

घटाटोप m. 1. overcasting of dark and dense clouds. 2. clothcovering of a vehicle or palanquin.

घटाना vt. 1. to subtract. 2. to reduce/diminish. 3. to decrease/lessen.

घटाव m. abatement.

घटित adj. occurred, happened.

घटिया adj. of inferior/low quality.

घट्ठा m. callosity, callus.

घड़घड़ाना vt. & vi. to rattle, to make a rattling sound.

घड़घड़ाहट f. rattling sound.

घड़ा m. earthen water-pot for storing purposes etc..

घड़ियाल m. alligator, crocodile.

घड़ी f. 1. a period of 24 minutes. 2. a moment. 3. watch, timepiece or clock.

घड़ीसाज़ m. watch-maker.

घन m. 1. cloud. 2. (big) hammer. 3. (Maths.) cube (solid). 4. third power of a quantity.

घनघनाहट f. tinkling.

घनघोर adj. 1. very dense. 2. heavy. 3. fearful, fierce, terrible.

घनचक्कर m. stupid fellow, blockhead.

घनत्व m. density.

घनफल m. (Maths.) result of cubing.

घनमूल m. (Maths.) cube-root.

घनश्याम m. 1. dark cloud. 2. Lord Krishna.

घना adj. dense, compact, thick.

घनात्मक adj. cubic.

घनिष्ठ adj. intimate, very close.

घनिष्ठता f. intimacy, intimate friendship, rapport.

घनीभूत adj. 1. condensed. 2. solidified.

घपला m. 1. bungled action. 2. bungled piece of work, scam.

घबराना vi. to be non-plussed/perplexed/nervous/confused/puzzled.

घबराहट f. perplexity, nervousness.

घमंड m. conceit, pride, vanity.

घमंडी adj. conceited.

घमस f. sultriness.

घमाका m. sound produced by a heavy blow.

घमाघम adv. with heavy blows, one after another.

घमासान adj. fierce.

घमौरी f. prickly heat.

घर m. 1. home, house. 2. place, space, room. 3. office; डाक ~ post office.

घर-गँवाऊ adj. prodigal, spendthrift, extravagant.

घर-गृहस्थी f. household, family set-up.

घरघराना vi. to wheeze.

घरघालू m. a person who ruins his family or house, a blackguard.

घर-घुस्सू m. stay-at-home.

घर-जँवाई m. son-in-law living with and depending on the in-laws.

घर-द्वार m. 1. whereabouts of the family. 2. household.

घरनी f. 1. mistress of a house. 2. wife.

घर-बार m. = घर-द्वार।

घर-बारी m. householder, family man.

घरवाला m. 1. husband. 2. member of the family.

घरवाली f. wife, the lady of the house.

घराती m. one belonging to a bridal party.

घराना m. family, dynasty.

घरिया f. small earthen cup in which goldsmith melts gold, crucible.

घरेलू adj. 1. domestic. 2. private. 3. homely.

घरौंदा m. 1. toy home. 2. mini house.

घर्रा m. rattling sound made by the throat.

घर्राटा m. = खर्राटा।

घर्षण m. 1. friction, abrasion. 2. rubbing.

घलुआ m. quantity of a com- modity given in gratis (in excess of a purchase).

घसिटना vi. to be dragged.

घसियारा m. hay-trusser, grass-cutter.

घसियारिन f. 1. woman who cuts or sells grass. 2. wife of a hay-trusser/grass-cutter.

घसीट f. illegible scrawling or scribbling.

घसीटना vt. 1. to drag. 2. to scrawl.

घहराना vi. to thunder, to roar.

घाँटी f. uvula.

घाई f. gap (between two fingers).

घाऊघप adj. & m. 1. greedy in eating, voracious. 2. grabber.

घाघ adj. & m. sharper, cunning (fellow), crafty.

घाघरा m. a variety of petticoat.

घाट m. 1. landing or bathing

place on the bank of a river. 2. flight of steps leading to a landing place on a river bank, ghat.

घाटबंदी f. ban on embarkation or disembarkation.

घाट-शुल्क m. ferriage.

घाटा m. 1. loss. 2. deficit.

घाटिया m. a person who sits at a ghat, takes charge of bather's clothes etc. and renders other petty services.

घाटी f. 1. valley. 2. pass. 3. gorge.

घात m. 1. blow, stroke. 2. oppor- tunity of fulfilling one's object, ambush, ambuscade. 3. (Maths.) power; २ का तृतीय घात ८ है The third power of 2 is 8. 4. slaughter.

घातक adj. 1. fatal. 2. malignant, pernicious.

घातकी m. = घाती।

घाती m. killer, assassin, murderer.

घान m. quantity of something crushed, ground, cooked or fried in one lot.

घानी f. establishment where crushing is carried out.

घाम m. 1. sunshine, sunlight. 2. heat of the sun.

घामड़ adj. & m. blockhead, idiot.

घायल adj. wounded, injured.

घालक adj. & m. 1. destroyer. 2. killer.

घालना vt. to destroy.

घाल-मेल m. 1. jumble, hotch-potch, mess, medley. 2. illicit relationship.

घाव m. 1. wound. 2. injury.

घास (ghAS) f. grass.

घास-पात m. 1. grass leaves and the like. 2. rubbish.

घासलेट m. 1. kerosene oil. 2. trash.

घिग्घी f. ~ बँधना—उसकी घिग्घी बँध गई His throat was choked.

घिघियाना vi. to supplicate abjectly.

घिचपिच adj. = गिचपिच।

घिन f. feeling of odiousness/abhorrence.

घिनौना adj. squalid, odious, abhorring.

घिरना vt. to be surrounded/encircled/beset.

घिरनी f. pulley.

घिरवाना vt. to cause to surround/encircle.

घिराव m. = घेराव।

घिसघिस f. 1. dilatoriness, undue delay. 2. indetermination, undue delay in taking a decision.

घिसना vi. 1. to be rubbed. 2. to wear out.

घिसना-पिटना vt. घिस-पिट जाना to fray out.

घिसपिस f. close contact, intimacy.

घिसवाना vt. to cause to rub.

घिसाई f. 1. abrasion. 2. friction. 3. charges paid for polishing etc.

घिसा-पिटा adj. 1. old and worn, thin, threadbare. 2. stereotyped, hackneyed. 3. frayed.

घिस्सा m. 1. friction. 2. hard rub. 3. push. 4. dodge.

घी m. ghee, clarified butter.

घुँइयाँ f. a root vegetable.

घुँघनी f. fried and seasoned corn.

घुँघराला adj. curly.

घुँघरू m. jingling bell usually worn by dancing girls.

घुंडी f. 1. knot. 2. knot-like button made of cloth.

घुग्घू m. 1. owl. 2. stupid fellow.

घुघुआना vi. to hoot like an owl.

घुटन f. suffocation.

घुटना m. knee. vi. to be ground. ख़ूब ~—उन दोनों में ख़ूब घुटती है They are chummy with each other. दम ~ to feel suffocated.

घुटन्ना m. half pants, shorts, knickers.

घुटवाना vt. 1. to cause to be rubbed. 2. to cause to be cleanshaven or tonsured.

घुटाना vt. = घुटवाना।

घुट्टी f. a medicinal liquid given to infants.

घुड़कना vt. 1. to reprimand. 2. to admonish. 3. to intimidate.

घुड़की f. 1. reprimand. 2. admonition.

घुड़चढ़ा m. rider.

घुड़चढ़ी f. a ceremony immediately preceding marriage in which the bridegroom goes to the bride's house on horse-back.

घुड़दौड़ f. horse-race.

घुड़नाल f. 1. an old type of small cannon drawn by horses. 2. horseshoe.

घुड़सवारी f. horse-riding.

घुड़साल f. stable.

घुन m. weevil, cankar, wood-worm and the like.

घुनना vi. to be eaten by lice or pests, to be infested with worms.

घुन्ना adj. maliciously secretive.

घुप्प m. intense; ~ अँधेरा pitch dark.

घुमक्कड़ adj. roving, wand- ering.

घुमड़ना vi. to gather and overcast (like clouds).

घुमाना vt. 1. to turn round. 2. to show round. 3. spin. 4. to circulate.

घुमाव m. 1. a single turn made is winding something. 2. turn, specially a bend or corner in a road.

घुमावदार adj. 1. winding, roundabout. 2.complicated.

घुरघुराना vi. to produce a rattling sound from the throat.

घुलना vi. to get dissolved; घुल-घुलकर जान देना / मर जाना to languish to death; घुल-घुलकर बातें करना to have a tete-a-tete.

घुलवाना vt. to cause to be dissolved or mixed.

घुलाना vt. 1. to dissolve in the mouth. 2. to dissolve something solid in some liquid.

घुसना vi. 1. to break in (to), to burst into, to thrust into. 2. to intrude/infiltrate.

घुसपैठ f. infiltration.

घुसपैठिया m. infiltrator.

घुसाना vt. to thrust in.

घुसेड़ना vt. to thrust into.

घूँघट m. veil.

घूँट m. a large sip.

घूँटना vt. to sip a large mouthful.

घूँसा m. fist-blow, box.

घूमना vi. 1. to stroll. 2. to rotate/gyrate/spin. 3. to go round, revolve.

घूर m. dunghill.

घूरना vt. to stare.

घूरा m. rubbish-heap.

घूर्णन m. rotation, gyration.

घूस f. bribe.

घूसख़ोर adj. & m. (one) given to taking bribes.

घृणा f. hatred, scorn, disgust, aversion.

घृणित adj. hated, abhorred, odious.

घृत m. ghee, clarified butter.

घेघा m. goitre.

घेर m. enclosure, circumference.

घेरना vt. 1. to enclose/fence. 2. to encircle/surround.

घेरा m. 1. circle. 2. fence, enclosure, ambit.

घेराबंदी f. = घेरेबंदी।

घेराव m. surrounding of a person as a means of coercion, gherao.

घेरेबंदी f. 1. act of enclosing (space). 2. encirclement/siege. 3. blockade.

घोंघा m. small animal living in spiral shell, snail, oyster.

घोंघा-बसंत m. foolish, block-head.

घोंटना vi. = घोटना।

घोंपना vi to pierce/penetrate.

घोंसला m. nest.

घोखना vi. to learn by rote/ repetition, to cram up.

घोटना vt. 1. to pestle (in a mo-rtar). 2. to smoothen by intensive rubbing. 3. to shave. 4. to strangle. 5. to commit to memory, to cram up.

घोटा m. 1. act or tool of pestling. 2. gadget for rubbing; ~ लगाना to learn by rote.

घोटाई f. 1. act of pestling or rubbing or wages paid for the same.

घोटाला m. 1. bungling. 2. scam, misappropriation.

घोड़ा m. 1. horse. 2. trigger. 3. knight (chess).

घोड़ा-गाड़ी f. horse-carriage.

घोड़िया f. 1. mare, small mare. 2. peg. 3. a gadget used by handloom weavers.

घोड़ी f. 1. mare. 2. a kind of song sung at a marriage ceremony.

घोर adj. 1. terrible, dreadful, fierce, horrible, formidable. 2. excessive. 3. loud. 4. serious.

घोल m. 1. solution. 2. emulsion.

घोलना vt. to mix and dissolve.

घोष adj. voiced. m. 1. sound. 2. slogan.

घोषणा f. declaration, announcement, proclamation, promulgation.

घोषणा-पत्र m. 1. proclamation. 2. manifesto.

घोसी m. milkman.

घौद m. bunch.

घ्राण m. 1. act of smelling. 2. odour, fragrance.

घ्राणेंद्रिय f. organ of smelling, nose.

ङ

ङ m. fifth and the last consonant of the soft palatal pentad of the Nagari alphabet; its sound is like that of n in king.

च

च sixth consonant and first of the alveo-palatal pentad of the Nagari alphabet; its sound is like that of ch in chill.

चंग f. small timbrel.

चंगा adj. sound, nice, healthy.

चंगुल m. clutch, talons, claw.

चंचरीक m. buzzing bee.

चंचल adj. 1. agile, brisk, nimble, not stable or firm. 2. playful.

चंचलता f. 1. instability, unsteadiness. 2. playfulness.

चंचला f. 1. Lakshmi, the god- dess of wealth. 2. lightning.

चंचु m. beak, bill.

चंट adj. cunning, sly, wily, knave.

चंड adj. 1. fierce. 2. furious. 3. violent.

चंडता f. 1. fierceness. 2. furiousness. 3. violence.

चंडाल adj. 1. cruel. 2. wret-ched, wicked. m. a low Hindu caste.

चंडिका f. 1. Durga, the goddess of prowess. 2. cruel virago.

चंडी f. = चंडिका।

चंडू m. Chandu, an intoxicant prepared from opium.

चंडूख़ाना m. den of चंडू smokers.

चंडूल m. a kind of lark.

चंद adj. a few, some.

चंदन m. sandal.

चँदला adj. baldheaded.

चँदवा m. small canopy.

चंदा m. 1. coutribution, subscription. 2. moon.

चँदिया f. cranium.

चँदोवा m. small canopy.

चंद्र m. moon.

चंद्रकला f. crescent.

चंद्रग्रहण m. lunar eclipse.

चंद्रचूड़ m. Lord Shiv.

चंद्रबिंदु m. nasal vowel represented by ँ.

चंद्रमा m. moon.

चंद्रहास m. 1. sword. 2. moonshine.

चंद्रिका f. moonshine.

चंपई adj. yellow.

चंपत adj. suddenly disappeared, slipped out.

चँपना vi. to bow down due to weight.

चंपा f. a variety of tree and its fragrant flowers.

चंपाकली f. 1. bud of चंपा।2. necklace having beads of the shape of चंपाकली।

चंपी f. massage, shampoo.

चंपू m. a drama which is composed of pieces of prose and verse alternately.

चँवर m. 1. whisk, originally made of the hair on the tail of a yak. 2. quill.

चँवरी f. altar of marriage.

चक adj. ample, abundant, plentiful. m. 1. wheel. 2. big plot of agricultural land, holding.

चकई adj. round.
f. a plaything for children in the form of a pulley.

चकती f. patch.

चकत्ता m. (skin) rash, blotch.

चकनाचूर adj. broken into fragments, reduced to smithereens.

चकपकाना vi. to be flab-bergasted/ dumbfound.

चकबंदी f. consolidation of holdings.

चकमक m. flint.

चकमा m. ruse, trick, hoodwinking, deception.

चकराना vi. 1. to feel giddy. 2. to be confounded.

चकला m. 1. disc on which flour is rolled into cakes. 2. expansive habitation. 3. brothel.

चकली f. 1. small round board for rubbing things, especially sandal wood. 2. pulley.

चकल्लस f. mess, medley.

चकवा m. ruddy goose.

चकाचक adj. exuberant, abundant, plentiful.

चकाचौंध f. the light which dazzles the eyes.

चकार m. the consonant च or its sound.

चकित adj. amazed, astonished, bewildered.

चकोटना vt. to pinch.

चकोतरा m. a fruit of the citrus family, shaddock.

चकोर f. red-legged partridge.

चक्कर m. 1. round. 2. revolution, rotation. 3. sensation of dizziness.

चक्करदार adj. 1. circuitous, roundabout. 2. meandering.

चक्का m. 1. wheel. 2. chunk, pebble.

चक्की f. 1. a device for grinding, mill.

चक्र m. 1. wheel. 2. potter's wheel. 3. cycle, circle. 4. whirlpool. 5. whirlwind. 6. disc given as a prize; महावीर ~ disc of valour.

चक्रगति f. cyclic/circular motion.

चक्रमंडप m. amphitheatre.

चक्रवर्ती adj. universal.

चक्रवात m. cyclone, hurricane.

चक्रवातीय adj. cyclonic; ~ वर्षा cyclonic rain.

चक्रवृद्धि f. compound (inte-rest).

चक्रव्यूह m. strategic arrange-ment of troops, spl. circular.

चक्राकार adj. cyclic.

चक्रीय adj. 1. circular. 2. cyclic.

चक्षु m. eye.

चक्षुगोचर adj. perceptible, visible.

चख़चख़ f. noisy exchange of words, discordant discussion.

चखना vt. to relish/taste, to try.

चखाचखी f. quarrel, strife.

चखाना vt. to cause to taste.

चगड़ adj.= चघड़।

चघड़ adj. cunning, tricky.

चचा m. = चाचा।

चचिया adj. = चचेरा।

चचेरा adj. of or pertaining to a paternal uncle.

चट adv. hurriedly, sharply, quickly. f. clattering sound, snapping of stick, wood etc.

चटक adj. = चटकीला। m. sparrow.

चटकदार adj. gaudy, bright (said of colour).

चटकना vi. 1. to snap. 2. to crack. 3. to open out (said of a bud).

चटकनी f. bolt, latch.

चटक-मटक f. fascination of dress and gestures.

चटका m. slap.

चटकाना vt. to crack.

चटकारा adj. flit. m. relishing a dish ostensibly.

चटकीला adj. too bright or colourful, gaudy.

चटखना vi. = चटकना।

चटचटाना vi. to make a crackling sound while burning.

चटनी f. Indian type of sauce, chutney.

चटपट adv. in no time, very quickly.

चटपटा adj. flavoured with spice, spicy.

चटपटी f. undue haste, hurry.

चटवाना vt. to cause to be licked.

चटाई f. mat.

चटाका m. 1. crackling sound. 2. slap.

चटाना vt. 1. to cause to be licked. 2. to bribe. 3. to sharpen a tool.

चटोरा adj. over-fond of spicy dishes, gourmet, epicure.

चट्टा m. arranged block of bricks, tiles etc.

चट्टान f. rock, cliff.

चट्टा-बट्टा m.; एक ही थैली के चट्टे-बट्टे birds of the same feather.

चट्टी f. 1. wooden slippers. 2. halting place. 3. loss or damage.

चड्डी f. lower undergarment.

चढ़त f. 1. offering to deity or preceptor. 2. start of a marriage procession.

चढ़ता adj. rising.

चढ़ना vi. 1. to climb. 2. to ascend. 3. to mount, ride. 4. to rise.

चढ़वाना vt. causative form of चढ़ना।

चढ़ाई f. 1. ascent. 2. invasion.

चढ़ाना vt. 1. to cause/help to mount/go up. 2. to offer (to a deity etc.). 3. to record (in a register etc.); आग पर ~ to place

च

on fire for cooking.

चढ़ाव m. 1. ascent. 2. rise.

चढ़ावा m. 1. offering to a deity. 2. gifts to a bride from the bridegroom's side.

चतुरंगिनी f. army consisting of four divisions (in olden times).

चतुर adj. 1. clever, shrewd. 2. wise. 3. skilled.

चतुरता f. 1. cleverness, shrewdness. 2. wisdom. 3. skill.

चतुराई f. = चतुरता।

चतुर्थ adj. fourth.

चतुर्थांश m. one-fourth part.

चतुर्थी f. fourth day of the lunar fortnight.

चतुर्दशी f. fourteenth day of the lunar fortnight.

चतुर्दिक adj. many sided. adv. in all four directions.

चतुर्धाम m. the four places of pilgrimage of the Hindus : Badrinath (North), Rameshwaram (South), Dwarka (West) and Jagannath Puri (East).

चतुर्भुज m. (Maths.) quad-rilateral.

चतुर्मास m. the four months (June-Sep. i.e. आषाढ़-आश्विन) of the rainy season.

चतुर्मुख adj. four-faced. m. Lord Brahma.

चतुर्वर्ण m. the four castes among the Hindus : Brahman, Kshatriya, Vaishya and Shudra.

चतुर्विध adj. having all the four sides or forms. adv. in all the four ways.

चतुष्कोण m. quadrangle.

चतुष्पदी m. a verse form consisting of four lines, sonnet.

चतुष्फलक m. (Maths.) tetrahedron.

चना m. gram.

चना-चबैना m. 1. gram and parched grain (poor man's diet). 2.snacks.

चपकन f. 1. a long Indian coat of the ancient type. 2. V-shaped bolt.

चपटा adj. flat.

चपड़-चपड़ f. 1. prattle. 2. tapping sound.

चपड़ा m. shellac.

चपत f. a hit on the face with the palm of the hand, slap.

चपतियाना vt. to go on slapping.

चपना vi. to be crushed.

चपनी f. 1. shallow dish. 2. lid of a container. 3. bowl made of coconut shard. 4. kneecap.

चपरकनाती m. stupid and parasitical person.

चपरगट्टू adj. &. m. duffer.

चपरास f. plate worn by peons etc. on the belt (as a mark of their office).

चपरासी m. a personal attendant, peon.

चपल adj. nimble, agile and clever.

चपला f. 1. lightning. 2. Lakshmi—Goddess of wealth.

चपाती f. thin cake.

चपेट f. hitting range.

चपेटना vt. 1. to entangle/embroil. 2. to press from all sides, to squeeze. 3. to brow-beat.

चप्पल f. slipper, sandal.

चप्पा m. 1. one-fourth part. 2. tiny part. 3. measure of the breadth of four fingers. 4. small piece of land.

चप्पू m. oar.

चबवाना vt. causative of चबाना।

चबाना vt. to masticate.

चबूतरा m. raised platform, rostrum.

चबेना m. parched grain.

चबेनी f. 1. refreshment. 2. allowance for refreshment.

चबैना m. = चबेना।

चमक f. 1. shine, radiance. 2. lustre. 3. flash of pain.

चमक-दमक f. glitter, glamour, pomp and show, splendour.

चमकदार adj. 1. shining, radiant. 2. lustrous.

चमकना vi. 1. to shine. 2. to sparkle. 3. to flourish. 4. to startle.

चमकाना vt. 1. to make (something) shiny by rubbing, brighten, burnish, illumine. 2. to startle. 3.to tease. 4. to coax/instigate.

चमकी f. star-like tiny metallic objects (meant for decoration).

चमकीला adj. bright, shining, glittering.

चमकौवल f. pantomimic coquetry, ogling.

चमगादड़ m. bat, vampire.

चमचम adj. glittering, shining, gleaming, refulgent. adv. glamorously, brightly.

चमचमाना vi. to glitter/gleam/ sparkle. vt. to burnish, polish.

चमचा m. 1. spoon. 2. sycophant.

चमचागीरी f. sycophancy.

चमड़ा m. 1. leather. 2. hide.

चमड़ी f. skin.

चमत्कार m. miracle, marvel, wonder.

चमत्कारपूर्ण adj. miraculous.

चमत्कारी adj. miraculous, wonderful, astonishing.

चमत्कृत adj. wonderstruck, astounded.

चमन m. 1. flower-garden. 2. gay place or country.

चमर m. 1. yak. 2. long, soft brush made of the tail-hair of the yak used as a fan.

चमाचम adj. glazing, glitte- ring, shining, brilliant. adv. glazingly, glitteringly.

चमार m. 1. a scheduled caste among the Hindus, usually living on skinning, tanning etc. 2. person of a low order.

चमारिन f. fem. of चमार।

चमारी f. 1. wife of a चमार। 2. the calling of a चमार।

चमू f. body of troops, division of an army.

चमेली f. jasmine.

चमोटा m. razor-strop.

चम्मच m. spoon.

चयन m. 1. act of culling or selecting. 2. cull, selection.

चयनकर्ता m. selector.

चयनिका f. anthology, colle- ction.

चर m. 1. spy, emissary. 2. scout; बाल ~ boy scout. adj. & m. variable (Maths.), unsteady.

च

चरकटा m. 1. chaff-cutter. 2. riffraff.

चरख m. large, rotating wheel.

चरख़ा m. spinning wheel.

चरख़ी f. pulley, reel.

चरचराना vi. to crackle.

चरचराहट f. crackling sound.

चरण m. foot.

चरणचिह्न m. foot-print, mark of the foot.

चरणधूलि f. dust of the feet.

चरणामृत m. ambrosia of the feet (of a deity); sacred drink, mixture of milk, ghee, curd, sugar etc. with which the feet of a deity are washed.

चरती m. one who does not observe a fast on a day of fasting.

चरना vt. to graze.

चरनी f. manger.

चरपरा adj. pungent-cum-spicy.

चरपराहट f. irritation due to pungency.

चरबाँक adj. clever, crafty, cunning.

चरबी f. fat.

चरम adj. 1. absolute. 2. ultimate.

चरमपंथी adj. & m. extremist, ultra.

चरमर f. creaking sound.

चरमराना vi. to creak.

चरमावस्था f. ultimate stage.

चरवाई f. = चराई।

चरवाना vt. to cause to graze.

चरवाहा m. grazier, shepherd.

चरस f. 1. an Indian intoxicant. 2. big leather bucket for drawing water for irrigation.

चराई f. 1. act or state of grazing. 2. charges paid for the grazing of cattle.

चरागाह m. pasture.

चराचर adj. 1. movable and immovable. 2. animate and inanimate. m. universe, the entire creation.

चराना vt. to graze.

चरितार्थ adj. performed or realized.

चरित्र m. character, conduct.

चरित्र-चित्रण m. characterization, portrayal.

चरित्रवान, चरित्रवान् adj. possessing a character, of a good moral character.

चरित्र-हत्या f.; **चरित्र-हनन** m. character assassination.

चरित्रहीन adj. unprincipled, characterless.

चरी f. 1. green fodder. 2. pasture.

चर्च m. church.

चर्चा f. mention, rumour, talk.

चर्चित adj. talked of.

चर्म m. 1. skin on the body, dermis. 2. shield.

चर्मकार m. shoemaker, cobbler, tanner.

चर्या f. routine, usual course or procedure.

चर्राना vt. 1. to creak/crack/crackle. 2. to smart (said of skin).

चर्वण m. chewing, masticating.

चल adj. 1. moving, mobile. 2. fickle, unsteady. 3. movable. 4. variable.

चलचित्त adj. fickle-minded, unsteady.

चलचित्र m. motion picture, movie.

चलता adj. going, moving.

चलता पुरज़ा adj. & m. sharper, cunning fellow, dexterous, crafty, sly.

चलती भाषा f. colloquial language.

चलन m. 1. prevalence. 2. practice, custom. 3. fashion.

चलना vi. 1. to go/walk/move. 2. to work. 3. to be accepted or acceptable.

चलनी f. = छलनी।

चल-विचल adj. unsteady, fickle.

चल-वृत्तांत running commen-tary.

चल-संपत्ति f. 1. movable property. 2. floating assets.

चलाऊ adj. 1. lasting, durable, strong.

चलाचल adj. movable and immovable.

चलाचली f. 1. act of departing from the world. 2. successive emergence and evanescence.

चलान m. 1. consignment; ~ करना to consign. 2. challan, charge-sheet.

चलाना vt. 1. to cause to move/walk. 2. to operate or set in motion. 3. to drive. 4. to put into circulation. 5.to start/establish.

चलानी adj. 1. that which has come from some other place for being sold. 2. pertaining to challan.

चलायमान adj. 1. wavering, unsettled, fickle, unsteady. 2. moving.

चलित adj. current, usual.

चवन्नी f. a four-anna coin; in decimal currency its value is 25 paise.

चवर्ग m. class of five consonants beginning with च; viz. च, छ, ज, झ, ञ।

चश्मा m. 1. pair of spectacles, eye-glasses. 2. spring, fountain.

चषक m. 1. wine-glass. 2. honey. 3. farmer.

चसक f. throbbing pain.

चस्का m. overpowering procli-vity/fondness, passion, addiction.

चस्पाँ adj. ~ करना to affix.

चहक f. chirp, warble.

चहकना vi. to chirp/warble.

चहचहाना vi. to warble.

चहचहाहट f. chirping, warbling.

चहबच्चा m. sump, cesspool.

चहल-क़दमी f. stroll for pleasure, saunter.

चहलपहल f. gaiety, merry-making, mirth.

चहेता adj. pet, dearly loved.

चाँइयाँ m. 1. sharper. 2. swindler. 3. pickpocket, thief.

चाँईं m. = चाँइयाँ।

चाँटा m. slap.

चाँड़ f. abutment.

चांडाल m. = चंडाल।

चाँद m. moon. f. crown (of the head).

चाँदनी f. moonlight.

चाँदमारी f. shooting range.

चाँदा m. (Math.) protractor.

चाँदी f. silver.

चांद्र adj. lunar; ~ मास lunar month; ~ वर्ष lunar year.

च

चाँपना vt. to press.

चाइयाँ adj. & m. sharper.

चाक m. 1. wheel. 2. potter's wheel. 3. pulley.

चाकर m. 1. servant. 2. attendant. [Fem. चाकरानी]

चाकरी f. 1. service. 2. attendance.

चाकलेट f. chocolate.

चाक़ू m. knife.

चाक्षुष adj. 1. of or pertaining to the eye, ocular. 2. optical.

चाचा m. paternal uncle.

चाची f. paternal aunt.

चाट f. 1. relish, taste. 2. spicy preparation of cut fruit, vegetables pulses etc.

चाटना vt. to lick/lap.

चाटुकार m. flatterer.

चातक m. a typical Indian bird supposed to live only on raindrops.

चातुरी f. 1. cleverness. 2. trick, artifice, finesse.

चातुर्य m. cleverness.

चादर f. 1. bed-cover. 2. over-all cover (esp. of a woman). 3. sheet (of iron, glass, plastic etc.).

चाप m. 1. arc. 2. bow. 3. arch. f. 1. sound of footstep. 2. act or state of putting pressure.

चापकर्ण m. (Geom.) chord.

चापलूस adj. & m. trying to win favour by flattery, flatterer, wheedler.

चापलूसी f. flattery, blarney, wheedling.

चाबना vt. = चबाना।

चाबी f. key.

चाबुक m. flagellum, horsewhip.

चाभी f. = चाबी।

चाम m. skin, leather.

चामीकर m. 1. gold. 2. datura. (धतूरा)

चाय f. 1. dried leaves of a particular shrub used to make a beverage. 2. such a beverage, tea.

चायदानी f. tea-pot.

चाय-पानी m. light refreshment.

चार adj. & m. 1. four. 2. act of going. 3. spy.

चारख़ाना m. chequered cloth.

चारजामा m. saddle.

चारण m. bard, minstrel.

चारदीवारी f. boundary wall.

चारपाई f. bed, cot.

चारा m. 1. fodder. 2. bait, lure. 3. food of a mean type. 4. remedy, device.

चाराजोई f. 1. application for amends. 2. suit, proceedings.

चारित्रिक adj. 1. pertaining to character, characteristic. 2. possessing a good character.

चारी adj. 1. going, moving. 2. following a particular cult e.g. ब्रह्मचारी celebate. [Fem. चारिणी]

चारु adj. charming, pretty, elegant.

चारुता f. charm, prettiness, elegance.

चारुहासी adj. possessing a pleasing smile. [Fem. चारुहासिनी]

चार्ज m. charge.

चार्जशीट f. a list of charges framed against someone.

चार्टर m. charter.

चाल f. 1. manner of going/walking, gait. 2. speed. 3. way of moving/working, motion. 4. move. 5. trick. 6. tradition, custom.

चालक m. 1. driver. 2. conductor.

चालचलन m. conduct.

चालढाल f. ways, bearing, deportment, demeanour.

चालना vt. to sieve/sift.

चालबाज़ adj. &. m. skilled in deception, crafty, cunning, trickster.

चाला m. auspiciousness for departure.

चालाक adj. clever, cunning, crafty.

चालाकी f. craftiness, cunning.

चालान m. see चलान।

चालिया adj. see चालबाज़।

चाली adj. tricky. m. round worm.

चालीस adj. & m. forty.

चालीसा m. period of forty days.

चालू adj. 1. prevalent, current. 2. in working order. 3.cunning; ~ आदमी sharper.

चाव m. ardour, zeal, gusto, warm enthusiasm.

चावल m. rice.

चाशनी f. treacle, viscous syrup.

चाह f. 1. craving, cherished desire, longing. 2. love.

चाहत f. 1. craving, cherished desire, longing. 2. love.

चाहना vt. 1. to desire, crave or like. 2. to want. 3. to love.

चाहनेवाला adj. & m. one who is crazy after, lover.

चाहा m. marshland bird with a long straight bill, snipe.

चाहिए vi. a typical form of verb चाहना meaning (i) is necessary, wanted, required. (ii) should.

चाहे conj. 1. if you please. 2. whether... or, either... or.

चिंगड़ा m. prawn.

चिंगारी f. = चिनगारी।

चिंघाड़ f. trumpeting (of an elephant), trumpet.

चिंघाड़ना vt. 1. to trumpet. 2. to roar (in rage).

चिंतक m. thinker, meditator, contemplator.

चिंतन m. thinking, meditation, reflection, pondering, musing.

चिंतनीय adj. serious, grave.

चिंता f. worry, anxiety.

चिंताग्रस्त adj. worried, anxious.

चिंताजनक adj. causing anxiety/concern.

चिंतामग्न adj. deeply thoughtful, pensive.

चिंतामणि m. 1. a fabulous gem which fulfils all desires. 2. God.

चिंतित adj. anxious, worried, concerned, careworn.

चिंदी f. fragment, shamble, shred etc..

चिंपांजी m. chimpanzee.

चिउँटा m. see च्यूँटा।

चिउँटी f. see च्यूँटी।

चिउड़ा m. = चिड़वा।

चिक f. 1. screen (of bamboo sticks). 2. pain in back or loins. m. butcher.

चिकट adj. = चिक्कट।

च

चिकन f. a kind of embroidered cloth.

चिकना adj. oily, smooth.

चिकनाई f. 1. oiliness, greasiness, fattiness. 2. lubricant.

चिकनाना vt. 1. to smoothen. 2. to lubricate.

चिकनापन m. oiliness, smoothness.

चिकनाहट f. 1. oiliness, smoothness. 2. lubricity.

चिकनी मिट्टी f. 1. marl, viscous soil. 2. slippery ground.

चिकनी सुपारी f. boiled and flattened betel-nut.

चिकारा m. 1. a stringed instrument. 2. antelope. [Fem. चिकारी]

चिकित्सक m. physician.

चिकित्सा f. 1. medical treatment. 2. therapy.

चिकित्सालय m. 1. hospital. 2. clinic. 3. dispensary.

चिकित्सा-विज्ञान, चिकित्सा-शास्त्र m. medical science, medical therapy.

चिकित्सा-सहायता f. medical aid.

चिकुर m. hair (on the head).

चिकोटी f. pinch, painful squ- eeze, tweak.

चिक्कट adj. oiled, soiled, greasy.

चिक्कण adj. 1. smooth. 2. oily.

चिखुरना vt. to weed out.

चिचड़ा m. snake-gourd used as a vegetable and medicine.

चिचड़ी f. tick, cattle-louse.

चिचियाना vi. to cry aloud, to scream.

चिचियाहट f. cry, loud scream.

चिचोरना vt. to suck (to the bone).

चिट f. 1. chit. 2. rag.

चिटकना vi. 1. to creak. 2. to fret, to feel annoyed/irritated.

चिटकनी f. bolt.

चिटफ़ंड m. chit-fund.

चिट्टा adj. 1. white. 2. fair-complexioned. m. 1. rupee. 2. abetment; ~ लड़ाना to instigate/abet.

चिट्ठा m. 1. balance-sheet. 2. account-book. 3. account; कच्चा ~ (i) rough account, detailed account; (ii) detailed account (of the misdeeds of someone).

चिट्ठी f. letter.

चिट्ठी-पत्री f. correspondence.

चिट्ठीरसाँ m. postman.

चिड़चिड़ा adj. fretful, peevish, irritable.

चिड़चिड़ाहट f. fretfulness.

चिड़वा m. parched rice, wetted flattened rice.

चिड़िया f. 1. sparrow. 2. bird.

चिड़ियाख़ाना m. 1. aviary. 2. = चिड़ियाघर।

चिड़ियाघर m. zoo.

चिड़ीमार m. bird-catcher, fowler.

चिड़ीहार m. fowler, bird-catcher.

चिढ़ f. 1. strong aversion, repulsion. 2. derisory nickname given to a person.

चिढ़ना vi. to be irritated, to feel provoked.

चिढ़ाना vt. 1. to fret/irritate/tease. 2. to call by a nickname.

चित adj. 1. supine. 2. culled. 3. collected. 4. covered.

m. 1. experience. 2. consciousness. 3. intuition. 4. disposition. 5. mind. 6. soul.

चितकबरा adj. 1. piebald, vari-coloured. 2. spotted.

चितचोर m. stealer of the heart, extremely attractive person (in the eyes of the sweet-heart), beloved.

चित-पट m. 1. a game in which the result is based upon tossing of a coin (चित = head, पट = tail); ~ हो जाए Let it be decided by toss. 2. wrestling duel.

चितरना vt. to paint.

चितवन f. look, glance.

चिता f. funeral pyre.

चितेरा m. painter.

चित्त m. 1. heart. 2. mind.

चित्त-निवृत्ति f. state of desirelessness.

चित्तवृत्ति f. attitude, mental disposition, mentality, mood.

चित्ताकर्षक adj. attractive, fascinating, charming, alluring.

चित्ती f. 1. spot, small mark. 2. speck. 3. pip.

चित्तीदार adj. spotted, specked.

चित्र m. 1. picture. 2. diagram, drawing. 3. painting, portrait, photo.

चित्रकला f. 1. art of painting. 2. painting, drawing etc.

चित्रकार m. painter.

चित्रकारी f. 1. painter's vocation. 2. painting.

चित्रण m. 1. act of painting, drawing etc., depiction, portrayal, delineation. 2. graphic description.

चित्रपट m. screen, silver screen.

चित्रफलक m. canvas.

चित्रमय adj. pictorial.

चित्रलिखित adj. beautiful, like a picture.

चित्रलिपि f. 1. hieroglyphics. 2. = चित्रलेख।

चित्रलेख m. 1. hieroglyphic, pictograph. 2. screen-play.

चित्रवत adj. still, motionless like a picture.

चित्र-विचित्र adj. 1. variegated, motley. 2. multiform. 3. peculiar.

चित्रशाला f. 1. picture gallery. 2. art gallery.

चित्र-संग्रह m. album.

चित्रांकन m. 1. portrayal, delineation. 2. depiction.

चित्रांकित adj. portrayed, delineated.

चित्रात्मक adj. 1. of or pertaining to a picture. 2. like a picture, picturesque.

चित्रित adj. 1. portrayed. 2. pain-ted. 3. depicted.

चित्रोपम adj. 1. picturesque. 2. having attractive facial appearance, photogenic.

चिथड़ा m. rag, tatter, shred.

चिनक f. smarting pain.

चिनगारी f. spark, scintillation.

चिनगी f. 1. = चिनगारी। 2. boy assistant of a juggler.

चिनना vt. = चुनना।

चिनाई f. = चुनाई।

चिनार m. a tall Indian tree.

च

चिनिया बादाम m. groundnut.

चिन्मय adj. conscious. m. supreme or pure consciousness.

चिन्ह m. = चिह्न।

चिन्हानी f. 1. token of remembrance. 2. mark/sign of identity.

चिपकना vi. 1. to stick/adhere, to be attached. 2. to cling. adj. sticky.

चिपकाना vt. to paste/stick.

चिपकू adj. & m. hanger-on, tenacious.

चिपचिप f. (state of) stickiness, viscosity.

चिपचिपा adj. sticky, viscous.

चिपचिपाहट f. (state of) stickiness, viscosity.

चिपटना vi. 1. to stick/cling/adhere. 2. to embrace.

चिपटा adj. flat (more current चपटा)।

चिपटाना vt. to embrace.

चिप्पड़ m. 1. patch. 2. patch of crust.

चिप्पी f. 1. small patch. 2. label.

चिबुक f. chin.

चिमटना vi. 1. to cling. 2. to hold fast.

चिमटा m. pincers used as a kitchen gadget.

चिमटी f. tweezers, small pincers, forceps.

चिमड़ा adj. tenacious, sticking stiffly.

चिमनी f. 1. chimney (smoke passage). 2. glass tube (of an oil lamp).

चियाँ m. seed (stone) of tamarind.

चिरंजीव adj. long-lived.

चिरंतन adj. perpetual, everlasting.

चिर adj. 1. lasting, long-lived. 2. perpetual.

चिरकाल m. 1. long time. 2. infinite time, eternity.

चिरकालिक adj. 1. abiding, las-ting. 2. eternal, perpetual.

चिरकालीन adj. = चिरकालिक।

चिरजीवी adj. long-living, having a long life.

चिरना vi. 1. to be sawed. 2. to crack.

चिरनिद्रा f. eternal sleep.

चिरवाई f. charges paid for sawing.

चिर-समाधि f. eternal समाधि i.e. death.

चिरस्थायी adj. everlasting, permanent.

चिरस्मरणीय adj. ever memorable, worth remembering for long.

चिराई f. act or state of sawing wood, or charges paid for the same.

चिराग़ m. lamp.

चिरायु adj. ~ हो May you live long !

चिरौंजी f. a kind of dry fruit and its tree.

चिरौरी f. entreaty, imploring, beseeching.

चिलक f. sharp pain, smart.

चिलकना vi. to feel a sharp pain, to smart.

चिलगोज़ा m. a kind of dry fruit, (the nut of the pine tree).

चिलचिलाना vi. to shine scorchingly; चिलचिलाती धूप scorching heat/sun.

चिलड़ा m. an Indian type of cake

prepared from the flour of lentil or any pulse.

चिलबिला adj. hectic and restless (person).

चिलबिल्ला adj. = चिलबिला।

चिलम f. earthen funnel in which tobacco, hemp etc. are placed for smoking (purposes).

चिलमची f. basin (for washing purposes).

चिलमन f. curtain made of bam-boo strips.

चिल्लड़ m. 1. = चीलर। 2. small coins, change.

चिल्लपों f. clamour, scream, ballyhoo.

चिल्ला m. 1. period of forty days. 2. bowstring. 3. = चिलड़ा।

चिल्लाना vi. to cry, to shout.

चिल्लाहट f. loud cry, yell.

चिहुंक f. 1. state of being startled. 2. hesitation, shyness.

चिहुँकना vi. 1. to be startled. 2. to hesitate, to feel shy.

चिह्न m. sign, mark, symbol, symptom.

चिह्नित adj. 1. marked. 2. sing-led out.

चीं f. 1. chirping of birds, chirp. 2. cry of pain and helplessness.

चीं-चपड़ f. grumbling.

चीं-चीं f. 1. warbling of birds. 2. thrilling note of children. 3. squeaking. 4. (of wheel) creaking in movement.

चींटा m. big black ant.

चींटी f. ant.

चींटीख़ोर m. ant-eater.

चीकट adj. very dirty, esp. soiled or oiled.

चीकू m. sapodilla.

चीख f. scream, shriek.

चीखना vt. 1. to scream/shriek. 2. to taste.

चीज़ f. thing.

चीड़ m. pine tree or its wood.

चीतना vi. to think, contemplate.

चीतल m. spotted antelope.

चीता m. spotted panther, cheetah.

चीत्कार m. scream of pain or distress, screech, uproar.

चीथना vt. to tear to pieces/bits with the teeth.

चीन m. China.

चीनी adj. of or pertaining to China. f. sugar.

चीनी मिट्टी f. porcelain.

चीन्हना vt. 1. to recognize. 2. to identify (criminals in session trial).

चीपड़ m. = चिप्पड़।

चीमड़ adj. tenacious, tough.

चीर m. 1. cloth. 2. strip of cloth. 3. opening made by a knife etc., cut, splint. 4. a tear, rent, fissure.

चीरना vi. 1. to saw. 2. to rip, to cut along a line, to rend. 3. to cut open, to tear, to operate (wound etc.).

चीर-फाड़ f. 1. surgical opera- tion. 2. dissection.

चीरा m. incision.

चील f. kite (bird).

चीलर m. louse.

चीस f. rankling pain, smart.

चुंगी f. octroi.

च

चुँघाना vt. to cause to suck.
चुँधियाना vi. = चौंधियाना।
चुंबक m. magnet.
चुंबक-पत्थर m. loadstone.
चुंबन m. kiss; ~ लेना to kiss.
चुआना vt. 1. to cause to drip. 2. to distil.
चुक़ंदर m. beet-root.
चुकता adj. 1. paid up, settled.
चुकना vi. 1. to be finished. 2. to be paid up or adjusted, to be settled.
चुकाई f. act or state of settling/ paying up or charges paid for the same.
चुकाना vt. 1. to pay, repay or settle. 2. to compensate.
चुक्कड़ m. an earthen cup.
चुग़द m. 1. owl. 2. stupid person.
चुगना vt. to pick up, to peck.
चुग़लख़ोर m. backbiter.
चुग़ली f. backbiting.
चुगाई f. act or state of चुगाना, or wages paid for the same.
चुगाना vt. to cause to peck.
चुग्गा m. coarse grain given to birds.
चुचकना vi. to shrivel.
चुचुक f. nipple (of breast).
चुटकना vi. 1. see चुटकी बजाना। 2. to create a sound of चुटकी।
vt. 1. to pick out with the fingers. 2. to pinch. 3. to be bitten by a snake. 4. to whip.
चुटकी f. 1. snapping sound made by the thumb and middle finger; ~ बजाना to snap the fingers. 2. a pinch.
चुटकुला m. a witty remark, epigram, titbit, pleasantry.
चुटकुलेबाज़ m. epigrammatist.
चुटिया f. tuft of hair on the crown.
चुटीला adj. 1. capable of hur-ting. 2. wounded.
चुटैल adj. hurt, wounded.
चुड़िहारा m. maker or seller of bangles.
चुड़िहारिन f. fem. of चुड़िहारा।
चुड़ैल f. she-hobgoblin, witch.
चुदाई f. act or process of cohabitation.
चुनचुना adj. causing a burning sensation on being touched.
चुनचुनाना vi. to feel an irritating or pricking sensation.
चुनचुनाहट f. irritating or pricking sensation.
चुनट f. = चुन्नट।
चुनन f. = चुन्नट।
चुनना vt. 1. to choose/select. 2. to pluck. 3. to cull/gather. 4. to erect. 5. to pick over, to sort out. 6. to make ruffles, to ruffle. 7. to elect.
चुनरी f. coloured over cloth (worn by women on ceremonial occasions).
चुनवाँ adj. 1. selected, chosen. 2. excellent.
चुनवाना vt. causative of चुनना।
चुनाई f. 1. laying bricks in a wall etc. 2. charges for laying bricks.
चुनाव m. 1. selection, choice. 2. election.
चुनाव-क्षेत्र m. constituency.
चुनाव-मंडल m. electorate.

चुनावी adj. of or pertaining to the election.

चुनिंदा adj. 1. chosen, selected. 2. choicest.

चुनी f. ruby.

चुनौटी f. small case for keeping lime (for chewing with tobacco).

चुनौती f. 1. challenge. 2. a demanding situation.

चुन्नट f. ruffle.

चुन्नी f. 1. small ruby. 2. spangle. 3. filings of corn. 4. sawdust.

चुप adj. 1. quiet, silent. 2. secretive.

चुपका adj. totally silent. m. complete silence.

चुपके adv.; ~ से quietly, stealthily.

चुपके-चुपके adv. stealthily.

चुपचाप adv. silently, quietly.

चुपड़ना vt. 1. to apply (butter, ghee etc.). 2. to annoint.

चुपड़ा adj. coated with some oily substance; चिकना - ~ with a well made-up appearance.

चुपाना vt. to quieten.

चुप्पा adj. reticent, uncommunicative by nature.

चुप्पा-घुन्ना adj. secretive.

चुप्पी f. reticence, silence.

चुभकना vi. to duck and plunge out (again and again).

चुभन f. 1. pricking sensation. 2. throbbing pain (physical or mental). 3. punch line/sting of a joke. 4. a source of irritation.

चुभना vi. to prick/pinch.

चुभनेवाला adj. pinching, irrita-ting, hurtful.

चुभलाना vt. to mumble.

चुभाना vt. to prick/pinch.

चुभोना vt. = चुभाना।

चुमकार f. sound produced while kissing.

चुमकारना vt. to coo and fondle.

चुम्मा m. kiss

चुम्मा-चाटी f. kissing and lick ing.

चुरचुरा adj. crisp.

चुरट m. cheroot.

चुरना vi. to boil and bubble (as pulse in water).

चुरमुर f. sound produced by the cracking of a crisp or fragile substance.

चुरमुरा adj. crisp, fragile. m. spicy preparation of fried, crisp grain.

चुरवाना vi. 1. to cause to steal. 2. causative of चुरना।

चुराना vt. 1. to steal/pinch. 2. to take quickly; चुंबन ~ to steal a kiss.

चुरुट m. = चुरट।

चुल f. 1. propensity to be itched, titilation. 2. craving for a coitus, strong sexual urge.

चुलबुला adj. 1. restless by nature. 2. playful as a child, frolicsome.

चुलबुलाना vi. to be frolicsome, to be restless like a child.

चुलबुली f. 1. state of being panicky. 2. undue haste.

चुल्लू m. 1. hollow cup made by the palm of the hand. 2. quantity contained in the चुल्लू।

चुसकी f. sip, suck.

चुसना vi. 1. to be sucked. 2. to be absorbed. 3. to be sque-ezed.

चुसनी f. nipple.

च

चुसाना vt. to cause to be sucked.
चुस्की f. = चुसकी।
चुस्त adj. 1. tight, skin-tight. 2. alert, smart (person).
चुस्ती f. alertness, smartness.
चुहचुहाता adj. buddling with juice (mango etc.).
चुहल f. 1. frolicsome act or chat. 2. jollity, joviality. 3. merriment.
चुहलबाज़ adj. frolicsome.
चुहलबाज़ी f. frolicsome gaiety.
चुहिया f. 1. female mouse. 2. small rat.
चूँ f. sharp and shrill tone, chirp.
चूँकि conj. because, as, since.
चूँ-चूँ f. chirping of birds; ~ का मुरब्बा hotch-potch of heterogeneous elements.
चूक f. 1. slip, lapse, error. 2. omission. fault, default. 3. blunder.
चूकना vi. 1. to miss/lose. 2. to default, to fail. 3. to make a mistake.
चूची f. 1. teat, nipple.
चूज़ा m. chicken.
चूड़ा m. 1. tuft of hair on the crown. 2. crest on the head of a bird.
चूड़ाकरण m. ceremonial shaving of the head of a child for the first time, tonsure.
चूड़ाकर्म m. see चूड़ाकरण।
चूड़ामणि m. 1. an ornament worn on the head. 2. crown, shining star.
चूड़ी f. 1. bangle of glass, lac etc. 2. thread.
चूड़ीदार adj. threaded, grooved.
चूत f. vagina.
चूतड़ m. buttocks.
चूतिया m. & adj. (pej.) dolt, stupid (fellow), blockhead.
चूनरी f. = चुनरी।
चूना m. lime. vi. to leak.
चूना-पत्थर m. limestone.
चूनेदानी f. mini lime-container.
चूमना vt. to kiss.
चूमना-चाटना vt. to kiss and lick. m. act of kissing and licking/caressing, slobbering.
चूमा m. kiss.
चूमाचाटी f. slobbering.
चूर m. 1. filings. 2. small fragments; थककर ~ हो जाना to be tired and exhausted; नशे में ~ dead drunk.
चूर-चूर adj. broken into bits/fragments, shattered to pieces.
चूरन m. digestive powder.
चूरा m. 1. filings. 2. small fragments.
चूर्ण m. 1. powder. 2. digestive powder.
चूल f. 1. a projection of wood fitting into a mortice, tenon into mortice. 2. pivot (of a door).
चूल्हा m. hearth, oven, fireplace.
चूषण m. act of sucking.
चूसना vt. to suck.
चूहा m. rat, mouse; पेट में चूहे कूदना to feel/bear the pangs of hunger. [Fem. चुहिया, चूही]
चूहेदानी f. mouse-trap, rat-trap.
चें-चें f. chirping of birds.
चेंप f. viscous substance (spl. of a mango).

चेंपदार adj. viscous.

चेंपना vt. to paste.

चेक m. cheque.

चेकबुक f. a book containing cheques.

चेचक f. pox, smallpox.

चेटा m. servant. [Fem. चेटी]

चेत m. 1. consciousness, sen-ses. 2. knowledge. 3. caution, prudence. 4. memory, remembrance. 5. mind.

चेतन adj. 1. animate. 2. conscious.

चेतनता f. consciousness.

चेतना f. awareness, consciousness.

चेतनाशून्य adj. numb, sensationless.

चेताना vt. 1. to remind. 2. to warn. 3. to kindle (a fire).

चेतावनी f. warning, admoni-tion.

चेन f. chain.

चेप f. = चेंप।

चेरा m. 1. servant. 2. = चेला।

चेरी f. female servant.

चेला m. pupil, disciple.

चेली f. female disciple.

चेले-चाँटे m. (plu.) pupils and followers (collectively).

चेष्टा f. 1. effort, endeavour. 2. act. 3. demeanour, carriage. 4. gesture, motion.

चेहरा m. 1. face, countenance. 2. mask.

चेहरा-मोहरा m. facial outline or feature, lineament.

चैत m. = चैत्र.

चैतन्य adj. conscious. m. consciousness.

चैत्र m. first month of the Hindu calendar.

चैन m. 1. mental ease, carefreeness. 2. relief.

चैला m. sliver, splinter.

चैली f. sliver.

चोंगा m. 1. funnel. 2. big envelope.

चोंगी f. tube of the bellows.

चोंच f. beak, bill.

चोंचला m. = चोचला।

चोंधना vt. to peck.

चोंधर adj. 1. having very small eyes. 2. very short-sighted. 3. foolish, stupid.

चोकर m. outer covering of grain, husk, bran.

चोखा adj. 1. sharp, well-honed. 2. pure, unadulterated. 3. candid, sincere, honest.

चोग़ा m. a kind of garment like cassock or toga.

चोचला m. artificiality of manner, affectation, coquetish behaviour.

चोचलेबाज़ m. one given to affectation.

चोट f. 1. hurt, injury. 2. hurting remark. 3. pleasing hurt.

चोटी f. 1. apex, top. 2. braid or plait of hair (of woman).

चोट्टा adj. thievish. m. pilferer. [Fem. चोट्टी]

चोथ m. lump of dung.

चोदना vt. to copulate/cohabit.

चोब f. 1. tent-pin. 2. drum-stick. 3. mace.

चोबदार m. watchman, spl. mace-bearer.

चोर m. one who steals, thief, burglar.

च

चोरकट m. 1. swindler. 2. petty thief.

चोर ताला m. 1. hidden or secret lock. 2. lock with some secret device.

चोर-बाज़ार m. black market.

चोर शिकारी m. poacher.

चोरी f. act of stealing, theft, thievery.

चोरी-छिपे adv. quietly and secretly, clandestinely, steal-thily, surreptitiously.

चोला m. 1. long robe. 2. new cloth ceremoniously put on a babe for the first time.

चोली f. 1. bodice. 2. blouse.

चौंकना vi. to be startled.

चौंकाना vt. to startle.

चौंतीस adj. & m. thirty-four.

चौंधियाना vi. to dazzle.

चौंरी f. 1. fly-flapper. 2. hank of thread with which women braid their hair. 3. tassel. 4. cow with a white tail.

चौंसठ adj. & m. sixty-four; ~ घड़ी whole day and night.

चौआ m. 1. quadruped. 2. the four fingers. 3. a measure (the breadth of the four fingers). 4. the four of cards.

चौक m. 1. courtyard. 2. market place.

चौकड़ी f. 1. group of four. 2. leap.

चौकन्ना adj. vigilant, cautious, alert.

चौकस adj. 1. fully prepared. 2. watchful. 3. just, proper.

चौकसी f. watchfulness, vigi-lance.

चौका m. 1. quadruple. 2. the four of cards. 3. fourer, set of four. 4. a shot scoring four runs, four. 5. kitchen/kitchen room.

चौका-बरतन m. act of cleaning the kitchen and utensils.

चौकी f. 1. an Indian bench/stool. 2. police station. 3. post, outpost, custom house. 4. watch, guard.

चौकीदार m. 1. watchman. 2. guard.

चौकीदारी f. 1. watchfulness. 2. the calling of a guard/watchman. 3. charges paid for keeping guard.

चौकोर adj. quadrangular, four sided.

चौखट f. 1. door-sill. 2. door-frame.

चौखटा m. four-cornered frame.

चौगड़ा m. hare.

चौगान m. 1. a kind of old game resembling hockey and polo. 2. field where the game is played. 3. drum-stick.

चौगुना adj. four times.

चौघड़ा m. container, having four compartments for serving vegetables.

चौड़ा adj. wide, broad.

चौड़ाई f. breadth.

चौड़ान f. see चौड़ाई।

चौतरा m. see चबूतरा।

चौथ f. 1. one-fourth part. 2. tribute levied by Marathas on subordinate kingships. 3. fourth day of the lunar fortnight.

चौथपन m. fourth stage of life, beginning after the seventy-fifth year.

चौथा adj. fourth.

चौथाई adj. & m. one-fourth part, quarter.

चौदंता adj. 1. having four teeth. 2. young (beast). 3. juvenile.

चौदस f. fourteenth day of the lunar fortnight.

चौदह adj. & m. fourteen.

चौदहवीं f. fourteenth lunar night; ~ का चाँद (i) moon of the fourteenth night; (ii) extremely handsome person.

चौधराई f. office, calling or status of a headman/chieftain.

चौधरी m. 1. headman. 2. chieftain. [Fem. चौधरानी]

चौधरीपना m. headmanship, leadership.

चौपट adj. 1. spoilt. 2. ruined. adv. completely, entirely; दरवाजा ~ खुला था The door was wide open.

चौपड़ m. an Indian game played with three dice or kauris.

चौपन्ना m. pamphlet.

चौपहिया adj. four-wheeled.

चौपाया m. four-footed animal, quadruped.

चौपाल m. canopy.

चौबच्चा m. tank, pool.

चौबीस adj. & m. twenty-four.

चौमासा m. rainy season comprising of four months.

चौमुहानी m. intersection, cros-sing.

चौरस adj. plane, flat or smooth.

चौरानबे adj. & m. ninety-four.

चौरासी adj. & m. eigthy-four.

चौराहा m. intersection, crossing.

चौर्य m. 1. act of stealing. 2. theft.

चौर्य-वृत्ति f. habit of stealing.

चौवन adj. & m. fifty-four.

चौवालीस adj. & m. forty-four. [M.C. चवालीस]

चौहत्तर adj. & m. seventy-four.

चौहद्दी f. boundary.

चौहरा adj. 1. fourfold. 2. quadruplicate.

च्युत adj. deviated from a course, standard etc.

च्युति f. 1. deviation from a course, standard etc. 2. lapse.

छ

छ m. second of the alveo-palatal pentad of consonants of the Nagari alphabet; aspirated form of letter च।

छंगा adj. & m. (person) having six fingers (or toes) in one or each of the hands (or feet).

छँगुली f. the little finger.

छँटना vi. 1. to be removed/separated, to be weeded out. 2. to scatter/diffuse. 3. to be retrenched. 4. to be sorted.

छँटनी f. 1. retrenchment. 2. act of pruning or trimming. 3. weeding out.

छँटवाना vt. causative of छाँटना।

छँटाई f. 1. act or state of pruning. 2. charges paid for pruning. 3. retrenchment.

छंद m. metre, stanza.

छंदशास्त्र m. prosody.

छः adj. & m. = छह

छकड़ा m. carrier vehicle drag-ged by men or bullocks.

छकड़ी f. set of six, group of six.

छकना vi. 1. to be satiated. 2. to be harassed, vexed.

छकाना vt. 1. to satiate. 2. to defeat in tactics.

छकार m. the letter छ or its sound.

छक्का m. 1. the six of cards. 2. dice with six pips. 3. sixer (in cricket).

छक्का-पंजा m. cunning tactics.

छगन m. baby, young one.

छगुनी f. little finger.

छछिया f. a pot for keeping whey.

छछूँदर f. musk-rat, shrew-mouse, mole.

छजली f. sun-shade.

छज्जा m. balcony, projection.

छटंकी f. = छटाँक।

छटकना vi. 1. to jump off, to shoot off. 2. to be separa-ted from a group/class.

छटकाना vt. to cause to jump or shoot off, to scatter.

छटपटाना vi. 1. to be listless due to pain, to writhe. 2. to feel extremely uneasy due to anxiety. 3. to pant for.

छटपटाहट f. listlessness, uneasiness, restlessness.

छटाँक m. an old Indian measure of weight roughly equivalent to 58 grams.

छटा f. beauty, charm, efful-gence, brilliance.

छठ f. sixth day of the lunar fortnight.

छठवाँ adj. = छठा।

छठा adj. sixth.

छठी adj. fem. of छठा।
f. ceremony performed on the sixth day of child-birth.

छड़ m. rod, bar.

छड़ा adj. young but unmarried. [Fem. छड़ी] m. an Indian foot ornament.

छड़ी f. stick.

छत f. 1. roof. 2. ceiling.

छतना vt. to put a roof (on a room or house). m. big umbrella made of leaves.

छतरी f. umbrella.

छत्ता m. 1. hive. 2. covered lane. 3. thick, shady tree.

छत्तीस adj. & m. thirty-six, 36.

छत्र m. royal umbrella.

छत्रक m. mushroom, fungus.

छत्र-छाया f. patronage, protec- tion, aegis.

छत्रधारी m. umbrella-holder.

छत्रपति m. sovereign king/mo-narch.

छत्री f. = क्षत्री।

छदाम m. one-fourth part of an old pice.

छद्म m. deceit, stratagem, fraud. adj. deceitful, inscrutable.

छद्मवेश m. disguise.

छद्मावरण m. camouflage.

छन m. = क्षण।

छनक f. tinkling/jingling sound.

छनकना vi. to jingle. m. = झुनझुना।

छनकाना vt. causative of छनकना।

छनछन f. series of tinkling/ringing sounds, jingle.

छनछनाना vi. to make a hissing sound, to hiss.

छनना vi. 1. to be sieved. 2. to be filtered. 3. to be fried in hot oil.

छनाछन adv. with a jingling sound.

छन्ना m. piece of cloth for siev-ing purposes.

छप f. splashing sound, splash.

छपकना vt. = छपछपाना।

छपका m. 1. thin stick. 2. (one) splash of water. 3. spot of water on cloth. 4. block attached to the lid of a wooden box. 5. a head ornament.

छपछप f. recurring, splashing sound.

छपछपाना vt. to make a splashing sound.

छपते-छपते m. stop press, latest news.

छपना vi. 1. to be printed. 2. to be imprinted/stamped.

छपरखट f. bed-stead fitted with a structure for a mosquito net.

छपवाना vt. to get (something) printed/imprinted/stamped.

छपाई f. 1. act of printing. 2. printing charges.

छपाका m. intense splashing sound.

छपाछप adv. with a series of splashing sounds.

छपाना vt. = छपवाना।

छप्पन adj. & m. fifty-six, 56.

छप्पन छुरी f. (woman) sharper.

छप्पय m. a Hindi poetic metre running into six lines.

छप्पर m. thatched roof.

छबि f. = छवि।

छबीला adj. foppish, handsome, graceful.

छब्बीस adj. & m. twenty-six, 26.

छम f. tinkling sound like that of a set of bells in dancing, jingle.

छमक f. jingling/tinkling sound.

छमकना vi. 1. to tinkle like bells. 2. to move to and fro like a glamour girl.

छ

छमछम f. 1. tinkling sound of ornaments (bangles, bells etc.). 2. sound of pouring rains.

छमछमाना vi. 1. production of a tinkling sound. 2. to shine.

छमा f. = क्षमा।

छमाछम adv. with a tinkling sound.

छमाही f. period of six months.

छरकीला adj. slim, slender.

छरहरा adj. slender, slim.

छर्रा m. 1. any of the tiny balls packed inside the cartridge, shot. 2. small pebble.

छल m. deception, deceit, fraud, subterfuge.

छलक f. act or state of spilling.

छलकना vi. to spill, to run over the side of the container.

छल-कपट m. fraudulent deception.

छलकाना vt. to cause to spill.

छलछंद m. trickery, craftiness.

छलछिद्र m. malicious fault-finding.

छलना vt. to deceive/cheat.

छलनी f. sieve.

छल-बल m. tactics, trickery.

छलाँग f. leap, jump.

छलावा m. apparition, will-o-the-wisp, anything which deceives.

छलिया adj. & m. treacherous, tricky, cheat.

छली adj. treacherous, tricky.

छल्ला m. 1. ring. 2. loop.

छल्ली f. 1. ulcer. 2. creeper. 3. pannier; basket. 4. an assay of sacks of grain. 5. ear of maize.

छल्लेदार adj. ringed, curly.

छवि f. winsomeness, (comely) sight, splendour, beauty of features.

छविगृह m. cinema-house.

छवैया m. one who thatches a roof.

छह adj. & m. six, 6.

छहराना vt. to spread/scatter.

छाँगुर adj. & m. = छंगा।

छाँट f. 1. act of pruning/ trimming. 2. cuttings, prunings, trimmings. 3. vomit.

छाँटन f. cuttings, prunings, trimmings.

छाँटना vt. 1. to cut and separate. 2. to cull, to pick out.

छाँदना vi. to hobble/fasten.

छाँव f. = छाँह।

छाँह f. 1. shade.

छाई f. 1. ashes. 2. fragments of (burnt) coal.

छाग m. he-goat.

छागल m. he-goat.

f. 1. leather water-bag. 2. an ornament worn on feet.

छागी f. she-goat.

छाछ f. whey, butter-milk.

छाछठ adj. & m. = छियासठ।

छाज m. 1. winnowing basket. 2.act or state of winnowing. 3. thatch.

छाजन f. 1. act or state of thatching, or wages paid for the same. 2. thatch. 3. covering of a room or tenement.

छाजना vi to suit, to befit.

छाता m. umbrella.

छाताधारी सेना f. paratroops.

छाती f. chest, breast.

छात्र m. student, disciple, pupil.

छात्रवृत्ति f. scholarship.

छात्रा f. girl student.

छात्रालय m. = छात्रावास।

छात्रावास m. hostel, students' lodge.

छादन m. 1. act or state of thatching. 2. thatch, cover. 3. screen, concealment. 4. cloth. 5. outer covering.

छादित adj. 1. thatched, covered. 2. concealed.

छानना vt. 1. to sieve. 2. to filter, to sift. 3. to percolate.

छान-बीन f. probe, scrutiny, search, investigation.

छाना vt. 1. to thatch/cover. 2. to construct. vi. 1. to spread out, gather. 2. to reside and almost settle down.

छाप f. 1. deep lasting effect, impression. 2. print. 3. a written or printed symbol, mark, seal. 4. stamp.

छापना vt. 1. to print. 2. to imprint.

छापा m. 1. raid. 2. imprint, impression. 3. block for printing purposes.

छापाख़ाना m. printing press.

छापामार adj. & m. (one) who attacks suddenly, raider.

छाबड़ी f. = खोंचा।

छाया f. 1. shade. 2. shadow, reflection. 3. shelter. 4. strong influence.

छायाकार m. photographer.

छायाचित्र m. 1. photo. 2. shadowgraph, silhoutte.

छायानुवाद m. adaptation.

छायापथ m. galaxy.

छायाभास m. 1. minor similarity; resemblance. 2. illusion, phantasm.

छायावाद m. a romantic movement in Hindi poetry.

छार m. = क्षार।

छाल f. bark, rind, peel.

छाला m. blister.

छाली f. betelnut or its paring.

छावनी f. cantonment.

छि interj. pooh, tut, pish !

छिक्का m. = छींका। f. = छींक।

छिछड़ा m. = छीछड़ा।

छिछला adj. shallow.

छिछलापन m. shallowness.

छिछोरा adj. mean/petty (said of a person), childish.

छिछोरापन m. meanness.

छिटकना vi. to be scattered/ dispersed/diffused.

छिटपुट adj. sporadic, hapha-zard, stray.

छिड़कना vt. 1. to sprinkle/splash. 2. spray.

छिड़काव m. watering by sprin-kling.

छिड़ना vi. to start/commence.

छितराना vt. to scatter/disperse.

छिदना vi. 1. to be pierced. 2. to be perforated.

छिदवाना vt. to cause to be pie-rced.

छिद्र m. 1. hole. 2. pore. 3. aperture, opening, gap. 4. fault.

छिद्रान्वेषण m. fault-finding, carping.

छिद्रित adj. bored, perforated.

छिनकना vi. to blow out the nose.

छिनना vi. to be snatched.

छ

छिनाल adj. & f. dissolute (woman), adulterous, harlot.

छिन्न adj. 1. separated away, severed. 2. divided, rent. 3. separate. 4. destroyed. 5. tired, exhausted.

छिन्न-भिन्न adj. broken and scattered, shattered.

छिपकली f. lizard.

छिपना vi. 1. to be concealed/hidden. 2. to set. m. act of hiding, taking shelter.

छिपाना vt. to keep secret, to conceal/hide.

छिपाव m. concealment, hiding, secrecy.

छिपे-छिपे adv. stealthily/secretly.

छिया f. excrement, faeces; ~ करना to detest and keep (something) away.

छियानबे adj. & m. ninety-six, 96.

छियालीस adj. & m. forty-six, 46.

छियासठ adj. & m. sixty-six, 66.

छियासी adj. & m. eighty-six, 86.

छिलका m. 1. peel (of fruit etc.). 2. husk (of rice etc.).

छिलना vi. 1. to take the skin of fruit, vegetables etc, to be peeled off. 2. (bark) to be taken off. 3. to be excoriated skinned. 4. to be rubbed off, to be bruised.

छिलवाना vt. causative of छीलना।

छिहत्तर adj. seventy-six, 76.

छींक f. sneeze, sternutation.

छींकना vi. to make a sneeze.

छींका m. 1. network of string for hanging things in. 2. mouth-cover (made of strings) of an ox.

छींट f. 1. drop of a liquid. 2. spot made on cloth etc. by a drop of liquid. 3. a kind of cloth spotted with figures of leaves and flowers, chintz.

छींटना vt. to scatter.

छींटा m. 1. splash. 2. drizzle. 3. sarcastic remark.

छींबी f. = छीमी।

छी interj. pooh, pish, tut ! ~ छी करना to pooh pooh.

छीछड़ा m. bit of tough flesh.

छीछालेदर f. 1. miserable plight, predicament. 2. muck, mess. 3. ruin, destruction.

छीज f. 1. decay. 2. wearing away, loss (due to handling), wastage.

छीजन f. 1. = छीज। 2. state or process of decay.

छीजना vi. 1. to dwindle/wear away. 2. to be diminished. 3. to be destroyed. 4. to be lessened.

छीनना vt. to snatch/wrench/grab/wrest/seize.

छीना-झपटी f. mugging.

छीमी f. pod of pea.

छीया m. = छिया।

छीलन f. 1. shavings, parings. 2. scrap, scrapings.

छीलना vt. 1. to peel (fruit etc.). 2. to shave (wood etc.). 3. to scrape.

छुआई f. act or state of touching or charges paid for the same.

छुआछूत f. 1. rigid adherence to conventions regarding eating and drinking. 2. institution of untouchability.

छुई-मुई f. 1. touch-me-not.

2. extremely touchy person. 3. mimosa (sensitive plant).

छुच्छी f. 1. nose-pipe. 2. funnel.

छुट m. alomorph of छोटा, as in छुटभैया।

छुटकारा m. 1. riddance, release, discharge, acquittal. 2. relief. 3. exemption.

छुटपन m. childhood, boyhood.

छुटपुट adj. sporadic, stray.

छुटभैया m. insignificant/petty person.

छुट्टा adj. 1. untethered (domestic) animal. 2. alone, lonely. m. money in small units, change, small coin.

छुट्टी f. 1. holiday. 2. leave. 3. vacation.

छुड़वाना vt. causative of छोड़ना.

छुड़ाना vt. 1. to get released, to extricate, to disentangle. 2. to cause to set free. 3. to discharge/ dismiss. 4. to take delivery of.

छुतहा adj. contagious.

छुरा m. 1. dagger, big knife. 2. razor.

छुरी f. small dagger, knife.

छुरेबाज़ m. one given to dagger-stabbing, knifer.

छुरेबाज़ी f. 1. stabbing (with a dagger). 2. exchange of dagger blows.

छुलछुलाना vi. to urinate slowly.

छुलाना vt. to get (something) touched.

छुवाना vt. = छुलाना।

छुहारा m. date-palm.

छूआछूत f. = छुआछूत।

छूछा adj. 1. (container) empty. 2. (person) empty-handed. 3. hollow, without substance.

छूट f. 1. freedom. 2. concession, relaxation, remission. 3. discount; commission. 4. rebate, abatement, exemption.

छूटना vi. 1. to be left/omitted. 2. to be separated.

छूत f. 1. act or state of touching. 2. contagion, infection.

छूतछात f. = छुआछूत।

छूना vt. to touch/contact.

छू-मंतर m. ~ हो जाना to vanish away/ to disappear.

छेंकना vt. 1. to surround/occupy (land). 2. to demarcate. 3. to prevent/obstruct. 4. to cancel (someone's name etc.).

छेड़ f. 1. act or state of छेड़ना, teasing. 2. = चिढ़ (teasing nickname).

छेड़खानी f. teasing.

छेड़छाड़ f. unbecoming (spl. indecent) behaviour calculated to provoke.

छेड़ना vt. 1. to tease/vex/irritate/ instigate/provoke (person). 2. to excite/disturb (snake, animal etc.). 3. to touch/stir for starting operation. 4. to create an obstruction in someone's work.

छेद m. 1. hole. 2. bore. 3. opening. 4. perforation, puncture, aperture.

छेददार adj. having holes, perforated.

छ

छेदना vt. to drill/perforate/broach.

छेना m. cheese.

छेनी f. chisel.

छेव m. act or state of छेवना।

छेवना vt. 1. to broach/scrape. 2. to attack. 3. to hurt. 4. to suffer patiently. 5. to throw.

छैल-छबीला, छैला m. fop, beau, cockscomb.

छोकरा m. lad, boy (pej.), urchin.

छोटा adj. 1. small, short. 2. younger. 3. of little importance, unimportant, inferior.

छोटाई f. 1. smallness, shortness. 2. inferiority.

छोटापन m. = छोटाई।

छोटा-मोटा adj. trivial, petty, minor.

छोड़ना vt. 1. to let off, to set free (as a prisoner). 2. to acquit (as an accused). 3. to give up, to abandon. 4. to omit, to leave out, to exclude.

छोड़वाना vt. causative of छोड़ना।

छोपना vt. 1. to paint/dye. 2. to cover. 3. to grab/grip.

छोर m. 1. end, extremity. 2. limit, boundary. 3. edge, border.

छोरा m. lad, brat.

छोरी f. lass.

छोलदारी f. small tent.

छोला m. = चना।

छौंक f. 1. act or state of spicing/ seasoning. 2. spices with which food is seasoned.

छौंकना vt. to spice/season.

छौना m. young one.

छौलदारी f. = छोलदारी।

ज

ज eighth consonant of the Nagari alphabet, third of the alveo-palatal pentad; its sound resembles that of j in jug. suffix. denoting origin as in जलज, अंडज।

जंग f. war, battle.

ज़ंग m. rust.

ज़ंगदार adj. rusted.

जंगम adj. movable.

जंगल m. jungle, forest.

जंगला m. 1. railing. 2. grating. 3. window. 4. lattice-work.

जंगली adj. wild, savage, uncivilized.

जंगली सुअर m. boar.

जंगाल m. rust.

जंघा f. thigh.

जँचना vi. 1. to be examined/tested. 2. to come out successful in a test.

जँचा adj. 1. examined and tested. 2. measured.

जंजाल m. entanglement, botheration, embarrassment.

जंजालिया adj. & m. mischievous, troublesome, trou-blemaker.

जंजाली adj. & m. = जंजालिया।

ज़ंजीर f. 1. chain. 2. shackle.

जंतर m. amulet.

जंतर-मंतर m. 1. occult science, witchcraft. 2. observatory. 3. amulet.

जंतरी f. 1. wire gauze used by goldsmiths for lengthening a wire. 2. calendar, almanac. 3. conjurer. 4. organ-player.

जंतु m. creature.

जँबीरी नीबू m. big sour lemon.

जंबू द्वीप m. one of the seven mythological divisions of the world which included India.

जंबूर m. pliers.

जँबूरा m. 1. large pliers. 2. boy-assistant of a juggler.

जँभाई f. yawn, yawning.

जँभाना vi. to yawn.

जँवाई m. son-in-law.

जई f. oat (s).

ज़ईफ़ adj. old, aged.

जकड़ f. firm grip, tight hold.

जकड़न f. rigidity (of limbs).

जकड़ना vi. to grip firmly, to bind tightly.

जकार m. the letter ज or its sound.

जकारांत adj. (word) ending in ज।

ज़ख़म m. = ज़ख़्म।

ज़ख़ीरा (za KHee rA) m. 1. stock. 2. store.

ज़ख़्म m. 1. wound. 2. injury.

ज़ख़्मी adj. wounded, hurt, injured.

जग m. world, universe.

जगत m. world.

जगत-पिता m. creator of the universe.

जगदंबा f. Durga, the goddess of Prowess.

जगदीश m. God.

जगदीश्वर m. God.

जगद्गुरु m. archpreceptor.

जगना vi. to be awake.

ज

जगन्नाथ m. Lord Vishnu.

जगमग adj. glittering, shining.

जगमगाना vi. to glitter/shine/gleam.

जगमगाहट f. glittering, glimmering, gleam, shine.

जगवाना vt. to cause to awake.

जग-हँसाई f. scoff/ridicule/mockery of the community at large.

जगह f. 1. place, room. 2. position, rank, place. 3. post.

जगाना vi. 1. to rouse from sleep, to awaken (someone). 2. to arouse (feeling), to invoke.

जघन्य adj. heinous, dastardly, despicable.

जच्चा f. a woman who has been delivered of a child.

जच्चाख़ाना m. 1. child-delivery chamber. 2. maternity home..

जच्चा-बच्चा m. mother and the new-born (baby).

जजमान m. = यजमान।

जज़िया m. a special tax levied by Muslim rulers on non-muslims, jaziya.

जज़्ब adj. 1. absorbed. 2. assimilated. 3. usurped.

जज़्बा m. emotion, sentiment, passion.

जज़्बाती adj. emotional, sentimental.

जटना vt. to rob by cheating.

जटा f. 1. tress (as of sadhus, hermits), matted hair. 2. coir (of a coconut). 3. network of roots (of a tree).

जटाजूट m. matted hair (of the head).

जटाधारी adj. & m. (usually a Sadhu) putting on a जटा customarily.

जटामासी f. nard.

जटित adj. studded.

जटिल adj. complex, arduous, intricate, complicated.

जटिलता f. 1. complexity, intricacy. 2. complication.

जठर m. stomach.

जठराग्नि f. power of digesting food.

जड़ adj. 1. inanimate, inert. 2. idiotic, stupid. f. 1. root (of a tree etc.). 2. the origin or basis of something.

जड़ता f. 1. state of being inanimate, inertia. 2. idiocy, stupidity. 3. rigidity.

जड़ना vt. 1. to inlay/imbed/embed/fit/inset. 2. to mount (as a picture).

जड़मति m. idiot.

जड़वाना vt. causative of जड़ना।

जड़हन m. paddy seedlings transplanted to another place.

जड़ाई f. 1. insetting, embedding, inlaying. 2. charges paid therefor.

जड़ाऊ adj. studded/inset with jewels.

जड़ाना vi. to get something inset, studded or framed.

जड़ाव m. act or state of setting jewels in an ornament.

जड़ित adj. studded with jewels.

जड़िया m. one who is an expert in insetting/embedding.

जड़ी-बूटी f. herb.

जड़ीभूत adj. stunned, dazed, stupefied.

जताना vt. 1. to inform pointedly, to apprise. 2. to put (someone) wise, to caution, to warn.

जत्था m. 1. batch. 2. band, gang.

जत्थेदार m. 1. leader of a batch. 2. group-leader.

ज़दा suff. inflicted; as in ख़ौफ़ ~ terrified; मुसीबत ~ distressed.

जद्दी adj. ancestral.

जद्दोजहद f. hard struggle.

जन m. (plu.) people, public, mass.

ज़न f. woman.

जनक m. 1. originator, producer (male). 2. father.

जनकल्याण m. public welfare.

ज़नख़ा adj. 1. womanish. 2. impotent. m. eunuch.

जनगणना f. the official counting of a country's population, census.

जनजाति f. tribe.

जनतंत्र m. democracy.

जनतांत्रिक adj. democratic.

जनता f. public, masses.

जनन m. 1. procreation. 2. production. 3. birth.

जनन-क्षमता f. procreative power, potency.

जनना vt. to give birth to.

जननायक m. (undisputed) leader of the masses.

जननिक adj. genetic.

जननी f. 1. originator, producer (female). 2. mother.

जननेंद्रिय m. genital/sex organ.

जनपद m. 1. habitation, populated piece of land. 2. district.

जन-प्रतिनिधि m. people's representative.

जनप्रिय adj. popular.

जनभावना f. the will of the people.

जनम m. = जन्म।

जनमघूँटी f. a medicine given to babies for sometime since birth.

जनमत m. public opinion.

जनमत-संग्रह m. plebiscite, referendum.

जनरल m. The General.

जनरव m. talk of the town, clamour.

जनवध m. genocide.

जनवरी f. January.

जनवाना vt. 1. to help in the delivery (of a child). 2. to help in knowing something, to inform.

जनवासा m. lodging place of a marriage party.

जनश्रुति f. rumour, hearsay.

जनसंख्या f. population.

जनसंचार m. the main means of communicating with large numbers of people, media.

जनसंपर्क m. public relation.

जनसमुदाय m. community.

जनहित m. common good.

जनांदोलन m. 1. public agitation. 2. people's movement.

जना m. person. adj. born.

जनाकीर्ण adj. 1. densely populated, populous. 2. crowded.

जनाज़ा m. bier.

जनादेश m. people's verdict.

ज़नानख़ाना m. 1. seraglio, harem. 2. female apartment.

जनाना vt. 1. to help deliver (a child).

ज

2. to draw pointed attention (of).

ज़नाना adj. 1. feminine. 2. pertaining to women, womanish. f. 1. woman. 2. wife. m. 1. eunuch. 2. female apartment.

जनाब m. Sire, Sir, Mr. [Fem. जनाबा]

जनार्दन m. Lord Vishnu, the maintainer.

जनित adj. born of, caused by.

जनून m. overpowering passion, craze, mania, madness.

जनेऊ m. sacred thread (Hindus).

जनोपयोगी adj. beneficial to public, of public utility.

जन्नत f. heaven.

जन्म m. birth.

जन्म-कुंडली f. horoscope.

जन्म-जन्मांतर adj. birth and re-birth.

जन्मजात adj. existing from birth, inborn.

जन्मतिथि f. date of birth.

जन्म-दर f. birth-rate.

जन्मदाता m. 1. progenitor, father. 2. originator, founder.

जन्मदिन m. 1. birth anniversary. 2. birthday.

जन्म-दिवस m. = जन्म-दिन।

जन्मना vi. 1. to be born. 2. to come into being. adv. according to birth, by birth.

जन्मपत्री f. horoscope.

जन्मपूर्व adj. prenatal, antenatal.

जन्मभूमि f. motherland.

जन्मसिद्ध adj. inborn, innate; ~ अधिकार birth-right.

जन्मांतर m. another birth, re-birth.

जन्माष्टमी f. birthday of Lord Krishna.

जन्मोत्तर adj. post-natal, after-birth.

जन्मोत्सव m. birthday cere-mony.

जन्य suffix. denoting born, produced, caused; परिस्थिति~ caused by circumstances.

जप m. repetition of the name of, or prayer to, a deity.

जप-तप m. habitual worship, study of religious books etc.

जपना vt. to repeat/muttering the name of, or prayer to, a deity.

जपमाला f. rosary for keeping count of prayers.

जब adv. at or during the time that, when; ~ कभी whenever; ~ - जब whenever (more frequently); ~ तक as long as, till, until; ~ - तब occasionally; ~ देखो तब oft, very often, frequently; ~ भी whenever; ~ से since.

जबकि adv. when, while, whereas.

जबड़ा m. jaw.

ज़बर adj. more than a match.

ज़बरदस्त adj. forceful, strong, violent, mighty.

ज़बरदस्ती f. force/coercion. adv. forcefully.

जबरन adv. forcefully, by force.

ज़बाँ f. = ज़बान।

ज़बान f. 1. tongue. 2. language.

ज़बानदराज़ adj. sharp-tongued.

ज़बानी adj. oral, verbal.

ज़ब्त adj. confiscated, forfeited.

ज़ब्ती f. confiscation.

जमघट m. concourse, conglomeration, assembly.

जमना vi. 1. to freeze, as ice, to

congeal. 2. to solidify, as curd. f. = यमुना (river).

जमहाई f. yawning, gaping.

जमा adj. 1. collected. 2. deposited. 3. added to. m. money or valuables deposited, credit, deposit.

जमाई m. son-in-law.

जमाकर्ता m. depositor.

जमा-ख़र्च m. credit and debit.

जमा खाता m. credit account.

जमाख़ोर m. one who holds essential commodities, hoar-der.

जमा-जथा f. = जमा-पूँजी।

जमात f. 1. category or group of people. 2. a group of students taught together, class.

जमादार m. 1. group leader, as of sweepers, peons etc. 2. head constable. 3. watchman. 4. sweeper.

ज़मानत f. security, surety, bail.

ज़मानती adj. pertaining to a bail, bailable. m. surety (person).

जमाना vt. 1. to freeze. 2. to solidify. 3. to get settled.

ज़माना m. 1. times, ages. 2. people, masses.

जमा-पूँजी f. 1. total assets. 2. total accumulations, val-uables, riches. 3. capital.

जमाबंदी f. a village register containing the names of tenants, their holdings, the amount of rent they pay etc.

जमा-बाक़ी f. credit balance.

जमाल m. 1. lustre, glory, pret-tiness, splendour. 2. loveliness.

जमालगोटा m. a purgative nut, croten tiglium.

जमाव m. 1. settling down. 2. gathering, assemblage.

जमावट f. = जमाव।

जमावड़ा m. 1. jamboree, large gathering, assemblage. 2. log-jam.

ज़मींक़ंद f. yam.

ज़मींदार m. 1. landlord. 2. cultivator.

ज़मींदारी f. 1. landlordism, feudal system. 2. land/estate belonging to a landlord.

ज़मीन f. 1. land. 2. floor, ground; earthen floor. 3. background, setting, as of a picture. 4. base.

ज़मीनी adj. 1. of, or pertaining to land. 2. perceptible, clearly visible; ~ सचाई perceptible reality.

ज़मीर m. conscience.

जमुना f. = यमुना (river).

जम्हाई f. = जँभाई।

जम्हाना vt. to yawn, to gap.

जयंत adj. victorious.

जयंती f. 1. jubilee; रजत ~ siver jubilee; स्वर्ण ~ golden jubilee; हीरक ~ diamond jubilee. 2. anniversary; तुलसी ~ Tulsi anniversary.

जय f. triumph, victory, conquest.

जयकारा m. a set phrase denoting devotional acclaim.

जयघोष m. acclamation.

जय-जयकार f. devotional acclaim.

जय-पराजय f. victory and defeat.

जयमाला f. 1. garland of victory. 2. garland which the bride

ज

puts round the neck of the bridegroom.

जयश्री f. 1. victory. 2. goddess of victory.

जयी adj. victorious.

जरठ adj. old. m. old age.

ज़रदा m. 1. scented tobacco. 2. a sweet dish of rice. 3. a yellow horse.

ज़रदी f. 1. yellowness. 2. yellow of the egg.

ज़रब f. 1. injury, blow. 2. multiplication; ~ देना to multiply.

जरमन adj. of Germany. m. inhabitant of Germany.

जरमनी f. 1. Germany. 2. lan-guage of the Germans.

जरसी f. jersey.

जरा f. 1. old age. 2. senility.

ज़रा adv. a bit, a little, slight.

जराग्रस्त adj. suffering from old age.

जरायु m. 1. placenta. 2. womb.

जरासीम m. (plu.) germs.

ज़रिया m. means, source.

ज़री f. 1. cloth woven with gold thread. 2. gold thread used for the above purpose.

ज़रीब f. land-measuring chain.

ज़रूर adv. 1. certainly, positively. 2. assuredly.

ज़रूरत f. necessity, need.

ज़रूरतन adv. of necessity.

ज़रूरतमंद adj. needy.

ज़रूरी adj. necessary, needful.

जर्जर adj. 1. decrepit, ramshackle. 2. almost collapsing, on the verge of collapse.

जर्जरता f. decrepitude.

जर्जरित adj. worn out, shattered, almost collapsing.

ज़र्दी f. = ज़रदी।

जर्मन adj. = जरमन।

ज़र्रा m. particle.

जर्राह m. surgeon.

जल m. water, aqua.

जलकल m. 1. plant of water- works. 2. waterworks.

जलक्रीड़ा f. aquatic play.

जलघड़ी f. water-clock.

जलचर adj. & m. aquatic creature.

जल-चिह्न m. water-mark.

जल-जंतु m. aquatic animal.

जलज adj. produced in water, aquatic. m. 1. lotus. 2. aquatic animal. 3. pearl. 4. conch.

जलजात m. lotus.

जलडमरूमध्य m. isthmus.

जलतरंग m. a kind of xyloph- one.

जलद m. cloud.

जलदस्यु m. pirate, buccaneer.

जलधर m. cloud.

जलधरी f. cup in which the phallus of Lord Shiv is fixed.

जलधारा f. stream, water current.

जलधि m. ocean.

जलन f. 1. burning sensation, 2. envy. 3. grudge.

जलना vi. 1. to burn. 2. to emit light, as lamp. 3. to feel burning sensation. 4. to feel jealous.

जलपथ m. waterway (s).

जलपरी f. siren, mermaid, water nymph.

जलपान m. light refreshment, repast.

जलप्रपात m. water-fall, cataract.

जलप्रवाह m. 1. water-flow. 2. immersion.

जलप्लावन m. flooding, inundation.

जलभीति f. hydrophobia.

जलमग्न adj. submerged.

जलमय adj. 1. submerged in water, inundated. 2. hydrous, watery.

जलमार्ग m. 1. waterway. 2. sea-route.

जल-यात्रा f. voyage, sailing.

जलयान m. ship, vessel.

जल-युद्ध m. naval war.

जलराशि f. expanse of water.

जलवाना vt. to cause to be burnt.

जलवायु m. climate.

जलवायु विज्ञान m. climatology.

जलविद्युत m. hydroelectricity.

जल-समाधि f. watery grave.

जलसह adj. water-proof.

जलसा m. 1. celebration, festive occasion. 2. ceremonious assemblage. 3. session.

जलस्तंभ m. 1. waterspout. 2. sea.

जलस्तर m. water-level.

जल-स्थलचर adj. amphibious. m. amphibian.

जलस्रोत m. 1. water-spring. 2. water-hole.

जलहीन adj. waterless; without water.

जलाऊ adj. 1. that which causes to burn. 2. that which burns (like wood).

जलाना vt. 1. to burn/ignite. 2. to light. 3. to set on fire. 4. to tease/annoy.

जला-भुना adj. burning with rage, infuriated, ireful.

जलार्णव m. ocean.

जलाल m. glory, lustre.

ज़लालत f. 1. meanness, lowliness. 2. humiliation.

जलावतरण m. launching.

जलावन m. fuel, sp. wood, coal etc.

जलावर्त m. whirlpool.

जलाशय m. water-reservoir, water-pool, body of water.

जलीय adj. watery, aquatic.

ज़लील adj. 1. mean, base. 2. humiliated.

जलूस m. procession, pageant.

जलेबी f. 1. an Indian sweet. 2. a lattice like firework. 3. anything of the shape of lattice.

जलोढ़ adj. alluvial.

जलोदर m. dropsy.

जलौका f. leech.

जल्द adv. quickly.

जल्दबाज़ adj. acting without thought, given to haste, hasty, rash.

जल्दबाज़ी f. hastiness, hurriedness.

जल्दी f. haste, hurry.

जल्प m. meaningless talk/prattle.

जल्पना vi. to prattle.

जल्लाद adj. cruel. m. 1. hangman. 2. butcher.

जवाँ allomorph of जवान।

जवाँमर्द adj. & m. gallant, youthfully brave.

जवान adj. youthful. m. 1. youth. 2. Indian soldier.

जवानी f. youth, youthfulness.

जवाब m. 1. answer in speech or writing. 2. reply (of a letter). 3. the answer to a mathematical problem. 4. match; तुम्हारा ~ नहीं You have no match/equal.

जवाब-दावा m. written statement of a defendent.

जवाबदेह adj. answerable, responsible.

जवाबदेही f. answerability, responsibility.

जवाबी adj. 1. pertaining to reply. 2. in the nature of a reply, opposite or contrary.

ज़वाल m. decline.

जवाहर m. jewel.

जशन m. festivity.

जस m. = यश।

जस्ता m. zinc, pewter.

जहन्नुम m. hell, gehenna, inferno.

ज़हमत f. 1. botheration. 2. trouble.

ज़हर m. poison.

ज़हरबाद m. carbuncle.

ज़हरमोहरा m. a kind of stone which absorbs poison.

ज़हरीला adj. poisonous, venomous.

जहाँ adv. where; ~ कहीं (i) wherever, (ii) everywhere; ~ का तहाँ at the same place as before; ~ वहाँ at whatever place, wherever; ~ तक so far as.

m. = जहान।

जहाँपनाह m. 1. God. 2. king.

जहाज़ m. ship, vessel.

जहाज़रानी f. sailing, navigation.

जहाज़ी adj. 1. pertaining to a ship, naval. 2. living on a ship.

जहान m. world.

जहालत f. illiteracy; the quality or state of being जाहिल।

ज़हीन adj. intelligent, sharp.

जहेज़ m. dowry. [H.E. दहेज]

जाँ allomorph of जान।

जाँगर m. 1. body. 2. bodily strength, vigour.

जाँगलू adj. = जंगली।

जाँघ f. thigh.

जाँघिया m. lower underwear, drawers.

जाँच f. 1. test. 2. verification. 3. investigation.

जाँचकर्ता m. 1. one who tests, examines, verifies etc. 2. auditor.

जाँचना vt. 1. to test. 2. to verify. 3. to examine.

जाँच-पड़ताल f. 1. fact finding, investigation. 2. scrutiny.

जाँता m. biggish grindstone.

जाँबाज़ adj. & m. brave, gallant (man).

जाकड़ m. 1. purchase of an article subject to apporval. 2. a thing so purchased.

जाकेट f. = jacket.

जाग f. state of being awakened.

जागना vt. 1. to wake up. 2. to become aware and alert, to be vigilant.

जागरण m. 1. state of keeping awake. 2. a sitting of devotional singing all through the night.

जागरूक adj. vigilant.

जागरूकता f. vigilance.

जागीर f. estate (received from a ruler as a gift or reward), jagir.

जागीरदार m. owner of an estate, jagirdar.

जागृत adj. 1. awakened. 2. cautious, alert.

जाग्रति f. 1. awakening. 2. awareness.

जाग्रत adj. = जागृत।

जाज़िम f. multicoloured floor-sheet.

जाज्वल्यमान adj. shining, resplendent.

जाट m. a caste of cultivators.

जाड़ा m. 1. winter. 2. cold.

ज़ात f. 1. caste. 2. race.

जातक m. 1. child, usu. a son. 2. Buddhistic tale.

जातकर्म m. ceremony performed on the birth of a child, one of the sixteen Hindu संस्कार (s).

जात-पाँत f. distinctions of caste and community.

जाति f. 1. caste.

जातिगत adj. 1. pertaining to caste or race, racial. 2. communal.

जाति-पाँति f. = जात-पाँत।

जाति-प्रथा f. the caste system.

जाति-बहिष्कार m. excommunication.

जाति-बहिष्कृत m. outcast, excommunicated.

जातिभेद m. caste distinction.

जातिभ्रष्ट adj. (one who has) fallen according to the standard of the caste/community.

जातिवाचक संज्ञा f. common noun.

जातिवाद m. casteism.

जाति-व्यवस्था f. caste system.

ज़ाती adj. personal.

जातीय adj. 1. of or pertaining to caste. 2. racial.

जातीयता f. 1. casteism. 2. racialism, racism.

जातुधान m. devil, demon.

जात्रा f. = यात्रा।

जादुई adj. 1. of magic, pertaining to magic. 2. magical.

जादू m. magic, magical power, sorcery.

जादूगर m. magician, sorcerer.

जादूगरनी f. sorceress.

जादूगरी f. sorcery, black magic.

जादू-टोना f. sorcery, obeahism.

जान f. 1. life. 2. livliness. 3. energy. 4. spirit. 5. strength.

जानकार adj. knowledgeable, well-informed.

जानकारी f. knowledge, information about facts.

जानकी f. Sita, wife of Lord Ram.

जानदार adj. 1. animate, having life. 2. full of life, vigorous. 3. weighty.

जानना vt. to know; जानकर knowingly, deliberately.

जानना-बूझना vt. to understand.

जान-पहचान f. acquaintance.

जान-बख़्शी f. 1. pardon (to a person fit to be hanged). 2. promise to give such a pardon.

जान-बूझकर adv. deliberately, intentionally.

जान-लेवा adj. life-killing (work).

जानवर m. 1. animal, creature. 2. beast.

जाना vi. to go.

जाना-अनजाना adj. practically unknown.

जाना-पहचाना adj. familiar.

जानी adj. of or pertaining to life; ~ दुश्मन sworn enemy.

जाने adv. = न जाने; ~ कौन आया था God knows who came.

जाने-अनजाने adj. unknown; ~ रास्ते unknown ways/routes. adv. knowingly or unknowingly.

जानो adv. 1. it appears, as if. 2. to wit, that is to say, suppose that.

जाप m. = जप।

जापा m. delivery of a child.

ज़ाफ़रान m. saffron.

जाफ़री f. wooden support for plants, trellis.

जा-बेजा adj. 1. improper. 2. in-opportune.

ज़ाब्ता m. 1. rule, law or code. 2. procedural formality.

जाम m. a glass for drinking wine from, wineglass. adj. jammed.

जामन m. rennet (used in coagulating milk into curd).

जामा m. robe.

जामाता m. son-in-law.

ज़ामिन m. surety, security.

जामुन m. jambolan, jambu.

जामुनी adj. of the colour of जामुन, dark blue, blackish blue.

ज़ायक़ा m. taste.

ज़ायक़ेदार adj. tasty, delicious, tasteful.

जायज़ adj. right, proper.

जायदाद f. property, effects, estate.

जायफल m. nutmeg.

जाया f. lawfully wedded wife (who has given birth to children). adj. born (of).

जार m. 1. adulterer. 2. container of jam, pickles etc., jar.

जारकर्म m. adultery, adulterous conduct.

जारज adj. adulterine, illegitimate. m. bastard.

जारजता f. illegitimacy.

जारण m. act of burning.

जारिणी f. adulteress, a woman of easy morals.

जारी adj. 1. continued. 2. current, in force. 3. issued.

जाल m. 1. net. 2. snare, trap. 3. dragnet, network for catching criminals. 4. net-like embroidered pattern.

जालदार adj. netted.

जालसाज़ m. forger, schemer.

जालसाज़ी f. forgery, fabrication.

जाला m. 1. spider's web. 2. cobweb. 3. cataract (of the eyes).

ज़ालिम adj. 1. cruel. 2. oppressive. m. tyrant.

जालिया m. forger.

जाली adj. forged, fabricated. f. 1. small net. 2. network, gauze, grating. 3. sieve.

जालीदार adj. meshed.

जावक outward, outgoing. m. 1. export. 2. despatch register.

जावित्री f. mace (spice).

जासूस m. spy, detective.

जासूसी adj. pertaining to detection. f. 1. spying. 2. espionage.

ज़ाहिर adj. apparent, evident, clear.

जाहिल adj. 1. having no sense, uncivilised, uncultured. 2. illiterate.

जाह्नवी f. Ganga (Ganges).

ज़िंदगानी f. life.

ज़िंदगी f. 1. life. 2. lifetime, span of life.

ज़िंदा adj. alive.

ज़िंदाबाद interj. Long live!

जिंस f. 1. commodity, thing. 2. goods, things.

ज़िक्र m. mention, reference to (some) topic.

जिगर m. liver.

जिगरा m. courage.

जिगरी adj. intimate, close.

जिगीषा f. lust for war.

जिगीषु adj. having lust for war, belligerent.

ज़िच f. 1. stalemate. 2. deadlock, impasse.

जिजीविषा f. strong desire to live.

जिज्ञासा f. curiosity, eagerness to know/learn.

जिज्ञासु adj. & m. 1. (one) with an enquiring/inquisitive mind. 2. (one) who is eager to know.

जिठानी f. = जेठानी।

जितना adj. 1. as many as. 2. as much as. adv. to a great extent or degree.

जिताना vt. to help/cause to win.

जितेंद्रिय adj. & m. (one) who has control over his senses.

ज़िद f. insistence, obstinacy.

ज़िद्दी adj. stubborn, obstinate, unyielding.

जिधर adv. at which side, in which direction.

जिन pron. plu. of जिस।

जिन्न m. ghost.

जिप्सी m. 1. an ancient tribe, gipsy. 2. a person belonging to this tribe, a gipsy.

जिमख़ाना m. gymkhana. gymnasium.

जिमाना vt. to feed (with respect).

ज़िम्मा m. responsibility.

ज़िम्मेदार adj. responsible.

ज़िम्मेदारी f. 1. responsibility. 2. liability.

जिरह f. cross-examination.

ज़िरहबक्तर m. armour.

जिराफ़ m. giraffe.

ज़िला m. 1. district. 2. territory.

ज़िलाधीश m. collector, district magistrate.

जिलाना vt. to bring to life.

जिल्द f. 1. strong covering holding the book, binding. 2. volume, part.

जिल्दबंद m. = जिल्दसाज़।

जिल्दसाज़ m. bookbinder.

जिल्दसाज़ी f. bookbinding.

ज़िल्लत f. 1. humiliation. 2. pli-ght.

जिस pron. & adj. which; ~ का whose; ~ को whom; ~ जगह where; ~ में wherein.

जिस्ता m. a quire.

जिस्म m. body.

जिस्मानी adj. bodily, corporal, corporeal.

जिहाद m. crusade, religious war.

जिहादी m. one taking part in a crusade.

जिह्वा f. tongue.

जिह्वाग्र m. front of the tongue.

जी m. heart. ~ का जंजाल (i) embarrassing botheration;

(ii) terrible nuisance; ~ का ग़ुब्बार निकालना to release or give vent to (one's) pent-up feelings; ~ खोलकर (i) without any reserve/ hitch; (ii) wholeheartedly; ~ चुराना (i) to shirk; (ii) to charm/ fascinate. interj. 1. term of respect; as पिता जी (Respected Father !). 2. What did you say? 3. an answer of yes.

जीजा m. sister's husband, brother-in-law.

जी-जान f. heart and soul.

जीजी f. elder sister.

जीत f. victory, triumph, conquest.

जीतना vi. to be successful. vt. 1. to conquer. 2. to win.

जीता हुआ adj. 1. alive. 2. already won.

जीतोड़ adj. using one's maximum power, all-out.

जीन m. gene.

ज़ीन f. 1. saddle. 2. a kind of thick, cotton cloth.

जीना vi. 1. to live, to be alive. 2. to remain alive.
m. act of living.

ज़ीना m. staircase.

जीभ f. tongue.

जीभी f. 1. a gadget for scraping the tongue, tongue-cleaner. 2. nib of a pen.

जीमना vt. to dine (spl. at ease).

ज़ीरा m. cummin seed.

जीर्ण adj. 1. worn-out, withered. 2. decayed.

जीर्णशीर्ण adj. tattered.

जीर्णोद्धार m. resurrection, restoration.

जीवंत adj. 1. lively, energetic, animated. 2. alive. 3. stirring.

जीव m. 1. living being, creature, animal. 2. soul.

जीव-जंतु m. (plu.) creatures, tiny creatures.

जीव-जगत m. animate world.

जीवट m. quality of courage and endurance, grit, stamina.

जीवधारी adj. animate, alive. m. living being.

जीवन m. 1. life, existence. 2. living. 3. lifetime.

जीवन-कथा f. life-history.

जीवनकाल m. life-time, life-span.

जीवनचरित m. biography.

जीवनदायक adj. life-giving.

जीवन-नौका f. 1. life-boat. 2. life as compared to a boat.

जीवन-पद्धति f. way of life, life-style.

जीवन-मुक्त adj. above the bonds of worldly connections, free from all bonds of life.

जीवन-वृत्त m. life-history.

जीवन-संगी m. 1. life compan- ion. 2. spouse.

जीवन-संघर्ष m. struggle for existence.

जीवन-साथी m. lifelong partner, life companion, spouse.

जीवन-स्तर m. standard of living.

जीवनी f. biography.

जीवनीकार m. biographer.

जीवलोक m. world of living beings, the earth.

जीवविज्ञान m. Biology.

जीववैज्ञानिक m. Biologist.

जीव-हत्या f. killing, slaughter.

जीवाणु m. bacteria.

जीवात्मा f. the individual soul.

जीवाश्म m. fossil.

जीविका f. livelihood.

जीवित adj. 1. living, alive, live.

जीवी adj. & m. (used as a suffix) subsisting on; श्रम ~ labourer.

जी-हुज़ूर m. submissive associate, yesman, sycophant.

जी-हुज़ूरी f. sycophancy.

जुआ m. 1. the practice of playing games for money, gambling. 2. the taking of risk for possible advantage. 3. yoke.

जुआ-घर m. gambling den.

जुआरी m. gambler.

ज़ुकाम m. catarrh, cold.

जुग m. = युग।

जुगत f. 1. device. 2. skill, tact, skilfulness.

जुगती adj. tactful, resourceful.

जुगनूँ m. 1. firefly, glowworm. 2. pendant (ornament).

जुगल m. pair, couple.

जुगल-जोड़ी f. duo, harmonious pair.

जुगलबंदी f. duet.

जुगाड़ m. 1. = जुगत। 2. procurement.

जुगालना vt. to chew the cud, to ruminate.

जुगाली f. rumination.

जुगुप्सा f. 1. repugnance, hat-red. 2. censure, reproach.

जुगुप्सित adj. repugnant.

जुज़ m. 1. part, portion. 2. prin-ted form of a book.

जुज़बंदी f. form-wise sewing of a book.

जुझार m. 1. warrior, fighter. 2. war, battle.

जुझारू adj. aggressive, belligerent.

जुट m. 1. pair. 2. set. 3. match. 4. batch, group.

जुटना vi. 1. to get engaged/engrossed. 2. to assemble/gather. 3. to unite.

जुटाना vt. 1. to collect/bring together. 2. to procure.

जुठारना vt. to make (some-thing edible) impure and unfit for eating (from other's point of view) by tasting; मुँह ~ to eat just a little for taste.

जुड़ना vi. 1. to be attached/jointed/fastened. 2. to be stuck. 3. to be collected/accumulated (as wealth.) 4. to be procured/got. 5. to be yoked.

जुड़पित्ती f. urticaria.

जुड़वाँ adj. twin.

जुड़वाई f. act or state of जुड़वाना or charges to be paid for the same.

जुड़वाना vt. to have (some ob-jects) set or joined.

जुड़ाई f. joinery.

जुतना vi. 1. to be yoked. 2. to be ploughed/tilled. 3. to be engaged/harnessed to some work.

जुतवाना vt. causative of जोतना।

जुताई f. act or state of जुतना, or wages to be paid for the same.

जुतियाना vt. 1. to beat with shoes.

2. to insult by using harsh language.

जुदा adj. separate.

जुदाई f. separation.

जुनून m. madness, craziness, mania.

जुमा m. Friday.

जुमेरात f. Thursday.

जुरमाना m. = जुर्माना।

जुर्म m. crime, offence.

जुर्माना m. fine, monetary pen-alty.

जुर्रत f. courage.

जुर्राब f. stockings, socks.

जुल m. dodge, deceit.

जुलबाज़ m. dodger, deceiver.

जुलाई f. July.

जुलाब m. purgative, cathartic.

जुलाहा m. weaver. [Fem. जुलाहिन]

जुलूस m. = जलूस।

ज़ुल्फ़ f. a lock of lovely hair.

ज़ुल्म m. 1. cruelty, tyranny. 2. oppression.

जुहाना vt. 1. to collect/procure. 2. to coordinate, to adjust (things).

जुहार f. greeting, salutation.

जुहारना vt. 1. to greet. 2. to take an obligation.

जूँ f. louse.

जूआ m. = जुआ।

जूजू m. 1. hooligan. 2. an imaginary animal whose name is used to frighten children.

जूझना vt. 1. to combat. 2. to cope/tackle.

जूट m. 1. jute. 2. matted hair.

जूठन f. leavings of food.

जूठा adj. (food) rendered unusable by improperly touching or eating.

जूड़ा m. lock of braid (s), round hair-do.

जूड़ी f. ague, malaria.

जूत-पैज़ार f. fighting with shoes.

जूता m. a shoe or a pair of shoes.

जूती f. 1. an Indian pumpshoe. 2. slipper.

जून m. 1. time. 2. June. 3. straw. f. life, existence.

जूरी f. jury.

जूस m. 1. juice. 2. soup.

जूसी f. molasses.

जूही f. 1. a kind of jasmine (flower). 2. the fruit of jasmine.

जेंवना vt. = जीमना।

जेठ m. elder brother of the husband.

जेठा adj. 1. elder. 2. better.

जेठानी f. wife of husband's elder brother.

जेते adj. as many.

जेनरेटर m. a machine for produ-cing electrical energy, generator.

जेब m. pocket.

जेबकतरा m. a pickpocket.

जेब-ख़र्च m. pocket money.

जेबघड़ी f. pocket watch.

जेबी adj. handy, which can be kept in the pocket.

जेय adj. conquerable.

जेल m. jail.

जेलख़ाना m. prison, jail.

जेलर m. jailor.

जेली f. 1. gadget for collecting grass. 2. jelly.

जेवनार f. feast (spl. one given on a ceremonial occasion).

ज़ेवर m. ornament.

ज़ेहन m. intellect.

जेहाद m. = जिहाद।

ज़ैतून m. olive.

जैन m. a Jain.

जैव adj. 1.pertaining to animate object. 2. born of an animal.

जैव विष m. toxin.

जैविक adj. having life, animate.

जैसा adj. 1. similar to, like. 2. as.

जैसे adv. 1. as. 2. as if.

जोंक f. leech.

जोंधरी f. millet.

जो pron. who, which; ~ कुछ भी हो come what may; ~ कुछ (i) what. (ii) whatever; ~ कोई whoever; ~ भी हो In any case.

जोख f. weighing.

जोखना vt. 1. to weigh. 2. to weigh the pros and cons (of something).

जोख़िम f. risk, hazard.

जोख़िमी adj. risky, full of danger.

जोगिन f. female ascetic or wife of an ascetic.

जोगिनी f. = जोगिन।

जोगिया adj. pertaining to an ascetic/mendicant.

जोगी m. saint, ascetic.

जोड़ m. 1. sum, total. 2. match, peer, compeer. 3. joint.

जोड़-तोड़ m. unscrupulous man-oeuvres, manipulation.

जोड़दार adj. having joint (s), jointed.

जोड़ना vt.1. to add. 2. to total. 3. to hoard/amass. 4. to connect/ join/unite. 5. to set.

जोड़-पट्‌टी f. fish-plate.

जोड़-बाक़ी f. addition and subtraction.

जोड़वाना vt. जुड़वाना।

जोड़ा m. 1. couple, pair. 2. set, suit.

जोड़ाई f. joinery.

जोड़ी f. 1. pair, couple. 2. pair of cymbals, dumb-bells etc. 3. carriage drawn by two horses.

जोड़ीदार m. 1. colleague, co-worker. 2. match.

जोत f. 1. act or state of yoking. 2. right to till a land. 3. yoke (strap). 4. strings of a balance. 5. flame. 6. holding.

जोतना vt. 1. to plough. 2. to till. 3. to yoke. 4. to harness.

जोताई f. ploughing or remuneration paid for it.

जोबन m. = यौवन।

ज़ोम m. 1. zeal, enthusiasm. 2. pride, vanity.

ज़ोर m. 1. force, power, strength. 2. emphasis. 3. influence. 4. height, intensity, momentum; ~ का ज्वर high fever. 5. strength.

ज़ोर-आज़माई f. trial of strength.

ज़ोर-ज़बरदस्ती f. duress, coercion.

ज़ोरदार adj. 1. forceful. 2. effective.

ज़ोर-शोर m. vigour and zest, gusto.

जोरू f. wife; ~ का गुलाम henpec-ked husband.

जोश m. 1. excitement. 2. fer-vour, zeal, enthusiasm.

जोशाँदा m. decoction.

जोशीला adj. 1. full of spirits, spirited. 2. zealous, enthusiastic.

जोशीलापन m. zealousness.

जोहना vt. to search minutely, to look for.

जौ m. barley.

जौहर m. 1. jewel. 2. real merit, skill, excellence. 3. suicide for self-respect. (annals of Rajasthan).

जौहरी m. 1. jeweller. 2. connoisseur.

ज्ञ m. letter of the Nagari alphabet which is a compound of ज् and ञ; its modern pronunciation is gy.

ज्ञप्ति f. 1. act or state of knowing. 2. a known thing. 3. wisdom.

ज्ञात adj. known.

ज्ञात यौवना f. a belle who is conscious of her youthful bloom.

ज्ञाता m. one who knows, scholar, learned person.

ज्ञाति f. person related by blood or birth.

ज्ञान m. knowledge, learning.

ज्ञानचक्षु m. inner vision.

ज्ञान-पिपासा f. thirst for knowledge.

ज्ञानवान, ज्ञानवान् adj. profound (spl. in spiritual knowledge).

ज्ञानाश्रयी adj. 1. dependent upon knowledge.
2. pertaining to knowledge.

ज्ञानिक adj. academic.

ज्ञानी adj. 1. learned, wise. 2. learned (in spiritual subjects).

ज्ञानेंद्रिय m. sense organ.

ज्ञापक adj. informative, instructive.

ज्ञापन m. 1. act or state of giving information/instruction. 2. memorandum.

ज्ञापित adj. informed, communicated.

ज्ञेय adj. knowable.

ज्ञेयता f. knowability.

ज्या f. 1. bow-string. 2. sine (of an angle) (Maths.). 3. mother. 4. earth.

ज़्यादती f. high-handedness, excess, overdoing.

ज़्यादा adj. & adv. more.

ज़्यादातर adv. mostly.

ज्यामिति f. Geometry.

ज्यूरी f. jury.

ज्येष्ठ adj. 1. seniormost, senior. 2. eldest, elder. m. 1. third month of the Hindu calendar. 2. = जेठ।

ज्येष्ठता f. seniority.

ज्यों adv. as, in the manner of; ~ का त्यों exactly as it was.

ज्योति f. 1. flame, light, lustre. 2. fire. 3. vision, view.

ज्योतित adj. flooded with light/lustre.

ज्योतिर्मय adj. lustrous, brilliant, glittering.

ज्योतिर्लिंग m. emblem of Lord Shiva.

ज्योतिष m. 1. Astronomy. 2. Astrology.

ज्योतिषी m. 1. astronomer. 2. astrologer. 3. fortune-teller.

ज्योत्स्ना f. moonlight.

ज्योनार f. feast.

ज्वर m. fever.

ज्वलंत adj. 1. shining, lustrous,

sparkling. 2. glaring, shocking or fierce.

ज्वलन m. 1. act or state of burning. 2. burning sensation. 3. fire. 4. flame. 5. inflammation.

ज्वलनशील adj. combustible, flammable, inflammable.

ज्वार f. 1. millet. 2. flow tide.

ज्वाला f. 1. flame. 2. extremely burning sensation. 3. pang, agony.

ज्वालामुखी adj. volcanic.

m. volcano; ~ फूटना eruption of a volcano.

झ

झ m. fourth of the alveo-palatal pentad of consonants of the Nagari alphabet; aspirated form of letter ज।

झंकार f. 1. sharp ringing sound. 2. twang.

झंकृत adj. 1. tinkled, jingled. 2. tinkling, jingling.

झंकृति f. = झंकार।

झंखाड़ m. big thorny bush.

झँगुला m. = झगा।

झंझट f. 1. complicated situation, fuss, imbroglio. 2. difficulty, trouble.

झंझटी adj. cantankerous, troublesome, quarrelsome.

झँझरी f. 1. lattice, network. 2. latticed window. 3. gauze of an oven. 4. hole, cavity. 5. sieve. 6. ladle with holes.

झंझा m. gale, tempest.

झंझावात m. storm.

झँझोड़ना vt. to give a violent shaking.

झंडा m. flag, banner.

झंडाभिवादन m. salutation of a flag.

झंडी f. small flag, bunting.

झँपना vi. to be closed.

झँवाना vi. 1. to become dusky (as of the sun). 2. fading of the fire. 3. to fade. 4. to be rubbed with pumice and cleaned. vt. 1. to blacken and make (something) dusky. 2. to extinguish fire (slowly). 3. to cause to fade. 4. to rub with pumice.

झँसना vt. to rub oil on some parts of the body; झँस लेना to grab something by trickery.

झक f. craze, whim.

झकझोरना vt. to give a shake up, to give a violent shaking, to rack up.

झकाझक adj. shining, glittering.

झकोरना vi. (air) to gush through.

झकोरा m. 1. gush of wind. 2. a swing.

झक्कड़ m. hurricane.

झक्की adj. crazy, whimsical.

झख f. = झक।

झगड़ना vi. to quarrel/altercate.

झगड़ा m. 1. quarrelling. 2. quarrel.

झगड़ा-टंटा m. troublesome af-fair, imbroglio.

झगड़ालू adj. fond of starting quarrels, quarrelsome.

झगा m. a loose garment for babies.

झगुली f. = झगा।

झझक f. = झिझक।

झट adv. ~ से instantly, forthwith, immediately, quic-kly.

झटकना vt. 1. to jerk rapidly, 2. to snatch; झटक लेना to grab.
vi. झटक जाना to be physically reduced.

झटका m. 1. sudden jerk, blow. 2. shock. 3. tremor. 4. an act of cutting animal's head with a one stroke. 5. the meat of such an animal.

झटकारना vt. to give a violent jerk, to shake off, to jerk off, to twitch.

झटपट adv. forthwith, instantaneously.

झड़ m. = झड़ी।

झड़न f. 1. act or state of झड़ना। 2. thing so fallen, as dust from clothes. 3. brokerage, interest etc. which is deducted from the principal sum.

झड़ना vi. to fall off, falling/shedding off.

झड़प f. wordy duel, altercation.

झड़पना vt. to browbeat, to tell off.

झड़पा-झड़पी f. high words.

झड़बेरी f. wild plum, jujube.

झड़वाई f. act or state of झड़वाना, or remuneration paid for the same.

झड़वाना vt. 1. to have (some-thing) dusted. 2. to get (someone) exorcized.

झड़ाझड़ adv. in quick succes- sion, continually.

झड़ी f. continuous fall.

झनक f. jingling/clinking sound.

झनकना vi. to jingle/clink.

झनझन f. jingling/tinkling sound.

झनझनाना vi. to jingle/clink.

झनझनाहट f. jingling, clinking.

झपक f. 1. act or state of win-king. 2. a twinkle. 3. nap.

झपकना vi. 1. to wink (repeatedly). 2. to doze.

झपकी f. doze, nap.

झपटना vi. to make a sudden attack; झपट लेना to snatch/grab.

झपटाझपटी f. pouncing by many at a time.

झपट्टा m. swoop, pounce.

झपना vi. to wink/blink.

झपेट f. striking range.

झपेटा m. = झपेट।

झबरा (jhab rA) adj. having or covered with long coarse hair, shaggy.

झबरीला adj. = झबरा।

झब्बा m. tassel.

झमक f. lustre, light.

झमकना vi. 1. to glitter off and on. 2. to make a jingling sound. 3. to walk with a jingling sound. 4. to strut.

झमझमाना vi. 1. to produce a jingling sound. 2. to shine/glitter.

झमाझम adv. 1. (continuously) with a jingling sound (as the falling of rain). 2. with lustre.

झमेला m. problem, complicated affair, turmoil, disturbance.

झमेलिया adj. & m. one given to creating problems, problematic, quarrelsome.

झरझर f. sound produced by the flow of water, air etc.

झरना m. 1. spring, streamlet. 2.sievelike big spoon. vi. to fall.

झरी f. 1. waterfall. 2. a tax realised from shopkeepers. 3. orifice, clink. 4. = झड़ी।

झरोखा m. smallish window, oriel.

झल m. craziness, eccentricity.

झलक f. glimpse, glance.

झलकना vi. to appear (faintly).

झ

झलझलाना vi. to sparkle with brilliance.

झलना vt. 1. to fan. 2. to solder.

झलवाना vt. causative of झलना।

झलाई f. 1. act of fanning or wages paid for the same. 2. soldering.

झलाना vt. = झलवाना।

झल्ल m. madness, eccentricity.

झल्ला adj. 1. eccentric, crank. 2. very soupy. m. 1. large basket. 2. light shower, drizzle.

झल्लाना vi. to be irritated/annoyed, to fret.

झल्लाहट f. fretting and fuming.

झाँई f. 1. black-out. 2. semblance. 3. shadow.

झाँई-झप्पा m. trickery.

झाँकना vi. to peep into.

झाँकी f. 1. public display of go-rgeously decorated idols of Hindu Gods. 2. tableau. 3. glimpse.

झाँझ f. sistrum.

झाँट f. pubic hair.

झाँप f. window or door shade.

झाँपना vt. to cover/shade.

झाँवाँ m. earthen pumice for scrubbing hands and feet.

झाँसा m. dodge, hoodwink.

झाँसा-पट्टी f. trickery.

झाड़ m. 1. bush, shrub. 2. small tree. 3. chandelier. 4. rebuff, reprimand, chiding.

झाड़-झंखाड़ m. jumble of bushes and shrubs.

झाड़न f. duster.

झाड़ना vt. 1. to dust, to shake off dust. 2. to upbraid/scold. 3. to treat with occult science; ज्ञान / विद्वत्ता ~ to make a pedantic show of one's learning.

झाड़-फ़ानूस m. ornamental candle-sticks hung from the roof, chandelier.

झाड़-फूँक f. exorcism, practice of occult arts.

झाड़ा m. 1. stool, excreta. 2. = झाड़-फूँक।

झाड़ी f. shrub, scrub, thicket.

झाड़ू f. broom.

झाड़ूवाला m. 1. sweeper. 2. bro-om-seller.

झापड़ m. slap.

झाबा m. pannier, large basket.

झायँ झायँ f. tinkling sound.

झारखंड m. 1. forest of bushes, spl. thorny. 2. an Indian State.

झारी f. small pitcher with a spout.

झाल f. 1. pungency. 2. soldering. 3. act or state of झालना।

झालदार adj. pungent.

झालना vt. to solder.

झालर f. frill, festoon.

झालरदार adj. frilled, fimbriate.

झिंगवा f. a kind of small fish.

झिझक f. 1. hesitation. 2. hitch (due to nervousness).

झिझकना vi. to hesitate.

झिड़क f. = झिड़की।

झिड़कना vt. to chide/admonish/ snub.

झिड़की f. chide, snub.

झिपना vi. = झपना।

झिरझिर adv. 1. slowly. 2. with

a whispering sound (as the movement of a breeze).

झिरझिरा adj. thinly woven.

झिरी f. 1. aperture, chink, slit. 2. pit. 3. streamlet.

झिरीदार adj. slitted, having apertures.

झिलम f. frill of a helmet.

झिलमिल adj. twinkling.
f. 1. shimmer. 2. twinkle.

झिलमिला adj. thinly woven.

झिलमिलाना vi. 1. to shimmer. 2. to twinkle.

झिलमिलाहट f. twinkling.

झिलमिली f. 1. a louvre to let air in. 2. screen.

झिल्ली f. membrane.

झींगा m. 1. a variety of small fish. 2. a kind of paddy. 3. an insect which eats into a cotton plant.

झींगुर m. cricket (insect).

झींसी f. drizzle.

झीखना vi. to grumble/grouse.

झीना adj. thinly/sparsely woven.

झील f. lake.

झुँझलाना vi. to fret, to be annoyed/ irritated.

झुँझलाहट f. irritation, petulance.

झुंड m. 1. herd, flock. 2. group.

झुकना vi. 1. to bend. 2. to be inclined. 3. to bow down.

झुकवाना vt. causative of झुकना।

झुकाना vt. 1. to bend/tilt. 2. to bow.

झुकाव m. 1. bend, tilt. 2. inclination, proclivity. 3. tendency.

झुग्गी f. hut.

झुटपुटा m. twilight.

झुठलाना vt. to prove false, to falsify.

झुठाना vt. = झुठलाना।

झुनझुन f. jingle, jingling sou- nd.

झुनझुना m. (child's) rattle.

झुनझुनाना vi. to produce a jingling sound.

झुनझुनी f. numbness.

झुमका m. 1. a kind of earring. 2. pendant of an ear-ring.

झुमाना vt. causative of झूमना।

झुरकुट adj. 1. withered, dried up. 2. lean and thin, emaciated.

झुरमुट m. 1. mess of shrubs, shrubbery. 2. cluster of trees, bushes etc.

झुर्री f. wrinkle.

झुलवाना vt. to cause to swing.

झुलसना vi. to be scorched/charred.

झुलाना vt. 1. to swing/rock. 2. to put off.

झूँटा m. swing.

झूठ m. lie, falsity, falsehood.

झूठ-मूठ adv. without any real cause, without any rhyme or reason, falsely.

झूठ-सच m. a lie or truth.

झूठा adj. false. m. liar.

झूमक m. 1. a variety of folk dance. 2. a song sung with the dance or in other festivities. 3. = झुमका।

झूमना vi. to move to and fro, to wave, to sway like leaves on a tree.

झूमर m. 1. a kind of earring. 2. a variety of folk dance. 3. a song sung with the dance or in other festivities.

झूरा m. 1. drought. 2. shortage.

झूल f. 1. sheet of cloth hung over the body of an elephant etc. for decoration. 2. loose and cumbersome garment.

झूलना vi. to swing.

झूला m. 1. swing. 2. swinging rope, ropeway.

झेंपना vi. to blush.

झेंपू adj. blushing.

झेलना vi. to endure/undergo/suffer/bear.

झोंक f. 1. impulse. 2. bent, inclination.

झोंकना vt. to throw (into an oven, furnace etc.) with a jerk.

झोंकवाना vt. causative of झोंकना।

झोंका m. gust, blast (of wind).

झोंकाई f. act or state of झोंकना, or wages paid therefor.

झोंटा m. 1. body of dishevelled hair on the head (spl. of a woman). 2. handy bundle.

झोंटा-झोंटी f. tussle in which two women pull each other by the hair.

झोंपड़ा m. biggish hut, cottage.

झोंपड़ी f. hut, crib.

झोरना vt. 1. to give a shaking. 2. to grab money deceitfully.

झोल m. 1. broth. 2. soup. 3. sag. 4. pucker; क़मीज कंधे पर ~ खा रही है The shirt puckers (up) at the shoulder.

झोलदार adj. 1. brothy. 2. soupy. 3. metal-coated. 4. sagging, loose.

झोला m. 1. knapsack, kit, wallet, handy/smallish bag. 2. loose shirt. 3. a disease of plants. 4. blow. 5. gust.

झोली f. 1. border of a cloth used as a mendicant's bag, wearing apparel (spl. its border) used as a bag. 2. alms bag.

झौर m. wrangle, altercation, uproar.

झौहाना vi. to talk fretfully and loudly.

ञ

ञ fifth of the alveo-palatal pentad of consonants of the Nagari alphabet; its sound resembles that of n in punch.

ट

ट

ट m. first of the five cerebral consonants of the Nagari alphabet; its sound resembles that of t in take, cut etc.

टँकना vi. 1. to be stitched or sewn. 2. to be noted/recorded.

टँकवाना vt. causative of टाँकना।

टँकाई f. 1. soldering. 2. charges paid for soldering.

टँकाना vt. = टँकवाना।

टंकार f. 1. twang of a bow. 2. tinkling sound.

टंकारना vt. 1. to twang a bow. 2. to make a tinkling sound.

टंकी f. 1. tank. 2. cistern, reservoir.

टँगड़ी f. leg (pej.).

टँगना vi. to be hung.

टंच adj. & m. sharper, crafty guy.

टंटा m. 1. meaningless complication. 2. botheration, trouble. 3. altercation, turmoil.

टक f. = टकटकी.

टकटकी f. steady/intent look, gaze.

टकराना vi. 1. to collide, to ram. 2. to clash/dash against.

टकराव m. 1. collision. 2. encounter, confrontation.

टकसाल f. mint, mint-house.

टकसाली adj. 1. of or pertaining to a mint. 2. standard, genuine.

टका m. an old Indian copper coin, equivalent of two (old) pice.

टकासी f. system of charging interest at the rate of two pice per rupee per month.

टकुआ m. 1. spindle. 2. pointed tool. [Fem. टकुई, टकुली]

टकुली f. diminutive of टकुआ।

टकैया adj. cheap as a farthing.

टकोर f. light fomentation.

टकोरना vt. 1. to foment lightly. 2. to give a light blow, to strike. 3. to pass a hurtful remark.

टक्कर f. 1. collision. 2. confrontation.

टखना m. ankle-joint.

ट

टटका adj. fresh.

टटोलना vt. to feel with the hands, to grope/probe.

टट्टर m. bamboo fence.

टट्टी f. 1. screen (made of st-raw). 2. faeces, stool. 3. latrine.

टट्टू m. pony.

टन f. tinkling sound. m. ton (measure of weight).

टनकना vi. 1. to tinkle. 2. to feel dizzy.

टनटन f. tinkling sound, sound of bells.

टनटनाना vi. to ring/tinkle.

टनमना adj. 1. perfectly healthy. 2. hale and hearty.

टनाटन f. tinkling sound, sound of peal. adv. with a tinkling sound.

टप f. 1. hood of a carriage. 2. cover of a lamp. 3. tub.

टपक f. throbbing pain.

टपकना vi. to fall as drops, to trickle/drip.

टपका m. falling in droplets/ driplets; टपके का आम mango fallen from the tree.

टपका-टपकी f. drizzle.

टपकाना vt. to cause to drip/trickle.

टपकाव m. act or state of टपकाना।

टपटप f. sound made by dripping water.

टपना vi. 1. to leap or jump across. 2. to remain without food. 3. to go on waiting without any tangible result.

टपाटप adv. with incessant sound of falling rain drops.

टपाना vt. 1. to cause (someone) to leap or jump across. 2. to cause to remain without food. 3. to cause (someone) to wait unnecessarily.

टप्पा m. 1. small tract of land. 2. bounce. 3. range of bouncing. 4. a type of folk song of the Punjab.

टब m. tub, vat.

टमटम f. tumtum.

टमाटर m. tomato.

टर f. 1. harsh sound. 2. obstinacy.

टरकाना vt. to put off, to post-pone.

टरटराना vi. to prattle/chatter.

टर्रटर्र f. 1. croak. 2. croaking sound.

टर्रा adj. obstinate and ill-tempered, obdurate.

टर्राना vi. 1. to croak. 2. to talk impertinently/aggressively.

टलना vi. to be postponed.

टवर्ग m. a group of five cerebral consonants of the Nagari alphabet, i.e. ट, ठ, ड, ढ and ण.

टस f. sound produced by the movement of a heavy object; ~ से मस न होना (i) not to budge an inch; (ii) not to yield even a fraction.

टसक f. act or state of टसकना।

टसकना vi. 1. to slip/move/budge. 2. to have a throbbing pain.

टसर m. 1. a kind of silk of light, grey colour. 2. cloth made of the same.

टहकना vi. 1. to have a throbbing pain (in the parts of the body). 2. to melt.

टहनी f. twig, spray, sprig.

टहल f. attendance, menial service.

टहलना vi. to take a walk, to stroll/saunter/walk.

टहलान f. (morning) walk.

टहलाना vt. to help (someone) walk.

टहलुआ m. lacky, man-servant.

टहोका m. jerk with a hand or foot.

टाँक f. 1. act or state of टाँकना। 2. part, portion. 3. han-dwriting. 4. point of a pen. 5. estimation of weight, value etc.

टाँकना vt. 1. to stitch or sew. 2. to cobble. 3. to solder. 4. to powder (as on a grindstone and thereby roughen). 5. to record/write down. 6. go grab improperly.

टाँका m. 1. stitch. 2. part stitched/sewn, patch. 3. solder.

टाँकी f. 1. chisel. 2. small piece cut out. 3. piece scooped out (of a fruit etc.).

टाँग f. leg.

टाँगन m. pony.

टाँगना vt. to hang.

टाँगा m. tonga, one-horse carriage.

टाँच f. stitching, sewing.

टाँचना vt. to stitch/sew.

टाँड़ f. projecting overhead rack/shelf.

टाँड़ा m. 1. flock of pack beasts. 2. goods carried by the flock. 3. caravan of travelling merchants. 4. halting place/camp of such a caravan. 5. family (pej.).

टाँय-टाँय f. 1. jabber, prattle. 2. hoarse sounds; ~ फिस होना to result in a fiasco, to come to nought.

टाँस f. tension in hands or feet due to being bent, or pain resulting therefrom.

टांसिल m. tonsil.

टाइप f. type (printing).

टाइपराइटर m. typewriter.

टाइपिस्ट m. typist.

टाई f. tie, necktie.

टाउनहाल m. townhall.

टाट m. sackcloth, gunny.

टान f. tension.

टाप f. hoof-beat.

टापना vi. to jump over; टापते रह जाना (i) to go on waiting fruitlessly; (ii) to have to stay without food.

टापा m. 1. = टप्पा (expanse of land, esp. barren land). 2. step in walking.

टापू m. island, isle.

टाफ़टा m. a shiny fabric like silk, taffeta.

टारकोल m. coal-tar.

टारपीडो m. torpedo.

टार्च f. torch.

टाल m. 1. big heap/pile (of wood, straw etc.). 2. shop having such piles.

टालटूल f. = टालमटोल।

टालना vt. 1. to put off. 2. to postpone.

टालमटोल f. procrastination, prevarication.

टाली f. bell tied to the neck of an animal.

टिंचर m. tincture.

टिंडा m. an Indian vegetable; round-gourd.

ट

टिकट m. 1. ticket. 2. stamp (postage or revenue). 3. party's permission to fight an election as its candidate, ticket.

टिकट-घर m. booking office.

टिकट-परीक्षक m. ticket-inspector, ticket-examiner.

टिकट-बाबू m. booking clerk.

टिकट-संकलक m. philatelist.

टिकट-संकलन m. the act of collecting postage stamps, philately.

टिक-टिक f. tick-tick (of a clock).

टिकठी f. 1. gallows, gibbet. 2. bier. 3. tea-poy, wooden bench.

टिकड़ा m. 1. disc. 2. pendant. 3. thick loaf baked on fire.

टिकड़ी f. small thick loaf baked on fire.

टिकना vi. 1. to stay. 2. to last. 3. to stand/rest.

टिकाऊ adj. likely to last for a long time; durable, lasting.

टिकान f. 1. halting place. 2. halt.

टिकाना vi. to lodge someone at someplace.

टिकाव m. 1. act or state of halting. 2. halting place. 3. halt. 4. stability.

टिकिया f. tablet, pill.

टिकुली f. spangle affixed on the forehead (by Indian women).

टिकैत m. 1. crown prince. 2. chief. 3. founder.

टिचन adj. 1. fit, spick and span. 2. ever-ready.

टिटकारना vt. to make a ticking sound for driving an animal.

टिटकारी f. 1. act or state of टिटकारना। 2. sound so produced.

टिटिहरी f. sandpiper.

टिड्डा m. grasshopper.

टिड्डी f. locust.

टिन m. tin.

टिप f. tip.

टिप-टिप. f. 1. sound produced by falling rain drops. 2. drizzle making such a sound.

टिपवाना vt. causative of टीपना।

टिप्पणी f. note, comment, remark.

टिप्पन m. 1. commentary. 2. horoscope.

टिप्पस m. a useful piece of advice.

टिमटिमाना vi. to glimmer twin-kle/ scintillate.

टिमटिमाहट f. glimmer, scintillation.

टिल्ला m. 1. hurt. 2. push.

टिहुनी f. 1. knee. 2. elbow.

टीका m. 1. a mark (of an unguent) put on the forehead. 2. inoculation. 3. vaccination. 4. comment, remark. 5. commentary, annotation. 6. ceremony performed before marriage at which the engagement is confirmed. 7. an ornament worn on the forehead.

टीकाकार m. 1. commentator. 2. annotator.

टीका टिप्पणी f. comments/criti-cism regarding merits and demerits of something.

टीन m. tin.

टीप f. 1. act or state of टीपना। 2. act or state of tapping. 3. act or state of filling in the gaps between bricks with cement instead of plastering, pointing. 3. loud sound. 4. something jotted down, note, document. 5. bond. 6. horoscope. 7. thumb-impression.

टीपटाप f. 1. embellishment, outward embellishment. 2. empty show.

टीपना vt. 1. to press with a finger. 2. to point (masonry). 3. to enter in record-book, to record, to jot down.

टीम f. team.

टीमटाम f. ostentation.

टीला m. 1. mound. 2. hillock.

टीस f. 1. smarting pain. 2. mental agony, anguish.

टीसना vi. to smart.

टुंड adj. 1. (tree) which is short of its branches. 2. (person) whose hands are cut off. 3. (beast) whose horns have fallen off.

टुंडा adj. = टुंड।

टुइयाँ adj. 1. tiny, very small. 2. dwarfish. f. small parrot.

टुक adj. a little.

टुकड़ allomorph of टुकड़ा as in टुकड़ख़ोर।

टुकड़ख़ोर m. hanger on, parasite.

टुकड़-तोड़ m. hanger-on, parasite.

टुकड़ा m. 1. piece, fragment. 2. part, portion. 3. morsel.

टुकड़ी f. 1. small piece, bit. 2. detachment (of troops).

टुकुर-टुकुर adv. ~ देखना to gaze with longing looks; to look wistfully.

टुक्कड़ m. piece of bread.

टुच्चा adj. lowly, low-minded, ignoble.

टुटपुँजिया adj. & m. (person) having very little capital/means.

टुटरूँ f. small dove; ~ टूँ voice of a dove.

adj. 1. alone, solitary. 2. very little. 3. lean and thin. 4. insignificant, trivial.

टूँगना vt. 1. to eat slowly and bit by bit. (sarcastic) 2. to graze to.

टूँड़ m. 1. long hair on the mo-uth of an insect. 2. pointed portion of an ear of corn/vergetable/fruit.

टूक m. bit, fragment; दो ~ जवाब देना to give a clearcut refusal.

टूट f. 1. breakage. 2. loss due to breakage.

टूटन f. broken fragments.

टूटना vi. to break, to crack, to burst.

टूट-फूट f. breakage, wear and tear.

टूटा adj. broken.

टूटा-फूटा adj. broken, rams-hackle.

टूटी-फ्रूटी f. fruit ice-cream.

टूम f. ornament.

टूरनामेंट f. tournament.

टें f. screech (of a parrot); ~ बोल जाना to pop off, to collapse.

टेंट f. fold in the loin-cloth for keeping money.

टें-टें f. prattle, useless talk.

टेंडर m. tender.

टेक f. 1. prop, support, fulcrum. 2.

ट

resolve. 3. opening line/burden/refrain of a song.

टेकना vt. 1. to prop, support. 2. to rest/lean.

टेकरी f. ridge, bump.

टेकान f. 1. act or state of टेकना। 2. support, prop. 3. platform on which to rest things.

टेकाना vt. 1. to provide a prop/support. 2. to rest (a heavy thing) on some prop.

टेकी adj. obstinate.

टेकुआ m. = तकला।

टेढ़ f.1. curve, bend. 2. crookedness.

टेढ़ा adj. 1. bent, twisted. 2. crooked. 3. difficult, abtruse.

टेढ़ापन m. 1. bent. 2. crookedness.

टेढ़ा-मेढ़ा adj. 1. sinuous. 2. zig-zag. 3. (work) arduous or difficult.

टेनिस m. tennis.

टेम f. flame.

टेर f. 1. act or state of टेरना। 2. loud call. 3. high note in vocal music.

टेरना vt. 1. to call loudly. 2. to sing in a loud tone.

टेरीकाट m. terricott.

टेलिप्रिंटर m. teleprinter.

टेलिफ़ोन m. telephone.

टेव f. wont, habit, custom.

टेवा m. skeleton horoscope.

टेसू m. the plant Bhutia frondosa and its blossoms.

टैंक m. tank (military science).

टैक्सी f. taxi.

टोंटी f. nozzle, spout.

टोंटीदार adj. nozzled, spouted.

टोक f. inauspicious interrogation.

टोकन m. token.

टोकना vt. to interrogate inauspiciously.

टोकरा m. large basket, crop.

टोकरी f. 1. (small) basket. 2. waste-basket.

टोका m. chaff-cutter.

टोटका m. superstitious remedy/device/spell.

टोटा m. 1. loss. 2. shortage.

टोनहा m. one who practises black magic, enchanter.

टोनही f. woman who practises black magic.

टोना m. witchcraft, enchantment.

टोना-टोटका m. superstitious device.

टोप m. 1. hat. 2. helmet.

टोपा m. 1. big cap. 2. basket.

टोपी f. cap, beret.

टोला m. locality, quarter.

टोली f. 1. team. 2. batch, group.

टोह f. search, hunt.

टोहना vt. 1. to sound/probe. 2.to feel with the fingers, to touch.

टोहिया m. a secret agent, spy.

ट्रस्ट m. trust. [H. E. न्यास]

ट्रस्टी m. trustee. [H. E. न्यासी]

ट्रेडमार्क m. trade mark.

ट्रेडिल m. treadle.

ठ

ठ m. second letter of the cerebral pentad of consonants of the Nagari alphabet, aspirated form of letter ट।

ठंड f. 1. cold. 2. peace, calm.

ठंडक f. 1. coolness. 2. cooling effect.

ठंडा adj. 1. cold. 2. wintry, chilly. 3. passionless.

ठक adj. stunned, thunder-struck, astounded.
f. tapping sound.

ठक-ठक f. 1. repeated tapping sound/knock. 2. altercation.

ठकठौआ m. 1. cymbal used by beggars. 2. a kind of small boat.

ठकार m. letter ठ or its sound.

ठकारांत adj. (word) having ठ at the end.

ठकुरसुहाती f. insincere praise, flattery.

ठकुराइन f. = ठकुरानी।

ठकुराई f. 1. act or state of being a ठाकुर। 2. sway, regime. 3. estate of a ठाकुर (landlord). 4. importance, eminence.

ठकुरानी f. 1. wife of a ठाकुर (chief). 2. lady proprietor.

ठग m. cheat, swindler.

ठगई f. cheating, swindling.

ठगना vt. to cheat or deceive, to dupe.

ठगनी f. woman swindler/cheat.

ठगपना m. cheating, swindling.

ठगवाना vt. to cause to be chea-ted.

ठगा-सा adj. flabbergasted.

ठगी f. cheating, swindling, thuggee.

ठट्ठ m. throng.

ठट्ठा m. 1. joke, wag. 2. lau- ghter.

ठट्ठेबाज़ m. wag, jester, joker.

ठठरी f. skeleton.

ठठेरा m. brazier.

ठठेरिन f. 1. brazier's wife. 2. woman brazier.

ठठेरी f. brazier's calling.

ठठोल m. jester, joker.

ठठोली f. jest, derision.

ठन f. jingling sound.

ठनक f. 1. jingling sound (of silver coin). 2. intermittent pain.

ठनकना vi. 1. to jingle. 2. playing on tabla, drum etc.

ठनका m. jingling sound.

ठनकाना vt. 1. to cause a jingling sound by beating on tambourine etc. 2. to play on musical instruments which create such a sound.

ठनठन f. clinking/jingling sound.

ठनठन गोपाल adj. & m. 1. (person) who possesses nothing, penniless. 2. (object) worthless, insignificant.

ठनठनाना vt. to tinkle/jingle.

ठनना vi. to start to take place.

ठनाका m. loud tinkling sound.

ठप adj. closed, suspended, finished.

ठप्पा m. 1. die, matrix. 2. impression made by a die or matrix.

ठमक f. halt.

ठ

ठमकना vi. to halt suddenly due to fear etc.

ठर्रा m. 1. a kind of cheap country liquor. 2. twisted, thick yarn. 3. big, half-baked brick.

ठवन f. pose, posture, stance, gait.

ठस adj. 1. miserly (person). 2. thick-woven (cloth). 3. strong, rigid, compact (thing). 4. too heavy to be moved (object).

ठसक f. affected manner, disdainful air.

ठसका f. 1. = ठसक। 2. dry cough.

ठसाठस adv. 1. full to the brim. 2. overcrowded. 3. overpacked.

ठस्सा m. = ठसक।

ठहरना vi. 1. to stop (as a train at a station). 2. to reside temporarily. 3. to wait (as for somebody). 4. to remain motionless for a while (as wind). 5. to be settled (as price or transaction).

ठहराना vt. 1. to cause to stay/stop. 2. to consider or regard.

ठहराव m. act or state of ठहरना; cessation of activities, pause.

ठहाका m. a loud deep hearty laugh, guffaw.

ठाँठ adj. 1. dry (cow etc.), not giving milk. 2. sapless.

ठाँय-ठाँय f. breeze, altercation.

ठाँव m. 1. place, residence, station. 2. rendezvous.

ठाँसना vt. to fill to the brim.

ठाकुर m. 1. deity, god, idol. 2. Lord, Master. 3. Chief, leader. 4. landlord. 5. highly honoured person. 6. a title of Kshatriyas.

ठाट m. = ठाठ।

ठाठ m. 1. splendour, splendid display. 2. frame, structure.

ठाठ-बाट m. pomp and show.

ठाठें fem. (plu). rising and rolling waves.

ठानना vt. 1. to start (something) with determination (as a war). 2. to resolve/determine.

ठाला m. 1. idler, person without any work. 2. unemployment. 3. want, scarcity, dearth, shortage.

ठिंगना adj. = ठिगना।

ठिकाना m. 1. place to stay. 2. destination. 3. rendezvous.

ठिगना adj. short-statured, dwarfish, petite.

ठिठक f. act or state of ठिठकना।

ठिठकना vi. 1. to stop suddenly (due to fear, as a horse at the appearance of a lion). 2. to hesitate, to fight shy.

ठिठुरना vi. to shiver with cold.

ठिठोली f. banter, jesting.

ठिया m. station, permanent seat.

ठिलना vi. 1. to be pushed (as a car by men). 2. to penetrate (on being forced).

ठीक adj. 1. right, proper. 2. correct. 3. just, exact.

ठीक-ठाक adj. & adv. 1. all right, okay. 2. satisfactory.

ठीकड़ा m. = ठीकरा।

ठीकमठीक adv. quite right.

ठीकरा m. 1. potsherd. 2. worthless article.

ठीकरी f. 1. a broken piece of clay or pot, shard, potsherd.

2. worthless object. 3. peb-ble.

ठीका m. contract.

ठीकेदार m. contractor.

ठीकेदारी f. calling of a contra- ctor.

ठीठी f. derisive/discourteous laugh.

ठीहा m. 1. working bench (of a carpenter, blacksmith etc.). 2. support (to prevent something from falling). 3. raised platform.

ठुकना vi. 1. to be beaten. 2. to be forced to penetrate. 3. to be spent unnecessarily/ involuntarily.

ठुकराना vt. 1. to kick. 2. to turn down, rejcet, spurn (with contemp).

ठुकाई f. beating, thrashing.

ठुड्डी f. chin.

ठुनकना vi. 1. to make a tinkl-ing sound. 2. to whimper/sob.

ठुनठुन f. 1. tinkling sound of a metallic vessel. 2. sound, act etc. of a child's sobbing.

ठुमक f. act or state or gait of toddling.

ठुमकना vi. to toddle.

ठुमका m. small jerk as that given to a kite to cause it to fly. adj. dwarfish.

ठुमकारना vi. to give or make a small jerk.

ठुमकी f. fem. of ठुमका।

ठुमरी f. a kind of short folk song.

ठुसकना vi. to sob.

ठुसकी f. sound produced in breaking wind (passing wind from the abdomen).

ठुसना vi. to be stuffed/cram-med in a small place.

ठुसाना vt. 1. to cause to be stuffed/crammed. 2. to feed by insistence (fig.)

ठूँठ m. stub, stump.

ठूँठा adj. (tree) leafless, having the branches lopped off.

ठूँसना vt. to stuff, to cram, to press tightly into (throat, mouth, stomach etc.), to huddle up.

ठेंगा m. thumb.

ठेकेदार m. = ठीकेदार।

ठेठ adj. 1. pristine, unalloyed. 2. typical.

ठेपी f. stopper.

ठेलना vt. to push and move.

ठेलमठेल f. jostling.

ठेला m. 1. pushcart, trolley. 2. wheel barrow. 3. push.

ठेस f. 1. light knock. 2. set-back. 3. shock.

ठोंकना vt. = ठोकना।

ठोंग f. a peck.

ठोंगना vt. to strike with the beak, to peck.

ठोंठी f. outer shell of a gram, husk.

ठोकना vt. to beat with hammer.

ठोकना-पीटना vt. to beat and hammer.

ठोकर f. 1. kick. 2. block, stoppage.

ठोड़ी f. chin.

ठोस adj. 1. solid. 2. profound, sound.

ठौर m. place; ~ हो जाना to die instantaneously.

ठौर-ठिकाना m. whereabouts.

ड

ड m. third consonant of the cerebral pentad of the Nagari alphabet; its sound resembles that of d in doll.

डंक m. sting.

डंका m. kettledrum.

डंठल m. stalk, stem.

डंठी f. fem. of डंठल।

डंड m. an Indian type of exercise.

डंडा m. 1. staff, club, bar. 2. stave; पुलिस का ~ the stave of a policeman. 3. rung (of a ladder).

डंडी f. 1. handle. 2. beam of a pair of scales.

डंस m. डाँस।

डँसना vi. = डसना।

डकार m. an act or sound of belching, belch.

डकारना vi. to belch. vt. to swallow; डकार जाना to grab.

डकारांत adj. (word) ending in ड।

डकैत m. dacoit, robber.

डकैती f. dacoity, robbery.

डग m. step, stride.

डगमग adj. 1. lurching. 2. staggering, wavering.

डगमगाना vi. 1. to lurch. 2. to waver.

डगर f. pathway.

डटना vi. 1. to hold on. 2. to hold one's own.

डट्टा m. stopper, cork.

डपट f. objuration, reprimand.

डपटना vt. to objurate/reprimand/scold/rebuke.

डपोरसंख m. one who talks big and does nothing; extremely shallow person.

डफ f. big tambourine.

डफली f. tambourine.

डबकौंहा adj. tearful.

डबडबाना vi. (eyes) to be filled with tears.

डबल रोटी f. loaf.

डमरू m. tabor.

डमरूमध्य adj. tabor-shaped; जल ~ strait; स्थल ~ isthmus.

डर m. 1. fear, dread, fright. 2. scare.

डरना vi. to fear, to be afraid.

डरपोक adj. timid, cowardly.

डरवाना vt. to frighten.

डराना vt. 1. to frighten/terrify/appal. 2. to scare/threaten.

डरावना adj. dreadful, frightening, scary.

डलना vi. to be poured/passed into.

डलवाना vi. to cause to be poured/put/dropped/passed into.

डला m. 1. lump. 2. biggish wicker-basket.

डलिया f. small wicker basket, hamper.

डली f. small lump.

डसना vt. to sting/bite.

डसवाना vt. = डसाना।

डसाना vt. to cause to sting.

डहकना vi. 1. to cry loudly. 2. to be cheated/deceived. vt. 1. to cheat/defraud/deceive. 2. to tantalise.

डहडहा adj. 1. (plant) blooming, green. 2. (plant) fresh. 3. (person) jolly, cheerful.

डहना vi. 1. to burn out, to be reduced to ashes. 2. to be irritated/vexed/annoyed. vt. 1. to burn, to reduce to ashes. 2. to irritate/vex/annoy.

डहर f. = डगर।

डाँक f. 1. scaling (of wall etc.). 2. vomiting.

डाँकना = डाकना।

डाँट f. scolding, rebuke.

डाँटना vt. to scold/reprimand.

डाँड़ m. penalty.

डाँड़ा m. 1. ridge, boundary. 2. oar. 3. staff pole.

डाँड़ी f. beam of a pair of scales.

डाँवाँडोल adj. not firm or steady, shaky, uncertain, lurching.

डाँस m. gnat.

डाइटिंग f. act of living on a restricted food.

डाइन f. 1. witch. 2. ugly wo-man. 3. quarrelsome woman.

डाक f. mail, dak, post.

डाकगाड़ी f. mail train.

डाकघर m. Post Office.

डाकटरी f. 1. medical practice. 2. medical check-up.

डाकना vt. to scale/cross over. vi. to vomit.

डाक बँगला m. Dak Bungalow.

डाका m. dacoity.

डाकिनी f. witch.

डाकिया m. postman.

डाकू m. dacoit, robber.

डॉक्टर m. doctor.

डाट f. 1. stopper. 2. cork. 3. prop. 4. archway. 5. = डाँट।

डाबर m. 1. low ground, marsh. 2. pond. 3. dirty water.

डाभ m. green coconut.

डामर m. 1. pomp and show, ostentation. 2. a type of small bee.

डामल m. 1. life sentence. 2. transportation for life.

डायरी f. diary.

डार f. = डाल।

डाल f. branch (of a tree).

डालना vt. 1. to pour. 2. to put. 3. to throw/cast away.

डालर m. dollar.

डाली f. 1. branch. 2. basket. 3. present (esp. in the form of a basketful of sweets, fruit etc.).

डाह f. envy, jealousy.

डिंगल f. a dialect of Rajasthan.

डिंब m. foetus.

डिक्री f. decree. [H.E. डिग्री]

डिगना vi. to deviate/deflect/swerve.

डिगरी f. degree.

डिज़ाइन m. design.

डिठौना m. black mark made on a child's forehead as protection against an evil eye.

डिपो m. depot.

डिप्टी m. one who does the head's job when the head is away, deputy.

डिबिया f. small box, casket.

डिब्बा m. 1. chest, case, smallish box. 2. a carriage of a railway train.

ड

डिब्बाबंद adj. tinned, canned.

डींग f. bragging, boasting.

डीठ f. sight, vision.

डील-डौल m. structure of the body.

डीह m. 1. habitation. 2. small village. 3. ruins of a dilapidated village.

डुगडुगाना vt. to beat a drum.

डुगडुगी f. = डुग्गी।

डुग्गी f. tabor.

डुबकी f. a dip or dive.

डुबवाना vt. to cause of sink.

डुबाव m. depth (of water) en-ough for drowning.

डुबोना vt. 1. to drown/sink. 2. to immerse (in some liquid). 3. to destroy/ruin/spoil.

डुलाना vt. 1. to move to and fro.

डूबना vi. 1. to be drowned/ immersed, to sink. 2. to set. 3. to be ruined/lost.

डेढ़ adj. & m. one and a half.

डेरा m. 1. dwelling, abode. 2. camp. 3. tent.

डेरा-डंडा m. bag and baggage.

डेरी f. dairy.

डेरीफ़ार्म m. dairy farm.

डेला m. 1. eye-ball. 2. = ढेला।

डेल्टा m. delta. [H.E. मुहाना]

डेवढ़ m. method, device, wor-king plan.

डेस्क m. desk.

डेहरी f. threshold, doorsill.

डैना m. wing of a bird, pinion.

डैमरेज m. demurrage.

डैश m. dash.

डोंगर m. hillock.

डोंगा m. serving bowl.

डोंगी f. small-boat.

डोंडी f. 1. = टोंटी। 2. = डौंड़ी।

डोई f. wooden ladle.

डोकरा m. old man.

डोकरी f. old woman.

डोगरा m. a caste among the Hindus living in Jammu and Kangra regions.

डोगरी f. the dialect of Dogras.

डोडा m. large blossom.

डोब m. dip, immersion.

डोम m. the lowest caste among the Hindus.

डोमकौआ m. raven, a kind of big crow.

डोमड़ा m. = डोम।

डोमनी f. fem of डोम।

डोमिन f. fem of डोम।

डोर f. 1. thread (esp. for kite-flying). 2. string.

डोरा m. thread.

डोरिया m. 1. a kind of striped cloth. 2. a type of heron.

डोरियाना vt. to tie with a cord.

डोरी f. string, cord.

डोल m. 1. act or state of डोलना। 2. bucket.

डोलची f. 1. small pail. 2. wic-ker basket.

डोलना vi. 1. to oscillate/swing. 2. to move about, ramble. 3. to waver/swerve.

डोला m. closed palanquin, sedan, litter.

डोली f. 1. small palanquin. 2. formal departure of a bride after marriage from the paternal home.

डौंडी f. drum.

डौल m. 1. shape, form. 2. method, device.

डौल-डाल m. device, strategy.

ड्यूटी f. duty. [H.E. 1. कर्तव्य। 2. कर, महसूल]

ड्योढ़ा adj. one and a half times (as big, as large etc.).

ड्योढ़ी f. passage way from the main entrance into a house, gateway, threshold.

ड्योढ़ीदार m. gatekeeper, doorkeeper.

ड्रम m. drum.

ड्रामेबाज़ी f. exaggerated (emotional) behaviour or act.

ढ

ढ m. fourth consonant of the cerebral pentad of the Nagari alphabet; its sound resem-bles that of dh in mudhole.

ढंग m. 1. method, mode, knack, way. 2. procedure.

ढंगी adv. cunning, crafty.

ढँढोर m. flame.

ढँढोरची m. announcer, one who announces by beat of drum.

ढँढोरना vt. to make a thorough search.

ढँढोरा m. 1. action of announcing publicly. 2. drum which is used by a public announcer.

ढँपना vt. = ढकना।

ढई f. picketing.

ढकना vt. 1. to cover. 2. to hide/conceal. m. lid, cover.

ढकनी f. small lid or cover.

ढका m. large drum.

ढकार m. letter ढ or its sound.

ढकेलना vt. to push.

ढकेला-ढकेली f. pushing and jostling.

ढकोसला m. hypocritical act/cant.

ढक्कन m. lid, cover.

ढड्ढा m. 1. scaffolding. 2. false show. adj. big and clumsy.

ढनमनाना vi. = लुढ़कना।

ढपना m. = ढक्कन।

ढब m. 1. method. 2. procedure. 3. manner. 4. knack.

ढमढम m. sound like that of a big drum.

ढरकना vi. 1. to roll down. 2. to trickle down.

ढरकी f. weaver's shuttle.

ढर्रा m. 1. mode, style. 2. device. 3. method or manner of doing something, way.

ढलकना vi. = ढरकना।

ढलका m. 1. disease of the eyes, in which they water continuously. 2. bamboo funnel.

ढलकाना vt. 1. to pour. 2. to shed. 3. to cause to roll down. 4. to spill (milk etc.).

ढलना vi. 1. to be poured into. 2. to be moulded. 3. to decline (physically).

ढलवाँ adj. 1. moulded, cast. 2. sloping.

ढलवाना vt. to cause to be cast/moulded.

ढलाई f. act or state of casting/moulding, or charges paid for the same.

ढलान f. slope, ramp.

ढलुआँ adj. 1. = ढलवाँ। 2. ढालुआँ।

ढहना vi. 1. to fall or tumble down. 2. to crash down.

ढहवाना vt. causative of ढाना, to cause to be demolished.

ढाँचा m. 1. frame. 2. structure, framework.

ढाँस f. = ढाँसी।

ढाँसना vi. to cough.

ढाँसी f. whooping cough.

ढाई adj. two and a half.

ढाक m. Butea frondosa.

ढाड f. bellowing, loud cry.

ढाढ़स f. = ढारस।

ढाना vt. to demolish, to pull down, to raze to the ground.

ढाबा m. 1. thatched roofing. 2. an Indian type of restaurant.

ढारस f. consolation, solace.

ढाल f. 1. downward slope, declivity. 2. shield.

ढालना vt. 1. to cast/mould. 2. to pour out. 3. to drink.

ढालवाँ adj. sloping, descending.

ढालुआँ adj. = ढालू।

ढालू adj. sloping, declivous.

ढासना m. pillow (for support).

ढाहना vt. = ढाना।

ढिंढोरना vt. = ढँढोरना।

ढिग adv. near, close to.

ढिठाई f. impudence, obduracy.

ढिबरी f. 1. spouted lamp. 2. nut, socket.

ढिमका adj. & m. such a one.

ढिलढिला adj. 1. loose, unfirm. 2. (liquid) thin, not dense.

ढिलाई f. 1. looseness, let-up. 2. sloth, indolence, idleness, slackness.

ढिलाना vt. to cause to be loosened.

ढिल्लड़ adj. indolent, lazy.

ढिसरना vt. 1. to slip down. 2. to be inclined/bent/prone.

ढींगर m. paramour.

ढींढा m. bulging stomach, tu-mmy.

ढीठ adj. impertinent, obdurate.

ढीम adj. 1. big piece of stone. 2. big lump.

ढील f. 1. head louse. 2. looseness.

ढीलना vt. to loosen.

ढीला adj. 1. loose, not tight. 2. thin. 3. sluggish. 4. not strict (as an officer).

ढीलापन m. act or state of looseness/sluggishness.

ढुँढ़वाना vt. to cause to be searched out.

ढुँढिराज m. Lord Ganesh.

ढुलकना vi. 1. to roll down. 2. to be inclined (towards someone).

ढुलकाना vt. causative of ढुलकना।

ढुलना vi. 1. to be moved/carried (to some other place). 2. = ढुलकना।

ढुलमुल adj. unsteady, not firm.

ढुलवाना vt. = ढुलाना।

ढुलाई f. act or state of carrying goods (luggage, load etc.) or charges paid therefor.

ढुलाना vt. to cause to be mov-ed/carried.

ढूँढ़ना vt. to search/investigate.

ढूह m. mould.

ढेंकली f. 1. appliance for pounding corn. 2. appliance for drawing water.

ढेंका m. = ढेंकली।

ढेर m. 1. heap, pile, bulk. 2. accumulation.

ढेरी f. small pile.

ढेरों adv. in heaps, in a huge quantity. adj. a lot of.

ढेला m. 1. lump/clod of earth. 2. piece of brick, stone etc.

ढैया m. 1. a weight of 2½ seers (roughly 2 1/3 kg.). 2. the number 2½ times a given natural number.

ढोंग m. (act of) hypocrisy, dissemblance, dissimulation.

ढोंगी adj. hypocritical, crafty, deceitful.

ढोना vt. 1. to carry on one's body. 2. to carry/transport. 3. (somehow) to pull on/carry on.

ढोर m. cattle.

ढोल m. drum, kettledrum.

ढोलक f. small drum.

ढोलकी f. = ढोलक।

ढोला m. 1. a kind of worm found in rotten articles. 2. mark of demarcation. 3. a kind of song (sung in marriages).

ढोली f. a pile, collection of 200 betel leaves.

ढौंचा m. a number 4½ times a given natural number.

ञ

ञ m. the nasal consonant of the cerebral pentad of the Nagari alphabet; its sound resembles that of rn in burnt.

त

त m. first consonant of the dental pentad of the Nagari alphabet; its sound resembles that of t in french matron.

तंग adj. 1. narrow. 2. tight. 3. harried, distressed. 4. short of, wanting.

तंगदिल adj. 1. miserly, close-fisted. 2. small-hearted.

तंगहाल adj. hard up, tight.

तंगी f. want.

तंज़ेब f. a type of muslin.

तंडुल m. rice.

तंतु m. 1. fibre, thread. 2. filament. 3. tissue.

तंतुवाद्य m. stringed instrument.

तंत्र m. 1. system. 2. machinery.

तंत्रशास्त्र m. occult science of charms and incantations.

तंत्रवाय m. weaver.

तंत्रिका f. nerve.

तंत्री m. one who plays on a stringed instrument.

तंदुरुस्त adj. 1. having a good health, healthy, hale and hearty. 2. stout.

तंदुरुस्ती f. 1. health. 2. heal-thiness.

तंदूर m. Indian oven.

तंदूरी adj. baked in a tandoor.

तंद्रा f. 1. sleepiness, dormancy. 2. lethargy.

तंद्रालु adj. 1. sleepy, drowsy. 2. lethargic.

तंबा m. kind of loose trousers.

तंबाकू m. tobacco.

तंबीह f. 1. advice, instruction. 2. admonition, reproof.

तंबू m. tent.

तंबूरा m. Indian type of guitar.

तँबोली m. betel-leaf seller. [Fem. तँबोलिन]

तईं post. for.

तक adv. 1. to, upto, until. 2. as far as, to. 3. even.

तक़दीर f. fate, lot, luck.

तकना vt. 1. to see/look. 2. to wait or wait for.

तकनीक f. technique.

त

तकनीकी adj. technical.

तकमा m. medal.

तकरार f. quarrel, wrangle.

तक़रीबन adv. almost, about, approximately.

तक़रीर f. speech, lecture.

तकला m. spindle.

तकली f. small spindle.

तकलीफ़ f. 1. trouble. 2. hardship, difficulty. 3. dearth.

तकल्लुफ़ m. formal procedure, formality.

तक़सीम f. division (maths.).

तक़ाज़ा f. 1. very strong request. 2. demand(s).

तक़ावी f. advance given to peasants.

तकिया m. 1. pillow, cushion. 2. support. 3. abode of a mendicant, shelter.

तकिया-कलाम m. an irrelevant word/phrase used habitually (by someone), prop word.

तकुआ m. spindle, distaff.

तक्र m. buttermilk.

तक्षण m. act of sculpting wood, stone etc.

तख़्त m. 1. plank. 2. throne.

तख़्तपोश m. bed-spread.

तख़्ता m. 1. plank. 2. board.

तख़्ती f. small plank/board.

तगड़ा adj. 1. strong, powerful. 2. sturdy, hard-built.

तग़मा m. medal.

तगादा m. तक़ाज़ा।

तगार m. reservoir of water used for watering bricks, preparing mortar etc.

तजना vt. to abandon/give up.

तजर्बा m. 1. experience. 2. experiment.

तजवीज़ f. 1. plan. 2. proposal.

तजुरबा m. = तजर्बा।

तट m. bank, shore, coast.

तटबंध m. embankment.

तटरक्षक m. coastguard.

तटवर्ती adj. situated on a bank/coast, coastal, littoral.

तटस्थ adj. 1. (lit). situated on a bank/coast. 2. neutral.

तटस्थता f. neutrality, nonalignment.

तटीय adj. of or pertaining to a bank/coast.

तड़कना vi. 1. to crack. 2. = छौंकना।

तड़क-भड़क f. 1. pomp and show. 2. pompousness, ostentation.

तड़का m. 1. dawn, daybreak. 2. seasoning (with spices).

तड़के adv. early in the morning.

तड़तड़ाना vi. to split/break with a cracking noise.

तड़तड़ाहट f. 1. act or state of तड़तड़ाना। 2. noise made thereby.

तड़प f. 1. agonizing pain. 2. pining. 3. instantaneous reaction. 4. glittering splendour.

तड़पना vi. 1. to feel agonizing pain, to writhe in pain. 2. to pine for. 3. to react instantaneously (of infuriated beasts).

तड़पाना vt. to cause writhing pain.

तड़फड़ाना vi. = छटपटाना।

तड़ाक f. snap, cracking sound. adv. 1. instantly. 2. successively.

तड़ाका m. cracking noise made

by something splitting/breaking, loud report.

तड़ाग m. pond, tank.

तड़ातड़ adv. in quick succession.

तड़ित f. lightning.

तड़ी f. 1. slap. 2. dodge.

ततैया f. wasp.

तत्काल ind. immediately, instantaneously, on the spur of the moment.

तत्कालीन adj. contemporary.

तत्क्षण adv. 1. at once, immediately. 2. instantly.

तत्त्व m. 1. element, substance. 2. factor. 3. truth, reality.

तत्त्वज्ञान m. 1. knowledge of reality, metaphysical knowledge. 2. philosophy.

तत्त्वज्ञानी m. 1. seer of the ultimate truth, metaphysician. 2. philosopher.

तत्त्वतः adv. substantially.

तत्त्व-मीमांसा f. metaphysics.

तत्त्वहीन adj. hollow, unsubstantial.

तत्त्वावधान m. auspices.

तत्पर adj. prepared and ready.

तत्परता f. 1. act/state/quality of readiness, preparedness. 2. application (to work).

तत्पश्चात, तत्पश्चात् adv. after-wards, thereafter.

तत्पुरुष m. 1. God. 2. a kind of compound in Sanskrit Grammar.

तत्रभवान m. His/Her Majesty.

तत्संबंधी adj. concerned.

तत्सम m. 1. same as that. 2. a word borrowed from another language without any alteration as मंत्र from Sanskrit.

तथा conj. 1. and. 2. so.

तथाकथित adj. so-called.

तथागत m. Lord Buddha.

तथापि conj. yet, even then, still.

तथास्तु interj. amen, so be it !

तथैव adv. similarly.

तथ्य m. 1. fact. 2. data. 3. reality, truth. 4. substance.

तथ्यतः adv. de facto, in fact, factually.

तदनंतर adv. thereafter, after- that, thereupon.

तदनुरूप adj. alike, similar (in form, shape etc.) (to), according (to).

तदनुसार adv. accordingly, according to that.

तदपि adv. nevertheless, even then, still.

तदबीर f. way, device, means, plan.

तदर्थ m. ad hoc.

तदाकार adj. 1. similar. 2. engrossed.

तदुपरांत adv. afterwards, thereafter, therupon.

तद्धित m. 1. secondary derivatives in Grammar. 2. suffixes which form such derivatives.

तद्‌भव adj. born of that. m. a word of some other language accepted in a modified form, as लालटेन from (English) 'lantern'.

तद्रूप adj. 1. alike, similar. 2. identical.

तद्वत् adj. alike, similar (to that etc.)1

त

तन m. body.

तनख़्वाह f. pay, salary.

तनना vi. to be stretched.

तनय m. son.

तनया f. daughter.

तनवाना vt. to cause to be stretched.

तनहा adj. single, alone, solitary.

तनहाई f. loneliness, solitude.

तना m. stem, trunk.

तनातनी f. 1. tension, tenseness. 2. strained relationship.

तनाव m. 1. state or quality of being stretched, tenseness. 2. tension.

तनावग्रस्त adj. strained, worried, tense.

तनावपूर्ण adj. tense.

तनिक adj. a little, slight.

तनिया f. = तनी।

तनी f. string for tying garments etc. adj. = तनिक।

तनु adj. lean and thin. m. body.

तनूकरण m. dilution.

तन्मय adj. absorbed, engrossed.

तन्मयता f. absorption, concentration.

तन्य adj. ductile, elastic.

तन्यता f. ductility, elasticity.

तन्वंगी f. = तन्वी।

तन्वी fem. a slender woman, sylph.

तप m. 1. austerity, practice of austerity. 2. penance. 3. fire. 4. heat. 5. summer season. 6. fever.

तपकना vi. to throb/palpitate/pulsate.

तपन f. 1. heat. 2. burning sensation.

तपना vi. 1. to be heated. 2. to shine out.

तपवाना vt. to cause to be heated.

तपश्चर्या f. practice of austerity, asceticism.

तपसी m. = तपस्वी।

तपस्या f. penance, austerities, self-mortification.

तपस्विनी f. fem. of तपस्वी।

तपस्वी m. ascetic, hermit.

तपाक m. ~ से with enthusiasm and promptitude.

तपा-तपाया adj. tried and seasoned.

तपाना vi. 1. to heat. 2. to inflict suffering on one's body (to gain spiritual ends).

तपित adj. heated, hot.

तपिश f. heat.

तपेदिक f. tuberculosis.

तपोधन m. austerity person- ified, a great ascetic.

तपोनिधि m. a great ascetic.

तपोनिष्ठ adj. engrossed in austerities.

तपोबल m. prowess attained by austerity, power (esp. spiritual).

तपोमय adj. ascetical.

तपोमूर्ति m. austerity person- ified, a great ascetic.

तपोवन m. forest sanctified by austerities.

तप्त adj. 1. heated. 2. flushed with rage.

तफ़तीश f. probe.

तफ़रीह f. amusement, merriment, recreation.

तफ़सील f. particulars, details.

तब adv. 1. then. 2. at that time. 3. therefore, for this reason.

तबक़ा m. 1. large piece of land. 2. layer. 3. any class of men.

तबदील adj. 1. (object) altered or changed. 2. (person) transferred.

तबदीली f. 1. change, alteration. 2. transfer.

तबल m. large drum.

तबलची m. one who plays on a tambourine, a Tabla-player.

तबला m. a two piece drum.

तबलावादक m. tabla player.

तबादला m. transfer.

तबाह adj. ruined, destroyed.

तबाही f. ruination, havoc, mayhem.

तबीयत f. 1. mood. 2. condition.

तबेला m. stable.

तभी m. 1. at that time, right then. 2. only if.

तमंचा m. revolver.

तम m. darkness.

तमक f. act or state of तमकना।

तमकना vi. 1. to be enraged. 2. (face) to be reddened with anger.

तमग़ा m. medal.

तमचर m. demon.

तमतमाना vi. to become red due to anger, sun etc.

तमतमाहट f. reddening (of the face) due to heat/rage.

तमन्ना f. aspiration

तमस m. darkness.

तमाकू m. tobacco.

तमाखू m. = तमाकू।

तमाचा m. slap.

तमाम adj. entire, whole, all.

तमाल m. an Indian tree.

तमाशबीन m. 1. viewer, spectator, one who is fond of seeing shows. 2. womaniser.

तमाशा m. 1. show, display. 2. fun.

तमिल f. Tamil, a major South Indian language.

तमिलनाडु m. a South Indian state (former name Madras).

तमीचर m. demon.

तमीज़ f. 1. manners, etiquette. 2. power of discrimination.

तमोगुण m. last of the three qualitites of nature, the one relating to darkness/ignorance.

तमोगुणी adj. (one) in whom तमोगुण predominates.

तमोली m. betel-leaf seller.

तय्यार adj. = तैयार।

तरंग f. 1. wave, ripple. 2. rise and fall of voice in music. 3. fancy, impulse.

तरंगित adj. full of waves, rip-pling.

तरंगी adj. impulsive, emotional, fantastic.

तर adj. 1. wet. 2.juicy. 3 damp, moist. suffix. denoting comparative degree; उच्च ~ higher.

तरकस m. quiver.

तरकारी f. 1. vegetable. 2. vegetable preparation.

तरकीब f. 1. device, plan, trick. 2. tact.

तरक़्क़ी f. 1. increase, incre- ment. 2. promotion (in service, exam. etc.). 3. progress.

तरख़ान m. carpenter.

तरजना vt. 1. to censure/admo-nish. 2. to warn/threaten.

तरण m. 1. crossing over. 2. means of crossing over (as a boat). 3. deliverance, riddance.

तरणि m. Sun.

तरणी f. boat.

तरतराना vt. = तड़तड़ाना।

तरतीब f. arrangement, order.

तरनतारन m. 1. salvation, emancipation from worldly bondage. 2. The Almighty.

तरना vi. 1. to swim across. 2. to attain salvation.

तरनी f. boat.

तरफ़ f. 1. direction. 2. side.

तरफ़, की postposition. in the direction of, towards.

तरफ़दार adj. partial. m. supporter, partisan.

तरबतर adj. drenched, soaked.

तरबूज़ m. watermelon.

तरल adj. 1. fluid, liquid. 2. watery.

तरलता f. fluidity, liquidity.

तरवन m. an ornament of the ears.

तरवर m. tree.

तरस m. pity.

तरसना vi. to pine for.

तरसाना vt. to tantalize.

तरह f. 1. kind. 2. way. ~ देना to give latitude, to overlook, to pass over.

तरह, की postposition. as, like.

तरहदार adj. 1. elegant, graceful. 2. fashionable.

तराई f. 1. valley, marshy ground, meadow. 2. (act of) wetting, watering.

तराज़ू m. weighing scale, bala-nce; ~ का पलड़ा scale-pan.

तराना m. a kind of song.

तरावट f. 1. delightful coolness, freshness. 2. moisture, humidity.

तराशना vt. 1. to cut/pare. 2. to clip/trim. 3. to chisel.

तरी f. 1. delightful coolness. 2. freshness. 3. riverside land. 4. boat.

तरीक़ा m. 1. method, way, mode. 2. device. 3. custom, practice.

तरु m. tree.

तरुण adj. youthful, young, adult. m. youth.

तरुणाई f. youth.

तरुणी f. young woman.

तरेंदा m. buoy.

तरे adv. = तले।

तरेड़ f. crack, crevice.

तरेरना vt. 1. to stare angrily. 2. to look askance.

तरैला m. step-son.

तरोई f. an Indian green vege- table.

तरोताज़ा adj. refreshed.

तरौंछ f. sediment.

तरौना m. an ornament for the ears.

तर्क m. 1. argument. 2. logic, reasoning.

तर्कणा f. 1. discussion. 2. an argument.

तर्क-वितर्क m. argument and counter-argument.

तर्कसंगत adj. 1. logical. 2. rational, reasonable.

तर्कसिद्ध adj. proved by reasoning.

तर्कहीन adj. illogical.

तर्कित adj. (topic) argued about.

तर्क्य adj. arguable, debatable.

तर्ज़ f. 1. manner, method. 2. tune (music).

तर्जन m. 1. chiding, snubbing. 2. threat, warning.

तर्जना vt. 1. chide/snub. 2. to threat/warn.

तर्जनी f. forefinger.

तर्पण m. offering libation.

तर्पित adj. offered.

तल m. 1. surface, level. 2. bed. 3. lens.

तलक adv. = तक।

तलख़ adj. 1. bitter. 2. aggressive.

तलघरा m. basement.

तलछट f. sediment, dregs.

तलना vt. to fry.

तलपट m. balance sheet.

तलफ़ी f. 1. ruin, destruction. 2. loss. 3. infringement.

तलब f. 1. search. 2. necessity. 3. demand. 4. call. 5. salary, wages.

तलबी f. summons, call, order to appear.

तलवा m. 1. the bottom part of the foot, sole. 2. the bottom part of the shoe, sock etc.

तलवार f. sword.

तलहटी f. vale, valley.

तला m. 1. bottom. 2. sole of a shoe. 3. = तलवा।

तलाई f. 1. small pond. 2. act or state of frying or charges paid therefor.

तलाक़ m. the legal ending of a marriage, divorce.

तलातल m. one of the nether regions according to Hindu mythology.

तलाश f. search, quest, investigation.

तलाशना vt. to search/investigate.

तलाशी f. a search.

तली f. 1. bottom. 2. sediment

तले adv. immediately under, beneath, below; ~ ऊपर का (i) one after the other; (ii) upside down, topsy-turvy.

तलैया f. small pond.

तलौंछ f. sediment, dregs.

तल्ला m. 1. storey. 2. = तलवा।

तल्लीन adj. engrossed, absorbed.

तल्लीनता f. engrossment, absorption (mental), concentration.

तवर्ग m. (the letters). त, थ, द, ध, and न।

तवा m. 1. a circular iron plate used for cooking purposes, griddle, disc. 2. gramophone record.

तवायफ़ f. prostitute, harlot.

तवालत f. 1. elongation, lengthening. 2. botheration, entanglement.

तवी f. small disc.

तशरीफ़ f. ~ रखना—तशरीफ़ रखिए Please be seated. ~ लाना—तशरीफ़ लाइए Grace us with your presence, please. अपना ~ का टोकरा यहाँ से ले जाओ Walk out of here. (pej.)

त

तश्तरी f. plate, saucer.

तसदीक़ f. attestation, confirmation.

तसमा m. shoe-lace.

तसला m. big shallow pan.

तसल्ली f. 1. solace, consolation. 2. satisfaction.

तस्कर m. smuggler.

तस्करी f. smuggling.

तस्वीर f. 1. picture, painting. 2. photograph.

तह f. 1. layer, fold. 2. bottom. 3. bed.

तहक़ीक़ात f. probe, investiga- tion.

तहख़ाना m. basement, cellar.

तहज़ीब f. 1. civilisation. 2. mannerliness.

तहत m. के तहत working in the control of somebody, under.

तहमत m. loincloth.

तहरी f. a dish made of rice cooked with vegetables etc.

तहलका m. furore, turmoil.

तहस-नहस adj. ruined, destroyed, devastated.

तहसील f. 1. an administrative division of a district. 2. office of such a division.

तहसीलदार m. presiding officer of तहसील।

तहाँ adv. at that place, there only.

तहाना vi. to fold (up), to wrap.

ताँगा m. = टाँगा।

तांडव नृत्य m. violent dance (of Shiva).

ताँत f. 1. gut. 2. string, bowstring. 3. string of a musical instrument. 4. a weaver's appliance.

ताँता m. 1. chain, succession, train. 2. series.

तांत्रिक adj. pertaining to the Tantra Science/Art. m. one who practises the Tantra Art.

ताँबई adj. of the colour/hue of copper.

ताँबा m. copper.

ताँबिया m. big, shallow vessel of copper.

तांबूल m. betel-leaf.

ता suffix. to form abstract nouns from तत्सम adjectives as सुंदरता, मादकता।

ताई f. 1. slight fever. 2. fever accompanied by cold. 3. (fem. of ताऊ) aunt, wife of father's elder brother.

ताईद f. confirmation, support.

ताऊ m. uncle, father's elder brother; बछिया का ~ simpleton, stupid man.

ताऊन m. plague.

ताक f. look-out.

ताक़ m. niche, alcove.

ताक-झाँक f. act of snooping.

ताक़त f. strength, might, power, capacity.

ताक़तवर adj. strong, mighty, powerful.

ताकना vt. 1. to peep. 2. to snoop, stare. 3. to look to somebody to provide something.

ताकि conj. so that, in order that.

ताकीद f. enjoining, cautioning.

ताखा m. niche, alcove.

तागड़ी f. chain worn round the waist as an ornament.

तागना vt. 1. to stitch. 2. to sew in long stitches.

तागा m. thread.

ताज m. crown, diadem.

ताज़गी f. freshness.

ताजपोशी f. crowning, enth-ronement.

ताजमहल m. famous mausoleum of Agra built by the Mughal Emperor Shah Jehan in memory of his wife (Mumtaz Mahal).

ताज़ा adj. 1. newly made or pro-duced, fresh. 2. recently experienced, fresh. 3. cool, fresh.

ताज़िया m. model of the tomb of Imam Hussain carried in a procession by Muslims during the Muharram.

ताड़ m. 1. toddy tree. 2. a beating/ reprimand.

ताड़न m. 1. giving a blow. 2. upbraiding. 3. punishment. 4. admonition.

ताड़ना f. reprimand. vt. 1. to reprimand. 2. to guess.

ताड़पत्र m. leaf of a toddy tree.

ताड़ी f. toddy.

तात m. 1. father. 2. respectable person. 3. word of endearment for a close relation. adj. heated.

ताताथेई f. 1. timing with the feet in dance. 2. dance.

तात्कालिक adj. immediate, in-stantaneous.

तात्त्विक adj. substantial, elemental.

तात्पर्य m. 1. import, sum and substance. 2. meaning, significance, purport.

तादात्म्य m. identity, oneness.

तादाद f. number, count, quantity.

तादृश adj. similar, identical.

तान f. tune.

तानना vt. 1. to stretch as a string. 2. to erect as a tent.

तानपूरा m. = तंबूरा।

ताना m. 1. taunt, sarcasm. 2. warp.

ताना-बाना m. warp and woof.

तानाशाह m. dictator.

तानाशाही adj. dictatorial. f. dictatorship.

ताप f. 1. heat. 2. fever, warmth, grief.

तापचालक adj. & m. conductor of, or conducting heat.

तापन m. 1. act or state of heating. 2. sun.

तापना vi. to heat/warm one's body.

तापमान m. temperature.

ताप-लहरी f. heatwave.

तापविद्युत f. thermoelectricity.

तापस m. ascetic.

तापसी f. female ascetic.

तापित adj. 1. heated. 2. afflicted, troubled.

तापीय adj. thermal.

तापोपचार m. heat treatment.

ताब f. 1. heat, warmth. 2. gloss. 3. strength. 4. power of endurance.

ताबड़-तोड़ adv. in quick succ-ession, non-stop.

ताबूत m. coffin.

ताबेदार adj. subservient, servile.

ताबेदारी f. subservience, servil-ity.

तामचीनी f. enamel.

तामझाम m. 1. paraphernalia. 2. pomp and show.

तामड़ा adj. of the colour of copper. m. over-baked brick.

तामस adj. 1. dark. 2. = तामसी। m. ignorance.

तामसिक adj. = तामसी।

तामसी adj. pertaining to तमोगुण।

तामिस्र m. darkness of mind.

तामीर m. construction, building.

तामील f. 1. execution. 2. service.

ताम्र m. copper.

ताम्रपत्र m. plate made of copper.

ताया m. father's elder brother, uncle.

तार m. 1. wire, string. 2. telegram. 3. chain, series.

तारक m. 1. redeemer, saviour. 2. star. 3. asterisk.

तारकोल m. coal-tar, tarmac.

तारघर m. telegraph office.

तारजाली f. wire gauze.

तारण m. 1. crossing over. 2. getting over a difficulty. 3. redemption, deliverance from worldly worries, salvation.

तारतम्य m. sequence, continuity, order.

तारना vt. 1. to take across, to help cross over. 2. to deliver from worldly worries. 3. to exempt from future transmigration.

तारपीन m. turpentine.

तारांकित adj. starred.

तारा m. 1. star. 2. pupil (of the eye).

तारापथ m. path of a star, sky.

तारामंडल m. constellation.

तारिका f. 1. small star. 2. actress, film-actress.

तारित adj. redeemed, delivered.

तारीख़ f. date.

तारीफ़ f. 1. praise. 2. compliment. 3. definition.

तारुण्य m. youth, young age.

तार्किक adj. logical. m. logician.

ताल m. 1. palm of the hand. 2. clapping. 3. pool, pond, tank. f. (i) measure of time (Music), tune, rhythm; (ii) thigh.

तालबद्ध adj. rhythmic.

ताल-मेल m. cohesion, coordination, harmony, concord.

तालव्य adj. palatal.

ताला m. lock, padlock.

तालाबंदी f. lock-out.

तालाब m. tank, pond, pool.

तालिका f. 1. list. 2. inventory.

ताली f. 1. key. 2. clapping, applause.

तालीम f. education.

तालू m. palate.

ताल्लुक़ m. 1. relationship, connection. 2. illicit connection.

ताल्लुक़ा m. an area of land for a specific purpose, estate.

ताव m. 1. heat. 2. wrath, great anger. 3. sheet (of paper).

तावदार adj. 1. (person) impulsive. 2. (object) stiff and resplendent.

तावान m. penalty, compensation.

तावीज़ m. amulet, talisman.

ताश m. playing cards.

ताशा m. kettledrum.

तासीर f. effect, property (of some medicine, drug etc.).

तास्सुब m. fanaticism, bigotry.

ताहम adv. 1. yet, still. 2. even, in spite of this/that.

ताहरी f. = तहरी।

तिकड़म m. stratagem, trickery, knack.

तिकड़मबाज़ adj. & m. wily, manoeuvring, crafty, highly manipulative (person).

तिकड़मी adj. wily, crafty.

तिकड़ी f. trio, group of three.

तिकोना adj. triangular, three-cornered.

तिक्की f. three of cards.

तिक्त adj. pungent, acrid.

तिखारना vt. to urge pointedly.

तिगुना adj. triple, treble, thre- efold.

तिग्गी f. three of cards.

तिजरा m. intermittent fever, recurring every third day.

तिजारत f. trade, commerce.

तिजोरी f. safe, chest.

तिड़ी f. three of cards; ~ करना to purloin/pinch; ~ हो जाना to slip away, to flee.

तितर-बितर adj. helter-skelter, scattered, topsyturvy.

तितली f. 1. butterfly. 2. glamour girl, flirt, minx.

तितलौकी f. bitter gourd.

तितिक्षा f. endurance, fortitude.

तितिक्षु adj. 1. enduring. 2. forgiving.

तिथि f. date.

तिन pron. those. m. = तृण।

तिनकना vi. to flutter/flare up/throb.

तिनका m. straw.

तिनपहला adj. three-faced.

तिन्नी f. a kind of thin rice.

तिपाई f. tripod, tea-poy, three-legged stool.

तिबारा adv. (for the) third time. m. three-doored room.

तिब्बत m. Tibet.

तिमंज़िला adj. three-storeyed.

तिमाही adj. produced or occurring once every three months, quarterly. f. quarter (period of three months).

तिमिंगिल f. huge whale.

तिमिर m. darkness.

तिमिरारि m. the Sun.

तिमुहानी f. junction of three roads/ meeting place of three paths.

तिय f. 1. woman. 2. wife.

तिरंगा adj. tricoloured. m. Indian tricoloured flag, Tricolour.

तिरछा adj. slanting, oblique.

तिरछापन m. obliqueness, obliquity.

तिरछे adv. 1. in a state of obliquity. 2. crookedly.

तिरपट adj. 1. bent. 2. crooked.

तिरपाई f. = तिपाई।

तिरपाल m. tarpaulin, awning.

तिरसठ adj. & m. sixty-three, 63.

तिरस्कार m. 1. contempt, humiliation, disdain. 2. disregard.

तिरस्कृत adj. 1. humiliated, disdained. 2. disregarded.

तिरानबे adj. & m. ninety-three, 93.

तिरासी adj. & m. eighty-three, 83.

तिराहा m. junction of three paths/ roads.

तिरिया f. = त्रिया।

त

तिरेसठ adj. & m. = तिरसठ।

तिरोधान m. disappearance, vanishing.

तिरोभाव m. 1. disappearance, vanishing. 2. concealment.

तिरोभूत adj. 1. disappeared, vanished. 2. concealed, hidden.

तिरोहित adj. 1. disappeared, vanished. 2. concealed, hidden.

तिर्यक adj. 1. slanting. 2. (gram.) oblique.

तिलंगा m. 1. a soldier of the Indian army. 2. a kind of big kite.

तिलंगाना m. Telangana, a region in South India.

तिल m. 1. sesame. 2. mole (on skin).

तिलक m. 1. an ornamental mark on the forehead. 2. an ornament worn on the forehead. 3. outstanding person, almost unequalled. 4. a customary ceremony performed before marriage as a token of presettle-ment.

तिलकना vi. (clay) to crack on being dried.

तिलकुट m. a sweetmeat prepared of sesame seed and molasses/ sugar.

तिलचट्टा m. cockroach.

तिलचावली f. mixture of sesame seed and rice. adj. black and white.

तिलमिलाना vi. 1. to get wild with rage. 2. to be painfully restless. 3. to be dazzled.

तिलमिलाहट f. act or state of तिलमिलाना।

तिलहन m. oilseed.

तिलांजलि f. abandonment.

तिलिस्म m. 1. magical spell, enchantment. 2. a structure based on a spell, enchantment or subtle devices.

तिलिस्मी adj. 1. causing spell, magical. 2. talismanic.

तिलौटी f. a pudding made of sesame seed and urd pulse (horse-bean).

तिल्ला m. 1. gold or silver thread. 2. border made of such thread.

तिल्ली f. 1. spleen. 2. = तीली।

तिल्लेदार adj. having a border made of gold or silver thread.

तिस pron. that, which.

तिहत्तर adj. & m. seventy-three, 73.

तिहाई f. one-third.

तीक्ष्ण adj. 1. pungent. 2. sharp, severe. 3. piercing, incisive. 4. penetrating. 5. shrill, harsh. 6. acute. 7. keen.

तीक्ष्णता f. state or quality of being तीक्ष्ण।

तीखा adj. 1. sharp. 2. biting.

तीज f. third day of each half of the lunar month.

तीतर m. partridge.

तीता adj. 1. acrid. 2. bitter, pungent.

तीन adj. & m. three, 3.

तीमारदार m. an attendant (or a person attending) on a patient.

तीमारदारी f. nursing, atten- dance on a patient.

तीय f. woman.

तीरंदाज़ m. archer.

तीरंदाज़ी f. archery.

त

तीर m. 1. arrow. 2. bank.

तीर्थंकर m. title of the twenty-four preceptors of Jainism.

तीर्थ m. a sacred place of pilgrimage, a holy bathing place.

तीर्थयात्रा f. pilgrimage.

तीर्थाटन m. pilgrimage.

तीली f. 1. spoke (of a wheel etc.). 2. knitting needle. 3. thin rod. 4. matchstick.

तीव्र adj. 1. intense, terrible. 2. rapid. 3. sharp. 4. quick, brisk, energetic, nimble, violent.

तीव्रता f. 1. intensity. 2. sharpness. 3. keenness. 4. quickness, swiftness.

तीस adj. & m. thirty, 30.

तीसरा adj. 1. third. 2. other, unrelated, arbitrator.

तीसी f. linseed.

तुंग adj. lofty, high, tall.

तुंगता f. 1. height. 2. altitude. 3. eminence

तुंड m. 1. snout. 2. trunk (of an elephant).

तुंद m. belly, stomach.

तुंदिल adj. pot-bellied.

तुंबा m. 1. gourd. 2. scooped gourd used as a pot.

तुंबी f. dim. of तुंबा।

तुक f. 1. rhyme. 2. point.

तुकबंदी f. rhyming, versification. (pej.)

तुकांत adj. rhymed, having rhymes.

तुक्कड़ m. rhymster, rhymer. (pej.)

तुक्का m. 1. an arrow blunt at one end. 2. wild guess or venture.

तुच्छ adj. insignificant, mean, trifling, trivial, of little or no consequence, negligible.

तुच्छता f. insignificance, triviality.

तुझ pron. inflective form of तू (thou)—तुझको, तुझसे, तुझमें etc.

तुझे pron. (to) thee/you.

तुड़वाना vt. 1. to cause to break/ demolish. 2. to cause to pluck.

तुड़ाना vt. to break off.

तुतलाना vi. to lisp/stutter.

तुतलाहट f. lisping, stuttering.

तुनक-मिज़ाज adj. quick-temp- ered, petulant.

तुम pron. you.

तुमुल adj. tumultuous, uproarious. m. tumult of battle, uproar.

तुम्हारा pron. your, yours.

तुम्हीं pron. you alone, only you.

तुम्हें pron. 1. you. 2. to you.

तुरंग m. horse.

तुरंत adv. at once, immediately, forthwith, quickly.

तुरंती adj. urgent; ~ पत्र urgent letter.

तुरत adv. = तुरंत।

तुरपई f. = तुरपन।

तुरपन f. a kind of hand-stitching (with long stitches).

तुरपना vt. to stich with the hand (with long stitches).

तुरही f. clarion, trumpet, bugle.

तुरीय adj. fourth (stage).

तुरुप m. trump.

तुर्क m. Turk.

तुर्किन f. Turkish woman.

तुर्की adj. of Turkey; ~ ब ~ जवाब देना to give smashing retorts.

f. 1. Turkey. 2. Turkish language.

तुर्रा m. 1. crest, lock of curly hair. 2. ornamental tassel worn on a turban. 3. peculiarity, peculiar incongruity (fig.).

तुलना f. comparison. vi. 1. to be weighed. 2. to be balanced. 3. to be bent upon (to quarrel, fight etc.).

तुलनात्मक adj. involving comparison, comparative.

तुलनीय adj. suitable to be compared with, comparable.

तुलवाना vt. to cause to be weighed.

तुलसी f. basil.

तुला f. 1. scales, balance. 2. Libra, the seventh sign of the zodiac.

तुलाई f. 1. act or state of weighing or wages paid for the same. 2. light quilt.

तुलादंड m. beam of a balance.

तुलादान m. gift of metal or grain equivalent to one's weight.

तुल्य adj. equivalent, equal.

तुल्यता f. equivalence.

तुषार adj. frost, mist.

तुष्ट adj. 1. contented, satisfied. 2. appeased, pleased. 3. gratified.

तुष्टि f. 1. contentment, satisfaction. 2. appea-sement, gratification.

तुष्टीकरण m. appeasement.

तुहिन m. 1. frost. 2. snow. 3. mist.

तूँबा m. 1. bitter gourd. 2. hollowed out and dried bitter gourd used as a bowl.

तूँबी f. small तूँबा।

तू pron. thou.

तूणीर m. quiver.

तूतिया m. blue vitriol, copper sulphate.

तूती f. 1. a kind of small singing bird. 2. a kind of small musical pipe.

तूफ़ान m. storm, typhoon, hurricane.

तूफ़ानी adj. stormy, tempestuous.

तूमड़ी f. hollowed out gourd used by snake-charmers as a musical pipe.

तूमतड़ाक f. 1. pomp and show. 2. coquetry. 3. gaudiness, fashion.

तूमना vt. 1. to card (cotton). 2. to reduce to shreds by piecing cotton. 3. to rub down with fingers. 4. to disclose (a secret) completely.

तूर m. large drum.

तूर्य m. tabor, timbrel.

तूल m. prolongation.

तूलिका f. painter's brush.

तूली f. painter's brush.

तूस m. 1. husk. 2. a kind of fine wool. 3. blanket made of the same.

तृण m. blade of grass, straw.

तृणमय adj. grassy, made of straw.

तृणवत् adj. 1. like grass. 2. insignificant, trivial.

तृतीय adj. third.

तृतीया f. third day of each half of a lunar month.

तृप्त adj. satisfied, contented.

तृप्ति f. satisfaction, contentment.

तृषा f. thirst.

तृषित adj. thirsty.

तृष्णा f. 1. thirst. 2. greed, long- ing, craving.

तेंतालीस adj. & m. forty-three, 43.

तेंतीस adj. & m. thirty-three, 33.

तेंदुआ m. leopard.

तेईस adj. twenty-three, 23.

तेग़ f. sword, cutlass.

तेज m. 1. lustre, effulgence, glow. 2.verve, enthusiasm.

तेज़ adj. 1. sharp, sharp-edged. 2. piercing, penetrating. 3. loud. 4. fast. 5. violent, hard. 6. bright. adv. 1. heavily. 2. rapidly.

तेज़-तर्रार adj. 1. sharp and short-tempered. 2. fast-paced.

तेजपत्र m. = तेजपात।

तेजपात m. bay leaf.

तेजस्विता f. 1. glory, radiance, lustre. 2. stateliness.

तेजस्विनी f. fem. of तेजस्वी।

तेजस्वी adj. 1. glorious, radi- ant, lustrous. 2. stately.

तेज़ाब m. acid.

तेज़ी f. 1. sharpness. 2. quickness, swiftness. 3. intensity. 4. pungency. 5. dearness.

तेजोमय adj. brilliant, glorious, effulgent.

तेरस f. thirteenth day of each half of a lunar month.

तेरह adj. & m. thirteen, 13.

तेरहीं f. 1. thirteenth day after death. 2. rituals performed on the above day.

तेरा pron. & m. thy, thine.

तेल m. oil.

तेलकूप m. oil well.

तेलहन m. oilseed (s).

तेलहा adj. 1. oiled. 2. pertaining to oil. 3. (seed) containing oil.

तेलिन f. 1. wife of an oilman. 2. female oil-seller.

तेलिया adj. 1. oily. 2. pertaining to oil. 3. containing oil. 4. of a light dark oily colour.

तेली m. oilman, oil-seller.

तेलुगु f. Telegu, the language of Andhra region in South India. m. inhabitant of the region.

तेवर m. 1. eyebrow. 2. scowl.

तेहरा adj. 1. threefold. 2. triplicate.

तेहराना vt. 1. to triplicate. 2. to do a thing thrice, or for the third time.

तेहा m. 1. anger, wrath. 2. pride, vainglory. 3. vehemence.

तैंतालीस adj. & m. = तेंतालीस।

तैंतीस adj. & m. = तेंतीस।

तै adj. settled, decided; (दूरी) ~ करना to cover/traverse (distance).

तैनात adj. 1. appointed. 2. engaged. 3. posting (on guard).

तैनाती f. 1. appointment. 2. engagement. 3. posting (on guard).

तैयार adj. 1. ready. 2. prepared, in a state of preparedness. 3. ripened.

तैयारी f. 1. preparation. 2. preparedness, readiness.

तैरना vi. 1. to swim. 2. to float.

तैराक m. swimmer.

तैराना vt. to cause to swim/float.

त

तैलंगाना m. = तिलंगाना।
तैल adj. pertaining to oil. m. = तेल।
तैलचित्र m. oil painting.
तैलरंग m. oil colour.
तैश m. wrath, anger.
तैसा adj. similar, akin, like that.
तैसे adv. in a similar or same way.
तोंद f. tummy, pot-belly.
तोंदल adj. pot-bellied.
तो conj. then.
तोड़ f. 1. onslaught as of water or wind. 2. antidote. 3. encounter.
तोड़-जोड़ m. stratagem, device.
तोड़ना vt. 1. to break (stone, glass etc.). 2. to pluck (flowers, fruit etc.). 3. to damage (watch, machine etc.). 4. to violate (a law, principle, oath etc.). 5. to cancel (an office, post etc.). 6. to break off.
तोड़-फोड़ m. secretly carried-out damage to buildings, machines etc., sabotage.
तोड़-मरोड़ m. perversion, distortion, mutilation.
तोड़ा m. 1. scarcity, dearth. 2. a kind of bangle. 3. a bag containing a thousand rupees.
तोतला adj. lisping. m. lisper.
तोतलाना vi. = तुतलाना।
तोता m. parrot.
तोतेचश्म adj. faceless.
तोप f. cannon, gun.
तोपख़ाना m. artillery.
तोपगाड़ी f. gun-carriage.
तोपची m. gunner.
तोपना vt. 1. to cover (vessel, plate etc.). 2. to cover up (pit, cavity etc.), to bury.
तोफ़ा m. = तोहफ़ा।
तोबड़ा m. nose-bag.
तोबा f. vow to desist from doing something again.
तोय m. water.
तोरण m. festoon, arch.
तोल f. weight.
तोलना vt. to weigh.
तोला m. an Indian measure of weight equal to about 11.7 gms.
तोश f. mattress.
तोशक f. cushioned mattress.
तोष m. 1. satisfaction, contentment. 2. appe-asement, gratification.
तोहफ़ा m. present, gift.
तोहमत f. false accusation, charge.
तौक़ f. neck-ring.
तौबा f. = तोबा।
तौर m. way, manner.
तौलिया m. towel.
तौहीन f. contempt, insult, disrespect.
त्यक्त adj. 1. abandoned, forsaken. 2. abnegated, rejected.
त्यजन m. abandoning, forsaking, abnegation.
त्याग m. 1. abandonment, relinquishment. 2. abne-gation, sacrifice.
त्यागना vt. 1. to abandon/desert/relinquish. 2. to break off relationship.
त्यागपत्र m. (letter of) resignation.
त्यागी m. 1. one who sacrifices/

relinquishes/ renounces. 2. recluse.

त्याज्य adj. renounceable, worth relinquishing, fit to be given up.

त्यों adv. like that.

त्योरी f. angry look, frown.

त्योहार m. festival.

त्योहारी f. tip given on a festival.

त्रय adj. & m. 1. triad. 2. third. 3. all three. 4. the number 'three', 3.

त्रयी f. group of three.

त्रयोदशी f. thirteenth day of each half of a lunar month.

त्रस्त adj. 1. frightened, terror-struck, terrified. 2. tormented.

त्राण m. 1. shelter, protection.

त्राता m. protector, defender, redeemer, saviour.

त्रास m. dread, fear, terror.

त्रासदी f. 1. a terrible event that causes great sadness. 2. a play with sad ending, tragedy.

त्रासदीय adj. pertaining to a tragedy.

त्राहि interj. help ! help ! save !

त्रिक adj. three. m. trio.

त्रिकाल m. 1. all three times : past, present and future. 2. all three times: morning, noon and evening.

त्रिकालज्ञ m. the Omniscient God, the knower of the events of all times.

त्रिकालदर्शी m. seer.

त्रिकोण m. triangle.

त्रिकोणमिति f. Trigonometry.

त्रिगुण m. the three principal qualities of human nature : सत्त्व, रज, तम। adj. three times, three-fold.

त्रिगुणात्मक adj. possessing the three qualities.

त्रिगुणित adj. multiplied by three.

त्रिज्या f. radius.

त्रिदंड m. a staff which is an insignia of a hermit/recluse.

त्रिदंडी m. recluse.

त्रिदोष m. the three humours of the body : वात, पित्त, कफ़।

त्रिनेत्र m. (lit.) having three eyes, Lord Shiv.

त्रिपक्षीय adj. tripartite.

त्रिपथगा f. river Ganga.

त्रिपिटक m. a religious book of Buddhism containing the teachings of Lord Buddha.

त्रिपुंड m. a mark of three horiz- ontal lines made on the forehead.

त्रिपुरारि m. Lord Shiv.

त्रिभुज m. triangle.

त्रिभुवन m. the three worlds: स्वर्ग (Heaven), पृथ्वी (Earth), पाताल (Underworld).

त्रिया f. woman.

त्रिलोक m. the three worlds.

त्रिलोकीनाथ m. God, the Lord of the three worlds.

त्रिशूल m. 1. the trident of Lord Shiv. 2. a top or crest of the Himalayas.

त्रिस्तरीय adj. 1. having three stages. 2. having three strands or layers.

त्रुटि f. defect, deficiency, fault, error, flaw.

त्रुटिपूर्ण adj. defective, imperfect.

त

त्रुटिहीन adj. faultless, impeccable.

त्रेता m. second yug (era) of Hindu mythology.

त्रैमासिक adj. quarterly, three-monthly. m. a magazine published four times a year.

त्वचा f. skin.

त्वदीय pron. your, yours, thine.

त्वरण m. acceleration.

त्वरा f. quickness, nimbness.

त्वरित adj. accelerated, speedy.

थ m. second of the dental pentad of consonants of the Nagari alphabet; its sound resembles that of th in thin.

थंब m. 1. pillar. 2. prop, support.

थकना vi. be fatigued/tired/weary.

थकान f. = थकावट।

थकाना vt. to cause to be tired, to tire out, to exhaust.

थका-माँदा adj. weary and exhausted.

थकार m. the letter थ or its sound.

थकावट f. fatigue, weariness, exhaustion.

थकित adj. fatigued, tired.

थक्का m. 1. lump. 2. clot.

थन m. udder, nipple.

थनैत m. 1. headman of a village. 2. landlord's agent who collects rents for him.

थपक f. pat/tap.

थपकना vt. to pat/tap.

थपकी f. a pat.

थपथपाना vt. to pat gently (with the palm).

थपेड़ा m. blow given with the hand, buffet.

थप्पड़ m. slap.

थमना vi. 1. to stop/cease/stay. 2. to rest (on), to be supported (by).

थमाना vt. 1. to make one hold. 2. to hand over.

थर m. 1. layer. 2. den; बाघ का ~ tiger's den.

थरथर adv. shuddering, trembling.

थरथराना vi. to tremble /shudder.

थरथराहट f. trembling/shuddering/shivering.

थर्राना vi. = थरथराना।

थल m. 1. place. 2. land.

थलकना vi. (outer skin) to loosen.

थलचर m. land animal.

थल-सेना f. = स्थल-सेना।

थलीय adj. pertaining to land.

थवई f. mason.

थाँग f. place where thieves hide.

था vi. was, wast.

थाक m. pile.

थाती f. 1. something inherited, heritage. 2. all one's belongings, entire (movable) property. 3. something accepted as a responsibility or kept on trust.

थान m. 1. place, abode, residence. 2. pound (of cattle). 3. family, breed. 4. full length of cloth.

थाना m. police station.

थाप f. a light hit with an open hand, clap.

थापना vt. 1. to instal (a deity). 2. to imprint an impression of the palm.

थापा m. 1. impression of the palm of hand. 2. mould as that of a brick. 3. heap. 4. subscription given for worship.

थापी f. 1. flat mallet used by masons and potters. 2. patting

थ

on the back for encouragement.

थामना vt. 1. to hold, as a stick. 2. to catch, as a ball. 3. to support, as a roof. 4. to restrain/arrest, as high prices. 5. to stop, as a carriage.

थाल m. big flat metallic dish.

थाली f. flat metallic dish.

थाह f. depth.

थाहना vi. 1. to estimate the depth (of). 2. to probe into the depth (of).

थिएटर m. theatre.

थिगली f. patch stitched on clo-thes to cover holes.

थिर adj. 1. still, tranquil. 2. sta-ble, fixed.

थिरक f. gliding dance.

थिरकना vi. to dance lightly, to glide.

थिरता f. = स्थिरता।

थी vi. was. [fem. of था]

थुक्का-फ़ज़ीहत f. 1.scurrilous wrangling. 2. censure and calumny.

थुथकार f. calumny, public censure.

थुथना m. snout.

थुलथुल adj. flabby, corpulent.

थू interj. word of contempt/disdain, shame !

थूक m. spittle, sputum.

थूकना vi. to spit.

थूथन m. snout of an animal.

थूनी f. prop, support.

थैला m. bag, sack.

थैली f. small bag, pouch.

थोक adj. & m. wholesale, bulk.

थोक विक्रेता m. wholesaler.

थोड़ा adj. 1. little, not much, some, meagre, slight. 2. less, too little. 3. not many.

थोथा adj. 1. hollow. 2. worthless, insubstantial.

थोपना vt. 1. to plaster (roughly), as mud on a wall. 2. to throw the responsibility (on someone). 3. to impose or inflict.

थोबड़ा m. 1. snout. 2. a person's nose.

द

द (da) m. third of the dental pentad of consonants of the Nagari alphabet; its sound resembles that of th in the.

दंग adj. amazed, surprised, astonished.

दंगई adj. rowdy, turbulent, rio-tous. m. rioter.

दंगल m. 1. wrestling tournament.

दंगा m. riot, disturbance.

दंगाई adj. & m. = दंगई।

दंगाग्रस्त adj. violence-torn.

दंड m. 1. staff, rod, stick. 2. pu-nishment, fine, penalty. 3. a kind of (Indian) physical exercise.

दंडनीय adj. punishable, culpable.

दंडपाणि m. 1. one who maintains law and order. 2. Yama, the God of death.

दंडवत m. prostration, bowing reverential salutation.

दंड-संहिता f. penal code.

दंडात्मक adj. pertaining to punishment, punitive, penal.

दंडित adj. punished, penalized.

दंडी m. 1. one equipped with a staff. 2. an ascetic who always keeps a staff. 3. doorkeeper. 4. king.

दंड्य adj. = दंडनीय।

दंत m. tooth.

दंतकथा f. legend, hearsay.

दँतखोदनी f. toothpick.

दंत-चिकित्सक m. dentist.

दंत-चिकित्सा f. dentistry.

दंत-पीड़ा f. toothache.

दंत-विहीन adj. toothless.

दंती f. elephant.

दंतोष्ठ्य adj. dentilabial.

दंत्य adj. dental.

दंपति m. = दंपती

दंपती f. husband and wife.

दंभ m. vanity, conceit.

दंभी adj. vain, conceited.

दंश m. 1. sting. 2. spite. 3. bite.

दंशन m. 1. stinging. 2. biting.

दई m. destiny.

दकार m. the letter द or its sound.

दक़ियानूस adj. & m. obscu-rantist, old-fashioned, conservative.

दक़ियानूसी adj. & f. 1. = दक़ियानूस। 2. old-fashioned, age-old (custom, practice etc.).

दक्खिन m. South.

दक्ष adj. 1. adept, dexterous, adroit. 2. efficient, expert, skilful.

दक्षता f. 1. dexterity, adroitness. 2. efficiency, expertness.

दक्षिण m. 1. South. 2. right.

दक्षिण-पंथ m. right-wing. (Pol.)

दक्षिणा f. honorarium paid to a preceptor or priest.

दक्षिणायन m. heading of sun towards the tropic of capricorn.

दक्षिणावर्त adj. & adv. clockwise.

दक्षिणी adj. Southern.

दख़ल m. 1. occupation. 2. meddling, interference.

दख़लकार m. occupant.

द

दग़ना vi. 1. to be fired. 2. to be branded.

दग़वाना vt. cansative of दाग़ना।

दग़ा f. treachery, deception cheating.

दग़ेबाज़ adj. treacherous, deceitful. m. cheat, traitor.

दग़ैल adj. blemished, tainted, sullied (person or character).

दग्ध adj. burnt, scorched.

दचक f. jolt, jerk, bump.

दचकना m. to jolt/jerk (as a vehicle in motion).

दढ़ियल adj. bearded.

दतुअन, दतुवन f. = दातुन।

दत्त adj. given, donated, paid, presented.

दत्तक adj. adopted.

दत्तचित्त adj. concentrated, fully attentive (to some work).

ददिहाल m. family of paternal grandfather or his residence.

ददोड़ा, ददोरा m. swelling, bump.

दद्रु m. ringworm.

दधि m. curd, yoghurt.

दनदनाना vi. 1. to start produ-cing noise suddenly and continuously (said of guns and cannons). 2. to make merry.

दनादन adv. 1. with the sound of a cannonade. 2. in quick succession, incessantly.

दनुज m. demon.

दपटना vt. = डपटना।

दफ़न m. burial.

दफ़नाना vt. 1. to place a dead body into a grave, to bury. 2. to forget something completely.

दफ़ा f. 1. time. 2. section. adj. gone away.

दफ़्तर m. office.

दफ़्तरशाही f. bureaucracy.

दफ़्तरी m. book-binder, daftaree.

दफ़्ती f. card-board.

दबंग adj. bold, fearless, undaunted, strong-headed.

दबकना vi. = दुबकना।

दबदबा m. awe, overwhelming influence, dignity, sway, grandeur.

दबना vi. 1. to be pressed, as under a stone. 2. to be crushed/trampled as by a crowd. 3. to be over-awed/subdued as by a superior person. 4. to be lessened, as the incidence of an epidemic.

दबवाना vt. causative of दबाना।

दबाना vt. 1. to press down. 2.to suppress/repress/subdue.

दबाव m. 1. pressure. 2. coercion, duress.

दबैल adj. under influence/control/subjection.

दबोचना vt. 1. to seize suddenly. 2. to hide/conceal.

दब्बू adj. meek.

दम m. 1. breath. 2. instant, moment.

दमक f. glimmer, glitter, bri-lliance, glow.

दमकना vi. to glimmer/glitter/glow/shine.

दमकल f. 1. water-pump. 2. fire-brigade.

दमकला m. oven (in which coal is used).

दमख़म m. 1. strength, prowess. 2. staying power, stamina. 3. firmness. 4. sharpness (of the edge of a sword).

दमचूल्हा m. = दमकला।

दमड़ी f. mite, one-eighth of a pice (old Indian currency).

दमदमा m. bunker.

दमदार adj. 1. virile, powerful. 2. firm, strong. 3. stout.

दम-दिलासा m. 1. encourage-ment. 2. consolation.

दमन m. oppression, suppression, repression.

दमनकारी adj. oppressive, suppressive, repressive.

दमनशील adj. suppressive, repressive, coercive.

दमनीय adj. suppressible, repressible, tamable.

दमसाज़ m. pal, faithful friend.

दमा m. an illness which causes difficulty in breathing, asthma.

दमाद m. = दामाद।

दमादम adv. in quick succession.

दमित adj. 1. suppressed. 2. oppressed (person), pressuri-sed.

दम्य adj. = दमनीय।

दयनीय adj. pitiable, miserable, wretched.

दया f. mercy, pity.

दया-दृष्टि f. attitude of kind-ness/ favour.

दयानत f. honesty, fair-minded-ness.

दयानिधान m. (lit. store of kindness). 1. a very good person/ benefactor. 2. God.

दयापात्र m. object of pity/ favour.

दयामय adj. full of compassion, compassionate, merciful, benevolent.

दयालु adj. humane, kind, compassionate, kind-hearted, magnanimous.

दयालुता f. benignity, kind-heartedness, graciousness.

दयावान्, दयावान adj. kind, compassionate, tender-hearted.

दयासागर adj. & m. (ocean of kindness) extremely kind-hearted/noble.

दर f. rate.
m. door.

दरकना vi. to crack, to be split.

दरकार f. need, necessity.

दरकिनार adv. let alone.

दरख़ास्त f. 1. application.

दरख़्त m. tree.

दरगाह f. 1. doorsill, threshold. 2. tomb, place of worship.

दरज f. crack, cleft, fissure.

दरजन m. dozen.

दरजा m. 1. rank, standard. 2. class.

दरज़िन f. 1. female tailor. 2. wife of a tailor.

दरज़ी m. tailor.

दरद m. = दर्द।

दरदरा adj. half-grounded, coarse.

दरदराना vt. to grind coarsely.

दरदीला adj. 1. compassionate. 2. touching, pathetic.

दरना vt. 1. to grind coarsely.

2. to destroy/ruin/devastate/ ravage.

दरबा m. 1. pigeon-hole.

दरबान f. doorkeeper, watchman.

दरबार m. king's court, royal court.

दरबारी adj. of or pertaining to a दरबार। m. 1. courtier. 2. sycophant.

दरमियान m. middle.

दरमियान, के postposition. 1. between. 2. among.

दरवाज़ा m. 1. door, gate. 2. doorway.

दरशाना vt. 1. to show. 2. to explain. 3. to depict.

दराज़ f. drawer (of a table, wardrobe etc.).

दरार f. 1. crack, crevice. 2. split, fissure, rift.

दरिंदा m. flesh-eating animal, carnivore.

दरिद्र adj. poor, indigent, miserable.

दरिद्रता f. poverty.

दरिद्री adj. 1. poor, wretched. 2. shabby. 3. unfortunate.

दरिया m. river.

दरियाई adj. pertaining to a river; ~ घोड़ा hippopotamus, river-horse.

दरियादिल adj. liberal, kind, large-hearted, generous.

दरियाफ़्त adj. ~ करना (i) to inqu- ire and find out; (ii) to enquire; (iii) to investigate.

दरी f. 1. carpet. 2. ravine.

दरीबा m. wholesale market.

दरेसी f. dressing, preparing (ground, building) for final touches.

दरोग़ा m. = दारोग़ा।

दर्ज adj. entered, noted, recorded (in a book, register etc.). m. = दरज।

दर्जा m. 1. class. 2. grade, order or division, standard.

दर्ज़ी m. = दरज़ी।

दर्द m. 1. pain, ache, affliction, malady. 2. pathos. 3. sympathy.

दर्दनाक adj. pitiful, woeful, awful.

दर्दमंद adj. sympathetic, compassionate.

दर्प m. hauteur, arrogance.

दर्पण m. mirror, looking glass.

दर्रा m. 1. (mountian) pass. 2. coarse powder (as of cereals).

दर्शक m. spectator, on-looker.

दर्शक-दीर्घा f. visitor's gallery.

दर्शन m. 1. sight, view. 2. Philosophy.

दर्शनीय adj. 1. worth being seen, worth a visit. 2. handsome, beautiful, marvellous.

दर्शनी हुंडी f. draft, bill of exchange, payable on sight.

दर्शाना vt. = दरशाना।

दर्शी adj. observing, seeing.

दल m. 1. party, clique, group, assembly. 2. batch. 3. flock. 4. leaf. 5. thickness.

दलक f. quivering, tremor.

दलकना vi. to quiver.

दलगत adj. party wise.

दलदल f. bog, marsh, quagmire.

दलदार adj. plump, fleshy.

दलन m. crushing.

दलना vt. to grind coarsely.

दलबंदी f. party-politics, grou-pism, factionism.

दलबदल m. defection.

दलबादल m. 1. conglomeration/ mass of clouds. 2. contingent of followers and companions.

दलवाना vt. to have something ground coarsely.

दलहन m. cereals used as pulse.

दलान m. portico.

दलाल m. 1. commission agent, broker; middleman, tout. 2. pimp.

दलाली f. 1. commission of a broker, brokerage. 2. broker's vocation, touting.

दलित adj. depressed, downtrodden.

दलिया m. 1. coarsely ground wheat, hominy, porridge. 2. coarse meal.

दलील f. argument, plea.

दलेल f. 1. army exercises, drill. 2. penalty parade.

दवा f. 1. medicine. 2. drug.

दवाख़ाना m. dispensary.

दवात f. inkpot.

दवा-दारू m. medical treatment.

दवामी adj. permanent.

दश adj. & m. = दस।

दशक m. decade.

दशन m. tooth.

दशनच्छद m. lip.

दशभुज m. decagon.

दशम adj. tenth.

दशमलव m. decimal.

दशमांश m. tithe, one-tenth part.

दशमिक adj. decimal, denary.

दशमी f. tenth day of each half of a lunar month.

दशहरा m. = विजयदशमी।

दशा f. 1. state, condition. 2. plight.

दशानुकूलन m. acclimatization.

दशाब्दी f. period of ten years, decade.

दशावतार m. the ten incarna- tions of Lord Vishnu (Hindu Mythology).

दशाह m. 1. period of ten days. 2. tenth day after death.

दस adj. &. m. ten, 10.

दस्तंदाज़ adj. (one) who inter-feres/ meddles.

दस्त m. 1. hand. 2. loose motion.

दस्तक f. 1. slight blow with the hand. 2. a knock.

दस्तकार m. artisan, craftsman.

दस्तकारी f. handiwork, handicraft, artisanship.

दस्तख़त m. signature.

दस्तख़ती adj. signed.

दस्ता m. 1. handle. 2. squad, squadron.

दस्ताना m. hand-glove, gauntlet.

दस्तावर adj. purgative, cathartic.

दस्तावेज़ m. document, deed.

दस्तावेज़ी adj. documentary.

दस्ती adj. 1. pertaining to hand, handy. 2. sent through some person.

दस्तूर m. custom, practice.

दस्तूरी f. 1. commission, customary discount. 2. perquisite.

दस्यु m. bandit, robber.

दस्युवृत्ति f. banditry/robbery as a means of livelihood.

दहक f. blaze.

द

दहकना vi. to blaze, to burn with a redhot flame.

दहकाना vt. to cause to blaze, to agitate.

दहन m. combustion, burning.

दहनशील f. combustible.

दहना vi. & vt. to burn.

दहलना vi. to be frightened/over-awed.

दहला m. ten of playing cards.

दहलाना vt. to over-awe.

दहलीज़ f. doorsill, threshold.

दहशत f. terror, alarm, intimidation, fear, awe, dread.

दहाई f. 1. state of being ten times. 2. ten's place in writing numerals. 3. set of ten things.

दहाड़ f. 1. roar of a lion. 2. wail.

दहाड़ना vi. to roar, to cry aloud.

दहाना m. 1. (big) mouth (of a river). 2. mouth of a water bag. 3. curb of the bridle of a horse.

दही m. curd, yoghurt.

दहेज f. dowry.

दहेड़ी f. curd-pot.

दाँत m. tooth.

दाँता m. tooth of comb, saw etc., dent.

दाँती f. sickle.

दाँतेदार adj. dentate, dented, jagged.

दांपत्य m. marital relationship; adj. marital; ~ जीवन married life; ~ प्रेम marital love.

दाँव m. 1. stake. 2. device. 3. wrestling skill/trick.

दाँव-पेच m. tactics, manoeu-vres.

दाई f. nurse, midwife.

दाऊ m. elder brother.

दाक्षिणात्य adj. southern.

दाख f. 1. grape. 2. raisin, currant.

दाख़िल adj. entered, inserted, admitted.

दाख़िला m. 1. entrance, admission. 2. entrance fee.

दाग m. cremation.

दाग़ m. 1. dirty mark, stain, slur. 2.anything that damages reputation, stigma.

दाग़ना vt. 1. to fire (a gun). 2. to brand.

दाग़ी adj. having a blot/spot.

दाड़िम m. pomegranate.

दाढ़ f. molar (tooth), grinder.

दाढ़ी f. beard.

दाढ़ीवाला adj. having a beard, bearded.

दातव्य adj. 1. due or worth giving. 2. charitable. m. donation, charity.

दाता m. donor, giver.

दातार m. giver, a big donor.

दातुन, दातौन f. fibrous twig used as a tooth-brush.

दाद f. 1. ringworm. 2. complaint. 3. well-deserved praise.

दादरा m. a variety of Indian music.

दादा m. 1. paternal grandfather. 2. elder brother. 3. leader of a gang, hoodlum, gangster.

दादागीरी f. 1. gangsterism, hooliganism. 2. leadership.

दादी f. grandmother, father's mother.

दादुर m. frog.

दान m. 1. act of giving. 2. donation. 3. charity, alms. suffix. used to denote a container, as in क़लमदान।

दानपात्र m. offertory box.

दान-पेटी f. offertory box.

दानव m. demon, giant.

दानवी adj. demonic. f. female demon, giantess.

दानवीर adj. very generous, munificent as prince.

दानशीलता f. munificence.

दाना m. 1. grain. 2. bead. 3. pimple.

दाना-पानी m. food and fodder, sustenance, livelihood.

दानी adj. charitable, generous, munificent. f. small receptacle, as चूहेदानी mouse-trap. (used as suffix).

दानेदार adj. granular.

दाप m. overbearing display of superiority, arrogance, pride.

दाब f. 1. pressure. 2. weight.

दाबना vt. 1. to press. 2. to keep under (one's) control/restraint, to keep in check.

दाम m. 1. price. 2. a small old Indian coin. 3. the second of the four policies for effecting one's purpose as expatiated in ancient Indian polity, viz. साम, दाम, दंड, भेद; the policy of monetary gratification. 4. garland. 5. heap.

दामन m. the skirt of a garment.

दामाद m. son-in-law.

दामिनी f. lightning.

दामी adj. expensive, costly, precious.

दाय adj. due, worth giving. m. 1. charity. 2. liability. 3. inherited wealth. 4. dowry, wedding presents.

दायभाग m. portion of paternal property which one is to get on division.

दायभागी m. heir, inheritor.

दायर adj. 1. wandering, roaming. 2. current. 3. filed (as a law-suit).

दायाँ adj. right.

दायाधिकार m. inheritance.

दायित्व m. 1. liability. 2. obliga-tion. 3. onus.

दायिनी suffix. as सुखदायिनी bestowing pleasure.

दायी suffix. bestower, giver.

दार suffix. denoting possession or quality; छाया ~ shady; दुकान ~ shopkeeper.

दारचीनी f. cinnamon.

दारण m. 1. surgery, operation. 2. instrument of operation.

दारा f. wife.

दारिद्र्य m. poverty, pauperism, indigence.

दारु m. pine tree.

दारुण adj. 1. severe, extreme. 2. dreadful/ghastly; dreadful/ghastly sight. 3. horrible.

दारुहलदी f. a kind of turmeric/curcuma.

दारू m. 1. medicine. 2. alcohol, wine, liquor. 3. gunpowder.

दारोग़ा m. inspector, supervisor.

दार्शनिक adj. philosophical. m. philosopher.

दाल f. pulse, lentil.

दालचीनी m. cinnamon.

दाल-दलिया m. coarse food, poor man's diet.

दालमोठ f. mixture of fried pulses (a kind of snack).

दाल-रोटी f. livelihood, sustenance.

दालान m. covered inner terrace (usually facing a courtyard).

दाव m. 1. jungle, wood. 2. = दाँव।

दावत f. feast, banquet.

दावा m. 1. claim. 2. suit.

दावाग्नि f. forest conflagration, fire in a jungle.

दावेदार m. one who makes a claim, claimant.

दास m. 1. slave, serf. 2. servant.

दासता f. slavery, servility, serfdom, subjection.

दासप्रथा f. system of slavery, serfdom.

दासभाव m. servitude.

दासा m. projecting prop.

दासानुदास m. very humble servant.

दासी f. female slave, maid-servant, slave girl.

दास्ताँ, दास्तान f. 1. story, tale. 2. narrative.

दाह m. 1. burning. 2. burning sensation. 3. cremation. 4. mental agony.

दाहक adj. caustic, inflammatory.

दाहकर्म m. funeral rite(s).

दाहक्रिया f. दाहकर्म।

दाहन m. burning.

दाहना vt. 1. to burn. 2. to torment/torture.

दाहिना adj. right.

दाहिने adv. to the right.

दाह्य adj. combustible, inflammable.

दिअली f. = दिउली।

दिउली f. 1. small earthen cup. 2. tiny cup of tinsel used in embroidery. 3. scab of a wound.

दिक् f. direction.

दिक़ adj. vexed, embarrassed.

दिक़्क़त f. diffculty, hardship, trouble.

दिक्सूचक m. compass.

दिखना vi. to appear, to be in sight, to be seen, to be visible.

दिखलाई f. 1. act of showing.

दिखलाना vt. to show.

दिखाई f. act of showing.

दिखाऊ adj. showy, ostentatious.

दिखाना vt. 1. to show. 2. to display.

दिखावट f. mere show, ostentation, pomposity.

दिखावटी adj. showy, ostent- atious.

दिखावा m. ostentation, display, pomp, show.

दिखौआ adj. meant for show, showy, flashy, ostentatious, gaudy.

दिगंत m. horizon.

दिगंबर adj. naked. m. a sect of Jainism.

दिगंश m. azimuth.

दिग्गज m. one of the eight mythological elephants which support the earth. adj. 1. ponderous. 2. heavy. 3. high, majestic.

दिग्दर्शक m. 1. (mariner's) compass. 2. director.

दिग्दर्शन m. direction, guidance.

दिग्भ्रम m. error about direction, loss of bearing.

दिग्मंडल m. all the directions combined.

दिग्विंदु m. cardinal point.

दिग्विजय m. conquest of the world.

दिन m. 1. day. 2. daytime.

दिनकर m. Sun.

दिनचर्या f. daily routine.

दिन-ब-दिन adv. day by day.

दिनमान m. length/duration of the day (from Sunrise to Sunset).

दिनांक m. date.

दिनांकित adj. dated.

दिनांध adj. day-blind.

दिनी adj. old, that which has been kept for a long time, as दिनी घी।

दिनेश m. Sun.

दिनौंधी f. day-blindness.

दिमाग़ m. brain.

दिमाग़दार adj. 1. brainy, very intelligent, intellectual. 2. proud, vain.

दिमाग़ी adj. mental.

दिया vt. past tense of देना। m. = दीया।

दिल m. heart.

दिलकश adj. alluring, attractive.

दिलचस्प f. interesting, amusing.

दिलचस्पी f. interest.

दिलजला adj. afflicted, tormented.

दिलजोई f. consolation.

दिलदार adj.1. affectionate. 2. generous, liberal.

दिलपसंद adj. pleasing to the heart, attractive, charming.

दिलबर adj. beloved, dearly loved. m. loved one, beloved one.

दिलरुबा m. 1. loved one, beloved one. 2. a stringed musical instrument.

दिलवाना vt. = दिलाना।

दिलवाला adj. large-hearted and courageous.

दिलाना vt. to cause to be given.

दिलावर adj. courageous, brave.

दिलासा m. solace, consolation.

दिली adj. 1. pertaining to the heart. 2. hearty, cordial. 3. intimate.

दिलेर adj. bold, courageous, brave.

दिलेरी f. 1. courage, bravery. 2. boldness.

दिल्लगी f. jest, joke, fun.

दिल्ला m. panel of a door.

दिल्लेदार adj. panelled.

दिवंगत adj. no longer alive, late, deceased.

दिवस m. day.

दिवांध adj. day-blind.

दिवाकर m. Sun.

दिवाल adj. & m. one who gives, giver.

दिवाला m. bankruptcy, insolvency.

दिवालिया adj. & m. bankrupt, insolvent.

दिवालियापन m. insolvency, bankruptcy.

दिवाली f. = दीवाली।

दिवास्वप्न m. 1. day-dream. 2. musing.

दिव्य adj. 1. heavenly, divine, celestial. 2. brilliant. 3. charming, attractive, fascinating.

दिव्यदृष्टि f. divine insight.

दिव्यपुरुष m. divine being.

दिव्यमूर्ति f. divine figure.
दिशा f. direction.
दिशानिर्देश m. direction, guidance.
दिशाभ्रम m. loss of direction.
दिशाशूल m. inauspicious time for starting on a journey in a particular direction.
दिशाहीन adj. without any line of action.
दिसंबर m. December.
दिसावर m. 1. foreign country. 2. place from which goods are ordered for.
दिहाड़ी f. 1. day. 2. period of time during the day a labourer is expected to work. 3. remuneration paid for the same.
दीक्षक m. preceptor.
दीक्षण m. initiation.
दीक्षांत adj. & m. (concerning) end of an academic session.
दीक्षा f. initiation, ceremonial introduction into some cult, sect etc.
दीक्षित adj. initiated, consecrated.
दीखना vi. 1. to be visible. 2. to appear.
दीठ f. look, glance, sight.
दीदा m. eye.
दीदार m. sight, vision.
दीदी f. elder sister.
दीन adj. 1. humble. 2. indigent, destitute.
दीनता f. 1. humility. 2. indigence, destitution.
दीनदयालु adj. merciful.
दीन-दुनिया f. this world and the next.
दीनबंधु m. 1. friend of the poor. 2. God.
दीनानाथ m. protector of the poor, God.
दीनार m. ancient Greek gold coin, drachma.
दीप m. lamp.
दीपक m. lamp.
दीपघर m. lamp-house.
दीपमाला f. row/series of lights.
दीपशिखा f. flame of a lamp.
दीपावली f. 1. row of lights. 2. दीवाली।
दीपित adj. = दीप्त।
दीप्त adj. illuminated.
दीप्ति f. 1. luminosity, glow. 2. lustre. 3. brightness.
दीमक f. white ant, termite.
दीयट f. = दीवट।
दीया m. lamp.
दीयासलाई f. match stick.
दीर्घ adj. long, sustained; ~ स्वर long vowel.
दीर्घकाय adj. tall and bulky, gigantic.
दीर्घकालीन adj. of a long term.
दीर्घजीवी adj. long-lived.
दीर्घवृत्त m. ellipse (Maths.)
दीर्घसूत्रता f. dilatoriness, procrastination.
दीर्घसूत्री adj. dilatory, slow, lethargic.
दीर्घा f. gallery.
दीर्घायु adj. long-lived.
दीवट f. lampstand.
दीवान m. 1. royal assembly. 2. minister of a state. 3. Prime Minister. 4. collected works of a poet.

दीवाना adj. nympholeptic, crazy.

दीवानापन m. nympholepsy, craziness.

दीवानी adj. 1. fem. of दीवाना। 2. civil.

दीवार f. wall.

दीवाली f. the Hindu festival of lights.

दुंदुभि f. kettledrum.

दुंबा m. a kind of ram.

दुःख, दुख m. 1. sorrow, grief, distress. 2. regret.

दुःखकर, दुखकर adj. = दुःखद।

दुःखद, दुखद adj. 1. unfortunate, painful. 2. sorrowful. 3. distressing.

दुःखदायक, दुःखदायी adj. = दुःखद।

दुःख-भरा adj. painful, sorrow-ful.

दुःखभोग m. suffering.

दुःखमय adj. full of sorrow/grief/agony.

दुःखांत adj. tragic, with a tragic end.

दुःखित adj. distressed, grief-stricken.

दुःखी, दुखी adj. & m. 1. grief-stricken, distressed. 2. melancholic, sad, gloomy. 3. (a person) who suffers (from an illness or deficiency).

दुःस्वप्न m. nightmare.

दुअन्नी f. two-anna coin (old currency).

दुआ f. 1. benediction, blessing. 2. prayer.

दुआबा m. region lying between two rivers.

दुकड़ी f. 1. pair. 2. carriage drawn by two horses. 3. two rupees. 4. the two of cards.

दुकान f. shop.

दुकानदार m. shopkeeper.

दुकानदारी f. vocation of a shopkeeper, shopkeeping.

दुकाल m. paucity, scarcity, famine.

दुकूल m. cloth, fine cloth.

दुकेला adj. having a companion.

दुक्कड़ m. 1. a kind of drum. 2. a pair of large boats tied together.

दुक्की f. the two of a suit of cards.

दुख m. = दुःख।

दुखड़ा m. sorrowful story, saga of suffering.

दुखता adj. painful, sore.

दुखना vi. to hurt/ache.

दुखाना vt. to cause pain, to inflict suffering.

दुखिया adj. (one) who has suffered, afflicted with sorrow.

दुखी adj. distressed, miserable.

दुगना adj. double.

दुगाना m. duet.

दुग्ध m. milk.

दुग्धमापक m. lactometer.

दुग्धशाला f. dairy.

दुग्धशर्करा m. lactose.

दुचित्ता adj. fickle-minded, not firm, wavering, of two minds, distracted.

दुटूक adj. ~ बात proposal/reply in concise, plain words.

दुढालू adj. having two slopes.

दुत interj. Off ! Away ! Be gone !

दुतकार f. reproof, reprimand, upbraiding.

दुतकारना vt. to reproach/reprimand/reprove/upbraid/scold.

दुतरफ़ा adj. 1. two-way. 2. bilateral.

दुतल्ला adj. two-storeyed.

दुद्धी f. a type of grass.

दुधमुँहा adj. unweaned.

दुधार adj. giving milk.

दुधारू adj. = दुधार।

दुधिया adj. 1. of or pertainintg to milk. 2. containing a good dose of milk, as दुधिया भाँग। 3. like milk, milky as दुधिया पत्थर। m. 1. chalk. 2. a kind of grass, also called दुद्धी।

दुनाली adj. double-barrelled.

दुनिया f. world.

दुनियादार adj. 1. worldly. 2. worldly-wise, pragmatic.

दुनियादारी f. 1. worldly beha-viour/worldliness. 2. prag-maticalness.

दुपट्टा m. linen wrapper.

दुपहर m. noon.

दुफ़सला adj. 1. yielding two crops. 2. having two meanings, ambiguous.

दुबकना vi. to quail.

दुबला adj. lean.

दुबलाना vt. to become lean/emaciated.

दुबलापन m. leanness.

दुबारा adv. once more, for a second time, again.

दुभाषिया m. 1. one who knows two languages, bilingual. 2. an interpreter.

दुमंज़िला adj. double-storeyed.

दुम f. 1. tail. 2. a thing like a tail.

दुमदार adj. having a tail, tailed.

दुमुँहाँ adj. having two mouths.

दुरंगा adj. 1. of two colours, bicoloured. 2. (person) double-faced, cunning, deceitful; दुरंगी चाल double game.

दुर्, दुर interj. pooh ! tut !

दुरदुराना vt. to pooh-pooh.

दुरभिसंधि f. conspiracy, collusion.

दुरमुट, दुरमुस m. an implement for pounding pavements, rammer.

दुरवस्था f. 1. sad plight, sorry state. 2. bad shape.

दुराग्रह m. intransigence, wilfulness.

दुराचरण m. 1. misconduct. 2. immorality, depravity.

दुराचार m. bad or immoral behaviour, misconduct.

दुराचारी adj. immoral, wicked, licentious, vile.

दुरात्मा adj. vile, wicked.

दुराना vt. 1. to keep away. 2. to hide.

दुरारोह adj. steep.

दुराव m. concealment.

दुराशय m. malevolence, bad motive, malafides.

दुराशा f. 1. false hope. 2. a thing that is impossible to catch or reach, will-o-the-wisp.

दुरुख़ा adj. double-edged, two-faced.

दुरुपयोग m. misuse, ill-use, abuse.

दुरुस्त adj. 1. right, correct. 2. in a proper condition.

दुरूह adj. abstruse, difficult to understand, obscure.

दुर्गंध f. foul smell, stink, stench.

दुर्ग m. fort, citadel.

दुर्गत adj. 1. troubled, oppressed. 2. poor. 3. calamitous.

दुर्गति f. plight, terrible plight, catastrophe, misery.

दुर्गपाल m. principal officer of a fort, fort-guard.

दुर्गम adj. 1. impassable, unapproachable, inaccessible. 2. abstruse, difficult. 3. impregnable.

दुर्गा f. Durga, goddess of prowess.

दुर्गुण m. characteristic flaw, demerit, vice, shortcoming.

दुर्घटना f. mishap, accident, disaster, tragedy.

दुर्जन m. villain, scoundrel, rascal, base fellow.

दुर्जेय adj. 1. impregnable. 2. formidable, invincible, unconquerable.

दुर्दमनीय adj. impregnable, invincible.

दुर्दशा f. adversity, misery, sad condition, plight.

दुर्दिन m. 1. bad days, hard times. 2. a day overcast with clouds, cloudy day.

दुर्दैव m. disaster, mishap, bad luck, misfortune.

दुर्बल adj. 1. weak. 2. lean, slender. 3. infirm.

दुर्बलता f. 1. weakness. 2. leanness.

दुर्बुद्धि adj. 1. foolish, stupid. 2. evil-minded, wicked, perverse.

दुर्बोध adj. incomprehensible, abstruse, obscure.

दुर्भाग्य m. ill-luck, misfortune.

दुर्भाव m. ill-will, antagonism, malevolence.

दुर्भावना f. ill-will, hostile feeling.

दुर्भावपूर्ण adj. malevolent.

दुर्भिक्ष m. 1. famine. 2. paucity, scarcity.

दुर्भेद्य adj. difficult to penetrate, impregnable, invulnerable.

दुर्मति adj. 1. foolish, stupid, silly, 2. evil-minded, wicked. m. evil-mindedness, wickedness.

दुर्मुख adj. 1. foul-mouthed, foul-tongued. 2. ugly. m. 1. horse. 2. spy. 3. a house facing north (considered inauspicious).

दुर्लभ adj. 1. scarce, unavailable. 2. rare.

दुर्वचन m. abuse, scurrilous language, reproach.

दुर्वह adj. onerous, difficult to carry.

दुर्वृत्ति f. depravity, wickedness, evil-mindedness.

दुर्व्यवस्था f. mismanagement.

दुर्व्यवहार m. 1. ill-treatment. 2. misbehaviour.

दुर्व्यसन m. vice, bad habit, addiction.

दुलकी f. trot.

दुलड़ा adj. of two strings. m. a necklace of two strings.

दुलड़ी adj. & f. fem. of दुलड़ा।

दुलत्ती f. (quadruped) kick with the two hind legs.

दुलराना vt. to caress/fondle.

दुलहन f. bride.

दुलहा m. bridegroom.

दुलहिन f. = दुलहन।

दुलाई f. quilt.

दुलार m. fondling, caressing.

दुलारना vt. to fondle/caress.

दुलारा adj. darling, beloved.

दुविधा f. dilemma, uncertainty, fix.

दुशवार adj. arduous, difficult, tedious.

दुशाला m. shawl.

दुश्चक्र m. vicious circle.

दुश्चरित्र adj. of bad character. m. misconduct, immorality, depravity.

दुश्मन m. enemy, foe.

दुश्मनी f. animosity, enmity, hostility.

दुष्कर adj. difficult to execute/ perform, arduous, hard.

दुष्कर्म m. 1. misdeed, wrong. 2. vice, sin.

दुष्कृत्य m. misdeed, wrong.

दुष्ट adj. 1. wicked, evilminded, knavish. 2. vicious, vile.

दुष्प्रभाव m. bad influence, ill effect.

दुष्प्रयोग m. misapplication, misuse.

दुष्प्राप्य adj. scarce, rare.

दुसूती f. a thick cloth of two sheets.

दुस्तर adj. 1. arduous, difficult. 2. difficult to cross, impassable, insurmountable.

दुहत्था adj. provided with two handles.

दुहना vt. 1. to milk. 2. to squeeze out.

दुहराना vt. 1. to revise. 2. to repeat.

दुहाई f. 1. invocation. 2. act of milking. 3. wages paid for milking.

दुहाजू adj. (one) who marries a second time (when the first spouse is dead).

दुहाना vt. to cause (a cow etc.) to be milked.

दुहाव m. 1. period of lactation of a milch cattle. 2. wages paid for milking.

दुहिता f. daughter.

दूज f. second day of each half of a lunar month.

दूत m. envoy, emissary, messenger.

दूतकर्म m. office or duty of an envoy.

दूतावास m. legation, consulate, embassy.

दूतिका f. = दूती।

दूती f. 1. female messenger. 2. go-between, procuress.

दूध m. 1. milk.

दूध-पूत m. wealth and progeny.

दूधवाला m. milk-vendor, milk-man.

दूधिया adj. 1. made of milk, milky. 2. milk-white. 3. lactiferous, juicy; ~ पत्थर opal.

दून f. act or state of doubling. m. vale, valley.

दूना adj. double, two-fold.

दूब f. a kind of grass.

दूबर adv. wanting vigour, weak, feeble.

दूभर adj. uncomfortable, difficult.

दूरंदेश adj. farsighted, sagacious.

दूर adv. far away, remote, distant.

दूरगामी adj. which can go far, far-reaching.

दूरदर्शिता f. farsight, farsightedness, sagacity.

दूरदर्शी adj. farsighted, sagacious.

दूरदृष्टि f. farsight, farsighted-ness.

दूरबीन f. 1. binocular. 2. telescope.

दूरभाष m. telephone.

दूरमुद्रक m. teleprinter.

दूरलेखी adj. telegraphic.

दूरवर्ती adj. distant, remote.

दूरवीक्षक m. telescope.

दूरसंचार m. telecommunication.

दूरस्थ adj. distant, remote.

दूरी f. 1. distance. 2. lack of friendly feelings in relationship.

दूरीकरण m. act or state of removing/turning away.

दूर्वा f. = दूब ।

दूल्हा m. = दुलहा ।

दूषण m. 1. fault, blame. 2. contamination, pollution.

दूषित adj. 1. faulty, defective. 2. defiled, polluted, contaminated. 3. blemished, sullied.

दूसरा adj. 1. second. 2. other, another, next. m. someone else.

दूहना vt. to milk (a cow etc.).

दृग m. 1. eye. 2. power of vision.

दृढ़ adj. 1. firm, steady. 2. rigid, inflexible.

दृढ़ता f. 1. firmness, steadiness. 2. rigidity, inflexibility.

दृढ़ांग adj. firm-bodied, stout, corpulent.

दृढ़ोक्ति f. assertion, averment.

दृश्य adj. 1. visible. 2. visual. m. 1. scene, view. 2. scenery.

दृश्यता f. visibility, visuality.

दृश्यमान adj. 1. visible, perceptible. 2. visual.

दृष्ट adj. seen, visible, apparent.

दृष्टांत m. instance, example, illustration.

दृष्टि f. 1. eyesight, vision; दिव्य ~ divine vision. 2. look.

दृष्टिकोण m. 1. viewpoint. 2. aspect.

दृष्टिगत adj. viewed, seen.

दृष्टिगोचर adj. perceptible, visible.

दृष्टिदोष m. 1. defect in sight. 2. oversight.

दृष्टिपटल m. retina.

दृष्टिपात m. glance.

दृष्टिभ्रम m. optical illusion.

दृष्टिहीन adj. sightless, blind.

देखनहारा m. one who looks after or takes care of.

देखना vt. 1. to see/look/notice. 2.to watch. 3. to look after. 4. to search, to look into.

देखभाल f. care, supervision.

देखा-देखी f. 1. nodding acquaintance. 2. blind imitation.

देखो interj. look, behold !

देखौवा adj. = दिखौआ ।

देग़ f. cauldron, big cooking pot, kettle.

देग़चा m. kettle, cooking pot.

देग़ची f. small cauldron, small kettle.

देदीप्यमान adj. refulgent, brilliant,

resplendent, splendid, glorious.

देन f. 1. act of giving. 2. gift.

देनदार m. debtor.

देनदारी f. liability, indebtedness.

देनहारा adj. (one) who gives.

देना vt. 1. to give, provide, grant or bestow. 2. to pay. 3. to confer. m. liability.

देना-पावना m. assets and liabi-lities (in cash).

देय adj. due, payable.

देयता f. liability.

देर f. 1. delay. 2. time.

देर-सबेर adv. sooner or later.

देरी f. delay, tardiness.

देव m. 1. God. 2. deity. 3. giant.

देवकन्या f. nymph.

देवगण m. 1. pantheon. 2. assistants of gods.

देवगृह m. abode/residence of a deity, temple.

देवता m. deity.

देवतुल्य adj. godlike, deific.

देवत्व m. divinity, godliness.

देवदार m. cedar.

देवदासी f. 1. dancing girl. 2. harlot, prostitute.

देवदूत m. messenger of gods, angel.

देवनागरी f. original name of Nagari alphabet.

देवभाषा f. language of gods, Sanskrit.

देजयोनि f. divine form of life.

देवर m. husband's younger brother.

देवरानी f. wife of देवर ।

देवलोक m. abode of gods, heaven, paradise.

देववाणी f. 1. oracle. 2. tongue of gods, Sanskrit.

देवांगना f. wife of a deity or celestial damsel.

देवाल m. giver, one who pays.

देवालय m. seat of a deity, temple.

देवी f. 1. goddess. 2. lady.

देवोत्थान m. the eleverth day of the bright fortnight of the month of Kartik when Lord Vishu is supposed to be awakened.

देवोपासना f. worship of gods.

देश m. 1. country. 2. region. 3. space.

देशज adj. indigenous, native.

देशद्रोह m. sedition, treason.

देशद्रोही m. traitor to the country, fifth columnist.

देशधर्म m. (i) religion of the country; (ii) public conduct/practices prevalent in the country.

देश-निकाला m. exile, transportation.

देशभक्त m. patriot.

देशभक्ति f. patriotism.

देशवासी m. inhabitant of (one's) country, fellow countryman.

देशांतर m. 1. longitude. 2. foreign/ other country.

देशाचार m. tradition of the land, native custom/practice.

देशाटन m. travel/wandering round the country.

देशी adj. native, indigenous.

देस m. = देश।

देसावर m. = दिसावर।

देह f. body.

देहत्याग m. end of the physical existence, death.

देहधारी m. possessing a body, corporeal.

देहरी f. = देहली।

देहली f. threshold.

देह-व्यापार m. prostitution.

देहांत m. 1. demise, death. 2. expiry.

देहात m. village, country.

देहाती adj. 1. of a village. 2. rustic, rural. m. 1. villager. [Fem. देहातिन] 2. bumpkin.

देहात्मवाद m. materialism.

देहावसान m. demise, death.

दैत्य m. demon, giant.

दैनिक adj. daily.

दैनिकी f. diary.

दैन्य m. 1. poverty, pauperism. 2. humility.

दैया f. destiny, fate; ~ रे दैया Oh God! Gosh!

दैव adj. godly. m. fate, destiny.

दैवगति f. course of events as ordained by destiny, providence.

दैवज्ञ m. fortune-teller, astro-loger, diviner.

दैवयोग m. chance, contingency.

दैववश adv. = दैवात्।

दैवात् adv. by chance, accidentally.

दैवी adj. 1. pertaining to gods, godly. 2. divine, celestial.

दैहिक adj. physical, bodily. corporeal.

दो adj. 1. two. 2. ~ एक just a few, one or two.

दोग़ला adj. 1. cross-breed, born out of wedlock, illegitimate. 2. not pure, mixed, bastard. 3. two-faced. m. bastard.

दोचित्ता adj. = दुचित्ता।

दोज़ख़ m. hell.

दोटूक adj. categorical, clear and definite.

दोतरफ़ा adj. = दुतरफ़ा।

दोतल्ला adj. = दुतल्ला।

दोदिला adj. having two minds, of a divided mind.

दोनली adj. double-barrelled.

दोना m. leaf-cup, leaf-bowl.

दोनों pron. the two, both.

दोपहर m. = दुपहर।

दोबारा adv. = दुबारा।

दोमट m. loam.

दोमुँहा adj. two-mouthed, deceitful.

दोयम adj. 1. second-rate. 2. second (in serial order or merit).

दोरंगा adj. = दुरंगा।

दोरसा adj. having two kinds of flavour or taste.

दोरुख़ा adj. = दुरुख़ा।

दोलक m. pendulum.

दोलन vi. oscillation.

दोलायमान adj. 1. oscillating, oscillatory. 2. wavering, swinging.

दोष m. 1. harm, blemish, defect, flaw. 2. fault. 3. charge, blame. 4. guilt.

दोषमुक्त adj. guiltless.

दोषारोपण m. accusation, allegation, charging, blaming.

दोषी adj. 1. at fault. 2. guilty, culprit. m. culprit.

दोसाला adj. biennial.

दोसूती adj. = दुसूती।

दोस्त m. friend.

दोस्ताना adj. friendly. m. friendship, friendliness.

दोस्ती f. friendship, friendliness.

दोहन vt. 1. milking. 2. exploitation.

दोहरा adj. having two folds, double.

दोहराना vi. 1. to make (something) two-fold. 2. to revise, to recapitulate. 3. to repeat/ reiterate.

दोहराव m. 1. revision. 2. repetition.

दोहा m. couplet.

दोहाई f. = दुहाई।

दौंचना vt. 1. to crush/pound. 2. to thrash/beat.

दौड़ f. 1. race, 2. run.

दौड़-धूप f. bustle, hectic activity.

दौड़ना vt. 1. to run. 2. to rush, to run about.

दौड़ादौड़ी f. hurry and scurry.

दौड़ाना vt. 1. to cause to run, to make (someone) run. 2. to despatch on errand.

दौर m. 1. cycle of times, wheel of fortune, turn in life. 2. stage, phase. 3. course (wine).

दौरा m. 1. tour. 2. paroxysm, fit (of swoon etc.). 3. a large basket. 4. session (s).

दौरान m. duration, period.

दौरी f. small basket.

दौर्बल्य m. weakness, debility.

दौलत f. wealth, riches.

दौलतख़ाना m. residence (euphemistic).

दौहित्र m. daughter's son. [Fem. दौहित्री]

द्युति f. light, lustre, glow, radiance, brilliance, splendour.

द्युतिमान adj. radiant, lustrous, brilliant.

द्यूत m. gambling.

द्यूतक्रीड़ा f. gambling (as a sport).

द्योतक adj. indicative, illustrative, depicting, explaining.

द्रव adj. & m. liquid, fluid.

द्रवण m. melting.

द्रवणशील adj. prone to liquefy, liquefiable.

द्रवता f. liquidity, fluidity.

द्रविड़ m. 1. Dravid, a region in South India. 2. an inhabitant of the region, a Dravidian.

द्रवित pp. 1. melted. 2. moved (by emotion).

द्रवीभूत pp. = द्रवित।

द्रव्य m. 1. matter, substance. 2. money. 3. wealth.

द्रव्यमान m. mass.

द्रष्टव्य adj. 1. worth seeing. 2. worth taking a note of, notable, worth consulting.

द्रष्टा m. 1. spectator, seer, looker-on. 2. sage, visionist.

द्राक्षा f. grape.

द्रावक adj. liquefying. m. thinner.
द्रुत adj. fast, swift, quick, rapid.
द्रुतगामी adj. going fast, swift.
द्रुम m. tree.
द्रोणी f. trough, basin.
द्रोह m. rebellion, revolt, hostility.
द्रोही adj. rebellious, revolting, hostile.
द्वंद्व m. 1. duel. 2. struggle, conflict. 3. hubbub, hulla-baloo, uproar. 4. quarrel.
द्वय adj. two.
द्वादश adj. & m. twelve, 12.
द्वादशी f. twelfth day of each half of a lunar month.
द्वापर m. the third era of Hindu mythology.
द्वार m. 1. door, gate. 2. entrance. 3. opening, outlet. 4. means.
द्वारपाल m. doorkeeper, warder, gatekeeper.
द्वारा, के postposition. by, thro-ugh, through the agency of.
द्वि pref. two.
द्विगुण adj. double, two-fold.
द्विज adj. twice-born. m. 1. one born of an egg, bird. 2. one belonging to the Brahman, Kshatriya or Vaishya caste.
द्वितीय adj. second.
द्वितीया f. 1. second day of each half of a lunar month. 2. accusative case. (Gram.)
द्वित्व m. 1. duplication. 2. duplication of a consonant in a word. 3. repetition.
द्विधा adv. 1. in two ways. 2. in two parts.
द्विपक्षी adj. = द्विपक्षीय।
द्विपक्षीय adj. bilateral, bipartite.
द्विपद adj. 1. having two feet, e.g., a human being. 2. comprising two words, compound word. 3. (Maths.) binomial.
द्विपदी f. couplet.
द्विभाजन m. dividing into two equal parts, bisection.
द्विभाषी adj. having or using two languages, bilingual.
द्विरागमन m. = गौना।
द्विरुक्ति f. repetition, reiteration.
द्विलिंगी adj. hermaphrodite, bisexual.
द्विवार्षिक adj. biennial.
द्विविध adj. of two kinds.
द्विविवाह m. bigamy.
द्विशताब्दी f. bicentenary.
द्विसदनी adj. bicameral.
द्वीप m. island.
द्वीपसमूह m. a group of many islands, archipelago.
द्वीपी adj. 1. insular. 2. living in an island. m. tiger.
द्वेष m. ill-will, malice, animosity.
द्वेषवश adv. out of malice.
द्वेषी adj. filled with ill-will, malicious, inimical, hostile.
द्वैत m. dualism, duality.
द्वैध m. 1. distinction between two things. 2. double-dealing.
द्वैध शासन m. government vested is two supreme rulers, diarchy.

ध

ध m. fourth of the dental pentad of consonants of the Nagari alphabet; aspirated form of द।

धंधा m. 1. profession, vocation. 2. occupation, employment.

धँसना vi. 1. to get thrust/stuck into, to penetrate into. 2. to subside/sink.

धँसान f. 1. sinking/subsidence of land. 2. peneteration.

धँसाना vt. to thrust into.

धँसाव m. = धँसान।

धक f. palpitation; ~ से रह जाना to be wonderstruck/awestruck.

धकापेल f. pell-mell, jostling.

धकियाना vt. = धकेलना।

धकेलना vt. to push (down), to shove.

धक्कमधक्का m. shoving and pushing, jostling.

धक्का m. 1. push, shove. 2. impact, shock. 3. setback.

धक्कामुक्की f. pushing and jostling, elbowing and shoving.

धगड़ा m. paramour. (pej.)

धगड़ी f. paramour (woman).

धचका m. jerk.

धज f. outward appearance, mien.

धज्जी f. shred, smithereen, lath.

धड़ m. the main part of the human body apart from the head, trunk. adv. ~ से instantaneously, hurriedly.

धड़क f. fright (as on the stage), shyness.

धड़कन f. palpitation, throbbing, pulsation.

धड़कना vi. to palpitate/throb/flutter.

धड़का m. 1. palpitation of the heart. 2. apprehension. 3. sca-recrow.

धड़धड़ f. thudding sound. adv. with a thudding sound.

धड़धड़ाना vt. 1. to do something with a thudding sound. 2. to do something all of a sudden.

धड़ल्ला m. thudding sound. 2. huge crowd. 3. pomp and show.

धड़ा m. 1. a substitute for a weight. 2. balancing substance.

धड़ाका m. 1. bang, crash. 2. explosion.

धड़ाधड़ adv. in quick succes-sion.

धड़ाबंदी f. = धड़ेबंदी।

धड़ाम m. banging sound, thud; ~ से suddenly, and with a bang/flop.

धड़ी f. a weight of five seers, roughly equal to 4½ kg.

धड़ेबंदी f. arraying armies for a show-down.

धत, धत् interj. pooh! pooh!

धता m. shunting off.

धतूरा m. thorn-apple.

धधक f. blaze.

धधकना vi. to blaze/flare up.

धनंजय m. Arjun (Mahabharat).

धन m. 1. money, wealth, riches. 2. property.

धनकुबेर m. multi-millionaire.
धनचिह्न m. plus sign (+).
धन-दौलत f. wealth, pelf, money and possessions.
धनधान्य m. wealth and plenty, affluence, prosperity.
धन-पक्ष m. credit side.
धनपति m. god of wealth.
धन-पिशाच adj. extremely stingy, over-greedy.
धनमद m. intoxication/pride of wealth.
धनलोलुप adj. greedy, avaricious.
धनवंत adj. = धनवान।
धनवान, धनवान् adj. rich, wealthy, made of money, moneyed.
धन-विधेयक m. money bill.
धन-संपत्ति f. wealth, money and possessions.
धनहीन adj. poor, moneyless.
धनाढ्य adj. rich, wealthy, moneyed.
धनात्मक adj. 1. positive (as an electric charge). 2. plus.
धनाना vi. (cow, etc.) to get sired.
धनिक = धनी।
धनिया m. coriander seed.
धनी adj. rich, wealthy, moneyed, well-to-do.
धनु m. 1. bow. 2. ninth sign of the zodiac.
धनुर्धारी adj & m. skilled in archery, bowman.
धनुर्वात m. tetanus.
धनुर्विद्या f. archery.
धनुष m. bow, arch.
धन्ना सेठ m. moneyed/wealthy man.
धन्य adj. blessed, blissful.
धन्यवाद m. an expression of thanks, thank you.
धन्वा m. bow.
धन्वी adj. & m. bowman, archer.
धप f. light thud.
धब्बा m. 1. stain, spot. 2. blemish; slur, blot.
धम f. bang, thud.
धमक f. thudding/thumping sound.
धमकना vi. 1. to thump. 2. to have a shooting pain.
धमकाना vt. to intimidate/threaten.
धमकी f. intimidation, threat.
धमधमाना vt. to bang, to produce a thumping sound repeatedly.
धमन m. 1. pumping of air. 2. bellows.
धमन-भट्ठी f. blast furnace.
धमनी f. artery.
धमाका m. 1. loud bang/report. 2. blast.
धमाचौकड़ी f. furore, frisk, gambols.
धमाधम adv. 1. with a thumping sound. 2. in quick succession.
धर adj. (one) who holds/supports; e.g. जलधर, गिरिधर।
धरणि f. = धरणी।
धरणी f. earth.
धरता adj. one who holds.
धरती f. earth.
धरन m. beam.
धरना vt. to place, to hold, to pledge. m. sitdown strike, picketing.
धरनी f. beam.
धर-पकड़ f. rounding up, arrest.
धरवाना vt. = धराना।

ध

धरहरा m. minaret.

धरा f. earth.

धराऊ adj. 1. old, kept for a long time 2. kept only to be used on special occasion.

धरातल m. 1. surface. 2. earth.

धराना vt. to knock out (some-thing out of someone).

धराशायी adj. 1. floored, fallen flat. 2. razed to the ground.

धरित्री f. = धरती।

धरोहर m. 1. anything given or kept in trust. 2. pledge.

धर्म m. 1. duty. 2. function, intrinsic quality or property. 3. religion.

धर्म-कर्म m. religious or virtuous acts/conduct.

धर्मगुरु m. religious preceptor, priest.

धर्मग्रंथ m. religious/sacred book, holy scripture.

धर्मज्ञ adj. well-versed in the principles of religion.

धर्मतंत्र m. hierarchy, theocracy.

धर्मदर्शन m. philosophy of religion, theology.

धर्मध्वजी adj. hypocrite.

धर्मनिरपेक्ष adj. secular.

धर्मनिरपेक्षता f. secularism.

धर्मनिष्ठ adj. pious, devout, virtuous.

धर्मपत्नी f. wife (legally married).

धर्मपरायण adj. deeply religious, devoted to religious obser-vances, religious minded.

धर्मपरायणता f. religiousness, devoutness.

धर्म-परिवर्तन m. (religious) conversion.

धर्मपिता m. godfather.

धर्मपुत्र m. godson.

धर्मभीरु adj. god-fearing, very religious, scrupulous.

धर्ममाता f. godmother.

धर्मयुद्ध m. 1. war of righteous-ness, crusade. 2. just war.

धर्मवीर m. dauntless fighter for a religious cause.

धर्मशाला f. 1. pilgrim's rest house. 2. inn.

धर्मशास्त्र m. (books of) theology.

धर्मशास्त्री m. theologian, theo-logist.

धर्मसंकट m. dilemma, quan- dary.

धर्मसभा f. synod.

धर्माचार्य m. high priest, pre-ceptor.

धर्मात्मा adj. pious, virtuous. m. saint.

धर्मादा m. money set apart for charitable purposes, charitable endowment.

धर्माधिकारी m. prelate.

धर्मार्थ adj. charitable.

धर्मिष्ठ adj. pious, religious, virtuous.

धर्मी adj. religious, religious minded.

धर्मोपदेश m. sermon, religious discourse.

धर्मोपदेशक m. religious pre-acher, ecclesiastic.

धवल adj. 1. white. 2. clear, bright. 3. without blemish, fair.

धवला f. white cow.

धवलित adj. white (ned), brightened.

धसक f. 1. constant dry cough due to pungent smell as of tobacco powder. 2. pungent smell.

धसकना vi. 1. to subside. 2. to feel depressed. 3. (heart) to sink due to fear, jealousy, etc.

धसका m. 1. (of animals) a disease of lungs. 2. dry cough, bronchitis.

धसना vi. 1. to be ruined or destroyed. 2. = धँसना।

धसान f. = धँसान।

धाँधली f. a dishonest act, unfair/improper/arbitrary conduct.

धाँय-धाँय f. thumping sound as that produced in cannonading, connonade.

धाँस f. irritating smell like that of tobacco powder or leaves.

धाँसना vi. to cough like a horse.

धाक f. sway, predominance, commanding influence.

धागा m. thread.

धाड़ f. full-throated cry/lamentation.

धाता m. preserver, sustainer, protector.

धातु f. 1. metal. 2. root (of a verb).

धातुकर्म m. metalwork.

धातुकर्मी m. metallurgist.

धातु-विज्ञान m. metallurgy.

धातृका f. nurse.

धात्री f. wet nurse.

धात्री-विद्या f. obstetrics.

धात्विक adj. metallic. m. metallurgist.

धान m. paddy, rice in the husk.

धाना vi. to run.

धानी adj. light green. f. 1. receptacle. 2. stand.

धान्य m. grain.

धान्यागार m. granary, barn.

धाप m. 1. a non-standard measure of distance, which varies from 2 to 3 kilometres. 2. an expansive field/plane.

धाम m. 1. abode, residence, dwelling. 2. seat of a deity.

धायँ-धायँ f. = धाँय-धाँय।

धाय f. wet nurse.

धार f. 1. edge of a weapon. 2. sharpness. 3. current, flow.

धारक m. 1. one who holds, holder. 2. bearer.

धारण m. 1. supporting, as a stick in hand. 2. putting on, wearing; as clothes on the body. 3. retention.

धारण-शक्ति f. power of reten- tion, retentiveness.

धारणा f. 1. assumption, notion, opinion. 2. belief.

धारदार adj. sharp-edged.

धारना vt. 1. to put on, to wear. 2. to borrow.

धारा f. 1. current. 2. stream, river. 3. article, section; ~ 144 section 144.

धाराप्रवाह adj. glib, fluent.

धारावाहिक adj. serialised, serial.

धारित adj. that/which has been held.

धारिता f. 1. capacity. 2. retentiveness.

धारी adj. (one) who holds. f. stripe, line, streak.

धारोष्ण adj. (milk) fresh from the udders, fresh and tepid.

ध

धार्मिक adj. 1. religious. 2. pious.
धार्य adj. 1. that which can be held. 2. that wihch should be held.
धावक m. runner.
धावन m. running.
धावा m. attack, raid, charge.
धिक, धिक् interj. term of contempt, pooh! fie!
धिक्कार f. upbraid, rebuke, reproach, disdain, condemnation.
धिक्कारना vt. to upbraid/reproach/rebuke/curse/censure.
धींगाधींगी f = धींगामुश्ती ।
धींगामुश्ती f. coercive dealing, high-handedness.
धी f. 1. intellect, knowledge, erudition. 2. daughter.
धीमर m. fisherman.
धीमा adj. 1. slow. 2. dim. 3. low, soft.
धीमान, धीमान् adj. wise, sharp-witted, intelligent.
धीर adj. 1. patient. 2. steady, firm.
धीरज f. patience.
धीरे adv. 1. slowly. 2. gently. 3. softly.
धीरे-धीरे adv. (i) slowly. (ii) softly, in a low tone; (iii) gradually.
धीवर m. fisherman.
धीवरी f. 1. fisherwoman. 2. fish-line.
धुँआ m. = धुआँ ।
धुंध f. 1. fog, mist. 2. haze.
धुँधलका m. 1. twilight. 2. haziness.
धुँधला adj. 1. hazy, misty. 2. obscure.
धुआँ m. smoke.
धुआँकश m. chimney.
धुआँधार adj. & adv. like a stream of smoke, fast and furious.
धुआँसा m. smoky.
धुकधुकी f. trepidation, palpitation, heart-throb.
धुकर-पुकर f. palpitation, perplexity, suspense.
धुत्त adj. besotted (with).
धुन f. 1. obsession, ruling passion; propensity, mania. 2. tune.
धुनकना vt. to card. (cotton).
धुनकी m. carder.
f. carding bow/gadget.
धुनना vt. 1. to card. 2. to knock, cudgel.
धुनवाना vt. to cause to be carded.
धुनाई f. 1. act of carding. 2. charges for carding.
धुनिया m. carder.
धुनी adj. tenaciously persevering, faddish.
धुपाना vt. to dry (something) in the sun.
धुप्पल f. dodge, bluff.
धुरंधर adj. topping, outstan ding, having mastery.
धुर adj. extreme. m. 1. axle. 2. beginning.
धुरा m. axle.
धुरी f. axis.
धुर्रा m. particle.
धुलना vi. to be washed/cleansed.
धुलवाना vi. causative of धोना, to get washed, to have cleansed.

धुलाई f. work of washing, or charges paid for the same.

धुलाना vt. to get washed.

धुवाँस m. ground meal of vetch.

धुस्स m. 1. mound. 2. embankment, dam.

धूआँ m. = धुआँ।

धूतू m. gong, whistle.

धू-धू m. ~ करके जलना to burn like wild fire.

धूनी f. 1. incense. 2. ascetic's fire.

धूप f. 1. sunshine, the sun. 2. incense.

धूप-घड़ी f. sun-dial.

धूप-चश्मा m. sun-glasses.

धूप-छाँह f. 1. sun and shade. 2. a kind of cloth in which the warp and the woof are of prismatic colours.

धूपदानी f. small censer, in-censory.

धूपन m. fumigation.

धूपबत्ती f. incense-stick.

धूप-स्नान m. sunbath.

धूम m. smoke, fume. f. furore, tumult.

धूमकेतु m. a star with a tail, comet.

धूम-धड़क्का m. ballyhoo, hullabaloo.

धूमधाम f. pomp and show, eclat, fanfare.

धूमिल adj. 1. smoke coloured, fumigated. 2. dim, blurred.

धूम्र m. smoke, fume.

धूम्रपान m. smoking.

धूर्जटी m. Lord Shiva.

धूर्त adj. not honest or straightforward, crafty, cunning, crooked.

धूर्तता f. wiliness, craftiness, cunningness, crookedness.

धूल f. dust, dirt.

धूल-धक्कड़ m. dust and din.

धूल-धूसरित adj. steeped in dust, filled with dust.

धूलि f. dust.

धूसर adj. of the colour of ashes, grey.

धृतराष्ट्र m. king of Kauravas in the epic Mahabharat.

धृष्ट adj. insolent, impertinent, impudent, rude, reckless.

धृष्टता f. insolence, impertinence, impudence.

धेनु f. (milch) cow.

धेला m. = अधेला।

धैर्य m. patience, endurance.

धैर्यवान adj. having or showing patience, patient.

धोंधा m. 1. lump/clod of earth. 2. grotesque body.

धोखा m. 1. deceit, deception, fraud. 2. illusion. 3. scarecrow.

धोखेबाज़ adj. & m. treacherous, trickster, fraudulent, cheat.

धोती f. loin-cloth, dhoti.

धोना vt. 1. to wash/launder. 2. to apply water to something, bathe.

धोबिन f. washerwoman.

धोबी m. washerman.

धोबी-घाट m. washing place on the bank of a river, pond etc.

धोरी m. 1. general controller. 2. chief. 3. eminent person. 4. bullock.

धोरे adv. near, close by.

ध

धौंकना vt. 1. to blow with bellows. 2. to chastise.

धौंकनी f. 1. bellows. 2. blowpipe.

धौंकिया m. bellowman.

धौंस f. browbeating, threat.

धौंसा m. large kettledrum.

धौरा adj. 1. white. 2. clean.

धौल f. slap, buffet.

धौल-धप्पड़ m. = धौल-धप्पा।

धौल-धप्पा m. slapping and boxing, exchange of blows.

ध्यान m. 1. attention (of mind), concentration. 2. meditation, contemplation. 3. middle stage of Yoga which comes after धारणा and before समाधि।

ध्यानमग्न adj. absorbed/engrossed/lost in meditation.

ध्याना vt. to contemplate.

ध्यानावस्थित adj. lost in meditation.

ध्येय m. goal, aim.

ध्रुपद m. a form of classical Indian music.

ध्रुव m. Pole. adj. firm, unchanging, fixed.

ध्रुवतारा m. North star, Pole star.

ध्रुवीय adj. polar.

ध्वंस m. destruction, devastation, ruination.

ध्वंसक adj. causing great destruction, devastating.

ध्वंसावशेष m. remains, relics, ruins.

ध्वज m. flag, banner.

ध्वजपोत m. flag-ship.

ध्वजा f. flag, ensign, banner.

ध्वजारोहण m. flag-hoisting.

ध्वनि f. 1. sound. 2. implied/suggested meaning.

ध्वनित adj. implied/suggested (meaning).

ध्वनिविज्ञान m. phonetics, phonology.

ध्वनिसह adj. soundproof.

ध्वस्त adj. destroyed, devastated, ruined.

ध्वानिक adj. acoustic.

न

न m. fifth of the dental pentad of consonants of the Nagari alphabet; its sound resem-bles that of n in not. adv. a sign of disagreement; no, not.

नंग m. nakedness; ~ धड़ंग stark naked, nude.

नंगा adj. 1. uncovered, exposed. 2. nude, naked. 3. bare. 4. shameless.

नंगा-झोली f. thorough search (of a person).

नंगापन m. 1. nakedness. 2. shamelessness.

नंगा-बूचा adj. penniless.

नंगा-लुच्चा adj. penniless and wicked.

नंद m. joy, happiness.

नंदकिशोर m. Lord Krishna.

नंदन m. son.

नंदनकानन m. garden of Lord Indra.

नंदित adj. pleased, delighted.

नंदिनी f. 1. daughter. 2. goddess Durga.

नंदी m. 1. the (carrier) bull of Lord Shiva. 2. banyan tree.

नंदोई m. = ननदोई ।

नंबरदार m. headman.

नंबरवार adv. 1. by turn. 2. serially.

नंबरी adj. 1. bearing a number, numbered. 2. standard, patent.

नई adj. new.

नकचढ़ा adj. finicky, peevish, hard to please, fastidious.

नकटा adj. & m. one with a nose chopped off.

नकटी f. fem. form of नकटा ।

नक़द m. cash, ready money.

नक़दी-रसीद f. cash receipt.

नक़ब f. house-breaking, burgl- ary.

नक़ल f. 1. imitation. 2. mimicry. 3. copy, duplicate.

नक़लची m. one who imitates.

नक़ली adj. 1. artificial. 2. fake. 3. forged, counterfeit. 4. mock.

नक़्शा m. 1. map, chart. 2. drawing. 3. sketch, rough drawing.

नक़शेबाज़ m. coquet.

नकसीर f. nose-bleed.

नक़ाब f. mask, veil.

नकार f. 1. the letter न or its sound. 2. denial, refusal.

नकारना vt. 1. to deny/refuse. 2. to dishonour (a cheque). 3. to negate.

नकारात्मक adj. negative, implying denial/refusal.

नक़ाशना vt. to engrave.

नकियाना vi. to speak with a nasal accent.

नकुल m. mongoose.

नकेल f. nosering, bridle.

नक्का m. the eye of a needle.

नक़्क़ारख़ाना m. kettledrum house.

नक़्क़ारा m. huge drum.

नक़्क़ाली f. 1. imitation. 2. mimicry.

नक़्क़ाश m. engraver, carver.

न

नक़्क़ाशी f. engraving, carving.

नक्की f. 'one' or 'ace' of a gambling game. adj. clear, free.

नक्कू adj. 1. having a large nose. 2. conspicuously nonconforming/ unconventional.

नक्र m. crocodile.

नक़्श adj. imprinted. m. 1. signs and designs which are engraved. 2. stamp. 3. figure of the face.

नक्षत्र m. constellation (of stars), planet.

नक्षत्र-विद्या f. astrology.

नक्षत्री adj. having good fortune, lucky, fortunate.

नख m. nail of a finger.

नख़ m. string used for kite flying.

नखक्षत m. injury caused by finger nails.

नख़रा m. flirtatious behaviour, coquetry.

नख़रीला adj. coquetish, prude.

नख़लिस्तान m. Oasis.

नख-शिख m. from head to foot, cap-a-pie.

नख़ास m. market.

नखियाना vt, to cause hurt with the finger nails.

नखी adj. having large nails.

नग m. 1. gem, jewel. 2. mountain. 3. piece, item.

नगण्य adj. almost negligible, trifling, insignificant.

नगद adj. & m. = नक़द।

नगपति m. Himalayas.

नगर m. 1. city. 2. all the people living in a city.

नगर-निगम m. municipal corporation.

नगरपालिका f. municipality.

नगरप्रमुख m. mayor.

नगरवासी m. citizen.

नगरी f. town.

नगरीकरण f. urbanisation.

नगरीय adj. of or pertaining to the city, urban.

नगाड़ा m. tymbal, huge drum.

नगीना m. jewel, gem.

नगेंद्र m. Himalayas.

नग्न adj. nude, naked.

नग्नता f. nudity, nakedness.

नचना m. dancer.

नचनी f. woman dancer.

नचाना vt. 1. to make one dance. 2. to harass/tease.

नज़दीक adj. & adv. near, adjacent, close.

नज़दीकी adj. near.

नज़र f. 1. the power or ability to see, eyesight. 2. look, glance. 3. view. 4. care. 5. gift, present. 6. evil eye.

नज़रबंद adj. interned, detained.

नज़रसानी f. 1. revision. 2. reconsideration.

नज़राना m. present, gift. vi. (usually नज़रा जाना) to be a victim of (someone's) evil eye.

नज़रिया m. point of view, viewpoint.

नज़ला m. catarrh.

नज़ाकत f. delicacy or tender-ness (of body).

नजात f. deliverance, riddance, liberation.

नज़ारा m. spectacle, scene, view.

नज़ीर f. 1. instance, example. 2. precedent.

नजूमी m. 1. astrologer. 2. astronomer.

नज़ूल m. land belonging to Government.

नज़्म f. poem.

नट m. 1. dancer, rope-dancer, acrobat. 2. actor. 3. impresario, stage-manager.

नटखट adj. 1. mischievous, naughty. 2. impish.

नटखटी f. mischief, naughtiness.

नटना vi. to go back by one's word, to negate.

नटनी f. actress.

नटी f. 1. actress. 2. stage manager's wife.

नत adj. 1. inclined, tilted. 2. bent, curved.

नतमस्तक adj. having head bowed down (in reverence).

नति f. inclination, bent.

नतिनी f. daughter's daughter.

नतीजा m. the effect or outcome of something, result, consequence.

नतोदर adj. concave.

नत्थ f. = नथ।

नत्थी f. file.

नथ f. nosering, nose-rope.

नथना m. nostril, nares.

नथनी f. nosering.

नथुना m. = नथना।

नद m. big river.

नदारद adj. missing, disappe- ared, absent.

नदी f. river, stream.

नदीतल m. river-bed.

नदीमुख m. mouth of a river, estuary.

ननद f. husband's sister.

ननदोई m. husband of husband's sister, husband of the ननद।

ननसाल f. = ननिहाल।

ननिहाल m. mother's paternal home.

ननुनच m. 1. hitch, hesitation. 2. objection.

नन्हा adj. tiny, wee.

नपाई f. act or process of measurement, or charges paid therefor.

नपा-तुला adj. 1. measured, exact to the core. 2. precisely to the point.

नपुंसक adj. & m. 1. impotent, emasculated. 2. coward.

नफ़रत f. very strong dislike, hatred.

नफ़री f. 1. one day's work of a labourer. 2. wages paid for the same.

नफ़ा m. 1. money gained in a business, profit, gain. 2. benefit gained from something, advantage.

नफ़ासत f. 1. sophistication, refinement, nicety. 2. delicacy.

नफ़ीरी f. clairnet.

नफ़ीस m. excellent, fine, nice.

नबी m. prophet, divine messenger.

नब्ज़ f. pulse.

नब्बे adj. & m. ninety, 90.

नभ m. sky, firmament.

नभचर adj. & m. (one) who moves in the sky, a bird.

नम adj. wet, damp.

न

नमक m. salt.

नमकदान m. salt-pot.

नमकहराम adj. & m. ungrateful, faithless.

नमकहलाल adj. & m. practically loyal/faithful/grateful, true to (someone's) salt.

नमकीन adj. 1. salty, saltish, salted, saline. 2. handsome, beautiful. m. dish of salty snacks.

नमदा m. a kind of woollen blanket, felt.

नमन m. 1. bowing, bending. 2. obeisance.

नमना vi. 1. to bow/bend. 2. to pay homage (to).

नमस्कार m. term of salutation.

नमस्ते f. term of salutation/greeting.

नमाज़ f. (Muslim's) prayer.

नमित adj. 1. bent, inclined. 2. bowed.

नमी f. 1. wetness, moisture, humidity. 2. dampness.

नमूना m. 1. sample. 2. example. 3. an awkward figure.

नम्य adj. (that) which can be bent, flexible.

नम्यता f. flexibility.

नम्र adj. quiet and modest, submissive, humble.

नम्रता f. modesty, humility, meekness, submissiveness.

नय m. policy.

नयन m. eye.

नयनगोचर adj. perceptible, visi- ble.

नया adj. 1. not existing before, new. 2. fresh, freshly produced. 3. different. 4. modern, of new fashion, recent, novel. 5. young.

नयापन m. 1. newness. 2. modernism, new fashion, novelty.

नर m. man.

नरक m. hell, inferno.

नरकट m. reed.

नरकवास m. living in hell.

नरगिस f. narcissus.

नरगिसी adj. of the colour of narcissus.

नरपति m. king.

नरपिशाच m. 1. ogre. 2. cannibal.

नरपुंगव m. topping/best man.

नरबलि f. human sacrifice.

नरभक्षी adj & m. cannibal, man-eater.

नरम adj. 1. soft, gentle, moderate. 2. smooth and delicate.

नरमा f. a kind of cotton.

नरमी f. softness, gentleness.

नरमेध m. sacrifice of a human being.

नरसिंहा m. a kind of copper horn.

नरसों adv. 1. the day, two days after tomorrow. 2. the day, two days before yesterday.

नरहत्या f. 1. murder, homicide. 2. genocide.

नरिया f. a kind of clay tile.

नरेंद्र m. king, prince.

नरेली f. outer covering of a coconut.

नरेश m. king.

नर्तक m. male dancer.

नर्तकी f. female dancer, dancing girl.

नर्स f. nurse.

नल m. 1. tap. 2. pipe, tube.

नलका m. 1. hand-pump. 2. water-tap.
नलकूप m. tubewell.
नलिका f. 1. thin tube. 2. quiver.
नलिन m. lotus, lily.
नलिनी f. lotus, lily.
नली f. 1. tube, pipe. 2. spout.
नवंबर m. November.
नव adj. 1. new, novel. 2. nine, 9.
नवग्रह m. the nine planets (Hindu Astrology).
नवजागरण m. renaissance.
नवजात adj. newborn, nascent.
नवधा adj. of nine kinds.
नवनीत m. butter.
नवम adj. ninth.
नवमल्लिका f. jasmine.
नवयुवक m. youth, young man.
नवयुवती f. young/youthful girl.
नवयौवन m. adolescence, youth.
नवरंग adj. novel, of a new design.
नवरत्न m. 1. nine (kinds of) precious stones. 2. the nine gems (learned men) of the court of king Vikramaditya.
नवल adj. novel, new.
नववधू f. newly married girl.
नवविवाहित adj. newly-married.
नवशिक्षु m. novice.
नवसाक्षर m. neo-literate.
नवागत m. newcomer, guest.
नवान्न m. new corn of a harvest.
नवाब m. baron, Nawab (Muslim feudal Lord).
नवासा m. daughter's son.
नवासी adj. & m. eighty-nine. f. daughter's daughter.
नवीकरण m. renovation.
नवीकृत adj. renovated.
नवीन m. new, novel.
नवीनता f. newness, novelty, recency, modernity.
नवेद m. 1. good news. 2. invitation.
नवेला adj. new and handsome, fresh and young.
नवेली f. young lady.
नवोढ़ा adj. & f. newly married woman.
नव्य adj. 1. new, novel. 2. modern, recent.
नशा m. intoxication.
नशा-पानी m. intoxicants and concomitant snacks.
नशाबंदी f. prohibition.
नशीला adj. intoxicating, inebriating.
नश्तर m. lancet, surgical knife.
नश्वर adj. 1. mortal, destructible, perishable. 2. transitory, ephemeral, short-lived.
नश्वरता f. 1. mortality, destructibility.
नष्ट adj. destroyed, ruined, annihilated.
नष्टप्राय adj. almost destoyed/ruined/annihilated/asunder.
नष्टभ्रष्ट adj. completely destroyed or ruined.
नस f. vein, sinew, nerve, thews.
नसबंदी f. vasectomy.
नसल (na sal) f. 1. lineage. 2. breed. 3. race.
नसवार f. snuff.
नसीब m. destiny, fortune, luck.
नसीबोंजला adj. ill-fated.

न

नसीम f. gentle breeze.

नसीहत f. advice, teaching, precept, preaching.

नसूड़िया adj. ill-omened, inauspicious.

नसैनी f. ladder, staircase.

नस्य m. snuff.

नहर f. canal.

नहरनी f. an Indian type of nail-cutter.

नहरी adj. of or pertaining to a canal.

नहरुआ m. guinea worm.

नहला m. nine of cards.

नहलाना vt. to give a bath to somebody, bathe.

नहान m. ablation, bathing.

नहाना vi. to bathe, to take a bath.

नहिक adj. negative.

नहीं adv. a sign of disagreement, no, not.

नहूसत f. 1. inauspiciousness. 2. gloominess.

नाँद f. tub, manger.

ना adv. no.

नाइत्तिफ़ाक़ी f. disunity, discord, disagreement.

नाइन f. barber's wife.

नाईं adv. like, as.

नाई m. barber.

नाक f. 1. nose. 2. heaven. 3. (fig.) prestige.

नाक़दरी f. 1. lack of appreciation, want of proper respect. 2. humiliation.

नाक-नक़शा m. the cut of the face, features.

नाकवाला adj. & m. prestigious (person).

नाका m. 1. entrance (to fort, city etc.). 2. check-post. 3. eye (of a needle) 4. crocodile.

नाक़ाबिल adj. unfit, undeser- ving, unworthy.

नाकारा adj. good-for-nothing, worthless.

नाक़िस adj. 1. defective (object), deficient. 2. worthless (person).

नाकेबंदी f. blockade, siege.

नाख़ून m. nail (of the finger).

नाग m. 1. cobra, snake, serpent.

नागपाश m. a noose-like weapon.

नागफनी f. a kind of thorny bush, cactus.

नागफेन m. 1. saliva of a snake. 2. opium.

नागर adj. 1. civil, civic. 2. urban.

नागराज m. king cobra.

नागरिक adj. civil. m. citizen.

नागरिकता f. citizenship.

नागरिक शास्त्र m. civics.

नागरी f. Devnagari script, Nagari characters.

नागवार adj. unbearable, intolerable.

नागा m. 1. one belonging to the Naga tribe. 2. a nude ascetic.

नाग़ा m. gap, absence from work.

नागालैंड m. a state in the north-east of India.

नागिन f. a 1. female serpent. 2. a line of hair on the back, considered inauspicious.

नागेंद्र m. 1. large snake. 2. big elephant.

नागेश m. = नागेंद्र।

नागेश्वर m. = नागेंद्र।

नाच m. dance.

नाच-गाना m. dancing and singing.

नाच-घर m. dancing hall.

नाचना vi. to dance.

नाच-रंग m. dancing and merry-making.

नाचीज़ adj. insignificant, trifling.

नाज़ m. 1. pride, vanity. 2. airs, charming gestures. 3. fondness.

नाज़-नख़रा m. coquetishness.

नाजायज़ adj. 1. illegitimate, illegal. 2. improper, unjust.

नाज़ी adj. very cruel, harsh, severe. m. nazi (German natse).

नाज़ीवाद m. nazism.

नाज़ुक adj. 1. soft, delicate, tender. 2. sensitive, vulnerable. 3. critical. 4. precarious.

नाज़ुकमिज़ाज adj. touchy, pee-vish, irritable.

नाटक m. drama, play, dramatic performance.

नाटकबाज़ी f. exaggerated emotional behaviour, dramatics.

नाटकीय adj. 1. dramatic. 2. deliberately affected.

नाटना vt. 1. to negate/refuse. 2. to deny.

नाटा adj. dwarfish, short statured.

नाटिका f. short drama.

नाट्य m. = नाटक।

नाट्यकला f. histrionics, dramatic art.

नाट्यकार m. 1. actor. 2. playwright, dramatist.

नाट्यशाला f. theatre.

नाट्यशास्त्र m. dramaturgy.

नाड़ा m. trouser string.

नाड़ी f. 1. pulse, nerve, blood vessel. 2. vein, artery

नाड़ी-व्रण m. sinus.

नाता m. relation, relationship.

नाती m. daughter's son. [Fem. नातिन, नतिनी]

नाते, के postposition. 1. due to relationship, status, position. 2. for, on behalf of.

नातेदार m. relative, kinsman.

नातेदारी f. relationship.

नाथ m. 1. master, Lord. 2. nose-rope.

नाथना vt. 1. to pierce a nostril of a bullock, etc. and pass a string through it for driving. 2. to bring under control. 3. to sew/string together.

नाद m. 1. sound, esp. musical. 2. noise.

नादान adj. 1. ignorant. 2. slow to understand, unintelligent.

नादानी f. 1. ignorance. 2. silliness.

नादिरशाही adj. tyrannous, high-handed. f. tyranny, high-handedness.

नादिहंद adj. & m. defaulting or defaulter in payment.

नान f. big, thick type of bread.

नानखताई f. a kind of sweet.

नानबाई m. baker.

नाना m. mother's father, maternal grandfather. adj. varied, divine, different, several.

नानार्थ adj. (word) homonym, (object) multi-purpose.

न

नानी f. maternal grandmother, mother's mother.

ना-नुकर f. 'no', negative reply.

नाप f. measure, measurement, dimension.

नापना vt. to measure.

नापसंद adj. not to one's liking, unacceptable.

नापाक adj. impure, unclean, dirty, uncouth.

नापित m. barber.

नाफ़ा m. navel of a musk-deer.

नाबदान m. gutter.

नाबालिग़ adj. minor, underage.

नाभि f. navel, hub.

नाभिक adj. nuclear. m. nucleus.

नाभिकीय adj. = नाभिक।

नामंज़ूर adj. 1. disallowed. 2. re-jected, not accepted. 3. refused.

नाम m. 1. name. 2. reputation, fame.

नामक adj. bearing/having the name, called.

नामकरण m. ceremony of naming a child, denomination, nomenclature.

नामज़द adj. nominated.

नाम-धातु m. denominative verb.

नामधारी adj. bearing the name, named.

नामपट्ट m. 1. signboard. 2. nameplate

नामराशि adj. & m. namesake.

नामर्द adj. 1. impotent 2. effemi-nate.

नामलेवा m. heir.

नामवर adj. famous, renowned, reputed.

नामांकन m. nomination.

नामांकित adj. nominated.

नामांतर m. alias, second name.

नामांतरण m. change of name, mutation.

नामावली f. nomenclature.

नामिका f. panel (of names).

नामी adj. famous.

नामे-बाक़ी f. debit balance.

नामोनिशान m. trace, mark.

नाम्ना adj. bearing/having the name.

नायक m. 1. leader, chief. 2. hero.

नायन f. नाइन।

नायब adj. deputy.

नायाब adj. 1. not easily available. 2. excellent, of a very high quality.

नायिका f. 1. heroine (of a story, novel etc.). 2. damsel, belle.

नायिका-भेद m. classification of heroines in Indian literature.

नारंगी f. orange.

नारकी adj. = नारकीय।

नारकीय adj. hellish, diabolical.

नारा m. 1. slogan; ~ देना to provide/ give a slogan. 2. (पाजामे का) tape (for fastening trousers).

नाराज़ adj. displeased, angry.

नारायण m. Lord Vishnu.

नारियल m. coconut; ~ की जटा coir.

नारी f. woman.

नारू m. louse.

नाल f. 1. pedicel, tubular stalk. 2. tube. 3. barrel of a gun.

4. weaver's spindle. 5. navel string. 6. horse-shoe. 7. ring of stone used for weight-lifting. 8. charges realised by the owner of a gambling den.

नाल-कटाई f. act of cutting the navel string of a newborn child, or wages paid therefor.

नाला m. 1. big drain, gutter. 2. rivulet, water-course, water-channel.

नालायक़ adj. unfit, worthless, incapable, unworthy.

नालिश f. lawsuit, complaint, report.

नाली f. drain, sewer.

नाव f. boat, ferry.

नाविक m. boatman, sailor.

नाश m. annihilation, destruction, ruination.

नाशक adj. causing destruction, ruinous, destructive.

नाशपाती f. pear.

नाशवान, नाशवान् adj. perishable.

नाशी adj. = नाशक।

नाश्ता m. breakfast, refreshment.

नास f. snuff.

नास-पीटा adj. totally worthless, good-for-nothing (fig.).

नासमझ adj. 1. innocent. 2. unintelligent.

नासमझी f. 1. lack of understanding/ intellingence. 2. foolish act.

नासा f. 1. nose. 2. nostril.

नासाज़ adj. out of sorts.

नासिका f. nose.

नासिक्य adj. nasal, pertaining to the nose.

नासूर m. sinus, fistula.

नास्तिक m. one who disbelieves in the existence of God, atheist.

नास्तिकता f. the belief that God does not exist, atheism.

नास्तिवाद m. atheism.

नाहक़ adv. in vain, to no purpose.

नाह-नूँह f. negation, expression of reluctance.

नाहर m. 1. lion. 2. lion-hearted person.

निंदक m. backbiter, slanderer, calumniator.

निंदना vt. to backbite/abuse/ defame.

निंदनीय adj. censurable, reprehensible, condemnable.

निंदा f. backbiting, censure, slander, opprobrium, reproof.

निंदा-प्रस्ताव m. censure motion.

निंद्य adj. = निंदनीय।

निः pref. denoting negation.

निःशंक adj. fearless, dauntless.

निःशेष adj 1. without any remainder/residue. 2. whole, entire. 3. complete all-round, exhaustive.

निःश्वास m. expiration, brea-thing out.

निःसंकोच adv. unhesitatingly, boldly.

निःस्पंद adj. motionless, still.

निःस्पृह adj. 1. above all desires. 2. selfless.

निःस्वार्थ adj. selfless, unselfish.

नि pref. denoting down, in, into, within etc.

निअराना vi. to come near.

निकट adj. proximate, near, close. adv. near.

निकटवर्ती adj. situated near, close-at-hand, adjacent, adjoining.

निकम्मा adj. 1. idle, inert. 2. good-for-nothing, worthless.

निकर m. half-pants, shorts.

निकलना vi. 1. to come out. 2. to rise. 3. to appear. 4. to pass. 5. to pass out, to turn out. 6. to prove. 7. to be subtracted.

निकलवाना vt. causative of निकालना।

निकष m. 1. touchstone. 2. criterion.

निकाय m. 1. body; शासी ~ governing body. 2. system; ग्रह ~ planetary system.

निकालना vt. 1. to take or draw out. 2. to bring out or publish. 3. to find. 4. to dismiss. 5. to put away, banish. 6. to cause to be issued, as a summons. 7. to solve, as a question.

निकाला m. expulsion, banishment.

निकास m. 1. act or state of coming out. 2. source of income. 3. outlet, egress. 4. exit. 5. exhaust.

निकासी f. 1. act or state of going out. 2. manufacture and sale of goods. 3. income. 4. toll. 5. clearance.

निकाह m. marriage (Muslim).

निकुंज m. bower, arbour, grove, thicket.

निकृष्ट adj. 1. very inferior, of a low order, worse, worthless. 2. vile, base.

निकृष्टता f. lowliness, worthlessness.

निकेतन m. residence, abode.

निक्षिप्त adj. 1. thrown. 2. abandoned. 3. deposited. 4. con-signed, pledged.

निक्षेप m. 1. throwing. 2. despatch. 3. deposit. 4. pledge, consignment.

निक्षेपण m. act or state of throwing.

निखट्टू adj. (one) who earns nothing, jobless, unemployed.

निखरना vi. to brighten up, to blossom out.

निखरवाना vt. causative of निखारना।

निखार m. lustre, brightening up, blossoming out, elegance.

निखारना vi. to clean/cleanse.

निख़ालिस adj. = ख़ालिस।

निखिल adj. entire, whole, all.

निगंदना vi. to sew (provisio-nally) with long stitches.

निगड़ m. fetters.

निगम m. 1. corporation. 2. Vedas.

निगमन m. 1. deduction. 2. incorporation.

निगमागम m. (Hindu) holy scriptures.

निगरानी f. 1. vigil, surveillance, supervision. 2. custody.

निगलना vi. to swallow up, to gulp down.

निगाली f. smoking pipe (of a हुक्का).

निगाह f. 1. eyesight. 2. vision. 3. watch, guard.

निगुरा adj. uninitiated.

निगूढ़ adj. 1. abstruse, obscure. 2. latent, secret, hidden.

निगोड़ा adj. & m. idler, lazy, worthless.

निग्रह m. 1. restraint. 2. self-control.

निघरा adj. homeless.

निचय m. 1. collection. 2. fund.

निचला adj. lowly, lower.

निचाई f. 1. lowness. 2. depth. 3. meanness.

निचान f. slope, state of being low.

निचुड़ना vi. to be squeezed.

निचोड़ m. epitome, extract, essence.

निचोड़ना vt. to squeeze/wring/extort.

निछत्र adj. dethroned.

निछल adj. निश्छल।

निछावर f. 1. something (sply. coins) offered for warding off evil influences. 2. sacrifice.

निज adj. own.

निज़ाम m. 1. Nizam (title of the ruler of the state of Hyderabad.) 2. administration, mana-gement. 3. order.

निजी adj. 1. own. 2. personal.

निजीकरण m. privatization, denationalization.

निठल्ला adj & m. 1. idler, lazy. 2. unemployed, lounger.

निठुर adj. hard-hearted, cruel.

निठुरता f. hard-heartedness, cruelty.

निठुराई f. = निठुरता।

निडर adj. fearless, undaunted.

निढाल adj. exhausted, languid.

नितंब m. buttocks, hips.

नित adv. = नित्य।

नितांत adj. 1. excessive, extreme. 2. absolute, downright.

नित्य adv. 1. every day. 2. always. adj. daily.

नित्यकर्म m. ceremonial routine.

नित्यचर्या f. daily routine.

नित्यता f. eternity, permanence.

नित्यसंबंध m. perpetual/permanent relation.

निथरना vi. to be decanted/purified.

निथार m. 1. decantation. 2. decanted substance (liquid).

निथारना vt. 1. to purify by decanting. 2. to filter (water).

निदरना vt. 1. to insult/humiliate. 2. to neglect/ignore.

निदर्शक adj. illustrating.

निदर्शन m. illustration, example.

निदान m. 1. diagnosis. 2. end. 3. conclusion.

निदानशाला f. clinic.

निदान-शास्त्र m. diagnostics.

निदेश m. 1. direction. 2. directive. 3. instruction.

निदेशक adj. directive. m. director.

निदेशक मंडल adj. board of directors.

निदेशालय m. directorate.

निदेशिका f. directory.

निद्रा f. sleep, slumber.

निद्रालस m. drowsiness, sleepiness.

निद्रालु adj. sleepy, drowsy, slumberous.

निद्रित adj. sleeping, asleep.

निधड़क adj. fearless, undaunted. adv. fearlessly, undauntedly.

निधन m. demise, decease, death.

निधान m. store, reservoir.

निधि f. 1. fund. 2. treasure.

निनाद m. 1. sound (especially loud). 2. humming sound.

निनादित adj. full of sound. echoing, resonant.

निन्यानबे adj. & m. ninety-nine, 99.

निपट adj. absolutely.

निपटना vi. 1. to be finished off. 2. to be free after some work. 3. to settle accounts. 4. to evacuate.

निपटान m. evacuation.

निपटाना vt. to dispose of, to settle.

निपटारा m. settlement, disposal.

निपत्र adj. without leaves.

निपात m. 1. fall, degradation, ruin. 2. destruction. 3. death. 4. particle. (Gram.)

निपुण adj. adept, proficient, skilful, expert, dextrous.

निपुणता f. efficiency, proficiency, skill, sagacity, acumen.

निपूता adj. issueless, childless.

निपूती f. woman having no issue.

निबंध m. essay, treatise.

निबंधन m. 1. tying/joining/fastening together. 2. registration.

निब f. nib.

निबटना vi. = निपटना।

निबटाना vt. = निपटाना।

निबद्ध adj. 1. tied/joined/fastened together. 2. registered.

निबाह m. = निर्वाह।

निबाहना vt. = निभाना।

निबिड़ adj. = निविड़।

निबेड़ना vt. = निपटाना।

निबेड़ा m. disposal, settlement, solution.

निभना vi. to be carried out, to pull on.

निभाना vt. 1. to fulfil (one's) responsibility/duty/order promise. 2. to get along, to carry on/pull on.

निभाव m. = निर्वाह।

निमंत्रण m. invitation.

निमंत्रित adj. invited.

निमकी f. 1. lemon-pickle. 2. fried salty smallish snacks.

निमकौड़ी f. seed of नीम (margosa) tree.

निमग्न adj. 1. immersed, submerged. 2. absorbed, engrossed.

निमज्जन m. 1. bathing. 2. immersion, submersion.

निमित्त m. 1. cause, reason. 2. purpose.

निमित्त, के postposition. for, for the sake of.

निमिष m. 1. blinking (of an eye), twinkle. 2. time taken in the twinkling of an eye, jiffy.

निमीलन m. winking.

निमीलित adj. closed, shut up.

निमेष m. = निमिष।

निमोनिया m. pneumonia.

निम्न adj. 1. low. 2. under.

निम्नलिखित adj. undermen-tioned, following.

नियंता m. 1. controller. 2. Supreme Controller, God.

नियंत्रक m. controller.

नियंत्रण m. control, rustraint.

नियंत्रित adj. controlled, rest-rained.

नियत adj. 1. destined, fated. 2. prescribed, specified. 3. appointed, posted, allotted.

नियतन m. allotment, fixation.

नियति f. destiny, fate.

नियम m. 1. rule. 2. usual practice.

नियमतः adv. 1. as a rule. 2. according to rule/law. 3. formally.

नियमन m. act of regulating/ controlling.

नियमानुसार adv. as per rule.

नियमावली f. manual (of rules and regulations), set of rules.

नियमित adj. regulated, regular.

नियमितता f. regularity.

नियामक m. one who lays down rules, regulator.

नियामत f. blessing, boon, bounty, favour, benevolence.

नियुक्त adj. 1. appointed. 2. posted, engaged, employed.

नियुक्ति f. 1. appointment. 2. posting, employment.

नियोक्ता m. employer.

नियोजक m. 1. employer. 2. planner

नियोजन m. 1. act of employing. 2. planning.

नियोजित adj. 1. employed. 2. planned.

नियोज्य adj. 1. employable. 2. which can be planned.

निरंकुश adj. 1. unrestrained, absolute. 2. despotic; ~ शासक despot.

निरंजन adj. 1. (eyes or person) without collyrium. 2. untainted, faultless, spotless, unstained.

निरंतर adj. continual, continuous. adv. incessantly, continuously, non-stop.

निरक्षर adj. illiterate, unlettered, uneducated.

निरखना vt. 1. to behold/view/see/ look. 2. to examine.

निरत adj. engrossed, absorbed.

निरनुनासिक adj. non-nasal, pronounced without a nasal touch.

निरन्न adj. 1. without food, hungry, 2. without cereals.

निरपराध adj. innocent, guiltless, not guilty.

निरपवाद adj. without exception.

निरपेक्ष adj. 1. absolute. 2. unconcerned. 3. indifferent.

निरपेक्षित adj. unconcerned.

निरभिमान adj. without pride, humble.

निरभिलाष adj. without any desire, above all desires, disinterested.

निरर्थक adj. 1. meaningless. 2. useless, worthless, futile.

निरवधि adj. 1. having no fixed period. 2. limitless, endless. 3. perennial.

निरवलंब adj. 1. without support/ prop. 2. helpless.

निरसन m. cancellation, repeal.

निरस्त्र adj. unarmed, disarmed.

निरस्त्रीकरण m. disarmament.

निरहंकार adj. prideless, without vanity.

निरा adj. sheer, absolute, pure.

निराई f. act of weeding out, or charges paid therefor.

निराकरण m. repudiation, contradiction, abrogation.

निराकार adj. formless, shape-less, incorporeal.

निरादर m. disrespect, insult, disgrace.

निराधार adj. 1. baseless, unfounded. 2. without support/ prop.

निराना vt. to weed out.

निरापद adj. immune, safe, secure.

निरामय adj. sound, healthy.

निरामिष adj. (food) without meat, egg or fish, vegetarian (food).

निरालंब adj. = निरवलंब।

निराला adj. 1. strange, queer. 2. unique. 3. peculiar, extraordinary. m. solitary or lonely place.

निरावरण adj. unveiled, uncovered.

निरावृत adj. unveiled, uncovered.

निराश adj. 1. disappointed, frustrated, hopeless. 2. dismayed, dejected.

निराशा f. 1. disappointment, frustration. despair. 2. dismay, pessimism.

निराशावाद m. pessimism.

निराश्रय adj. without refuge/shelter/ protection.

निराहार adj. abstaining from food.

निरीक्षक m. inspector, invigila-tor, supervisor.

निरीक्षण m. 1. observation, viewing. 2. inspection.

निरीक्षित adj. 1. inspected. 2. observed.

निरीश्वरवाद m. atheism.

निरीह adj. innocent, harmless.

निरुक्त m. etymology.

निरुक्ति f. derivation.

निरुत्तर adj. at a loss to answer.

निरुत्साह adj. without enthu- siasm/ zeal/spirit.

निरुद्देश्य adj. aimless, purposeless. adv. aimlessly, purposelessly.

निरुद्ध adj. obstructed, choked.

निरुद्यम adj. not industrious, lazy, indolent.

निरुपम adj. matchless, peerless, incomparable.

निरुपाधि adj. 1. without any attribute. 2. above all attributes. 3. unconditioned.

निरुपाय adj. resourceless, helpless.

निरूपण m. exposition, elucidation.

निरूपित adj. explained, elucidated.

निरोग adj. = नीरोग।

निरोध m. 1. constraint, control, restriction, check, prevention. 2. condom

निर्ख़ m. rate.

निर्गंध adj. odourless, smell-less.

निर्गत adj. issued.

निर्गम m. 1. issue, egress. 2. exit, outlet.

निर्गुण adj. 1. without attributes. 2. without (good or bad) qualities. 3. absolute.

निर्जन adj. desolate (place), un-inhabited, solitary, lonely, deserted.

निर्जनता f. loneliness, desolation.

निर्जर adj. having no old age, everyoung, possessing perennial youth.

निर्जल adj. dry.

निर्जीव adj. 1. lifeless, without life, inanimate, dead. 2. insipid, spiritless.

निर्झर m. fall, waterfall, torrent.

निर्झरिणी f. small waterfall.

निर्णय m. decision, judgment, verdict, finding.

निर्णायक adj. deciding, decisive, conclusive, determinative. m. referee, judge, umpire.

निर्णायक मत m. 1. decisive vote. 2. casting vote.

निर्णीत adj. decided, judged.

निर्दयता f. cruelty, pitilessness, mercilessness, ruthlessness.

निर्दयी adj. pitiless, merciless, ruthless.

निर्दलीय adj. not belonging to any party, independent.

निर्दिष्ट adj. assigned, determined, specified.

निर्देश m. 1. instruction. 2. direction. 3. reference.

निर्देशक m. 1. instructor. 2. dire- ctor.

निर्दोष adj. 1. innocent, blameless, guiltless, not guilty (person). 2. unblemished, flawless.

निर्दोषता f. innocence, guiltlessness.

निर्द्वंद्व adj. 1. (object) without dispute, uncontested. 2. carefree, above pleasure and pain. 3. (person) without a rival or opposer.

निर्धन adj. poor, have-not, indigent.

निर्धनता f. poverty, indigence, penury.

निर्धारण m. 1. assessment, ascertainment. 2. fixation, determination.

निर्धारित adj. 1. ascertai-ned, assessed. 2. fixed, determined. 3. scheduled.

निर्निमेष adv. without blinking/ winking.

निर्बल adj. weak, infirm, feeble.

निर्बाध adj. 1. unrestricted, un-obstructed. 2. without anything blocking, free.

निर्बीज adj. seedless.

निर्बुद्धि adj. foolish, stupid.

निर्भय adj. fearless, intrepid, valiant, dauntless.

निर्भयता f. fearlessness, intrepidity, dauntlessness.

निर्भर adj. dependent.

निर्भीक adj. = निर्भय।

निर्भ्रांत adj. (person) who has no

doubts, free from doubts.

निर्मम adj. merciless, cruel, harsh, ruthless.

निर्ममता f. heartlessness, ruthlessness, cruelty.

निर्मल adj. 1. pure, clear, clean. 2. spotless, stainless.

निर्माण m. 1. act of building. 2. construction, erection. 3. manufacturing, production. 4. making, creation.

निर्माता m. 1. builder. 2. constructor. 3. manufacturer. 4. creator; 5. producer.

निर्मित adj. 1. built. 2. constructed. 3. manu-factured. 4. created, produced.

निर्मुक्त adj. enjoying liberty, free.

निर्मूल adj. 1. rootless, without root. 2. baseless, unfounded.

निर्मोही adj. not responsive to love, loveless, cold-hearted, harsh, cruel.

निर्यात m. export.

निर्यातक m. exporter.

निर्यास m. 1. exudation from plants. 2. gum.

निर्लज्ज adj. shameless, brazen-faced, immodest.

निर्लज्जता f. shamelessness, brazen-facedness, immodesty; ~ से shamelessly.

निर्लिप्त adj. unattached, detached.

निर्लोभ m. unselfishness. adj. uncovetous.

निर्वंश adj. issueless, childless.

निर्वचन m. interpretation.

निर्वसन adj. naked, nude.

निर्वहन m. discharge.

निर्वाचक m. elector. ~ मंडल electoral college.

निर्वाचन m. election; ~ अधिकारी returning officer; ~ क्षेत्र constituency.

निर्वाचित adj. elected.

निर्वाण m. salvation, liberation.

निर्वात adj. devoid of air or gas. m. vacuum.

निर्वापण m. extinction.

निर्वासन m. deportation, banishment, exile, expulsion.

निर्वाह m. subsistence, sustenance, maintenance.

निर्विकल्प adj. 1. without any alternative/option. 2. concentrated.

निर्विकार adj. 1. changeless, invariable. 2. unmoved, dispassionate, stolid.

निर्विघ्न adj. uninterrupted, un-obstructed, troublefree, unimpeded.

निर्विरोध adj. unopposed, uncontested.

निर्विवाद adj. indisputable, in-controvertible, irrefutable, undeniable.

निर्वेद m. 1. disgust. 2. indifference (to the world), resignation.

निलंबन m. suspension.

निलय m. residence, mansion, abode.

निवर्तन m. 1. act of returning.

2. conclusion, closure. 3. repeal.

निवारक adj. deterrent, pre-ventive.

निवारण m. 1. clearance or removal (of something undesirable). 2. prevention, preclusion.

निवाला m. morsel, mouthful.

निवास m. 1. abode, dwelling, residence. 2. act of residing.

निवासी m. inhabitant, dweller, resident. [Fem. निवासिनी]

निविड़ adj. deep, dense, thick, pitch.

निविड़ता f. density, thickness.

निविदा f. tender.

निविष्ट adj. 1. entered, pene-trated. 2. situated.

निवृत्त adj. 1. freed (after doing some work), liberated. 2. retired.

निवृत्ति f. 1. freedom (after doing some work). 2. retirement. 3. abstinence, abstention.

निवेदक m. applicant, petitioner.

निवेदन m. 1. submission, petition. 2. request.

निवेश m. 1. camp. 2. house, residence. 3. entry. 4. investment.

निशा f. night.

निशाकर m. the moon.

निशाचर m. 1. nightwanderer, demon. 2. goblin, hobgoblin.

निशान m. 1. mark, sign, impres-sion. 2. flag standard. 3. emblem. 4. trace, clue, spot, scar.

निशानची m. a good shot, marksman.

निशाना m. aim, target, bull's eye.

निशानी f. 1. sign, token. 2. gift that evokes someone memories, keepsake.

निशानेबाज़ adj. & m. good shot, marksman, shooter.

निशास्ता m. essence of wheat.

निशि f. night.

निशिदिन adv. day and night, ever, almost always.

निश्चय m. 1. determination, resolution. 2. decision. 3. certitude, certainty.
adv. certainly, surely, really.

निश्चयात्मक adj. positive, definite, certain, absolute.

निश्चल adj. 1. motionless, stationary. 2. immobile, immovable. 3. firm, calm, steady, unwavering.

निश्चायक adj. conclusive, decisive.

निश्चिंत adj. carefree, without worries, free from anxiety.

निश्चित adj. 1. certain, definite. 2. determined. 3. settled, fixed, resolved.

निश्चेष्ट adj. 1. motionless, still, stagnant. 2. inactive, inert. 3. unconscious.

निश्चेष्टता f. 1. inertia. 2. uncon-sciousness.

निश्छल adj. without wile, sinc- ere, guileless, honest.

निश्वास m. = निःश्वास।

निश्शंक adj. = निःशंक।

निषंग m. quiver.

निषाद m. a primitive non-Aryan

tribe of India; a person belonging to this tribe.

निषिद्ध adj. prohibited, forbid- den, tabooed.

निषेध m. forbiddance, prohibi-tion, ban, taboo, restriction.

निषेधाज्ञा f. injunction, stay order.

निषेधात्मक adj. 1. prohibitive. 2. negative.

निषेधाधिकार m. veto.

निष्कंटक adj. 1. free from thorns. 2. unobstructed, free from troubles or dangers.

निष्कपट adj. 1. guileless, unpretentious. 2. honest, sincere.

निष्कपटता f. artlessness, honesty, guilelessness, candour.

निष्कर्ष m. 1. conclusion, result, substance, essence. 2. finding. 3. extract, epitome.

निष्कलंक adj. blameless, spotless, stainless, immaculate. innocent, pure.

निष्काम adj. 1. (person) unattached. 2. (act) done without any desire or attachment, motiveless.

निष्कासन m. expulsion, eject- ment, rustication.

निष्क्रमण m. evacuation, exit.

निष्क्रांत adj. evacuee.

निष्क्रिय adj. 1. not active, inactive. 2. idle. 3. passive.

निष्क्रियता f. 1. inactivity, inertia, inaction. 2. passivity.

निष्ठ adj. faithful, loyal.

निष्ठा f. 1. loyalty, allegiance, fidelity. 2. devotion, faith.

निष्ठुर adj. heartless, cruel, callous, ruthless.

निष्णात adj. accomplished, skilled, adept.

निष्पंद adj. = निस्पंद।

निष्पक्ष adj. impartial, unbiased.

निष्पक्षता f. impartiality, unbiasedness.

निष्पत्ति f. 1. completion, accomplishment. 2. execution (of order, instruction or decision).

निष्पन्न adj. 1. completed, accomplished.

निष्पादक m. executive.

निष्पादन m. execution.

निष्पाप adj. sinless (person or act), without guilt, innocent.

निष्प्रभ adj. 1. (object) without glitter, dull, pale, lustreless. 2. (person) disconcerted, out of countenance.

निष्प्रभाव adj. 1. ineffectual, ineffective. 2. defunct.

निष्प्रयोजन adv. & adj. without purpose, aimless.

निष्प्राण adj. lifeless, soulless

निष्फल adj. futile, fruitless, infructuous, ineffective, unproductive.

निसर्ग m. nature.

निसर्गतः adv. naturally, in the natural/primitive form.

निसार adj. sacrificed.

निस्तत्त्व adj. without any substance, worthless, unsubstantial.

निस्तब्ध adj. 1. stationary, still, inert. 2. quiet, without noise, silent.

निस्तार m. deliverance, redemption, riddance.

निस्तारण m. 1. rescue, delivery. 2. going across.

निस्तारना vt. 1. to take across. 2. to rescue, to be instrumental in getting over difficulties. 3. to release.

निस्तेज adj. 1. lifeless, lustreless, pallid, insipid. 2. dull.

निस्पंद adj. 1. without vibration, motionless, 2. unwavering, steady.

निस्पृह adj. = निःस्पृह।

निस्बत f. comparison; की ~ in comparison with, compared to.

निस्संकोच adv. = निःसंकोच।

निस्संग adj. 1. lonesome, lonely. 2. without any desires.

निस्संतान adj. issueless, childless.

निस्संदेह adv. = निःसंदेह।

निस्सरण m. excretion, outflow.

निस्सहाय adj. helpless, without support.

निस्सार adj. without any substance, worthless, unsubstantial.

निस्सारित adj. turned out.

निस्सीम adj. limitless, boundless.

निस्सृत adj. extracted/drawn out.

निस्स्वार्थ adj. = निःस्वार्थ।

निहंग adj. 1. alone, solitary. 2. celibate. 3. naked.

निहत्था adj. unarmed.

निहाई f. anvil.

निहानी f. instrument used for scratching letters on wax-covered surfaces, style.

निहारना vt. to look intently, to behold.

निहाल adj. perfectly satisfied, exalted, contented, happy.

निहित adj. vested, inherent, implied.

निहोरना vi. to entreat/solicit/beseech.

निहोरा m. 1. obligation. 2. entreaty, solicitation. 3. support, prop.

नींद f. sleep, slumber.

नींबू m. = नीबू।

नींव f. foundation.

नीक adj. = नीका।

नीका adj. good.

नीच adj. mean, low, base, vulgar, abject.

नीचता f. 1. meanness, baseness, lowliness. 2. act of meanness.

नीचा adj. 1. low, below the average level, not high, sloping. 2. mean, base. 3. not loud.

नीचाई f. lowness, depth, low level.

नीचे adv. below, underneath, under.

नीचे, के postposition. under.

नीड़ m. nest.

नीति f. 1. ethical principle. 2. policy.

नीतिकुशल adj. tactful, politic, shrewd.

नीतिज्ञ m. 1. one who tells people how to behave ethically. 2. statesman.

न

नीति-निर्धारण m. policy-making.

नीतिशास्त्र m. ethics.

नीबू m. lemon.

नीम हकीम m. quack.

नीयत f. intention, motive.

नीर m. water.

नीरज adj. born out of water. m. lotus.

नीरद m. cloud.

नीरव adj. still, quiet, silent.

नीरस adj. 1. juiceless. 2. insipid. 3. dry. 4. prosaic, uninteresting, tedious.

नीरोग adj. without ailment, sound, healthy.

नील adj. blue. m. 1. indigo. 2. blue scar (on the skin).

नीलकंठ m. 1. jay (bird). 2. Lord Shiv.

नीलगाय f. antelope, yak.

नीलम m. sapphire.

नीलमणि m. sapphire.

नीला adj. blue.

नीलाक्ष adj. blue-eyed.

नीला थोथा m. blue vitriol, copper sulphate.

नीलाम m. auction.

नीलामी f. state of being auctioned.

नीलिमा f. bluishness, blueness.

नीलोत्पल m. blue lotus.

नीहार m. fog, mist.

नीहारिका f. nebula.

नुक़्ता m. 1. point, dot. 2. point, issue.

नुक़्ताचीं m. fault-finder.

नुक़्ताचीनी f. fault-finding, carp.

नुक़सान m. 1. loss, damage. 2. harm.

नुकीला adj. having a sharp tip, pointed.

नुक्कड़ m. corner, especially turn of a street.

नुक़्स m. defect, fault, flaw.

नुचना vt. 1. to be plucked up. 2. to be scratched.

नुचवाना vi. causative of नोचना, to get scratched.

नुनखरा adj. saltish, saline.

नुनेरा m. one who prepares salt.

नुमाइश f. exhibition, display, show.

नुस्ख़ा m. prescription, recipe.

नूतन adj. 1. new, novel. 2. modern. 3. fresh, recent.

नूतनता f. 1. newness, novelty. 2. modernity.

नून m. salt.

नूपुर m. anklet, an ornament for the ankles.

नूर m. splendour, light, lustre.

नृ m. man, human being.

नृत्य m. dance.

नृत्यकला f. art of dancing.

नृत्यशाला f. dancing hall.

नृप m. king, monarch.

नृशंस adj. atrocious, cruel, barbarous.

नृशंसता f. atrocity, cruelty.

नृसिंह m. 1. a pre-eminent person. 2. the fourth incarnation of Lord Vishnu. 3. lion-like man.

ने postposition. attached to the

nominative case in the past tense etc., of a transitive verb.

नेक adj. good and virtuous, goody.

नेकनीयती f. good faith, honesty of purpose.

नेकी f. goodness.

नेकी-बदी f. good and evil.

नेग m. ceremonial tip/due present.

नेज़ा m. spear, lance.

नेज़ाबरदार m. lancer, lance bearer.

नेता m. leader, pioneer.

नेति phrase. There is no end to this; This (God) is infinite.

नेती f. cord used for churning.

नेतृत्व m. leadership, hegemony.

नेत्र m. eye.

नेत्र-जल m. tear (s).

नेत्रविज्ञान m. ophthalmology.

नेत्री f. woman leader.

नेपथ्य m. green room of a theatre.

नेमत f. = नियामत।

नेम-धर्म m. religious practices.

नेमी adj. (a person) who observes religious rites punctiliously.

नेवला m. mongoose.

नेस्त adj. non-existent; ~ नाबूद utterly ruined/destroyed/devastated.

नेस्ती f. 1. non-existence. 2. laziness.

नैचा m. main body (pipes etc.) of a hubble-bubble.

नैज adj. one's own, personal.

नैतिक adj. 1. ethical. 2. moral.

नैतिकता f. morality.

नैत्रिक adj. ocular.

नैदानिक adj. clinical.

नैन m. = नयन।

नैपुण्य m. skill, adroitness, dexterity.

नैमित्तिक adj. causal, occasional.

नैया f. boat.

नैयायिक m. logician.

नैराश्य m. = निराशा।

नैवेद्य m. offering made to a deity, oblation.

नैसर्गिक adj. natural, innate, inherent.

नैहर m. parental home (of a woman).

नोक f. point, tip.

नोक-झोंक f. wordy encounter/skirmish/taunt.

नोकदार adj. pointed, sharp.

नोच-खसोट f. 1. pinching and snatching. 2. grabbing.

नोचना vt. to claw.

नोट m. 1. currency note, bank note, paper currency. 2. footnote.

नोटिस f. notice.

नोन m. = नून।

नोना adj. saline saltish. m. 1. saltpetre. 2. decaying earth of mud walls, bricks etc.

नौ adj. nine. m. boat, ship.

नौकर m. a person employed to perform household duties, servant.

नौकर-चाकर m. retinue of servants.

नौकरशाही f. bureaucracy.

न

नौकरानी f. maid servant.

नौकरी f. 1. service. 2. job.

नौका f. boat.

नौका-विहार m. boating.

नौचालन m. navigation.

नौजवान m. youth, youngman.

नौटंकी f. village drama.

नौनिहाल adj. promising (boy).

नौबत f. 1. situation, state of affairs. 2. small drum.

नौबहार m. spring season.

नौरत्न m. 1. (collection of) nine gems. 2. necklace containing nine gems. 3. a kind of sweet sauce.

नौलखा adj. worth nine lakhs of rupees, very precious.

नौसादर m. ammonium chloride.

नौसिखुआ adj. inexperienced. m. novice, fresher.

नौ-सेना f. navy, armada, naval force.

नौ-सेनापति m. admiral, Chief of Naval Staff.

नौ-सैनिक adj. & m. of or pertaining to navy, one in naval service.

न्यस्त adj. 1. arranged. 2. deposited, invested.

न्याय m. justice, fairness, impartiality.

न्यायतः adv. judicially, justly, honestly, equitably.

न्यायपरायण adj. just, equitable, judicious.

न्यायपालिका f. judiciary.

न्यायपीठ m. 1. bench. 2. seat of justice.

न्यायपूर्ण adj. justified.

न्यायमूर्ति f. a Supreme Court Judge.

न्यायवादी m. attorney.

न्यायशास्त्र m. jurisprudence.

न्यायसंगत adj. just, equitable.

न्यायाधीश m. judge.

न्यायालय m. court of justice.

न्यायिक adj. judicial.

न्यायी adj. proper, reasonable and fair (person).

न्यायोचित adj. that can be justi-fied, justifiable.

न्यारा adj. 1. unique. 2. queer, uncommon. 3. somewhat different, peculiar.

न्यास m. 1. trust, endowment. 2. act of arranging or placing. 3. deposit, investment.

न्यासधारी m. trustee.

न्यासभंग m. breach of trust.

न्यून adj. less, insufficient, lack-ing, deficient; ~ कोण acute angle. (Geom.)

न्यूनतम adj. & m. minimum.

न्यूनता f. shortage, deficiency.

न्योछावर f. = निछावर।

न्योतना vt. to invite.

न्योता m. invitation.

प

प m. the first of the bilabial pentad of consonants, pronounced as p in picture.

पंक m. slime, mud, mire, bog.

पंकज adj. born in slime. m. lotus.

पंकिल adj. slimy, muddy, boggy.

पंक्ति f. 1. line, queue. 2. a line of houses, seats, chairs etc., row. 3. rank.

पंख m. 1. a feather. 2. a wing. 3. an arm of a fan.

पंखड़ी f. flower-petal, blade.

पंखा m. fan.

पंगत f. a sitting for common dinner.

पंगु adj. cripple, invalid, lame.

पँच adj. allo. of पाँच (five).

पंच adj. five. m. 1. arbitrator. 2. set of five.

पंचक m. 1. group/set of five. 2. inauspicious period during which five particular stars are in conjunction.

पँचगुना adj. five times.

पंचतत्त्व m. = पंचभूत।

पंचत्व m. demise, death.

पंचनामा m. 1. written award. 2. declaration given by five (prominent) persons.

पंचनिर्णय m. judgement of an arbitrator, award.

पंचभुज m. pentagon.

पंचभूत m. the five primary elements—earth, water, air, fire, ether.

पंचम adj. fifth.

पंचमांग m. an organisation working secretly for the enemy within the country, fifth column.

पंचमाक्षर m. fifth letter of any pentad of consonants of the Nagari alphabet, any of the nasal consonants : ङ, ञ, ण, न, म।

पंचमी f. fifth day of each half of the lunar month.

पंचमुखी adj. possessing five mouths.

पँचमेल adj. 1. of five sorts. 2. assorted.

पँचरंगा adj. five-coloured, multi-coloured.

पंचरत्न m. the five sacred jewels.

पँचलड़ा adj. of five strings.

पँचहरा adj. 1. of five layers, folded five times. 2. fivefold.

पंचांग m. Hindu calendar, almanac.

पंचाट m. award.

पंचानन m. 1. lion. 2. Lord Shiv. 3. a profound scholar.

पंचानबे adj. & m. ninety-five, 95.

पंचामृत m. sacred drink consisting of milk, yoghurt, sugar, ghee and honey.

पंचायत f. 1. a court of arbitrators, usually of five, panchayat. 2. assemblage.

पंचायती adj. public, common.

पंचेंद्रिय f. the five organs of

sense—eye, ear, nose, tongue, skin.

पंछा m. 1. aqueous discharge from a wound, incision etc. 2. lymph.

पंछी m. bird.

पंजर m. skeleton, frame, cage.

पंजा m. 1. set of five. 2. hand or its impression. 3. claw, talon. 4. पैर का ~ tiptoe.

पंजाब m. Punjab, a state in India, land of five rivers.

पंजिका f. small register.

पंजी f. register.

पंजीकरण m. registration.

पँजीरी f. a kind of Indian sweet, usually given as a medicine.

पंडा m. a Brahmin guide for conducting rituals (in pilgrimage).

पंडाल m. pandal, a theatre for meetings, big pavilion.

पंडित m. 1. a Brahmin. 2. lear-ned person, scholar.

पंडिताई f. 1. priesthood. 2. sc-holarship, erudition. 3. pedantry.

पंडिताऊ adj. 1. scholarly, befitting a पंडित। 2. pedantic.

पंडितानी f. 1. wife of a Brahmin/ learned man. 2. a woman priest.

पंथ m. 1. way, path. 2. cult, creed, sect, school.

पंथी m. 1. traveller. 2. follower of a sect/cult.

पंद्रह adj. & m. fifteen, 15.

पँवाड़ा m. 1. saga. 2. exaggerated description.

पंसारी m. grocer.

पँसेरी f. a weight of five seers, roughly 4½ kg.

पकड़ f. 1. hold, catch. 2. firm grip.

पकड़ना vt. 1. to hold/seize. 2. to nab/apprehend/arrest. 3. to entrap/snare/entangle. 4. to catch.

पकड़वाना vt. causative of पकड़ना।

पकना vt. 1. to ripe/ripen. 2. to be cooked.

पकवान m. Indian type of pudding/ cookie.

पकाई f. act or process of ripening.

पकाना vt. 1. to cook. 2. to ripen, as fruit. 3. bake, as pots in fire. 4. to cause to suppurate, as a boil.

पकौड़ा m. a piece of vegetable fried in batter.

पकौड़ी f. dim. of पकौड़ा।

पक्का adj. 1. ripe. 2. mature. 3. brickbuilt. 4. settled, confirmed.

पक्व adj. 1. cooked. 2. mature.

पक्वता f. ripeness, maturity.

पक्ष m. 1. wing. 2. fortnight. 3. aspect, side. 4. phase, aspect. 5. party to a suit.

पक्षधर adj. & m. partisan, supporter.

पक्षपात m. partiality, favouri-tism.

पक्ष-विपक्ष m. the two parties/sides to a dispute.

पक्षांतर m. 1. the other fortnight. 2. the other party/side.

पक्षाघात m. paralysis.

पक्षी m. bird.

पक्षीराज m. eagle..

पक्षी-विज्ञान m. Ornithology.

पख f. 1. impediment, hindra-nce, obstacle. 2. flaw, defect.

पखवाड़ा m. a period of two weeks, fortnight.

पखारना vt. to wash/cleanse.

पखावज f. drum, timbrel.

पखेरू m. bird.

पग m. 1. foot. 2. step. 3. pace.

पगडंडी f. footpath.

पगड़ी f. 1. turban. 2. black money, given for obtaining possession of a premises.

पगना vt. to be impregnated with some syrup.

पगला adj. mad, insane.

पगली f. mad, insane (woman).

पगहा m. a rope or chain by which an animal is tied to a peg, tether.

पगार m. 1. mud prepared for building purposes. 2. fordable river or rivulet. 3. wages.

पगुराना vt. to chew the cud, to ruminate.

पगोड़ा m. Buddha temple, pag-oda.

पचकना vt. = पिचकना।

पचड़ा m. ado, fuss, pother, affray.

पचना vi. to be digested.

पचपन adj. & m. fifty-five, 55.

पचहत्तर adj. & m. seventy-five, 75.

पचाना vt. to digest.

पचाव m. digestion.

पचास adj. & m. fifty, 50.

पचासा m. 1. set of fifty similar things, half a century. 2. alarm bell of a jail.

पचासी adj. & m. eighty-five, 85.

पचीस adj. & m. twenty-five, 25.

पचीसी f. 1. set of twenty-five similar things. 2. first twenty-five years of (someone's) life.

पच्चर f. 1. wedged chip. 2. anything that prevents progress.

पच्चीकारी f. inlaying work.

पछड़ना vi. 1. to be beaten down/ defeated. 2. to be floored, to be knocked down.

पछताना vi. to repent/rue.

पछतावा m. sorrow for wrong doing, repentance, remorse.

पछना vi. to be scarified/tattooed.

पछवाँ adj. Western, coming from the West.

पछाँहीं adj. belonging or pertaining to the West.

पछाड़ f. falling down in a trance.

पछाड़ना vt. 1. to beat down/defeat. 2. to floor, to knock down. 3. to beat out dust from a cloth.

पछुआ f. = पछवाँ।

पछोड़ना vt. to winnow, to separate out.

पछोरना vt. = पछोड़ना।

पटंबर m. silken cloth.

पट m. 1. cloth, fabric. 2. screen. 3. gate, door. 4. covering. 5. pitpat sound. adj. upside down.

पटकना vt. to knock/throw down.

प

पटकनी f. a knock-down.

पटका m. 1. sash. 2. belt, girdle, cincture.

पटकान f. a flooring, a knock- down.

पटतर adj. & adv. equal, equivalent. m. equality, equivalence.

पटना vi. 1. to be covered. 2. to be filled up. 3. to be dumped. 4. pulling on. 5. completion of a transaction. 6. balancing, squaring.

पट-परिवर्तन m. change of the screen or scene.

पटरा m. 1. low wooden seat, stave. 2. plank.

पटरानी f. cheif queen, queen consort.

पटरी f. 1. rail. 2. footpath, sidewalk, pavement. 3. flat ruler.

पटल m. 1. screen. 2. roof. 3. layer. 4. side. 5. wooden plank, table. 6. counter.

पटवा m. embroiderer. [Fem. पटइन]

पटवाना vt. causative of पाटना।

पटवारी m. patwari, village official who maintains land records.

पटसन m. jute.

पटा m. 1. an Indian weapon (of wood or iron), cudgel. 2. = पटरा।

पटाई f. 1. act or state of पाटना, or wages paid for the same. 2. dumping.

पटाक f. sharp sound, thump, crash.

पटाका m. 1. cracker. 2. slap.

पटाक्षेप m. drop-scene.

पटाख़ा m. = पटाका।

पटाना vt. 1. to cause to cover as a pit. 2. to settle as a transaction, an account, purchase etc.

पटापट adv. 1. with a continuous tapping sound. 2. briskly.

पटाव m. 1. act or state of पाटना। 2. rubbish etc., with which a pit is covered. 3. covering.

पटिया f. slate, tile, board.

पटीलना vt. 1. to bring (someone) round, to make someone agree to one's point of view. 2. to cheat. 3. to accomplish.

पटु adj. 1. clever. 2. skilful, adept, dexterous, expert, diligent.

पटुआ m. jute.

पटुता f. cleverness, skill, dexterity.

पटेबाज़ adj. & m. skilful in wielding पटा।

पटेल m. headman of a village.

पटेला m. flat boat.

पटैला m. papyrus.

पटोला m. a kind of silken cloth.

पट्ट m. 1. = पटरा। 2. board or plank of wood. 3. = पट्टी। 4. scarf. 5. shield.

पट्ट-महिषी f. queen consort.

पट्टरानी f. = पटरानी।

पट्टशिष्य m. favourite disciple.

पट्टा m. 1. lease, lease deed; (किसी के नाम) ~ करना to execute a lease. 2. band of leather, put around an animal's ncek, collar.

पट्टाधारी m. lessee, lease-holder.

पट्टी f. 1. wooden board (used by children as slate to write on). 2. bandage. 3. instruction. 4. misguidance. 5. belt (of land).

पट्टीदार m. 1. lessee. 2. co-sharer, co-partner.

पट्टीदारी f. partnership, coparcenary, coparceny.

पट्टू m. a type of coarse woo-llen cloth.

पट्ठा m. 1. sinew. 2. robust youth.

पठन m. 1. reading, studying. 2. recitation.

पठनीय adj. readable, worth reading.

पठार m. plateau, tableland.

पठित adj. studied, read.

पड़ता m. manufacturing cost.

पड़ताल f. investigation, search, survey.

पड़ती f. fallow land.

पड़ना vi. 1. to be laid. 2. to fall on something.

पड़पड़ाना vt. 1. to crack. 2. to prattle/clatter.

पड़वा m. calf of a buffalo. f. the first day of a lunar fortnight.

पड़ाव m. camp, halting place, halt.

पड़िया f. she-calf of a buffalo.

पड़ोस m. neighbourhood, vicinity.

पड़ोसी m. neighbour. [Fem. पड़ोसिन]

पढ़त f. reading.

पढ़ना vt. 1. to read. 2. to read out. 3. to study, to receive education. 4. to recite.

पढ़वाना vt. to cause to be read.

पढ़ाई f. 1. reading, studying, learning at school. 2. teac-hing.

पढ़ाना vt. 1. to teach. 2. to coach/educate/instruct.

पढ़ा-लिखा adj. educated.

पण m. 1. wager. 2. stake, bet.

पण्यवस्तु f. commodity.

पतंग m. 1. moth, insect. 2. paper-kite.

पतंगबाज़ m. kite-flier.

पतंगा m. moth, insect.

पत f. prestige, honour, dignity; ~ उतारना to dishonour.

पतझड़ m. autumn, the fall of leaves.

पतझर f. = पतझड़।

पतन m. 1. fall. 2. downfall, decline, ruin.

पतनशील adj. tending to fall, falling.

पतनोन्मुख adj. tending to fall, falling.

पतला adj. 1. thin. 2. lean.

पतलापन m. 1. thinness. 2. leanness. 3. tenuousness, wateriness.

पतलून f. pantaloon, trousers.

पतवार f. helm, rudder.

पता m. 1. address. 2. knowing.

पताका f. flag, banner.

पति m. 1. husband. 2. lord, master.

पतित adj. fallen, degraded, corrupted.

पतितपावन adj. & m. one who uplifts the downtrodden.

पतिता f. fallen, degraded (woman).

पतियाना vt. to trust/rely.

प

पतियारा m. trust, faith.

पतिव्रता adj. faithful to the husband.

पतीला m. (large) kettle.

पतीली f. 1. container. 2. small पतीला।

पतुरिया f. 1. prostitute. 2. dancing girl. 3. woman of easy morals.

पतोखा m. a cup made of leaves.

पतोहू f. daughter-in-law.

पत्तन m. 1. town. 2. port-town.

पत्तर m. sheet of metal.

पत्तल f. leaf-plate.

पत्ता m. 1. leaf. 2. a playing card; पत्ते खेलना to play cards.

पत्ती f. 1. leaf, especially small leaf. 2. share.

पत्तीदार m. shareholder, partner.

पत्थर m. stone.

पत्थरबाज़ी f. stone-throwing.

पत्नी f. wife.

पत्र m. 1. leaf. 2. letter. 3. paper.

पत्रक m. 1. leaflet, chit. 2. card.

पत्रकार m. journalist.

पत्रकारिता f. journalism.

पत्रपुष्प m. 1. leaves and flowers. 2. (fig.) token' (representing something greater).

पत्र-मित्र m. pen-friend.

पत्रवाहक m. letter-bearer.

पत्रव्यवहार m. the act of exchanging letters, correspondence.

पत्रा m. Hindu calendar, almanac.

पत्राचार m. correspondence.

पत्रिका f. periodical, magazine.

पत्री f. horoscope.

पथ m. path, way, route, course.

पथगामी m. pedestrian.

पथप्रदर्शक m. 1. guide. 2. leader.

पथभ्रष्ट adj. deviated from the right path.

पथरना vt. to be stoned/sharpened on stone/honed.

पथराना vi. to petrify, to be come hard like stone.

पथराव m. pelting with stones.

पथरी f. 1. bladder-stone. 2. sto-ne cup or bowl.

पथरीला adj. stony, littered with stones.

पथिक m. wayfarer, traveller, passenger.

पथेरा m. 1. brick-maker. 2. tile-maker.

पथ्य m. wholesome diet, prescribed diet.

पद m. 1. post, office, rank. 2. word as used in a phrase or sentence. 3. word or phrase. 4. foot, verse-line.

पदक m. medal.

पदकधारी m. medallist.

पदचाप m. footfall.

पदचारी m. pedestrian.

पदचिह्न m. 1. foot-print, foot-mark, insignia. 2. trail.

पदच्युत adj. & pp. 1. dismissed, fired. 2. degraded.

पदतल m. sole (of foot).

पदत्राण m. shoe, footwear.

पददलित adj. depressed (classes),

oppressed, down-trodden.

पदधारी m. office-bearer, incumbent.

पदनाम m. designation.

पदबंध m. phrase.

पदवी f. 1. title/degree. 2. rank.

पद-व्याख्या f. parsing.

पदाघात m. blow with the feet, kick.

पदाति m. foot-soldier, infantryman.

पदाधिकारी m. office-bearer, official.

पदाना vt. 1. to tire out. 2. to harass/vex.

पदारविंद m. lotus-like feet (an expression of respect).

पदार्थ m. 1. matter. 2. substance, material. 3. word meaning.

पदार्थवाद m. = भौतिकवाद।

पदार्पण m. the act of arriving (something or someone auspicious).

पदावधि f. tenure, regime.

पदावनति f. demotion.

पदावली f. phraseology.

पदासीन adj. occupying (an) office.

पदिक m. foot-soldier, infantryman.

पदेन adv. ex-officio, because of one's position.

पदोन्नत adj. promoted.

पदोन्नति f. promotion.

पद्धति f. 1. orderly system or arrangement, method. 2. methodology. 3. practice, custom.

पद्म m. lotus.

पद्मा f. goddess of wealth, Lakshmi.

पद्माकर m. lotus lake.

पद्मासन m. a particular type of cross-legged seating posture. (Yog)

पद्मिनी f. 1. small lotus. 2. beautiful woman, belle.

पद्य m. 1. verse. 2. a stanza of a poem.

पद्यात्मक adj. in the form of a verse.

पधारना vi. 1. to arrive. 2. to proceed.

पन m. suffix. meaning quality or state; पीलापन yellowness.

पनघट m. the public place wherefrom people (usually women) draw water.

पनचक्की f. watermill.

पनडुब्बा m. diver.

पनडुब्बी f. submarine.

पनपना vi. 1. to grow. 2. to flourish/thrive.

पनबिजली f. hydroelectricity.

पनवाड़ी m. betelseller.

पनसारी m. = पंसारी।

पनसाल f. store of drinking water, from where water is distributed to travellers.

पनही f. footwear.

पना m. 1. beverage prepared from mango juice or tamarind etc. 2. width of a cloth.

पनाला m. gutter/drain.

पनाह f. shelter, refuge.

पनियाँ adj. 1. pertaining to water. 2. containing water. 3. living in water, aquatic.

प

पनिहार m. water-carrier.
पनिहारिन f. female water-carrier.
पनीर m. cheese.
पन्ना m. 1. emerald. 2. leaf (of a book etc.), folio.
पन्नी m. 1. leaf of a metal. 2. tin-foil. 3. coloured, shining thin paper.
पपड़ियाना vi. to become covered with a crust.
पपड़ी f. 1. crust, scab. 2. thin cake of some cereal.
पपड़ीला adj. scabby, flaky.
पपीता m. papaya fruit.
पपीहा m. an Indian type of cuckoo.
पय m. milk.
पयस्विनी f. 1. milch cow. 2. wet nurse.
पयोधर m. udder, a woman's breast.
पयोधि m. ocean, sea.
परंतु conj. 1. on the contrary, but. 2. in spite of this, however.
परंपरा f. 1. tradition. 2. the passing of beliefs or customs from one generation to the next.
परंपरागत adj. traditional.
पर adj. other, not one's own. postposition. 1. at. 2. on, upon. 3. over. 4. after. m. feather.
परई f. earthen bowl.
परकटा adj. with feathers cut off, wing-clipped.
परकाजी adj. fond of helping others, benignant, benevolent.
परकार m. pair of compasses/ callipers.
परकीय adj. belonging or pertaining to someone else.
परकीया f. a woman with whom a married man is having a love affair outside marriage, other woman.
परकोटा m. rampart.
परख f. 1. test, examination, assay. 2. the ability to judge correctly.
परख़चा m. particle, fragment, shred.
परखना vt. to test/examine critically, assay.
परखवाना vt. causative of परखना।
परगना m. a unit of several villages.
परगामिनी f. adulteress.
परचना vi. also; परच जाना to be familiarised/acquainted/ habituated.
परचा m. 1. piece of paper, chit. 2. question paper. 3. newspaper. 4. handbill.
परचाना vt. 1. to acquaint/familiarise/habituate. 2. to tame, to domesticate.
परची f. slip, chit.
परचून m. grocery, provisions.
परचूनिया m. grocer, retailer of provisions.
परछत्ती f. a roofing (below the roof) meant for storage.
परछाईं f. shadow, reflection.
परजवट m. a system of renting out land.
परजाता m. coral tree.
परजीवी m. parasite.

परतंत्र adj. subjugated, dependent.

परतंत्रता f. 1. subjugation. 2. dependence.

परत f. layer, veneer, fold.

परतल m. packsaddle.

परतला m. shoulder belt.

परती f. fallow land, uncultivated land.

परदा m. 1. screen, curtain. 2. veil.

परदादा m. great grandfather.

परदानशीन adj. (a woman) who observes purdah.

परदेश m. foreign country.

परदेशी adj. belonging to a foreign country, alien, exotic. m. foreigner, alien, stranger.

परनाना m. (maternal) great grandfather. [Fem. परनानी]

परनाला m. drain pipe, gutter.

परपीड़न m. sadism.

परपुरुष m. a person other than someone's own husband.

परपोता m. great grandson.

परब्रह्म m. The Supreme.

परम adj. 1. absolute. 2. ultimate.

परमाणु m. atom.

परमात्मा m. Supreme Soul, God.

परमादेश m. writ of mandamus.

परमानंद m. bliss, blessedness.

परमार्थ m. supreme good, ultimate good.

परमेश्वर m. God, the Almighty.

परराष्ट्र m. foreign country.

परला adj. of the other side.

परलोक m. next/other world, Heaven.

परलोकवास m. 1. existence in the next world. 2. demise.

परवरदिगार m. maintainer of all, God.

परवरिश f. maintenance, nurture.

परवर्ती adj. later, subsequent.

परवल m. an Indian green vegetable.

परवश adj. 1. dependent, subservient. 2. helpless.

परवान m. limit, boundary.

परवाना m. 1. written command/order. 2. warrant. 3. moth. 4. ardent/dedicated lover.

परवाह f. care, heed.

परशु m. battle-axe, halberd.

परसना vt. to serve (food).

परसर्ग m. postposition (e.g. ने, को, से, में).

परसों adv. 1. day after tomorrow. 2. day before yesterday.

परस्त्रीगमन m. adultery.

परस्पर adv. mutually. adj. mutual, reciprocal.

परस्पर-विरोधी adj. conflicting, contradictory, incompatible.

परहित m. benevolence, benefaction.

परहेज़ m. 1. abstinence. 2. avoidance, abstention.

पराँठा m. a kind of semifried Indian pan-cake.

पराँदा m. string/ribbon for tying चोटी।

पराकाष्ठा f. climax, apogee, zenith, acme.

प

पराक्रम m. valour, bravery, prowess.

पराक्रमी adj. valorous, valiant, intrepid, brave.

पराग m. pollen.

परागण m. pollination.

पराङ्मुख adj. 1. looking the other way. 2. disinclined, indifferent. 3. opposed, averse.

पराजय m. defeat, rout, repulse.

पराजित adj. defeated, subju-gated, vanquished.

परात f. large metal dish.

पराधीन adj. dependent, subservient, subject.

पराधीनता f. subjection, subservience, dependence.

परान्न m. food provided by oth- ers.

पराभव m. 1. defeat, subjection. 2. humiliation.

पराभूत adj. 1. defeated, sub-jected. 2. humiliated.

परामर्श m. 1. consultation. 2. advice, counsel.

परामर्शदाता m. adviser, consultant, counsel.

परामर्श मंडल m. adisory board.

परायण adj. & suffix. sticking/ adhering to, fulfilling, discharging; कर्तव्य ~ fulfilling (one's) duties.

पराया adj. someone else's, other's.

परार्थ m. others' good, benevolence, altruism. adv. for someone else.

परार्थी m. benevolent man, altruist.

परावर्तन m. 1. retreat, with-drawal. 2. rebounding, turning back. 3. reflection.

पराश्रयी adj. & m. dependent on others.

परास m. range.

परास्त adj. defeated, vanquished.

परिंदा m. bird.

परि prefix. 1. round, round about. 2. intensive. 3. well, very well. 4. fully, completely.

परिकथा f. narrative story (especially re. the vicinity).

परिकलन m. calculation.

परिकल्पना f. presumption, hypothesis. (Maths.)

परिक्रमण m. revolution, going around.

परिक्रमा f. round, circumambulation.

परिखा f. moat.

परिगणक m. calculator.

परिगणन m. calculation, enumeration.

परिचय m. 1. introduction. 2. acquaintance. 3. the beginning part of a book. 4. a book which gives important facts about something.

परिचय-पत्र m. 1. letter of introduction. 2. identity card.

परिचर m. attendant, retainer.

परिचर्चा f. all-round discussion.

परिचर्या f. nursing, attendance.

परिचायक adj. 1. indicative, illustrative. 2. introductory.

परिचारक m. attendant, male nurse.

परिचालक m. conductor.

परिचालन m. act of conducting, steering, operation.

परिचित adj. acquainted, known.

परिच्छन्न adj. covered all-round, fully covered.

परिच्छादित adj. covered.

परिच्छेद m. 1. chapter. 2. sec- tion.

परिजन m. 1. retinue. 2. kith and kin.

परिणत adj. 1. transformed, changed. 2. culminated.

परिणति f. 1. transformation. 2. finale, end, culmination.

परिणय m. marriage, wedding.

परिणाम m. 1. consequence. 2. outcome, result.

परिणामी adj. resultant.

परिणीत adj. married.

परित: adv. on all sides, around.

परिताप m. 1. heat. 2. anguish.

परितुष्ट adj. satisfied, gratified, satiated, pleased.

परितुष्टि f. = परितोष।

परितोष m. satisfaction, gratification, satiation.

परित्यक्त adj. abandoned, renounced, forsaken, rejected.

परित्यक्ता adj. abandoned (woman).

परित्याग m. abandoning, de-sertion, abandonment, renunciation.

परित्राण m. saving, deliverance, riddance, protection.

परित्राता m. saviour, deliverer.

परिदृश्य m. perspective, view.

परिधान m. clothes, costume, garment.

परिधि f. 1. circumference, periphery. 2. boundary, perimeter.

परिपक्व adj. 1. ripe. 2. mature.

परिपक्वता f. 1. ripeness. 2. maturity.

परिपत्र m. circular, circular letter.

परिपथ m. circuit.

परिपाक m. 1. assimilation, digestion. 2. perfection, accomplishment.

परिपाटी f. convention, system, method, order, tradition.

परिपालन m. 1. compliance; observance. 2. execution, implementation.

परिपुष्ट adj. well-nourished, well-built, well-developed.

परिपूर्ण adj. 1. replete, brimful. 2. perfect.

परिपृच्छा f. 1. enquiry, investigation. 2. curiosity.

परिपोषण m. 1. act of nourishing. 2. nourishment.

परिप्रेक्ष्य m. perspective.

परिभाषा f. 1. definition. 2. technical language.

परिभाषित adj. defined.

परिभोग m. easement.

परिभ्रमण m. 1. rotation. 2. touring.

परिमंडल m. 1. globe. 2. halo.

परिमल m. fragrance, aroma, sweet smell.

परिमाण m. magnitude, quantity.

परिमाणवाचक adj. quantitative.

परिमार्जन m. complete purification, refinement, cleansing.

परिमित adj. limited, finite.

प

परिमिति f. 1. limit. 2. perimeter.

परियोजना f. project, scheme.

परिरक्षण m. 1. preservation. 2. custody.

परिरूप m. design.

परिरेखा f. periphery, outline.

परिवर्तन m. 1. change. 2. alter-ation. 3. variation. 4. transformation.

परिवर्तनशील adj. changing, alterable, convertible.

परिवर्ती adj. 1. changing. 2. variable.

परिवर्धन m. enlargement, growth, development.

परिवहन m. 1. transport. 2. transportation. 3. conveyance

परिवाद m. complaint.

परिवादी m. complainant.

परिवार m. 1. family. 2. a group of things related by common characteristics, group, family.

परिवार-नियोजन m. family planning, birth control.

परिवेश m. environment, surroundings.

परिवेष्टन m. enclosing, encircling, wrapping.

परिव्यय m. cost, outlay, expenditure.

परिव्याप्त adj. 1. all-pervaded, all-pervading. 2. overlapped. (Maths.)

परिव्राजक m. roving ascetic.

परिशिष्ट m. appendix, addenda.

परिशीलन m. study from all angles, critical study.

परिशुद्ध adj. accurate, precise.

परिशुद्धता f. accuracy, precision.

परिशोध m. 1. repayment. 2. cleaning.

परिशोधन m. repayment.

परिश्रम m. labour, hard work, toil, exertion.

परिश्रमी adj. laborious, hard-working, diligent.

परिश्रांत adj. exhausted, tired, weary, fatigued.

परिषद, परिषद् f. council, board.

परिष्करण m. = परिष्कार।

परिष्कार m. refinement, purification.

परिष्कृत adj. refined, purified.

परिसंपत्ति f. assets.

परिसमापन m. liquidation.

परिसीमन m. delimitation, demarcation.

परिसीमित adj. limited, demarcated.

परिस्थिति f. circumstances, situation.

परिहार m. 1. avoidance, evasion. 2. atonement, expiation.

परिहार्य adj. avoidable.

परिहास m. a remark with a good humour or for amusement.

परिहासात्मक adj. humorous, full of humour.

परी f. 1. nymph, fairy, elf. 2. dream girl.

परीक्षक m. examiner.

परीक्षण m. testing, examining.

परीक्षा f. examination, test.

परीक्षार्थी m. examinee.

परीक्षित adj. examined, tested, tried.

परीलोक m. fairy land.

परुष adj. 1. hard, harsh. 2. rigid.

परे adv. away.

परे, से postposition. beyond.

परेई f. dove.

परेता m. big reel.

परेशान adj. distressed, vexed, coufused, harassed, worried.

परेशानी f. 1. worry, harassment. 2. discomfort.

परोक्ष adj. 1. indirect. 2. invisible, imperceptible.

परोपकार m. act of benevolence/munificence.

परोपकारी adj. benevolent, munificent.

परोसना vt. to dish up, to serve.

परोसा m. a dish of one man's meal.

पर्चा m. = परचा।

पर्ची f. 1. slip. 2. prescription.

पर्ण m. leaf.

पर्णकुटी f. hut made of leaves, bower.

पर्दा m. = परदा।

पर्यंक m. bed, bedstead, couch.

पर्यटक m. tourist, traveller.

पर्यटन m. tourism, travelling.

पर्यवलोकन m. comprehensive view.

पर्यवसान m. end, termination.

पर्यवेक्षक m. supervisor.

पर्याप्त adj. 1. enough, adequate, sufficient. 2. ample, plentiful.

पर्याप्तता m. sufficiency.

पर्याय m. synonym.

पर्यायवाची adj. synonymous.

पर्यालोचन m. critical obser-vation.

पर्यावरण m. environment.

पर्यावरणिक adj. environmental.

पर्व m. 1. festival. 2. chapter.

पर्वत m. mountain.

पर्वतमाला f. mountain chain/range.

पर्वतवासी m. hillman, highlander

पर्वतारोहण m. mountaineering.

पर्वतीय adj. mountainous, hilly.

पलंग m. bed, bedstead, couch.

पलंगपोश m. bedsheet.

पलंगिया f. small bed.

पल m. moment, instant.

पलक f. eyelid.

पलटन f. platoon, battalion.

पलटना vt. to turn about or over.

पलटा m. 1. turn, return. 2. relapse.

पलड़ा m. scale-pan.

पलथी f. squatting.

पलना m. = पालना। vi. to be brought up/reared.

पलस्तर m. plaster.

पलायन m. act of absconding/fleeing.

पलायनवाद m. escapism.

पलायमान, पलायमान् adj. absconding, fleeing.

पलाश m. name of a tree, Butea fondosa.

पलास m. 1. = पलाश। 2. pliers.

पली f. ladle for measuring liquids.

पलीता m. fuse, igniter, wick.

पलीद adj. unclean, dirty, polluted.

पलेट f. pleat.

प

पलेथन m. dry flour used to help (to) roll kneaded flour into a cake.

पल्लव m. sprout, shoot.

पल्लवित adj. 1. full of new sp-routs/ green foliage. 2. flo-urishing, thriving.

पल्ला m. 1. veil, purdah. 2. the skirt of a garment. 3. plank. 4. shutter of a door.

पल्लू m. end of a woman's wear, used as a head-cover.

पल्लेदार m. labourer, porter, grain porter.

पवन m. wind, air, breeze.

पवनचक्की f. windmill.

पवन-पुत्र m. Hanuman.

पवर्ग m. the five labial consonants of the Nagari alphabet: प, फ, ब, भ & म।

पवाड़ा m. bother, trouble, fuss.

पवित्र adj. holy, sacred, pious.

पवित्रात्मा adj. pious/holy (person), devout, godly.

पशम m. 1. soft fine wool. 2. pubic hair.

पशमीना m. cloth made of soft fine wool.

पशु m. 1. animal, beast, cattle. 2. cruel person, brute.

पशु-चिकित्सक m. veterinary doctor.

पशु-चिकित्सालय m. veterinary hospital.

पशु-जगत m. animal world.

पशुता f. 1. beastliness. 2. brutality, savagery, cruelty.

पशुधन m. livestock, cattle-wealth.

पशुपति m. Lord Shiv.

पशुपालन m. animal husbandry, cattle breeding.

पश्च adj. 1. back. 2. later. 3. western.

पश्चात, के postposition. after, afterwards, following in time.

पश्चात्ताप m. repentance, remorse, contrition.

पश्चिम m. west.

पश्चिमी adj. western.

पश्चिमोत्तर adj. northwest (ern).

पश्तो m. Pashto, the language of Afghanistan.

पसंगा m. = पासंग।

पसंद f. 1. liking. 2. choice.

पस m. pus.

पसरना vi. to squat or lie stret-ched, to stretch full length.

पसली f. rib.

पसार m. 1. expansion, act or state of पसरना। 2. expanse.

पसारना vt. to stretch out, to spread.

पसीजना vi. 1. to melt, to be compassionate. 2. to ooze.

पसीना m. perspiration, sweat.

पसेरी f. = पँसेरी।

पसोपेश m. hitch, fix.

पस्त adj. completely fatigued and exhausted.

पहचनवाना vt. to cause to be recognised.

पहचान f. 1. identification, identity. 2. acquaintance.

पहचानना vt. 1. to recognise. 2. to know.

पहनना vt. 1. to put on (clothing), to wear. 2. to have it on one's body.

पहनाना vt. to clothe, to cause to dress.

पहनावा m. dress, costume, vestment, robe.

पहर m. one-eighth part of a day, a three-hour period.

पहरा m. guard, patrol.

पहरेदार m. watchman, guard.

पहल m. facet. f. initiative.

पहलवान m. 1. wrestler, grappler. 2. a stout person. 3. athlete.

पहला adj. 1. first. 2. former.

पहलू m. 1. facet, aspect. 2. side, flank.

पहले adv. 1. first of all. 2. before.

पहलौटा adj. first-born.

पहलौटी f. first delivery.

पहाड़ m. 1. hill, mountain. 2. herculean task, a heap of anything.

पहाड़ा m. multiplication table.

पहाड़ी adj. hilly, mountainous. f. hill, hillock.

पहिया m. wheel.

पहुँच f. 1. access, reach. 2. arrival.

पहुँचना vi. 1. to reach/arrive. 2. to approach.

पहुँचा m. wrist.

पहुँचाना vt. 1. to carry/convey. 2. to see out, to conduct. 3. to see off, to reach.

पहुँची f. an ornament worn on the wrist.

पहेली f. riddle, puzzle, enigma.

पाँच adj. & m. five, 5.

पांचजन्य m. a conch of Lord Vishnu.

पाँचा m. a gadget used for collecting grains etc., in the grainyard.

पांचाल m. old name of a region situated in the northwest of India.

पांडव m. Pandavas, the five sons of king Pandu (Mahabharat).

पांडित्य m. scholarship, erudi- tion, learning, wisdom.

पांडित्यपूर्ण adj. scholarly.

पांडु m. dim yellow colour.

पांडुर m. jaundice.

पांडुलिपि f. manuscript.

पाँति f. = पंक्ति।

पाँयचा m. 1. a leg of a pair of trousers. 2. foot-rest.

पाँव m. foot.

पाँवड़ा m. foot-rug.

पाँवड़ी f. 1. sandal, footwear. 2. ladder. 3. threshold.

पाइप m. pipe.

पाई f. 1. pie, smallest old Indian coin, 1/192th part of a rupee. 2. vertical stroke, the sign of the fullstop in the Nagari alphabet.

पाउंड m. = पौंड।

पाउडर m. 1. powder. 2. face-powder.

पाक adj. pure, sacred, holy.

पाकदामन adj. chaste, virtuous (woman).

पाकशाला f. kitchen.

पाकशास्त्र m. science of cooking.

पाका m. = पक्का।

पाक्षिक adj. appearing or happening after two weeks, fortnightly.

पाखंड m. sanctimoniousness, hypocrisy.

पाखंडी adj. sanctimonious, hypocritical.

पाख़ाना m. 1. latrine, lavatory. 2. excreta.

पाग m. sweet or medicine prepared in some syrup.

पागना vt. to boil in syrup. 2. crazy.

पागल adj. 1. mad, lunatic. m. maniac, lunatic.

पागलख़ाना m. 1. an insane asylum, lunatic asylum. 2. mental hospital.

पागलपन m. madness, insanity, lunacy.

पागुर m. chewing of the cud by the animals.

पाचक adj. digestive. m. cook.

पाचन m. digestion.

पाछ f. incision.

पाछना vt. to incise.

पाजामा m. Indian trousers, pyjama.

पाजी adj. wicked, mean, vile, crooked.

पाज़ेब f. an ornament worn on the ankles, anklet.

पाट m. 1. jute. 2. span (of a river). 3. plank.

पाटन f. roof.

पाटना vt. 1. to cover up (a pit etc. with earth, debris, dirt and filth etc.). 2. to heap/pile.

पाटल m. rose.

पाटा m. wooden plank.

पाटी f. 1. the longer beam of a bed. 2. slate.

पाठ m. 1. lesson. 2. reading. 3. recitation. 4. text. 5. version.

पाठक m. one who reads, reader.

पाठचर्या f. course.

पाठशाला f. school.

पाठांतर m. different version.

पाठा adj. sound, healthy, stout. m. stout, young man.

पाठ्य adj. 1. readable, legible. 2. fit to be read, worth reading.

पाठ्यक्रम m. curriculum.

पाड़ m. 1. border of a length of cloth. 2. scaffolding. 3. framework placed on the mouth of a well.

पाड़ा m. 1. a group of dwelling houses, locality, enclave. 2. boundary of a field.

पाढ़ा m. hogdeer.

पाणि m. hand; ~ ग्रहण marriage, wedding.

पाणिनि m. famous Sanskrit grammarian of India.

पात m. 1. fall. 2. shedding. 3. collapse, destruction. 4. node. (Maths.). 5. leaf.

पातक m. 1. sin, guilt. 2. misdeed.

पातकी adj. sinful, misdoer. m. sinner, evil-doer.

पातर adj. lean and thin.

पाताल m. nether world, hell, hades.

पातिव्रत्य m. faithful devotion (to husband).

पाती f. 1. leaf, dried leaf. 2. letter.

पात्र m. 1. deserving or eligible person. 2. pot, vessel, receptacle. 3. basin, vessel. 4. character (in a drama).

पात्रता f. 1. eligibility. 2. propriety.

पाथना vt. to daub/beat into shape/ construct.

पाथेय m. provision for a journey.

पाद m. 1. foot, leg. 2. line or fourth part of a stanza. 3. quadrant, fourth part of a figure. 4. wind from bowels.

पाद-टिप्पणी f. footnote.

पादना vi. to break/pass wind.

पादप m. tree.

पादपूरण m. act of filling in a required/missing line of a poem.

पादपूर्ति f. = पादपूरण।

पाद-प्रहार m. kick.

पादरी m. clergyman, missionary.

पादशाह m. king, emperor.

पादाक्रांत adj. crushed with feet.

पादाघात m. kick.

पादुका f. footwear, sandal.

पाधा m. Hindu priest.

पान m. 1. drinking. 2. betel leaf.

पानदान m. a box for keeping betel leaves, tobacco etc.

पाना vt. 1. to get, to obtain, acquire, achieve. 2. to find.

पानी m. 1. water. 2. lustre. 3. juice.

पानीदार adj. 1. lustrous. 2. sensitive to honour, word, etc. 3. honourable.

पानेवाला m. recipient, payee.

पाप m. sin, evil.

पापकर्म m. sinful deed.

पापड़ m. a thin crisp and saltish bread.

पापपूर्ण adj. sinful.

पापलेन m. poplin.

पापाचार m. sinful conduct/way of living.

पापी adj. 1. sinning, sinful. 2. immoral. m. sinner.

पाबंद adj. bound; वक़्त का ~ punctual.

पाबंदी f. restriction, binding.

पामर adj. 1. mean, wicked. 2. crooked. 3. sinful.

पामा m. eczema.

पायँता m. part of a bedstead towards the feet.

पायजामा m. = पाजामा।

पायताबा m. inner sole.

पायदान m. foot-rest, foot-board.

पायदार adj. durable, lasting.

पायल f. an ornament worn on the ankles, anklet.

पायस m. a sweet milky dish.

पाया m. 1. leg of a chair, cot etc. 2. pillar. 3. foundation, prop, support.

पारंगत adj. well-versed, lear- ned, adept.

पारंपरिक adj. based on tradition, traditional.

पार m. opposite bank or shore.

पारखी adj. & m. connoisseur, expert, assayer.

पारचा m. 1. bit, fragment. 2. cloth. 3. dress.

प

पारण m. passing; ~ करना to pass.

पारद m. mercury, quicksilver.

पारदर्शक adj. 1. transparent. 2. evident, obvious. 3. frank.

पारना vt. to dump.

पारपत्र m. passport.

पारभासक adj. translucent.

पारलौकिक adj. other worldly, pertaining to the other world.

पारस m. philosopher's stone.

पारसल m. parcel.

पार साल m. last year.

पारसी m. Persee.

पारस्परिक adj. mutual, reciprocal.

पारस्परिकता f. 1. mutuality, reciprocity. 2. familiarity.

पारा m. quicksilver, mercury.

पारायण m. 1. finale. 2. complete reading of a (religious) book.

पारावार m. 1. limit, boundary. 2. ocean.

पारिजात m. coral tree, one of the trees of paradise.

पारित adj. passed.

पारितोषिक m. prize, reward, gift.

पारिभाषिक adj. technical.

पारिवारिक adj. familial.

पारिश्रमिक m. remuneration, emolument.

पारिस्थितिक adj. circumstantial, ecological.

पारिस्थितिकी f. ecology.

पारी f. 1. turn, shift. 2. a player's or team's turn at batting, innings.

पारेषक m. transmitter.

पारेषण m. transmission.

पार्थ m. Arjuna.

पार्थक्य m. 1. separation. 2. segregation. 3. secession. 4. di-stinction.

पार्थिव adj. earthly, terrestrial.

पार्वती f. wife of Lord Shiva.

पार्श्व m. 1. side, flank. 2. siding. 3. vicinity, neighbourhood. 4. aspect, facet. adj. adjacent.

पार्श्वगत adj. gone aside.

पार्श्वगायन m. background singing, playback singing.

पार्श्ववर्ती adj. 1. lying alongside. 2. adjacent.

पार्श्व-संगीत m. background music, playback music.

पार्षद m. councillor, senator.

पाल suffix. denoting (one) who maintains, governs etc.; राज्य ~ Governor. m. 1. sail. 2. process of ripening fruit by keeping them under leaves, straw etc.

पालक adj. & m. (one) who maintains and preserves. m. spinach.

पालकी f. palanquin, sedan chair.

पालट m. adopted son.

पालतू adj. domestic/tame/pet (animal).

पालथी f. = पलथी।

पालन m. 1. maintaining, main-tenance. 2. abidance. 3. ob-servance. 4. discharge, performance.

पालना vi. to maintain/bring up. m. 1. swing. 2. cradle.

पालना-पोसना vt. to bring up/nurture/foster.

पाला m. 1. frost. 2. dealing.

पालागन m. reverential greeting, asking for benediction of some venerable person by touching his feet.

पालिश f. polish.

पालिसी f. 1. policy. 2. insurance policy.

पाली f. 1. पारी। 2. an Indo-Aryan language in which most of the Buddhist scriptures are written.

पाव m. 1. quarter of a seer. 2. one fourth part.

पावक m. fire.

पावती f. 1. receipt. 2. acknowledgement.

पावती सहित f. with acknowledgement due.

पावदान m. पायदान।

पावन adj. holy, sacred.

पावनता f. holiness, sanctity, purity.

पावना m. dues. vt. to receive.

पावरोटी f. loaf of bread.

पावस m. rainy season.

पावा m. leg of a chair, cot etc.

पाश m. 1. cord, chain, noose etc., for tying, net. 2. snare, trap.

पाशव adj. = पाशविक।

पाशविक adj. 1. of or pertaining to animals. 2. beastly, brutal.

पाशा m. a title of Muslim (Turkish) nobles.

पाश्चात्य adj. of or representing west, western, occidental.

पाषंड m. = पाखंड।

पाषाण m. stone.

पाषाण युग m. stone age.

पाषाण-हृदय adj. stone-hearted, hardhearted, cruel.

पासंग m. 1. difference between the weights of the two pans of a balance. 2. weight attached to counterbalance the above difference.

पास adv. near. m. pass.

पास, के postposition. 1. in possession. 2. close to.

पासबान m. watchman, guard.

पासा m. dice, die.

पाहन m. stone.

पाहुना m. guest.

पाहुनी f. 1. female guest. 2. reception.

पिंगल m. prosody.

पिंजर m. skeleton.

पिंजरा m. cage, trap.

पिंजरापोल m. cow-pan.

पिंड m. 1. body. 2. lump. 3. orb, globe.

पिंडज adj. born from the body, viviparous.

पिंडदान m. offering/oblation of cooked rice balls to the manes.

पिंडली f. calf (of the leg).

पिंडा m. = पिंड।

पिंडिका f. small body.

पिंडी f. 1. small round lump. 2. round skein of thread.

पिघलना vi. 1. to melt. 2. to soften, to be moved.

पिघलाना vt. 1. to melt. 2. to soften, to move (one's heart).

पिचकना vi. to subside, to de-flate/ shrink/squeeze.

पिचकारी f. an Indian type of syringe.

पिचपिचा adj. adhesive, sticky, flabby, watery.

पिछड़ना vi. to lag behind.

पिछड़ा adj. 1. backward. 2. under-developed.

पिछलगा m. = पिछलग्गू।

पिछलग्गू m. minion, henchman, follower, hanger-on.

पिछला adj. 1. back, rear. 2. last. 3. old, previous.

पिछवाड़ा m. 1. rear, hind part. 2. backyard.

पिटंत f. a beating.

पिटक f. basket, small box.

पिटना vi. to be beaten/thrashed.

पिटवाना vt. to cause to be beaten.

पिटाई f. 1. thorough beating/ thrashing. 2. charges paid for the above.

पिटारा m. a wicker-box provided with cover, pannier, chest.

पिटारी f. small pannier/basket.

पिट्ठू m. stooge, blind follower, minion, puppet.

पितर m. manes, past ancestors.

पिता m. father.

पितामह m. paternal grandfather.

पितामही f. paternal grandmother.

पितृ m. 1. paternal ancestor. 2. father (पिता).

पितृऋण m. debt owed to the ancestors.

पितृगृह m. paternal home.

पितृतंत्र m. patriarchical system.

पितृपक्ष m. dark fortnight of the lunar month of आश्विन during which period oblations are offered to the forefathers.

पितृभक्त adj. devoted to the father.

पितृहत्या f. patricide.

पित्त m. bile, gall.

पित्ता m. = पित्ताशय।

पित्ताशय m. gall bladder.

पित्ती f. prickly heat.

पित्तोन्माद m. hypochondria.

पिद्दी f. a tiny bird of the sparrow family.

पिन f. pin.

पिनक f. lethargy due to intoxi-cation.

पिनकी m. 1. jittery. 2. opium-addict.

पिनपिनाना vi. to go on lamenting like a sickly child.

पिनाक m. bow of Lord Shiva.

पिन्नी f. a kind of sweetmeat.

पिन्हाना vt. = पहनाना।

पिपरमेंट m. peppermint.

पिपासा f. thirst, craving, year- ning.

पिपासु adj. thirsty, having a craving/ yearning.

पिय m. = पिया।

पियक्कड़ adj. & m. drunkard, boozy.

पिया m. 1. lover. 2. husband.

पिराना vi. to ache, to be painful.

पिरोना vt. to thread.

पिलना vi. to be crushed in a crusher etc.

पिलपिला adj. limp, not stiff (specially fruit etc.), flaccid, soft, flabby.

पिलपिलाना vt. to press and turn flaccid.

पिलपिलाहट f. flaccidity.

पिलवाना vt. to cause to drink.

पिलाई f. act or state of पिलाना, or charges paid for the same.

पिलाना vi. 1. to cause to drink. 2. to let (animal) drink. 3. to suckle. 4. to pour (liquid) in a hole.

पिल्ला m. a young dog, puppy.

पिल्लू m. a worm.

पिशाच m. devil, demon, evil spirit, fiend, satan.

पिशाच-पूजा f. devil worship.

पिशाच-विद्या f. necromancy.

पिशुन m. backbiter, slanderer.

पिष्ट adj. ground, powdered.

पिष्टपेषण m. grinding what is already ground, doing a thing/repeating over again, repetitiousness.

पिसनहारा m. one whose calling is grinding.

पिसना vi. 1. to be ground/ powdered. 2. to be overworked.

पिसवाना vt. to cause to grind.

पिसाई f. 1. grinding. 2. charges paid for grinding.

पिसान m. flour.

पिसाना vt. = पिसवाना।

पिस्तई adj. of the colour of pistachio, light green.

पिस्ता m. pistachio nut.

पिस्तौल f. pistol, revolver.

पिस्सू m. flea.

पिहकना vi. singing of birds like the peacock or the nightingale.

पींजना vt. to card (cotton).

पी m. = पिया। f. melodious note of a cuckoo.

पीक f. spittle

पीकदान m. spittoon, cuspidor.

पीच f. starch usually of rice.

पीछा m. 1. back side. 2. chase, following.

पीछे adv. behind, at the back.

पीछे, के postposition. 1. after. 2. behind.

पीटना vt. to beat/thrash.

पीठ f. back. m. 1. bench. 2. chair.

पीठ-पीछे adv. behind one's back.

पीठी f. ground (wetted) pulse/ lentils.

पीड़क adj. causing or inflicting pain. m. oppressor, tormenter.

पीड़न m. tormenting, oppressing.

पीड़ा f. pain, ache, distress.

पीड़ानाशक adj. analgesic, pain-relieving.

पीड़ित adj. afflicted, distressed, oppressed. m. one who is harmed or injured, victim.

पीढ़ा m. low stool, pedestal.

पीढ़ी f. 1. generation. 2. small पीढ़ा।

पीत adj. 1. yellow. 2. pallid (due to illness).

पीतल m. brass.

पीतांबर m. 1. yellow cloth. 2. one who wears yellow clothes, Lord Krishna.

पीन adj. corpulent.

पीनक f. = पिनक।

पीनता f. bulkiness, fatness.

पीनस m. 1. a kind of cold. 2. palanquin.

पीना vt. 1. to drink. 2. to suck. 3. to smoke.

पीना-पिलाना vt. to indulge in drinking in company.

पीप f. pus.

पीपल m. the peepal tree.

पीपा m. 1. cask, barrel. 2. drum, pontoon.

पीब f. = पीप।

पीयूष m. nectar, ambrosia.

पीर m. Muslim saint. f. = पीड़ा।

पीला adj. 1. yellow. 2. pale.

पीलिया m. jaundice.

पीसना vt. to grind, to pound.

पीहर m. parental residence (of a married woman).

पुंकेसर m. stamen.

पुंगव adj. 1. best. 2. great.

पुंगीफल f. betel-nut.

पुंज m. group, heap or collection.

पुंजातीय adj. male.

पुंजित adj. accumulated, collected.

पुंजीभूत adj. पुंजित।

पुंडरीक m. lotus (white).

पुंलिंग adj. masculine gender, masculine.

पुंश्चली f. unchaste woman, woman of loose morals, adulteress.

पुंसत्व m. manliness, virility.

पुआ m. a variety of Indian sweet, flour-cake.

पुआल m. dried stems of rice plants, straw.

पुकार f. call.

पुकारना vt. to call (by name), to call out.

पुखराज m. a yellow sapphire, topaz.

पुगना vi. to be completed/finished.

पुगाना vt. 1. to complete. 2. to lead/take a draughtsman to the goal.

पुचकार f. coddling, fondling.

पुचकारना vi. to coddle/fondle/caress.

पुचारना vi. to cleanse/wipe with a wet cloth.

पुचारा m. cloth used for cleansing/wiping out.

पुच्छ m. 1. tail. 2. rear.

पुच्छल adj. having a tail, tailed.

पुच्छलतारा m. comet.

पुछना vi. to be cleaned/dried.

पुछल्ला m. 1. long tail, tail piece. 2. lackey, toady, sycophant.

पुजना vi. to be worshipped/adored/extolled.

पुजवाना vt. to get (oneself) worshipped/respected.

पुजाई f. 1. act of worship. 2. remuneration paid for the same.

पुजाना vt. 1. to cause to worship. 2. = पुजवाना।

पुजापा m. paraphernelia/articles

used in worship; ~ फैलाना to put on a show of worship.

पुजारी m. 1. (Hindu) priest. 2. worshipper, adorer.

पुट m. dash, seasoning.

पुटाश m. potash.

पुटी f. 1. capsule, vesicle. 2. small packet.

पुटीन f. a paste for filling holes in wood, putty.

पुट्ठा m. hip, buttock.

पुड़िया f. small paper packet.

पुण्य m. 1. spiritual reward of any good act. 2. virtue, merit.

पुण्यकर्म m. holy or sacred act.

पुण्यकाल m. auspicious time.

पुण्यक्षेत्र m. holy place.

पुण्यतिथि f. death anniversary.

पुण्यात्मा adj. & m. virtuous/pious/righteous (soul).

पुतला m. 1. effigy. 2. scarecrow.

पुतली f. 1. puppet. 2. doll. 3. pupil (of the eye).

पुतली-घर m. textile factory.

पुताई f. 1. act of whitewashing, cowdung plastering etc. 2. wages paid for the same.

पुत्र m. son.

पुत्र-पौत्र m. sons and grandsons.

पुत्रवत, पुत्रवत् adv. like a son.

पुत्रवती f. (woman) blessed with a son.

पुत्री f. daughter.

पुत्रेष्टि यज्ञ m. यज्ञ performed for begetting a son.

पुदीना m. mint (plant and its leaves).

पुनः adv. again.

पुनना vt. 1. to filter. 2. to abuse.

पुनरपि adv. 1. again and again, time and again. 2. even then.

पुनरवलोकन m. revision.

पुनरस्त्रीकरण m. rearmament.

पुनरागमन m. 1. coming again. 2. reincarnation.

पुनरारंभ m. resumption.

पुनरावर्ती adj. recurring, relapsing.

पुनरावृत्ति f. repetition, recurrence, revision.

पुनरीक्षण m. review, revision.

पुनरुक्ति f. 1. repetition, reiteration.

पुनरुत्थान m. resurrection, renaissance.

पुनरुत्पादन m. reproduction, regeneration.

पुनरुद्धार m. renovation, restoration, resurrection.

पुनर्गठन m. reorganisation, reconstitution.

पुनर्ग्रहण m. retaking, resump-tion.

पुनर्जनन m. reproduction.

पुनर्जन्म m. rebirth. reincarnation.

पुनर्जागरण m. 1. reawakening. 2. renaissance.

पुनर्जीवन m. rejuvenation, resurrection.

पुनर्निर्माण m. rebuilding, reconstruction, reshuffling.

पुनर्मिलन m. act of reuniting, reunion.

पुनर्मूल्यांकन m. reassessment.

पुनर्वास m. rehabilitation, resettlement.

पुनर्विचार m. reconsideration, revision, review.

पुनर्स्थापन m. restoration, re-establishing, reinstallation.

पुनश्च adv. further more (used as equivalent to postscript).

पुनश्चर्या m. refresher course.

पुनि adv. again.

पुनीत adj. holy, sacred, pious, pure.

पुरंदर m. Lord Indra, king of gods.

पुर m. town, city.

पुरखा m. ancestor, forefather.

पुरजन m. (plu.) inhabitants of a town.

पुरज़ा m. 1. chit, slip. 2. prescription. 3. part of a machine.

पुरना vi. 1. to be completed/filled. 2. to be spun.

पुरनारी f. prostitute.

पुरनिया m. an aged man. adj. old, aged.

पुरबिया adj. belonging to the east, eastern.

पुरवट m. leather bucket (used in drawing water in well irrigation).

पुरवा m. 1. small village. 2. small earthen pot. f. = पुरवाई।

पुरवाई f. east wind, easterly.

पुरवासी m. inhabitant of a town.

पुरवैया f. = पुरवाई।

पुरश्चरण m. 1. observing some religious ritual. 2. undergoing sacrifice with some religious objective.

पुरसा m. a measure of five cubits.

पुरस्कार m. reward, prize.

पुरस्कृत adj. rewarded.

पुरा m. small village.

पुराकाल m. antiquity.

पुराकालीन adj. ancient, antique.

पुराण adj. ancient, old. m. 1. Hindu mythology. 2. scriptures so named.

पुराण-कथा f. myth.

पुरातत्त्व m. Archaeology.

पुरातत्त्वज्ञ m. archaeologist.

पुरातन adj. ancient, very old.

पुराना adj. 1. old. 2. old-fashioned, out of date. 3. ancient, olden. 4. experienced, veteran. 5. chronic. m. oldster.

पुरालिपि f. palaeography.

पुरावशेष m. antiquities, remnants, ruins, relics.

पुरावृत्त m. chronicle, annals.

पुरी f. town, city.

पुरीष m. excrement, stool, faeces.

पुरुष m. 1. man. 2. person (Gram.).

पुरुषत्व m. = पुंसत्व।

पुरुषवाचक adj. relating to masculine gender.

पुरुषार्थ m. 1. man's objective. 2. valour. 3. capacity.

पुरुषार्थी adj. self-exerting, painstaking, industrious, energetic.

पुरुषोत्तम m. Supreme Being, The Almighty.

पुरोगामी adj. going ahead, pioneering, progressive.

पुरोहित m. Hindu priest, chap- lain.

पुरोहित-तंत्र m. hierarchy.

पुरोहिताई f. priesthood, prie-stcraft.

पुरोहितानी f. fem. of पुरोहित।

पुर्ज़ा m. = पुरज़ा।

पुल m. bridge.

पुलक m. thrill (of joy or terror).

पुलकना vi. to be thrilled.

पुलकावली f. row of hair standing on end due to rapture.

पुलटिस f. poultice.

पुलपुला adj. = पिलपिला।

पुलाव m. a delicious rice preparation.

पुलिंदा m. bundle.

पुलिन m. bank (of a river).

पुलिया f. a small bridge.

पुली f. pulley.

पुश्त f. 1. back (पीठ)। 2. back part (पिछला भाग)। 3. generation.

पुश्ता m. 1. embankment. 2. prop, buttress.

पुश्तैनी adj. 1. hereditary. 2. ancestral.

पुष्कर m. 1. pond, water-pond. 2. lotus.

पुष्ट adj. 1. well-nourished, maintained, stout, robust, energetic. 2. healthy and powerful. 3. confirmed.

पुष्टि f. 1. confirmation. 2. ratification. 3. nourishment.

पुष्टिकर adj. 1. confirmatory. 2. nutrient, nutritious.

पुष्प m. flower.

पुष्पधन्वा m. Kamdeva, cupid.

पुष्पवर्षा f. shower of flowers.

पुष्पांजलि f. 1. (offering of) handful of flowers. 2. floral tribute.

पुष्पित adj. flowered, flowering.

पुष्पोद्यान m. flower-garden.

पुस्तक f. book.

पुस्तकाकार adj. book-form. adv. in the form of a book.

पुस्तकालय m. library.

पुस्तकालयाध्यक्ष m. librarian.

पुस्तिका f. 1. booklet, handbook. 2. pamphlet.

पूँछ f. tail (also fig.).

पूँजी f. capital, wealth, fund.

पूँजीपति m. capitalist.

पूँजीवाद m. capitalism.

पूँजीवादी adj. capitalistic.

पूआ m. = पुआ।

पूगना vi. to be completed/ accomplished.

पूछ f. 1. enquiry. 2.respect, esteem.

पूछताछ f. enquiry, interrogation.

पूछना vt. 1. to ask. 2. to enquire/ interrogate. 3. to respect.

पूजक m. worshipper, votary.

पूजन m. worship (ping), adoration.

पूजना vt. to worship/adore/revere.

पूजनीय adj. revered, venerable, august.

पूजा f. worship, veneration.

पूजित adj. worshipped.

पूज्य adj. revered, venerable, honourable.

पूज्यपाद adj. venerable, revered.

पूड़ी f. = पूरी।

पूत adj. holy, sacred. m. son.

पूति f. 1. piety. 2. septicity, contamination.

पूनी f. cotton-roll (for spinning).

पूय m. pus.

पूर m. pulverized fillings (for cookies).

पूरक adj. complementary, supplementary.

पूरण m. 1. completion. 2. filling the gaps.

पूरना vt. to fill to the brim.

पूरब m. east.

पूरा adj. 1. full, complete, entire. 2. all, total.

पूरित adj. filled, completed, fulfilled.

पूरी adj. fem. of पूरा। f. an Indian variety of unleavened bread fried in fat.

पूर्ण adj. 1. complete, full. 2. whole, entire.

पूर्णकालिक adj. whole-time.

पूर्णतः adv. totally, fully, entirely, completely, downright.

पूर्णतया adv. = पूर्णतः।

पूर्णता f. 1. fullness, completeness. 2. perfection.

पूर्णमासी f. = पूर्णिमा।

पूर्णयोग m. grand total, sum.

पूर्णविराम m. fullstop (।).

पूर्णांक m. 1. maximum marks. 2. whole number, integer.

पूर्णाहुति f. finishing touch of a Yaggya or project, holocaust.

पूर्णिमा f. full-moon day.

पूर्णेंदु m. full-moon.

पूर्ति f. 1. supply. 2. fulfilment, completion.

पूर्व adj. former. adv. before, prior to. m. east.

पूर्वक suffix. with; विश्वास ~ with confidence.

पूर्वकथित adj. aforesaid, above-mentioned.

पूर्वकल्पित adj. presupposed.

पूर्वकालिक adj. belonging to pervious times; ~ क्रिया past tense.

पूर्वकृत adj. accomplished/committed previously.

पूर्वग्रह m. prejudice, bias.

पूर्वज m. ancestor (s), forefather (s).

पूर्वज्ञान m. pre-knowledge, foreknowledge, foresight.

पूर्वदत्त adj. prepaid.

पूर्वपीठिका f. 1. background. 2. prolegomenon.

पूर्वपुरुष m. (plu.) 1. forefathers, ancestors. 2. predecessors.

पूर्ववत् adv. as before/as it was.

पूर्ववर्ती adj. 1. former, previous, foregoing, preceding. 2. pre-existing. m. predecessor.

पूर्वसर्ग m. preposition.

पूर्वाग्रह m. prejudice, bias.

पूर्वानुमान m. forecast.

पूर्वाभ्यास m. 1. rehearsal. 2. (in game) practice.

पूर्वार्ध m. first/former half.

पूर्वाह्न m. forenoon.

पूर्वी adj. eastern. f. 1. eastern

dialect. 2. a kind of folk music.

पूर्वोक्त adj. aforesaid, above-mentioned.

पूर्वोत्तर adj. & m. northeast.

पूर्वोपाय m. precautionary measure.

पूला m. bundle of straw etc., sheaf.

पूस m. = पौष।

पृथक् adj. apart, separate, distinct.

पृथक्करण m. 1. act of separating. 2. segregation.

पृथक्ता f. secession.

पृथक्तावाद m. secessionism, separatism.

पृथु adj. 1. wide, large. 2. great.

पृथ्वी f. earth.

पृष्ट adj. 1. asked, enquired. 2. irrigated.

पृष्ठ m. 1. page. 2. back. 3. outer surface.

पृष्ठपोषक adj. & m. supporter, patronizer.

पृष्ठभूमि f. background.

पृष्ठांकन m. endorsement.

पेंग f. swing, oscillation (of a swing).

पेंडुकी f. dove.

पेंदा m. bottom, base, [Fem. पेंदी]

पेंशन f. pension.

पेंसिल f. pencil.

पेच m. 1. screw. 2. twist. 3. complication.

पेचकस m. screw-driver.

पेचदार adj. 1. twisted. 2. complicated. 3. wily.

पेचिश m. gripes, dysentery.

पेचीदा adj. complicated, intricate, complex.

पेट m. belly, stomach, abdomen.

पेटा m. 1. main part of an object. 2. middle part of an object which is to be filled up. 3. subhead. 4. details of an account. 5. detailed description.

पेटी m. 1. box, cummerbund, girdle. 2. bag, small box, chest.

पेटीकोट m. petticoat.

पेटू adj. greedy eater, gluttonous, voracious, ravenous.

पेठा m. 1. a kind of gourd. 2. sweet/comfit made from this.

पेड़ m. tree.

पेड़ा m. 1. a roundish lump (of cheese, flour etc.). 2. a comfit of the same.

पेड़ू m. pelvis.

पेनीसिलिन f. penicillin.

पेपर m. 1. paper (काग़ज़)। 2. newspaper. 3. question paper.

पेमेंट f. payment (भुगतान)।

पेय adj. potable, drinkable. m. drink, beverage.

पेरना vt. 1. to crush (sugarcane, oilseeds etc.) in crushers, to press hard. 2. to torment, to exploit, to tease, to harass.

पेलना vt. to labour hard to penetrate.

पेश adj. 1. presented, forwarded. 2. put forth.

पेशकार m. reader, a clerk of court.

पेशगी f. money paid in advance, earnest money.

प

पेशतर, से postposition. before, prior to.

पेशबंदी f. 1. pre-arrangement. 2. anticipation.

पेशवा m. 1. leader, chief. 2. title of the prime ministers of the Maratha kings.

पेशा m. profession, calling.

पेशानी f. forehead.

पेशाब m. urine; ~ करना to urinate.

पेशाब-घर m. urinal.

पेशी f. 1. hearing (of a lawsuit). 2. presentation. 3. muscle.

पेशेवर adj. professional.

पेषण m. pulverisation, grinding, milling.

पेस्ट f. paste.

पैंजनी f. tinkling ornament worn on the ankles.

पैंट f. trousers.

पैंठ f. market.

पैंतरा m. tactics, manoeuvre, strategic move.

पैंतरेबाज़ m. tactician, strategist.

पैंतालीस adj. & m. forty-five, 45.

पैंतीस adj & m. thirty-five, 35.

पैंया f. foot.

पैंसठ adj. & m. sixty-five, 65.

पै prep. on, upon, yet, but, definitely.

पैग़ंबर m. prophet, divine messenger.

पैग़ाम m. message.

पैजामा m. = पाजामा।

पैजार f. shoe.

पैठ f. 1. access, reach. 2. insight.

पैठना vi. 1. to enter. 2. to go/dive deep (also fig.).

पैड m. pad, writing pad.

पैड़ी f. stair, step.

पैताना m. lower end of a bedstead/ cot.

पैतृक adj. 1. hereditary, ances-tral. 2. paternal. 3. patriarchal.

पैतृक संपत्ति m. patrimony.

पैत्तिक adj. bilious.

पैदल adj. going on foot, wal-king. m. 1. pedestrian. 2. foot soldier, infantryman. adv. on foot.

पैदा adj. 1. born, created. 2. to be produced/grown. 3. earned.

पैदाइश f. birth.

पैदाइशी adj. inborn, inherent, innate.

पैदावार f. 1. produce, harvest, yield. 2. production.

पैना adj. sharp, pointed.

पैबंद m. 1. patch, botch. 2. graft.

पैमाइश f. measurement, survey.

पैमाना m. 1. scale. 2. measure, measuring glass.

पैयाँ f. foot. adv. on foot.

पैर m. foot.

पैरना vi. = तैरना।

पैरवी f. pursuit.

पैरा m. paragraph, para.

पैराशूट m. parachute.

पैरोल m. parole.

पैशाच adj. = पैशाचिक।

पैशाचिक adj. devilish, dia-bolical, satanic.

पैशून्य m. backbiting, slander.

पैसा m. 1. paisa, one-hundredth part of a rupee. 2. money, wealth.

पों f. 1. a kind of long horn. 2. the sound produced by blowing it.

पोंकना vi. to suffer from loose stools.

पोंगा adj. stupid, foolish.

पोंछन f. 1. wipings, sweepings. 2. duster.

पोंछना vt. 1. to wipe, to cleanse. 2. to rub out, to efface.

पोआ m. young one of a snake.

पोखरा m. pond, tank.

पोखरी f. small pond, puddle.

पोच adj. 1. mean. 2. worthless. 3. weak. 4. timid.

पोटली f. bundle.

पोटा m. capacity.

पोटाश m. potash.

पोत m. 1. ship. 2. texture. 3. young one of a bird/beast.

पोतड़ा m. baby's clout, diaper.

पोतध्वंस m. shipwreck.

पोतध्वंसक m. torpedo.

पोतना vt. 1. to daub, to whitewash. 2. to besmear.

पोतभार m. cargo.

पोता m. 1. grandson, son's son. 2. testicle. 3. daubing clout.

पोताई f. act, state, quality, etc., of पोतना; or wages paid therefor.

पोती f. grandduaghter, son's daughter.

पोथा m. 1. big/voluminous book. 2. bundle of papers.

पोथी f. book, specially a reli-gious book.

पोदीना m. = पुदीना।

पोप m. Pope.

पोपला adj. shrivelled.

पोर m. 1. knuckle, gnarl. 2. part of a limb between two joints. 3. digit of finger.

पोल f. 1. hollowness. 2. weakness.

पोला adj. 1. hollow. 2. worthless, weak.

पोशाक f. uniform, dress, apparel.

पोशीदगी f. 1. concealment. 2. secrecy, privacy.

पोशीदा adj. secret, hidden, concealed.

पोषक adj. nutritive. m. one who brings up/maintains, patron.

पोषण m. 1. bringing up, rearing. 2. nutrition, nourishment.

पोषित adj. 1. reared, supported. 2. brought up. 3. nourished.

पोष्य adj. fit to be supported/reared; ~ पुत्र adopted/foster son.

पोस m. 1. love born of gratefulness. 2. tameness.

पोसना vt. 1. to rear/support/bring up. 2. to tame/domesticate.

पोस्टर m. poster.

पोस्त m. poppy flower from which opium is extracted.

पोस्ता m. = पोस्त।

पौंचा m. 1. five and a half times. 2. multiplication table consisting of 5½ times of integers.

पौंड m. 1. pound sterling. 2. pound weight.

पौ f. 1. first ray of sunlight. 2. an ace in dice.

पौआ m. quarter of a seer, roughly, .23 of a kg.

पौढ़ना vi. to lie and relax.

पौत्र m. grandson, son's son.

पौत्री f. granddaughter.

पौद f. 1. sapling. 2. seedling.

पौधा m. plant.

पौन adj. three-fourth, 3/4th. m. = पवन (wind).

पौना m. 1. three-fourth, 3/4th. 2. multiplication tables of 3/4ths of integers. 3. ladle with a long handle.

पौनी f. small ladle.

पौर adj. pertaining or relating to city, urban.

पौरा m. incoming.

पौराणिक adj. mythological.

पौरी m. = ड्योढ़ी।

पौरुष m. 1. manliness, manhood. 2. prowess, valour, vigour, strength.

पौरोहित्य m. priesthood.

पौष m. tenth month of Hindu calendar.

पौष्टिक adj. nutritive, nutritious, restorative, alimentary.

पौसरा m. = प्याऊ।

पौहारी adj. & m. (one) living on milk.

प्याऊ m. water-booth, free water-booth (for passers-by).

प्याज़ m. onion, scallion.

प्यादा m. 1. footman, pedestrian. 2. foot-soldier. 3. pawn (chess).

प्यार m. love, affection.

प्यारा adj. 1. dear, beloved, pleasing. 2. lovely. 3. beautiful, attractive.

प्याला m. cup.

प्याली f. small cup.

प्यास f. 1. thirst. 2. longing, crave, desire.

प्यासा adj. thirsty.

प्र prefix. indicating : 1. in front, forward. 2. abundantly, excessively.

प्रकंप m. shivering, trembling.

प्रकट adj. 1. apparent, obvious, clear, manifest. 2. disclosed. 3. express.

प्रकटन m. 1. manifestation, appearance. 2. revelation.

प्रकरण m. 1. topic. 2. chapter. 3. subject.

प्रकर्ष m. 1. eminence, distinction, excellence. 2. plenty.

प्रकल्पना f. 1. presumption. 2. supposition.

प्रकांड adj. profound, outstan- ding.

प्रकार m. 1. kind, type. 2. manner, way, method.

प्रकार्य m. 1. special work. 2. fun-ction.

प्रकार्यात्मक adj. functional.

प्रकाश m. light.

प्रकाशक adj. bringing to light. m. publisher.

प्रकाशन m. 1. bringing to light. 2. the act of publishing, publication. 3. a published book or magazine.

प्रकाशमान्, प्रकाशमान adj. lu-minous, shining, brilliant.

प्रकाश-स्तंभ m. 1. lighthouse. 2. beacon-light.

प्रकाशिकी f. optics.

प्रकाशिकीय adj. optical.

प्रकाशित adj. 1. brought to light. 2. published.

प्रकीर्ण adj. miscellaneous.

प्रकृत adj. 1. natural, normal. 2. real, true.

प्रकृति f. 1. nature. 2. temperament, habit.

प्रकृतिवादी adj. & m. naturalist.

प्रकृतिस्थ adj. 1. in the natural state. 2. calm and cool, composed.

प्रकोप m. wrath, fury.

प्रकोष्ठ m. 1. lobby. 2. chamber.

प्रक्रम m. 1. order. 2. process.

प्रक्रिया f. 1. procedure, mode. 2. process.

प्रक्षालन m. 1. washing, clean- sing. 2. bleaching.

प्रक्षालित adj. 1. washed, clean-sed. 2. bleached.

प्रक्षिप्त adj. hurled, thrown, projected. (Maths.)

प्रक्षेप m. 1, hurling, throwing. 2. interpolation.

प्रक्षेपण m. = प्रक्षेप।

प्रक्षेपास्त्र m. ballistic missile.

प्रखंड m. 1. part. 2. division, section, part, block.

प्रखर adj. 1. fierce, terrific, acute, acrid. 2. keen, sharp.

प्रख्यात adj. famous, reputed, renowned, well-known.

प्रख्यापन m. 1. promulgation. 2. declaration.

प्रगट adj. = प्रकट।

प्रगति f. progress, advancement, development.

प्रगतिवाद m. progressivism.

प्रगतिशील adj. progressive.

प्रगल्भ adj. unabashed, unhes-itant, impertinent, courageous.

प्रगाढ़ adj. 1. very thick and deep (colour). 2. dense. 3. firm, tight.

प्रगीत m. lyric, song.

प्रचंड adj. 1. terrific, violent, terrible. 2. fierce, direful, furious.

प्रचंडता f. the state of being प्रचंड।

प्रचलन m. 1. prevalence, curr-ency. 2. vogue.

प्रचलित adj. 1. current, prevalent. 2. in use, in force, in vogue.

प्रचार m. propaganda.

प्रचारक m. 1. propagandist, propagator. 2. publiciser, publicist.

प्रचारित adj. propagated, pubi-cized, made known.

प्रचालक m. starter, operator.

प्रचालन m. operation.

प्रचुर adj. plentiful, abundant.

प्रचुरता f. plenty, abundance.

प्रच्छन्न adj. hidden, latent, obscure, concealed.

प्रच्छाया f. umbra.

प्रजनन m. procreation, reproduction.

प्रजा f. 1. citizen. 2. the people who are ruled by a monarch, dictator, government etc., subjects.

प्रजातंत्र m. democracy.

प्रजातांत्रिक adj. democratic.

प्रजापति m. maintainer of subjects, king.

प्रज्ञ adj. 1. wise. 2. intelligent. 3. learned.

प्रज्ञा f. intellect.

प्रज्ञाचक्षु adj. physically blind, but gifted with the inner eye of wisdom.

प्रज्वलन m. 1. ignition, setting on fire. 2. burning, blazing.

प्रज्वलित adj. 1. ignited, set on fire. 2. burnt, blazed.

प्रण m. resolution, vow, promise, pledge.

प्रणत adj. bent, bowed (down).

प्रणतपाल m. protector of one who seeks shelter.

प्रणय m. love, affection.

प्रणयन m. 1. creation. 2. compostition (of a literary work), writing.

प्रणयिनी f. beloved.

प्रणयी m. lover, master, lord.

प्रणव m. Om, the Almighty.

प्रणाम m. respectful greeting/ salutation, bow.

प्रणाली f. 1. channel. 2. mode, way, system, custom, manner, course.

प्रणिधान m. religious meditation/ concentration.

प्रणेता m. 1. creator. 2. author, composer, writer.

प्रतनु adj. lean and thin.

प्रताड़ना f. admonition, chiding.

प्रताप m. glory, dignity, splen-dour.

प्रतापवान्, प्रतापवान adj. = प्रतापी ।

प्रतापी adj. august, glorious, illustrious.

प्रति f. copy. prefix. 1. every, per. 2. in opposition to something. 3. in reverse, in opposite direction.

प्रति, के postposition. in the direction of, towards; उसके प्रति towards him.

प्रतिकार m. 1. retaliation. 2. revenge.

प्रतिकूल adj. 1. opposite, contrary, perverse, against, adverse. 2. hostile.

प्रतिकृति f. copy of the shape of something or somebody, facsimile.

प्रतिक्रम m. reverse order.

प्रतिक्रिया f. 1. reaction, repercussion. 2 retaliation.

प्रतिक्रियात्मक adj. reactionary, reacting.

प्रतिक्रियावादी adj. reactionary.

प्रतिक्षण adv. happening every moment.

प्रतिगामी adj. regressive, retrogressive.

प्रतिग्रहण m. acceptance.

प्रतिग्राह्य adj. acceptable.

प्रतिघात m. counter-blow, coun-ter-stroke, repercussion.

प्रतिच्छाया f. 1. reflection. 2. image, picture.

प्रतिच्छेद m. intersection.

प्रतिज्ञा f. solemn promise, pledge, assertion.

प्रतिज्ञापत्र m. written pledge/ agreement, covenant, indenture.

प्रतिदत्त adj. returned, refunded.

प्रतिदान m. return, repayment, redemption.

प्रतिदिन adv. daily, day by day, everyday.

प्रतिद्वंद्व m. contest, conflict, duel.

प्रतिद्वंद्वी m. rival, competitor, opponent.

प्रतिध्वनि f. echo, resonance, reverberation.

प्रतिनिधि m. 1. representative, delegate. 2. agent.

प्रतिनिधित्व m. representation.

प्रतिनिर्देश m. cross-reference.

प्रतिपक्ष m. opposite party, opposition, hostile camp, rival side.

प्रतिपक्षी m. opponent, rival, contestant.

प्रतिपत्ति f. 1. exposition, expounding. 2. accomplishment, execution.

प्रतिपदा f. first day of a lunar fortnight.

प्रतिपन्न adj. 1. expounded. 2. accomplished, executed.

प्रतिपादक m. exponent (person), expositor.

प्रतिपादन m. exposition, presentation, treatment.

प्रतिपादित adj. expounded.

प्रतिपालक adj. maintaining. m. maintainer, patron.

प्रतिपालन m. 1. maintenance. 2. execution.

प्रतिपुरुष m. 1. substitute. 2. effigy. 3. proxy.

प्रतिपूरक adj. 1. complementary. 2. compensatory.

प्रतिफल m. requital, reward, retribution, result.

प्रतिबंध m. 1. restriction, ban, prohibition. 2. condition, stipulation.

प्रतिबद्ध adj. committed (to).

प्रतिबिंब m. reflection, image, shadow.

प्रतिबिंबित adj. reflected.

प्रतिबोध m. 1. awakening. 2. sense, comprehension.

प्रतिभा f. genius, talent, intellect; ~ संपन्न talented.

प्रतिभावान्, प्रतिभावान adj. talented.

प्रतिभू m. surety (person).

प्रतिभूति f. bail, security.

प्रतिमा f. idol, statue, icon, image, figure.

प्रतिमान m. 1. model, pattern. 2. an accepted way of behaving, norm.

प्रतिमूर्ति f. replica, prototype.

प्रतियोगिता f. competition, rivalry, contest.

प्रतियोगी m. competitor, rival, contestant, opponent. adj. competitive.

प्रतिरूप m. 1. counterpart, image.

प

2. representative. 3. specimen.

प्रतिरोध m. 1. resistance. 2. obstruction.

प्रतिरोधी adj. resisting.

प्रतिलिपि f. copy, duplicate, facsimile.

प्रतिलोम adj. 1. converse, reverse, inverted. 2. inverse, opposite.

प्रतिवर्तन m. reversion, rebounding.

प्रतिवर्ष adv. each year, once a year, yearly.

प्रतिवाद m. 1. refutation, contradiction. 2. protest.

प्रतिवादी m. defendant, respondent.

प्रतिवेदन m. report, represen-tation.

प्रतिवेश m. 1. neighbourhood. 2. environment.

प्रतिशत adv. & adj. percent.

प्रतिशब्द m. echo, resonance, averberation

प्रतिशोध m. revenge, reprisal, retaliation.

प्रतिश्याय m. cold, catarrh.

प्रतिश्रुत adj. 1. heard. 2. promi- sed, pledged.

प्रतिषेध m. denial, rejection.

प्रतिष्ठा f. prestige, dignity, respectability.

प्रतिष्ठान m. establishment, installation.

प्रतिष्ठापन m. establishing, establishment, installation.

प्रतिष्ठावान्, प्रतिष्ठावान adj. prestigious.

प्रतिष्ठित adj. 1. reputed, renow- ned. 2. distinguished, respected, prestigious. 3. established, installed.

प्रतिस्थापन m. 1. replacement. 2. substitution.

प्रतिस्पर्धा f. rivalry, competition, contest.

प्रतिस्पर्धी adj. & m. rival, competitor, contestant.

प्रतिहस्ताक्षर m. countersignature.

प्रतिहार m. = प्रतिहारी।

प्रतिहारी m. 1. chamberlain. 2. gate-keeper, watchman, porter.

प्रतिहिंसा f. counter-violence, reprisal.

प्रतीक m. symbol, mark, emblem.

प्रतीकवाद m. symbolism.

प्रतीकात्मक adj. symbolic.

प्रतीक्षा f. wait, waiting.

प्रतीक्षालय m. waiting room.

प्रतीक्षा-सूची f. waiting list.

प्रतीक्षित adj. awaited.

प्रतीची f. west.

प्रतीत adj. clear to the eye or mind.

प्रतीप adj. inverse, counter.

प्रतीयमान adj. apparent, evident.

प्रत्यंचा f. bow-string.

प्रत्यक्ष adj. 1. obvious, apparent, visible, evident, perceivable. 2. ocular, eye. 3. direct.

प्रत्यक्षत: adv. on the evidence available, prima facie.

प्रत्यक्षीकरण m. ocular demonstration, direct perception; बंदी ~ habeas corpus.

प्रत्यभियोग m. indictment, counter-accusation.

प्रत्यय m. 1. desinence, suffix. 2. idea, concept. 3. confidence, faith. 4. testimony.

प्रत्यर्पण m. extradition.

प्रत्यागमन m. coming back, return.

प्रत्यारोप m. counter-charge, counter-accusation.

प्रत्याशा f. anticipation, expectation.

प्रत्याशी m. 1. candidate. 2. applicant.

प्रत्याहार m. control of the senses.

प्रत्याह्वान m. recalling, recall, calling back.

प्रत्युत conj. 1. however, but. 2. on the contrary, on the other hand.

प्रत्युत्तर m. rejoinder, repartee.

प्रत्युत्पन्न adj. 1. reborn. 2. ready-witted, prompt; ~ मति one who has presence of mind.

प्रत्युपकार m. requital of obligation.

प्रत्यूष m. dawn, day-break.

प्रत्येक adj. each, every one.

प्रथम adj. 1. before all others, first. 2. foremost, most important.

प्रथमतः adv. firstly, in the first place, first of all.

प्रथमा f. nominative case. (Gram.)

प्रथा f. custom, practice, usage, rule.

प्रथागत adj. customary.

प्रद adj. suffix. used for denoting 'giver' as in सुखप्रद।

प्रदक्षिणा f. going round the shrine of a deity or sacred place, circumambulation.

प्रदत्त adj. given, bestowed.

प्रदर m. leucorrhoea.

प्रदर्शक m. 1. exhibitor, showman. 2. demonstrator, performer.

प्रदर्शन m. 1. exhibition. 2. demonstration.

प्रदर्शनकारी m. demonstrator.

प्रदर्शनी f. exhibition.

प्रदर्शित adj. 1. exhibited, displayed. 2. demonstrated.

प्रदान m. act of giving or donating.

प्रदायी adj. providing, supply-ing.

प्रदाह m. burning sensation.

प्रदीप m. 1. lamp. 2. light.

प्रदीपन m. 1. act of lighting/igniting. 2. excitement, stimulation.

प्रदीप्त adj. lighted, ignited.

प्रदीप्ति f. light, glow.

प्रदेश m. 1. region, province. 2. state.

प्रदेशीय adj. regional, provincial.

प्रदोष m. time of sunset.

प्रद्युम्न m. Cupid, God of love.

प्रधान adj. head, prime, general. m. 1. headman. 2. president (of an institution).

प्रधानता f. 1. importance, prominence, supremacy, primacy. 2. headship, leadership.

प्रधानाचार्य m. principal.

प्रधानाध्यापक m. headmaster.

प्रपंच m. 1. worldly affairs, mun-dane affairs. 2. trickery. 3. detailed ceremonials.

प्रपंची adj. deceitful, fraudulent, scheming.

प्रपत्र m. form (of application etc).

प्रपन्न adj. 1. obtained. 2. refugee.

प्रपात m. 1. waterfall. 2. cataract.

प्रपितामह m. paternal great grandfather. [Fem. प्रपितामही]

प्रपुत्र m. grandson, son's son.

प्रपौत्र m. great grandson, son's grandson. [Fem. प्रपौत्री]

प्रफुल्ल adj. 1. blossomed blooming. 2. delighted, joyful.

प्रबंध m. 1. management, organisation, contrivance. 2. thesis, dissertation; ~ - काव्य epic.

प्रबंधक m. manager, organiser, executive.

प्रबल adj. 1. powerful, strong, mighty. 2. forceful or influential. 3. staunch; ~ समर्थक staunch supporter.

प्रबुद्ध adj. enlightened, awakened.

प्रबोध m. enlightenment, awakening.

प्रभंजन m. 1. act of breaking, ruin, destruction. 2. hurricane, storm.

प्रभव m. 1. creation, production. 2. origin, source.

प्रभा f. 1. light, effulgence. 2. glory.

प्रभाकर m. Sun.

प्रभाग m. division.

प्रभात m. dawn, early morning.

प्रभाती f. morning song.

प्रभामंडल m. halo.

प्रभार m. charge.

प्रभारी adj. in-charge.

प्रभाव m. 1. influence. 2. effect, impact.

प्रभावशाली adj. 1. influential, potential. 2. effective. 3. impressive, fascinating.

प्रभावित adj. impressed, influenced.

प्रभावी adj. 1. influential. 2. effective. 3. impressive.

प्रभावोत्पादक adj. effective.

प्रभु m. 1. god. 2. master. 3. sovereign.

प्रभुता f. 1. sway, sovereignty. 2. glory. 3. supremacy.

प्रभुत्व m. = प्रभुता।

प्रभु-सत्ता f. sovereignty.

प्रभूत adj. plentiful, abundant, ample.

प्रभृति conj. et cetera.

प्रभेद m. distinction, difference.

प्रभेदी adj. distinctive.

प्रमत्त adj. drunk, insane, senseless.

प्रमा f. authoritative knowledge.

प्रमाण m. 1. testimony. 2. proof. 3. evidence.

प्रमाणन m. act of certifying, certification.

प्रमाणपत्र m. certificate.

प्रमाणित adj. 1. proved. 2. certi-fied.

प्रमाद m. 1. intoxication (speci- ally with power, pelf and money). 2. carelessness, negligence.

प्रमादी adj. 1. vain, intoxicated due to power and money. 2. careless, negligent. [Fem. प्रमादिनी]

प्रमाप m. measure, weight.

प्रमुख adj. 1. main, chief.

2. pro-minent, outstanding, predominant, excellent.

प्रमुखता f. eminence, importance, prominence.

प्रमुदित adj. delighted, full of joy, glad, pleased.

प्रमेय m. theorem.

प्रमेह m. diabetes.

प्रमोद m. entertainment, recreation, enjoyment.

प्रयत्न m. effort, attempt, endeavour.

प्रयत्नशील adj. endeavouring.

प्रयाण m. 1. march. 2. going, departure.

प्रयास m. attempt, endeavour, effort.

प्रयुक्त adj. used, applied.

प्रयोक्ता m. user, experimenter.

प्रयोग m. 1. use, application. 2. usage. 3. experiment.

प्रयोगवाद m. experimentalism, empiricism.

प्रयोगवादी adj. empirical. m. empiricist.

प्रयोगशाला f. laboratory.

प्रयोगी adj. & m. experimenter.

प्रयोजन m. 1. purpose, aim. 2. intention, motive.

प्रयोजनीय adj. applicable, usable, requisite, suitable.

प्रयोज्य adj. applicable, usable.

प्ररूप m. type, form.

प्रलंब adj. & m. 1. that which hangs vertically, vertical. 2. long.

प्रलयंकर adj. (that) which causes deluge, catastrophic, calamitous, disastrous.

प्रलय m. 1. annihilation, total devastation, end of all existence. 2. deluge, devastating flood.

प्रलयकारी adj. = प्रलयंकर।

प्रलाप m. incoherent talk (especially due to sorrow or grief), prattle.

प्रलेख m. document, deed.

प्रलेप m. ointment, salve.

प्रलोभन m. temptation, allurement, seduction, inducement.

प्रवंचक m. deceiver, cheat.

प्रवंचन m. deception, deceitfulness.

प्रवंचना f. = प्रवंचन।

प्रवंचित adj. deceived, cheated.

प्रवक्ता m. 1. spokesman. 2. lec-turer.

प्रवचन m. discourse.

प्रवण adj. 1. inclined, bent. 2. disposed.

प्रवर adj. 1. superior. 2. senior; ~ समिति select committee.

प्रवर्तक m. 1. promoter. 2. foun-der. 3. innovator.

प्रवर्तन m. 1. initiation. 2. setting in motion, starting. 3. founding. 4. innovation. 5. enforcement.

प्रवर्धन m. magnification, enlargement.

प्रवसन m. migration.

प्रवात m. gale.

प्रवाद m. 1. conversation. 2. hearsay. 3. rumour (especially of a bad name).

प

प्रवाल m. coral.

प्रवास m. emigration.

प्रवासी adj. migratory.

प्रवाह m. flow, fluency.

प्रवाहमान adj. fluent, flowing.

प्रवाहित adj. set in flow.

प्रविधि f. technique.

प्रविधिज्ञ m. technician.

प्रविष्ट adj. 1. entered. 2. admitted.

प्रविष्टि f. 1. entry. 2. admission.

प्रवीण adj. proficient, skilful, expert.

प्रवीणता f. proficiency, skilfulness.

प्रवृत्त pp. 1. inclined. 2. engaged.

प्रवृत्ति f. inclination, tendency, trend.

प्रवेश m. 1. admission. 2. entry, entrance. 3. access.

प्रवेशद्वार m. doorways, portal, entrance.

प्रवेशपत्र m. pass, admission ticket/ card, admit card.

प्रवेशिका f. primer, first reader, elementary book (on subject).

प्रव्रजन m. migration.

प्रव्राजक m. wandering mendi- cant.

प्रशंसक m. one who praises, eulogist, admirer.

प्रशंसनीय adj. praiseworthy, commendable, laudable.

प्रशंसा f. praise, admiration.

प्रशंसित adj. praised, admired.

प्रशमन m. pacification, soothing.

प्रशस्त adj. broad, expansive.

प्रशस्ति f. eulogy.

प्रशांत adj. tranquil, calm, quiet.

प्रशाखा f. sub-branch, off-shoot, twig.

प्रशासक m. administrator.

प्रशासन m. administration.

प्रशासनिक adj. administrative.

प्रशिक्षण m. training.

प्रशिक्षणार्थी m. trainee.

प्रश्न m. question.

प्रश्नचिह्न m. sign/note of interrogation (?).

प्रश्नवाचक adj. interrogative.

प्रश्नावली f. questionnaire.

प्रश्नोत्तरी f. catechism, quiz.

प्रश्रय m. backing, support.

प्रश्रयदाता supporter.

प्रसंग m. 1. context. 2. topic. 3. subjcet, theme.

प्रसंविदा f. covenant.

प्रसन्न adj. happy, pleased, glad.

प्रसन्नता f. happiness, pleasure, gladness, delight.

प्रसरण m. expansion, extension.

प्रसव m. delivery (of a child).

प्रसाद m. 1. gift (from a deity), favour. 2. blessing, benediction, boon, grace.

प्रसादी f. offering made to a deity.

प्रसाधन m. beauty/make-up aids.

प्रसार m. 1. extension, expansion, dissemination. 2. dispersion, scattering, spreading.

प्रसारित adj. 1. broadcast, transmitted. 2. dispersed, propagated, scattered.

प्रसिद्ध adj. well-known, famous, renowned, reputed.

प्रसिद्धि f. fame, renown, esteem, repute.

प्रसुप्त pp. 1. dormant, asleep. 2. hibernated.

प्रसूत adj. delivered, born.

प्रसूता f. a woman who has recently delivered a baby.

प्रसूति f. labour (of delivery), progeny, maternity.

प्रसून m. flower, blossom.

प्रस्तर m. stone, rock.

प्रस्ताव m. 1. proposal. 2. motion. 3. offer (in contract).

प्रस्तावक m. 1. proposer. 2. mo-ver (of a resolution). 3. offerer (in a contract).

प्रस्तावना f. preface, preamble, foreword.

प्रस्ताविती m. offeree.

प्रस्तुत adj. 1. presented, submitted.

प्रस्तुति f. 1. readiness. 2. presentation. 3. the production of a play.

प्रस्तुतीकरण m. presentation.

प्रस्थान m. departure, setting out.

प्रस्थापन m. installation, establishment.

प्रस्थापना f. = प्रस्थापन।

प्रस्थापित adj. installed, established.

प्रस्फुटन m. 1. blossoming. 2. manifestation.

प्रस्वेद m. sweat, perspiration.

प्रहर m. eighth part of a day, period of three hours.

प्रहरी m. sentry, watchman, gu-ard.

प्रहसन m. farce, caricature, mockery, satire, skit.

प्रहार m. 1. blow. 2. assault, attack.

प्रहेलिका f. riddle, conundrum, puzzle, enigma.

प्रांगण m. courtyard.

प्रांजल adj. straight, plain, simple, crystal clear (idea or language), lucid.

प्रांत m. 1. province, prefecture. 2. territory, region.

प्रांतीय adj. provincial.

प्राइमरी adj. 1. primary. 2. elementary.

प्राकार m. boundary, fencing.

प्राकृत adj. natural, innate, inborn.

प्राकृतिक adj. natural, innate.

प्राक्कथन m. foreword.

प्राक्कलन m. estimation.

प्राक्कल्पना f. assumption, supposition.

प्रागैतिहासिक adj. prehistoric.

प्राचार्य m. principal of a college.

प्राची f. east, orient.

प्राचीन adj. very old, ancient.

प्राचीनता f. antiquity.

प्राचीर m. rampart, boundary wall.

प्राचुर्य m. abundance.

प्राच्य adj. 1. eastern. 2. oriental.

प्राज्ञ adj. clever, wise, learned.

प्राण m. (usually plu.) 1. winds of the body. 2. life. 3. liveliness, energy.

प्राणघात m. killing, murder.

प्राणदंड m. capital punishment.

प्राणदान m. saving someone's life.

प्राणनाथ m. husband, lord, beloved one.

प

प्राणप्रतिष्ठा f. deification of an idol.

प्राणवान्, प्राणवान adj. full of life/ vitality, lively.

प्राणांत m. death, end of life.

प्राणायाम m. breathing exercise.

प्राणी m. living being, animal.

प्रातः m. morning.

प्रातःकाल m. early part of the day.

प्राथमिक adj. 1. primary, initial, elementary. 2. preliminary.

प्राथमिकता f. priority, precedence, preference.

प्रादुर्भाव m. 1. origin, birth. 2. manifestation, appea-rance, advent.

प्रादुर्भूत adj. 1. born. 2. mani-fested, appeared.

प्रादेशिक adj. provincial, regional, territorial.

प्राधान्य m. predominance, preponderance, supremacy.

प्राधिकार m. authority.

प्राधिकारी m. authority (person).

प्राधिकृत adj. authorised.

प्राध्यापक m. professor, lecturer.

प्रापक m. receiver.

प्राप्त adj. 1. received, secured. 2. acquired, obtained.

प्राप्ति f. 1. receipt, act of receiving. 2. income. 3. gain. 4. realisation, acquisition.

प्राप्य adj. 1. due. 2. obtainable, attainable, procurable, available.

प्राबल्य m. 1. dominance. 2. fo-rce, intensity.

प्रामाणिक adj. 1. authentic. 2. reliable, credible, genuine.

प्रामाणिकता f. 1. authenticity. 2. reliability, credibility.

प्रायः adv. 1. often, quite often. 2. usually, generally, mostly.

प्राय adj. used as a suffix, almost; नष्ट ~ almost destroyed.

प्रायद्वीप m. peninsula.

प्रायशः adv. very often, usually.

प्रायश्चित्त m. atonement, expiation.

प्रायिक adj. probable.

प्रायिकता f. probability.

प्रायोगिक adj. tentative.

प्रारंभ m. 1. beginning, comme-ncement. 2. debut.

प्रारंभिक adj. 1. preliminary. 2. elementary. 3. initial.

प्रारब्ध m. destiny, fate.

प्रारूप m. draft, proforma.

प्रार्थना f. 1. prayer. 2. request, petition.

प्रार्थना-पत्र m. application.

प्रार्थनीय adj. worth praying/ applying/soliciting for.

प्रार्थी m. 1. applicant. 2. petitioner. 3. candidate.

प्रालेख m. draft, proforma.

प्राविधिक adj. technical.

प्रासंगिक adj. 1. relevant. 2. contingent, incidental.

प्रासाद m. mansion, palace.

प्रिंट f. printed design.

प्रिय adj. 1. dear. 2. lovely, comely.

प्रियजन m. dear ones.

प्रियतम adj. 1. dearest, most loved. 2. husband.

प्रियतमा f. dearest lady.

प्रिया f. beloved, lovely, sweetheart.

प्रीतम m. = प्रियतम।

प्रीति f. love, affection, fondness.

प्रीतिभोज m. social dinner, banquet.

प्रूफ़ m. proof (printing).

प्रेक्षक m. observer, spectator, onlooker.

प्रेक्षण m. act of observing/viewing/beholding.

प्रेक्षागृह m. auditorium.

प्रेत m. spirit (of the dead), ghost, poltergeist, spectre.

प्रेतनी f. woman spirit.

प्रेतबाधा f. poltergeistic disturbance.

प्रेतात्मा f. spirit of the dead.

प्रेम m. love, affection.

प्रेमपात्र m. beloved one, love.

प्रेमपूर्वक adv. with love.

प्रेमलीला f. romance.

प्रेमविह्वल adj. overwhelmed with emotion of love.

प्रेमिका f. beloved one.

प्रेमी m. lover.

प्रेय adj. dear, loved. m. 1. loved one. 2. desired object.

प्रेयसी f. beloved one, darling, dearie.

प्रेरक adj. inspiring. motivating.

प्रेरणा f. impetus, inspiration, urge, initiative.

प्रेरणादायक adj. = प्रेरक।

प्रेरणार्थक adj. causative; ~ क्रिया causative verb.

प्रेरित adj. inspired, motivated, instigated, prompted.

प्रेषक m. sender, despatcher.

प्रेषण m. sending, remittance, transmission.

प्रेषित pp. sent, despatched.

प्रोक्त adj. declared, announced, spoken, uttered.

प्रोटीन m. protein.

प्रोत्साहन m. encouragement, boosting up, stimulation.

प्रोत्साहित adj. encouraged, inspired.

प्रोन्नत adj. promoted.

प्रोन्नति f. promotion.

प्रौढ़ adj. 1. mature, matured. 2. middle-aged. m. adult

प्रौढ़ता f. 1. maturity. 2. adulthood.

प्रौढ़ा f. adult/elderly woman.

प्लवन m. floating.

प्लावन m. submersion, plunging.

प्लावित adj. flooded, inundated.

प्लुत adj. long-drawn (sound of a vowel).

प्लेग m. plague.

फ

फ m. the second consonant of the bilabial pentad; its sound resembles that of ph in philosophy.

फंका m. a quantity of an edible powder or medicine which can be contained in hollow of the palm.

फंकी f. diminutive of फंका।

फंदा m. snare, noose, trap.

फँसना vt. 1. to be entrapped/ensnared. 2. to get stuck up.

फँसाना vt. 1. to entrap/ensnare. 2. to decoy.

फक f. ~ से suddenly.

फ़क़ adj. pale, white.

फकार m. the letter फ or its sound.

फ़क़ीर m. Muslim or Sikh mendicant.

फ़क़ीरी f. 1. mendicancy. 2. poverty.

फक्कड़ m. ribald.

फ़ख़्र m. pride.

फगुआ m. Holi festival.

फगुनाहट f. the breeze of the coming spring.

फ़ज़्ल m. grace, blessing.

फ़ज़ीहत f. feeling of being harried and maltreated.

फ़ज़ूल adj. 1. useless. 2. unnecessary.

फ़ज़ूलख़र्च adj. spendthrift, extravagant.

फट m. thud; ~ से suddenly and quickly.

फटकन f. chaff separated from grain in winnowing.

फटकना vt. 1. to winnow. 2. to reach.

फटकार f. scolding, upbraiding.

फटकारना vt. 1. to scold/upbraid/rebuke. 2. to snap. 3. to beat clothes for washing or cleaning.

फटन f. cleavage, fissure, split, gap, crack, rift.

फटना vt. to be torn/split.

फटफटाना vi. to make a flut- tering sound, to flutter, to flap.

फटा adj. torn.

फटीचर adj. & m. 1. shabbily dressed (person). 2. an insignificant (person), of no consequence.

फटेहाल adj. down and out, in a sorry plight, in a miserable condition.

फड़ m. a cloth used as a gambling board.

फड़क f. throbbing, palpitation, pulsation.

फड़कना vi. to pulsate.

फड़फड़ाना vt. & vi. to flutter/flap/flicker.

फड़फड़ाहट f. flutter, excitement.

फण m. hood of a snake.

फणधर m. cobra.

फ़तवा m. a (religious) ruling given by a (Muslim) judge.

फ़तह f. victory.

फतिंगा m. moth, flying insect, hopper.

फतुही f. waist-coat stuffed with cotton.

फन m. = फण।

फ़न m. 1. skill. 2. art. 3. cunning.

फनफनाना vi. to make a hissing sound.

फफूँदी f. fungus.

फफोला m. blister, blotch.

फबती f. befitting remark, jest, sarcasm, fling.

फबन f. state or quality of फबना, befittingness, suitability.

फबना vi. to suit nicely/fine, to become.

फ़र f. fur.

फरफंद m. trickery, fraud.

फरफर adv. swiftly, rapidly.

फ़रमा m. frame, format, forme (printing).

फ़रमान m. edict, command.

फ़रमाना vt. to speak out.

फ़रलाँग m. furlong.

फ़रवरी f. February.

फरसा m. pick-axe, spade.

फरहरा m. flag, banner, pennant.

फ़रामोशी f. oblivion, forgetfulness.

फ़रार m. absconder.

फ़रियाद f. complaint, plaint.

फ़रियादी m. 1. complainant. 2. accuser.

फ़रिश्ता m. angel.

फ़रेब m. fraud, deception, treachery.

फ़रेबी adj. fraudulent, treacherous, cheater.

फ़र्क़ m. difference, distinction.

फ़र्ज़ m. duty, obligation.

फ़र्ज़ी adj. 1. nominal. 2. fictitious, artificial. m. queen (in chess)

फ़र्द f. 1. account book. 2. list. m. 1. a single person. 2. a single piece. 3. top sheet of a covering.

फ़र्म m. firm, concern.

फ़र्माइश f. (specific) request.

फ़र्माइशी adj. on request, made to order.

फर्राटा m. fluency.

फ़र्श m. floor.

फ़र्शी सलाम m. deferential greeting.

फल m. 1. fruit. 2. result, consequence. 3. effect.

फलक m. sheet, board, counter.

फलतः adv. consequently, therefore.

फलद adj. 1. fruitful. 2. bearing fruit, fructiferous.

फलदायक adj. fruitful.

फलदार adj. bearing fruit.

फलना vt. 1. to bear fruit; ~ - फूलना to flourish/thrive. 2. to prove auspicious. 3. appearance of granules on any part of the body.

फलप्रद adj. 1. fruitful. 2. bearing fruit. 3. effective, advantageous.

फलभोग m. undergoing/enjoying the result of (one's) deed.

फलवती adj. & f. fruitful.

फलस्वरूप adv. consequently.

फलहीन adj. fruitless.

फ़लाँ adj. that (specified), so and so.

फलाँग m. = छलाँग।

फलाँगना vt. to jump/cross over.

फ़लाना adj. = फ़लाँ।

फ़लालैन f. flannel.

फलाहार m. fruit diet.

फलाहारी m. fruitarian.
adj. prepared with fruits only.

फलित adj. 1. resulted. 2. resultant; ~ ज्योतिष Astrology.

फली f. bean, bean-like vegetable.

फलीदार adj. (plant) bearing beans.

फलीभूत adj. fructified, succe-ssful.

फलोत्पादक adj. capable of bearing fruit.

फ़व्वारा m. fountain.

फ़सल f. 1. crop. 2. harvest.

फ़सली adj. seasonal.

फ़साद m. affray, brawl.

फ़सादी adj. & m. quarrelsome, given to quarrels.

फहरना vi. to flutter in the air.

फहराना vi. to hoist.
vi. to wave/flutter.

फाँक f. slice of melon, mango, orange etc.

फाँकना vt. to put something powdered into mouth.

फाँद f. jump, jumping.

फाँदना vt. to jump/leap over.

फाँस f. 1. thorn, splinter. 2. trap, noose.

फाँसना vt. to trap/entrap/ensnare.

फाँसी f. hanging.

फ़ाइल f. file.

फ़ाइलेरिया m. filaria.

फ़ाक़ा m. 1. starvation. 2. fast.

फ़ाक़ेमस्त adj. (one) who keeps cheerful even when starving.

फ़ाख़्ता f. dove.

फाग m. 1. Holi festival. 2. a song sung during the Holi festival.

फागुन m. = फाल्गुन।

फाटक m. 1. gate. 2. entrance.

फाटका m. speculation.

फाड़न f. 1. piece (of cloth, paper etc.) torn out of a bigger piece. 2. buttermilk left over when butter is taken out fresh from yoghurt.

फाड़ना vt. to tear/rend/chop/split.

फ़ानूस f. chandelier.

फ़ायदा m. 1. profit, gain. 2. advantage, benefit, use, utility.

फ़ायदेमंद adj. profitable, advantageous, useful.

फ़ायर m. fire, shooting.

फ़ारम m. farm.

फ़ारमूला m. formula.

फ़ारसी f. Persian (language).

फ़ारिग़ adj. relieved.

फ़ार्म m. form.

फाल m. step, stride.

फ़ालतू adj. 1. useless, good for nothing. 2. superfluous.

फालसई adj. brownish red.

फ़ालसा m. a tiny fruit of the summer season.

फ़ालिज m. paralysis.

फाल्गुन m. last month of the Hindu calendar.

फावड़ा m. spade, mattock.

फावड़ी f. small spade.

फ़ाश adj. exposed.

फ़ासला m. distance.

फ़ासिज़्म m. fascism.

फाहा m. 1. fluffy piece of cotton (usually soaked in perfume or medicine). 2. a piece of cotton for cleaning wounds, swab.

फ़िकर f. = फ़िक्र ।

फ़िक़रा m. sentence.

फ़िक्र f. anxiety, worry, perplexity.

फ़िक्रमंद adj. worried, anxious.

फिटकरी f. alum.

फ़ितना adj. budding (sharper), wily.

फ़ितरत f. 1. disposition, nature. 2. mischief. 3. wily disposition, wiliness, cunningness.

फ़ितरती adj. mischievous, wily, crafty, cunning.

फ़ितूर m. defect.

फ़िदा adj. enamoured, infatuated, enchanted, fascinated, charmed.

फ़िनाइल f. phenyl.

फ़िरंगी m. European.

फ़िरंट adj. opposed, angry.

फिर adv. 1. afterwards. 2. again. 3. moreover.

फ़िरका m. tribe, clan.

फिरकी f. reel.

फ़िरक़ेवाराना adj. communal.

फिरना vi. 1. to go back, to return. 2. to go round. 3. to turn.

फिरनी f. a sweet preparation of milk, powdered rice etc.

फिरवाना vt. to have (something) returned.

फिराऊ adj. 1. returnable. 2. returning.

फ़िराक़ m. 1. purpose; वह किस ~ में है What is he after? 2. search.

फिराना vt. 1. to take around. 2. to cause to change.

फिरोजी adj. violet blue.

फ़िरौती f. ransom.

फ़िलहाल adv. for the time being, for the present.

फ़िल्म f. 1. film, reel. 2. movie.

फ़िल्माना vt. to film.

फ़िल्मी adj. filmic.

फिस adj. nought.

फिसड्डी adj. sluggish, always lagging behind.

फिसलन f. slipperiness.

फिसलना vi. 1. to slip. 2. to slide/skid. adj. slippery.

फ़ी adj. each.

फीका adj. 1. tasteless. 2. without saltiness or sweetness, insipid. 3. dim.

फ़ीता m. 1. a narrow strip of cloth, tape. 2. lace, ribbon. 3. strap.

फ़ीरोज़ा m. amethyst, violet blue gem.

फ़ील m. 1. elephant. 2. bishop (chess).

फ़ीलपाँव m. elephantiasis.

फ़ीस f. fee.

फुँकना vi. to burn.

फुँकनी f. blow-pipe.

फुँकवाना vt. causative of फुँकना ।

फुंकार f. hissing sound.

फुँदना m. tassel.

फ

फुंसी f. boil.

फुट m. foot (measurement).

फुटकर adj. 1. retail. 2. miscellaneous, sundry.

फुटबाल m. football.

फुटा m. foot-rule.

फुड़िया f. smallish boil.

फुदकना vi. to jump/skip.

फुनगी f. 1. top, summit. 2. cockade. 3. sprout.

फुप्फुस m. lung.

फुफकार f. hiss (of a snake).

फुफकारना vi. to hiss.

फुफेरा adj. pertaining to फूफा or फूफी / बुआ (father's sister).

फुर f. flutter; ~ हो जाना to move/fly away quickly.

फुरतीला adj. 1. agile, nimble. 2. prompt, quick.

फुर्ती f. agility, promptness, ha-ste, hurry.

फ़ुर्सत f. 1. free time. 2. respite. 3. spare time, leisure.

फुलका m. thin loaf, muffin.

फुलझड़ी f. 1. a type of firework. 2. provocative remark.

फुलवारी f. flower garden.

फुलाना vt. to inflate, to pump in air.

फुलाव m. inflation, puffing up.

फुलेल f. scented oil.

फुलौरी f. a fried dish made of cereal flour.

फुसफुसाना vt. to whisper, to speak in a hushed up/subdued tone.

फुसफुसाहट f. whispering sound.

फुसलाना vt. to wheedle/seduce/lure/cajole.

फुहार f. drizzle.

फुहारा m. fountain.

फूँक f. a current of air sent out of the mouth, blow.

फूँकना vt. 1. to blow. 2. to turn to ashes.

फूँकनी f. blow-pipe.

फूँ-फाँ f. pomp and show.

फूट f. 1. split, rift. 2. discord, disunity.

फूटना vt. 1. to be smashed/broken. 2. to burst.

फूफा m. husband of father's sister.

फूफी f. father's sister.

फूल m. 1. flower. 2. a white metal.

फूल-गोभी f. cauliflower, broccoli.

फूलदान m. flower pot/vase.

फूलदार adj. flowery.

फूलना vi. 1. to flower/blossom. 2. to swell/inflate/be puffed up.

फूली f. white outgrowth in the pupil of the eye.

फूस f. hay, straw.

फूहड़ adj. sluttish, uncouth, sloven, awkward, ludicrous, stupid, mannerless.

फेंकना vt. 1. to cast, throw or hurl. 2. to emit. 3. to offer.

फेंट f. part of the धोती folded up round the waist. m. shake.

फेंटना vt. 1. to beat up (as espresso coffee). 2. to shuffle (as a pack of cards).

फेंटा m. 1. circumference of the waist. 2. short turban.

फेन f. foam, froth, lather.

फेनी f. a type of Indian sweet.

फेफड़ा m. lung.

फेर m. 1. detour, circuitous route, curvature. 2. complication. 3. misconception, misunderstanding, ambiguity, miscalculation.

फेरना vt. to turn, twist.

फेर-बदल m. f. reshuffle, shake-up.

फेरा m. 1. round, circumambulation, alteration. 2. one round of the sacred fire (as a matrimonial rite).

फेरी f. 1. round. 2. hawking.

फेरीवाला m. hawker, pedlar.

फ़ेल adj. failed.

फ़ेहरिस्त f. list, inventory.

फैलना vi. 1. to spread, pervade, permeate. 2. to spill over. 3. to radiate (as rays). 4. to be prevalent (as fashion). 5. to spread (as a rumour). 6. to extend (as a hand), to saturate.

फैलाना vt. causative of फैलना।

फैलाव m. expansion, stretch, span.

फ़ैसला m. adjudication, judgement, decision, settlement.

फोक m. residue left after extraction.

फोकट adj. 1. without any substance. 2. without any labour or charge.

फोकटी adj. costing nothing.

फ़ोटो m. photo.

फोड़ना vt. 1. to break/smash. 2. to burst.

फोड़ा m. suppurated sore, abscess, boil, ulcer.

फ़ोता m. testicle.

फ़ौज f. army, military force.

फ़ौजदारी adj. criminal, penal.

फ़ौजी adj. pertaining to the army/military, martial. m. a soldier.

फ़ौरन adv. forthwith, immediately, at once, instantly.

फ़ौलाद m. steel.

फ़ौलादी adj. 1. made of or pertaining to steel. 2. stout, sturdy.

फ़ौवारा m. fountain, artificial spring of water.

फ्रांसीसी adj. of France, French.

फ्रॉक m. frock.

फ्री adj. free, without any charge.

फ्रेम m. frame (of picture, painting etc.).

ब

ब m. third of the bilabial pentad of consonants of the Nagari aphabet; its sound resembles that of b in ball.

बंक adj. 1. curved, bent. 2. crooked.

बंकिम adj. 1. curved, bent. 2. crooked.

बंकिमा f. 1. curvature, bent. 2. crookedness.

बँगला adj. of or pertaining to Bengal. f. Bengali language. m. bungalow.

बंगाल m. Bengal (a state in the Indain Union).

बंगाली adj. of or pertaining to Bengal. m. inhabitant of Bengal.

बंजर adj. barren.

बंजारा m. nomad.

बँटना vi. 1. to be shared. 2. to be divided.

बँटवारा m. 1. distribution. 2. partition.

बँटाई f. 1. distribution. 2. crop-sharing, partnership in crops.

बंटाधार m. spoilage, destructive effect.

बंडा m. vegetable of the taro family.

बंडी f. jacket.

बंद adj. 1. shut. 2. closed. 3. stopped. 4. blocked. 5. locked up. m. 1. strap; कमर ~ band, belt. 2. metal strap. 3. stanza (in Urdu poetry). 4. joint of the body. 5. a cessation of work as a protest against something unusual, strike, band; क़लम ~ हड़ताल pen-down strike.

बंद गली f. 1. blind lane, culde-sac. 2. (fig.) impasse.

बंदगी f. salutation, expression of respect/homage.

बंद गोभी f. cabbage.

बंदनवार f. arch, festoon of flowers/green leaves.

बंदर m. monkey, ape.

बंदरगाह f. harbour, port.

बंदर-घुड़की f. bluff, hollow threat.

बंदर-भभकी f. = बंदर-घुड़की।

बँदरिया f. female monkey.

बंदरी f. female monkey.

बंदा m. human being.

बंदापरवर m. protector of the human beings.

बंदिश f. 1. restriction. 2. precautionary measure. 3. musical pattern.

बंदी[1] m. 1. prisoner, captive, convict. 2. bard.

बंदी[2] f. 1. shut-down. 2. closure. 3. holiday.

बंदीगृह m. prison.

बंदूक़ f. gun.

बंदूक़ची m. gunner, gunman.

बंदूक़बाज़ी f. 1. firing. 2. marksmanship.

बंदोबस्त m. 1. management, arrangement. 2. survey and settlement.

बंध m. 1. = बंधन। 2. = बाँध।

बंधक m. 1. mortgage, pledge. 2. hostage.

बंधन m. 1. tie. 2. bond. 3. restriction, confinement, binding. 4. bondage. 5. joint (of the body).

बंधनकारी adj. binding (restric-tion, obligation etc.).

बँधना vi. 1. to be tied/fastened/ imprisoned. 2. to be bound. m. string, cord, anything used for tying.

बँधवाना vt. to cause (someone) to tie.

बँधा adj. tied, fastened, bound.

बंधान m. 1. (binding) tradition. 2. stipulation. 3. embankment.

बँधी लीक f. beaten track.

बंधु m. brother.

बँधुआ adj. & m. captive, bond-man.

बंधुता f. brotherhood, fraternity.

बंधुत्व m. = बंधुता।

बंधुभाव m. kinship, frater-nalism.

बंधेज m. 1. binding tradition. 2. amount paid due to such a tradition. 3. restriction, hindrance.

बंध्य adj. sterile.

बंध्या adj. & f. barren woman.

बंपुलिस m. public lavatory.

बंब m. 1. sound of bam bam. 2. bomb.

बंबा m. waterpipe.

बँसवाड़ा m. 1. bamboo market. 2. grove of bamboos.

बंसी f. 1. flute. 2. fishing hook.

बंसीधर m. one who plays on a flute, Lord Krishna.

बँहगी f. = बहँगी।

बक m. heron. f. prattle, gossip.

बक-झक f. babbling, jabbering.

बकना vi. to jabber/babble.

बकबक f. prattle.

बकरम f. a kind of stiff cloth, buckram.

बकरा m. he-goat.

बक़रीद f. an important Muslim festival.

बकलस m. buckle.

बकवाद f. foolish, useless or confused talk, babble, prattle.

बकवास f. = बकवाद।

बकसुआ m. buckle.

बक़ाया adj. & m. arrear (s).

बक्की adj. talkative, chatty.

बक्स m. box.

बखान m. 1. description. 2. pr-aise, eulogy.

बखानना vt. 1. to describe in detail. 2. to eulogise at length.

बखार m. barn, grain-store, gra-nary.

बख़िया m. back-stitching.

बख़ूबी adv. 1. beautifully. 2. thoroughly.

बखेड़ा m. complication, mess, uproar, tumult, row.

ब

बखेड़िया adj. & m. one who starts a row.

बख़्तर m. armour.

बख़्शना vt. to forgive/excuse/ pardon.

बख़्शीश f. tip.

बग़ल f. 1. armpit. 2. side.

बग़लगीर adj. 1. seated by the side. 2. in the embrace.

बग़लबंदी f. an old-fashioned Indian jacket.

बगला m. heron.

बगला-भगत m. hypocrite.

बग़ली adj. pertaining to the armpit/ flank. f. 1. a trick in wrestling. 2. hole made in a wall for burglary. 3. tailor's bag for keeping gadgets etc.

बग़ावत f. rebellion, revolt.

बगिया f. small garden.

बगीचा m. small garden, orc-hard.

बगुला m. = बगला।

बगूला m. whirlwind.

बग़ैर, के postposition. without.

बग्घी f. four-wheeled horse carriage.

बघनखा m. tiger-claw, a weapon of the shape of a tiger-claw.

बघार m. seasoning (of vegetables, lentils etc.) in the process of cooking.

बघारना vt. 1. to season (vegetables, lentils etc.) in the process of cooking. 2. to talk big/tall.

बचकाना adj. childish.

बचकानापन m. childishness.

बचत f. 1. money saved, saving. 2. something saved.

बचत खाता m. savings account.

बचना vi. 1. to be saved. 2. to remain unused. 3. to escape. 4. to avoid, shun.

बचपन m. 1. childhood. 2. childishness, puerility.

बचपना m. = बचपन।

बचा-खुचा adj. left over.

बचाना vt. 1. to save. 2. to spare. 3. to defend/protect. 4. to avoid.

बचाव m. 1. rescue, protection, safety. 2. escape.

बचाव-कार्य m. rescue operation.

बच्चा m. 1. (usu. male) child, baby. 2. kid.

बच्ची f. female child, small girl.

बच्चेदानी f. the female reproductive organ, ovary.

बछड़ा m. he-calf.

बछिया f. she-calf.

बजकना vi. = बजबजाना।

बजट m. budget.

बजड़ा m. 1. = बाजरा। 2. = बजरा।

बजना vi. to ring/tinkle. m. sounding of a bell; आठ बजने में पाँच मिनट हैं It is five to eight. दस बजने को हैं It is close to ten/It is almost ten.

बजबजाना vi. to form gas and bubbles.

बजरंग adj. very stout; ~ बली (Mighty) Hanuman.

बजरबट्टू m. a seed used (as a talisman) for warding off the evil eye.

बजरा m. 1. double-deck boat. 2. = बाजरा।

बजरी f. gravel.

बजवाना vt. causative of बजाना।

बजवैया m. one who plays on musical instruments.

बजा adj. right, proper.

बज़ाज़ m. clothier, cloth-merchant, draper.

बज़ाज़ा m. cloth-market, dra-pery.

बजाना vt. 1. to play, to toot. 2. to toll, to ring.

बजाय, के postposition. instead of, in place of.

बजे adv. at... o'clock.

बझना vt. be tied/entangled.

बझाऊ adj. entangling.

बझाना vt. to tie/entangle.

बट m. = वट (tree).

बटखरा m. weight.

बटन m. button.

बटना vt. to twist as a cord, rope, etc.

बटमार m. one who robs tra-vellers, highwayman.

बटलोई f. a round vessel used for cooking.

बटवारा m. division, partition.

बटा m. divided by (Maths.); दो ~ तीन 2/3, two (divided) by three.

बटाई f. sharing of crop.

बटाऊ m. traveller, wayfarer.

बटालियन f. battalion.

बटिया f. 1. small, smooth mass of stone or clay. 2. small pestle.

बटी f. 1. pill or tablet.

बटुआ m. money-bag, purse.

बटुरना vi. to be accumulated.

बटेर m. he-quail.

बटेरी f. she-quail.

बटोरन f. sweepings.

बटोरना vt. 1. to gather or collect. 2. to accumulate.

बटोही m. traveller, wayfarer.

बट्टा m. 1. piece of stone.2. stone pestle. 3. rebate, discount, brokerage, commission.

बट्टी f. cake.

बड़ m. 1. banyan tree. 2. allomorph of बड़ा, used in compound words. f. brag.

बड़प्पन m. 1. elderliness, greatness, generosity. 2. magnanimity, dignity.

बड़बड़ f. foolish talk, grumble.

बड़बड़ाना vi. to talk foolishly or too much, to blab.

बड़बोल = बड़बोला।

बड़बोला adj. braggart.

बड़भागी adj. lucky, fortunate.

बड़वाग्नि f. = बड़वानल।

बड़वानल m. marine fire.

बड़हार m. marriage feast given by the bridal party.

बड़ा adj. 1. big, large, huge. 2. great, grand. 3. major. 4. elder. 5. older. 6. very much, extremely. m. biscuit of ground pulse fried in oil etc. adv. too much, very.

बड़ाई f. 1. greatness. 2. praise.

बड़ी f. preparation of ground pulse.

ब

बड़ी इलायची f. black cardamom.

बढ़ई m. carpenter.

बढ़ती f. 1. increase. 2. increment. 3. surplus.

बढ़ना vi. 1. to grow. 2. to rise. 3. to increase. 4. to exceed. 5. to advance/progress. 6. to be extended.

बढ़नी f. broom.

बढ़ा-चढ़ा adj. surpassing, excelling.

बढ़ाना vt. 1. to increase. 2. to raise. 3. to extend, to lengthen. 4. to magnify/enlarge as a photograph.

बढ़ाव m. act or state of बढ़ाना।

बढ़ावा m. incentive, encouragement.

बढ़िया adj. 1. good, nice, of a high quality. 2. excellent, splendid.

बढ़ोतरी f. 1. increase, increment. 2. rise, hike. 3. progress.

बतंगड़ m. बात का ~ storm in a teacup, much ado about nothing.

बत f. an allomorph of बात (see बतकही, बतरस)।

बतकही f. conversation.

बतक्कड़ adj. & m. talkative, garrulous, chatty.

बतरस m. relish/fondness for talk.

बतलाना vt. = बताना।

बताना vt. 1. to tell. 2. to state. 3. to indicate, to point out.

बतासा m. a. roundish sugar-cake.

बतियाना vt. to talk/converse.

बतौर conj. like, just like.

बत्ती f. 1. wick. 2. candle. 3. light.

बत्तीदान m. candlestand.

बत्तीस adj. & m. thirty-two, 32.

बत्तीसी f. a full set of teeth, denture.

बथुआ m. a leafy vegetable.

बद adj. bad.

बदइंतज़ामी f. mismanagement.

बदक़िस्मत adj. unlucky, unfortunate.

बदचलन adj. of loose morals, depraved, corrupted.

बदज़बान adj. evil-tongued, foul-mouthed.

बदज़ात adj. vile, wicked.

बदतमीज़ adj. rude, unmannerly.

बदतर adj. worse.

बददुआ f. curse.

बदन m. body.

बदनसीब adj. unlucky, unfortunate.

बदना vt. to bet/wager.

बदनाम adj. defamed, ill-famed.

बदनामी f. defame, ill-fame.

बदनीयत adj. of ill-intent, malevolent, ill-motived.

बदपरहेज़ी f. intemperance, indulgence in wrong or unbalanced diet.

बदबू f. foul/bad smell, reek.

बदबूदार adj. reeking, stinking, foul-smelling, smelly.

बदमाश adj. & m. wicked (per- son), scoundrel, rascal, hooligan.

बदमिज़ाज adj. short/ill-tem- pered.

बदरंग adj. 1. of a faded colour, discoloured. 2. of a grotesque colour. 3. of a different/another colour (cards).

बदल m. change.

बदलना vt. 1. to change, alter. 2. to exchange or replace.

बदलवाना vt. causative of बदलना।

बदला m. revenge, reprisal, retaliation; बदले में in lieu of, in exchange for, in return.

बदलाव m. 1. change. 2. replacement.

बदली f. 1. cloudiness. 2. transfer.

बदले, के postposition. in place of, instead of.

बदसुलूकी f. maltreatment, misbehaviour.

बदसूरत adj. ugly, clumsy.

बदस्तूर ind. as usual, as ever before, in the customary manner.

बदहज़मी f. indigestion.

बदहवास adj. out of one's wits, bewildered, confused, perplexed.

बदा adj. fated, destined.

बदा-बदी f. rivalry.

बदी f. 1. dark fortnight of the lunar month. 2. evil.

बदौलत, की postposition. by the grace of, through the kindness of, by virtue of.

बद्ध adj. bound, tied, fixed.

बद्धकोष्ठ adj. suffering from constipation.

बधाई f. congratulation, gree-tings, felicitation.

बधावा m. presents sent ceremoniously as a mark of felicitation.

बधिक m. = वधिक।

बधिया adj. castrated.

बधिर adj. unable to hear, deaf.

बधिरता f. deafness.

बन m. = वन.

बनत f. design.

बनना vi. 1. to become. 2. to be made. 3. to be built/constructed. 4. to come into existence. 5. to be repaired.

बनना-बिगड़ना vi. to be made and unmade.

बनफ़्शा m. a type of medicinal herb.

बनबिलाव m. a wild animal of the cat family, lynx.

बनवाई f. act or state of बनवाना, or charges paid for the same.

बनवाना vt. causative of बनाना।

बनाना vt. 1. to make (physical or conceptual), to build/erect/construct. 2. to befool.

बना-बनाया adj. 1. readymade. 2. well-made.

बनाम conj. versus.

बनाव m. = बनावट; ~- सिंगार make-up.

बनावट f. 1. formation, structure, construction. 2. affectation.

बनावटी adj. artificial, showy, unreal.

बनिया m. grocer, trader.

बनियाइन f. an undergarment.

बनिस्बत, की postposition. in comparison with.

बनैला adj. wild, belonging to or living in the forest.

ब

बन्ना m. bridegroom.

बन्नी f. bride.

बपौती f. inheritance, heritage, patrimony.

बफारा m. medicated steam.

बबुआ m. 1. toy (in the shape of a boy). 2. boy-child.

बबूल m. acacia tree.

बबूला m. 1. bubble. 2. whirl-wind.

बम m. bomb.

बमगोला m. bomb shell.

बमपुलिस m. public latrine.

बमबारी f. bombing.

बमवर्षक m. bomber.

बयनामा m. sale-deed.

बया m. weaver bird.

बयान m. 1. statement. 2. account, description.

बयाना m. earnest money.

बयालीस adj. & m. forty-two, 42.

बयासी adj. & m. eighty-two, 82.

बरई m. one who sells betel leaves.

बरकत f. 1. grace; ख़ुदा की ~ Grace of God. 2. affluence.

बरक़रार adj. in tact.

बरख़ास्त adj. dismissed.

बरख़ास्तगी f. sack, dismissal.

बरगद m. banyan tree.

बरछा m. spear.

बरछी f. dagger.

बरज़ोर adj. 1. strong. 2. coercive, oppressive.

बरतन m. utensil, vessel.

बरतन-चौका m. act of cleaning the kitchen and kitchen-wares.

बरतना vt. 1. to use. 2. to exercise. 3. to deal with.

बरताव m. treatment, behaviour, dealing.

बरदाश्त f. = बर्दाश्त।

बरबस adv. 1. forcefully, willy-nilly. 2. spontaneously.

बरबाद adj. 1. ruined, destroyed. 2. wasted.

बरबादी f. 1. ruination, ruin. 2. waste, wastage.

बरमा m. 1. drill (for making holes). 2. Burma, old name of Myanmar, a country in Asia.

बरस m. = वर्ष।

बरसना vi. to rain, to shower.

बरसात f. 1. rain. 2. rainy season.

बरसाती adj. rainy, of or pertaining to rains. f. 1. porch. 2. raincoat.

बरसाना vt. to rain, to shower (upon).

बरसी f. first death anniversary.

बरात f. 1. marriage procession. 2. marriage party.

बरात घर m. the place where marriage parties stay.

बराती m. a member of a marriage party.

बराबर adj. 1. of the same age or size, equal. 2. adjoining. adv. 1. regularly. 2. non-stop.

बराबर, के postposition. equal to, upto.

बराबरी f. equality, parity.

बरामद adj. seized, recovered.

बरामदा m. verandah.

बरास्ता adv. via.

बरी adj. acquitted, released.

बरौनी f. eyelash.

बर्तन m. = बरतन।

बर्ताव m. = बरताव।

बर्थ m. berth, seat.

बर्दाश्त f. power of endurance, tolerance, forbearance.

बर्फ़ f. snow, ice.

बर्फ़ानी adj. snowy.

बर्फ़ी f. a sweetmeat of rectangular shape.

बर्फ़ीला adj. icy, snowy.

बर्बर adj. barbaric, savage.

बर्बरता f. barbarism, savagery.

बर्र f. wasp.

बर्राना vi. 1. to gabble. 2. to talk in one's sleep, fever etc.

बल m. 1. force. 2. strength, power, might. 3. vigour. 4. stress, emphasis. 5. direction; आड़े ~ slantingly, obliquely. 6. twirl.

बलकना vi. to be visibly excited, to boil, to simmer.

बलकारक adj. invigorating, vitalising, restorative.

बलग़म f. phlegm.

बलतोड़ m. boil caused by the uprooting of a hair.

बल-प्रयोग m. 1. use of force. 2. application of force (Maths.).

बल-बूता m. strength.

बलवती adj. fem. of बलवान, strong.

बलवर्धक adj. tonic, invigora-ting, restorative.

बलवा m. riot.

बलवाई m. rioter.

बलवान्, बलवान adj. powerful, stout, strong.

बलशाली adj. powerful, vig-orous.

बलहीन adj. powerless, weak.

बला f. 1. evil, calamity, adversity. 2. trouble, affliction, misery.

बलाघात m. emphasis, stress.

बलात् adv. by force, forcibly.

बलात्कार m. 1. rape. 2. The act of spoiling something.

बलात्कारी m. rapist.

बलि f. something offered as a sacrifice.

बलिदान m. act of sacrificing, sacrifice.

बलिष्ठ adj. very strong, stout, powerful.

बलिहारी adj. & f. (किसी पर) ~ जाना to bestow affectionate blessings (on someone).

बली adj. powerful, strong.

बलीवर्द m. ox, bull.

बलुआ adj. sandy.

बल्कि conj. 1. but. 2. rather. 3. on the contrary.

बल्ब m. bulb.

बल्लम m. lance, spear.

बल्ला m. 1. (cricket) bat. 2. (tennis) racket.

बल्ली f. long wooden staff.

बल्लेबाज़ m. batsman.

बवंडर m. cyclone, typhoon, whirlwind.

बवासीर f. piles.

बशर्ते conj. provided that, only if.

ब

बसंत m. spring.

बसंती adj. 1. pertaining to the spring season. 2. yellow.

बस interj. 1. no more please, that's all, enough, sufficient. 2. just. m. = वश। f. bus

बसना vi. 1. to dwell/inhabit/ live. 2. to settle (down). 3. to permeate.

बसाना vt. causative of बसना। vi. to emit bad odour.

बसूला m. adze.

बसूली f. small adze.

बसेरा m. shelter, dwelling.

बस्ता m. bag, school bag, portmanteau.

बस्ती f. 1. habitation. 2. colony.

बहँगी f. load-carrying device in the shape of a scale-pan.

बहक f. raving, going astray, irrelevant talking.

बहकना vt. to rave, to go astray.

बहकाना vt. to lead astray, to seduce, to entice, to allure, to mislead.

बहकावा m. enticement.

बहत्तर adj. & m. seventy-two, 72.

बहन f. sister.

बहना vi. 1. to flow. 2. to be swept by the current.

बहनापा m. 1. sister-like relationship. 2. sisterhood.

बहनोई m. sister's husband, brother-in-law.

बहरा adj. unable to hear, deaf.

बहरापन m. deafness.

बहरी f. a bird of the hawk family.

बहरूपिया m. = बहुरूपिया।

बहलना vi. to be agreeably diverted/ amused.

बहलाना vt. to amuse, recreate.

बहलाव m. entertainment, recreation.

बहस f. 1. discussion. 2. argument.

बहादुर adj. brave, bold, valorous, adventurous.

बहादुरी f. bravery, boldness, valour.

बहाना[1] m. pretext, pretence.

बहाना[2] vt. 1. to cause to flow. 2. to set afloat.

बहानेबाज़ adj. (one) who is given to making excuses/pretences.

बहार f. 1. spring. 2. season of delight/affluence. 3. charm.

बहाल adj. 1. reinstated. 2. maintained.

बहाली f. 1. reinstatement, restoration (to the original status). 2. happiness.

बहाव m. drift, flow.

बहिरंग adj. external.

बहिर्गत adj. outward.

बहिर्गमन m. 1. an act of going out. 2. an act of leaving a meeting, conference etc., as a protest.

बहिर्मुखी adj. extrovert.

बहिश्त m. heaven.

बहिष्करण m. boycotting.

बहिष्कार m. boycott, ban, taboo.

बहिष्कृत adj. boycotted, excommunicated.

बही f. an account book.

बही-खाता m. account book.
बहु adj. many.
बहु-आयामी adj. multidi-mensional.
बहुखंडीय adj. 1. multistoried. 2. having many compart-ments.
बहुजातीय adj. multi-ethnic.
बहुज्ञ adj. & m. (a person) of wide knowledge, versatile, erudite, scholarly.
बहुत adj. 1. much, too much, abundant, plentiful. adv. very. m. many people.
बहुतायत f. abundance, plenty, excess.
बहुतेरा adj. = बहुत।
बहुदर्शी adj. versatile, learned.
बहुदलीय adj. multiparty.
बहुधर्मी adj. multireligious.
बहुधा adv. 1. generally, frequently, quite often, very often. 2. in many ways.
बहुपक्षीय adj. multilateral.
बहुपतित्व m. polyandry.
बहुपत्नीक m. polygamist.
बहुभाषी adj. multilingual. m. multilinguist.
बहुमत m. majority.
बहुमुखी adj. versatile, well-rounded/versed.
बहुमूल्य adj. 1. precious. 2. cos-tly, invaluable.
बहुरना vi. to come back/return.
बहुराष्ट्रीय adj. multinational.
बहुरूप adj. multiform.
बहुरूपिया m. an expert in many different forms of disguise, impostor.
बहुल adj. abundant, plentiful, copious.
बहुलता f. abundance, plenty, plentitude.
बहुवचन m. plural.
बहुविवाह m. polygamy, polyandry.
बहुश्रुत adj. widely informed/heard.
बहुसंख्यक adj. numerous, majority.
बहू f. 1. daughter-in-law. 2. wife.
बहेलिया m. fowler, hunter.
बाँक f. (graceful) curvature/bend.
बाँकपन m. = बाँकापन।
बाँका adj. foppish.
बाँकापन m. foppishness.
बाँग f. 1. cock-a-doodle-doo, a long cry of a cock. 2. prayer call (by the chief of a mosque).
बाँगड़ू adj. uncivilized.
बाँचना vt. to read aloud.
बाँझ adj. barren (woman).
बाँझपन m. barrenness (of a woman).
बाँट f. division, partition.
बाँटना vt. 1. to distribute. 2. to divide/partition. 3. to share out.
बांड m. bond.
बाँदी f. odalisque.
बाँध m. dam, dike, embankment.
बाँधना vt. 1. to bind/tie/fasten. 2. to wrap around.
बाँधनू m. preplanned approach.
बांधव m. fraternal relation.
बाँबी f. snake-bill, ant-hill.
बाँस m. bamboo.
बाँसुरी f. flute.
बाँसुरीवादक m. flute player, flutist.

ब

बाँह f. 1. arm. 2. sleeve.

बाइसिकिल f. bicycle.

बाई f. 1. lady. 2. delirium.

बाईस adj. & m. twenty-two, 22.

बाएँ adv. towards the left, to the left.

बाएँ, के postposition. on the left side.

बाक़ी f. 1. subtraction. 2. remainder. 3. balance. 4. arrears. adj. remaining.

बाग़ m. garden.

बागडोर f. reins.

बाग़बान m. gardener.

बाग़बानी f. gardening.

बाग़ी adj. & m. rebel, insurgent.

बाग़ीचा m. बग़ीचा।

बाघंबर m. tiger skin.

बाघ m. tiger.

बाछ f. tip of the lip; उसकी बाछें खिल गईं He felt extremely happy.

बाछा m. calf.

बाज़ m. hawk, falcon. suffix. doer; पतंग ~ kite-flier. adv. bereft of, without; ~ आना to refrain, to desist from. adj. a few, some.

बाजरा m. millet.

बाजा m. musical instrument.

बाजा-गाजा m. fanfare band.

बाज़ार m. market, shopping area.

बाज़ार-भाव adj. 1. market rate, kerb rate. 2. market value.

बाज़ारी adj. pertaining to the market, commonplace, rude.

बाज़ारू adj. cheap and third-rate.

बाज़ी f. 1. bet, stake. 2. turn.

बाज़ीगर m. juggler, conjurer.

बाज़ीगरी f. jugglery.

बाजू m. arm.

बाजूबंद m. armlet.

बाट m. 1. way, path, passage.

बाटी f. roasted, round thick dough bread.

बाड़ f. hedge, fence.

बाड़ी f. 1. small garden. 2. house.

बाढ़ f. 1. growth. 2. flood. 3. a great quantity of something.

बाण m. arrow.

बाण-विद्या f. archery.

बात f. 1. talk. 2. matter. 3. thing.

बातचीत f. conversation.

बाती f. wick.

बातूनी adj. talkative, chatty, garrulous.

बाद adj. deducted, subtracted.

बाद, के postposition. after.

बादबान m. sail.

बादल m. cloud.

बादवाला adj. next, following.

बादशाह m. 1. king, ruler. 2. king (chessman).

बादशाहत f. reign, government, sovereignty.

बादाम m. almond.

बादामी adj. of the colour of almond.

बादी adj. flatulent. f. flatulence, fat.

बाधक adj. obstructive.

बाधा f. 1. hurdle, obstruction. 2. interruption.

बाधित adj. 1. obstructed. 2. barred.

बाध्य adj. compelled, forced.

बाध्यता f. obligation, compulsion.

बान m. 1. = बाण। 2. cord of twisted grass.

बानक m. shape of things.

बानगी f. sample, specimen, example.

बानबे adj. & m. ninety-two, 92.

बानर m. = वानर।

बाना m. 1. woof. 2. dress, guise. vt. to open out.

बाप m. father.

बाप-दादा m. (plu.) forefathers, ancestors.

बापुरा adj. & m. = बेचारा।

बापू m. father.

बाबत, की postposition. about, in respect of, pertaining to.

बाबा m. 1. grandfather. 2. old man. 3. ascetic.

बाबा आदम m. primitive man.

बाबुल m. father.

बाबू m. 1. educated man. 2. clerk.

बाबू जी m. 1. (form of addressing) Father! 2. (respectable form of addressing) an elderly man.

बायकाट m. boycott.

बायन m. present, gift.

बायबी adj. strange.

बायाँ adj. left.

बायें adv. = बाएँ।

बारंबार adv. again and again, repeatedly.

बारंबारता f. frequency.

बार f. time.

बारजा m. balcony.

बारदाना m. 1. fare, food. 2. miscellany.

बार-बार adv. time after time, repeatedly, time and again.

बारह adj. & m. twelve, 12; ~ खड़ी set of consonants of the Nagari alphabet in combination with the vowels.

बारहदरी f. a structure having twelve entrances.

बारहमासा m. a particular type of Hindi poetry.

बारहमासी adj. 1. perennial, all-weather. 2. flower (s) bloo-ming all the year round.

बारहसिंगा m. stag, reindeer.

बारात f. = बरात।

बारिश f. rain, rainfall.

बारी f. 1. turn. 2. inning. 3. gro-ve, small garden.

बारीक adj. 1. thin. 2. minute, subtle.

बारूद m. gunpowder.

बारूद-घर m. ammunition store.

बारूदी सुरंग f. a land-mine.

बारे में, के postposition. relating to, pertaining to, about.

बार्डर m. border.

बाल m. 1. hair. 2. infant, child. 3. ear of corn. 4. ball.

बालक m. 1. a boy. 2. a child.

बालकपन m. boyhood.

बालगोपाल m. (plu.) children.

बालचर m. boy scout.

बालटी f. bucket.

ब

बालडांस m. ball dance, orga-nised dance programme.

बालतोड़ m. = बलतोड़।

बालना vt. 1. to burn. 2. to light.

बालपन m. the state or time of being a boy, childhood.

बाल-बच्चा m. offspring.

बाल-ब्रह्मचारी m. lifelong celibate.

बालम m. darling, sweet lover.

बालरवि m. morning sun.

बालवध m. infanticide.

बाल-विधवा f. child widow, widow since childhood.

बाल-सफ़ा adj. depilatory, hair-removing.

बाल-साहित्य m. juvenile lit-erature.

बालसुलभ adj. childlike.

बालहठ m. childish insistence.

बाला f. adolescent girl. m. earornament.

बालानशीन adj. prestigious.

बालापन m. childhood.

बालिका f. female child, girl.

बालिग़ adj. adult.

बालिश्त m. hand-span.

बाली adj. young. f. 1. ear-ring. 2. ear of corn.

बालुका f. sand.

बालुकामय adj. sandy.

बालू m. sand.

बालूशाही f. a kind of sweet.

बालेंदु m. new moon, the second night rising moon.

बालोचित adj. childlike.

बाल्टी f. bucket, pail.

बाल्य adj. of or pertaining to a child.

बाल्यकाल m. childhood, adoles-cence.

बाल्यावस्था f. infancy, childhood.

बावजूद, के postposition. in spite of.

बावड़ी f. broad well with a low surface of water provided with flight of stairs.

बावन adj. & m. fifty-two, 52.

बावरची m. cook.

बावरा adj. = बावला।

बावला adj. 1. insane, mad. 2. crazy.

बावली adj. fem. of बावला। f. = बावड़ी।

बावेला m. furore, tumult, uproar.

बाशिंदा adj. & m. dweller.

बास m. = वास। f. smell.

बासठ adj. & m. sixty-two, 62.

बासन m. vessel, utensil.

बासा m. abode, habitat.

बासी adj. 1. having lost freshness. 2. stale.

बाहर adv. out, outside. m. foreign land; ~ के लोग foreigners.

बाहर, के postposition. outside.

बाहरवाला adj. & m. outsider.

बाहर, से postposition. out of, beyond.

बाहरी adj. 1. outward, outer. 2. external, outside. m. outsider, external.

बाहु f. arm.

बाहुबल m. physical force/str-ength.

बाहुमूल m. shoulder-joint.

बाहुल्य m. exuberance, plenty, abundance.

बाह्य adj. outward, external.

बाह्यतः adv. externally.

बाह्यांचल m. outskirts.

बिंदी f. 1. dot, point. 2. cypher. 3. vermilion mark on the forehead.

बिंदु m. 1. dot, point. 2. cypher.

बिंदु-चित्रण m. stippling.

बिंधना vi. 1. to be pierced. 2. to be engrossed/tied up.

बिंब m. 1. disc. 2. = प्रतिबिंब।

बिआना vt. to give birth to, to be delivered of (said of animals).

बिकना vi. to be sold.

बिकल adj. = विकल।

बिकवाना vi. to cause to sell.

बिकसना vi. = विकसना।

बिकाऊ adj. for sale.

बिक्री f. sale.

बिखरना vi. to be scattered/diffused.

बिखराव m. act or state of being scattered/diffused.

बिखेरना vt. to scatter/diffuse.

बिगड़ना vi. 1. to be angry/annoyed. 2. to deteriorate.

बिगड़ा adj. 1. worsened, spoilt, pampered. 2. damaged.

बिगड़ी f. serious and difficult condition.

बिगड़ैल adj. short-tempered, peevish.

बिगाड़ m. rift, discord.

बिगाड़ना vt. 1. to spoil, to damage, to vitiate. 2. to ruin.

बिगाड़ू adj. (one) who spoils/destroys.

बिगुल m. bugle.

बिचकना vi. to falter.

बिचकाना vt. to sneer.

बिचला adj. middle, mid.

बिचवई m. mediator.

बिचौलिया m. go-between, middleman.

बिच्छू m. scorpion.

बिछड़ना vi. to cease to be together.

बिछना vi. to be spread out.

बिछलन f. = फिसलन।

बिछाना vt. to spread out.

बिछावन f. 1. bed-sheet. 2. bedding.

बिछिया f. fem. of बिछुआ।

बिछुआ m. an ornament worn on the toe.

बिछुड़ना vi. = बिछड़ना।

बिछोड़ा m. = बिछोह।

बिछोह m. painful separation, bereavement.

बिछोही adj. painfully separa-ted, bereaved.

बिछौना m. bedding.

बिजली f. 1. lightning. 2. electricity. 3. electric light.

बिजली घर m. powerhouse.

बिजूखा m. scarecrow.

बिजैला adj. seedy.

बिज्जू m. an animal of the wild cat family.

बिटिया f. 1. daughter. 2. girlie.

बिठाना vt. = बैठाना।

बिड़ाल m. he-cat

बिताना vt. to spend (time).

ब

बित्ता m. hand span.

बिथरना vi. to scatter.

बिदकना vi. to shy, to be alar- med.

बिदेश m. = विदेश।

बिदेसिया m. dweller in a foreign land, foreigner.

बिध f. concordance.

बिधना m. fate, destiny.

बिन adv. = बिना।

बिनन f. texture.

बिनना vt. 1. to pick out (bad ones). 2. to knit/weave. 3. to select.

बिनवाना vi. to cause to be knit- ted.

बिना adv. without. f. cause, plea.

बिनाई f. the work of knitting and/or charges paid for the same.

बिना, के postposition. without.

बिनावट f. texture.

बिनौला m. cotton-seed.

बिपता f. = विपत्ति।

बिफरना vi. to be visibly anno- yed.

बियाबान m. wilderness, deser- ted spot.

बिरला adj. rare.

बिरवा m. plant.

बिरह m. = विरह।

बिरहा m. a folk song of separa- tion, ballad.

बिराजना vi. विराजना।

बिरादर m. brother.

बिरादरी f. community.

बिराना vt. to jeer, to mock.

बिल m. 1. hole. 2. bill (for payment).

बिलकुल adv. = बिल्कुल।

बिलखना vt. to wail/lament.

बिलटना vi. 1. to be spoiled. 2.to be reversed.

बिलटी f. railway receipt.

बिलना vi. to be rolled into flat cakes.

बिलनी f. sty.

बिलपना vi. to wail/lament.

बिलबिलाना vi. 1. to whine. 2. to wriggle.

बिलसना vi. to look fine, to suit admirably.

बिला adj. without.

बिलाई f. cat.

बिलाना vi. to be gone out of sight.

बिलार m. tom-cat.

बिलाव m. tom-cat.

बिलैया f. 1. cat. 2. bolt.

बिलोड़ना vt. = बिलोना।

बिलोना vt. to churn (milk, curd etc.).

बिलौटा m. kitten.

बिल्कुल adv. totally, absolutely, perfectly, wholly.

बिल्ला m. 1. tom-cat. 2. badge.

बिल्ली f. 1. cat. 2. = सिटकनी।

बिल्लौर m. 1. crystal. 2. quartz.

बिल्लौरी adj. 1. crystalline. 2. quartziferous.

बिवाई f. chilblain(s).

बिस m. = विष।

बिसखोपड़ा m. chamelion.

बिसमिल्ला m. beginning.

बिसरना vi. to be forgotten.

बिसात f. 1. capacity. 2. board

for displaying goods or playing chess etc.

बिसातख़ाना m. 1. general merchandise. 2. haberda-shery/ drapery.

बिसाती m. general merchant, haberdasher/draper.

बिसायँध f. stench.

बिसारना vt. to forget.

बिसूरना vi. to sob/wail.

बिस्कुट m. biscuit.

बिस्तर m. bedding.

बिस्तरबंद m. holdall.

बिस्वा m. a measure of land, one-twentieth of a बीघा।

बिही f. quince, smallish guava.

बींधना vi. to bore/perforate.

बी f. = बीबी।

बीघा m. a measure of land, five-eighth of an acre.

बीच m. centre, middle part.

बीच, के postposition. 1. amidst. 2. between.

बीच-बचाव m. mediation.

बीचोबीच, के postposition. exactly or just in the middle or midway.

बीछी f. female scorpion.

बीज m. 1. seed. 2. the cause or beginning of something.

बीजक m. invoice.

बीजगणित m. Algebra.

बीजारोपण m. sowing (seeds).

बीजी adj. = बीजू।

बीजू adj. produced from seed (i.e. not grafted).

बीट f. bird droppings.

बीड़ा m. seasoned and folded betel leaf, prepared for being taken; ~ उठाना solemnly to undertake a difficult assignment/contract.

बीड़ी f. Indian substitute for cigarette with tobacco rolled in spl. kinds of leaves.

बीतना vi. 1. to pass. 2. to be spent. 3. to elapse.

बीन f. 1. a classical Indian st-ringed instrument. 2. sna-kecharmer's flute.

बीनना vt. to pick up/select/choose.

बीनाई f. vision, eyesight.

बीबी f. 1. lady. 2. elder sister. 3. = बीवी।

बीभत्स adj. horrid, loathsome, abhorrent, frightful, hideous.

बीभत्सता f. horridness, loathsomeness, fright-fulness.

बीम m. beam (शहतीर)।

बीमा m. insurance.

बीमाकर्ता m. insurer.

बीमाकृत adj. insured.

बीमार adj. sick, ill.

बीमारी f. disease, illness, sic-kness.

बीर adj. = वीर। m. brother.

बीरन m. brother.

बीर-बहूटी f. velvety insect, lady-cow, lady-fly.

बीवी f. wife.

बीस adj. & m. twenty, 20.

बीसी f. set of twenty.

बीहड़ adj. 1. rough and rugged, hazardous. 2. difficult to do,

ब

arduous; 3. difficult to tackle.
बुँदकी f. dot.
बुंदा m. ear-top.
बुँदिया f. a small globular Indian sweet.
बुंदीदार adj. dotted, spotted.
बुंदेला m. subcaste among Rajputs.
बुआ f. = फूफी।
बुकचा m. bundle (usually of clothes).
बुकनी f. powder.
बुक्का m. pulverized mica.
बुख़ार m. 1. fever. 2. irritation.
बुज़दिल m. coward.
बुज़दिली f. cowardice.
बुज़ुर्ग adj. & m. an elderly (person), venerable.
बुझना vi. 1. to be extinguished. 2. to be quenched/slaked.
बुझाना vt. 1. to extinguish, to put out. 2. to slake.
बुझौवल f. enigma, riddle.
बुड़बुड़ाना vi. = बड़बड़ाना।
बुड्ढा adj. & m. old, aged, old man.
बुढ़ाना vi. to get/grow old.
बुढ़ापा m. the latter part of the life, old age.
बुढ़िया f. old woman.
बुत adj. dumb and motionless. m. icon, idol.
बुतपरस्त m. idolator.
बुताना vt. = बुझाना।
बुताम m. button.
बुत्ता m. dodge.
बुदबुदाना vi 1. to effervesce/ bu-bble, to be bubbling. 2. to mumble.
बुदबुदाहट f. effervescence.
बुद्ध adj. 1. awakened, enlightened. 2. scholarly. m. Lord Buddha.
बुद्धि f. 1. intelligence. 2. wisdom, sense, wit, knowledge.
बुद्धिजीवी m. an intellectual.
बुद्धिबल m. intellectual power.
बुद्धिमत्ता f. wisdom, intelligence.
बुद्धिमान, बुद्धिमान् adj. wise, learned, sharp-witted.
बुद्धिमानी f. 1. wisdom. 2. an act of wisdom, sagacity, prudence.
बुद्धिहीन adj. void of sagacity, senseless, stupid, foolish.
बुद्धू adj. & m. simpleton, dul- lard.
बुध m. Mercury (planet).
बुधजन m. scholarly people, the wise, learned.
बुधवार m. Wednesday.
बुनकर m. weaver.
बुनना vt. 1. to knit. 2. to weave.
बुनवाई f. 1. act of knitting/weaving. 2. charges paid for knitting/ weaving.
बुनवाना vt. causative of बुनना।
बुनाई f. 1. texture. 2. charges paid for knitting/weaving.
बुनावट f. texture.
बुनियाद f. 1. foundation. 2. basis.
बुनियादी adj. 1. basic. 2. serving as a foundation.
बुनियादी ढाँचा m. infrastructure.
बुभुक्षा f. hunger, appetite.
बुभुक्षित adj. hungry.
बुरकना vt. to spray/sprinkle.

बुरक़ा m. veil.

बुरकी f. enchanted dust.

बुरबक adj. senile.

बुरा adj. 1. bad, untoward, harmful, faulty; evil. 2. wicked.

बुराई f. 1. defect, flaw. 2. evil, vice. 3. discredit, bad name.

बुरादा m. saw-dust.

बुरा-भला m. good side and bad; ~ कहना to reprimand/upbraid.

बुरुश m. brush.

बुर्ज m. bastion, turret, tower.

बुर्जुआ adj. & m. bourgeois.

बुर्द m. 1. additional income. 2. competition.

बुर्दाफ़रोश m. slave-dealer.

बुलंद adj. 1. lofty. 2. loud.

बुलंदी f. loftiness, height.

बुलबुल f. nightingale.

बुलबुला m. 1. bubble. 2. transi-tory thing. 3. unrealistic scheme.

बुलवाना vt. 1. to send for. 2. to make one speak.

बुलाक़ m. nose-pendant.

बुलाना vt. 1. to call. 2. to invite. 3. to convene.

बुलावा m. 1. call. 2. invitation.

बुलेटिन m. bulletin.

बुसना vi. to become stale.

बुहारना vt. to sweep.

बुहारी f. broom.

बूँद m. drop.

बूँदा-बाँदी f. raindropping, drizzling.

बूँदी f. 1. a kind of sweet or saltish dish in the form of droplets. 2. small circular designs printed and embroidered on cloth.

बू f. foul smell.

बूआ f. = फूफी।

बूकना vi. to powder.

बूचड़ m. butcher.

बूचड़ख़ाना m. slaghter-house.

बूचा adj. maimed, mutilated.

बूझ f. faculty of guessing the future or factuality correctly, comprehension.

बूझना vt. 1. to infer/guess correctly. 2. to pose a riddle for solution.

बूट m. boot.

बूटा m. 1. plant. 2. design (usually on cloth).

बूटी f. 1. herb. 2. design. (fem. of बूटा) । 3. pip (on a playing card).

बूटेदार adj. embroidered or printed (cloth).

बूढ़ा adj. aged, old. m. old man.

बूढ़ी f. old woman.

बूता f. capacity to do, hold or contain something.

बू-बास f. 1. smell. 2. characteristics.

बूरा m. unrefined sugar.

बृहत् adj. great, large.

बृहत्तर adj. greater.

बृहद् adj. = बृहत्।

बृहस्पति m. 1. Jupiter. 2. (~वार) Thursday.

बेंच m. bench.

बेंट f. handle (of knife etc.).

बेंत m. cane.

बे prefix. without, lacking, void.

बेअक़्ल adj. void of wisdom, foolish, idiot, stupid.

बेअदब adj. lacking in proper respect, impertinent.

बेआबरू adj. dishonoured.

बेइंसाफ़ी f. lack of justice, injustice.

बेइज़्ज़त adj. dishonoured, disgraced.

बेईमान adj. dishonest, corrupt, fraudulent, insincere.

बेउसूल adj. unprincipled.

बेऐब adj. 1. faultless. 2. flawless.

बेक़द्री f. 1. non-appreciation, lack of appreciation. 2. disrespect.

बेक़रार adj. disconsolate, uneasy, restless.

बेकस adj. helpless.

बेक़सूर adj. guiltless, innocent.

बेक़ाबू adj. uncontrollable.

बेकाम adj. 1. idle, good for nothing, ineffectual. 2. unemployed (person). 3. having no practical use.

बेक़ायदा adj. 1. irregular. 2. improper, unmannerly. 3. unlawful, illegal.

बेकार adj. 1. good-for-nothing, hopeless, useless, worthless. 2. unemployed. adv. to no purpose, unnecessarily.

बेखटके adv. without hitch or apprehension, unhesitatin-gly.

बेख़बर adj. 1. oblivious, unwary, heedless. 2. uninformed, unaware.

बेख़ुदी f. selflessness.

बेख़ौफ़ adj. fearless, dauntless. adv. fearlessly.

बेगम f. queen.

बेग़म adj. having no sorrow.

बेगाना adj. & m. not belonging or related to oneself, outsider, stranger.

बेगार f. forced ,or involuntary labour, careless work.

बेगुनाह adj. guiltless, innocent, faultless.

बेघर adj. homeless, without home and hearth.

बेचना vt. to sell/dispose.

बेचारा adj. helpless, poor.

बेचैन m. restless, uneasy.

बेजा adj. improper, unfair, unjust.

बेजान adj. 1. having no life, lifeless. 2. lacking liveliness. 3. dead.

बेज़ार adj. fed up, tired.

बेजोड़ adj. 1. without joints. 2. matchless, unique, ideal.

बेटा m. son.

बेटिकट adj. ticketless. adv. without ticket.

बेटी f. daughter.

बेठन m. 1. wrapper. 2. covering.

बेठिकाने adv. at a wrong place.

बेड़ा m. 1. fleet. 2. raft.

बेड़ी f. 1. boat. 2. fetters, shackles.

बेडौल adj. disproportionate, unsymmetrical, ugly, clumsy.

बेढंगा adj. 1. uncouth. 2. rough and shaggy, unsystematic, unmethodical.

बेढब adj. deformed, uncanny.

बेतकल्लुफ़ adj. observing no formality, informal.

बेतरतीब adj. unsystematic, unmethodical.

बेतहाशा adv. at breakneck speed, recklessly, wildly.

बेताब adj. = बेचैन।

बेतार adj. wireless.

बेताल adj. out of tune. m. = बैताल।

बेतुका adj. 1. unrhymed. 2. absurd, irrelevant, bizarre, pointless.

बेदख़ल adj. ejected, dispossessed.

बेदम adj. 1. breathless. 2. totally exhausted.

बेदर्द adj. hard-hearted, merciless, harsh, cruel.

बेदाग़ adj. spotless, stainless.

बेदाना adj. without seeds.

बेदिल adj. heartless, unkind.

बेध m. hole.

बेधड़क adv. without hitch or hesitation, dauntlessly, fearlessly.

बेधना vt. to pierce a hole into.

बेनज़ीर adj. without precedent, unprecedented.

बेनाम adj. without name, nameless.

बेपनाह adj. without shelter/support, shelterless.

बेपर adj. without feathers/wings; ~ की उड़ाना to talk tall.

बेपरदा adj. unveiled, uncovered, exposed.

बेपेंदा adj. bottomless.

बेफ़ायदा adj. without any gain/profit, fruitless, useless.

बेफ़िक्र adj. 1. careless. 2. carefree. happy-go-lucky

बेबस adj. helpless.

बेबसी f. helplessness, subjugation.

बेबाक adj. fully paid up, cleared off.

बेबुनियाद adj. unfounded, baseless.

बेभाव adj. unbounded, unlimi-ted.

बेमतलब adj. pointless, meaningless.

बेमन adj. uninterested, unwilling.

बेमिसाल adj. unparalleled, unique, marvellous.

बेमुरव्वत adj. not caring about someone's feelings, inconsiderate.

बेमेल adj. 1. incongruous, odd, incoherent. 2. mismatched.

बेमौक़े adv. at a wrong occasion.

बेमौसमी adj. 1. unseasonal. 2. off-season.

बेरंग adj. lacklustre.

बेर m. jujube.

बेरहम adj. merciless, ruthless, heartless, cruel.

बेरी f. jujube tree.

बेरी-बेरी f. beri beri (a disease).

बेरुख़ी f. indifference, neglect.

बेरोक adj. unobstructed, unhindered.

बेरोज़गार adj. unemployed.

बेरोज़गारी f. unemployment.

बेरौनक़ adj. lacklustre, dull.

बेल m. wood-apple. f. creeper.

बेलगाम adj. & adv. unbridled.

बेलचा m. shovel.

बेलदार m. manual labourer, digger.

बेलन m. 1. rolling pin. 2. cylinder, roller.

बेलना vt. to roll (kneaded flour into flat cakes).

ब

बेला m. 1. a kind of jasmine. 2. time, period of time. 3. wave. 4. seashore. 5. a variety of stringed instrument.

बेलाग adj. 1. straightforward, frank. 2. impartial, detached. 3. evident.

बेलिहाज़ adj. having no regard and consideration.

बेली m. friend, companion.

बेवक़ूफ़ adj. foolish, stupid, idiot.

बेवक़्त adv. untimely.

बेवफ़ा adj. disloyal, faithless.

बेवा f. widow.

बेवाई f. = बिवाई।

बेशक adv. of course, indeed, definitely, undoubtedly.

बेशक़ीमत adj. 1. precious, costly. 2. very useful or important, valuable.

बेशर्म adj. shameless.

बेशर्मी f. shamelessness.

बेशुमार adj. countless, innumerable, numberless, plenty.

बेसन m. gram flour, pulverised gram.

बेसनी f. cake made of gram flour.

बेसबरा adj. impatient.

बेसलीक़ा adj. mannerless, unmannerly, impolite, rude.

बेसहारा adj. helpless, without support/shelter.

बेसिर adj. ~ पैर का having no basis, illogical.

बेसी adj. & adv. much, more, excessive.

बेसुध adj. 1. unconscious. 2. absent-minded.

बेसुरा adj. discordant, out of tune.

बेस्वाद adj. tasteless, insipid.

बेहतर adj. better.

बेहतरी f. betterment.

बेहद adj. excessive.

बेहन m. seedling.

बेहया adj. shameless, obsti- nately shameless.

बेहयाई f. shamelessness.

बेहाल adj. afflicted, distressed.

बेहूदगी f. smuttiness, obscenity.

बेहूदा adj. smutty, obscene or offensive, absurd.

बेहोश adj. unconscious, fainted.

बेहोशी f. unconsciousness, swoon.

बैंक m. bank.

बैंगन m. eggplant, brinjal, aubergine.

बैंगनी adj. purple.

बैंड m. band.

बैकुंठ m. paradise.

बैज m. badge.

बैट m. bat (cricket).

बैटरी f. battery.

बैठक f. 1. sitting/drawing room, parlour. 2. sitting. 3. an Indian athletic posture.

बैठकबाज़ adj. & m. 1. associative/companionable, habituated to gossiping. 2. tricky (fellow), sharper.

बैठका m. spacious sitting room.

बैठकी f. = बैठक।

बैठना vi. 1. to sit, to take a seat.

बैठाना vt. 1. to seat. 2. to set (fracture of a bone etc.).

बैठे-ठाले adv. = बैठे-बैठाए।

बैठे-बैठाए adv. unexpectedly, without any warning.

बैताल m. evil spirit, goblin.

बैनामा m. sale-deed.

बैरंग adj. bearing.

बैर m. = वैर।

बैरक f. barrack.

बैरा m. bearer (in a hotel).

बैराग m. = वैराग्य।

बैरागी m. one who has renou- nced all, recluse.

बैरिस्टर m. barrister-at-law.

बैरोमीटर m. barometer.

बैल m. bullock.

बैसाख m. second month of the Hindu calendar.

बैसाखी f. 1. crutches. 2. festival observed in the month of बैसाख।

बोआई f. 1. act or process of sowing. 2. wages paid for sowing.

बोझ m. load, burden.

बोझिल adj. burdensome, heavy, loaded.

बोटी f. slice of flesh.

बोड़ा m. a kind of Indian bean.

बोतल f. bottle.

बोदा adj. 1. dull-headed, stupid. 2. timid.

बोध m. 1. perception. 2. sense.

बोधक adj. & m. 1. indicating. 2. who imparts knowledge. 3. signifying.

बोधगम्य adj. intelligible, understandable.

बोनसाई m. potted dwarf tree.

बोना vt. to sow.

बोरना vt. = डुबोना।

बोरसी f. earthen firepot.

बोरा m. sack, bag, burlap.

बोरिया m. 1. small sack/bag. 2. mat.

बोरिया-बिस्तर m. bag and bagg- age; lock, stock and barrel.

बोरी f. small sack/bag.

बोर्जुआ adj. & m. = बुर्जुआ।

बोर्ड m. board.

बोल m. utterance.

बोलचाल f. colloquial parlance.

बोलता सिनेमा m. talkie.

बोलती f. power of speech.

बोलना vt. to speak.

बोलना-चालना vi. to converse.

बोलनेवाला adj. speaking. m. speaker.

बोलबाला m. sway.

बोली f. 1. dialect. 2. bid. 3. sarcastic remark.

बोहनी f. the first cash sale of the day (which is considered auspicious).

बौखलाना vi. to speak too loudly and angrily.

बौखलाहट f. state of बौखलाना।

बौछार f. shower, volley.

बौड़म adj. & m. mad cap, stupid.

बौद्ध adj. pertaining to Bud-dhism. m. Buddhist.

बौद्धिक adj. of person's power of

reasoning, intellectual.

बौद्धिकता f. intellectualism.

बौना adj. dwarfish. m. dwarf.

बौर m. blossom.

बौरा adj. crazy.

बौराना vi. to go off one's head, to become crazy. vt. & vi. to blossom.

ब्याज m. interest.

ब्याजख़ोर m. usurer.

ब्याज-मुक्त adj. interest-free.

ब्यान m. delivery (only in relation to animals).

ब्याना vi. to give birth to (said of an animal).

ब्यालू m. dinner.

ब्याह m. marriage, wedding.

ब्याहता adj. & f. married (woman).

ब्याहना vi. to wed/marry.

ब्योंत f. planning.

ब्योंतना vi. to cut the cloth as per measurements.

ब्योरा m. 1. description. 2. details.

ब्योरेवार adv. in details.

ब्रह्म m. 1. the eternal spirit. 2. the voice of conscience.

ब्रह्मचर्य m. celibacy.

ब्रह्मचर्य आश्रम m. the first of the four stages in the life of a Hindu devoted to learning and preparation of life (characterised by celibacy).

ब्रह्मचारी m. celibate. [Fem. ब्रह्मचारिणी]

ब्रह्मज्ञान m. knowledge of the Supreme.

ब्रह्मभोज m. collective feeding (of Brahmins or ascetics).

ब्रह्मरेखा f. line of fate (on forehead).

ब्रह्मर्षि m. Seer of the Spiritual Reality.

ब्रह्मलेख m. line of fate (which is ineffaceable).

ब्रह्मविद्या f. knowledge divine.

ब्रह्मांड m. universe, cosmos.

ब्रह्मांड-विद्या f. cosmology.

ब्रह्मा m. Lord Brahma, the Creator/Prajapati.

ब्राह्म adj. of or pertaining to Brahma; ~ मुहूर्त time before dawn, early dawn.

ब्राह्मण m. Brahman, the first caste among the Hindus.

ब्राह्मणी f. 1. wife of a Brahman. 2. woman of the Brahman caste.

ब्राह्मी f. 1. a medicinal herb. 2. an ancient Hindu script from which most of the Indian scripts are believed to be evolved.

ब्रेक (brek) m. brake.

भ

भ m. the fourth of the bilabial pentad of consonants of the Nagari alphabet; its sound is like that of bh in abhor.

भंग m. 1. breaking up, dissolution. 2. breach. 3. disbandment. 4. breakage, fracture. f. = भाँग।

भंगड़ m. addict of भाँग।

भंगड़ा m. typical Punjabi folk dance.

भंगिमा f. posture, pose.

भंगी m. sweeper, scavenger. [Fem. भंगिन]

भंगुर adj. brittle, frail, fragile.

भंगेड़ी m. = भंगड़।

भंजक adj. & m. (one) who breaks/destroys.

भंजन m. breaking, demolition, destruction.

भँजना vi. 1. to be broken. 2. to be folded. 3. to be changed into smaller coins. 4. to be divided.

भंजना vt. to break.

भँजाई f. act or state of भाँजना, or charges paid for the same.

भँजाना vi. causative of भाँजना।

भंटा m. brinjal, aubergine, egg-plant.

भँड़साल f. utensil-store.

भंडा m. = भांड (बरतन)।

भंडाफोड़ m. exposure/disclosure (of someone's secrets).

भंडार m. 1. store. 2. stock. 3. depot.

भंडार-घर m. store-house.

भंडारा m. the feast open to all, community feast.

भंडारी m. 1. store-keeper. 2. co-ok. 3. steward.

भँडैती f. buffoonery.

भँभीरी f. = फिरकी।

भँवर m. whirlpool.

भँवरा (m. = भौंरा।

भइया m. = भैया।

भई m. a form of address indicating familiarity.

भक f. sound produced by a sudden outburst into a flame.

भकभकाना vi. (i) to glow intermittently with a noise; (ii) to fret and fume.

भकुआ m. fumbler, tomfool.

भकुआना vi. to fumble.

भकोसना vt. to eat greedily, to devour, to eat up, to gobble up.

भक्त m. devotee.

भक्तवत्सल adj. fondly affec-tionate towards devotees.

भक्ति f. devotion.

भक्तिमार्ग m. path of devotion.

भक्षक m. devourer.

भक्षण m. devouring.

भक्षणीय adj. = भक्ष्य।

भक्षित adj. 1. eaten. 2. devoured, eaten up.

भक्षी m. eater.

भक्ष्य adj. edible, eatable.

भक्ष्याभक्ष्य adj. edible and inedible.

भगंदर m. fistula.

भग f. vulva.

भगत m. भक्त।

भगदड़ f. sudden rush of frightened people or animals, stampede, panic.

भगल m. swindling, stratagem.

भगवत् m. God.

भगवती f. goddess.

भगवा adj. saffron-coloured.

भगवाकरण m. saffronisation.

भगवान m. God.

भगाना vt. to cause to run away, to drive off, to dispel.

भगिनी f. sister.

भगीरथ m. an ancient Indian king who brought Ganga to the earth.

भगीरथ-प्रयत्न m. Herculean or heroic effort.

भगोड़ा m. 1. absconder, fugitive, truant. 2. coward, shirker.

भग्न adj. 1. broken. 2. interrupted.

भग्नावशेष m. ruins, debris, remains.

भचक f. limp.

भचकना vi. to limp.

भजन m. hymn, devotional song, prayer.

भजना vt. to repeat God's name with a devotional attitude.

भजनावली f. hymnal, hymn book.

भजनीक m. a singer of hymns.

भजनोपदेशक m. one who prea-ches through hymns.

भट m. = भट्ट।

भटक f. state of भटकना।

भटकना vi. 1. to go astray, to stroll. 2. to wander about.

भटकाना vt. to mislead, causa-tive of भटकना।

भटकाव m. the state of being off the track.

भटियारख़ाना m. 1. abode of an inn-keeper. 2. centre of noise and tumult. 3. rendezvous of vulgar people.

भटियारा m. inn-keeper (of a low order).

भटियारिन f. 1. wife of an inn-keeper. 2. (woman) inn-keeper.

भट्ट m. 1. a sub-caste among Brahmians. 2. = भाट।

भट्ठा m. 1. brick kiln. 2. large भट्ठी।

भट्ठी f. 1. big oven, fireplace, furnace. 2. distillery. 3. liquor shop, wine shop.

भठियारख़ाना m. = भटियारख़ाना।

भठियारा m. = भटियारा। [Fem. भठियारिन]

भड़क f. 1. ostentation, grand show. 2. warmth.

भड़कना vi. 1. to flare up. 2. to get enraged/provoked.

भड़काना vt. to excite, to incite.

भड़कीला adj. 1. ostentatious, gaudy, showy. 2. cheap, tawdry. 3. causing excitement.

भड़कीलापन m. ostentation, tawdriness, gaudiness.

भड़भड़ f. 1. dull thudding sound. 2. discordant or tumultuous noise.

भड़भड़ाना vi. causation of a dull heavy sound. vt. to produce a thumping sound.

भड़भड़िया adj. & m. 1. prattler. 2. one who can't retain a secret.

भड़भूँजा m. parcher.

भड़ास f. pent-up feeling.

भड़ुआ m. 1. a musician companion of a dancing girl. 2. broker of a prostitute, pimp, pander. 3. a good-for-nothing fellow.

भणित adj. (that which is) said/uttered.

भतार m. husband.

भतीजा m. brother's son, nephew.

भतीजी f. brother's daughter, niece.

भत्ता m. allowance.

भदंत adj. revered, adored.

भदई adj. of or pertaining to the month of भादों।

भद्द f. ridicule, humiliation.

भद्दा adj. 1. awkward, clumsy, uncouth, vulgar. 2. dirty.

भद्दापन m. awkwardness, clumsiness, ugliness.

भद्र adj. 1. courteous. 2. affable.

भद्रता f. nobility, generosity, politeness.

भद्रपुरुष m. gentleman.

भद्रा f. evil conjunction of stars.

भद्राभद्र adj. good and evil.

भद्रे f. O noble lady!

भनक f. low or faint ring/sound.

भनभनाहट f. hum, buzz.

भब्भड़ f. disorderly crowd, turmoil.

भभक f. 1. flare (of a lamp, lantern etc.). 2. foul smell, stench.

भभकना vi. 1. to flare up. 2. to emit/come out forcefully.

भभका m. 1. still, distillation plant. 2. foul smell, stench. 3. flare (of a lamp, lantern etc.)

भभकी f. bluff, menace, threat.

भभूका adj. red hot. m. blaze.

भभूत f. sacred ashes.

भयंकर adj. terrible, dreadful, awful, precarious.

भयंकरता f. dreadfulness, fierceness.

भय m. fear, dread, scare.

भयत्रस्त adj. terror-stricken, frightened, scared.

भयप्रद adj. alarming, terrifying.

भयभीत adj. afraid, frightened, scared, terrified.

भयाक्रांत adj. horror-stricken, terrified, frightened.

भयादोहन m. blackmail.

भयानक adj. terrible, dreadful, dangerous.

भयानकता f. dreadfulness.

भयावना adj. terrifying, frightening.

भयावह adj. vicious, alarming.

भर adv. 1. fully. 2. only.

भरण m. feeding.

भरण-पोषण m. maintenance, support.

भरत-वाक्य m. epilogue.

भरता m. 1. mash. 2. sustainer, husband.

भरतार m. husband.

भरती f. 1. recruitment, enrolment.

2. admission. 3. filling.

भरना vt. to fill in; घाव ~ to heal up (wound, sore etc.); चाभी ~ (मशीन में) to wind (a machine); दंड ~ to pay off by way of penalty; हामी ~ to give assent (to). vi. to be filled; भर जाना to become full.

भरपाई f. receipt acknowledging payment in full.

भरपूर adj. 1. completely full/ overflowing. 2. plentiful.

भरभराना vi. to crash down.

भरम m. 1. = भ्रम।

भरमना vi. to roam/doubt/confuse.

भरमाना vt. 1. to mislead/misdirect. 2. to delude. 3. to perplex.

भरमार adj. abundant, plenteous, excessive. f. abundance, plenty.

भरवाई f. act of भरवाना, or charges paid for the same.

भरवाना vt. causative of भरना।

भरसक adv. to one's utmost.

भरसाईं f. parcher's oven.

भरा adj. 1. full. 2. loaded. 3. fleshy.

भराई f. act or state of filling up, or charges paid for the same.

भराव m. 1. act or state of filling. 2. filling, stuffing.

भरी f. an Indian measure for weighing gold, silver etc., approximately equal to 11 grams.

भरोसा m. reliance, trust, hope, faith, confidence.

भर्ता m. sustainer, husband, lord.

भर्त्सना f. admonition, reproach, upbraiding, reprimand.

भर्राटा m. dull, rattling sound.

भर्राना vi.; आवाज़ ~ — उसकी आवाज़ भर्रा गई His voice turned hoarse.

भलमनसाहत f. goodness, gentle-manliness, benevolence, generosity, nobility.

भला adj. 1. good, gentle, noble. 2. pleasing. m. good.

भलाई f. 1. goodness.

भलाई-बुराई f. 1. good or bad. 2. pros and cons.

भला-चंगा adj. hale and hearty, stout.

भलामानस m. good man/person, gentleman.

भली-भाँति adv. thoroughly.

भले adv. good, well; ~ ही even if.

भव m. 1. entity, existence. 2. world.

भवजाल m. (mesh of) worldly affairs, snares of life.

भवदीय pron. yours, yours faith-fully. [Fem. भवदीया]

भवन m. 1. building, mansion, house, premises. 2. palace.

भवसागर m. the world viewed as an ocean.

भवानी f. Durga, goddess of prowess.

भवितव्य adj. destined, fated.

भवितव्यता f. fate, the inevitable, destiny.

भविष्य m. 1. future. 2. future tense.

भविष्य कथन m. augury.

भविष्यदर्शी m. seer.

भविष्य निधि f. provident fund.

भविष्यवक्ता m. fortune-teller, prophet.

भविष्यवाणी f. prediction, prophecy.

भव्य adj. splendid, magnificent, grand, superb, marvellous.

भव्यता f. splendour, magnificence, grandeur.

भसींड़ m. lotus stem.

भस्म m. 1. ash, cinders. 2. calx, the ash of metal, precious stone and the like.

भस्मसात् adj. turned/reduced to ashes.

भस्मावशेष m. residue in the form of ashes.

भस्मीकरण m. incineration.

भस्सी f. dust of lime, coal etc.

भहराना vi. to collapse/crash down.

भाँग f. Indian intoxicating leafy drug.

भाँज f. 1. fold. 2. small change (specially in coins).

भाँजना vt. 1. to fold, twist. 2. to brandish (sword etc.).

भाँजा m. = भानजा।

भाँजी f. ~ मारना to talk ill, to impede (someone's) plan, to interrupt.

भांड m. pot, vessel.

भाँड़ m. jester, clown, buffoon.

भांडार m. 1. stock. 2. stock-room, godown, warehouse.

भाँत f. = भाँति।

भाँति f. 1. type. 2. design.

भाँपना vt. to guess, to see through, to divine.

भाँय-भाँय f. sound of wind produced in a desolate place.

भाँवर f. circumambulation of a matrimonial fire.

भाई m. brother.

भाईचारा m. social dealings between people.

भाई-दूज f. = भैया-दूज।

भाई-बंद m. (plu.) = भाई-बंधु।

भाई-बंधु m. (plu.) kith and kin, near relations.

भाई-भतीजावाद m. nepotism.

भाखा f. = भाषा।

भाग m. 1. part. 2. divison. 3. = भाग्य।

भाग-दौड़ f. 1. running about. 2. hustle and bustle.

भागना vi. 1. to run. 2. (कर्तव्य, दायित्व से) भाग जाना to welsh.

भागफल m. quotient, result of dividing.

भागमभाग adv. 1. with a running speed; in hot haste. 2. running/fleeing about.

भागिनेय m. sister's son.

भागीदार m. co-partner, partner.

भागीदारी f. 1. partnership.

भागीरथी f. the river Ganga.

भाग्य m. fate, destiny, luck.

भाग्यवादी m. fatalist.

भाग्यवान adj. lucky, fortunate.

भाग्यविधाता m. controller of destiny/fate.

भाग्याधीन adj. depending on fate, destined.

भाग्योदय m. advent of luck.

भ

भाजक m. divisor.

भाजन m. 1. pot, vessel. 2. receptacle. 3. act of dividing (Maths.).

भाजी f. vegetable.

भाज्य adj. divisible.

भाट m. bard.

भाटा m. low tide.

भाड़ m. parcher's oven.

भाड़ा m. 1. fare. 2. freight. 3. hire.

भात m. boiled rice.

भाथा m. 1. quiver. 2. big bellows.

भाथी f. bellows.

भादों m. sixth month of the Hindu calendar.

भाद्रपद m. = भादों।

भान m. knowledge, consciousness; ~ होना to be conscious of.

भानजा m. sister's son.

भानजी f. sister's daughter.

भानमती f. sorceress.

भाना vi. to be appealing/plea- sing.

भानु m. Sun.

भानुजा f. = यमुना।

भाप f. steam, vapour.

भाभी f. brother's wife.

भामंडल m. halo.

भामा f. woman.

भामिनी f. 1. pretty and attractive lady. 2. peevish woman.

भार m. 1. load, burden. 2. responsibility.

भारत m. India.

भारतवर्ष m. India.

भारतवासी m. an Indian.

भारती f. 1. सरस्वती (goddess of learning). 2. Mother India.

भारतीय adj. & m. Indian.

भारमुक्त adj. disburdened.

भारी adj. 1. heavy. 2. hefty. 3. huge, vast. 4. great. 5. ov-erwhelming, massive/ ponderous.

भारीपन m. heaviness, weightiness.

भारी-भरकम adj. massive, voluminous and heavy, hefty.

भारोपीय adj. Indo-Eurpoean.

भार्या f. wife.

भाल m. forehead.

भालना vt. to look intently.

भाला m. spear, lance.

भालू m. bear.

भाव m. 1. existence (lit.). 2. idea, purport, gist. 3. sentiment, emotion.

भावचित्र m. ideogram, ideograph.

भावज f. brother's wife.

भाव-ताव m.; ~ करना to haggle/ bargain.

भावना f. 1. mental attitude. 2. sentiment, imagination.

भावनात्मक adj. sentimental, fanciful, emotional.

भावप्रधान adj. primarily emo-tional, sentimental.

भावभंगी f. gesture and posture.

भावभीनी adj. steeped in emotion, hearty.

भाववाचक adj. (gram.) abstract.

भावविभोर adj. overwhelmed with emotion, steeped in emotion.

भावव्यंजक adj. expressive.

भावशून्य adj. devoid of emo- tion,

unemotional, expressionless.

भावहीन adj. = भावशून्य

भावांकन m. ideography.

भावातिरेक m. exuberance of emotion.

भावात्मक adj. 1. sentimental. 2. emotional.

भावार्थ m. substance, purport.

भावावेश m. impulse (of emotion).

भावी adj. 1. coming, would be. 2. pertaining to future, predestined, upcoming. m. destiny.

भावुक adj. sentimental, emotional.

भावुकता f. sentimentality, thoughtfulness.

भावोत्तेजक adj. emotive/exciting.

भावोन्मत्त adj. wild with emotion, wildly emotional.

भाषण m. speech, lecture, ora-tion.

भाषण-स्वातंत्र्य m. liberty/freedom of speech.

भाषांतर m. translation.

भाषा f. language.

भाषाई adj. lingual, linguistic.

भाषायी adj. = भाषाई।

भाषावार adj. lingusitic.

भाषाविज्ञान m. Philology, Linguistics.

भाषाविद् m. linguist.

भाषित adj. spoken, said, uttered, told.

भाषी m. speaker.

भाष्य m. annotation, an explanatory treatise, commentary.

भाष्यकार m. one who interprets/ explains or advocates, exponent, commentator.

भास m. 1. effulgence, radiance. 2. inkling.

भासना vi. 1. to glitter/sparkle/ gleam. 2. to appear, to seem.

भासमान adj. appearing.

भासित adj. appeared, seemed.

भास्कर m. Sun.

भास्वर adj. radiant, effulgent.

भिंडी f. ladyfinger, okra.

भिक्षा f. alms.

भिक्षापात्र m. beggar's bowl.

भिक्षावृत्ति f. mendicancy.

भिक्षु m. 1. beggar. 2. mendicant, monk.

भिक्षुक m. mendicant, beggar.

भिक्षुणी f. fem. of भिक्षु।

भिखमंगा m. beggar.

भिखमंगी f. beggary.

भिखारिन f. female beggar.

भिखारी m. beggar.

भिगोना vt. to wet, to make wet; भिगो-भिगोकर मारना to give a thorough beating.

भिजवाना vt. 1. to cause to wet. 2. to cause to send.

भिड़ंत f. 1. grappling, encounter, confrontation. 2. collision. 3. bout.

भिड़ f. wasp.

भिड़ना vi. 1. to collide. 2. to grapple (with).

भिड़ाना vt. 1. causative of grap-ple. 2. to collide.

भितल्ला m. lining (of a cloth).

भित्ति f. wall.

भित्तिचित्र m. fresco, wall painting.

भिदुर adj. thunderbolt.

भिनकना vi. to buzz.

भिनभिन f. buzzing sound.

भिनभिनाना vi. to buzz.

भिन्न adj. different. m. fraction (Math.).

भिन्नता f. 1. difference. 2. dissimilarity.

भिन्नात्मक adj. fractional.

भिन्नाना vi. to appear indignant.

भिश्ती m. water-carrier, sply. one who carries water in a leather bag.

भींचना vt. 1. to embrace tightly. 2. to close tightly.

भींजना vi. = भीगना।

भी adv. 1. too, also. 2. denoting emphasis.

भीख f. 1. alms. 2. beggings.

भीगना vi. to get soaked, to get wet/drenched.

भीटा m. mound.

भीड़ f. crowd, mob, throng.

भीड़-भड़क्का m. thick of a crowd.

भीड़-भाड़ f. thick of a crowd, multitude.

भीत adj. afraid. f. wall.

भीतर adv. in, within, inside.

भीतर, के postposition. inside.

भीतरी adj. 1. internal, inner. 2. secret.

भीति f. phobia, scare.

भीना adj. light and delightful.

भीम adj. huge, of very great size, gigantic.

भीमकाय adj. enormous in size and strength, titanic.

भीरु adj. fearful, timid, coward.

भीरुता f. timidity, shyness.

भील m. a jungle tribe of central India.

भीषण adj. terrible, horrible, awful.

भीषणता f. gruesomeness, awfulness.

भीषिका f. panic.

भीष्म adj. dreadful, terrible, horrible.

भुकड़ी f. mould, fungus.

भुक्खड़ adj. 1. famished (with hunger). 2. gluttonous. m. glutton.

भुक्तभोगी adj. having experience of sufferings.

भुखमरा adj. famished, dying of starvation.

भुखमरी f. collective starvation, famine.

भुगतना vt. to suffer, face or undergo.

भुगतान m. payment, disbursement.

भुगताना vt. to pay up.

भुच्च adj. idiotic, stupid.

भुजंग m. snake.

भुज m. 1. arm. 2. side of a geometrical figure.

भुजपाश m. arm-embrace.

भुजबंध m. armlet.

भुजबल m. 1. strength of the arms, physical power. 2. prowess.

भुजा f. 1. arm. 2. side.

भुजाली f. small dagger.

भुजिया adj. roasted. f. a roasted vegetable.

भुट्टा m. ear of corn.

भुतहा adj. haunted.

भुनगा m. gnat, maggot, a kind of tiny flying insect.

भुनना vi. 1. to be roasted; जलना - ~ to fret and fume. 2. to be changed into smaller coins.

भुनभुनाना vi. to fret and fume, to mutter.

भुनवाई f. act or state of भुनवाना or charges paid for the same.

भुनवाना vt. causative of भुनाना।

भुनाना vt. 1. to get or cause (something) to be parched. 2. to get (cheque etc.) cashed, to encash. 3. to get (a coin or currency note) changed into smaller coins.

भुरकस m. pulp.

भुरभुरा adj. friable, crisp.

भुरभुरापन m. friability, crispness.

भुलक्कड़ adj. forgetful, absentminded.

भुलवाना vt. to cause to forget.

भुलाना vt. to forget.

भुलावा m. 1. dodge, feint. 2. illusion.

भुवन m. world.

भुवनेश्वर m. Lord of the world, God.

भुस m. chaff.

भुसौरा m. barn.

भूँकना vt. to bark/yelp.

भूँजना vt. to parch.

भूँजा m. parched gram.

भू f. 1. earth. 2. land.

भू-अभिलेख m. land records.

भूकंप m. earthquake.

भूखंड m. 1. an extended area, tract. 2. a piece of land, plot.

भूख f. appetite, hunger.

भूख-हड़ताल f. hunger strike.

भूखा adj. hungry.

भूगर्भ m. interior/bowels of the earth.

भूगोल m. Geography.

भूचाल m. = भूकंप।

भूत m. 1. past. 2. ghost, revenant.

भूतकाल m. past tense.

भूतकृदंत adj. past participle.

भूतनी f. female ghost.

भूतपूर्व adj. pristine, ex-, former.

भूत-प्रेत m. (plu.) evil spirits.

भूतल m. 1. surface of the earth. 2. this world.

भूदान m. gift of land.

भूधर m. mountain.

भूनना vt. to roast/parch.

भूप m. king, monarch.

भूभल f. hot ash.

भूभाग m. territory.

भूमंडल m. globe.

भूमध्य रेखा f. equator.

भूमध्य सागर m. Mediterranean Sea.

भूमि f. 1. land. 2. soil. 3. ground.

भूमिका f. 1. introduction, preamble, prelude, preface. 2. role, part.

भूमिगत adj. 1. underground. 2. acting in secret.

भूमिधर m. a farmer who owns his own land.

भ

भूरा adj. brown.

भूराजस्व m. land revenue.

भूरि adj. very much.

भूल f. 1. mistake, error. 2. slip.

भूलचूक f. errors and omissions.

भूलना vt. to forget.

भूलभुलैया f. labyrinth, maze.

भूलाभटका adj. strayed.

भूलोक m. earth, region mun- dane.

भूविज्ञान m. Geology.

भूशायी adj. (one) whose bed is earth, lying on the ground.

भूषण m. 1. ornament. 2. ornamentation, decoration, embellishment.

भूषित adj. ornamented, decorated, embellished.

भूसंपत्ति f. estate.

भूसा m. husk, hay.

भूसी f. husk.

भूस्खलन m. landslide.

भूस्वामी m. landlord.

भृंग m. black bee.

भृकुटी f. eyebrow; ~ चढ़ाना / तानना to frown.

भृति f. 1. service. 2. salary.

भेंगा adj. squint-eyed.

भेंट f. 1. gift, present. 2. meeting.

भेंटना vt. 1. to meet. 2. to embrace.

भेंटवार्ता f. interview.

भेजना vt. 1. to send. 2. to despatch.

भेजवाना vt. to cause to send.

भेजा m. brain.

भेड़ f. sheep.

भेड़-चाल f. tendency to follow unthinkingly, mob-mentality.

भेड़ना vt. to shut/close.

भेड़ा m. male-sheep, ram.

भेड़िया m. wolf.

भेड़िया-धसान f. propensity to follow others blindly, mob-mentality.

भेड़ी f. sheep, ewe.

भेद m. 1. secret, mystery. 2. difference, discrimination.

भेदक adj. 1. piercing, intersecting. 2. discriminative.

भेदन m. act of piercing, intersection.

भेदना vt. to pierce.

भेदबुद्धि f. faculty of discri-mination, discriminating power.

भेदभाव m. the feeling of difference, discrimination.

भेदिया m. 1. one who knows the secret of others. 2. spy, confidant.

भेदी adj. piercing. m. one who knows the secret.

भेद्य adj. pierceable, permeable, vulnerable.

भेरी f. siren, drum.

भेला m. lump.

भेली f. small lump.

भेष m. = भेस।

भेषज m. drug.

भेस m. dress, garb, guise.

भैंस f. buffalo.

भैंसा m. male-buffalo.

भैया m. brother.

भैरव m. 1. one of the melodies of

Indian music. 2. Lord Shiva.

भैरवी f. one of the morning melodies of Indian music.

भैषजिकी f. Pharmacology.

भोंकना vt. to thrust/stab/pierce.

भोंदू adj. dullard, stupid.

भोंपू m. 1. siren. 2. horn.

भोंभों m. the sound of the barking of dogs.

भोक्ता m. consumer, one who uses/utilises.

भोग m. 1. enjoyment. 2. suffering, pain. 3. offering (to gods).

भोगना vt. 1. to pay for, to suffer. 2. to enjoy.

भोगबंधक m. mortgage with possession.

भोगलिप्सा f. sensuous enjoyment, ludeness.

भोगविलास m. indulgence in luxury.

भोगाधिकार m. right of occupancy, right of easement.

भोगी m. enjoyer.

भोग्य adj. 1. worth consuming/ using. 2. worth enjoying.

भोज m. feast, community dinner, banquet.

भोजन m. 1. food, meal. 2. diet.

भोजन-कक्ष m. a room where meals are eaten/served, dining room.

भोजनभट्ट m. one who eats too much, gourmand, glutton.

भोजनालय m. restaurant, eating-house, mess.

भोजी m. eater.

भोज्य adj. eatable, edible.

भोथरा adj. obtuse, blunt, dull.

भोर m. morning, early morning, dawn.

भोला adj. simple and artless, simple-hearted.

भोलापन m. simplicity and artlessness.

भोलेनाथ m. Lord Shiva.

भौं f. eyebrow.

भौंकना vi. 1. to bark, yelp. 2. to howl (pej.).

भौंरा m. black bee, beetle.

भौंरी f. female black bee.

भौंह f. eyebrow.

भौगोलिक adj. geographical.

भौचक्का adj. flabbergasted, aghast, wonderstruck, stun-ned.

भौजाई f. = भाभी।

भौजी f. = भाभी।

भौतिक adj. 1. material. 2. physical. 3. mundane.

भौतिकवाद m. materialism.

भौतिकवादी adj. materialistic. m. materialist.

भौतिकी f. Physics.

भौमिक adj. 1. geological. 2. earthly, terrestrial.

भ्रंश m. 1. fall. 2. ruin, destruc- tion. 3. sabotage. 4. breach.

भ्रकुटि f. = भृकुटी।

भ्रम m. 1. illusion, fallacy. 2. misuderstanding, misconception. 3. confusion.

भ्रमजाल m. snares of illusions, worldly affairs.

भ्रमण m. roving, travelling (widely), roaming.

भ्रमणशील adj. roving, rambling; ~ कलाकार itinerant artist.

भ्रममूलक adj. illusory, misleading.

भ्रमर m. black bee.

भ्रमरी f. fem. of भ्रमर।

भ्रमात्मक adj. illusory.

भ्रमित adj. 1. illusioned. 2. mistaken. 3. confused.

भ्रष्ट adj. 1. corrupt, deprave. 2. immoral.

भ्रष्टता f. corruptness, corruption, depravity.

भ्रष्टाचार m: corruption.

भ्रष्टाचारी adj. corrupt.

भ्रांत adj. misled, mistaken.

भ्रांति f. 1. illusion. 2. confusion.

भ्रांतिमूलक adj. 1. confusing. 2. illusory, illusive, misleading.

भ्राता m. brother.

भ्रातृ m. = भ्राता।

भ्रातृभाव m. feeling of brotherhood, fraternity.

भ्रामक adj. confusing, illusive.

भ्रू m. eyebrow, pleasing movement of the eyebrow.

भ्रूण m. foetus, embryo.

भ्रूणहत्या f. foeticide.

भ्रूभंगिमा f. the movement of the eyebrow, specially fascinating.

म m. fifth of the bilabial pentad of consonants of the Nagari alphabet; its sound is like that of m in man.

मँगता m. beggar.

मँगनी f. 1. betrothal, espousal. 2. loan.

मंगल adj. auspicious. m. 1. Tuesday. 2. Mars. 3. welfare.

मंगलकारी adj. auspicious.

मंगलगान m. song sung on ceremonial occasions.

मंगलध्वनि f. auspicious sound.

मंगलभाषण m. euphemism.

मंगलमय adj. auspicious.

मंगलवार m. Tuesday.

मंगलसूत्र m. lucky thread (worn by a woman whose husband is alive).

मंगलाचरण m. invocatory/benedictory prologue.

मंगलाचार m. benedictory prologue.

मंगलामुखी f. harlot, prostitute.

मंगली adj. (in Astrology) (a person) on whom Mars (planet) is casting an evil influence.

मंगलोत्सव m. festivity.

मँगवाना vt. to cause to be sent for, to be brought by someone.

मँगाना vt. to send for, to ask for.

मँगेतर m. fiance. f. fiancee.

मंच m. 1. stage, dais, podium, platform, stadium. 2. forum.

मंचन m. way of presenting a play on the stage, staging.

मंच-संकोच m. stage shyness.

मंजन m. tooth-powder.

मँजना vi. to get proficient/seasoned.

मंजरी f. sprout.

मँजवाना vt. to cause to be cleansed.

मंज़िल f. 1. storey, floor. 2. destination.

मँजीरा m. cymbal.

मंजु adj. = मंजुल।

मंजुल adj. beautiful, pretty.

मंजुलता f. beauty, prettiness.

मंज़ूर adj. 1. approved, accepted. 2. granted, sanctioned.

मंज़ूरी f. acceptance, sanction.

मंजूषा f. casket.

मँझधार f. midstream.

मंझा m. cot.

मंड m. starch.

मंडन m. 1. embellishing. 2. corroboration, support.

मंडना vt. 1. to embellish/decorate. 2. to corroborate.

मंडप m. pavilion.

मँडराना vi. to hover.

मंडल m. 1. circle. 2. halo, ring. 3. zone. 4. commissionary. 5. monastery.

मंडलाकार adj. circular, ring-shaped.

मंडली f. 1. party. 2. team, society, association, club.

म

मंडलीय adj. pertaining to a zone, zonal.

मंडलेश्वर m. head of a monastery.

मँडवा m. = मँडुआ।

मंडित adj. 1. adorned, embel-lished, decorated. 2. corroborated.

मंडी f. 1. market place. trade centre, bazaar.

मँडुआ m. 1. pavilion. 2. mobile theatre.

मंडूक m. frog.

मंतर m. = मंत्र। छू ~ हो जाना to vanish/ disappear.

मंतव्य m. objective, intent.

मंत्र m. 1. vedic hymn. 2. any sacred verse. 3. incantation, spell, charm, magic. 4. esoteric formula.

मंत्रकार m. composer of मंत्र।

मंत्रणा f. 1. counsel, advice. 2. deliberation.

मंत्र-तंत्र m. incantations accompanied by rituals.

मंत्रपाठ m. recitation of mantras.

मंत्रमुग्ध adj. enchanted, spell-bound.

मंत्रसिद्धि f. power to obtain success through मंत्र।

मंत्रालय m. ministry.

मंत्रित adj. consecrated by मंत्र।

मंत्रि-परिषद् f. ministry, council of ministers.

मंत्रिमंडल m. cabinet.

मंत्री m. 1. minister. 2. secretary.

मंथन m. 1. churning. 2. contemplation.

मंथर adj. slow, sluggish, tardy.

मंद adj. 1. slow, sluggish. 2. dim, dull, feeble. 3. low; ~ ज्वर low fever.

मंदता f. 1. slowness. 2. dimness. 3. dullness, feebleness.

मंदबुद्धि adj. dull, stupid, moron, imbecile.

मंदभाग्य adj. not favoured by luck, unfortunate, wretched.

मंदमति adj. of sluggish intellect, moron, dullard.

मंदा adj. 1. slow, tardy. 2. dull.

मंदाकिनी f. galaxy.

मंदाग्नि f. dyspepsia, indigestion.

मंदित adj. retarded.

मंदिर m. 1. temple. 2. house.

मंदी f. slump, recession, depres-sion.

मंद्र adj. deep. m. deep note.

मंशा f. intent, intention/desire/ willingness.

मंसूख़ adj. annulled, revoked; ~ करना to annul/revoke.

मई f. (month of) May.

मकई f. maize.

मकड़जाल m. spider's web, cobweb.

मकड़ा m. male spider.

मकड़ी f. female spider.

मक़बरा m. mausoleum.

मकरंद m. fragrance.

मकर m. 1. crocodile. 2. capri-corn; ~ रेखा Tropic of Capricorn.

मक़सद m. purpose, intention.

मकान m. house.

मकान-मालिक m. house owner.

मकुर m. looking glass.

मकोड़ा m. large ant.

मकोय m. a small Indian fruit.

मक्का m. maize.

मक्कार adj. sly, cunning, deceitful, crafty.

मक्कारी f. slyness, deception.

मक्की f. maize, corn.

मक्खन m. butter.

मक्खी f. fly.

मक्खीचूस adj. & m. (person) extremely niggardly.

मक्षिका f. fly.

मख m. = यज्ञ।

मखनिया adj. skimmed. m. butter-seller.

मख़मल f. velvet.

मख़मली adj. velvety.

मखाना m. parched lotus seed.

मख़ौल m. ridicule, derision.

मग m. 1. = मार्ग। 2. mug.

मग़ज़ m. 1. brain. 2. kernel, seed.

मग़ज़ी f. hem, border.

मगद m. a variety of sweetmeat.

मगदल m. an Indian sweet prepared from powdered pulse.

मगध m. ancient name of South Bihar.

मगन adj. = मग्न।

मगर conj. but; अगर- ~ ifs and buts. m. alligator, crocodile.

मगरमच्छ m. crocodile.

मग़रिब m. west.

मग़रूर adj. proud, vain, arrogant.

मग्न adj. 1. engrossed, delightfully absorbed. 2. immersed, sunk.

मघवा m. = इंद्र।

मचना vi. to be perpetrated/ occasioned; to happen.

मचलना vi. to indulge in chil- dish insistence, to pester.

मचला adj. prone to मचलना।

मचलापन m. childish insistence, pestering.

मचान f. raised structure/plat-form usually for guarding farms or for gamehunting, scaffold.

मचाना vt. to make/create.

मचिया f. a low wicker stool to sit on.

मच्छ m. a very big fish.

मच्छड़ m. = मच्छर।

मच्छर m. mosquito.

मच्छरदानी f. mosquito net/curtain.

मछली f. fish.

मछलीमार m. angler, fisherman.

मछुआ m. fisherman.

मछुआरा m. = मछुआ।

मज़दूर m. labourer.

मज़दूर संघ m. trade union, labour union.

मज़दूरी f. 1. wages. 2. labour charges. 3. calling of a labourer.

मजनूँ m. 1. celebrated lover of Laila of Arabian tales. 2. love-lorn person. 3. very lean and thin person.

मज़बूत adj. 1. strong. 2. stout, sturdy (person).

मज़बूती f. 1. strength, sturdiness. 2. firmness.

म

मजबूर adj. 1. helpless. 2. compelled.

मजबूरन adv. under compulsion, in a state of helplessness.

मजबूरी f. 1. helplessness. 2. compulsion.

मजमा m. gathering.

मज़मून m. 1. subject. 2. essay, article.

मजलिस f. assembly.

मज़हब m. religion.

मज़ा m. fun, delight, pleasure, enjoyment.

मज़ाक़ m. 1. joke, ridicule. 2. spoof.

मज़ाक़िया adj. fun-loving, witty, humorous.

मज़ार m. grave, tomb.

मजाल f. courage, guts.

मजिस्ट्रेट m. magistrate.

मजीठ f. a creeper from which red colour is prepared.

मजीठी adj. red.

मज़ेदार adj. 1. enjoyable, pleasurable. 2. delicious, full of relish.

मज्जन m. 1. bath. 2. dipping, immersion.

मज्जा f. marrow.

मझधार f. mid-stream.

मझला adj. middle, of the middle.

मझोला adj. medium.

मटक f. strut, coquetry.

मटकना vi. to strut, to coquet, to ogle.

मटका m. large earthen pitcher.

मटकाना vt. to make coquettish gestures by strutting one's limbs.

मटकी f. small earthen pitcher.

मटकौअल f. मटका।

मटमैला adj. of the colour of earth, dust-coloured, dim.

मटर m. pea.

मटरगश्त adj. roaming, wandering.

मटरगश्ती f. roaming, wander- ing.

मटियामेट adj. completely ruined, devastated.

मटीला adj. 1. dusty. 2. dust-coloured.

मट्ठर adj. slow and sluggish.

मट्ठा m. = मठा।

मट्ठी f. thin fried saltish pan-cake.

मठ m. Hindu convent/monastery, abbey.

मठा m. buttermilk.

मठाधीश m. head of a mona- stery.

मड़ई f. hutment, cottage.

मड़ैया f. hutment, cottage.

मढ़ना vt. 1. to frame/mount/cover. 2. to inflict.

मढ़वाना vt. causative of मढ़ना।

मढ़ाई f. act of मढ़ना or charges paid for it.

मढ़ी f. 1. hutment. 2. small monastery or temple.

मणि f. gem, jewel.

मणिमाला f. string of jewels.

मत m. 1. opinion, belief, view. 2. vote. 3. theory, doctrine. 4. sect, creed. जैन ~ sect of Jains. adv. denoting forbiddance, 'don't'.

मतगणना f. counting of votes.

मतदाता m. voter.

मतदान m. voting, polling.

मतदान-केंद्र m. polling station.

मतदान-पेटिका f. ballot-box.

मतपत्र m. a printed slip used in secret voting, ballot paper.

मतभेद m. difference of opinion, disagreement.

मतलब m. 1. meaning, purport, motive, object. 2. self-interest, concern.

मतलबी adj. selfish.

मतली f. nausea.

मतवाला adj. 1. drunk, intoxi- cated, insane, tipsy. 2. (one) who is off his head.

मतांध adj. fanatic.

मतांधता f. fanaticism.

माताधिकार m. franchise, suffrage.

मतानुयायी m. follower of a creed/ tenet.

मतारी f. mother.

मति f. 1. intellect. 2. opinion, view.

मतिभ्रम m. 1. hallucination. 2. mental aberration.

मतिभ्रष्ट adj. lost to all sense of wisdom, foolish, stupid, idiot.

मतिमंद adj. foolish, stupid. m. dunce.

मतिमान adj. wise.

मतिहीन adj. foolish.

मतैक्य m. unanimity, unison.

मत्त adj. intoxicated, drunk.

मत्था m. forehead.

मत्सर m. jealousy, envy.

मत्स्य m. fish.

मत्स्य-उद्योग m. fishing industry, fishery.

मत्स्यन्याय m. the law of 'might is right'.

मत्स्यपालन m. pisciculture.

मथना vt. to churn, to beat to skim.

मथानी f. churn-staff.

मद m. 1. intoxication. 2. pride, vanity, madness. f. item, head.

मदकाल m. a period of sexual excitement.

मदद f. help, aid, assistance.

मददगार m. helper.

मदन m. Cupid.

मदनोत्सव m. an ancient festival held in the month of चैत्र and dedicated to the god of love.

मदमत्त adj. 1. intoxicated. 2. power-drunk.

मदरसा m. school.

मदहोश adj. heavily intoxicated, dead drunk.

मदार m. 1. elephant. 2. a plant, also called आक।

मदारी m. 1. juggler, trickster. 2. showman of animals trained to perform tricks.

मदिरा f. wine, liquor.

मदिरालय m. public drinking house, bar.

मदोन्मत्त adj. 1. drunk, intox- icated. 2. arrogant, power-blind.

मदोन्मत्तता f. 1. drunkenness. 2. arrogance.

मद्धिम adj. moderate, slow.

मद्धे adv. in/to the account of, on behalf of.

मद्य m. wine, liquor.

मद्यत्याग m. temperance.

मद्य-निषेध m. prohibition.

मद्यप m. drunkard.

मद्यपायी m. drunkard.

मद्यसेवन m. alcoholism.

मधु m. honey.

मधुऋतु f. spring (season).

मधुकर m. black bee, mellifer.

मधुकरी f. cooked articles collected as alms from different houses.

मधुबाला f. wine-maid, lady wine server.

मधुमक्खी f. honey-bee.

मधुमक्खी पालन m. bee keeping; apiculture.

मधुमास m. the month which heralds the advent of spring, चैत्र।

मधुमेह m. diabetes.

मधुयामिनी f. the first night of newly married couple.

मधुर adj. sweet, pleasant, melodious.

मधुरता f. 1. sweetness. 2. harmony, gaiety.

मधुरिमा f. 1. sweetness. 2. charm, comeliness, gracefulness.

मधुशाला f. public drinking house, bar, pub.

मध्य adj. & m. middle, mid, central.

मध्यकाल m. Middle Age, Medieval Period.

मध्यकालीन adj. medieval.

मध्यपूर्व m. the Middle East.

मध्यम adj. 1. medium. 2. intermediate.

मध्यम पुरुष m. second person (Gram.).

मध्यमा f. middle finger.

मध्यमान m. mean, average.

मध्यमार्ग m. middle path/course.

मध्ययुग m. मध्यकाल।

मध्यवर्ग m. middle class, bourgeois.

मध्यवर्ती adj. 1. middle, central. 2. intermediary.

मध्यस्थ adj. situated in the middle, medial, intermediate. m. 1. intermediary. 2. mediator.

मध्यस्थता f. mediation.

मध्यांतर m. interval (of time).

मध्यावकाश m. recess.

मध्याह्न m. noon, midday.

मनःस्थिति f. state of mind.

मन m. 1. Indian weight equal to forty seers, maund, roughly equal to 37 kg. 2. mind. 3. heart; ~ आना—मेरा उस पर ~ आ गया है I have taken a fancy for her. ~ उखड़ना—अब मेरा ~ उखड़ गया है Now I am fed-up with the matter. ~ खट्टा हो जाना to be sore/estranged; ~ बना लेना to make up one's mind; ~ मारना to suppress one's desires, to deny oneself; ~ में चोर बैठा होना to have a lurking suspicion.

मनका m. 1. bead. 2. rosary.

मनगढ़ंत adj. fictitious, con-cocted, fabricated.

मनचला adj. flirtatious.

मनचाहा adj. longed/wished/cherished for.

मनन m. reflection, meditation.

मनबहलाव m. 1. amusement, merriment, recreation. 2. diversion, distraction.

मनभाया adj. after (one's) heart, gratifying, pleasing, agreeable.

मनमाना adj. arbitrary, spontaneous, according to one's own free will.

मनमानी f. arbitrary conduct, arbitrariness, entirely voluntary.

मनमुटाव m. estrangement, strained relations.

मनमोदक m. day-dreaming, wishful thinking.

मनमोहन m. charm personified, Lord Krishna.

मनमौजी adj. temperamental, capricious, fantastical.

मनवांछित adj. = मनोवांछित।

मनवाना vt. causative of मनाना।

मनशा f. = मंशा।

मनश्चिकित्सा f. psychotherapy.

मनसा adv. mentally.

मनसिज m. name of कामदेव।

मनसूबा m. plan, design.

मनस्ताप m. remorse, mental agony, sorrow.

मनस्वी adj. determined to achieve an object, strong willed. [Fem. मनस्विनी]

मनहरण adj. lovely, extremely attractive, marvellous.

मनहूस adj. 1. ominous, inauspicious. 2. gloomy. 3. abominable.

मना adj. prohibited, forbidden.

मनाना vt. 1. to persuade, to bring round. 2. to carry out, to perform.

मनाही f. forbiddance, prohi-bition.

मनिहार m. bangle-seller.

मनिहारिन f. woman bangle-seller.

मनीआर्डर m. money order.

मनीषा f. 1. mental faculty, intellect. 2. wisdom.

मनीषी m. 1. a profound thinker. 2. wise man, scholar.

मनु m. Manu, the progenitor of the human race.

मनुज m. man, offspring of Manu.

मनुजाद adj. cannibal.

मनुष्य m. man, human.

मनुष्य जाति f. mankind, human race.

मनुष्यता f. the quality of being human, humanity.

मनुष्योचित adj. fit or suitable for people, humane.

मनुहार f. appeasement.

मनुहारना vt. to appease.

मनोकामना f. longing, desire.

मनोगत m. idea.

मनोगति f. tendency of the mind.

मनोदशा f. condition of the mind.

मनोनयन m. nomination.

मनोनीत adj. nominated.

मनोबल m. morale, tempo.

मनोमय adj. mental.

मनोयोग m. single-mindedness.

मनोरंजक adj. recreative, amu-sing, entertaining.

मनोरंजन m. entertainment, recreation, amusement.

म

मनोरथ m. long cherished desire.

मनोरम adj. charming, lovely, comely, attractive.

मनोरोग m. mental disease, psychopathy.

मनोवांछित adj. longed for, aspired after.

मनोविकार m. 1. emotion, passion. 2. psychopathy, mental disorder.

मनोविज्ञान m. Psychology.

मनोविनोद m. amusement, recreation, merriment.

मनोविश्लेषण m. psychoanalysis.

मनोवृत्ति f. mentality, disposi- tion.

मनोवेग m. impulse.

मनोवैज्ञानिक adj. psychological. m. psychologist.

मनोव्यथा f. mental agony.

मनोहर adj. attractive, alluring, charming.

मनोहारी adj. = मनोहर।

मनौअल f. appeasement.

मनौती f. vow of offering (to a deity).

मन्नत f. = मनौती।

मन्वंतर m. tenure of Manu (in Puranas).

मम pron. my, mine, of me.

ममता f. parental/filial affection.

ममेरा adj. of or pertaining to the maternal uncle.

मयंक m. moon.

मय suffix. denoting fulness, e.g. आनन्दमय blissful.

मयस्सर adj. available.

मयूख m. beam, ray, flame.

मयूर m. peacock.

मयूरी f. she-peacock/peahen.

मरक m. epidemic.

मरकज़ m. centre.

मरकत m. emerald.

मरकहा adj. prone to attack (usually with horns).

मरघट m. cremation ground.

मरज़ m. = मर्ज़।

मरण m. death.

मरणासन्न adj. (one) on the point of death, dying, moribund.

मरणोन्मुख adj. dying, facing death, heading towards death/end.

मरणोपरांत adj. posthumous, after death.

मरतबा m. post, rank, status. f. time.

मरतबान m. jar.

मरता adj. on the verge of death, dying.

मरदना vt. 1. to crush, to trample upon. 2. to knead.

मरदानगी f. bravery, masculinity.

मरदाना adj. manly, brave.

मरदूद adj. 1. condemned. 2. contemptible.

मरन m. = मरण।

मरना vi. 1. to die. 2. to sacrifice (oneself). 3. to long keenly; मरे जाना to show unreasonable eagerness.

मरनी f. death.

मरनी-करनी f. obsequies, funeral rites.

मरभुक्खा adj. 1. famished with hunger. 2. indigent, ravenous.

मरमर m. marble.

मरम्मत f. 1. repair, mending. 2. thrashing.

मरम्मती adj. (things) for being repaired, or needing repairs.

मरसिया m. elegy, song of lamentation.

मरहम m. = मलहम।

मरहूम adj. late, deceased.

मराल m. swan.

मरियम f. Mary, mother of Christ.

मरियल adj. gaunt, lean, emaciated, rickety, sickly.

मरी f. epidemic (resulting in many fatalities).

मरीचिका f. 1. mirage. 2. illusion.

मरीची m. Sun.

मरीज़ m. patient.

मरु m. desert, barren land.

मरुद्वीप m. oasis.

मरुभूमि f. dersert land.

मरुस्थल m. desert land.

मरोड़ m. twist, contortion.

मरोड़ना vt. to twist/contort/wring.

मर्कट m. monkey.

मर्ज़ m. ailment, disease.

मर्ज़ी f. wish, desire, will, pleasure.

मर्तबान m. = मरतबान।

मर्त्य adj. mortal. m. 1. man. 2. body.

मर्त्यता f. mortality.

मर्त्यलोक m. mortal world, the earthly world.

मर्द m. man.

मर्दन m. 1. massaging, rubbing vigorously. 2. crushing/trampling.

मर्दाना adj. = मरदाना।

मर्दुमशुमारी f. census.

मर्म m. 1. quintessence; essential meaning, secret. 2. vital organ.

मर्मज्ञ m. one who knows the quintessence of things, connoisseur.

मर्मभेदी adj. heart-rending.

मर्मर m. rustling sound.

मर्मवेदना f. deep anguish.

मर्मव्यथा f. agony in the vitals.

मर्मस्थल m. 1. vital spot. 2. vulnerable point.

मर्मस्पर्शी adj. touching, moving.

मर्माहत adj. hit in the vitals.

मर्यादा f. 1. limit, boundary line. 2. ethical propriety, decorum, status, dignity.

मर्यादापूर्ण adj. decorous.

मर्यादित adj. 1. limited. 2. limited/restricted by propriety.

मलंग m. carefree person.

मल m. 1. filth, waste matter. 2. faecal matter, excrement.

मलत्याग m. defecation.

मलद्वार m. anus.

मलना vt. 1. to rub. 2. to massage.

मलबा m. 1. debris from a ruined building, rubble. 2. wreckage.

मलमल f. a fine cotton cloth, muslin.

मलमास m. intercalary month.

मलय m. a region in South India, famous for sandal-wood trees.

मलयज m. sandal.

मलवाना vt. causative of मलना।

मलहम m. ointment.

म

मलहम-पट्टी f. dressing.

मलाई f. cream, fatty part of milk.

मलाट m. coarse thick packing paper.

मलामत f. reproof.

मलाल m. bitter regret, anguish, remorse.

मलाशय m. rectum.

मलिक m. king, lord.

मलिका f. queen.

मलिन adj. 1. unclean, dirty 2. sad.

मलिनता f. uncleanliness, dirtiness.

मलीदा m. 1. a sweet dish made usually of flour. 2. a soft woollen cloth.

मलेरिया m. malaria.

मल्ल m. wrestler, athlete.

मल्लयुद्ध m. wrestling bout.

मल्लशाला f. wrestling arena.

मल्लाह m. boatman.

मल्लिका f. a fragrant flower.

मल्हार m. an Indian melody sung during the rainy season.

मवक्किल m. client.

मवाद m. pus.

मवेशी m. cattle.

मशक f. big leathern water bag. m. mosquito, gnat.

मशक़्क़त f. toil, hard labour.

मशग़ूल adj. occupied, busy, engaged.

मशरिक़ m. east.

मशविरा m. counsel, advice.

मशहूर adj. famous.

मशान m. = श्मशान।

मशाल f. torch.

मशालची m. ṭorch-bearer.

मशीन f. machine.

मशीनगन m. machine-gun.

मशीनरी m. 1. machinery. 2. mechanism.

मश्क़ f. practice, exercise.

मस f. the soft hair on the top lip, the beginning of moustaches. adj. टस से ~ न होना not to budge at all.

मसक m. = मशक (mosquito).

मसकना vi. to give way (said of cloth).

मसका m. butter.

मसकाना vt. to tear, to separate, to split.

मसख़रा m. jester, buffoon.

मसख़रापन m. jesting.

मसख़री f. 1. jesting. 2. jestful remark.

मसजिद f. mosque.

मसनद f. roundish pillow for reclining and/or cushioned seat.

मसरूफ़ adj. occupied, busy.

मसल f. maxim, proverb.

मसलन conj. for instance/example.

मसलना vt. to press with great force.

मसला m. problem, issue.

मसहरी f. mosquito net.

मसा m. wart.

मसान m. = श्मशान।

मसाना m. urinary bladder.

मसाला m. 1. condiment, spice. 2. something requisite, material, matter.

मसालेदार adj. 1. spiced. 2. exciting

or interesting, spicy.

मसि f. ink.

मसीह m. Christ.

मसीहा m. messiah, angel.

मसूड़ा m. the gums.

मसूर m. lentil.

मसूरिका f. measles, chicken-pox.

मसोसना vi. दिल मसोसकर रह जाना to feel woefully frustrated/helpless.

मसौदा m. draft, written preliminary sketch.

मस्जिद f. = मसजिद।

मस्त adj. 1. carefree. 2. engrossed in. 3. intoxicated.

मस्तक m. 1. forehead. 2. head, summit.

मस्तमौला adj. happy-go-lucky, easy-going.

मस्ताना adj. easy-going, unworrying, happy-go-lucky. vi. 1. to be intoxicated/inebriated. 2. to be in heat.

मस्तिष्क m. brain.

मस्ती f. 1. state of being self-contained. 2. gaiety. 3. inebriety, inebriation.

मस्तूल m. mast.

मस्सा m. wart, mole.

महँगा adj. dear, expensive, costly.

महँगाई f. dearness.

महँगी f. = महँगाई।

महंत m. high priest.

महंती f. priesthood.

महक f. smell.

महकदार adj. (sweet) smelling, fragrant.

महकमा m. department.

महज़ adv. 1. only. 2. sheer.

महत, महत् adj. great, excellent, eminent.

महताब m. moon.

महतारी f. mother.

महती adj. fem. form of महत्।

महतो m. headman.

महत्तम adj. greatest.

महत्तर adj. greater.

महत्ता f. greatness.

महत्त्व m. importance, significance.

महत्त्वपूर्ण adj. important, significant, key, vital.

महत्त्वाकांक्षा f. ambition, aspiration.

महत्त्वाकांक्षी adj. ambitious.

महफ़िल f. recreational assemblage.

महफ़ूज़ adj. 1. safe. 2. protected.

महबूब m. one's beloved.

महबूबा f. beloved (woman).

महरा m. servant who performs household chores.

महरूम adj. deprived.

महर्षि m. sage.

महल m. palace, mansion, edifice.

मह़ल्ला m. = मुहल्ला।

महसूल m. freight.

महसूस adj. felt, experienced; ~ करना—(i) to feel. (ii) to realize.

महा adj. great, large, big.

महाकाय adj. gigantic.

महाकाली f. goddess Durga in the form of a destroyer.

महाकाव्य m. epic.

म

महाजन m. 1. high personage, great man. 2. money-lender, banker.

महाजनी f. 1. money-lending business. 2. accountancy, banking. 3. script used by money-lenders.

महात्मा m. high-souled personage, saint.

महाद्वीप adj. continent.

महाद्वीपीय adj. continental.

महाधिवक्ता m. Advocate General.

महान, महान् adj. great, eminent.

महानगर m. metropolis.

महानगरीय adj. metropolitan.

महानिद्रा f. Sleep Eternal.

महानुभाव m. person of high and noble ideas, a highly respected person.

महान्यायवादी m. Attorney General.

महापाप m. great sin.

महापुरुष m. great man, dignitary.

महाप्रयाण m. life's journey's end.

महाप्राण adj. & m. 1. aspirate. (Gram.) 2. noble soul.

महाबाहु adj. valorous.

महाब्राह्मण m.a Brahman who conducts funeral obsequies (for payment).

महाभाग m. lucky person, happy.

महाभारत m. 1. one of the two great epics of India. 2. the war described therein. 3. a big fight, a great struggle.

महामंत्री m. general secretary.

महामहिम m. His Excellency.

महामात्य m. Prime Minister.

महामारी f. pestilence, epidemic.

महायुद्ध m. great war.

महारत f. skill obtained by training or practice.

महारथी m. the great warrior.

महाराज m. 1. emperor. 2. cook. [Fem. महाराजिन]

महाराजा m. king of kings, emperor.

महाराजाधिराज m. Emperor, the Great.

महारानी f. empress.

महार्घ adj. 1. valuable, precious. 2. too costly.

महार्णव m great ocean.

महाल m. locality.

महालय m. a fortnight in which Hindus offer oblations to their deceased ancestors.

महालेखापाल m. Accountant General.

महावत m. elephant driver.

महाविद्यालय m. college.

महाविपत्ति f. catastrophe.

महाशक्ति f. 1. Prowess Personified, Goddess Durga. 2. Super power.

महाशय m. 1. a polite form of address. 2. gentleman.

महासभा f. congress.

महासागर m. ocean.

महि f. earth.

महिमा f. greatness, glory, dignity.

महिमान्वित adj. dignified.

महिला f. a woman with dignity and good manners, lady.

महिषी f. queen consort.

मही f. earth.

महीन adj. 1. thin. 2. fine. 3. sharp.

महीना m. 1. month. 2. monthly wages/salary. 3. menses.

महीप m. king.

महुआ m. an Indian tree bearing yellow flowers which are used for preparing liquor.

महोत्सव m. gala festival.

महोदय m. a polite form of address (for gentleman).

महोदया f. a polite form of address (for ladies).

महौषधि f. remedy for all ills, panacea.

माँ f. mother.

माँग f. 1. demand. 2. hair-parting.

माँगना vt. 1. to beg, to claim, to demand, to request (for). 2. to ask (for). 3. to borrow.

माँगपत्र m. 1. order form, indent. 2. memorandum of demands.

मांगलिक adj. auspicious, propitious.

माँझा m. substance used for sharpening the kite-flying thread, size; ~ लगाना act or process of sizing.

माँझी m. boatman.

माँड़ m. (boiled) rice-water, scum.

माँड़ना vt. 1. to knead (flour). 2. to separate grain from chaff.

माँड़ा m. a disease of the eye.

माँड़ी f = माँड़ ।

माँद f. den, lair.

माँदगी f. 1. illness. 2. fatigue.

मांस m. meat, flesh.

मांसपेशी f. muscle.

मांसल adj. of or like flesh, fleshy.

मांसलता f. fleshiness.

मांसाहार m. non-vegetarian food.

मांसाहारी adj. 1. non-vegetarian (person). 2. carnivorous (animal).

माई f. 1. = माता । 2. elderly woman.

माई-बाप m. all in all.

माक़ूल adj. appropriate, proper, reasonable, fit.

माखन m. butter.

मागधी f. ancient Prakrit lan- guage of मगध ।

माघ m. eleventh month of the Hindu calendar.

माचिस f. matches (match-box).

माछ m. fish.

माजरा m. matter, affair, happening.

माटी f. = मिट्टी ।

माठा m. whey.

माणिक m. ruby.

मात f. mate, checkmate.

मातदिल adj. 1. temperate. 2. moderate.

मातबर adj. reliable, trustworthy.

मातम m. mourning.

मातहत adj. subordinate, dependent.

माता f. 1. mother. 2. smallpox.

मातामह f. mother's father.

मातामही f. mother's mother.

मातुल m. mother's brother.

मातृ f. mother.

म

मातृतंत्र m. matriarchy.

मातृत्व m. motherhood, mater- nity.

मातृभाषा f. mother tongue.

मातृभूमि f. one's native country, motherland.

मातृहत्या f. matricide.

मात्र adj. only.

मात्रा f. 1. quantity. 2. dosage, dose. 3. sign, sply. vowel mark. 4. a unit of measurement (as in music, prosody etc.).

मात्रात्मक adj. quantitative.

मात्रिक adj. unitary.

मात्सर्य m. jealousy.

माथा m. forehead.

माथापच्ची f. taxing of brain.

मादक adj. intoxicating, spiri-tuous.

मादकता f. inebriety, intoxication.

मादा f. female (animal).

माधवी f. a creeper bearing fragrant flowers.

माधुरी f. sweetness.

माधुर्य m. 1. sweetness. 2. melo-diousness. 3. pleasantness.

माध्य m. average, mean.

माध्यम m. medium.

माध्यमिक adj. middle, secondary, intermediary.

मान m. 1. respect, regard, dignity, reputation. 2. quantity, value. 3. feigned anger.

मानक adj. standard.

मानकीकरण m. standardization.

मानकीकृत adj. standardized.

मानचित्र m. 1. map. 2. chart.

मानचित्रण m. mapping.

मानता f. मनौती।

मानदंड m. criterion.

मानद adj. given as an honour, honorary.

मानदेय m. honorarium.

मानना vt. 1. to admit. 2. to accede/accept.

माननीय adj. honourable, esteemed, revered.

मानपत्र m. address (of welcome or greeting).

मानभंग m. dishonour, disres-pect, humiliation.

मानमंदिर m. observatory.

मानमर्दन m. subduing of (some-one's) vanity, humiliation.

मान-मर्यादा f. established prestige.

मानव adj. human. m. man, human being.

मानवता m. human race, humanity.

मानवतावाद m. humanism.

मानवती f. beloved, feigning to be angry.

मानवप्रेम m. philanthropy.

मानवशास्त्र m. humanities.

मानवाधिकार m. human right (s).

मानवीकरण m. humanisation.

मानवीय adj. 1. human. 2. humane.

मानस m. mind.

मानसरोवर m. a time-honoured lake in Tibet.

मानसिक adj. mental.

मानसून m. monsoon.

मानहानि f. defamation.

मानाभिषेक m. investiture.

मानार्थ adj. complimentary.

मानिंद adj. like, similar.

मानिक m. ruby.

मानिक्य m. = मानिक।

मानिनी f. wife or beloved who feigns to be angry.

मानी m. meaning, purport.

मानुषिक adj. human.

मानुषी adj. human.

माने m. meaning, purport.

मानो conj. as if, as it were.

मानोपाधि f. title of honour.

मान्य adj. 1. prestigious, hon-ourable, respected. 2. acceptable.

मान्यता f. 1. recognition, accre-dition. 2. tenet. 3. assumption.

मान्यताप्राप्त adj. recognised.

माप m. measure.

मापना vt. to measure.

मापनी f. scale.

माफ़ adj. forgiven, pardoned.

माफ़िक़ adj. 1. favourably inclined/ disposed. 2. agreeable.

माफ़िया m. a secret terrorist or criminal group, mafia.

माफ़ी f. 1. forgiveness, pardon. 2. freehold land.

मामला m. 1. case. 2. affair, matter.

मामा m. maternal uncle.

मामी f. maternal aunt.

मामूली adj. ordinary, com-monplace.

मायका m. mother's home (of a married woman).

माया f. 1. God's play. 2. illusion.

मायाजाल m. web of worldly attachments.

मायाविनी f. fem. of मायावी।

मायावी adj. 1. illusory, illusive. 2. magical. m. magician.

मायूस adj. 1. disappointed. 2. dejected.

मायूसी f. 1. disappointment, frustration. 2. dejection, gloom.

मार f. 1. beating. 2. range.

मारक m. antidote.

मारका m. mark.

मारकाट f. bloody affray, bloody scuffle, carnage.

मारकीन m. a kind of coarse (unbleached) cloth.

मारजार f. pussy, cat.

मारण m. killing.

मारधाड़ f. 1. fighting and killing, fracas, affray. 2. onslaught.

मारना vt. 1. to beat. 2. to kill (मार डालना)। 3. to strike, to hit. 4. to snatch; मार लेना to grab; मक्खियाँ ~ to idle away time.

मारपीट f. exchange of blows, scuffle, battery, assault.

मारफ़त, की postposition. 1. through. 2. care of.

मारा adj. stricken, beaten, smitten.

मारामारी f. 1. scuffle, affray. 2. hot haste.

मारी f. = महामारी।

मारुत m. wind.

मारू m. martial music.

मारे, के postposition. on account of, because of, due to.

मार्क्सवाद m. Marxism.

मार्केट f. market.

मार्ग m. 1. way. 2. route. 3. road.

मार्ग-कर m. toll-tax.

मार्गच्युत adj. deviated, deflected.

मार्गदर्शन m. guidance.

मार्गरक्षक m. escort.

मार्गशीर्ष m. अगहन, the ninth month of Hindu calendar.

मार्च m. March (month).

मार्जन m. 1. cleansing, cleaning. 2. purifying, purification. 3. rectification, correction.

मार्जनी f. broom.

मार्जित adj. 1. cleansed. 2. purified. 3. rectified, corrected, refined.

मार्तंड m. Sun.

मार्मिक adj. 1. touching, appealing, moving. 2. pathetic, stirring, poignant. 3.vital.

मार्शल adj. martial. m. Marshal

माल m. 1. valuable property, merchandise, stock, material. 2. commodities, goods, revenue. 3. stuff.

माल-असबाब m. luggage.

मालकिन f. lady of the house.

मालगाड़ी f. goods train, freight train.

मालगुज़ारी f. land revenue.

मालगोदाम m. (railway) godown, goods shed.

मालटा m. a kind of citrus fruit.

माल-टाल m. 1. valuables, riches. 2. cash money.

मालती f. a creeper yielding sweet-smelling flowers.

मालदार adj. wealthy, rich.

मालपुआ m. pancake.

माल-मता m. 1. effects, assets. 2. wealth.

माल-महकमा m. department of revenue.

माल-सूची inventory of property.

माला f. 1. garland, wreath. 2. rosary.

मालामाल adj. very affluent, immensely rich, opulent, wealthy.

मालिक m. owner, master, boss.

मालिकाना adj. 1. of or pertaining to an owner. 2. in the capacity of an owner, like an owner. 3. proprietory.

मालिन f. 1. woman gardener. 2. wife of a gardener. 3. flowerselling maid.

मालिन्य m. = मलिनता।

मालियत f. 1. value. 2. wealth.

मालिश f. massage.

माली adj. pertaining to finance, financial, economic. m. gardener.

मालूम adj. known.

मालूमात f. 1. pieces of infor-mation. 2. knowledge.

मावा m. = खोआ।

माश m. = उरद।

माशा m. an Indian measure of weight, equivalent to one-twelfth of a tola, approx. 1 gm.

माशाअल्लाह interj. Good God!

माशूक़ m. beloved.

माशूक़ा f. beloved (woman).

मास m. month.

मासांत m. end of the month.

मासिक adj. of or pertaining to a month.

मासूम adj. innocent, guileless.

मास्टर m. 1. master. 2. teacher.

मास्टरी f. 1. profession/job of a teacher. 2. expert knowledge, expertise.

माह m. month.

माहवारी adj. occurring or appearing once every month, monthly. m. 1. monthly wages/remuneration. 2. menses.

माहात्म्य m. greatness, glory.

माहिर adj. 1. expert, dexterous, proficient.

माहुर m. poison, venom.

माहेश्वरी f. goddess Durga.

मिचकना vi. to wink.

मिचकाना vt. to wink/blink the eyes over and again.

मिचना vi. to close, sply. closing of the eyes.

मिचलाना vi.; जी ~ to feel like vomiting, to nauseate.

मिचली f. nausea, qualm.

मिचोली f. आँख - ~ hide and seek.

मिचौनी f. = मिचोली।

मिज़ाज m. 1. temperament, disposition. 2. mood.

मिज़ाजी adj. proud, vainglorious, conceited.

मिटना vi. 1. to be erased/effaced. 2. to be destroyed/ruined.

मिटाना vt. 1. to erase/efface/ abolish. 2. to destroy.

मिट्टी f. 1. earth. 2. clay. 3. corpse.

मिट्टी का तेल m. kerosene oil.

मिट्टी का दीया m. mud lamp.

मिट्ठू m. 1. parrot. 2. sweet-tongued person.

मिठबोला adj. sweet-tongued.

मिठलोना adj. mild/pleasantly saltish.

मिठाई f. sweet (s).

मिठास f. sweetness.

मितभाषी adj. taciturn, one who speaks little.

मितव्ययी adj. thrifty, econo- mical, frugal.

मिताई f. friendship.

मिताहारी adj. austere in food.

मिति f. 1. (system of) measurement. 2. = तिथि।

मिती f. date according to the lunar month.

मित्र m. friend.

मित्रता f. friendship.

मित्रतापूर्ण adj. friendly, showing good will.

मित्रभाव m. 1. friendship. 2. friendly attitude, cordiality.

मिथुन m. 1. Gemini (sign of the zodiac). 2. mating. 3. couple.

मिथ्या adj. false, spurious, untrue.

मिथ्याचार m. deceitful conduct.

मिथ्याभिमान m. false pride, vainglory.

मिथ्यावादी adj. & m. (one) who tells a lie, liar.

मिनट m. minute.

मिनमिन f. utterance, almost inaudible.

म

मिन्नत f. supplication, entreaty.

मिमियाना vi. 1. to bleat. 2. to supplicate with servility, to grovel.

मियाँ m. 1. a Mohammedan form of address. 2. husband.

मियाँ-मिट्ठू adj. self-complacent; अपने मुँह ~ बनना to indulge in self-praise.

मियाद f. time limit, validity period.

मियादी adj. extending over a fixed period.

मियान f. scabbard, sheath.

मियाना m. 1. medium. 2. open palanquin.

मियानी f. 1. a small storey between two main floors, mezzanine. 2. gusset in a pyjama.

मिर्गी f. epilepsy.

मिर्च f. chilli.

मिर्जई f. an Indian type of jacket.

मिलकर adv. together, jointly.

मिलता-जुलता adj. very much alike, resembling, akin.

मिलन m. 1. union. 2. meet, meeting.

मिलनसार adj. social, sociable, companionable.

मिलना vi. 1. to meet, unite. 2. to be found. 3. to be mixed/ mingled; नदियों का ~ confl-uence of rivers. जन्मपत्री ~ matching of horoscopes.

मिलना-जुलना vi. to mix, to have social intercourse.

मिलनी f. a ceremonial meet.

मिलवाना vt. to cause to meet.

मिला-जुला adj. 1. mixed. 2. collective.

मिलान m. 1. act or state of colla-tion. 2. comparison.

मिलाना vt. 1. to mix, to blend. 2. to connect/join.

मिलाप m. 1. reunion. 2. reconciliation.

मिलावट f. 1. act of mixing. 2. adulteration, mixture. 3. the thing admixed.

मिलावटी adj. adulterated.

मिलीभगत f. collusion.

मिल्कियत f. 1. ownership. 2. property, estate.

मिशन m. 1. specific purpose. 2. group of missionaries.

मिशनरी m. one engaged in charitable works and religious teaching, missionary.

मिश्र adj. mixed; ~ - धातु alloy.

मिश्रण m. 1. mixture. 2. adulteration.

मिश्रित adj. mixed, mingled.

मिष्ट adj. sweet.

मिष्टभाषी adj. sweet-tongued.

मिष्टान्न m. sweets.

मिस m. pretext.

मिस, के postposition. on behalf of.

मिसरा m. one-half of a couplet.

मिसरी f. sugar-candy.

मिसल f. = मिसिल।

मिसाल f. example.

मिसिल f. case-file.

मिस्तरी m. 1. artisan, mechanic. 2. mason.

मिस्री f. sugar-candy.

मिस्सा m. mixed flour.

मिस्सी f. a powder used by women for tinging their lips.

मिस्सी रोटी f. bread prepared with mixed flour.

मींजना vt. to rub with the hands.

मींडना vt. 1. मींजना। 2. to knead.

मीचना vt. to close/shut/wink (e.g. eyes).

मीज़ान f. total.

मीटर m. meter.

मीटिंग f. meeting.

मीठा adj. sweet-tasting, sweet; मीठी आँच slow fire.

मीत m. friend.

मीन f. 1. fish. 2. twelfth sign of the zodiac, Pisces.

मीन-मेख m. fault, error, uncharitable criticism.

मीना m. 1. multicoloured glass. 2. goblet of wine. 3. precious stone of a blue colour. 4. enamel.

मीनाकार m. enameller.

मीनाक्षी adj. (woman) having fish-shaped eyes.

मीना बाज़ार m. fancy fair, gala fete.

मीनार f. tower, minaret, turret.

मीमांसा f. commentation, interpretative exposition, scholarly commentary; उत्तर ~ Vedantic Philosophy of वादरायण; पूर्व ~ Philosophy of Jaimini.

मीमांसित adj. thoroughly expounded, commented upon.

मीर m. 1. leader, chief. 2. nobleman. 3. winner in a game/sport.

मील m. a unit of length equal to 1760 yards, mile.

मीलन m. 1. act of closing. 2. act of contracting/resiling.

मीलित adj. closed, shut.

मीसना adj. uncommunicative, usually self-agonising. vt. 1. to mix. 2. to crush by rubbing.

मुँगरा m. wooden hammer. [Fem. मुँगरी]

मुँगौरी f. tiny roundish eatable, prepared of ground moong pulse.

मुंड m. 1. head. 2. skull.

मुंडन m. 1. the act of shaving the head. 2. ceremonious tonsure.

मुँडना vi. 1. to have the head shaved. 2. to be fleeced/cheated.

मुंडमाल f. garland of skulls.

मुंडा adj. 1. shaven-headed. 2. bald-headed. 3. without a head/cover. m. lad, boy.

मुँड़ाई f. the act of shaving the head or charges paid for the same.

मुँडाना vt. to get shaven.

मुंडित adj. shaved, tonsured.

मुंडी f. shaven-headed woman.

मुँडेर f. = मुँडेरा।

मुँडेरा m. parapet, battlement.

मुँदना vi. 1. to be closed. 2. to come to an end.

मुँदरी f. finger-ring.

मुंशी m. clerk, scribe.

मुंसिफ़ m. presiding officer in a lower court.

मुँह m. 1. mouth. 2. face. 3. front part of a thing. 4. opening (of pots, vessels etc.); ~ अँधेरे before dawn; ~ की खाना to be knocked out; ~ डालना to poke one's nose (into).

मुँहचढ़ा adj. = मुँहलगा।

मुँहचोर adj. shy, unwilling to be seen, bashful.

मुँहचोरी f. shyness.

मुँह-ज़बानी adv. orally, verbally.

मुँहज़ोर adj. impudent, insolent, obstinate, rude.

मुँहतोड़ adj. ~ उत्तर / जवाब crushing/smashing retort.

मुँहदिखाई f. present offered to the bride on the occasion of मुँहदेखनी।

मुँहदेखनी f. an Indian ritual after marriage when kinswomen see the bride formally.

मुँहफट adj. speaking roughly and plainly, blunt, abusive.

मुँहभराई f. 1. hush money, bribe, sop. 2. process of giving hush money.

मुँहमाँगा adj. asked for.

मुँहलगा adj. cheeky, imperti- nent.

मुँहाँ adj. & suffix. having a mouth; दु ~ having a mouth at either end.

मुँहाँमुँह adv. 1. to the brim. 2. face to face.

मुँहासा m. pimple, acne.

मुअत्तल adj. suspended (from service).

मुआ adj. dead.

मुआफ़िक़ adj. = माफ़िक़।

मुआयना m. inspection.

मुआवज़ा m. compensation.

मुक़दमा m. law-suit.

मुक़दमेबाज़ी f. litigation.

मुक़द्दर m. destiny, fate, luck.

मुकद्दस adj. holy, sacred, pious.

मुकम्मल adj. 1. complete/ completed. 2. complete and perfect.

मुकरना vt. to go back upon one's word, to deny, to refuse.

मुकरी f. riddle in the form of a short couplet.

मुक़र्रर adj. 1. appointed. 2. fixed.

मुकलावा m. = गौना।

मुक़ाबला m. 1. comparison. 2. encounter.

मुक़ाम m. 1. halt, halting place. 2. site, place.

मुकियाना vt. to give light blows with the fists for giving relief, to pummel.

मुकुट m. coronet, crest, diadem, crown, tiara.

मुकुर m. mirror.

मुकुल m. bud.

मुकुलित adj. budded.

मुक्का m. punch, blow given with the fist.

मुक्का-मुक्की f. exchange of blows/ punches.

मुक्की f. light blow of fist.

मुक्केबाज़ m. boxer.

मुक्केबाज़ी f. boxing.

मुक्त adj. 1. freed, liberated, released, emancipated. 2. free, independent.

मुक्तकंठ adj.; ~ से without any reserve.

मुक्तक m. piece of poetry.

मुक्तकेश adj. having uncombed hair.

मुक्तछंद m. blank verse.

मुक्तद्वार m. open door, free excess.

मुक्तवसन adj. naked, nude.

मुक्तहस्त adj. bounteous, liberal.

मुक्ता f. pearl.

मुक्तावली f. 1. string of pearls. 2. collection of poetic gems.

मुक्ति f. 1. liberation, emancipation, release. 2. salvation. 3. riddance, deliverance. 4. acquittal, exemption.

मुक्तिदाता m. 1. liberator. 2. one who gives salvation, saviour.

मुक्तिपथ m. path of salvation.

मुक्तिमार्ग m. = मुक्तिपथ।

मुक्तिलाभ m. emancipation.

मुख m. 1. mouth. 2. face. 3. opening.

मुखकमल m. lotus-like face, pretty face.

मुखड़ा m. face.

मुख़तारनामा m. power of attorney.

मुखद्वार m. gateway.

मुखपत्र m. an organ of a particular party or group.

मुखपृष्ठ m. title page.

मुख़बिर m. informer, spy.

मुखमंडल m. countenance.

मुखर adj. 1. cheeky. 2. talkative, loquacious, vociferous.

मुखरित adj. voiced, expressed, resonant.

मुखशुद्धि f. 1. cleansing of the mouth (after a meal). 2. taking betel-leaf, clove, cardamom etc. after a meal.

मुखाकृति f. mien.

मुखापेक्षी adj. looking at others for help, depending on others.

मुखारविंद m. pretty/lovely face.

मुखिया m. 1. head, headman, kingpin.

मुखौटा m. mask, false face/ countenance.

मुख़्तलिफ़ adj. different.

मुख़्तसर adj. brief.

मुख्य adj. 1. chief. 2. main, key, primary, principal. 3. leading.

मुख्यतः adv. mainly, primarily, predominantly, chiefly, principally.

मुख्यतया adv. = मुख्यतः।

मुख्यालय m. head office, headquarters.

मुगदर m. Indian type of dumb-bells used in physical exercises, mallet.

मुग़ल m. Moghal.

मुग्ध adj. fascinated, infatuated, charmed, captivated.

मुग्धता f. fascination, infatuation.

मुचल्का m. personal bond.

मुछंदर adj. whiskered.

मुजरा m. musical sitting by a dancing girl.

म

मुजरिम adj. & m. accused, offender, criminal.

मुझ pron. me.

मुझे pron. me, to me.

मुटका adj. fat (person).

मुटाई f. fattiness, fat.

मुटाना vi. to fatten, to grow fat.

मुटापा m. fatness, plumpness, obesity.

मुटासा adj. vainglorious (due to affluence).

मुटियाना vi to get fat, to become arrogant.

मुट्ठा m. 1. bundle. 2. handle.

मुट्ठी f. fist; ~ गरम करना to bribe.

मुठभेड़ f. 1. confrontation. 2. encounter.

मुठिया f. haft, a handle or hilt.

मुठियाना vt. 1. massage with light strokes of the fist. 2. to hold in one's fist/grip/grasp.

मुड़कना vi. to bend/twist.

मुड़ना vt. 1. to turn (about). 2. to return. 3. to bend. 4. to be twisted.

मुड़िया m. one with a clean-shaven head.

मुतबन्ना adj. & m. adopted (son).

मुताबिक adv. according (to).

मुतास f. urge to urinate.

मुत्तफ़िक़ adj. in agreement with.

मुदा m. = मुद्दा।

मुदाख़लत f. interference.

मुदित adj. delighted, pleased, rejoiced.

मुद्गर m. = मुगदर।

मुद्दई m. plaintiff, suitor.

मुद्दत f. 1. duration. 2. long period/time.

मुद्दा m. 1. intention, purport, proposition. 2. issue.

मुद्दालेह m. defendant, accused.

मुद्रक m. printer.

मुद्रण m. printing.

मुद्रणालय m. printing press.

मुद्रा f. 1. seal. 2. money. 3. coin/ currency. 4. mien.

मुद्रास्फीति f. inflation of currency.

मुद्रिका f. 1. finger-ring. 2. seal.

मुद्रित adj. printed.

मुनक़्क़ा f. currant.

मुनादी f. announcement, proclamation.

मुनाफ़ा m. profit, gain, advantage.

मुनाफ़ाख़ोर m. profiteer.

मुनासिब adj. 1. proper, fit, just. 2. reasonable.

मुनि m. hermit, sage, saint.

मुनियाँ f. 1. a small red-coloured bird. 2. small girl.

मुनीम m. 1. accounts clerk, accountant. 2. clerk.

मुनीमी f. work or profession of a मुनीम।

मुनीश m. a great hermit/sage.

मुनीश्वर m. great hermit.

मुन्ना m. dear child. [Fem. मुन्नी]

मुफ़लिस adj. & m. poor, pauper.

मुफ़ीद adj. beneficial, useful, advantageous.

मुफ़्त adj. free (of charge).

मुफ़्तख़ोर adj. (social) parasite.

मुफ़्तख़ोरी f. habit of living on others, parasitic way of living.

मुफ़्ती f. plain clothes.

मुबारक adj. auspicious.

मुबारकबाद f. congratulations.

मुमकिन adj. possible.

मुमानियत f. forbiddance, prohibition.

मुमुक्षा f. aspiration for salvation.

मुमुक्षु adj. seeking/desiring Salvation/Deliverance.

मुमूर्षा f. pining for death, desire to die.

मुमूर्षु adj. (person) pining for death.

मुरंडा adj. 1. dried out. 2. very lean and thin. m. a sweet made of parched wheat.

मुरकी f. 1. ear-top, earring. 2. a kind of musical ornamentation around a note.

मुरग़ा m. cock, fowl.

मुरग़ाबी f. water-fowl.

मुरग़ी f. hen.

मुरग़ी-पालन m. poultry-farming.

मुरझाना vi. to fade/wither.

मुरदनी f. 1. lifeless/deadly/deathly stillness. 2. funeral.

मुरदा adj. dead. m. dead body.

मुरदाघर m. mortuary.

मुरदा-दिल adj. devoid of zest.

मुरब्बा m. jam, preserve.

मुरमुरा m. parched and puffed rice, maize etc.

मुरमुराना vi. to break with a clicking sound, to crack down.

मुरली f. flute.

मुरलीमनोहर m. Lord Krishna.

मुरव्वत f. consideration, affability, favour, obliging disposition.

मुराद f. longing, craving.

मुरीद m. 1. follower. 2. disciple.

मुरौअत f. = मुरव्वत।

मुर्ग़ m. = मुरग़ा; ~ मुसल्लम roasted whole fowl.

मुलमुलाना vi. to blink.

मुलम्मा m. veneer, coating.

मुलाक़ात f. 1. meeting. 2. acquaintance.

मुलाक़ाती m. visitor.

मुलाज़मत f. service, employ-ment.

मुलाज़िम m. 1. employee. 2. servant.

मुलायम adj. 1. delicate. 2. tender.

मुलाहिज़ा m. consideration, regard (for others).

मुलेठी f. liquorice.

मुल्क m. country.

मुल्ज़िम adj. accused. m. culprit.

मुल्तवी adj. postponed.

मुल्ला m. Muslim priest.

मुवक्किल m. client.

मुशायरा m. poets' meet, poetic symposium.

मुश्क f. 1. musk. 2. odour, smell. 3. arm.

मुश्किल adj. 1. not easy, diffi-cult. 2. hard, tough. f. difficulty.

मुश्की adj. musky.

मुष्टि f. fist.

मुष्टि-प्रहार m. hard punch, sock.

मुसम्मी f. a variety of orange.

मुसलमान m. Muslim.

मुसलिम adj. = मुस्लिम।

म

मुसाफ़िर m. 1. traveller, voyager. 2. passenger.

मुसाफ़िरख़ाना m. waiting room.

मुसाहब m. = मुसाहिब।

मुसाहबी adj. sycophancy.

मुसाहिब m. 1. counsellor. 2. sycophant.

मुसीबत f. 1. difficulty, trouble. 2. adversity, calamity, misfortune.

मुसीबतज़दा adj. struck by misfortune, calamity-stricken.

मुस्कराना vi. to smile.

मुस्कान f. smile.

मुस्टंडा adj. & m. boorish, hefty fellow.

मुस्तैद adj. 1. ever-ready, pro- mpt. 2. alert, vigilant.

मुस्लिम adj. Muslim.

मुहताज adj. 1. indigent, poor. 2. handicapped, needy. 3. wanting.

मुहब्बत f. love, deep affection.

मुहम्मद m. prophet Mohmmad.

मुहर f. 1. an Indian gold coin. 2. seal. 3. stamp.

मुहरबंद adj. Sealed.

मुहर्रम m. day of Imam Hussain's martyrdom—a Muslim festival.

मुहर्रमी adj. dismal, very glo- omy.

मुहलत f. 1. period of time allo-tted for finishing a job. 2. leisure. 3. leave of absence from work.

मुहल्ला m. locality.

मुहाना m. estuary, mouth.

मुहाल adj. difficult.

मुहावरा m. 1. idiom. 2. practice.

मुहावरेदार adj. idiomatic.

मुहासा m. = मुँहासा।

मुहिम f. 1. campaign, military expedition. 2. arduous job.

मुहूर्त m. auspicious moment.

मूँग m. green gram, kidney bean.

मूँगफली f. groundnut.

मूँगा m. coral.

मूँगिया adj. green.

मूँछ f. moustache (s).

मूँज f. a kind of reed.

मूँड़ m. head.

मूँड़ना vt. 1. to shave the head. 2. to fleece.

मूँड़ी f. = मूँड़।

मूँदना vt. to close/shut/cover.

मूआ adj. dead.

मूक adj. 1. dumb, speechless, mute. 2. silent.

मूज़ी adj. 1. tyrannical. 2. mean, lowly. 3. extremely miserly/stingy.

मूठ f. 1. handle. 2. black magic.

मूड m. mood.

मूढ़ adj. idiotic, stupid, foolish, ignorant.

मूढ़ता f. idiocy, stupidity, foolishness, folly, silliness.

मूत m. urine.

मूतना vi. to pass urine, to urinate.

मूत्र m. urine.

मूत्रालय m. urinal.

मूत्राशय m. urinary bladder.

मूर्ख adj. stupid, foolish.

मूर्खता f. 1. stupidity, foolishness, idiocy. 2. blunder.

मूर्च्छना, मूर्छना f. modulation.

मूर्च्छा, मूर्छा f. swoon, fainting.

मूर्च्छित, मूर्छित adj. & pp. fainted, out of senses, hysterical.

मूर्त adj. 1. concrete, tangible. 2. corporeal, statuesque. 3. personified.

मूर्तता f. concreteness.

मूर्ति f. idol, statue, icon. ~ - कला sculpture; ~ - पूजक idolater; ~ - भंजक iconoclast.

मूर्तिमान, मूर्तिमान् adj. personified.

मूर्द्धन्य, मूर्धन्य adj. 1. pertaining to the मूर्धा, cerebral. 2. top-ranking, renowned, leading.

मूर्द्धा, मूर्धा f. cerebrum.

मूल adj. 1. pertaining to the origin/ source. 2. original, pristine. 3. primitive. 4. fundamental. m. 1. root. 2. origin.

मूलतः adv. 1. originally. 2. basically, fundamentally.

मूलतत्त्व m. 1. basic element (s). 2. The Elements (of a subject).

मूलधन m. principal (amount).

मूलभूत adj. fundamental, basic.

मूल स्थान m. 1. original home. 2. starting point, source.

मूली f. radish.

मूल्य m. value, price.

मूल्य-नियंत्रण m. price control.

मूल्यवान adj. valuable, precious, costly.

मूल्यविहीन adj. 1. valueless. 2. worthless.

मूल्यवृद्धि f. hike/rise in price.

मूल्य-सूचकांक m. price index.

मूल्यांकन m. valuation, estimation.

मूल्यांकनकर्ता m. valuer.

मूल्यानुसार adj. ad valorem.

मूषक m. rat.

मूषिका f. she-rat.

मूस m. rat, mouse.

मूसदानी f. rat-trap.

मूसना vt. 1. to extort money (from someone). 2. to steal, pilfer.

मूसल m. pestle.

मूसलधार adj.; ~ पानी / वर्षा torrential rains.

मूसला f. tap-root.

मूसली f. small pestle.

मूसा m. 1. mouse. 2. moses.

मृग m. deer.

मृगछाला f. skin of deer, deerskin.

मृगछौना m. fawn.

मृगतृष्णा f. 1. mirage. 2. any hope that cannot be fulfilled.

मृगमरीचिका f. mirage.

मृगया f. hunting.

मृगी f. hind.

मृणाल m. stalk of the lotus plant.

मृण्मूर्ति f. clay model.

मृत adj. dead, deceased, extinct.

मृतक m. a dead person.

मृतक-कर्म m. obsequies, last rites.

मृतप्राय adj. about to come to an end, almost dead.

मृत्तिका f. earth, clay.

मृत्युंजय adj. immortal.

मृत्यु f. death.

मृत्युदंड m. capital punishment.

म

मृत्युलोक m. this world, mortal world.

मृदंग m. an Indian musical instrument of the percussion type.

मृदु adj. 1. soft. 2. tender, mild. 3. sweet, gentle.

मृदुता f. 1. softness. 2. tenderness. 3. sweetness, gentleness.

मृदुभाषी adj. sweet/soft-tongued.

मृदुल adj. = मृदु ।

में postposition. 1. in, into, at, on, between, among. 2. denoting possession.

मेंगनी f. dung-ball of cattle.

मेंड f. ridge (between two fields).

मेंडक m. frog.

मेंडकी f. she-frog.

मेंमें f. bleat (of a goat).

में से postposition. 1. from among. 2. from inside. 3. thro-ugh, from one side of an objcet to the other.

मेंह m. rain.

मेकप m. act of applying cosmetics, make-up.

मेख f. smallish nail.

मेखल f. 1. girdle. 2. = मेखला ।

मेखला f. belt.

मेगज़ीन f. magazine.

मेघ m. cloud.

मेघनाद m. thunder.

मेघाच्छन्न adj. over spread with clouds, clouded.

मेघालय m. a state in the east of India.

मेज़ f. table.

मेज़पोश m. table cloth.

मेज़बान m. 1. host. 2. one who introduces and interviews guests, presenter.

मेजर m. major (army).

मेट m. mate, foreman (of labourers).

मेट्रन f. matron.

मेढ़ा m. ram.

मेढ़ी f. small braid, braiding.

मेथी f. fenugreek, a green plant used as a vegetable.

मेद m. fat (inside the body).

मेदा m. stomach.

मेदिनी f. earth.

मेधा f. intellect.

मेधावी adj. intellectual, intelligent, wise, clever.

मेनू m. menu.

मेम f. madam, lady.

मेमना m. lamb.

मेरा adj. my. pron. mine.

मेरु m. a mythological mountain.

मेरुदंड m. backbone, spine.

मेरु-रज्जु m. spinal cord.

मेल m. match, concord.

मेल-गाड़ी f. mail train.

मेलजोल m. intimacy.

मेलना v. to collate.

मेल-मिलाप m. 1. unison. 2. reconciliation, coming back to friendship after estrangement.

मेला m. fair, fete.

मेवा m. dry fruit.

मेष m. 1. sheep. 2. Aries, the first sign of the zodiac.

मेहँदी f. myrtle.

मेह m. = प्रमेह।

मेहतर m. sweeper, scavenger. [Fem. मेहतरानी]

मेहनत f. labour, toil.

मेहनताना m. remuneration.

मेहनती adj. laborious.

मेहना m. taunt.

मेहमान m. guest.

मेहमानदारी f. hospitality.

मेहर f. grace.

मेहरबान adj. kind, benevolent, merciful.

मेहरबानी f. kindness, favour.

मेहरा m. servant who does household chores, e.g. drawing water, cleansing utensils.

मेहराब f. arch.

मेहरारू f. 1. woman. 2. wife.

मेहरी f. 1. wife of मेहरा। 2. maid-servant.

मैं pron. I. f. ego.

मैंगनीज़ m. manganese.

मै f. wine.

मैख़ाना m. liquor-shop, bar.

मैच m. match.

मैत्री f. 1. friendship. 2. alliance.

मैथुन m. coitus.

मैदा m. fine flour.

मैदान m. 1. ground. 2. plains.

मैदानी adj. pertaining to the plains.

मैना f. a black Indian bird with a melodious voice.

मैनाक m. a peak of the Himalayas.

मैयत f. death.

मैया f. mother.

मैल f. 1. dirt, filth.

मैलख़ोरा adj. dust/dirt absorbing.

मैला adj. dirty, filthy, nasty, defiled, foul. m. excreta.

मैला-कुचैला adj. dirty and untidy, slatternly.

मैलापन m. dirtiness, filthiness.

मोक्ष m. Salvation, Deliverance, Moksha.

मोखा m. opening, scuttle, peephole.

मोच f. sprain, twist.

मोचन m. deliverance, riddance, release, acquittal.

मोचना vt. to get rid of, to liberate.

मोची m. cobbler. [Fem. मोचिन]

मोज़ा m. sock, stocking.

मोट m. 1. bundle. 2. leathern bag.

मोटर f. motor.

मोटा adj. 1. fat. 2. rough.

मोटाई f. = मोटापा।

मोटाना vi. 1. to grow fat, to fatten. 2. to become swollen-headed.

मोटापन m. fatness, plumpness.

मोटापा m. obesity, fatness, plumpness, corpulence.

मोठ m. a kind of lentil.

मोड़ m. turn, bend, curve.

मोड़ना vt. to turn/bend/twist.

मोतिया adj. of the colour of pearl. m. jasmine flower.

मोतियाबिंद m. cataract.

मोती m. pearl.

मोतीचूर m. tiny sweetened balls of gram flour.

मोद m. delight, pleasure.

मोदक m. a type of Indian sweet.

मोदी m. grocer.

मोम f. wax.

मोमजामा m. oil-cloth.

मोमबत्ती f. candle-stick.

मोमिन m. 1. Muslim. 2. Muslim weaver class.

मोमिया f. mummy.

मोमी adj. made of wax; ~ काग़ज़ tracing paper.

मोयन m. ghee used in kneading flour.

मोर m. peacock.

मोर-चंद्रिका f. moon-like pattern at the end of a peacock's feather.

मोरचा m. 1. rust. 2. battle-front. 3. a particular area of activity, front. 4. alliance of political parties.

मोरचेबंदी f. battle-array, entrenchment.

मोरनी f. peahen.

मोरपंख m. peacock feather.

मोरपंखी adj. of the colour of the feather of a peacock. m. a kind of hand-fan.

मोरमुकुट m. crown made of peacock feathers.

मोरी f. 1. drain, sewer. 2. outlet for water.

मोल m. price, cost.

मोल-भाव m. bargaining, horse trading.

मोह m. infatuation, fascination, delusion, affection.

मोहक adj. attractive, charming, fascinating, stupifying.

मोहग्रस्त adj. infatuated, obsessed.

मोहन adj. extremely charming, enchanting, alluring.

मोहना vt. to charm/fascinate.

मोहभंग m. disenchantment, disillusionment.

मोहनी f. spell, enchantment.

मोह-ममता f. 1. deep attachment. 2. undue affection

मोहर f. = मुहर।

मोहरा m. 1. the mouth of a container. 2. chessman. 3. forepart of an army, vanguard.

मोहरी f. mouth-like forepart of trousers or bottle etc.

मोहलत f. 1. leisure. 2. moratorium, period of time.

मोहित adj. fascinated, captivated, charmed.

मोहिनी adj. charming, bewitching.

मोही adj. 1. fascinated, captivated. 2. under an illusion.

मौक़ा m. occasion, opportunity.

मौक्तिक adj. of pearls.

मौखिक adj. spoken, oral, verbal.

मौज f. 1. wave. 2. fancy, caprice.

मौज़ा m. village.

मौजी adj. capricious, fanciful, jovial.

मौज़ूँ adj. just, suitable, opportune, appropriate.

मौजूद adj. present.

मौत f. 1. end of life, death. 2. the power that destroys life.

मौन m. the state of non-speaking, silence.

मौनव्रत m. vow of silence.

मौर m. 1. crown, diadem, tiara, crest, coronet. 2. blossoming of mango.

मौरूसी adj. hereditary.

मौलसिरी f. the plant ninsops dengi.

मौला m. master, god; मस्त ~ carefree man.

मौलिक adj. original, basic, elementary, fundamental.

मौलिकता f. orginality.

मौसम m. 1. weather. 2. season. 3. suitable period.

मौसमी adv. seasonal.

मौसा m. husband of mother's sister.

मौसी f. mother's sister.

मौसेरा adj. related through मौसा। [Fem. मौसेरी]

म्याऊँ f. mewing (of a cat).

म्यान f. sheath, scabbard.

म्यानी f. = मियानी।

म्लान adj. 1. withered. 2. without energy or spirit, languid. 3. gloomy.

म्लानता f. 1. state of being withered. 2. langour. 3. gloom.

म्लेच्छ adj. 1. dirty, unclean. 2. (pej.) un-Indian. 3. pagan. m. 1. alien. 2. contemptuous term for a non-Aryan.

य

य m. The first of the four semi-vowels of the Nagari alphabet; its sound is like that of y in yoke.

यंत्र m. 1. machine, instrument, apparatus, implement. 2. talisman, amulet.

यंत्रकार m. machine-maker.

यंत्रचालित adj. machine-operated.

यंत्रणा f. torture, affliction, pain, anguish.

यंत्र-मंत्र m. black magic, sorcery.

यंत्र-मानव m. robot.

यंत्रवत् adj. like a machine.

यंत्र-विद्या f. mechanics.

यंत्रित adj. mechanized.

यंत्रीकरण m. mechanization.

यकायक adv. all of a sudden.

यकार m. the letter य or its sound.

यक़ीन m. 1. certainty, surety, confidence.

यकृत m. liver.

यक्ष m. mythological demigod.

यक्ष्मा m. tuberculosis.

यजमान m. patron of priest, host.

यजुर्वेद m. the third of the four Vedas.

यज्ञ m. religious sacrifice and oblation.

यज्ञ-मंडप m. a canopy prepared for performance of religious sacrifice and oblation.

यज्ञोपवीत m. the sacred thread worn by the caste Hindus.

यति m. 1. ascetic. 2. check, obstacle.

यतीम m. orphan.

यतीमख़ाना m. orphanage.

यत्किंचित् adv. & adj. somewhat, to a small degree.

यत्न m. effort, exertion, labour, device, care.

यत्नपूर्वक adv. with effort, with due care.

यत्र-तत्र adv. here and there, at several places.

यथा adv. as per, as.

यथाकथित adj. as mentioned, as aforesaid/stated.

यथाक्रम adv. 1. in (due) order, systematically. 2. as scheduled.

यथातथ्य adj. & adv. exact, as it is.

यथापूर्व स्थिति f. status quo.

यथामूल्य adv. & adj. ad valorem.

यथायोग्य adj. suitably.

यथार्थ adj. 1. real. 2. exact.

यथार्थतः adv. 1. really. 2. exactly.

यथार्थता f. 1. reality. 2. exactness, exactitude, accuracy.

यथार्थवाद m. realism.

यथावत् adv. as before.

यथासाध्य adv. as far as practicable.

यथेष्ट adj. sufficient, enough, as required.

यथोचित adj. proper, just, appropriate.

यदा adv. 1. when. 2. where.

यदा-कदा adv. occasionally, off and on.

यदि conj. if, in case, supposing.

यद्यपि conj. 1. though, although. 2. even though, in spite of.

यम m. god of Death.

यमक m. pun.

यमज adj. twin.

यमदूत m. messenger/angel of Death.

यमलोक m. infernal world.

यमुना f. river Yamuna.

यवन m. Mohammadan.

यवनिका f. curtain.

यश m. repute, renown.

यशस्वी adj. reputed, renowned, glorious, celebrated.

यशोगाथा f. narrative of glorious deeds.

यशोगान m. eulogy, encomium.

यष्टि f. rod, stick.

यह pron. this one. adj. this, it.

यहाँ adv. here.

यहाँ, के postposition. at his house/place.

यहीं adv. at this very place; ~ कहीं somewhere here.

यही adj. & pron. this very, this one.

यहूदिन f. Jewess.

यहूदी m. Jew/Hebrew.

यांत्रिक adj. mechanical.

यांत्रिकी f. Mechanics.

या conj. or; ~ तो...या either...or.

याचक adj. & m. 1. suppliant. 2. beggar.

याचना f. 1. supplication, suppliance. 2. begging.

याचिका f. petition.

याजक m. sacrificing priest.

यातना f. torture, bodily infliction.

यातायात m. traffic, transport.

यात्रा f. 1. journey. 2. march.

यात्री m. 1. traveller. 2. passenger.

याद f. memory.

यादगार f. keepsake, monument, memento.

याददाश्त f. memory.

यादृच्छिक adj. arbitrary, random.

यान m. vehicle; वायु ~ aeroplane.

यानी adv. that is.

यापन m. spending, passing.

यामिनी f. night.

याम्योत्तर m. meridian.

यायावर m. nomad.

यार m. 1. friend, companion. 2. boy friend, lover.

याराना adj. friendly. m. friendship.

यारी f. friendship.

यावज्जीवन adv. throughout life, lifelong.

यावत् adj. as much. adv. as far as.

युक्त adj. 1. combined, joined. 2. fitted.

युक्ति f. 1. plea. 2. argument. 3. device, trick.

युक्तिपूर्वक adv. tactfully, skilfully.

युक्तिसंगत adv. reasonable, rational.

युग m. age, era, epoch, long period.

युगपत् adj. simultaneous.

युग-प्रवर्तक adj. & m. moving spirit of the times, epoch-maker.

युगल m. 1. twins. 2. pair.

युगांतर m. new era.

युगांतरकारी adj. epoch-making.

युग्म m. pair, couple.

युति f. combination.

युद्ध m. war, warfare, battle.

युद्ध-कौशल m. tactics of war, stratagem.

युद्धघोष m. battle/war cry.

युद्धनीति f. war policy/strategy.

युद्धपोत m. warship.

युद्धबंदी m. prisoner of war.

युद्धरत adj. belligerent.

युद्धविराम m. ceasefire.

युयुत्सा f. belligerence, enmity.

युयुत्सु adj. & m. militant, belligerent, war monger.

युवक m. young boy/man, youth.

युवती f. young girl/woman.

युवराज m. heir apparent.

युवा adj. young, youthful.

युवावस्था f. 1. young age. 2. youth, youthfulness.

यूँ adv. = यों।

यूथ m. group.

यूनानी adj. Greek.

यूनियन m. union.

यूनिवर्सिटी f. University.

यूरोप m. Europe.

ये pron. they. adj. these.

यों adv. in this way, thus.

योग m. 1. total. 2. joining together, union. 3. system of meditation. 4. one of the six schools of Indian philosophy. 5. conjunction (of stars).

योगक्षेम m. welfare.

योगदान m. 1. participation. 2. contribution.

योगफल m. sum, result of addition.

योगबल m. power acquired through योग।

योगशास्त्र m. Patanjali's treatise on योग।

योगाभ्यास m. practice of योग।

योगासन m. posture adopted in practising योग।

योगिनी f. fem. of योगी।

योगी m. ascetic, yogi.

योग्य adj. 1. able. 2. capable. 3. worthy.

योग्य, के postposition. to be equal to or capable for, up to.

योग्यता f. 1. ability, capability. 2. fitness.

योजक adj. which unites/joins. m. connective, conjunction.

योजक-चिह्न m. hyphen.

योजन m. 1. joining, union. 2. a measure of distance, roughly 13 kilometers.

योजना f. 1. plan, project, scheme. 2. planning.

योजना आयोग m. Planning Commission.

योजनाबद्ध adj. planned, preplanned.

योद्धा m. warrior.

योनि f. 1. vagina, female organ. 2. form of life.

यौगिक adj. compound.

यौन adj. sexual.

यौनतृप्ति f. sexual gratification.

यौन-भावना f. sexual urge.

यौन-विकृति f. sexual perversion.

यौन-संबंध m. sexual relation.

यौनाकर्षण m. sex appeal, sexual attraction.

यौनाचार m. sex-indulgence, moral laxity.

यौनिकी f. Sexology.

यौवन m. 1. youth, adolescence.

यौवनारंभ m. beginning of youth, puberty.

र

र

र m. second of the semi-vowels of the Nagari alphabet; its sound resembles that of r in row.

रंक adj. poor, penniless.

रंग m. colour, hue, dye, complexion, paint.

रंगक्षेत्र m. stage.

रंग-ढंग m. ways, conduct.

रंगत f. 1. tint, tinge; चेहरे की ~ complexion. 2. shade.

रँगना vt. to colour/dye.

रंग-बिरंगा adj. multicoloured, of various colours, motley.

रंगभूमि f. theatre.

रंगभेद m. colour bar, apartheid.

रंगमंच m. stage.

रंगमहल m. theatre.

रंग-रँगीला adj. colourful and gay, jovial.

रंगरली f. revelry.

रंगरूट m. 1. recruit. 2. novice.

रंगरेज़ m. dyer.

रंगरेली f. = रंगरली।

रंग-रोग़न m. paint and varnish.

रँगवाना vt. to cause to be dyed.

रंगशाला f. stage, theatre.

रंगसाज़ m. painter.

रंगस्थापक m. mordant.

रँगाई f. 1. act or process of dying, or charges paid for the same. 2. colouring, painting.

रंगारंग adj. colourful, variegated.

रंगीन adj. 1. coloured. 2. co-lourful.

रँगीला adj. 1. colourful. 2. gay, sportive, jovial.

रंगोली f. pictures made on the ground with coloured powders.

रँगौधी f. colour-blindness.

रंज m. sorrow, grief.

रंजक m. pigment, dye-stuff. adj. colouring.

रंजन m. 1. dyeing. 2. entertainment.

रंजित adj. dyed, coloured.

रंजिश f. ill-feeling, malice.

रंजीदा adj. sad, gloomy.

रँडापा m. widowhood.

रंडी f. prostitute, harlot.

रंडीबाज़ m. one who wenches with prostitutes.

रँडुआ m. widower.

रँदना vt. to plane (carpentry).

रंदा m. planer.

रंधन m. cooking.

रंध्र m. pore, orifice.

रंभा f. 1. a celestial nymph. 2. prostitute, harlot. m. iron rod, chiselled at one end, used for digging holes.

रँभाना vi. to bellow (cow, buffalo etc.).

रइयत f. = रैयत।

रई f. churning stick.

रईस adj. wealthy, prosperous. m. 1. rich man. 2. nobleman.

रईसी f. 1. richness, riches. 2. nobility.

रक़म f. 1. amount, sum, capital.

2. goodly sum; चलती ~ sharper, cunning guy.

रकाब f. stirrup.

रकाबी f. disc, plate.

रकार m. the letter र or its sound.

रक्त m. blood. adj. blood-red.

रक्त-कणिका f. blood corpuscle.

रक्त-क्षीणता f. anaemia.

रक्तचाप m. blood pressure.

रक्तदाता m. blood donor.

रक्तदान m. donation of blood.

रक्तपात m. bloodshed, carnage.

रक्तपायी adj. blood-sucker. m. leech.

रक्तरंजित adj. 1. blood-stained. 2. bloody, involving bloodshed.

रक्तस्राव m. haemorrhage, bleeding.

रक्ताभ adj. ruddy, having a red tinge.

रक्तिम adj. = रक्ताभ।

रक्षक m. 1. defender. 2. protector, saviour. 3. guard.

रक्षण m. protection, defence.

रक्षा f. 1. protection. 2. defence.

रक्षा-कवच m. safeguard, armour.

रक्षात्मक adj. defensive, protective.

रक्षाबंधन m. a Hindu festival.

रक्षार्थ, के postposition. for protection or defence (of).

रक्षित adj. protected.

रक्ष्य adj. worth protecting/defending/lifelong protection.

रखना vt. 1. to put/place. 2. to lay. 3. to keep. 4. to appoint. 5. to maintain.

रखरखाव m. maintenance, upkeep.

रखवाना vt. to cause to place/appoint/maintain, etc.

रखवाला m. caretaker, guard, watchman.

रखवाली f. guarding, watch-manship.

रखेल f. = रखेली।

रखेली f. concubine, kept woman.

रग f. nerve, vein.

रगड़ f. friction, attrition.

रगड़ना vt. to rub.

रगड़वाना vt. causative of रगड़ना।

रगड़ा m. rub, rubbing.

रगेदना vt. to chase away.

रघुकुल m. the solar dyansty starting with रघु।

रघुनंदन m. Ram, the great-grandson of रघु।

रचना f. 1. construction. 2. composition. 3. formation. vt. 1. to construct. 2. to compose. 3. to fabricate.

रचनात्मक adj. constructive.

रचयिता m. author, composer, creator.

रचित adj. constructed, composed, compiled.

रज m. 1. dust. 2. blood of menstruation.

रजत m. silver.

रजत-जयंती f. silver jubilee.

रजनी f. night.

रजनीकर m. moon.

रजनीचर m. 1. nocturnal being. 2. demon.

र

रजनीश m. moon.

रजवाड़ा m. erstwhile princely state of India.

रजस्वला f. woman in her menstrual period.

रज़ा f. 1. wish, desire. 2. consent, permission.

रज़ाई f. quilt.

रज़ामंद adj. agreed, willing.

रजिस्ट्री f. registration.

रजोगुण m. the second of the three constituent qualities of all the material objects.

रजोधर्म m. menses.

रजोनिवृत्ति f. menopause.

रज्जु f. rope, cord, string.

रटंत f. learning by rote, repetitiousness.

रट f. continual repetition, reiteration.

रटन f. = रटंत।

रटना vt. to cram, to learn by rote.

रडार m. radar.

रड़क f. irritating sensation (due to some foreign matter).

रड़कना vi. to produce irritating pain.

रण m. battle, war, combat.

रणकौशल m. tactics of war, stratagem.

रणक्षेत्र m. battle-field.

रणचंडी f. Goddess of war—Durga.

रणछोड़ m. Lord Krishna.

रत adj. engaged, busy, absorbed.

रतजगा m. keeping awake the whole night usually for devotional purposes, singing etc.

रतनारा adj. ruddy, red.

रतनारी adj. (eyes) with veins reddened.

रति f. 1. conjugal love. 2. love. 3. cohabitation.

रतिक्रिया f. cohabitation, copulation.

रतिशास्त्र m. Sexology.

रतौंधी f. night-blindness, nyctalopia.

रत्ती f. an Indian weight, approximately equal to 1/8 mg.

रत्न m. jewel, gem. adj. the most extraordinary/talented.

रत्नाकर m. ocean, sea.

रथ m. chariot.

रथवान m. charioteer.

रथी m. charioteer.

रथ्या f. roadway.

रद m. tooth. adj. = रद्द।

रदक्षत m. tooth-mark.

रद्द adj. cancelled.

रद्दा m. layer.

रद्दी adj. of very poor/inferior quality, worthless. f. 1. waste paper. 2. something discarded as junk, waste material

रद्दोबदल m. alteration, modification, change.

रन m. run (cricket).

रनिवास m. harem, seraglio.

रपट f. report.

रपटना adj. slippery. vi. to slip/skid.

रपटीला adj. slippery.

रफ़्ता-रफ़्ता adv. gradually, slowly.

रफ़ल m. shawl, woollen wrapper.

रफ़ा adj. shunted away.

रफ़ा-दफ़ा adj. settled and finished, done away with.

रफ़ू m. darning.

रफ़ूगर m. darner.

रफ़ू-चक्कर adj. ~ हो जाना to show a clean pair of heels, to make good (one's escape).

रफ़्तार f. speed.

रब m. God.

रबड़ m. rubber.

रबड़ी f. thick sweetened milk.

रबी f. spring crop, rabi crop.

रमज़ान m. ninth month of the Muslim calendar.

रमण m. 1. amorous activity/dalliance. 2. cohabitation. 3. merriment

रमणी f. (lovely) young woman.

रमणीक adj. pleasing, attractive, inviting.

रमणीय adj. 1. pleasant and enjoyable, idyllic, elegant. 2. charming, fascinating.

रमता adj. roving, roaming, wandering.

रमना vi. 1. to rove. 2. to be engrossed. m. lawn, pleasant spot for roaming.

रमल m. future-telling by a throw of dice, geomancy.

रमा f. Goddess of wealth, Lakshmi.

रम्मी f. a game of cards, rummy.

रलना vi. to get mixed up, as a child in a crowd.

रव m. 1. sound. 2. noise, uproar, tumult.

रवन्ना m. passage/transit permit, way-bill.

रवाँ adj. मेरा हाथ इस मशीन पर ~ है I am used to this machine.

रवा m. crystal.

रवानगी f. departure.

रवाना adj. departed, set out.

रवानी f. 1. flow. 2. fluency.

रवि m. Sun.

रविवार m. Sunday.

रविश m. 1. aisle/path between flower beds. 2. movement.

रवेदार adj. granular, crystalline.

रवैया m. 1. way of doing something, style. 2. way of dealing with someone, behaviour, conduct.

रश्मि f. beam, ray.

रस m. 1. juice, essence. 2. sap (of tree). 3. extract. 4. relish. 5. flavour. 6. interest.

रसगुल्ला m. an Indian sweet made from cheese.

रसज्ञ m. connoisseur.

रसद f. 1. provisions. 2. supplies.

रसदार adj. juicy.

रसना f. tongue. vi. = रिसना।

रसभंग m. interruption of relish.

रसभरी f. raspberry.

रस-भीना adj. full of flavour, soaked in sentiment.

रसहीन adj. sapless.

रसा m. 1. soup of meat, vegetable etc., broth. 2. juice.

रसाई f. approach.

रसातल m. nether world, hell, Hades, underworld.

रसाभास m. semblance of रस।

रसायन m. chemistry.

रसायनज्ञ m. chemist.

रसायनशाला f. chemical laboratory.

रसाल m. mango.

रसास्वादन m. tasting, relishing.

रसिक adj. & m. 1. getting pleasure from poetry, drama etc. 2. jolly person.

रसिया m. 1. a man of taste, one with aesthetic sense. 2. a type of folk song.

रसीद f. receipt.

रसीदी टिकट f. revenue stamp.

रसीला adj. 1. juicy. 2. delicious.

रसूल m. divine messenger, prophet.

रसेदार adj. having broth.

रसोइया m. cook, chef.

रसोई f. 1. cooking. 2. cuisine. 3. kitchen.

रसोईघर m. kitchen.

रसौली f. tumour.

रस्म f. 1. custom, practice. 2. formality.

रस्मी adj. ceremonial.

रस्सा m. rope.

रस्साकशी f. tug-of-war.

रस्सी f. rope string, cord.

रहट m. Persian wheel (used for drawing water from a well).

रहन m. way of living.

रहन-सहन m. way of living.

रहना vi. 1. to live. 2. to stay. 3. to remain.

रहम m. kindness, pity, compassion, benevolence.

रहमदिल adj. kind, merciful, compassionate, benevolent.

रहस्य m. 1. secret. 2. inexplicable event, mystery.

रहस्यपूर्ण adj. mysterious, arcane, mystic.

रहस्यवाद m. mysticism.

रहस्यवादी adj. mystical, mystic.

रहस्योद्घाटन m. revelation of a mystery.

रहा-सहा adj. all that remained, residual, left over.

रहित adj. 1. bereft. 2. less, devoid.

रहीम adj. kind. m. God.

राँगा m. tin.

राँड f. widow.

राँधना vt. to cook (lentil, rice etc.).

राई f. small seeds of mustard used as condiment; ~ का पहाड़ करना to make a mountain of a mole hill.

राका f. the night of the full moon.

राकेट m. rocket.

राकेश m. moon.

राक्षस m. 1. goblin, devil, demon, giant, monster. 2. wicked person, badly behaved person.

राक्षसी adj. devilish, demoniac. f. demoness.

राख f. ash, ashes.

राखदान m. ash-tray.

राखी f. sacred thread tied by the sister on the wrist of her brother who guarantees life-long protection to her.

राग m. 1. melody, tune. 2. passion, attachment.

रागरंग m. merry-making, enjoyment.

रागिनी f. a kind of melody.

रागी m. filled with love/attachment.

राछ f. a weaver's tool.

राज m. 1. state, dominion, rule, administration, kingdom. 2. reign. 3. mason. 4. allomorph of राजा।

राजकाज m. state affairs.

राजकीय adj. 1. of the government, governmental. 2. managed by the state.

राजकुमार m. prince.

राजकुमारी f. princess.

राजकोष m. royal treasury.

राजगद्दी f. 1. throne. 2. enthronement.

राजगीर m. mason.

राजगृह m. palace, royal mansion.

राजचिह्न m. insignia of royalty.

राजतंत्र m. 1. monarchy. 2. polity.

राजतिलक m. coronation.

राजत्व m. 1. kingship. 2. reign.

राजदंड m. 1. sceptre. 2. punishment awarded by the king.

राजदूत m. ambassador.

राजदूतावास m. embassy, consulate.

राजद्रोह m. treason, sedition, disloyalty.

राजधानी f. capital, metropolis.

राजनयिक adj. diplomatic. m. diplomat.

राजनीति f. politics.

राजनीतिज्ञ m. politician, statesman.

राजनीति-शास्त्र m. Political Science.

राजनीतीकरण f. politicization.

राजनेता m. statesman.

राजपत्र m. gazette, charter.

राजपद m. state/goverment post.

राजपाट m. empire and its paraphernalia.

राजपुरुष m. state offficial.

राजप्रासाद m. palace.

राजभक्त adj. loyal to the ruler or country. m. loyalist.

राजभाषा f. official language of a country.

राजमद m. the vanity of being in power and pelf.

राजमहिषी f. queen.

राजमार्ग m. highway.

राजरोग m. long-drawn ailment.

राजर्षि m. saintly king.

राजलक्ष्मी f. goddess of royal grandeur, Maha Lakshmi.

राजविप्लव m. insurrection, anarchy.

राजवैद्य m. king's physician.

राजशाही adj. royal, kingly, stately.

राजसत्ता f. 1. regal power. 2. sovereignty.

राजसभा f. 1. royal court. 2. royal assembly.

राज-सिंहासन m. royal throne.

राजसी adj. 1. princely, royal, gaudy. 2. pertaining to रजोगुण।

राजस्व m. revenue.

राजा m. king.

राजाज्ञा f. royal/regal order.

राजाधिराज m. emperor.

राज़ी adj. 1. agreed. 2. agreeable, willing.

राज़ी-ख़ुशी adv. happily, peacefully.

राज़ीनामा m. agreement.

राजीव m. 1. lotus. 2. elephant.

राज्ञी f. queen consort.

राज्य m. 1. rule. 2. state.

राज्यकाल m. reign, ruling period.

राज्य-परिषद् m. council of state.

राज्यपाल m. governor; महा - ~ Governor General.

राज्यव्यवस्था f. polity.

राज्यसंघ m. confederation.

राज्यसभा f. Council of State, Upper House, Rajya Sabha.

राज्याभिषिक्त adj. enthroned; ~ करना to enthrone.

राज्याभिषेक m. coronation, enthronement.

राढ़ f. quarrel, fracas, dispute.

रात f. night.

रात की रानी f. queen of the night, a very fragrant flower which blooms in the night.

रातिब m. one day's food for cattle.

रात्रि f. night.

रात्रिचर adj. & m. demon, nocturnal being.

रानी f. 1. consort. 2. queen; पट ~ queen consort.

राब f. molasses.

राम m. Prophet king Ram, the hero of the Ramayan.

राम-कहानी f. episode of one's life.

रामनवमी f. ninth day of bright fortnight of चैत्र; birthday of God Ram.

रामबाण adj. unfailing (medicine). m. 1. a remedy of all diseases or evils, panacea. 2. unerring device.

राम भरोसे adv. to the mercy of god.

रामरज f. yellow ochre.

रामरस m. salt.

रामराज्य m. rule of Ram, ideal rule, utopia.

राम-राम m. 1. greeting. 2. valediction, valedictory remark. interj. showing disgust.

रामलीला f. dramatic pageant of the Ramayan.

रामायण m. Ramayan (Hindu epic).

राय f. opinion. m. king.

रायता m. a saltish dish prepared with curd and vegetables.

रायल m. royal size (of paper).

रार f. quarrel, dispute.

राल f. resin.

राव m. 1. king. 2. a member of a royal family.

रावटी f. small tent.

रावण m. demon king of Shri Lanka (Ramayan).

राशन m. ration.

राशि f. 1. amount, quantity. 2. zodiac sign.

राशिचक्र m. zodiac.

राष्ट्र m. nation.

राष्ट्रकवि m. national poet, poet-laureate.

राष्ट्रगान m. national anthem.

राष्ट्रचिह्न m. national emblem.

राष्ट्रध्वज m. national flag.

राष्ट्रपति m. President.

राष्ट्रभाषा f. national language.

राष्ट्रमंडल m. Commonwealth.

राष्ट्रवाद m. nationalism.

राष्ट्रवादी adj. nationalist.

राष्ट्रव्यापी adj. nation-wide.

राष्ट्रीय adj. national; ~ गान National Anthem

राष्ट्रीयकरण m. nationalization.

राष्ट्रीयता f. 1. nationality. 2. nationalism.

रास adj. favourable, beneficial; ~ आना to prove favourable/wholesome. m. 1. circular dance associated with Lord Krishna. 2. reins.

रास-मंडली f. band of performers of रास।

रासायनिक adj. chemical.

रासो m. poetic life history of a king.

रास्ता m. 1. path, way, road. 2. route. 3. passage. 4. (fig.) ploy.

रास्ती f. forbearance.

राह f. path, way.

राह-ख़र्च m. travelling expenses.

राहगीर m. wayfarer.

राहज़न m. highwayman.

राहज़नी f. highway robbery.

राहत f. respite, relief.

राही m. one who goes on a journey sply. by foot, wayfarer.

राहु m. 1. the mythical monster who swallows up the moon and the sun and thus causes their eclipses. 2. (someone) pestilent.

राहु-केतु m. (plu.) everpestering enemies.

रिंच m. wrench.

रिआयत f. 1. concession. 2. remission, relaxation.

रिआयती adj. concessional.

रिआया f. subjects, people.

रिकार्ड m. the best performance, or highest level ever reached, record.

रिक्त adj. empty, vacant, blank.

रिक्तता m. 1. void, vacuum. 2. vacancy.

रिक्ति f. = रिक्तता।

रिक्थ m. legacy.

रिक्शा m. rickshaw.

रिज़क m. livelihood.

रिज़र्व adj. reserved.

रिझाना vi. to allure/captivate/entice/please.

रिझाव m. captivation, lure.

रिटायर adj. retired.

रिड़कना vt. to churn.

रिपु m. enemy, foe, antagonist.

रिपुघ्न m. the destroyer of the enemy, God Ganesh.

रिपोर्ट f. report.

रिपोर्टर m. reporter.

रिबन m. ribbon.

रिम m. 1. ream. 2. edge of a wheel, rim.

रिमझिम f. light drizzle.

रियाज़ m. 1. exercise, exertion. 2. practice.

र

रियासत f. 1. former Indian princely state. 2. estate. 3. state. 4. regality.

रिरियाना vi. 1. to whimper. 2. to implore/entreat/beseech abjectly.

रिवाज m. custom, practice, vogue.

रिवाल्वर m. revolver.

रिश्वत f. bribe.

रिश्वतख़ोर adj. & m. (one) who is used to taking bribes, bribee.

रिश्वतख़ोरी f. bribery.

रिश्ता m. relation, relationship.

रिश्तेदार m. relative, relation, kinsman.

रिश्तेदारी f. kinship, relationship.

रिस m. anger, wrath, indignation.

रिसना vi. to ooze/drizzle/leak.

रिसाना vi. to get angry.

रिसाला m. 1. platoon. 2. journal.

रिहर्सल rehearsal

रिहा adj. released, aquitted, freed.

रिहाइश f. residence.

रिहाई f. release, discharge, acquittal.

रीं-रीं f. whimpering sound.

रीछ m. bear.

रीझ f. overbearing interest.

रीझना vi. to be allured/captivated/charmed.

रीठा m. soap-nut.

रीढ़ f. backbone, spine; ~ की हड्डी vertebral column.

रीता adj. 1. empty. 2. vacant.

रीति f. 1. usage, practice, custom, rite. 2. manner, system.

रीति-रिवाज m. customs and manners, rites and rituals.

रील f. reel (of thread etc.).

रुंड m. torso.

रुँधना vi. to be choked.

रुआँ m. fuzz, soft hair on the body.

रुई f. cotton.

रुईदार adj. stuffed with cotton.

रुकना vi. 1. to stop. 2. to stay.

रुकवाना vt. to cause to stop.

रुकाव m. = रुकावट।

रुकावट f. hindrance, obstacle, obstruction.

रुक़्क़ा m. 1. chit, note. 2. document.

रुक्ष adj. 1. harsh, rough. 2. ruffled, unkempt (hair).

रुख़ m. 1. attitude. 2. trend. 3. face, facet, frontage. 4. rook/castle (in chess).

रुख़सत f. 1. leave (of absence). 2. permission to leave.

रुखाई f. curtness, bluntness.

रुखानी f. chisel.

रुग्ण adj. indisposed, ailing, ill.

रुग्णता f. illness, indisposition.

रुचना vi. 1. to relish. 2. to derive interest.

रुचि f. 1. interest, liking, taste.

रुचिकर adj. 1. inspiring interest, extremely interesting. 2. relishing.

रुचिर adj. 1. sightly, winsome, attractive. 2. sweet, pleasing, winning.

रुझान m. bent, proclivity, inclination, propensity.

रुतबा m. 1. position, status. 2. rank.

रुदन m. lamentation, weeping, bewailing.

रुद्ध adj. 1. blocked. 2. choked. 3. impeded.

रुद्र adj. dreadful, awful, fearful. m. Lord Shiv.

रुद्राक्ष m. seed of a tree used for making rosaries.

रुद्राणी f. = पार्वती।

रुधिर m. blood.

रुनझुन f. tinkle/tinkling sound.

रुनाई f. redness, ruddiness.

रुपया m. 1. rupee. 2. money.

रुपल्ली m. = रुपया।

रुपहला adj. silvery.

रुलाई f. wailing, weeping.

रुलाना vt. to cause to weep.

रुष्ट adj. displeased, offended, angry, enraged, indignant.

रुसवाई f. ill-fame, disrepute.

रुसूख़ m. social contact (s).

रूई f. = रुई।

रूक्ष adj. = रुक्ष।

रूखा adj. 1. not smooth, rough. 2. dry, without personal warmth. 3. harsh, blunt.

रूखापन m. 1. roughness. 2. dryness (of person). 3. bluntness.

रूठना vi. to be displeased, to show displeasure.

रूढ़ adj. 1. conventional. 2. prevalent, traditional.

रूढ़ार्थ m. conventional mea- ning.

रूढ़ि f. convention, tradition.

रूढ़िगत adj. = रूढ़।

रूढ़िवाद m. conservatism, conventionalism, conformism.

रूढ़िवादी adj. conventionalist, conservative.

रूप m. 1. beauty, charm. 2. shape, form, size, appearance.

रूपक m. 1. metaphor. 2. bluff. 3. a kind of dramatic play, allegory.

रूपगर्वित adj. proud of (one's) beauty. [Fem. रूपगर्विता]

रूप-तालिका f. (Gram.) paradigm.

रूपरेखा f. 1. outline. 2. contour. 3. synopsis. 4. design.

रूपवती adj. & f. (woman) of beautiful features, a beauty, damsel.

रूपवान, रूपवान् adj. handsome, pretty.

रूप-विज्ञान m. morphology.

रूप-सज्जा f. make-up, beautification.

रूपसी adj. beautiful (woman).

रूपांतरण m. 1. transformation, transfiguration. 2. adaptation (of a literary piece).

रूपा m. silver.

रूपायन m. giving a shape.

रूपिम m. morpheme.

रूपी suffix. denoting shape or figure; बहु ~ multiform, multifaced.

रूबरू adv. in the presence of, in front of, face to face.

रूमाल m. handkerchief, scarf.

र

रू-रिआयत f. concession, leniency, consideration.

रूल m. 1. ruler. 2. rule, regulation.

रूलदार adj. ruled.

रूलर m. ruler, scale.

रूसी adj. Russian. m. 1. Russian language. 2. scurf, dandruff.

रूह f. soul, inner being.

रेंकना vi. to bray.

रेंगना vi. to creep/crawl/plod.

रेंट f. snot, mucus of nose, nasal discharge.

रेंड़ m. castor plant.

रेख (rekh) f. line, mark.

रेखांकन m. 1. underlining. 2. demarcation.

रेखा f. line.

रेखाकृति f. 1. line-drawing. 2. sketch.

रेखागणित m. = ज्यामिति।

रेखाचित्र m. 1. line-drawing, diagram. 2. sketch.

रेखाचित्रण m. 1. drawing a diagram. 2. sketching.

रेखित pp. lined, delineated, demarcated, furrowed.

रेखीय adj. linear.

रेगमाल m. sand-paper.

रेगिस्तान m. desert.

रेचक adj. & m. purgative.

रेचन m. purgation, purging (of bowels).

रेज़गारी f. money in small units.

रेज़गी f. = रेज़गारी।

रेट m. rate, price.

रेडियो m. radio.

रेढ़ f. ruin, devastation.

रेणु f. sand.

रेणुका f. 1. sand. 2. mother of Parasuram, a character in the Ramayan.

रेत f. sand.

रेतना vt. to file/rasp.

रेती f. 1. file. 2. sandbank. 3. (expanse of) sand.

रेतीला adj. sandy.

रेफ़ m. the sign (᳚) used to denote the sound of 'र' devoid of its vowel parts as in धर्म, सर्प।

रेल f. 1. railway. 2. rail.

रेलगाड़ी f. railway train.

रेलपथ m. rail track.

रेलपेल f. 1. melee, bustle. 2. exuberance.

रेलवे f. railway.

रेला m. a rush.

रेलिंग f. railing.

रेवड़ m. flock.

रेवड़ी f. a hard crisp sweetmeat.

रेशम m. silk; ~ का कीड़ा silk-worm.

रेशमी adj. silken.

रेशा m. fibre.

रेशेदार adj. made of fibres, fibrous.

रेह f. whitish soil for cleansing purposes.

रेहन m. pledge, hypothecation, mortgage.

रेहनदार m. mortgagee.

रेहननामा m. mortgage deed.

रैन f. night.

रैन-बसेरा m. night-shelter.

रैयत f. public, subjects.

रोंगटा m. small and soft hair on the body.

रोआँ m. small and soft hair on the body, fur.

रोआसा adj. on the point of weeping, almost in tears.

रोएँदार adj. hairy.

रोक f. 1. restraint. 2. restriction, ban, prohibition, prevention, embargo.

रोकटोक f. too much of restriction/ proscription.

रोकड़ f. cash in hand.

रोकड़-बाक़ी f. cash balance.

रोकड़िया m. cashier.

रोकथाम f. 1. prevention, check. 2. preventive measure.

रोकना vt. 1. to stop, stem. 2. to prevent/ hinder/check. 3. to detain. 4. to avert. 5. to restrain.

रोग m. disease, sickness, illness, malady.

रोगग्रस्त adj. diseased, ailing.

रोग़न m. paint, lacquer.

रोगनाशक adj. preventive, prophylactic.

रोगाणु n. germs of a diesease, microbe.

रोगी m. sick, patient.

रोगी-कक्ष m. patients' ward.

रोचक adj. interesting, pleasant, sweet.

रोचकता f. quality of being interesting, interest, sweetness.

रोज़ m. day. adv. daily.

रोज़गार m. business, occupation, profession.

रोज़नामचा m. diary.

रोज़मर्रा adv. daily, everyday.

रोज़ा m. fast.

रोज़ाना adv. daily.

रोज़ी f. livelihood.

रोटी f. 1. loaf (of bread). 2. meal.

रोड़ा m. 1. piece of stone/brick, pebble. 2. (fig.) impediment.

रोड़ी f. small pebble.

रोदन m. weeping, crying, lamentation.

रोध m. blockade.

रोना m. pathetic and painful episode of one's life. vi. to weep.

रोना-पीटना vi. to cry and wail loudly.

रोनी सूरत m. one who habitually expresses one's sorrow or disappointment for something.

रोपक m. planter, transplanter.

रोपण m. planting.

रोपना vi. to plant/implant/ transplant.

रोपनी f. transplanting.

रोपित adj. 1. planted, transplanted, sown. 2. affixed.

रोब m. overpowering influence, awe.

रोबीला adj. awe-inspiring.

रोम m. soft hair on the body, fur.

रोमहर्षक adj. horripilating, horrid.

रोमांच m. sensation, a feeling of excitement, thrill.

रोमांचक adj. causing excitement, thrilling.

रोमांचित adj. thrilled.

र

रोमानी n. romantic.

रोमावली f. soft hair on the body.

रोयाँ m. = रोआँ।

रोर m. hubbub, uproar, tumult.

रोरी f. = रोली।

रोली f. a mixture of turmeric and lime powder used for auspicious purposes.

रोशन adj. 1. lit up, lighted. 2. bright, shining. 3. manifest.

रोशनदान m. ventilator.

रोशनाई f. ink.

रोशनी f. 1. light. 2. illumination.

रोष m. resentment, anger.

रोहण m. ascending, mounting, climbing.

रोहू m. a kind of fish.

रोहे m. (plu.) trachoma.

रौंदना vt. to trample down, to crush down.

रौ m. 1. flow. 2. impulsive mood.

रौद्र adj. dreadful, fearful, horrible, terrible.

रौनक़ f. 1. lustre, brightness, shining. 2. hustle-bustle.

रौरव adj. dreadful, terrible, horrible.

रौला m. uproar, tumult.

ल

ल m. the third of the semi-vowels of the Nagari alphabet, pronounced like l in love.

लंक m. heap, pile.

लंकिनी f. witch, evil spirit.

लंग m. lameness, limp.

लंगड़ adj. = लँगड़ा। m. = लंगर (anchor).

लँगड़ा adj. lame, limp, crippled.

लँगड़ाना vi. to limp.

लंगर m. 1. anchor. 2. pendulum. 3. a thread with a weight at one end (toy). 4. a place where free meal is served to all and sundry.

लंगूर m. an Indian ape, gibbon, baboon.

लँगोट m. = लँगोटा।

लँगोटा m. a small loin-cloth used as an undergarment in India.

लँगोटिया adj. ~ यार pal, chum, a friend since childhood.

लँगोटी f. small लँगोट।

लंघन m. going without food, fast, abstinence.

लंघनीय adj. passable, trans-gressible.

लंठ adj. 1. boorish, rude. 2. foolish, stupid.

लंठई f. 1. boorishness. 2. stupidity

लंड m. penis.

लंतरानी f. empty boast, brag- ging, boasting.

लंपट adj. dissolute, lecherous, lewd, incontinent, licentious.

लंपटता f. lewdness, lechery, profligacy.

लंब m. perpendicular.

लंबतड़ंग adj. unusually tall.

लंबरदार m. a lambardar in the days of the zamindari system.

लंबा adj. 1. long. 2. tall. 3. lengthy.

लंबाई f. length.

लंबान f. length.

लंबायमान adj. 1. lengthened. 2. lying flat.

लंबित adj. suspended, pendent, kept in pending.

लंबू adj. & m. thin and bony, gaunt.

लंबोतरा adj. longish, somewhat long.

लंबोदर adj. fat-bellied. m. Ganesh.

लकड़ m. allomorph of लक्कड़।

लकड़बग्घा m. hyena.

लकड़हारा m. woodman, wood-cutter.

लकड़ी f. 1. wood. 2. firewood. 3. stick.

लक़वा m. paralysis.

लकीर f. line; ~ का फ़क़ीर blind imitator/conventionalist/follower.

लकुटी f. stick.

लक्कड़ m. log of wood.

लक्का m. fan-tailed pigeon.

लक्ष m. 1. one hundred thousand, lac (lakh). 2. target, aim, objective.

ल

लक्षण m. 1. symptom. 2. indication. 3. characteristic feature.

लक्षणा f. 1. metonymy. 2. figurative sense of a word.

लक्षणात्मक adj. 1. symptomatic. 2. figurative.

लक्षित adj. 1. indicated, hinted, marked, observed. 2. apparent.

लक्षितार्थ m. figurative/implied meaning.

लक्ष्मण-रेखा f. impregnable/formidable barrier.

लक्ष्मी f. Lakshmi, goddess of wealth.

लक्ष्य m. target, objective, aim, goal.

लक्ष्यवेध m. hitting the target.

लक्ष्यसिद्धि f. attainment of one's goal/target.

लखना vt. to spot/mark out, to keep an eye on, to behold/see/perceive.

लखपति m. millionaire.

लखेरा m. one who prepares bangles from लाख (shellac).

लखौरी f. small brick.

लगन f. 1. zest, devotion (to purpose). 2. assiduity, steadfast perseverance, attachment, gusto.

लगना vi. 1. to take. 2. to be attached/affixed. 3. to be contiguous/adjoining, to abut. 4. to be a relation of. 5. to engage (one's thought/idea, etc.). 6. to be engaged (in some work). 7. to apply oneself heart and soul (in some persuit). 8. to hit/strike (a target). 9. to seem/appear. 10. to feel hurt/offended. 11. to feel. 12. to bear (fruits/flowers etc.). 13. to begin (with infinitives). 14. to be held. 15. to be eaten away. 16. to cost. 17. to receive an offer.

लगभग adv. 1. approximately, nearly, about. 2. almost.

लगवाना vi. causative of लगाना।

लगातार adv. 1. continuously, incessantly, without break. 2. continually. 3. in a row.

लगान f. rent (of land).

लगाना vt. 1. to put on. 2. to apply. 3. to affix. 4. to impose. 5. to plant.

लगाम f. rein, bridle.

लगालगी f. 1. attachment, affection, deep intimacy. 2. rivalry, competition.

लगाव m. 1. attachment. 2. intimacy. 3. connection.

लगी f. 1. conflict. 2. attachment.

लग्गा m. 1. pole, a piece of beam used as a gadget for many purposes, such as pulling a boat, plucking a fruit etc. (Fem. लग्गी). 2. commencement of a work.

लग्गी f. 1. fishing rod. 2. see लग्गा।

लग्न adj. attached, annexed. m. auspicious moment.

लघिमा f. smallness, meagre-ness, littleness, shortness.

लघु adj. small.

लघुतम adj. 1. smallest. 2. lowest (common multiple).

लघुता f. 1. smallness. 2. inferiority.

लघुरूप m. short form, miniature.

लघुशंका f. urination.

लचक f. 1. elasticity (of objects). 2. flexibility, adaptability (of persons, laws, etc.).

लचकदार adj. 1. elastic. 2. flexible.

लचकना vi. 1. to resile, spring back. 2. to bend.

लचकाना vt. causative of लचकना।

लचना vi. 1. to bend. 2. to come down in one's attitude.

लचर adj. weak, loose.

लचीला adj. 1. elastic. 2. flexible (constitution).

लच्छा m. 1. hank, skein. 2. a kind of sweetmeat in the form of threads (thickly coiled).

लच्छी f. deminutive of लच्छा।

लच्छेदार adj. charming/fascin- ating (talk).

लजाना vi. 1. to be shy. 2. to blush. 3. to be ashamed.

लजालू adj. bashful.

लज़ीज़ adj. delicious, tasty.

लजीला adj. bashful.

लजीलापन m. bashfulness.

लज्जा f. 1. bashfulness. 2. modesty. 3. shame.

लज्जाजनक adj. shaming, shameful.

लज्जालु adj. bashful, shy, shameful.

लज्जावती adj. bashful, shy (woman).

लज्जावान, लज्जावान् adj. bashful.

लज्जाहीन adj. brazen, shameless, impudent.

लज्जित adj. shamefaced, blushing, ashamed.

लट f. lock of hair.

लटक f. 1. affected movement, bend. 2. impulse.

लटकन m. 1. pendant, pendulum, locket. 2. a kind of flower or its seed which yields a reddish colour.

लटकना vi. 1. to hang, swing. 2. to be in suspense. 3. to sag/bend.

लटका m. 1. device, compendious formula, tip. 2. mannerism, coquetry.

लटकाना vt. 1. to hang/suspend. 2. to keep waiting. 3. to delay, to keep in suspense, to dangle.

लटकौआ adj. that which can be suspended/hung.

लटना vi. to become lean and thin.

लटपटाना vi. to stagger, stum-ble, to falter while walking.

लट्टू m. 1. a toy that spins round and round whirling; (किसी पर) ~ होना to be fascinated by somebody. 2. (electric) bulb.

लट्ठ m. stick, cudgel.

लट्ठबाज़ adj. skilled in wielding a लाठी।

लट्ठमार adj. uncivil, crude.

लट्ठा m. 1. a rod measuring 5½ cubits. 2. = मारकीन (a kind of cloth). 3. log, raft.

लठैत m. one skilled in using/wielding a लाठी।

ल

लड़ m. strand, string.

लड़कपन m. 1. the state of being a baby, boyhood, childhood. 2. childishness, silliness.

लड़क-बुद्धि f. childish mentality.

लड़का m. boy.

लड़की f. girl.

लड़खड़ाना vi. 1. to stagger, to falter. 2. to fall or almost fall, stumble. 3. collapse.

लड़खड़ाहट f. staggering gait, tottering state.

लड़ना vi. 1. to fight. 2. to collide.

लड़ना-झगड़ना vi. to quarrel.

लड़ाई f. 1. fight. 2. battle, war. 3. clash.

लड़ाई-झगड़ा m. broil, quarrel.

लड़ाईबंदी f. cessation of hostilities and ceasefire.

लड़ाका adj. = लड़ाकू।

लड़ाकू adj. 1. quarrelsome. 2. militant, bellicose. m. a militant, fighter; ~ विमान fighter aeroplane.

लड़ाना vt. to cause to fight.

लड़ी f. string, chain.

लड़ैत adj. & m. 1. skilled fihgter. 2. quarrelsome.

लड़ैता adj. = 1. लाड़ला। 2. लड़ैत।

लड्डू m. a round Indian sweet. मन के ~ imaginary enjoyment.

लत f. 1. habit. 2. bad habit, addiction, whim.

लतख़ोर adj. used to receiving kicks, habituated to kicks, mean.

लतख़ोरा adj. = लतख़ोर। m. door-mat.

लतर f. = लता।

लता f. creeper.

लताड़ f. heavy scolding, upbraiding, reproof, insult.

लताड़ना vt. 1. to press with feet for relieving pain. 2, to scold/ upbraid/reprove.

लतियाना vt. to give a kicking, to kick, to trample by foot.

लतीफ़ा m. witticism, a joke.

लत्ता m. rag, tatter.

लथपथ adj. besmeared, wet.

लथाड़ f. = लताड़।

लथेड़ना vt. 1. to make dirty by rough and wrong use. 2. = लताड़ना।

लदन f. load.

लदना vi. 1. to be loaded. 2. to be sentenced to rigorous imprisonment. 3. to be laden (with fruits),

लदवाना vt. to cause to load.

लदाई f. act of loading or charges paid therefor.

लदान f. 1. process of loading. 2. load.

लदाव m. load, cargo.

लद्दू adj. & m. beast of burden.

लद्धड़ adj. slow, lethargic, lazy.

लनतरानी f. = लंतरानी।

लप m. elasticity; ~ मारना to shine while bending.

लपक f. state or quality of being elastic.

लपकना vi. to rush forward. to flash/spring. vt. to catch.

लपका m. pilferer.

लपझप adj. 1. unsteady. 2. odd and uncouth.

लपट f. flame, blaze.

लपटीला adj. sticky.

लपना vi. to bend/sag.

लपलपाना vi. to be bent again and again, to resile. vt. 1. to brandish (as a sword). 2. to bring out again and again (as the tongue).

लपसी f. 1. a variety of हलुआ (sweet dish). 2. a sticky substance, porridge.

लपेट f. 1. fold, twist, winding. 2. involvement. 3. ambiguity.

लपेटन f. 1. folding, winding. 2. cover, wrapper.

लपेटना vt. 1. to fold/roll up. 2. to implicate/entangle.

लपेटवाँ adj. which can be folded/ twisted/wound.

लप्पड़ m. slap with the full palm.

लफ़ंगा m. loafer, rogue, vagabond.

लफ़्ज़ m. word.

लब m. lip.

लबड़-धोंधों f. mess, confusion, row.

लबाड़ adj. = लबाड़िया।

लबाड़िया adj. used to talking unnecessarily.

लबादा m. over-garment, cloak, gown, robe.

लबालब adj. full to the brim, brimming.

लब्ध adj. got, attained, acquired.

लब्धप्रतिष्ठ adj. reputed, renowned.

लब्धि f. 1. attainment. 2. quotient. (Maths.)

लभ्य adj. available, attainable.

लमतड़ंग adj. lean and lanky, tall.

लमहा m. moment.

लय f. rhythm, tune. m. 1. deluge. 2. merger, fusion.

लयन m. act or state of being merged.

ललक f. longing, craving, intense desire.

ललकना vi. to long for, to crave.

ललकार f. challenge, gage.

ललकारना vt. 1. to challenge. 2. to abet (someone) to assault/ murder.

ललचना vi. to be tempted/allured.

ललचाना vt. to tempt, to allure, to entice.

ललचौहाँ adj. greedy.

ललना f. beautiful lady.

लला m. sweet child (boy).

ललाई f. redness, flush of face.

ललाट m. forehead.

ललाम adj. beautiful, charming.

ललित adj. fine, pretty, comely; ~ कला fine art.

लली f. sweet girl.

लल्ला m. an affectionate form of addressing a boy. [Fem. लल्ली]

लल्लो f. tongue.

लल्लो-चप्पो f. flattery, servility.

लवंग m. clove.

लवंग-लता f. 1. clove creeper. 2. a variety of Indian sweet.

लव adj. tiny.

ल

लवण m. salt.

लवणता f. 1. salinity. 2. comeliness.

लवना vt. to harvest a crop.

लवलासी f. yearning to establish a love connection.

लवलीन adj. absorbed, engrossed.

लवलेश adj. & m. iota.

लवा m. 1. a bird allied to the lark. 2. parched rice.

लवेरी f. milch cow.

लशकर m. 1. army. 2. host, multitude.

लस m. stickiness, adhesiveness.

लसदार adj. sticky, viscid, clammy.

लसना vt. to paste, as a stamp on an envelope.

लसलसा adj. gluey, sticky, adhesive.

लसलसाहट f. glueyness, stickiness, adhesiveness.

लसी f. 1.= लसलसाहट। 2. temptation.

लसीला adj. sticky, gluey, adhesive.

लसोड़ा m. a tree, Cordia dichotoma, or its fruit.

लस्टम-पस्टम adv. haphazardly, in a disorderly manner.

लस्त adj. fagged, fatigued, exhausted.

लस्त-पस्त adj. totally exhausted, weary.

लस्सी f. drink made of yogurt.

लहँगा m. a long loose skirt worn by women in India.

लहँड़ा m. flock, herd.

लहक f. blaze, glare.

लहकना vt. to blaze/glare.

लहकाना vt. causative of लहकना।

लहकारना vt. 1. to excite. 2. to excite a dog to attack someone.

लहजा m. 1. tone, intonation. 2. manner of speech.

लहर f. 1. wave. 2. impulse.

लहरदार adj. wavy, undulatory.

लहरा m. 1. wave. 2. merrymaking, enjoyment.

लहराना vi. & vt. to wave/undulate.

लहरिएदार adj. wavy, rippling, corrugated.

लहरिया m. wavy line, tilde (~).

लहरी adj. whimsical, fanciful. f. ripple.

लहलहाना vi. 1. to be verdant/bloom (said of fields and foliage). 2. to flourish/bloom.

लहसुन m. garlic, Allium sativum.

लहसुनिया m. cat's eye, a variety of grey-coloured precious stone.

लहालोट adj. enamoured, fascinated, extremely pleased.

लहू m. blood.

लहू-लुहान adj. smeared with/bathed in blood.

लाँग f. the part of the dhoti tucked up at the back.

लाँघना vt. 1. to cross over, to jump over. 2. to transgress/overstep.

लांछन m. stigma, stain, blemish.

लांछित adj. stigmatized, blamed.

लाइन f. 1. a long thin mark, line. 2. queue. 3. railway line. 4. a course of action. 5. business, profession.

लाइनदार adj. lined.

लाइलाज adj. 1. incurable. 2. irremediable.

लाई f. parched rice.

लाई-लुतरी f. 1. backbiting. 2. telltale.

लाकेट m. locket.

लाक्षणिक adj. figurative, metaphoric (al).

लाक्षा f. sealing wax, lac.

लाख adj. & m. a hundred thousand, lac. f. sealing wax.

लाग f. 1. approach. 2. subtle device.

लागत f. 1. cost. 2. investment.

लाग-लपेट f. hidden meaning/ implication.

लागू adj. 1. applicable (of rules). 2. accustomed to haunt.

लाघव m. brevity, shortness.

लाचार adj. helpless, poor.

लाचारी f. helplessness.

लाज f. 1. honour, prestige.

लाजवंत adj. shy, bashful.

लाजवंती f. 1. bashful (blonde), shy woman. 2. touch-me-not.

लाजवाब adj. 1. matchless, in-comparable, unique. 2. speechless, answerless.

लाज़िम adj. compulsory, obligatory.

लाट f. a tall tower, steeple. m. lord.

लाठी f. lathi, staff.

लाठी-चार्ज m. lathi-charge.

लाड़ (lAR) m. fondness, caressing.

लाड़ला adj. darling, beloved.

लात f. leg, kick.

लाद f. belly, tummy, entrails.

लादना vt. 1. to put a load on, to load. 2. to cause to do something under pressure, force.

लाद-फाँद f. parching and loa- ding.

लादी f. 1. load of a beast. 2. big lot, burden.

लानत f. damnation, reproach.

लानत-मलामत f. reproach, reproof.

लाना vt. to bring/fetch.

लापता adj. 1. missing, untraceable. 2. (person) whose whereabouts are unknown/missing.

लापरवाह adj. careless, negli- gent.

लापरवाही f. lack of proper care, carelessness, negligence.

लाभ m. 1. profit, gain, attainment. 2. benefit. 3. advantage.

लाभकर adj. 1. profitable. 2. worthwhile.

लाभदायक adj. 1. profitable, gainful. 2. lucrative, paying. 3. beneficial, advantageous.

लाभप्रद adj. = लाभदायक।

लाभांश m. dividend.

लाम m. 1. army. 2. war/battle front.

लामबंदी f. mobilization.

लायक़ adj. 1. able. 2. capable. 3. befitting. 4. worthy. 5. fit. 6. competent.

लार f. saliva.

लारी f. lorry.

लाल adj. red. m. 1. carbuncle (gem.). 2. son. 3. ruby. 4. a variety of a tender and small bird.

लालच m. greed, temptation, avarice.

लालची adj. greedy, avaricious.

लालटेन f. lantern, lamp.

लालन m. bringing up.

लाल फीता m. red tape; ~शाही red-tapism.

लाल बुझक्कड़ m. village wiseacre.

लाल मिर्च f. chilly.

लालसा f. yearning, craving, cherished desire, aspiration.

लाल सागर m. Red Sea.

लाला m. 1. a term of respect. 2. a form of respectful address. 3. a variety of red flower.

लालायित adj. eager, anxious, desirous.

लालित्य m. charm, winsomeness, grace.

लालिमा f. ruddiness, reddishness.

लाली f. 1. redness. 2. glow, radiance.

लाले m. (plu.) lack, shortage; ~ पड़ जाना to be deficient or lacking.

लावण्य m. charm, loveliness, elegance.

लावनी f. a kind of folk song.

लाव-लश्कर m. array of attendants, satellites, paraphernalia.

लावा m. 1. parched rice. 2. lava (volcano).

लावारिस adj. 1. (person) heirless. 2. (object) unclaimed.

लाश f. dead body, corpse, carcass.

लासा m. 1. an adhesive. 2. birdlime. 3. lure, bait.

लासानी adj. peerless, matchless, unique.

लास्य m. a spontaneous female dance.

लाही f. grain insect.

लिंग m. 1. gender. 2. sex. 3. male organ.

लिंग-पूजा f. phallus worship.

लिंटर m. lintel.

लिए, के postposition. for, for the sake of, in order to.

लिखत f. writing.

लिखत-पढ़त f. (written) deed, document.

लिखना vt. 1. to write. 2. to note down.

लिखना-पढ़ना vi. reading and writing.

लिखवाई f. causing to write or remuneration paid therefor.

लिखवाना vt. to cause to write.

लिखा adj. written; भाग्य का ~ destined.

लिखाई f. 1. = लिखावट। 2. = लिखवाई।

लिखाना vt. 1. to cause to write by giving dictation. 2. to cause to copy from a manuscript.

लिखा-पढ़ा adj. educated, literate.

लिखा-पढ़ी f. 1. reduction to written form. 2. corres-pondence (of letters).

लिखावट f. handwriting.

लिखित adj. 1. written, reduced to black and white. 2. documentary.

लिटर m. litre.

लिटाना vt. causative of लेटना।

लिट्टी f. small biscuit made of flour, spherical ball of flour baked on fire.

लिथड़ना vi. to be besmeared.

लिपटना vi 1. to cling (to). 2. to be engrossed. 3. to embrace.

लिपटाना vt. causative of लिपटना।

लिपना vi. 1. to be plastered/coated. 2. to be smeared.

लिपवाना vt. causative of लीपना।

लिपाई f. act/process of लीपना, or charges paid for the same.

लिपाई-पुताई f. plastering and whitewashing.

लिपि f. 1. script. 2. writing.

लिपिक m. clerk, writer.

लिपिबद्ध adj. written, reduced to black and white.

लिप्त adj. 1. closely connected, embroiled, involved. 2. engrossed. 3. united.

लिप्तता f. involvement, embroilment.

लिप्यंतरण m. transliteration.

लिप्सा f. greed, lure, lust.

लिफ़ाफ़ा m. 1. envelope. 2. outer covering.

लिफ़्ट f. lift.

लिबलिबा adj. too soft to touch.

लिबलिबी f. trigger.

लिबास m. dress, attire, uniform.

लियाक़त f. ability, capability.

लिवाना vt. to cause to bring.

लिसलिसा adj. viscous.

लिसोड़ा m. the fruit cordia myxa or its tree.

लिहाज़ m. 1. consideration. 2. considerateness. 3. respect. 4. point of view. 5. modesty.

लिहाज़ा adv. therefore, hence, and so.

लिहाड़ा adj. & m. rough and ready (person), mean, contemptible.

लिहाड़ी f. ridicule, mockery, derision.

लिहाफ़ m. quilt.

लीक f. 1. = लकीर (line). 2. track. 3. rut (of a wheel).

लीख f. a type of tiny whitish louse.

लीग f. 1. league (institution). 2. measure of distance, roughly equivalent to 5 kilometres.

लीचड़ adj. 1. sluggish, lethargic. 2. mean (in money matters). 3. stingy.

लीची f. a tree and its fruit.

लीथो m. litho.

लीन adj. 1. dissolved, merged, mingled, absorbed. 2. engrossed, rapt.

लीपना vt. 1. to plaster/coat/besmear. 2. to smear.

लीपना-पोतना vt. to plaster/coat and whitewash/paint.

लीलना vt. to swallow/devour.

लीला f. 1. frolicsome/illusory creation (of God). 2. sportive display, fun and frolic.

लीवर m. lever (of a gadget).

लुंगी f. an Indian type of loin cloth.

लुंचन m. pulling off (hair etc.); pulling out (feathers etc.).

ल

लुंज adj. crippled.

लुंठन m. rolling.

लुंठित adj. rolled; ~ व्यंजन rolled consonant.

लुंड m. torso, trunk, dead body without arms, legs or head.

लुंडा adj. tailless (lamb, bird etc.).

लुआठा m. a long piece of wood with one end burning, embers. (Dim. लुआठी)

लुआब m. sticky pith.

लुक m. 1. shining paint. 2. flame.

लुकना vi. 1. to hide. 2. to go underground.

लुक़मा m. morsel.

लुका-छिपी f. hide-and-seek.

लुकाट m. loquat, the tree or its fruit.

लुकाना vt. to conceal, to hide, to keep secret.

लुगदी f. pulp, paper pulp.

लुगाई f. 1. woman. 2. wife. 3. kept woman, concubine.

लुच्चा adj. & m. wicked (person), scoundrel, villain, rogue.

लुच्ची f. biscuit made of fine wheat flour.

लुटना vi. to be robbed/looted/plundered.

लुटाना vt. 1. to squander. 2. to spend lavishly. 3. to give away indiscriminately.

लुटिया f. diminutive of लोटा।

लुटेरा m. robber, bandit, plunderer.

लुढ़कना vi. 1. to roll down. 2. to die (fig.). 3. to be upset/toppled. 4. to tumble down.

लुढ़काना vt. causative of लुढ़कना।

लुतरा adj. & m. 1. tell-tale. 2. backbiter.

लुत्फ़ m. 1. enjoyment, pleasure. 2. fun.

लुनना vt. to reap.

लुनेरा m. reaper.

लुप्त adj. 1. disappeared, vanished. 2. extinct, obsolete. 3. omitted.

लुब्बे-लुबाब m. 1. essence, pith. 2. gist, sum and substance.

लुभाना vt. to charm/entice.

लुभावना adj. charming, fascinating, attractive.

लुहार m. blacksmith.

लू f. heatwave, sunstroke.

लूका m. 1. flame. 2. burning piece of wood. 3. meteor.

लूट f. pillage, loot.

लूटना vt. to rob/plunder/loot/despoil/ravage.

लूटमार f. plundering and massacre.

लूता m. spider.

लूम m. loom.

लूला adj. with a maimed/dismembered hand; ~ - लँगड़ा maimed and crippled.

लूलू adj. foolish. m. fool.

लेंस m. lens.

लेंहड़ा m. herd.

लेई f. an adhesive preparation of fine flour (used in book-binding), paste.

लेकिन conj. but, however.

लेक्चर m. lecture.

लेख m. 1. writing, handwriting. 2. article, treatise, composition, essay. 3. deed, document.

लेखक m. 1. writer, author. 2. clerk.

लेखन m. 1. act of writing. 2. profession of a writer.

लेखन सामग्री f. stationery.

लेखनी f. an instrument for writing sply. with ink, pen.

लेखपाल m. 1. record-keeper. 2. patwari.

लेखबद्ध adj. reduced to writing.

लेखमाला m. series of articles.

लेखा m. account, calculation.

लेखा-जोखा m. calculation of accounts.

लेखा-परीक्षक m. auditor.

लेखा-परीक्षण m. auditing.

लेखा-बही f. 1. account book. 2. ledger.

लेखिका f. woman writer, authoress.

लेख्य adj. worthy to be noted down. m. a written document.

लेट f. late.

लेटना vi. to lie (down), to lay oneself down.

लेनदार m. creditor.

लेन-देन f. 1. give-and-take. 2. social dealings. 3. financial transaction.

लेना vt. 1. to accept. 2. to take. 3. to claim. 4. to get.

लेना-देना m. 1. लेन-देन transac-tion. 2. relation.

लेप m. 1. liniment. 2. coating, plaster, ointment.

लेपन m. 1. anointing, applying liniment, plastering. 2. coating.

लेपना vt. to anoint/coat.

लेफ़्टिनेंट m. lieutenant.

लेवा m. one who takes.

लेवाल m. = लेवा।

लेश m. bit, whit, modicum.

लेस f. adhesiveness, stickiness.

लेसदार adj. adhesive, sticky, gluey.

लेह m. any jelly-type preparation.

लैंगिक adj. sexual.

लैस adj. fully-equipped, fitted.

लोंदा m. wet lump, dough.

लोई f. 1. dough. 2. a thin woollen shawl or wrapper.

लोक m. 1. world. 2. people.

लोककथा f. folk tale.

लोकगीत m. folk song.

लोकतंत्र m. democracy.

लोकतांत्रिक adj. democratic.

लोकना vt. to catch (a dropping ball, fruit etc.).

लोकनिंदा f. public censure.

लोकनृत्य m. folk dance.

लोकप्रिय adj. popular, in vogue.

लोकप्रियता f. popularity.

लोक-लज्जा f. regard for public opinion.

लोक-लाज f. = लोक-लज्जा।

लोकसंग्रह m. mobilisation of the people.

लोकसभा f. 1. House of the People. 2. the Lower House of the Indian Parliament, Lok Sabha.

लोकसेवा f. Public Service.

ल

लोकहित m. public interest.

लोकाचार m. popular custom, ethos.

लोकापवाद m. adverse public opinion, public slander.

लोकोक्ति f. popular saying, proverb.

लोकोत्तर adj. supernatural, unworldly, etheral.

लोकोपकारी adj. philanthropic. m. philanthropist.

लोग m. men, public, people, folk.

लोग-बाग m. common people.

लोच f. elasticity, flexibility, tenderness.

लोचदार adj. elastic, flexible.

लोचन m. eye.

लोट f. rolling.

लोटन m. a kind of pigeon.

लोटना vi. to roll/welter.

लोटा m. an Indian type of water vessel; बेपेंदी का ~ spineless person.

लोथ m. corpse, dead body.

लोथड़ा m. lump of flesh.

लोन m. salt.

लोना adj. saltish, saline.

लोप m. 1. The state of being vanished, disappearance. 2. a letter (of the alphabet) which is understood.

लोफ़र m. loafer, vagabond.

लोबान m. a tree gum used as incense.

लोबिया f. cow pea.

लोभ m. 1. greed. 2. rapacity.

लोभी adj. 1. greedy. 2. rapacious.

लोम m. = रोम।

लोमड़ी f. fox.

लोरी f. lullaby.

लोलक adj. pendant. m. pendulum.

लोलुप adj. covetous, avaricious, greedy.

लोहा m. iron.

लोहार m. blacksmith.

लोहारी f. blacksmith's work or calling.

लोहित adj. red, scarlet.

लोहू m. blood.

लौंग m. 1. clove. 2. nose-stud.

लौंडा m. lad, boy.

लौंडी f. servant/slave girl.

लौंडेबाज़ m. sodomite.

लौंद m. ~ का महीना intercalary month.

लौ f. 1. flame, glow. 2. love, devotion.

लौआ m. gourd, pumpkin.

लौकिक adj. worldly, mundane.

लौकी f. bottle gourd, pumpkin.

लौट f. return.

लौटना vi. to return, to come back.

लौट-फेर m. interchange, substantial derangement.

लौटाना vt. to give back, to return.

लौह m. iron.

लौहचूर्ण m. iron filings.

लौहपुरुष m. iron-man.

लौहयुग m. iron age.

व

व Fourth of the semi-vowels of the Nagari alphabet; usually its sound is like that of v in value; sometimes, in the middle or end of a syllable, it sounds like w in swarm.

वंग m. Bengal.

वंगभंग m. Partition of Bengal in pre-independence India.

वंचक adj. & m. deceitful, cheat crafty, swindler, fraudulent.

वंचन m. 1. deception. 2. deprivation.

वंचित adj. 1. deceived. 2. deprived. 3. cheated.

वंटन m. distribution.

वंदन m. obeisance, adoration.

वंदनवार f. wreathe of green leaves (hung up on auspicious occasions).

वंदना f. obeisance, adoration, salutation.

वंदनीय adj. worthy of obeisance/ reverence, adorable.

वंदी m. captive, prisoner.

वंदीगृह m. prison.

वंध्य adj. sterile.

वंध्या adj. sterile, unproductive, barren. f. unfertile woman.

वंश m. 1. dynasty. 2. bamboo. 3. race, clan, progeny.

वंशचरित m. family history.

वंशज m. 1. descendant. 2. a young member of one's family, scion.

वंशतालिका f. genealogical table.

वंशधर m. = वंशज।

वंश-परंपरा f. family tradition, lineage.

वंशवृक्ष m. family tree, pedigree.

वंशावली f. line of one's ancestors, genealogy.

वंशी f. flute, pipe.

वक m. crane (bird).

वकवृत्ति f. hypocrisy.

वकालत f. 1. legal practice, lawyer's/pleader's profession. 2. pleading.

वकालतनामा m. power of attor-ney.

वकील m. lawyer, vakil, pleader.

वक़्त m. time.

वक्तव्य m. statement, speech.

वक्ता m. speaker, orator, spokesman.

वक्तृता f. 1. speech, lecture. 2. oration.

वक़्फ़ m. waqf, charitable endowment.

वक्र adj. 1. curved. 2. oblique, slanting.3. crooked, sinister.

वक्रता f. 1. curvature. 2. obliq-ueness, obliquity. 3. crookedness.

वक्री adj. 1. deflected. 2. retrograde.

वक्रोक्ति f. remarkable satirical utterance, innuendo, circumlocution.

व

वक्ष m. 1. breast. 2. chest. 3. bosom.

वक्षस्थल m. = वक्ष।

वग़ैरह conj. et cetera.

वचन m. 1. utterance. 2. promise. 3. number (Grammar).

वचनबद्ध adj. committed (to one's words), bound (by one's words).

वचनभंग m. breach of promise.

वज़न m. 1. The amount of anything that weighs, weight. 2. importance, influence.

वज़नदार adj. 1. weighty. 2. important. 3. influential.

वजह f. reason.

वज़ीफ़ा m. 1. stipend. 2. scholarship.

वज़ीर m. minister.

वज़ू m. washing of hands and feet before prayer.

वज्र m. 1. Indra's thunderbolt. 2. impenetrable, solid or formidable.

वज्रपात m. a very terrible event, thunderbolt.

वज्रहृदय adj. stone-hearted, hard-hearted.

वज्राघात m. 1. thunderstroke. 2. severe blow, calamity.

वट m. banyan (tree).

वटिका f. pill, globule.

वटी f. tablet.

वटु m. bachelor, lad.

वणिक m. businessman, trader, merchant.

वतन m. motherland.

वत्स m. beloved child, dear young one.

वत्सर m. year.

वत्सल adj. affectionate towards children or young ones.

वत्सलता f. affection, parental love.

वदन m. face.

वध m. killing, murder, slaughter.

वधिक m. 1. executioner, assassin. 2. fowler, hunter.

वधू f. wife.

वध्य adj. deserving/meant to be killed.

वन m. forest, jungle, woods.

वनदेवी f. a wood goddess, dryad.

वनपाल m. forester.

वनमहोत्सव m. ceremony for plantation of trees.

वनमानुष m. chimpanzee.

वनराज m. 1. king of forest. 2. lion.

वनरोपण m. act of planting trees to form a forest, afforestation.

वनवास m. dwelling in the forest, exile.

वनस्थली f. land covered with trees, woodland.

वनस्पति f. 1. vegetation. 2. vegetable.

वनस्पति-विज्ञान m. Botany.

वनिता f. pretty woman.

वन्य adj. of the wilds, wild.

वपन m. sowing seed.

वफ़ा f. loyalty, faith, trust.

वफ़ादार adj. loyal, faithful, trustworthy.

वबाल m. fuss, ado.

वमन m. vomiting.

वयः संधि f. puberty.

वय m. age.

वयस m. age.

वयस्क adj. & m. major, adult.

वयस्कता f. adulthood.

वयोवृद्ध adj. aged, venerable, worthy of respect due to age.

वरंच conj. but.

वर m. 1. bridegroom. 2. boon.

वरक़ m. leaf.

वरज़िश f. physical exercise.

वरण m. selection, choice.

वरद adj. conferring a boon.

वरदी f. = वर्दी।

वरना vt. to choose. conj. or else, otherwise.

वरपक्ष m. group of persons related to the bridegroom present at the time of marriage.

वरांगना f. belle, pretty woman.

वराह m. 1. wild boar. 2. one of the incarnations of Lord Vishnu.

वरिष्ठ adj. senior.

वरिष्ठता f. seniority.

वरीय adj. preferable.

वरीयता f. preference.

वरुण m. Neptune, sea-god.

वर्ग m. 1. class, category, group, series, species. 2. a shape with four straight lines, square (Geom.). 3. second power. (Alg.)

वर्ग-पहेली f. crossword puzzle.

वर्गमूल m. square root.

वर्ग-संघर्ष m. class struggle.

वर्गाकार adj. of the shape of a square.

वर्गीकरण m. classification.

वर्गीकृत adj. arranged in groups or categories, classified.

वर्जन m. 1. forbiddance, ban. 2. prohibition, abandonment.

वर्जित adj. 1. forbidden, banned (by law, custom, etc.). 2. prohibited, disallowed.

वर्ण m. 1. colour. 2. class, race, tribe. 3. letter (alphabet).

वर्णक्रम m. 1. alphabetical order. 2. spectrum.

वर्णन m. description, narration, account.

वर्णनकर्ता m. narrator, relater.

वर्णनातीत adj. indescribable, beyond description.

वर्णनात्मक adj. descriptive.

वर्णभेद m. = रंगभेद।

वर्णमाला f. alphabet.

वर्ण-विचार m. orthography.

वर्ण-व्यवस्था f. Hindu classification of society into four castes.

वर्णसंकर adj. & m. crossbreed (among humans).

वर्णांध adj. colour blind.

वर्णागम m. addition of a letter to a word.

वर्णात्मक adj. alphabetic.

वर्णानुक्रमणिका f. alphabetical glossary.

वर्णाश्रम m. Hindu classification of society and life into four divisions/orders.

वर्णित adj. described.

व

वर्ण्य adj. fit to be described, describable.

वर्तन m. social dealings.

वर्तनी f. spelling.

वर्तमान adj. 1. present. 2. living, existing, being.

वर्ति f. = बत्ती।

वर्ती suffix. situated; तट ~ situated on the bank.

वर्तुल adj. circular, round.

वर्दी f. uniform, livery.

वर्धन m. increase, growth.

वर्धमान adj. increasing, grow-ing.

वर्धित adj. increased.

वर्ष m. year.

वर्षगाँठ f. birth anniversary.

वर्षा f. rain.

वर्षा-ऋतु f. rainy season.

वर्षामापक m. rain gauge.

वर्षीय adj. 1. aged. 2. of years; पंचवर्षीय योजना five year plan.

वलय m. ring.

वलयाकार adj. ringshaped.

वलित adj. coiled.

वल्कल m. bark.

वल्द adj. son of.

वल्लभ adj. & m. dear, dear one.

वल्लरी f. creeper.

वश m. control, authority, power, subjection. adv. suffix. caused by, due to; द्वेषवश out of malice.

वशीकरण m. charming (someone) into submission, bewitchment, enchantment; ~ यंत्र talisman.

वशीभूत adj. brought under control, smitten, subdued, fascinated.

वश्य adj. 1. worth controlling/ overpowering, submissive. 2. manageable.

वसंत m. spring (season).

वसंती adj. 1. vernal. 2. light yellow.

वसंतोत्सव m. spring festival.

वसन m. garment, clothing.

वसा f. fat.

वसीयत f. will.

वसुंधरा f. earth.

वसुधा f. earth.

वसूल adj. 1. realized, collected. 2. recovered.

वसूली f. 1. realization, colle- ction. 2. recovery.

वस्तु f. 1. object. 2. something of use, thing, article. 3. an article of trade.

वस्तुगत adj. objective.

वस्तुतः adv. in reality, actually, virtually, truly.

वस्तुनिष्ठ adj. objective.

वस्तुनिष्ठा f. objectivity.

वस्तु-स्थिति f. reality, actual position.

वस्त्र m. 1. clothes. 2. apparel.

वह adj. that. pron. 1. he/she/it. 2. that one.

वहन m. act of carrying, trans-portation.

वहम m. false notion, misconception, delusion.

वहमी adj. & m. 1. (one who is) prone to delusion. 2. superstitious (person).

वहशी adj. & m. savage, barbarous/ cruel (person).

वहाँ adv. there, thither, yonder.

वहीं adv. 1. at that very place. 2. right there.

वही adj. & m. the same.

वाँ suffix. denoting 'th' after numerical words, e.g. सातवाँ seventh.

वांछनीय adj. desirable.

वांछित adj. desired.

वा conj. or.

वाक़ई adv. in reality, really, indeed, infact, truly speaking.

वाक़ा m. 1. event, happening. 2. fact.

वाक़िफ़ adj. 1. familiar. 2. conversant.

वाक् f. speech.

वाक्चतुर adj. = वाक्पटु।

वाक्छल m. fraudulent talk/speech, a speech calculated to defraud/deceive, glibness, sophistry.

वाक्पटु adj. skilled in the art of talking, eloquent.

वाक्पटुता f. the art of using language in an impressive way, eloquence.

वाक्य m. sentence.

वाक्यांश m. phrase.

वाग्जाल m. 1. grand eloquence. 2. insincere but impressive speech or writing, rhetoric.

वाग्दत्ता adj. & f. (woman) betrothed/engaged.

वाग्दान m. betrothal, engagement.

वाग्मिता f. oratory.

वाग्विलास m. delightful conversation, grandiloquence.

वाङ्मय m. literature.

वाचक m. narrator.
suffix. as in गुण ~ qualitative.

वाचन m. reading.

वाचनालय m. reading room.

वाचस्पति m. profound scholar.

वाचाल adj. & m. talkative, prattler, garrulous.

वाच्य m. the form of the verb that shows the relation of the subject (or object) to the verb, voice कर्तृ ~ active voice; कर्म ~ passive voice.

वाच्यार्थ m. literal meaning.

वाजिब adj. proper, just, appropriate, reasonable.

वाजी m. horse.

वाटिका f. small garden.

वाणिज्य m. trade, commerce.

वाणी f. speech, voice, language.

वात m. one of the three/four humours of the body, wind.

वातज adj. (ailment) caused by वात।

वातानुकूलन m. airconditioning.

वातानुकूलित adj. airconditioned.

वातायन m. ventilator.

वातावरण m. atmosphere, environment.

वातुल adj. & m. talkative, gabbler, garrulous.

वात्या f. gale.

वात्सल्य m. parental affection.

वात्सल्यपूर्ण adj. affectionate.

वाद m. 1. ism. 2. suit (law court), argument.

वादक m. instrumentalist.

वादन m. playing on a musical instrument.

वाद-प्रतिवाद m. argument and counter-argument, discussion, debate, discourse.

वाद-विवाद m. 1. discussion, controversy. 2. debate.

वादा m. promise.

वादी m. 1. complainant. 2. plaintiff.

वाद्य m. musical instrument.

वाद्यवृंद m. orchestra.

वाद्यसंगीत m. insrtrumental music.

वान adj. suffix indicating possession as in भाग्यवान।

वानप्रस्थ m. a person in his third stage of life (Hindu system).

वानर m. 1. ape. 2. monkey. [Fem. वानरी]

वानस्पतिक adj. 1. vegetational. 2. botanical.

वापस adj. returned.

वापसी f. act of returning.

वापिका f. = वापी।

वापी f. tank.

वाम adj. left (side).

वामन m. 1. dwarf. 2. Vaman—(an incarnation of Lord Vishnu).

वामपक्ष m 1. left side. 2. left wing.

वामपक्षी adj. & m. leftist, left-winger.

वाममार्ग m. a Hindu Tantrik cult.

वामा f. woman.

वामावर्त adj. anti-clockwise, counter-clockwise.

वायदा m. promise.

वायन m. presents of sweets to relatives on auspicious occasions.

वायलिन m. violin.

वायव adj. aerial.

वायवीय adj. aerial, pneumatic.

वायस m. crow.

वायु f. air.

वायुमंडल m. atmosphere.

वायुमार्ग m. air-route.

वायुयान m. aeroplane.

वायुसेना f. airforce.

वायु-सेवा f. air-service.

वारंट m. warrant.

वारंवार adv. frequently, time and again, repeatedly.

वार m. 1. day. 2. stroke. suffix. signifying direction or manner; क्षेत्रवार sectorwise; हफ़्तेवार weekly.

वारण m. banning, prohibition.

वारदात f. mishap, accident.

वारना vt. to sacrifice (on someone).

वारनिश f. varnish.

वार-पार m. this end and that.

वारांगना f. harlot, prostitute.

वारा-न्यारा m. final settlement of issues.

वाराह m. wild boar.

वारि m. water.

वारिद m. cloud.

वारिधर m. cloud.

वारिधि m. ocean.

वारिस m. heir.

वारुणी f. wine.

वार्ता f. 1. conversation. 2. talk, negotiation.

वार्ताकार m. speaker, talker.

वार्तालाप m. parley, conversation.

वार्धक्य m. old age, senility.

वार्षिक adj. yearly, annual.

वार्षिकी f. annuity.

वार्षिकोत्सव m. anniversary.

वाला suffix. equivalent to 'er'; as in पानेवाला receiver.

वाष्प m. steam, vapour.

वासंतिक adj. pertaining to the spring season.

वास m. 1. abode, residence, habitation. 2. smell.

वासना f. 1. craving, longing. 2. sexual desire.

वासस्थान m. abode, residence.

वासित adj. perfumed.

वासी m. dweller, inhabitant.

वासुदेव m. 1. Lord Krishna, son of Vasudev. 2. Peepal tree.

वास्कट f. waist-coat.

वास्तव adj. factual, actual, real.

वास्तविक adj. real, actual, de facto.

वास्तविकता f. reality, actuality.

वास्ता m. dealing.

वास्तुकला f. architecture.

वास्ते, के postposition. for the sake of, for the purpose of.

वाह interj. excellent, well done, bravo!

वाहक adj. & m. 1. bearer. 2. conductor.

वाहन m. that which carries, vehicle.

वाहवाही f. applause, cheer.

वाहिका f. vessel, duct.

वाहिनी f. a division of the army.

वाहियात adj. 1. vulgar (talk). 2. undesirable (person). 3. worthless (object). m. nonsense.

वाह्य adj. portable.

विंदु m. 1. point, dot. 2. drop.

विंध्य m. a range of mountains in central India.

विंध्याचल m. = विंध्य।

वि prefix. denoting separation, contrariety, intensity etc., as in वियोग (separation), विषम (contrariety).

विकट adj. 1. horrible, monstrous, formidable. 2. onerous.

विकराल adj. monstrous, formidable.

विकर्ण m. diagonal (Geom.).

विकर्षण m. repulsion, aversion.

विकल adj. 1. restless, uneasy, not at ease. 2. agitated, perturbed.

विकलता f. restlessness.

विकलांग adj. handicapped, disabled.

विकल्प m. option, alternative.

विकसना vi. 1. to flourish, to develop. 2. to blossom/bloom.

विकसित adj. 1. developed. 2. blossomed/bloomed/budded.

विकार m. change (smacking of deterioration), deviation (from a natural state).

विकारी adj. 1. changeable, vari-able. 2. declinable; ~ रूप declinable form.

विकास m. 1. development, growth. 2. evolution.

विकासवाद m. (Theory of) Evolution, evolutionism.

विकासशील adj. developing.

विकासोन्मुख adj. developing.

विकिट f. wicket (cricket).

विकिरण m. radiation.

विकीर्ण adj. scattered, disseminated, diffused.

विकृत adj. 1. deformed, distorted. 2. changed. 3. impaired; ~ करना to impair.

विकृति f. 1. deformity. 2. distortion. 3. abnormality.

विकृष्ट adj. thrown back, repulsed.

विकेंद्रण m. decentralisation.

विकेंद्रीकरण m. decentralisation.

विक्रम m. valour, valiance.

विक्रमी adj. valorous, valiant.

विक्रय m. sale.

विक्रांत adj. valorous, valiant.

विक्रेता m. seller, salesman.

विक्रेय adj. saleable, marketable.

विक्षिप्त adj. insane, demented.

विक्षिप्तता f. insanity, dementia.

विक्षुब्ध adj. 1. agitated, perturbed, perplexed. 2. turbulent.

विक्षेप m. 1. projection. 2. deflection.

विक्षेपण m. 1. projection. (Math). 2. deflection.

विक्षोभ m. 1. agitation, perturbation. 2. turbulence.

विखंडन m. splitting, breaking up.

विखंडित adj. split up, divided into parts.

विख्यात adj. renowned, well-known, distinguished.

विख्याति f. renown, repute, fame, celebrity.

विगत adj. past, previous.

विगलन m. melting, fusion.

विगलित adj. melted, fused.

विगुण adj. devoid of merit, useless.

विग्रह m. 1. disintegration. 2. squabble, tiff.

विग्रही adj. quarrelsome, bellicose.

विघटन m. 1. decomposition. 2. disintegration. 3. dissolution.

विघटनकारी adj. causing disruption, disruptive.

विघटित adj. 1. decomposed. 2. disintegrated. 3. dissolved.

विघ्न m. 1. hindrance, obstacle, impediment. 2. interference.

विघ्नकारी adj. impeding, obstructing.

विचक्षण adj. very sagacious, farsagacious, farsighted, proficient.

विचरण m. 1. rambling, wandering. 2. variation (Maths.).

विचलन m. deviation.

विचलित adj. 1. deviated. 2. upset.

विचार m. 1. idea, thought. 2. view. 3. consideration.

विचारक m. thinker, ideologist, philosopher.

विचारगोष्ठी f. symposium or meeting for exchange of thoughts.

विचारणा f. contemplation, reasoning.

विचारणीय adj. worth consideration/considering, worth being given a thought to, ponderable.

विचारधारा f. ideology.

विचारना vi. to think (over).

विचारपूर्ण adj. thoughtful, well-considered.

विचारमग्न adj. absorbed/engrossed in thought, pensive, museful.

विचारवान, विचारवान् adj. & m. man of thought, thoughtful, sober.

विचार-विमर्श m. 1. deliberation. 2. consultation.

विचारशक्ति f. power of thinking, reasoning, intellect.

विचारशील adj. showing careful thought, rational, thoughtful, contemplative.

विचारशीलता f. thoughtfulness.

विचार-स्वातंत्र्य m. freedom of thought.

विचाराधीन adj. under consideration, pending.

विचारित adj. considered, thought, decided.

विचारोत्तेजक adj. thought-provoking/exciting/instigating.

विचार्य adj. worth considering.

विचित्र adj. 1. strange, fantastic, curious, peculiar, weird. 2. funny.

विचित्रता f. strangeness, queerness, oddity, peculiarity.

विच्छिन्न adj. 1. broken, cut off. 2. discontinued. 3. separated.

विच्छेद m. 1. break. 2. disconti-nuity. 3. separation. 4. dispersion.

विच्छेदन m. 1. disconnection. 2. amputation.

विछोह m. separation from a dear one.

विजन adj. lonely, solitary.

विजय f. triumph, success in game, contest, battle etc. win, conquest, victory.

विजयदशमी m. an Indian festival.

विजय-लक्ष्मी f. goddess of victory.

विजया f. an Indian herb known as भाँग which has an inebriating effect.

विजयादशमी f. = विजयदशमी।

विजयी adj. victorious, triumphant.

विजयोपहार m. trophy.

विजातीय adj. of foreign genus.

विजित adj. conquered.

विजेता m. The winner of a game, contest, battle etc., victor, conqueror.

विज्ञ m. one who knows, wise, learned.

विज्ञप्ति f. an official communication, comm-unique, bulletin, release.

विज्ञान m. science.

विज्ञानी m. scientist.

विज्ञापन m. advertisement; ~ करना to advertise.

विज्ञापित adj. advertised.

विज्ञेय adj. worth knowing, knowable.

विटप m. tree.

विटामिन m. vitamin.

विडंबना f. mockery, anomaly.

विडाल m. cat.

व

वितंडा m. 1. cavil. 2. imbroglio.

वितत adj. extended, expanded.

वितति f. extension.

वितरक m. distributor.

वितरण m. distribution.

वितर्क m. counter-argument.

वितान m. 1. canopy, baldachin, tent. 2. extension.

वितृष्णा f. 1. freedom from desire. 2. repulsion.

वित्त m. wealth, finance.

वित्तीय adj. financial.

विद् m. knower, scholar.

विदग्ध adj. 1. burnt up. 2. shrewd, clever.

विदा f. farewell, valediction, adieu.

विदाई f. leave-taking, farewell, send-off.

विदित adj. known.

विदीर्ण adj. lacerated, torn, split, asunder.

विदुषी f. scholarly/learned woman.

विदूषक m. buffoon, jester.

विदेश m. foreign country/land, abroad.

विदेशी adj. foreign, alien, exotic. m. foreigner.

विदेह adj. not bound by the physical body, incorporeal.

विद्ध adj. perforated, pierced.

विद्यमान, विद्यमान् adj. present, existent, alive.

विद्यमानता f. presence, existence.

विद्या f. 1. knowledge, learning. 2. know-how.

विद्यापीठ m. house of learning, school, abode of education.

विद्यार्थी m. student, learner.

विद्यालय m. school.

विद्युत f. 1. lightning. 2. electri-city.

विद्युतीकरण m. installation of electricity, electrification.

विद्रुम m. tree.

विद्रोह m. rebellion, revolt, in-surrection.

विद्रोही adj. rebellious, insurgent, revolting. m. an insurgent, rebel.

विद्वज्जन m. (plu). concourse of learned people, intelligentsia.

विद्वत्ता f. scholarship, learning, erudition.

विद्वान, विद्वान् adj. & m. learned, erudite, scholar.

विद्वेष m. ill-will, animus, animosity, malice, rancour.

विद्वेषी adj. malicious, rancorous, hostile, inimical.

विधना m. destiny, fate.

विधर्म m. a religion different from one's own.

विधर्मी adj. 1. belonging to a religion other than one's own. 2. heretic.

विधवा f. widow.

विधा f. form, type.

विधाता m. 1. creator. 2. providence. [Fem. विधात्री]

विधान m. 1. constitution. 2. le-gislation; ~ - परिषद् legislative council; ~ - मंडल legislature; ~ सभा legislative assembly.

विधायक m. lawmaker, legisla- tor.

विधायन m. legislation, enact-ment.

विधायिका f. legislature.

विधि f. 1. method, mode, system. 2. law. 3. ways, activities, movements.

विधिक adj. legal.

विधिपूर्वक adv. methodically.

विधिमान्य adj. legally acceptable, valid.

विधिवत् adv. 1. lawfully, legally. 2. duly, methodically.

विधिविहित adj. (as) prescribed by law.

विधिवेत्ता m. expert in law, jurist.

विधिशास्त्र m. Science of law, jurisprudence.

विधिशास्त्री m. jurist.

विधुर m. widower.

विधेय adj. to be done or performed. m. predicate (Gram.).

विधेयक m. bill (legislative).

विध्वंस m. destruction, devastation, demolition, desolation.

विध्वंसक adj. destructive, subversive. m. destroyer.

विनत adj. bowed low, modest.

विनति f. 1. act of bowing. 2. entreaty. 3. submission.

विनती f. entreaty.

विनम्र adj. modest, humble.

विनम्रतापूर्ण adj. full of modesty, modest, humble.

विनय m. modesty, humility.

विनयशील adj. modest, humble.

विनयी adj. polite, modest.

विनश्वर adj. perishable, destructible, transitory.

विनष्ट adj. perished, destroyed, ruined, devastated.

विनाश m. destruction all round, devastation, ruination.

विनाशकारी adj. destructive, devastating, deadly.

विनाशी adj. = विनाशकारी।

विनिधान m. allocation.

विनिमय m. exchange, barter.

विनियंत्रण m. decontrol.

विनियम m. regulation.

विनियोग m. 1. appropriation. 2. investment.

विनिवेश act of disinvesting, disinvestment.

विनिश्चय m. decision.

विनिश्चित adj. decided.

विनीत adj. bowing, modest, submissive, humble.

विनोद m. 1. amusement. 2. humour, wit.

विनोदप्रिय adj. humorous, jocular.

विनोदी adj. humorous, jocular, jocund. m. humorist.

विन्यास m. arrangement, setting, marshalling.

विपक्ष m. 1. opposite party, opponent. 2. opposition party.

विपक्षी m. opponent.

विपणन m. marketing.

विपत्ति f. 1. hardship, woe, adversity. 2. calamity, catastrophe.

विपथ m. wrong path.

विपद् f. = विपत्ति।

विपदा f. = विपत्ति।

व

विपन्न adj. distressed, afflicted.
विपरीत adj. contrary, opposite.
विपर्ण adj. without leaves.
विपर्यय m. transposition, revesr-sal.
विपर्याय m. antonym.
विपर्यास m. reversal, intercha- nge.
विपल m. one-sixtieth part of a पल ।
विपाक m. ripening, maturity.
विपिन m. forest, woods; ~ विहारी roamer of woods, i.e., Lord Krishna.
विपुत्र adj. issueless, childless.
विपुल adj. abundant, immense, ample, plenty, huge; ~ सम्पत्ति immense wealth.
विपुलता f. abundance, hugeness, immensity.
विप्र m. Brahman.
विप्रलंभ m. separation (of lov- ers).
विप्लव m. revolt, rebellion, uprising, panic, insurrection.
विप्लवी adj. revolting, rebellious.
विफल adj. 1. fruitless, futile. 2. failed, unsuccessful.
विफलता f. failure, ill-success.
विबुद्ध adj. & m. wise (man).
विबोधन m. awakening.
विभक्त adj. separated, divided, partitioned.
विभक्ति f. 1. postposition. 2. division, partition.
विभव m. 1. wealth, riches. 2. prosperity, affluence, pelf, pomp.
विभाग m. 1. division, portion. 2. department.
विभागीय adj. departmental.
विभाजक adj. dividing. m. divisor. (Maths.)
विभाजन m. division, partition.
विभाज्य adj. divisible.
विभावना f. imagination, supposition.
विभावरी f. night.
विभिन्न adj. of different kinds, diverse, various.
विभिन्नता f. diversity, variety.
विभीषिका f. dread, horror, terror, scarecrow.
विभु adj. 1. omnipresent, all pervading. 2. omnipotent, almighty. 3. onmiscient, extensively wise.
विभूति f. 1. (sacred) ash. 2. gra-ndeur. 3. great personality, personage.
विभूषण m. ornament, embellishment.
विभूषित adj. 1. ornamented, embellished. 2. adorned.
विभेद m. 1. sub-division. 2. di-visiveness
विभेदक adj. discriminating, discriminatory.
विभेदन m. 1. splitting. 2. dif-ferentiation.
विभेद्य adj. 1. pierceable. 2. dis-tinguishable.
विभोर adj. filled with joy.
विभ्रंश m. destruction.
विभ्रम m. 1. delusion. 2. confusion, perplexity, paranoia.
विभ्रांत adj. confused, perplexed.

विभ्रांति f. confusion, perplexity, hallucination.

विमत adj. dissenting, disagreeing. m. contrary view, dissenting opinion.

विमति f. dissent, disagreement.

विमर्दन m. pounding, crushing.

विमर्श m. 1. consultation, consideration. 2. deliberation.

विमल adj. 1. limpid, crystal clear. 2. pure, immaculate. 3. flawless, spotless.

विमा f. dimension.

विमाता f. step-mother.

विमान m. aeroplane.

विमानचालक m. pilot.

विमानपत्तन m. airport.

विमान-परिचारिका f. air-hostess.

विमीय adj. dimensional.

विमुक्त adj. 1. released, freed. 2. liberated, emancipated. 3. exempted.

विमुख adj. turned away (from), averse.

विमुग्ध adj. infatuated, char- med, hypnotised.

विमोचन m. 1. release. 2. liberation, emancipation.

वियुक्त adj. separated.

वियुक्ति f. separation.

वियोग m. 1. separation, parting from. 2. bereavement, detachment. 3. subtraction. (Maths.)

वियोगांत m. ending in separa- tion, having a tragic finale.

वियोगिनी f. fem. of वियोगी।

वियोगी adj. separated from the beloved one.

वियोजक adj. separative, caus- ing separation. m. subtrahend. (Maths.)

वियोजन m. 1. separation. 2. subtraction.

वियोजित adj. 1. separated. 2. subtracted. (Maths.)

वियोज्य adj. 1. separable. 2. (qu- antity) from which something is to be subtracted. (Math.).

विरंचि m. the name of ब्रह्मा।

विरंजक adj. bleaching.

विरंजित adj. bleached.

विरक्त (adj. detached (from worldly affairs).

विरक्ति f. detachment, aversion.

विरचित adj. composed, written, produced.

विरत adj. refrained, desisted.

विरति f. desistance, refrainment.

विरद m. = विरुद।

विरल adj. rare.

विरला adj. = विरल.

विरस adj. insipid, tasteless.

विरह m. separating, parting.

विरहाग्नि f. agony/anguish of separation.

विरहानल m. = विरहाग्नि।

विरहिणी f. fem. of विरही।

विरही adj. & m. (one) separated from the loved one.

विराग m. detachment.

विरागी adj. & m. (one) detached.

विराजना vi. to take seat, to be seated.

व

विराजमान adj. occupying a seat (of honour), present.

विराट् adj. large-scale, gigantic.

विराम m. 1. The action or act of stopping, stop, cessation. 2. rest. 3. an interval between periods of work, break, pause.

विराम-चिह्न m. punctuation mark.

विरासत f. heritage, inheritance.

विरुद m. eulogy, panegyric.

विरुदावली f. chain of pane- gyrics, long-drawn eulogy.

विरुद्ध adj. adverse, hostile, contrary, opposite.

विरुद्ध, के postposition. against.

विरूपण m. disfiguration, deformation.

विरूपता f. deformity.

विरूपित adj. disfigured, deformed.

विरेचक adj. laxative, purgative.

विरेचन m. purgation.

विरोध m. opposition, objection, hostility.

विरोधाभास m. paradox, apparent contradiction.

विरोधी adj. contrary, hostile.

विलंब m. delay.

विलंबन m. delaying, postponement.

विलंब-शुल्क m. late fee.

विलक्षण adj. 1. peculiar, queer. 2. odd. 3. remarkable.

विलग adj. separated, disjointed.

विलगाव m. 1. aloofness, isolation. 2. separation.

विलयन m. 1. dissolution. 2. merger.

विलाप m. wailing, lamentation, moaning.

विलायत f. 1. England. 2. any European country.

विलास m. indulgence and enjoyment of rich and comfortable living, merriment, luxury.

विलासमय adj. luxurious.

विलासी adj. pleasure-seeking.

विलीन adj. 1. absorbed, merged. 2. vanished, disappeared.

विलुप्त adj. 1. disappeared, vanished. 2. no longer used.

विलेख m. legal document, deed.

विलेप m. ointment.

विलेय adj. soluble.

विलोकन m. act of beholding.

विलोकनीय adj. worth behol- ding/ seeing.

विलोकित adj. beheld, seen, viewed.

विलोचन m. eye.

विलोड़न m. 1. act of churning. 2. thorough study.

विलोपन vt. 1. causing to disappear. 2. elimination.

विलोम adj. 1. converse, reverse. 2. inverse. 3. opposite, contrary.

विलोमक adj. depilatory.

विलोमता f. reversion.

विल्व m. wood-apple tree and its fruit.

विल्व-पत्र m. leaf of wood-apple tree.

विवक्षा f. implication, implied meaning.

विवक्षित adj. implied.

विवर m. cavity, hole.

विवरण m. 1. description, account. 2. particulars, statement, explanation.

विवरणिका f. brochure.

विवरणी f. return (of income tax etc.).

विवर्ण adj. faded, dimmed, pale.

विवर्त m. round.

विवर्तन m. going round.

विवश adj. 1. helpless. 2. compelled, forced.

विवशता f. 1. helplessness. 2. compulsion.

विवस्त्र adj. naked.

विवाचक m. arbitrator.

विवाचन m. arbitration.

विवाद m. 1. dispute. 2. controversy. 3. litigation.

विवादग्रस्त adj. controversial, disputed, under dispute/controversy.

विवादास्पद adj. controversial.

विवादी adj. discordant. m. disputant.

विवाद्य adj. 1. disputable. 2. questionable.

विवाह m. 1. marriage, wedding. 2. union.

विवाह-विच्छेद m. divorce.

विवाहोत्सव m. marriage celebration.

विविक्त adj. isolated.

विविक्ति f. isolation.

विविध adj. 1. miscellaneous. 2. diverse, various.

विविधता f. diversity, variety.

विवृत adj. open.

विवृति f. 1. interpretation. 2. commentary.

विवेक m. 1. faculty of reasoning. 2. discretion.

विवेकी adj. prudent, discreet.

विवेचन m. 1. discrimination. 2. critcal appreciation, evaluation. 3. discussion.

विवेचना f. expatiation, detailed discussion.

विवेचनीय adj. worth discussion, debatable.

विवेच्य adj. = विवेचनीय।

विशद adj. elaborate.

विशाख adj. without branches, branchless.

विशारद adj. proficient, versed in.

विशाल adj. grand, colossal, gigantic, huge.

विशालता f. 1. grandeur, hugeness. 2. enormity.

विशिष्ट adj. 1. particular, specific. 2. prominent, remarkable.

विशिष्टता f. 1. speciality, highlight. 2. singularity.

विशुद्ध adj. 1. pure, unmixed. 2. genuine.

विशुद्धि f. 1. purification. 2. purity.

विशूचिका f. cholera.

विशृंखल adj. disarrayed, disorderly, scattered.

विशेष adj. special, particular, specific.

व

विशेषक adj. & m. characteristic.

विशेषज्ञ adj. & m. specialist.

विशेषण m. 1. adjective. 2. epithet, attribute.

विशेषता f. 1. speciality. 2. characteristic feature, trait.

विशेषाधिकार m. privilege, prerogative.

विशेषीकरण m. specialization.

विशेष्य m. 1. that which is qualified. 2. a noun which is qualified by an adjective.

विश्रांत adj. reposed, relaxed.

विश्रांति f. relaxation.

विश्राम m. rest, repose, relaxation.

विश्राम-कक्ष m. 1. rest room. 2. lounge.

विश्रामालय m. retiring room.

विश्रुत adj. renowned, famous, reputed.

विश्लिष्ट adj. analysed.

विश्लेषण m. analysis.

विश्लेषणात्मक adj. analytical.

विश्लेषित adj. analysed.

विश्वंभरा f. the earth.

विश्व m. 1. universe. 2. world.

विश्वकर्मा m. God, the Architect of the universe.

विश्वकोश m. encyclopaedia.

विश्वजनीन adj. universal.

विश्वनाथ m. Lord Shiv.

विश्व-प्रसिद्ध adj. world-renowned.

विश्वविजय m. conquest of the world.

विश्वविद्यालय m. university.

विश्वव्यापी adj. world-wide, universal.

विश्वसनीय adj. credible, reliable, trustworthy.

विश्वसनीयता f. credibility, reliability.

विश्वस्त adj. relied on, reliable.

विश्वास m. 1. belief, confidence, trust. 2. faith. 3. assurance.

विश्वासघात m. perfidy, betrayal, treachery, deception.

विश्वासघाती adj. & m. betrayer, traitor.

विश्वासपात्र adj. & m. fit to be trusted, reliable, trustworthy (person).

विश्वासी adj. & m. 1. believer, trustful, faithful. 2. trustworthy, reliable.

विष m. poison, venom.

विषघ्न adj. antidote.

विषण्ण adj. gloomy, melanc- holy, saddening, depressing.

विषधर m. (poisonous) snake.

विषनाशक adj. alexipharmic.

विषम adj. 1. uneven, rough. 2. odd. 3. difficult, intricate, adverse.

विषमता f. 1. unevenness, roughness. 2. dissimilarity, contrast.

विषय m. 1. subject, subject matter. 2. theme, matter. 3. topic. 4. wordly pleasure.

विषयक adj. concerning, pertaining.

विषय-वस्तु m. subject matter.

विषय-वासना f. sensuality.

विषयांतर m. diversion, digression.

विषयी adj. sensual, carnal,

debauched, voluptuous, licentious.

विष विज्ञान m. toxicology.

विषहर adj. anti-venom.

विषहीन adj. non-poisonous.

विषाक्त adj. poisonous, toxic.

विषाण m. 1. horn (of a beast). 2. tusk (of a boar etc.).

विषाणु m. virus.

विषाद m. 1. despondency, gloom, sadness. 2. melan-choly, sorrow, grief.

विषादजनक adj. causing melancholy.

विषुव m. equinox.

विषुवत् adj. equatorial; ~ रेखा equator.

विषूचिका f. cholera.

विषैला adj. poisonous, venomous.

विष्ठा f. excrement, faeces.

विष्णु m. Lord Vishnu, the Preserver.

विसंगत adj. inconsistent, irrelevant, incoherent, discrepant.

विसंघटित adj. 1. disorganised. 2. disarranged.

विसम्मति f. dissent.

विसरण m. diffusion.

विसर्ग m. the colon-like sign (:) in Devanagri; it connotes a sound similar to the pure consonental sound of h.

विसर्जन m. 1. abandonment. 2. disposal. 3. dispersal.

विसर्जित adj. dispersed, dispo- sed.

विसैन्यीकरण m. demilitarisation.

विस्तार m. 1. extent, extension. 2. expansion, expanse.

विस्तारपूर्वक adv. in detail, extensively, elaborately.

विस्तीर्ण adj. = विस्तृत।

विस्तृत adj. 1. extensive, extended. 2. broad, spacious, wide. 3. detailed, all-round.

विस्तृति f. extension, expansion.

विस्थापन m. displacement.

विस्थापित adj. displaced.

विस्फारण m. spreading out.

विस्फीति f. deflation.

विस्फोट m. blast, explosion.

विस्फोटक adj. explosive.

विस्मय m. 1. amazement, astonishment, surprise. 2. wonder.

विस्मयकारी adj. causing amazement, amazing, astonishing, wonderful.

विस्मरण m. 1. forgetting, obli- vion. 2. forgetfulness.

विस्मरणशील adj. oblivious, forgetful.

विस्मित adj. amazed, astonished, wonderstruck.

विस्मृत adj. forgotten, lost to memory, gone into oblivion.

विस्मृति f. forgetfulness, oblivion.

विहंग m. bird.

विहंगम m. bird; ~ दृष्टि bird's eye-view.

विहग m. bird.

विहसन m. laughing.

व

विहान m. day-break, dawn.

विहार m. 1. roaming for pleasure. 2. merry-making, am-usement. 3. Buddhist monastery.

विहारी adj. & m. one who wanders for pleasure.

विहित adj. enjoined, ordained.

विहीन adj. bereft of, without.

विह्वल adj. agonisingly perturbed, vexed.

वीचि f. ripple, wave.

वीचिमाली m. ocean.

वीणा f. veena, harp, an Indian musical instrument like a lute.

वीतराग adj. = वीतरागी।

वीतरागी adj. having overcome attachment.

वीभत्स adj. & m. = बीभत्स।

वीर adj. brave, gallant, daring, valiant. m. hero, warrior.

वीरगति f. heroic end.

वीरचक्र m. an award given for gallantry in war.

वीरता f. 1. bravery, gallantry. 2. heroism.

वीरपूजा f. hero-worship.

वीरांगना f. valiant woman, heroine.

वीरान adj. desolate, deserted.

वीराना m. desolate/deserted place.

वीरोचित adj. befitting/becoming a hero.

वीर्य m. semen.

वीर्यवान् adj. virile, potent.

वुज़ू m. = वज़ू।

वुजूद m. existence, being.

वृंत m. stem, stalk.

वृंद m. congregation, assemblage, group.

वृंदगान m. chorus.

वृक्क m. kidney.

वृक्ष m. tree.

वृक्षरोपण m. plantation of tree.

वृक्षवासी adj. arboreal.

वृत्त m. 1. circle. 2. description, account.

वृत्तखंड m. sector of a circle.

वृत्तचित्र m. documentary film.

वृत्तांत m. 1. description, narra-tive. 2. account, story.

वृत्ताकार adj. circular.

वृत्ति f. 1. vocation, calling (for sustenance, livelihood). 2. disposition, mentality. 3. stipend.

वृत्ति-कर m. profession tax.

वृत्तीय adj. 1. pertaining to a circle. 2. vocational, professional.

वृथा adv. in vain, uselessly.

वृद्ध adj. aged, elderly.

वृद्धा f. old woman.

वृद्धावस्था f. old age, senility.

वृद्धि f. 1. increase, enhancement. 2. growth.

वृश्चिक m. 1. scorpion. 2. Scorpio, the eighth sign of zodiac.

वृष m. bull.

वृषभ m. 1. bull. 2. Taurus, the second sign of zodiac.

वृष्टि f. rain.

वृहत् adj. = बृहत्।

वृहस्पति m. = बृहस्पति।

वेंकटेश m. Lord Vishnu.

वे adj. those; ~ दिन those days. pron. they.

वेग m. velocity, speed.

वेगमापी m. speedometer.

वेगवान, वेगवान् adj. fleet, swift.

वेणी f. braid (of hair).

वेणु m. flute.

वेतन m. pay, salary.

वेतनभोगी adj. salaried, stipendiary.

वेतनमान m. seale of pay, pay-scale.

वेताल m. = बैताल।

वेत्ता m. a person having knowledge of something. suffix. proficient, well-versed; तत्त्व ~ well-versed in Metaphysics.

वेद m. 1. ancient Hindu scriptures, Vedas. 2. divine (knowledge).

वेदज्ञ m. one who is well-versed in the Vedas.

वेदना f. agony, afflication, tor-ment.

वेदपाठ m. recitation of the Vedas.

वेदमंत्र m. Vedic hymn.

वेदसम्मत adj. sanctioned by the Vedas.

वेदांत m. highest form of philosophy as per the Vedas.

वेदिका f. small altar.

वेदी f. altar.

वेदोक्त adj. ordained by the Vedas.

वेध m. = वेधन।

वेधन m. 1. act of piercing, perforation. 2. observation.

वेधशाला f. observatory.

वेधित adj. pierced, perforated.

वेधी adj. piercing.

वेला f. time, moment.

वेश m. 1. dress, costume, apparel. 2. guise.

वेशधारी adj. in the guise of.

वेशभूषा f. garments, apparel and get-up etc.

वेश्या f. prostitute.

वेश्यालय m. brothel.

वेश्यावृत्ति f. the practice of working as a prostitute, prostitution.

वेष m. = वेश।

वेष्टन m. 1. wrapping, enveloping. 2. wrapper, envelope.

वैकल्पिक adj. optional, alternative.

वैकुंठ m. 1. Vishnu's abode. 2. heaven.

वैकुंठ-लोक m. paradise.

वैचारिक adj. ideological.

वैजयंती f. trophy.

वैज्ञानिक adj. scientific. m. scientist.

वैतनिक adj. stipendiary, sala- ried, paid.

वैतरणी f. legendary river which flows between this world and the world hereafter.

वैताल m. = बैताल।

वैदिक adj. pertaining or related to the Vedas.

वैदूर्य m. a precious stone, beryl.

वैदेशिक adj. foreign, pertaining to a foreign country.

वैद्य m. Ayurvedic physician.

वैद्यक m. Ayurvedic system of medicine.

वैध adj. legally accepted, affected

व

or used, valid, legitimate.

वैधता f. validity, legitimacy.

वैधव्य m. widowhood.

वैधानिक adj. constitutional.

वैभव m. 1. grandeur, magnificence. 2. wealth and glory.

वैभवशाली adj. 1. grand, magnificent. 2. wealthy and glorious.

वैमनस्य m. animosity, rancour.

वैमानिक adj. aeronautical. m. pilot.

वैमानिकी f. aeronautics.

वैयक्तिक adj. 1. personal. 2. individual.

वैयक्तिकता f. individuality.

वैयाकरण m. an expert in grammar, grammarian.

वैर m. enmity.

वैरागी adj. & m. (one) who has renounced mundane affairs, recluse, mendicant.

वैराग्य m. dispassion, non-attachment, renunciation.

वैरी m. foe, enemy.

वैवाहिक adj. matrimonial.

वैशाख m. second month of the Hindu calendar.

वैशाखनंदन m. donkey, ass.

वैशेषिक m. one of the six sys-tems of Indian Philosophy.

वैश्य m. third of the four castes of Hindu social system.

वैश्वानर m. fire, the Almighty.

वैश्वीकरण m. globalization.

वैष्णव m. 1. devotee of Lord Vishnu. 2. an orthodox sect among the Hindus.

वैसा adj. of that kind, like that.

वैसे adv. in that way.

वोट m. vote.

व्यंग्य m. irony, sarcasm, satire.

व्यंग्य-चित्र m. cartoon.

व्यंग्यार्थ m. suggested meaning.

व्यंजक adj. 1. expressive. 2. suggestive. m. expression. (Maths.)

व्यंजन m. 1. consonant. 2. an article of food, usually cooked, dainty dish. 3. act of expressing.

व्यंजना f. suggested meaning.

व्यक्त adj. 1. explicit, expressed. 2. manifested.

व्यक्ति m. 1. person. 2. individual.

व्यक्तिगत adj. personal, indivi- dual.

व्यक्तित्व m. 1. personality. 2. individuality.

व्यक्तिनिष्ठ adj. subjective.

व्यक्तिवाचक संज्ञा f. Proper Noun.

व्यक्तीकरण m. individualisation, personalisation.

व्यग्र adj. restless, perturbed, bewildered, perplexed.

व्यग्रता f. restlessness, perturbation, perplexity.

व्यजन m. 1. hand fan. 2. act of fanning.

व्यतिक्रम m. 1. violation of established/traditional order. 2. deviation.

व्यतिरेक m. distinction by cont-rast, contradistinction.

व्यतिरेकी adj. contrastive.

व्यतीत adj. passed, past (time).

व्यथा f. anguish, agony.

व्यथित adj. in agony.

व्यभिचार m. 1. adultery. 2. fornication.

व्यभिचारिणी f. adultress, lewd woman.

व्यभिचारी m. one who commits adultery, lewd, adulterer, libertine.

व्यय m. expenditure, expense, expending.

व्यर्थ adj. useless, pointless, futile. adv. in vain.

व्यवकलन m. subtraction.

व्यवच्छेद m. separation.

व्यवधान m. 1. hindrance, impediment, obstruction. 2. interruption, intervention.

व्यवसाय m. 1. vocation, calling, profession, occupation. 2. trade, business.

व्यवसायिक adj. = व्यावसायिक।

व्यवसायी adj. 1. professional. 2. mercantile. m. merchant, trader, businessman, dealer.

व्यवस्था f. 1. arrangement. 2. system. 3. order. 4. ruling.

व्यवस्थापक m. 1. manager. 2. organiser.

व्यवस्थापन m. organisation, management.

व्यवस्थित adj. 1. organised, well-managed. 2. syste-matised, methodical.

व्यवहार m. 1. behaviour. 2. dealing. 3. use, practice.

व्यवहार-कुशल adj. practical, worldlywise, dextrous.

व्यवहार-बुद्धि f. practical wis- dom.

व्यवहार्य adj. practicable, feasible.

व्यवहृत adj. used, utilised.

व्यष्टि m. individual.

व्यसन m. 1. addiction, evil habit. 2. hobby; विद्या - ~ hobby of learning.

व्यसनी m. addict.

व्यस्त adj. busy, engaged, occupied.

व्याकरण m. Grammar.

व्याकरणिक adj. grammatical.

व्याकुल adj. agitated, perturbed, restless.

व्याकुलता f. perturbation, restlessness.

व्याख्या f. 1. explanation, elaboration, expatiation. 2. commentary, annotation.

व्याख्याकार m. 1. commentator. 2. interpreter.

व्याख्याता m. 1. exponent. 2. lecturer.

व्याख्यात्मक adj. explanatory, annotated.

व्याख्यान m. lecture, speech.

व्याघात m. 1. blow, stroke. 2. hindrance, obstruction, obstacle.

व्याघ्र m. tiger.

व्याज m. 1. pretext, pretence. 2. = ब्याज।

व्याजस्तुति f. ironical commendation.

व्याजोक्ति f. ironical statement.

व्याध m. hunter, fowler.

व

व्याधि f. ailment, malady, disease.

व्यापक adj. 1. pervading, pervasive. 2. extensive, widespread. 3. comp-rehensive.

व्यापना vt. to pervade, to spread through/over.

व्यापार m. business, trade, trading.

व्यापार-बुद्धि f. business apti- tude/ tact.

व्यापार-संघ m. mercantile association.

व्यापारिक adj. commercial, mercantile.

व्यापारी m. trader, tradesman, merchant, businessman, dealer.

व्यापी adj. pervading, pervasive.

व्याप्त adj. pervaded, permeated.

व्याप्ति f. pervasiveness, pervasion.

व्याप्य adj. pervasive.

व्यामोह m. 1. infatuation, fascination. 2. bewilderment, embarrassment.

व्यायाम m. physical exercise, bodily exercise, athletic.

व्यायामशाला f. gymnasium.

व्याल m. snake.

व्यावसायिक adj. professional, vocational, occupational, pertaining to business.

व्यावहारिक adj. 1. practical, realistic, down-to-earth. 2. applied.

व्यावहारिकता f. The state or quality of being practical or realistic, practicality.

व्यास m. diameter.

व्यासपीठ n. pulpit.

व्युत्क्रम m. 1. reversal (as 'dab' of 'bad'). 2. reciprocal (as $^3/2$ of $^2/3$).

व्युत्क्रमण m. 1. reversal. 2. reciprocation.

व्युत्पत्ति f. derivation, etymology.

व्युत्पत्तिक adj. derivative, etymological.

व्युत्पन्न adj. derived, derivative.

व्युत्पन्नमति adj. ready wit, witty.

व्यूह m. battle array, disposition of army.

व्योम m. sky, space.

व्योमचारी adj. sky-going/faring.

व्रजन m. roaming, wandering.

व्रण m. wound.

व्रत m. 1. vow, pledge. 2. fast.

व्रती adj. & m. 1. (one) who has taken a vow/pledge. 2. (one) who is observing/keeping a fast.

व्रीड़ा f. bashfulness, modesty.

श

श m. first sibilant of the Nagari alphabet; its sound resem-bles that of s in sugar.

शंकर m. Lord Shiv.

शंका f. 1. doubt, apprehension. 2. an objection started in disputation.

शंकाकुल adj. perturbed by doubt.

शंका-निवारण m. removing a doubt.

शंकालु adj. & m. (a person) of a suspicious disposition, inclined to doubt.

शंकित adj. 1. full of doubt/suspicion. 2. alarmed, apprehensive.

शंकु m. cone, peg.

शंख m. 1. conch. 2. hundred billions.

शंबु m. snail.

शऊर m. mannerliness, manners, wisdom, shrewdness.

शक m. 1. suspicion, uncertainty. 2. doubt.

शकट m. cart.

शकर f. = शक्कर।

शकरकंद m. sweet potato.

शकरकंदी f. sweet potato.

शकल f. = शक्ल।

शक संवत् m. an era introduced by emperor Shalivahan in 78A.D.

शकुंत m. bird.

शकुन m. 1. bird. 2. omen, augury.

शकुन-विचार m. augury.

शकुनी m. augur, soothsayer.

शक्कर f. sugar.

शक्की adj. of a doubting/ suspi- cious nature, sceptical, whimsical.

शक्की-मिज़ाज adj. = शक्की।

शक्ति f. 1. power. 2. physical strength, might, energy. 3. Goddess of power.

शक्ति-पूजा f. worship of Shakti, the Goddess of power.

शक्तिवर्धक adj. energy-giving, nutritive, invigorating.

शक्ति-संतुलन m. balance of power.

शक्तिसंपन्न adj. full of power/ strength/energy.

शक्तिहीन adj. powerless, devoid of energy, enervated.

शक्य adj. possible, feasible.

शक्ल f. 1. countenance, looks, appearance. 2. shape, form.

शक्ल-सूरत f. appearance, looks.

शख़्स m. person, individual.

शग़ल m. hobby, pastime, occupation.

शगुन m. an auspicious ceremony performed as a token, token of betrothal ceremony given by the bride's party.

शगुनिया m. augur, diviner.

शगूफ़ा m. 1. bud, blossom. 2. squib, utterance calculated to let off a quarrel; ~ छोड़ना set off a squib.

शजरा m. 1. geneological table/

श

tree. 2. map of rural holdings.

शठ adj. & m. wicked, rogue, knave, cunning.

शत adj. & m. hundred.

शतक m. 1. one hundred. 2. a century.

शतदल m. lotus.

शतपद m. centipede.

शतरंज f. chess.

शतरंजी f. 1. chessboard. 2. carpet with a chessboard design. m. good chess-player.

शतवार्षिकी f. centenary.

शतशः adv. in a hundred ways.

शतांश m. 1. hundredth part. 2. scanty, meagre.

शताब्दी f. 1. century, 100 years. 2. centenary.

शतायु adj. 100 years old, centenarian.

शती f. a period of 100 years, century.

शत्रु m. enemy, foe, opponent.

शत्रुता f. enmity, hostility, animosity; ~ बरतना to behave inimically.

शनाख़्त f. identification.

शनि m. 1. Saturn, the seventh of the nine planets. 2. = शनिवार।

शनिवार m. Saturday.

शनैः शनैः adv. gradually, by degrees.

शपथ f. oath, swearing.

शपथ-पत्र m. an affidavit.

शपथपूर्वक adv. on oath, under oath.

शफ़तालू m. a kind of peach, nectarine.

शबनम f. dew.

शब्द m. word.

शब्दकोश m. dictionary, lexicon.

शब्दचयन m. 1. act of collecting or selecting words. 2. words selected to express an idea, wording.

शब्दचित्र m. word-sketch.

शब्दजाल m. 1. word-trap. 2. circumlocution.

शब्दभेद m. part of speech.

शब्दवेधी बाण m. arrow which follows the track of a sound.

शब्दशः adv. verbatim.

शब्दशक्ति f. word-power, force of a word.

शब्दसंग्रह m. collection of words, glossary.

शब्दहीन adj. 1. speechless. 2. fin- ding no words to say.

शब्दातीत adj. beyond words/ description.

शब्दानुवाद m. literal translation.

शब्दान्वय m. parsing.

शब्दालंकार m. embellishment of language based on the arrangement of words.

शब्दावली f. 1. list of words in proper order. 2. terminology. 3. wording.

शम m. tranquillity/peace of mind.

शमन m. 1. act of extinguishing. 2. slaking, quenching, allaying.

शमशीर f. sword.

शमा f. burning candle/lamp.

शमित adj. 1. extinguished. 2. slaked, quenched, allayed.

शयन m. sleeping, turning in.
शयन-कक्ष m. bed-room.
शयनागार m. bed-chamber.
शयनिका f. bunk, sleeping berth.
शय्या f. 1. bedstead. 2. bed. 3. couch.
शय्याग्रस्त adj. bed-ridden.
शर (shar) m. arrow.
शरच्चंद्र m. autumnal moon.
शरण f. 1. refuge, shelter. 2. asylum.
शरणागत adj. & m. (one) who has come to seek shelter, refugee.
शरणार्थी m. refugee [Fem. शरणार्थिन]
शरत, शरत् f. autumn.
शरद, शरद् f. autumn.
शरबत m. 1. syrup. 2. sweet beverage.
शरबती adj. of the colour of शरबत, light rosy, pink.
शरम f. = शर्म।
शरमाना vi. to feel shy.
शरशय्या f. bed of arrows.
शराकत m. 1. participation. 2. partnership.
शरापना vt. to curse, to imprecate.
शराफ़त f. gentlemanlinesss.
शराब f. wine, liquor.
शराबख़ाना m. 1. distillery. 2. liquor bar.
शराबी adj. & m. drunkard.
शराबोर adj. soaked to the skin, drenched.
शरारत f. mischief, naughtiness.
शरारती adj. & m. 1. naughty (person). 2. mischievous or trouble-maker.
शरीक adj. participating, associating. m. 1. partner. 2. relative.
शरीफ़ adj. noble, gentlemanly.
शरीफ़ा m. custard apple.
शरीर adj. 1. naughty. 2. mischievous. m. body.
शरीरधारी adj. incarnate.
शरीरविज्ञान m. Physiology.
शरीरांत m. death, demise.
शरीरी adj. physical, corporal, corporeal.
शर्करा f. sugar.
शर्त f. 1. condition, terms. 2. wager, bet.
शर्तिया adv. surely, certainly, assuredly.
शर्म f. 1. shame. 2. shyness.
शर्मनाक adj. shameful, disgraceful.
शर्मिंदा adj. ashamed.
शर्मीला adj. shy, bashful, modest.
शलक m. scale (of fish).
शलग़म m. turnip.
शलजम m. = शलग़म।
शलभ m. moth.
शलाका f. rod, spoke.
शल्य m. 1. thorn. 2. surgical instrument.
शल्यचिकित्सा f. 1. surgery. 2. (surgical) operation.
शव m. dead body, corpse.
शवदाह m. cremation.
शव-परीक्षा f. postmortem examination.
शवसंस्कार m. (last) funeral rites.

श

शशक m. rabbit.

शशांक m. moon.

शशि m. moon.

शस्त्र m. weapon, arms.

शस्त्रधारी m. armed soldier, warrior.

शस्त्रविद्या f. science of arms, Military Science.

शस्त्रागार m. arsenal, armoury.

शस्त्रीकरण m. armament.

शस्य m. = सस्य।

शहंशाह m. king of kings, emperor.

शहंशाही adj. royal, regal, kingly. f. 1. state of being a शहंशाह। 2. reign of a शहंशाह।

शह f. 1. check (in chess). 2. lift, incitement.

शहज़ादा m. prince.

शहज़ादी f. princess.

शहतीर m. beam.

शहतूत m. mulberry tree and its fruit.

शहद m. honey.

शहनाई f. an Indian clarionet, oboe.

शहबाला m. a young boy who accompanies the bridegroom.

शहर m. town, city.

शहरी adj. belonging to a city or town, urban.

शहसवार m. horse-rider, horse-man.

शहादत f. 1. testimony, evidence. 2. martyr's suffering or death, martyrdom.

शहाना adj. 1. royal, regal. 2. majestic.

शहीद adj. & m. martyr.

शांत adj. 1. tranquil, calm, serene. 2. peaceful. 3. silent, quiet.

शांतचित्त adj. calm by nature, of a peaceful mind.

शांति f. 1. tranquillity, calm. 2. peace. 3. silence, quietude.

शांतिदायक adj. tranquillizing, pacifying, peace-giving.

शांतिपूर्ण adj. peaceful.

शांति-प्रक्रिया f. peace process.

शांतिभंग m. breach of peace.

शांति-संधि f. peace treaty.

शाक m. (leafy) vegetable.

शाकाहार m. 1. vegetarian food. 2. vegetarian diet.

शाकाहारी adj. & m. vegetarian.

शाक्त m. worshipper of Goddess of Power.

शाखा f. 1. a branch of a tree. 2. a branch of any business firm. 3. a division of a larger system. 4. offshoot.

शागिर्द adj. & m. pupil, disciple.

शातिर adj. extremely bad, vile.

शादी f. marriage.

शान m. 1. pomp. 2. splendour, grandeur. 3. grace.

शानदार adj. magnificent, splendid, grand, great.

शाप m. curse, imprecation.

शापग्रस्त adj. cursed, accursed.

शाबाश int. Bravo, Well Done.

शाबाशी f. applause (for chee- ring up).

शाब्दिक adj. verbal, literal.

शाम f. evening.

शामत f. ill-luck.
शामियाना m. canopy.
शामिल adj. included.
शायक m. arrow.
शायद adv. perhaps.
शायर m. poet.
शायरी f. poetry.
शायिका f. (Rly.) sleeper, sleeping berth.
शायी adj. prostrate, lying down.
शारदा f. Goddess of learning.
शारदीय adj. autumnal.
शारीर adj. bodily, physical.
शारीरिक adj. bodily, physical.
शार्क m. shark.
शार्दूल m. lion, tiger.
शाल m. shawl.
शाला f. house as in गोशाला, धर्मशाला।
शालिनी f. fem. of शाली।
शाली suffix. denoting possession; शक्ति ~ powerful.
शालीन adj. 1. graceful, serene. 2. decent.
शालीनता f. 1. grace, sobriety. 2. decency.
शावक m. young one of an animal or bird.
शाश्वत adj. eternal, perpetual, everlasting.
शासक m. ruler.
शासकीय adj. official, governmental.
शासन m. 1. governance. 2. government, rule.
शासन-व्यवस्था f. system of government.
शासनिक adj. governmental.
शासित adj. ruled, governed.
शास्ति f. sanction, provision for enforcing obedience to law.
शास्त्र m. 1. branch of knowledge. 2. scripture; ~ विरुद्ध opposed to the scriptures; ~ सम्मत sanctioned by the scriptures.
शास्त्रार्थ m. debate on the scriptures or interpretation there-of.
शास्त्री m. scholar of the scriptures.
शास्त्रीय adj. 1. classical. 2. scriptural. 3. academic.
शास्त्रोक्त adj. as ordained by the shastras.
शाहंशाह m. = शहंशाह।
शाह m. 1. king. 2. master.
शाहख़र्च m. spendthrift, prodigal, extravagant.
शाहज़ादा m. = शहज़ादा।
शाहाना adj. kingly, princely.
शाही adj. 1. kingly, royal. 2. majestic.
शिकंजा m. 1. clamp. 2. grip, clutches.
शिकन f. 1. crease. 2. wrinkle.
शिकमी m. subtenant.
शिकवा m. grouse, grumble, (sweet) complaint.
शिकस्त f. defeat, knock-down.
शिकस्ता adj. worn out, decrepit, crumbling.
शिकायत f. 1. complaint. 2. grievance. 3. trouble; पेट की ~ stomach trouble.
शिकार m. 1. victim, prey. 2. game; ~ करना to hunt.
शिकारा m. cosy boat (Kashmir).
शिकारी m. huntsman, hunter.
शिक्षक m. educator, teacher.
शिक्षण m. 1. teaching. 2. education.

श

शिक्षा f. 1. education. 2. instruction.
शिक्षा-परिषद् f. academic council, board of education.
शिक्षाप्रद adj. instructive, educative.
शिक्षार्थी m. 1. learner. 2. pupil, student.
शिक्षालय m. school, educational institution.
शिक्षाशास्त्र m. Pedagogy.
शिक्षित adj. 1. educated. 2. literate.
शिक्षु m. apprentice.
शिखंडी m. 1. an effeminate warrior. 2. effeminate man.
शिखर m. apex, summit, peak.
शिखा f. 1. tuft of hair on the crown. 2. pointed flame. 3. crown of a peacock. 4. pinnacle, apex.
शिखी m. peacock.
शिगूफ़ा = शगूफ़ा।
शिथिल adj. 1. lax, not strict/severe. 2. flaccid.
शिथिलता f. laxity.
शिथिलीकरण m. act or process of relaxation.
शिद्दत f. severity, intensity.
शिनाख़्त f. identification.
शिर m. head.
शिरस्त्राण m. helmet.
शिरस्थ adj. topping, outstanding.
शिरा f. vein.
शिरोधार्य adj. reverentially accepted.
शिरोमणि m. 1. crest jewel. 2. topping person.
शिरोरेखा f. headline of the letters (as in Devanagri Script), upper bar.
शिरोबिंदु m. apex, zenith.
शिला f. rock, piece of stone.
शिलान्यास m. laying a foundation stone.
शिलालेख m. petrograph, inscription.
शिल्प m. The skill at making particular things with the hands, craft.
शिल्पकार m. craftsman.
शिल्पकौशल m. craftsmanship.
शिल्पशाला f. school for teaching crafts.
शिल्पी m. craftsman.
शिव m. Lord Shiv, one of the three chief gods of the Hindus; God, the Destroyer.
शिवलिंग m. phallus, worshipped as a symbol of Shiva.
शिवालय m. temple dedicated to Lord Shiva.
शिवाला m. = शिवालय।
शिविका f. palanquin.
शिविर m. camp.
शिशिर m. latter half (the colder part) of winter.
शिशु m. infant, baby.
शिशु-बलि f. child sacrifice.
शिशु-हत्या f. infanticide.
शिश्न m. penis, male organ.
शिष्ट adj. civilised, courteous, mannerly.
शिष्टता f. civility, courtesy.
शिष्टमंडल m. delegation, deputation.
शिष्टाचार m. 1. etiquette, usual formality, good manners. 2. courtesy, comity.

शिष्य m. disciple, pupil.
शीघ्र adv. speedily, soon, quickly. adj. quick, prompt, rapid, speedy.
शीघ्रता f. quickness, swiftness, promptness.
शीत adj. 1. cold. 2. frigid.
शीतक m. cooler.
शीत कटिबंध m. frigid zone.
शीतकाल m. winter season.
शीतयुद्ध m. cold war.
शीतल adj. 1. cool. 2. cold.
शीतलता f. 1. coolness. 2. coldness.
शीत लहरी f. cold wave.
शीतला f. 1. smallpox. 2. goddess of smallpox.
शीतागार m. cold storage.
शीतोष्ण adj. temperate, moderate.
शीत्कार m. hissing sound.
शीरा m. 1. molasses, treacle. 2. syrup.
शीर्ष m. 1. apex, summit, top. 2. vertex.
शीर्षक m. 1. heading, title. 2. headline (in a newspaper).
शीर्षविंदु m. apex, vertical point, zenith.
शीर्षस्थ adj. highest in posi-tion, topmost, topranking.
शीर्षस्थान m. top position.
शील m. 1. disposition. 2. (deferential) modesty, propriety.
शीलभंग m. 1. outrage of mode- sty. 2. rape.
शीलवती adj. (woman) deferentially modest.
शीलवान, शीलवान् adj. deferentially modest.
शीश m. head.
शीशम m. rosewood.
शीशमहल m. house of mirrors.
शीशा m. 1. glass. 2. mirror, looking glass.
शीशी f. phial.
शुंड m. trunk (of an elephant).
शुक m. parrot.
शुक्ति f. oyster.
शुक्र m. 1. semen. 2. planet Venus. 3. Friday. 4. thanks.
शुक्रवार m. Friday.
शुक्राना m. money offered by way of thanksgiving.
शुक्रिया m. thanks.
शुक्ल adj. 1. white. 2. spotlessly clean.
शुचि adj. pure, sacred.
शुचिता f. 1. cleanliness. 2. purity, sanctity.
शुतुरमुर्ग m. ostrich.
शुद्ध adj. 1. pure, unadulterated, chaste, accurate, genuine. 2. correct, right. 3. net.
शुद्धता f. 1. purity. 2. accuracy.
शुद्धि f. 1. purification. 2. correction, rectitude.
शुद्धिपत्र m. errata, corrigendum.
शुभंकर m. mascot.
शुभ adj. 1. auspicious. 2. good.
शुभचिंतक adj. & m. benevolent, well-wisher.
शुभागमन m. gracious arrival.
शुभाशीष f. gracious benediction.
शुभ्र adj. white, bright, radiant.
शुमार m. count.
शुरुआत f. beginning.

श

शुरू m. beginning, start, commencement.
शुल्क m. 1. fee. 2. subscription. 3. duty.
शुश्रूषा f. nursing.
शुष्क adj. dry, arid.
शूकर m. pig, boar.
शूटिंग m. shooting of a film.
शूद्र m. a member of the lowest of the four classess of Hindu society.
शून्य adj. empty, vacant. m. 1. cypher, zero. 2. not hing-ness, void.
शून्यक m. vacuum.
शून्यभाव m. vacant look.
शूर adj. brave, valorous, gallant.
शूरता f. bravery, valour, gallantry.
शूरवीर adj. & m. valiant (person).
शूल m. 1. prong, thorn. 2. stabbing pain.
शूलना vt. to inflict pain, to torture.
शृंखला f. 1. chain. 2. series.
शृंखलाबद्ध adj. arrayed in series.
शृंग m. 1. summit, peak. 2. horn.
शृंगार m. 1. make-up, adornment. 2. ornamentation.
शृंगारिक adj. amatory, amorous, erotic.
शृंगी adj. horned.
शृगाल m. jackal. [Fem. शृगाली]
शेख़ m. one of the four subdivisions amongst Muslims.
शेख़चिल्ली m. a legendary foolish person.
शेखर m. apex, summit, top.
शेख़ी f. boasting, gasconade.
शेख़ीबाज़ m. boastful, vainglorious.
शेड m. 1. shed. 2. shade.
शेफाली f. Vitex negundo.
शेयर m. share.
शेर m. 1. tiger. 2. couplet in Urdu poetry.
शेरपा m. Sherpa.
शेरबच्चा m. dauntless, fearless person.
शेरबबर m. lion.
शेरवानी f. a long fitting coat.
शेष m. 1. remainder. 2. residue, rest, outstanding. 3. balance.
शेषनाग m. (in Hindu mythology) thousand-headed serpent who is supposed to support the earth on his head.
शेषशायी m. Lord Vishnu who is supposed to sleep over शेषनाग।
शेषांश m. remaining part.
शै f. thing.
शैक्षणिक adj. academic.
शैक्षिक adj. educational.
शैतान adj. naughty, mischievous. m. Satan, Lucifer.
शैतानी adj. Satanic, mischievous.
शैथिल्य m. laxity, looseness, lethargy, relaxation.
शैल m. rock.
शैली f. style, method, mode.
शैलेंद्र m. Himalayas.
शैव adj. of or pertaining to Lord Shiv. m. Lord Shiv's devotee.
शैवाल m. moss, algae.
शैशव m. infancy, childhood.
शोक m. 1. sorrow, grief, distress. 2. mourning, dolour.
शोकग्रस्त adj. grief-stricken, bereaved.

शोकमय adj. sorrowful, woeful, mournful.

शोकसंतप्त adj. bereaved.

शोकसंदेश m. message of condolence.

शोकसभा f. condolence meeting.

शोख़ adj. 1. impertinent, insolent, rude. 2. aggressive, offensive; ~ रंग aggressive colour.

शोख़ी f. impertinence, insolence.

शोच m. sorrow, grief.

शोचनीय adj. 1. critical, causing anxiety. 2. deplorable.

शोणित m. blood.

शोथ m. swelling.

शोध m. 1. research. 2. repayment.

शोधक m. 1. corrector. 2. purifier. 3. refiner.

शोध-क्षमता f. solvency.

शोधन m. 1. correction. 2. purification. 3. cleansing, refinement, expurgation.

शोधना vt. to correct/purify/cleanse.

शोभन adj. 1. graceful. 2. befi- tting, becoming, beautiful.

शोभनीय adj. = शोभन।

शोभा f. beauty, grace, splend-our, glory.

शोभामय adj. splendid, beautiful.

शोभायमान adj. graceful, lustrous, magnificent.

शोभित adj. radiant, embellished.

शोर m. noise.

शोरबा m. soup, broth.

शोरा m. saltpetre, sodium nitrate.

शोला m. flame of fire.

शोशा m. 1. projecting point. 2. raised point in some Arabic letters. 3. inciting topic.

शोषक m. 1. exploiter. 2. absorber. 3. withering.

शोषण m. 1. absorption. 2. exploitation.

शोषित adj. exploited.

शोहदा m. scoundrel, rogue.

शोहरत f. fame, renown.

शौक़ m. 1. hobby. 2. fondness.

शौक़ीन adj. 1. stylish, fashionable. 2. foppish.

शौच m. 1. evacuation, natural ablution. 2. purification.

शौचालय m. lavatory.

शौर्य m. chivalry, heroism, valour, bravado.

शौहर m. husband.

श्मशान m. cremation ground.

श्याम adj. dark-complexioned, black. m. Lord Krishna.

श्यामपट्ट m. black-board.

श्यामल adj. dark-complexioned.

श्यामला f. brunette.

श्रद्धांजलि f. homage.

श्रद्धा f. reverence, faith, venerability.

श्रद्धालु adj. devotional, reverent, faithful.

श्रद्धेय adj. reverend, venerable.

श्रम m. hard work, labour.

श्रमजीवी m. labourer.

श्रमदान m. contribution of labour (for some charitable purpose).

श्रम-विधि f. labour law (s).

श्रम-विभाजन m. division of labour.

श्रमशील adj. hard-working, laborious, assiduous.

श्रमसाध्य adj. arduous, strenuous.

श

श्रमिक m. labourer.

श्रवण m. 1. act of hearing. 2. ear, organ of hearing.

श्रवणेंद्रिय f. organ of hearing, ear.

श्रव्य adj. audible.

श्रांत adj. wearied, tired.

श्रांति f. weariness, fatigue, tiredness.

श्रावण m. = सावन।

श्रावणी f. festival of रक्षाबंधन celebrated on the full-moon day of श्रावण।

श्री f. wealth and glory.

श्रीगणेश m. debut, commencement (of some work), beginning.

श्रीमंत adj. prosperous, aristocratic, rich, wealthy.

श्रीमन m. = श्रीमान।

श्रीमान, श्रीमान् m. 1. respectful form of addressing someone, as Sir, Mr. etc. 2. title appended to a name for respect.

श्रीमुख m. glowing/radiant face (respectful form of referring to the face of someone).

श्रीयुत, श्रीयुत् m. = श्रीमान।

श्रीहीन adj. lacking in colour/lustre/glory, lustreless.

श्रुत adj. heard, perceived through the ear.

श्रुति f. 1. that which can be heard. 2. sound. 3. saying. 4. (gram.) glide.

श्रेणी f. 1. grade, class. 2. series, row, line.

श्रेय m. credit (for achieving some object).

श्रेष्ठ adj. 1. best. 2. prominent.

श्रेष्ठता f. prominence, primacy.

श्रोता m. listener.

श्लाघा f. admiration, commendation.

श्लाघ्य adj. admirable, commendable.

श्लिष्ट adj. united, joined together.

श्लील adj. refined, not vulgar.

श्लेष m. pun, equivoque, paronomasia.

श्लेष्मा f. phlegm, catarrh, mucus.

श्लोक m. couplet, hymn.

श्वदंत m. canine tooth.

श्वसन m. act of breathing/respiration.

श्वसुर m. father-in-law.

श्वान m. dog.

श्वास m. 1. breath. 2. asthma.

श्वास-नली f. bronchial pipe.

श्वास-प्रश्वास m. inhaling and exhaling.

श्वेत adj. & m. white.

श्वेतकुष्ठ m. leucoderma.

श्वेतपत्र m. white paper.

श्वेतांबर m. 1. one who dons white. 2. one of the two principal sects among Jains.

ष

ष m. second of the four sibilants of the Nagari alphabet. Its sound is like that of s in sugar.

षंड m. bull, bullock.

षकार m. the letter ष or its sound.

षट् adj. & m. six, 6.

षट्ऋतु f. the six seasons of the year.

षट्कोण m. hexagon.

षट्चक्र m. six mysterious cha-kras (cycles) of the body, according to हठयोग।

षट्रस m. six main tastes : मीठा (sweet), नमकीन (saline), कड़ुवा (bitter), तीता (pungent), कसैला (astringent), खट्टा (sour).

षड्यंत्र m. conspiracy, plot, intrigue.

षड्यंत्रकारी adj. & m. conspirator.

षण्मासिक adj. six-monthly.

षष्टि adj. & m. sixty, 60.

षष्टिपूर्ति f. completion of sixty years of age.

षष्ठी f. 1. sixth day after birth. 2. possessive case (Gram.).

षोडश adj. & m. sixteen, 16.

षोडशी f. belle of blooming sixteen.

स

स third of the four sibilants of the Nagari alphabet; its sound is like that of s in sin.

संकट m. 1. trouble, jeopardy, distress, adversity. 2. crisis.

संकटकाल m. period of crisis.

संकटापन्न adj. in distress, in trouble.

संकटावस्था f. condition of being in distress.

संकर adj. hybrid, cross.

संकरण m. cross-breeding.

संकरता f. hybridity, miscegenation, admixture.

सँकरा adj. narrow.

संकलन m. compilation, collection.

संकलनकर्ता m. compiler.

संकलित adj. compiled.

संकल्प m. resolve, determination, resolution.

संकल्पना f. concept, notion.

संकल्पित adj. resolved.

संकाय m. faculty (in an academic institution).

संकीर्ण adj. narrow, parochial.

संकीर्तन m. congregational singing (of devotional songs).

संकुचित adj. 1. contracted. 2. narrow, parochial.

संकुल adj. congested, crowded. m. complex (set of buildings).

संकेंद्रण m. concentration.

संकेत m. signal, hint.

संकेतक m. pointer.

संकेतन m. 1. signalling. 2. hin- ting, indicating. 3. notation. 4. token, sign, gesture.

संकेतित adj. 1. signalled. 2. hin-ted, indicated.

संकोच m. 1. contraction. 2. shyness, bashfulness. 3. hesitation, hitch.

संकोचवश adv. due to shyness/ hesitation.

संकोची adj. 1. shy, bashful. 2. hesitant.

संक्रमण m. 1. transition. 2. infection.

संक्रमणकाल m. period of transition, interregnum.

संक्रमणशील adj. transitional.

संक्रांति f. 1. transition. 2. transi-tion of the sun from one constellation to another.

संक्रामक adj. infectious.

संक्रिया f. operation, process.

संक्रियात्मक adj. operational.

संक्षिप्त adj. 1. brief, short, concise. 2. abridged. 3. abbreviated.

संक्षिप्ति f. brevity, abridgement.

संक्षेप m. 1. abridged form. 2. abbreviated form. 3. precis.

संक्षेपण m. 1. abridgement. 2. abbreviation. 3. precis-writing.

संक्षोभ m. perturbance, turbule-nce.

संखिया m. arsenic.

संख्यक adj. used as a suffix denoting number; अल्प ~ जाति minority community.

संख्यांक m. numeral.

संख्यांकित adj. numbered.

संख्या f. number.

संख्यावाचक adj. numerical; ~ विशेषण numerical adjective.

संग m. 1. accompaniment, company. 2. stone.

संगठन m. organisation.

संगठनात्मक adj. organisational.

संगठित adj. organised.

संगणन m. computation.

संगत adj. relevant, compatible, consistent. f. 1. association. 2. assemblage.

संगति f. 1. relevance, compatibility, consistency. 2. association, company.

संगदिल adj. cruel, merciless, hard-hearted.

संगम m. 1. confluence (of rivers). 2. junction, meeting place. 3. conjunction.

संगमन m. confluence, coming together.

संगमरमर m. marble.

संगरोध m. quarantine.

संगिनी adj. & m. female companion; जीवन ~ life-partner, wife.

संगी adj. & m. chum, companion.

संगीत m. music.

संगीतकार m. composer of music.

संगीत-नाटिका f. opera.

संगीतशास्त्री m. musicologist.

संगीतात्मक adj. musical.

संगीतालय m. house of music.

संगीन adj. grave. m. bayonet.

संगी-साथी m. (plu.) friends and companions.

संगृहीत adj. 1. collected, gat- hered. 2. compiled. 3. am-assed.

संगोष्ठी f. a conference for some discussion, symposium, seminar.

संग्रह m. 1. collection. 2. compilation.

संग्रहकर्ता m. 1. collector. 2. compiler.

संग्रहणी f. chronic diarrhoea, sprue.

संग्रहालय m. museum.

संग्राम m. 1. battle. 2. war.

संग्राहक m. one who collects things, collector.

संघ m. 1. federation. 2. union. 3. society, corporation.

संघटक m. component, constituent.

संघटन m. 1. formation, composition. 2. organisation. 3. constitution.

संघटनात्मक adj. of or pertaining to organisation, organisational.

संघ-भावना f. esprit de corps, team spirit.

संघर्ष m. 1. struggle, strife, collision, rivalry. 2. conflict. 3. fight.

संघर्षमय adj. full of struggle.

संघर्षशील adj. having a disposition of struggle.

संघर्षी adj. fricative; ~ व्यंजन fricative consonant.

स

संघात m. 1. impact. 2. blow.

संघाराम m. Buddhist monastery.

संघीय adj. 1. of or pertaining to the union. 2. federal.

संचय m. 1. accumulation. 2. collection.

संचयन m. act of accumulation/collection, storage.

संचयी adj. & m. (one) who accumulates/collects.

संचरण m. 1. movement. 2. transmission.

संचलन m. 1. movement. 2. locomotion.

संचार m. 1. communication. 2. circulation.

संचारण m. communication.

संचार-माध्यम m. media.

संचारी adj. communicable.

संचालक m. 1. conductor. 2. director.

संचालन m. 1. conduction. 2. direction.

संचित adj. accumulated, collected.

संजीदगी f. 1. sobriety. 2. seriousness, gravity.

संजीदा adj. sober, solemn.

संजीवनी f. elixir; ~ बूटी a mythological, life-giving herb.

संजोग m. = संयोग।

सँजोना vt. to keep things shipshape, to array.

संज्ञक adj. having the name.

संज्ञा f. 1. name; ~ देना to give a name. 2. Noun. 3. consciousness.

संज्ञान m. cognizance.

संज्ञापन m. act of informing, advice, communication.

सँझला adj. 1. younger than the middle (brother). 2. pertaining to evening.

संड m. bull.

संड-मुसंड adj. & m. stout & robust (fellow).

सँड़सी f. household forceps, pincers, pliers.

संडा adj. & m. stout, carefree fellow.

संडास m. latrine in the form of a pit.

संत adj. saintly. m. 1. saint. 2. ascetic, mendicant.

संतत adj. continuous (in space). [c.f. सतत continuous (in time)]

संतति f. progeny, offspring.

संतप्त adj. grieved, stricken (with grief).

संतरण m. thorough crossing.

संतरा m. 1. tangerine. 2. orange.

संतरी m. sentry, armed guard/watchman.

संतान m. issue, offspring, progeny.

संताप m. 1. grief, anguish, agony, woe. 2. remorse, compunction.

संतुलन m. 1. balance, counterbalance. 2. equilibrium.

संतुलित adj. 1. balanced. 2. even, level.

संतुष्ट adj. satisfied, gratified.

संतृप्त adj. 1. satiated, well-satisfied. 2. saturated.

संतोष m. satisfaction, contentment.

संतोषजनक adj. satisfactory, satisfying.

संतोषी adj. contented.

संत्रस्त adj. 1. tormented, tortured. 2. terrorised.

संत्रास m. 1. torment, torture. 2. terror.

संदर्भ m. 1. context. 2. reference.

संदर्भ-ग्रंथ m. reference book.

संदल m. sandal (wood).

संदिग्ध adj. 1. doubtful, dubious. 2. suspicious.

संदिग्धता f. doubtfulness, dubiety.

संदूक़ m. box.

संदूक़ची f. small box.

संदेश f. 1. message, tidings, information, news. 2. a kind of Bengali sweet.

संदेशवाहक m. messenger.

सँदेसा m. = संदेश।

संदेह m. 1. suspicion. 2. doubt, misgiving.

संदेहजनक adj. 1. suspicious. 2. doubtful.

संधान m. 1. aiming. 2. searching.

संधि f. 1. conjunction (of two different entities). 2. joint. 3. union of two sounds (Gram.). 4. treaty. 5. hole, knot.

संधिपत्र m. deed/document of treaty.

संधि-वार्ता f. negotiation for peace.

संधि-विच्छेद m. 1. annulment of treaty. 2. separation of the constituents in a conjunct word.

संधिशोथ m. arthritis.

संध्या f. 1. evening, twilight, dusk. 2. evening prayer.

संध्यावंदन m. evening prayer.

संनिविष्ट adj. 1. enclosed, attached, appended. 2. inserted.

संन्यास m. 1. the fourth and the last stage of a Hindu's life typifying renunciation of family, its affairs and also home. 2. renunciation.

संन्यासी m. ascetic, one who takes संन्यास। [Fem. संन्यासिनी]

संपत्ति f. 1. wealth, pelf, riches. 2. property, possession, effects. 3. attainments.

संपत्ति-कर m. wealth/property tax.

संपदा f. wealth, property, resources.

संपन्न adj. 1. endowed with ple-nty, prosperous, affluent. 2. accomplished, completed, fulfilled.

संपरीक्षण m. scrutiny.

संपर्क m. contact, liaison.

संपर्क-अधिकारी m. liaison officer.

संपात m. coincidence, contact.

संपाती adj. coincident.

संपादक m. editor. [Fem. संपादिका]

संपादक-मंडल m. editorial board.

संपादकीय adj. & m. editorial.

संपादन m. 1. editing. 2. accomplishment, carrying out.

संपीड़ित adj. compressed.

संपुट m. hollow of a receptacle, cavity.

संपुटिका f. capsule.

स

संपुष्ट adj. confirmed, certified.
संपूरक adj. complementary.
संपूर्ण adj. 1. entire, whole, complete. 2. completed, finished.
संपूर्णतः adv. entirely, wholly, completely.
संपूर्णता f. completion, completeness.
सँपेरा m. snake-charmer.
सँपोला m. young one of a snake.
संप्रति adv. for the time being, for the present.
संप्रदान m. 1. bestowing, giving. 2. ~ कारक dative case.
संप्रदाय m. 1. community. 2. (religious) sect. 3. school (of thought).
संप्रदायवाद m. communalism.
संप्रदायवादी adj. communalistic. m. communalist.
संप्रभु m. sovereign.
संप्रभुता f. sovereignty.
संप्रेषण m. transmission.
संप्रेषणीय adj. transmissible.
संप्रेषित adj. transmitted.
संबंध m. 1. relation, connection, relationship. 2. contact. 3. ~ कारक genitive case.
संबंधवाचक adj. possessive.
संबंधी adj. pertaining to, relating to. m. relative.
संबद्ध adj. 1. related, connected. 2. affiliated, joined.
संबल m. mainstay, support.
संबुद्ध adj. enlightened.
संबोधन m. 1. address. 2. ~ कारक vocative case.
संभरण m. supply.
सँभलना vi. 1. to pull oneself together, to come to one's self/senses. 2. to recover, to recuperate.
संभव adj. possible.
संभवतः adv. possibly, probably.
सँभाल f. looking after, care, upkeep.
सँभालना vt. to take care of, to look after.
संभावना f. possibility, likeli-hood.
संभावित adj. probable.
संभाषण m. discourse, dialogue, conversation.
संभाषी adj. speaker.
संभोग m. cohabitation, coitus.
संभोगी adj. & m. (one) who indulges in sex.
संभ्रम m. confusion, perplexity.
संभ्रांत adj. distinguished, esteemed, respectable, honourable.
संमुख, के postposition.= के सम्मुख।
संयंत्र m. fixed machinery, plant.
संयत adj. restrained, disciplined, controlled, subdued.
संयम m. restraint, discipline.
संयमी adj. & m. moderate, disciplined, sober, temperate.
संयुक्त adj. joint, united.
संयुक्त वाक्य m. compound sentence.
संयुक्त सरकार f. coalition government.
संयुत adj. conjunct.
संयोग m. coincidence, chance, accident.

संयोजक m. 1. convener. 2. = योजक, conjunction. (Gram.)

संयोजन m. combination.

संयोज्य adj. that which can be mixed/combined, combinable.

संरक्षक m. patron, guardian, supporter.

संरक्षण m. 1. patronage. 2. protection.

संरक्षित adj. 1. patronised. 2. protected, preserved.

संरक्षित राज्य m. protectorate.

संरचना f. 1. structure. 2. composition, construction.

संरचनात्मक adj. structural.

संरेखन m. alignment.

संरोध m. blockade.

संलग्न adj. 1. attached, appended, annexed. 2. adjacent, adjoining.

संवत् m. era, year, Vikram Samvat.

संवरण m. 1. choice, selection. 2. resistance.

सँवरना vi. to appear in a right/ choice make-up.

सँवरिया m. 1. the darkish one. 2. Lord Krishna, the darkish one.

संवर्ग m. cadre.

संवर्धक adj. magnifying. m. magnifier.

संवर्धन m. 1. enlargement, magnification, nourishment. 2. culture.

संवर्धित adj. 1. enlarged, magnified. 2. cultured.

संवहन m. 1. carrying. 2. conduction.

संवातन m. ventilation.

संवाद m. 1. message. 2. dialogue, conversation, news. 3. communication.

संवाददाता m. correspondent.

संवादहर m. messenger.

संवादी adj. 1. corresponding. 2. concordant.

सँवारना vt. 1. to make-up. 2. to arrange/put in proper order.

संवाहक m. conductor.

संवाहन m. conduction.

संवितरण m. disbursement.

संविदा f. contract.

संविधान m. constitution.

संविधानवाद m. constitutionalism.

संविधान-सभा f. constituent assembly, ensembly.

संविधानिक adj. = संवैधानिक।

संविधि f. a rule or law passed by an institution or Parliament, statute.

संविधिक adj. statutory.

संवीक्षक m. scrutinizer.

संवीक्षा f. scrutiny.

संवृत adj. closed.

संवृद्धि f. growth, development.

संवेग m. momentum.

संवेदन m. sensation.

संवेदनशील adj. sensitive.

संवेदनहारी adj. anaesthetic.

संवेदना f. 1. condolence. 2. the deep feeling of sharing the suffering of another, compassion.

संवेदित adj. perceived through senses.

स

संवेदी adj. sympathetic.

संवेद्य adj. perceptible through senses.

संवैधानिक adj. constitutional.

संवैधानिकता f. constitutionality, constitutionalism.

संशय m. doubt, suspicion, uncertainty.

संशयात्मक adj. doubtful, uncertain.

संशयी adj. given to doubting, sceptic.

संशोधक adj. corrective.

संशोधन m. 1. correction, modification. 2. amendment, revision.

संशोधित adj. 1. corrected, modified. 2. amended. 3. revised.

संश्रित adj. allied.

संश्लिष्ट adj. synthesised, synthetic.

संश्लेषण m. synthesis.

संश्लेषित adj. = संश्लिष्ट।

संसक्त adj. cohesive.

संसद f. parliament.

संसदीय adj. parliamentary.

संसर्ग m. contact, association.

संसर्गज adj. 1. born out of association. 2. contagious.

संसार m. world.

संसार-बंधन m. bondage mundane.

संसारी adj. mundane, worldly. m. worldly being.

संसृति f. world.

संसेचन m. insemination.

संस्करण m. edition.

संस्कार m. 1. ritual, rite, sacrament. 2. (cultural) tradition, which becomes a part of one's being. 3. refinement, purification.

संस्कारहीन adj. unrefined, uncultured.

संस्कारित adj. cultured.

संस्कृत adj. refined, cultured, purified. f. Sanskrit, the source language of India.

संस्कृति f. culture.

संस्तर m. bed.

संस्तुत adj. recommended.

संस्तुति f. recommendation.

संस्था f. 1. institution. 2. a very familiar person is some activity.

संस्थागत adj. institutional.

संस्थान m. institute.

संस्थापक m. founder.

संस्थापन m. founding, establishing, establishment.

संस्थापित adj. founded, established.

संस्पर्श m. 1. touch. 2. contact.

संस्मरण m. reminiscences, memoirs.

संहत adj. compact, consolidated.

संहति f. compactness, state of being consolidated.

संहार m. annihilation, carnage, mayhem.

संहारक m. annihilator.

संहित adj. 1. accumulated. 2. codified.

संहिता f. a set of rules or laws arranged in a system, statute-book, code.

संहिताकरण m. codification.

संहिताबद्ध adj. codified.

संहिति f. accumulation.

स prefix. denoting 1. 'with' as सप्रेम with love. 2. likeness or equality, as सदृश like, similar, समान equal.

सइयाँ m. 1. lover. 2. husband.

सईस m. one who cleans and looks after horses, groom.

सकंटक adj. thorny.

सकता m. state of being stunned/dumb-founded; सकते में आना to be stunned/dumb-founded.

सकना vi. can, may.

सकपकाना vi. to be non-plussed, to be confounded.

सकरकंद m. = शकरकंद।

सकरपारा m. a kind of lozenge-shaped sweet.

सकर्मक adj. transitive; ~ क्रिया transitive verb.

सकल adj. 1. all, whole, entire. 2. gross, total.

सकाम adj. impelled by desire, purposeful, motivated, purposive.

सकार m. the letter स or its sound.

सकारना vt. to honour.

सकारात्मक adj. 1. indicating agreement or assent, affirmative. 2. positive, i.e. constructive or optimistic.

सकारे adv. at day-break, in the early morning.

सकुचाना vi. 1. to feel embarrassed. 2. to hesitate, to feel shy.

सकुचाहट f. 1. embarrassment. 2. hesitation, shyness.

सकोरा m. earthen cup.

सक़्क़ा m. water-carrier.

सक्रिय adj. 1. full of engery, active. 2. operating or working.

सक्रियता f. activity.

सक्षम adj. competent, capable.

सखरा adj. cooked in water.

सखा m. chum, pal, intimate friend.

सखी f. chum (girl).

सख़्त adj. 1. hard. 2. rigorous. 3. strict. 4. harsh. 5. dire. 6. serious. 7. stiff.

सख़्ती f. quality or state of being सख़्त।

सख्य m. feeling of being chummy.

सगा adj. real, born of the same parents.

सगाई f. 1. betrothal, engagement. 2. remarriage of a widow or divorcee.

सगापन m. close kinship/affinity.

सगुण m. possessed of attributes, endowed with qualities.

सगुणोपासना f. worship of God possessed of attributes.

सगुन m. auspicious act for someone's welfare.

सगुनिया m. soothsayer.

सगोत्र adj. of the same गोत्र।

सघन adj. 1. dense, thick. 2. intensive.

सघनता f. 1. denseness, thickness. 2. intensity.

सच adj. true, real, right.
m. truth.

सचमुच adv. 1. truly, really, in fact,

स

verily. 2. actually. 3. indeed.

सचराचर adj. with animates and inanimates.

सचल adj. moving, movable, mobile.

सचाई f. 1. truthfulness. 2. truth, veracity.

सचान m. falcon, hawk.

सचित्र adj. 1. pictorial. 2. illustrated.

सचिव m. secretary.

सचिवालय m. secretariat.

सचेत adj. 1. alert, cautious. 2. conscious.

सचेतक m. an official of a political party who manitains discipline among its members in legislative debates, whip.

सचेतन adj. conscious.

सचेष्ट adj. active, endeavouring.

सच्चरित्र adj. of good moral character, virtuous.

सच्चा adj. 1. truthful. 2. true. 3. sincere. 4. real, genuine.

सच्चाई f. = सचाई।

सच्चापन m. = सचाई।

सच्चिदानंद m. The Supreme Being, the personification of three attributes—Truth, Consciousness, Bliss.

सज f. style, orientation.

सजग adj. 1. wakeful, awake. 2. cautious, attentive.

सजधज f. pomp and show, ornamentation.

सजना vi. 1. to appear in make-up, to be embellished/ador-ned/bedecked/decorated/dressed. 2. to shine forth.

सजनी f. sweet chum (fem. of साजन)।

सजल adj. 1. hydrous, aqueous. 2. tearful.

सज़ा f. punishment, penalty.

सज़ा-ए-मौत f. capital punis- hment.

सजाति adj. = सजातीय।

सजातीय adj. 1. of one and the same class/caste; ~ विवाह endogamous marriage. 2. homogeneous.

सजा-धजा adj. made-up and adorned.

सजाना vt. 1. to embellish/adorn/decorate. 2. to arrange in proper order, to put (things) shipshape.

सज़ायाफ़्ता adj. convicted. m. previous convict.

सजावट f. decoration, ornamentation.

सजावटी adj. that makes some-thing look more beautiful, decorative.

सजीला adj. winsome, graceful.

सजीव adj. live, full of life, vivacious.

सजीवता f. liveliness, vivacity.

सज्जन m. gentleman, good man.

सज्जनता f. gentlemanliness, goodness.

सज्जा f. 1. decoration. 2. equipment.

सज्जित adj. 1. decorated, adorned.

सज्जी f. saltpetre.

सझिया m. = साझेदार।

सटकना vi. to give the slip, to slip away.

सटना vi. 1. to be contiguous. 2. to stick/adhere.

सटपटाना vi. = सिटपिटाना।

सटाक m. sound made by a lash or a whip.

सटीक adj. 1. to the point, apt. 2. supplied with explanatory notes, annotated.

सटोरिया m. speculator.

सट्टा m. speculation.

सट्टी f. market-place.

सठियाना vi. to be in dotage, to be senile.

सठियाव m. dotage, senility.

सड़क f. road.

सड़न f. putrefaction, decomposition.

सड़ना vi. to rot/decompose.

सड़सठ adj. & m. sixty-seven.

सड़सी f. pair of tongs, forceps.

सड़ा adj. putrefied, decomposed.

सड़ाक m. = सटाक।

सड़ाना vt. 1. to cause to putrefy. 2. to decompose.

सड़ायँध f. stench, foul smell due to putrefaction.

सड़ियल adj. 1. rotten, decaying, putrid. 2. good for nothing, worthless.

सत abbreviation of सात used as prefix meaning seven; सतपहला seven-folded.

सतगुना adj. seven times.

सतत adj. 1. continual. 2. continuous (in time). [Cf. संतत continuous (in space)]. 3. constant, perpetual.

सतथ्य adj. with facts, factual.

सतनजा m. a mixture of seven kinds of grains.

सतमासा adj. of seven months; ~ बच्चा child born seven months after conception.

सतर f. line, row.

सतर्क adj. alert, cautious, careful, vigilant.

सतर्कता f. alertness, cautiousness.

सतलड़ा m. necklace with seven chains.

सतवंती adj. (woman) faithful to her husband and true to her duties.

सतसई f. collection of seven hundred verses of a poet.

सतह f. 1. the uppermost level of land, surface. 2. level.

सतहत्तर adj. & m. seventy-seven, 77.

सतही adj. 1. pertaining to the surface, skin-deep. 2. superficial.

सताना vt. to oppress/victimize/torment/torture.

सतालू m. peach.

सतावर f. asparagus.

सती f. chaste woman, especially true to her husband.

सतीत्व m. chastity, fidelity to one's husband.

सतीत्व-भंग f. loss of (one's) chastity.

सतुआ m. = सत्तू।

सतोगुण m. first of the three qualities according to the Hindu Philosophy of life, representing purity and goodness.

सत् adj. used as prefix denoting (i)

truth, (ii) piety and virtue.

सत्कर्म m. virtuous deed.

सत्कर्मी adj. virtuous in deed.

सत्कार m. courteous welcome.

सत्कीर्ति f. good name, renown, repute, fame.

सत्त m. 1. essence, extract. 2. power, strength.

सत्तर adj. & m. seventy, 70.

सत्तांतरण m. transference of power or authority.

सत्ता f. 1. existence. 2. power. m. the 'seven' of playing cards.

सत्ताईस adj. & m. twenty-seven.

सत्ताधारी adj. & m. (person) in power/authority.

सत्तानबे adj. & m. ninety-seven.

सत्तारूढ़ adj. in power or aut-hority.

सत्तावन adj. & m. fifty-seven.

सत्तासी adj. & m. eighty-seven.

सत्तू m. parched gram or barley, pulverised and used as an edible.

सत्त्व m. = सत्त।

सत्त्वहीन adj. void of essence.

सत्पथ m. path of truth, right path.

सत्पात्र m. deserving/worthy person.

सत्फल m. excellent result.

सत्य adj. true. m. truth, reality.

सत्यता f. truthfulness, reality.

सत्यनारायण m. God, the Truth.

सत्यनिष्ठा f. fidelity to Truth, integrity.

सत्यवादी f. scrupulously true in word.

सत्याग्रह m. 1. insistence on truth, Satyagrah. 2. a nonviolent struggle offered to uphold the truth, passive resistance.

सत्यानाश m. total ruination, destruction.

सत्यानाशी adj. & m. ruinous, completely destructive.

सत्यापन m. verification.

सत्यापित adj. verified.

सत्ययुग m. the first age accor-ding to Indian mythology, gloden age.

सत्र m. session, period of time having definite limits.

सत्रह adj. & m. seventeen, 17.

सत्रावसान m. 1. prorogation (of an assembly). 2. conclusion of a session.

सत्व m. = सत्त।

सत्वर adj. & adv. fast, swiftly, quickly.

सत्संग m. 1. company of the good. 2. religious assembly.

सत्संगी m. 1. one who belongs to the fraternity of the good. 2. one who attends सत्संग।

सदन m. house.

सदमा m. shock, trauma.

सदय adj. filled with kindness/ compassion.

सदर adj. main, head, principal. m. president, chairman.

सदरी f. sleeveless jacket.

सदस्य m. member.

सदस्यता f. membership.

सदा adv. always, ever. f. cry, spl. mendicant's cry.

सदाचरण m. good conduct.

सदाचार m. good conduct, righteousness.

सदाचारी adj. of good conduct, righteous. [Fem. सदाचारिणी]

सदाबहार adj. evergreen.

सदारत f. chairmanship, presidentship.

सदावर्त m. distributing food to the poor on a permanent basis.

सदाशय adj. of good faith, well-intentioned. m. good faith.

सदिश m. vector. (Maths.)

सदी f. century.

सदुपदेश m. good counsel.

सदुपयोग m. good use, proper use.

सदृश adj. 1. like, alike. 2. similar, analogous.

सदेह adv. bodily, physically.

सदैव adv. always, ever, forever.

सदोष adj. faulty, defective, having shortcomings.

सद्गति f. 1. better state/condi- tion. 2. salvation.

सद्गुण m. good trait, virtue.

सद्गुरु m. worthy preceptor.

सद्भाव m. 1. good will. 2. kin-dly feeling.

सद्भावना f. = सद्भाव।

सद्यः adv. 1. just a moment ago, a moment back. 2. forthwith.

सद्वृत्ति f. righteous disposition, right type of attitude.

सधना vi. 1. to be well accomplished. 2. to be well practised. 3. to be well-trained. 4. correct aiming.

सधन्यवाद adv. thankfully.

सधर्मी adj. & m. 1. co-religionist. 2. having similar function.

सधवा adj. & f. (woman) whose husband is alive. (opp. of विधवा)

सधाना vt. to cause to be trained.

सन m. 1. hemp. 2. sound (resembling a hissing noise) produced by an object moving swiftly. 3. Year.

सनई f. hemp.

सनक f. 1. fad, whim, vagary, mania. 2. craze.

सनकना vi. to go crazy.

सनकी adj. 1. eccentric, whimsical. 2. crazy.

सनद f. 1. certificate from a person in authority. 2. deed, document.

सनना vi. 1. to be besmeared. 2. to be kneaded.

सनम m. a person who is much loved, dear one, darling.

सनसन m. hissing/swishing sound.

सनसनाना vi. to produce a swishing sound, to rustle.

सनसनाहट f. 1. swishing sound. 2. thrill.

सनसनी f. sensation, thrill, excitement.

सनसनीख़ेज़ adj. sensational, thrilling, exciting, whizzing.

सनातन adj. eternal, perpetual, traditional.

सनातन धर्म m. 1. Religion Eternal. 2. conservative/orthodox Hinduism.

सनातनी adj. 1. eternal.

स

2. follower of सनातन धर्म।

सनाथ adj. endowed with a patron, blessed with a protector.

सनाय f. senna—a plant, the leaves of which serve as a purgative.

सनीचर m. = शनि।

सन् m. Anno Domini.

सन्न adj. stunned.

सन्नद्ध adj. 1. equipped, attached. 2. prepared, ready.

सन्नद्धता f. preparedness.

सन्नाटा m. stillness complete. सन्नाटे में आना to be stunned.

सन्निकट ind. close by, very near, in close proximity.

सन्निकर्ष m. close proximity.

सन्निपात m. disorder of the three humours.

सन्निविष्ट adj. inserted, inclu- ded.

सन्निवेश m. inclusion, insertion; ~ करना to include.

सन्निहित adj. 1. included. 2. implied.

सन्मान m. = सम्मान।

सन्मार्ग m. path of righteousness/ virtue, right/moral course.

सन्मुख adv. & adj. = सम्मुख।

सपक्ष adj. having wings, win- ged.

सपत्नी f. co-wife.

सपत्नीक adv. along with (one's) wife.

सपना m. dream.

सपरदायी m. accompanyist of a dancing girl.

सपरना vt. to pull through.

सपरिकर adv. with attendents/ paraphernalia.

सपरिश्रम कारावास m. rigorous imprisonment.

सपरेटा m. skimmed milk.

सपाट adj. flat, plane, smooth, even.

सपाटा m. speed.

सपिंड adj. collateral.

सपूत m. worthy son.

सपेरा m. snake-charmer.

सप्त adj. & m. seven, 7.

सप्तक m. 1. group of seven. 2. septat/septette, gamut (Music).

सप्तपदी f. seven bridal steps round the fire.

सप्तमी f. seventh day of each lunar half month.

सप्तमी विभक्ति f. sign of locative case. (Gram.)

सप्तर्षि m. Ursa Major, the Great Bear.

सप्तस्वर m. the seven notes of music.

सप्ताह m. week.

सप्ताहांत m. weekend.

सप्रमाण adv. with testimony.

सफ़र m. journey, travel.

सफ़र-मैना m. sappers and miners.

सफल adj. 1. successful. 2. fruitful.

सफलता f. 1. success. 2. fruitfulness. 3. achievement.

सफ़ा adj. clean. m. page, folio.

सफ़ाई f. 1. cleanliness, tidiness. 2. cleansing. 3. explanation, clarification. 4. defence.

सफ़ाई-पक्ष m. defence party/side.

सफ़ाया m. clean sweep.

सफ़ेद adj. white.

सफ़ेदा m. 1. white lead. 2. a variety of mango.

सब adj. all. pron. everybody or everything.

सबक़ m. lesson.

सबब m. cause, reason.

सबरी f. an iron-rod used for house breaking, jemmy.

सबल adj. strong, powerful.

सबूत m. proof, evidence.

सबेरा m. morning.

सबेरे adv. in the morning.

सब्ज़ adj. green; ~ बाग़ दिखाना to raise false hopes.

सब्ज़ी f. 1. herbage. 2. vegetable.

सब्बल m. crowbar.

सब्र m. patience.

सभा f. 1. assembly. 2. meeting.

सभापति m. chairman.

सभा-भवन m. assembly hall.

सभासद m. member of an assembly, councillor.

सभी adj. all. pron. everbody.

सभ्य adj. civilized, civil.

सभ्यता f. 1. civilization. 2. civility, courtesy.

समंजन m. adjustment.

समंजित adj. adjusted.

सम adj. 1. equal. 2. even.

समकक्ष adj. of the same level, on the same footing, of the same stature.

समकारी adj. equalising.

समकालिक adj. synchronous, contemporary, coeval.

समकालीन adj. = समकालिक।

समकोण m. right angle; ~ त्रिभुज right-angled triangle.

समक्ष adv. before.

समग्र adj. entire, whole.

समग्रता f. entirety, totality.

समजातीय adj. homogeneous, homologous, of the same species.

समझ f. intelligence, intellect, understanding, sense, comprehension.

समझदार adj. & m. sensible, wise.

समझना vt. 1. to understand/follow, to make out, to comprehend. 2. to realize. 3. to consider. 4. to know. m. act of understanding.

समझ-बूझ f. prudence, shrewdness.

समझाना vt. 1. to make (someone) understand, to explain, to instruct, to advise. 2. to bring round by persuasion.

समझौता m. compromise, agreement, pact, compounding.

समतल adj. level, even, plane, smooth.

समता f. 1. equality. 2. parity.

समदर्शी adj. even-eyed.

समदृष्टि f. 1. even-handedness. 2. neutrality.

समधिन f. mother-in-law of son/daughter.

समधियाना m. residence or household of the father-in-law of son/daughter.

समधी m. father-in-law of son/daughter.

स

समध्वनिक m. homonym.

समन m. सम्मन।

समन्वय m. coordination, harmony.

समन्वित adj. coordinated.

समबुद्धि adj. equanimous, level-headed. f. equanimity.

समभुज adj. equilateral. (Geom.)

सममित adj. symmetrical.

सममिति f. symmetry.

समय m. 1. time. 2. period, duration.

समय-कुसमय adv. at all odd hours.

समयनिष्ठ adj. punctual.

समयपालक m. time-keeper.

समय-सारणी f. timetable.

समय-सीमा f. time-limit.

समयविहीन adj. timeless.

समयांतर m. interval of time, time-lag.

समयानुसार adv. as per occasion, suitable for the occasion.

समयोचित adj. timely, opportune.

समयोपरि adj. overtime.

समर m. war, battle.

समरथ adj. = समर्थ।

समरस adj. 1. level-headed, equanimous. 2. harmonious, concordant.

समरांगण m. battle-field.

समरूप adj. similar. (Geom.)

समरूपता f. similarity.

समरोचित adj. appropriate in time of war, suitable for war purposes.

समर्थ adj. capable, competent.

समर्थक m. supporter.

समर्थता f. capability, competence.

समर्थन m. support.

समर्थन-मूल्य adj. support price.

समर्पण m. 1. dedication. 2. surrender.

समर्पित adj. 1. dedicated. 2. surrendered.

समवयस्क adj. equal in age, of the same age.

समवर्ण adj. of the same colour/caste.

समवर्ती adj. 1. concurrent, contemporary. 2. adjacent, contiguous.

समवाय m. 1. jumbled heap or collection. 2. concourse.

समवाय-संबंध m. inseparable relation.

समवेत adj. & adv. collectively.

समवेत-गान m. chorus.

समवेदना f. condolence.

समशीतोष्ण adj. temperate.

समष्टि f. 1. collection. 2. aggregate, totality.

समसामयिक adj. contemporary, contemporaneous.

समस्त adj. 1. entire, whole, all. 2. compound.

समस्या f. problem.

समस्या नाटक m. problem play.

समाँ m. 1. time. 2. atmosphere; ~ बाँधना to keep the audience spellbound.

समांग adj. homogeneous.

समांतर adj. parallel.

समाई f. 1. capacity. 2. room.

समाकलन m. integration. (Math.)

समागत adj. & m. welcome stranger.

समागम m. 1. arrival. 2. meeting,

assembly or gathering.

समाघात m. 1. blow. 2. combat.

समाचार m. news.

समाचारदाता m. news reporter.

समाचारपत्र m. newspaper.

समाचारवाचक m. newsreader.

समाज m. society, company.

समाजवाद m. socialism.

समाजवादी adj. socialistic, socialist.

समाज-विरोधी adj. anti-social.

समाजशास्त्र m. Sociology.

समाज-सेवक m. social worker.

समाज-सेवा f. social service, social work.

समाज-सेविका f. woman social worker.

समाज-सेवी m. social worker.

समाजीकरण m. socialization.

समादर m. reverence, veneration, respect.

समादरणीय adj. reverend.

समादेश m. 1. command. 2. writ.

समादेश-याचिका f. writ petition.

समाधान m. 1. solution (of a problem), satisfaction. 2. satisfying explanation.

समाधि f. 1. a state of total unity with God, transcendental meditation, trance. 2. tomb, grave.

समाधि-शिला f. tomb-stone.

समाधिस्थ adj. in a state of trance/meditation.

समान adj. 1. equal. 2. similar. 3. like, alike, same.

समानता f. 1. equality. 2. similarity. 3. likeness.

समानांतर adj. parallel.

समाना vi. to pervade in, to fill (in its entirety), to occupy all space in.

समानार्थ adj. (words) having similar meanings, equivalent, synonymous.

समानार्थक adj. = समानार्थ।

समानुपात m. proportion.

समानुपातिक adj. proportional.

समापन m. winding up, closing up, ending, completion.

समापवर्तक m. common factor. (Math.)

समापवर्त्य m. common multiple. (Math.)

समाप्त adj. finished, ended.

समाप्तप्राय adj. almost finished, moribund.

समाप्ति f. 1. conclusion, end, finish. 2. expiration, expiry.

समायोजक adj. & m. adjuster.

समायोजन m. adjustment.

समारंभ m. happy beginning, commencement, initiation.

समारोह m. 1. celebration, function. 2. festive event, ceremony.

समालोचक m. reviewer, critic.

समालोचना f. review, criticism.

समावर्तन m. returning from Gurukul after completion of studies.

समाविष्ट adj. 1. incorporated. 2. included, entered.

समावृत adj. enclosed, attached.

समावेश m. 1. incorporation. 2. inclusion.

समाशोधन m. clearing; ~ गृह clearing house.

स

समास m. compound, compound word. (Gram.)

समाहरण m. collecting.

समाहर्ता m. collector.

समाहार m. collection, accumulation.

समिति f. 1. committee. 2. society.

समिति-कक्ष m. commitee room.

समिधा f. fire-wood used as fuel in sacrificial fire.

समीकरण m. 1. equation. 2. equalisation. 3. assimilation. (Phon.)

समीकृत adj. equalised.

समीक्षक m. 1. reviewer, commentator. 2. critic.

समीक्षा f. 1. act of viewing again, review. 2. a critical discussion dealing with a book, review.

समीक्षाकार m. reviewer, commentator.

समीचीन adj. appropriate, proper, right, befitting.

समीप adj. near, close by.

समीपतम adj. nearest.

समीपता f. nearness, proximity.

समीपवर्ती adj. situated near by, neighbouring, proximate.

समीपस्थ adj. near (by), proximate.

समीर f. breeze.

समुंदर m. = समुद्र।

समुचित adj. appropriate, suitable.

समुच्चय m. 1. collection, set. 2. compilation.

समुच्चयबोधक m. conjunction. (Gram.)

समुज्ज्वल adj. effulgent.

समुदाय m. 1. association. 2. commune. 3. community. 4. group.

समुद्यत adj. just ready, quite ready.

समुद्र m. sea, ocean.

समुद्रकंप m. seaquake.

समुद्रतट m. coast, sea-beach, sea-shore, seaboard.

समुद्र-तल m. sea-level.

समुद्र-तली f. seabed, sea-bottom.

समुद्र-देवता m. Oceanus.

समुद्र-मंथन m. churning of the sea (Indian Mythology).

समुद्रयात्रा m. voyage.

समुद्रयात्री m. seafarer.

समुद्रविज्ञान m. Oceanography.

समुद्री adj. oceanic; ~ हवा sea breeze.

समुद्री घोड़ा m. hippopotamus, walrus.

समुद्री डाकू m. pirate, sea-robber.

समुद्री ताक़त f. sea power, a country with a strong navy.

समुद्री तार m. cable.

समुद्री शक्ति f. समुद्री ताक़त।

समुन्नत adj. 1. raised high, elevated. 2. developed.

समुन्नयन m. 1. elevation. 2. development, progress.

समूचा adj. whole, all entire.

समूल adv. from the root.

समूह m. 1. multitude, concourse, assemblage, crowd. 2. group.

समूहवाचक adj. collective; ~ संज्ञा collective noun.

समृद्ध adj. prosperous, rich, affluent.

समृद्धि f. prosperity, affluence, richness.

समेकन m. 1. fusion. 2. consolidation.

समेकित adj. consolidated.

समेटना vt. 1. to gather. 2. to roll up.

समेत adv. with, along with.

समोना vt. to mix together inextricably.

समोसा m. an Indian variety of saltish pastry, usually triangular in shape.

सम्मत adj. sanctioned by; धर्म ~ sanctioned by religion.

सम्मति f. 1. opinion, view. 2. assent, consent.

सम्मन m. summons.

सम्मान m. honour, esteem, respect.

सम्माननीय adj. honourable, respected.

सम्मानपूर्वक adv. 1. respectfully. 2. honourably.

सम्मानसूचक adj. honorific.

सम्मानार्थ adv. in honour (of).

सम्मानित adj. esteemed, respected, honoured, revered.

सम्मिलन m. 1. combining, joining, mingling. 2. meet, get-together.

सम्मिलित adj. 1. combined, joint, mingled. 2. included.

सम्मिश्र adj. complex (Maths.); ~ संख्या complex number.

सम्मिश्रण m. 1. compounding, combining. 2. admixture, mixing up.

सम्मुख, के postposition. 1. in front of, facing each other, face to face. 2. opposite to (Maths.).

सम्मेलन m. conference, convention.

सम्मोह m. fascination, charm.

सम्मोहक adj. fascinating, charming, attractive.

सम्मोहन m. charm, fascination.

सम्मोहन विद्या f. hypnotism.

सम्मोहित adj. hypnotised.

सम्यक, सम्यक् adj. 1. thorough, comprehensive, all around. 2. proper, appropriate.

सम्राज्ञी f. empress.

सम्राट, सम्राट् m. emperor.

सयानपन m. = सयानापन।

सयाना adj. 1. grown up. 2. shrewd, clever.

सयानापन m. shrewdness, cleverness.

सयापा n. a chant of lamentation for the dead, dirge.

सरंध्र adj. porous.

सर m. pond, lake. f. hand in game; उसकी तीन सरें बनी हैं He has three hands.

सरकंडा m. a kind of reed.

सरकना vi. 1. to move a little. 2. to crawl, to move slowly.

सरकस m. circus.

सरकार f. government. m. master, boss, lord.

सरकारी adj. official, pertaining to government, governmental.

सरग़ना m. (ring) leader, chieftain.

सरगम m. gamut. (Music)

सरगर्मी f. zeal and enthusiasm.

सरगी f. meal taken at early dawn

स

immediately before commencing a fast.

सरणी f. line, row.

सरताज m. = सिरताज।

सरदार m. 1. chief, chieftain. 2. leader. 3.member of Sikh community. [Fem. सरदारनी]

सरना vi. to be accomplished.

सरनाम adj. well-known, renowned, famed, reputed.

सरनामा m. form of addressing (on top of a letter).

सरपंच m. chief arbiter.

सरपट adj. gallopping.

सरपत m. a kind of reed.

सरपरस्त m. 1. guardian. 2. patron.

सरमाया m. 1. capital. 2. total assets, estate.

सरमायेदार m. capitalist.

सरल adj. 1. simple. 2. easy. 3. straight.

सरलता f. 1. simplicity. 2. easiness. 3. straightness.

सरल संगीत m. light music.

सरलीकरण m. simplification.

सरस adj. 1. juicy, watery.2. tasty, delicious. 3. full of tender sentiments.

सरसठ adj. & m. sixty-seven 67.

सरसना vi. 1. to flourish/prosper. 2. to look lovely/charming.

सरसब्ज़ adj. in full bloom, ver-dant.

सरसर f. sound produced by a snake, air etc. whilst in movement, rustle.

सरसराना vi. to rustle.

सरसराहट f. rustle.

सरसरी adj. cursory, summary.

सरसाम m. delirium.

सरसिज m. lotus.

सरसिरुह m. lotus.

सरसी f. waterpool, pond.

सरसों f. mustard (seed or plant).

सरस्वती f. Goddess of Learning.

सरहज f. = सलहज।

सरहद f. 1. border, boundary. 2. frontier.

सरहदी adj. pertaining to the frontier.

सरापना vt. to curse.

सरापा m. complete set of clothes.

सराफ़ m. = सर्राफ़।

सराबोर adj. fully soaked, completely drenched.

सराय f. inn, tavern, caravan-serai.

सरासर adv. in toto, totally, wholly.

सराहना vt. to praise/laud, to commend.

सराहनीय adj. praiseworthy, laudable, commendable.

सरिता f. stream, river.

सरिया m. iron bar.

सरिस adj. similar, alike, equal.

सरीखा, के postposition. like, similar to.

सरीसृप m. crawling/creeping insects or the like, reptiles.

सरूप adj. 1. alike, similar. 2. beautiful. m. guise.

सरूपता f. 1. likeness, similarity, semblance. 2. comeliness, beauty.

सरूर m. slight inebriation, intoxication.

सरेआम adv. publically.

सरेस m. gelatine, glue.

सरो m. cypress tree.

सरोकार m. concern, connection, dealings.

सरोज m. lotus.

सरोद m. an Indian musical instrument resembling a guitar.

सरोरुह m. lotus.

सरोवर m. 1. lake. 2. pond, pool.

सरोष adv. angrily, wrathfully.

सरौता m. instrument for cutting betel nuts, nut-cracker.

सर्ग m. canto, chapter.

सर्जन m. 1. creation. 2. surgeon.

सर्जनहार m. creator.

सर्द adj. cold; ~ आहें sorrowful sighs.

सर्दा m. a variety of melon.

सर्दी f. 1. cold; ~ खाना to catch cold. 2. winter.

सर्प m. snake.

सर्पण m. creeping/crawling.

सर्पदंश m. 1. snakebite. 2. wound caused by snakebite.

सर्पिणी f. female snake.

सर्पिल adj. serpentine, spiral.

सर्पी adj. crawling, creeping.

सर्फ़ adj. spent.

सर्राटा m. सर्राटे से fast, swiftly.

सर्राफ़ m. bullion merchant.

सर्राफ़ा m. bullion market.

सर्व adj. 1. all. 2. whole, entire.

सर्वगत adj. all-pervasive.

सर्वग्रास m. total eclipse.

सर्वचारी adj. rolling all round.

सर्वजनीन adj. pertaining to all.

सर्वजित adj. all-conquering.

सर्वज्ञ adj. omniscient.

सर्वतः adv. 1. all round, on all sides. 2. in every respect.

सर्वतोभद्र adj. auspicious all round.

सर्वतोमुखी adj. all-round, versatile.

सर्वत्र adv. everywhere, at every place, in all cases.

सर्वथा adv. totally, completely, entirely.

सर्वदलीय adj. of or pertaining to all parties, all-party.

सर्वदा adv. ever, ever more, always.

सर्वनाम m. pronoun.

सर्वनाश m. complete ruination, utter/total destruction.

सर्वनियंता m. Controller Supreme.

सर्वप्रयोज्य adj. all-purpose.

सर्वप्रिय adj. dear to all, loved by all, darling of one and all.

सर्वभक्षी adj. omnivorous, devouring anything.

सर्वमान्य adj. accepted by all.

सर्वव्यापक adj. omnipresent, all-pervading.

सर्वशक्तिमान, सर्वशक्तिमान् adj. all-powerful, almighty, omnipotent.

सर्वश्री adj. messrs, plu. of mr.

सर्वश्रेष्ठ adj. best of all.

सर्वसम्मत adj. unanimous.

सर्वसाधारण m. common people, public, populace.

सर्वस्व m. everything.

स

सर्वहारा m. member of proletariate, proletarian.

सर्वहित m. public good, common weal.

सर्वांग m. all components (of the body).

सर्वांगीण adj. all-round.

सर्वाधिक adj. 1. greatest in number. 2. surpassing every one.

सर्वाधिकार m. all rights, full powers; ~ सुरक्षित all rights reserved.

सर्वार्थ m. all purposes.

सर्वेक्षक m. surveyor.

सर्वेक्षण m. survey.

सर्वेश्वर m. Supreme Lord, Lord of all.

सर्वे-सर्वा adj. all in all.

सर्वोच्च adj. supreme; highest in place or rank.

सर्वोत्तम adj. supreme, best of all.

सर्वोपकारी adj. benevolent to all.

सर्वोपरि adj. above all, supreme.

सलई f. pine tree.

सलज्ज adj. coy, bashful.

सलना vi. to be bored/pierced.

सलमा m. gold or silver thread used in embroidery.

सलवार f. a kind of trousers (worn by women, especially in the Punjab).

सलसलाना vi. to feel itching sensation. vt. to rub gently with fingers.

सलहज f. wife of wife's brother.

सलाई f. 1. pointed longish stick rod for applying collyrium to the eyes. 2. match-stick.

सलाख़ f. thin long metallic bar.

सलाद m. salad.

सलाम m. Muslim form of salutation.

सलामत adj. (fully) alive, safe.

सलामी f. 1. salutation. 2. formal salutation (military in particular); ~ देना to present a guard of honour. 3. gratification (in cash).

सलामी बल्लेबाज़ m. an opening batsman.

सलाह f. advice, counsel.

सलाहकार m. counsellor, advisor.

सलिल m. water.

सलीक़ा m. etiquette, good manners.

सलीक़ेदार adj. mannerly, possessing good manners.

सलीता m. a kind of tough and stout cloth.

सलीपर m. (pair of) slippers.

सलीब f. cross.

सलूक m. 1. behaviour, social dealings, treatment. 2. the good done, obligation.

सलोना adj. 1. comely, winsome, charming. 2. saltish.

सल्तनत f. 1. sultanate, dominion, kingdom. 2. reign.

सवर्ण adj. 1. having the same colour. 2. (words) having the same spelling.

सवर्ण हिंदू m. a Hindu belonging to one of the upper three castes.

सवा adj. one and a quarter.

सवाक adj. gifted with the talking faculty/speech, which can talk.

सवाब m. = पुण्य।

सवाया adj. one and a quarter times.

सवार adj. mounted. m. rider.

सवारी f. 1. act or state of riding. 2. vehicle, animal or person meant to carry passengers. 3. passenger. 4. cavalcade.

सवाल m. 1. an inquiry to obtain information, question. 2. demand. 3. a subject of debate or dispute, issue, problem.

सवाल-जवाब m. 1. question and answer. 2. argumentation.

सवालिया adj. interrogative.

सवाली adj. = सवालिया।

सविता m. Sun.

सविनय adj. humble, modest. adv. humbly.

सविनय अवज्ञा f. civil disobedience.

सविस्तर ind. in detail.

सवेरा m. = सबेरा।

सवैया m. 1. one and a quarter. 2. multiplication table of one and a quarter times of natural numbers. 3. a kind of metre in Hindi poetry.

सशंक adj. = सशंकित।

सशंकित adj. alarmed due to suspicion.

सशक्त adj. 1. powerful. 2. dominant, forceful.

सशक्तीकरण m. an act of making powerful, empowerment.

सशस्त्र adj. armed.

सशुल्क adj. paying fee/subscription.

सश्रम adj. 1. fatigued, tired. 2. rigorous.

ससीम adj. limited, finite.

ससुर m. father-in-law. [Fem. सास]

ससुरा m. the expression 'father-in-law' used as a form of abuse.

ससुराल f. place or residence of the in-laws.

सस्ता adj. low in price, cheap, inexpensive.

सस्नेह adv. with love, with loving regards.

सस्मित adj. smiling, with a smile playing on the lips.

सस्य m. crop.

सह prefix. indicating 'with', 'along with', equivalent of 'co-'.

सह-अपराधी m. accomplice.

सह-अस्तित्व m. co-existence.

सहकारिता f. cooperation.

सहकारी adj. & m. cooperative.

सहगान m. chorus.

सहगामिनी adj. (woman) who goes along with (someone). f. wife, mate.

सहगामी adj. concomitant, concurrent. m. mate.

सहचरी f. fair sex associate or companion.

सहचारी adj. & m. associate, companion.

सहज adj. easy, which comes easily.

सहज ज्ञान m. instinctive/innate knowledge, intuition.

स

सहज बुद्धि f. natural wit, innate sense.

सहजवृत्ति f. instinct.

सहजीवन m. = सह–अस्तित्व।

सहधर्मिणी f. wife.

सहधर्मी adj. 1. having a common duty. 2. having the same intrinsic quality.

सहन m. 1. courtyard. 2. act or state of enduring/bearing/tolerating. रहन - ~ way of living.

सहनशक्ति f. power of forbearance, tolerance, endurance.

सहनशील adj. having tolerance, forbearing, tolerant.

सहना vt. to endure/bear/tolerate, to abide by, to suffer, to put up with.

सहनीय adj. bearable, tolerable.

सहपाठी m. class-fellow.

सहभोज m. a dinner, community dinner.

सहमत adj. concurred, agreed. ~ होना to concur/agree.

सहमति f. concurrence, assent.

सहमना vi. to get scared/alarmed/ frightened.

सहयात्री m. co-traveller, fellow passenger.

सहयोग m. cooperation, collaboration.

सहयोगी m. fellow-worker, associate, comrade.

सहयोजित adj. co-opted.

सहर f. morning.

सहरा m. jungle, forest.

सहराई adj. wild.

सहलाना vt. to rub gently; तलवे~ to indulge in abject flattery.

सहवर्ती adj. contemporaneous, contemporary.

सहवास m. 1. living together, co-dwelling. 2. cohabitation.

सहशिक्षा f. co-education.

सहसंबंध m. correlation.

सहसा adv. suddenly, all of a sudden.

सहस्र adj. & m. thousand.

सहस्राब्दि f. a millemium.

सहानुभूति f. sympathy.

सहाय m. help, support.

सहायक m. assistant, aide, helper. adj. helpful.

सहायक नदी f. tributary.

सहायता f. aid, help, assistance.

सहारना vt. to endure/tolerate.

सहारा m. support, prop.

सहारे, के postposition. with the support of.

सहालग m. period considered auspicious for (Hindu) weddings.

सहिजन m. a kind of large tree whose long beans and flowers are used as a vegetable.

सहित, के postposition. with, along with, together with.

सहिष्णु adj. meek and forbea- ring, tolerant.

सहिष्णुता f. tolerance.

सही adj. 1. right, correct. 2. true. 3. fit. m. 1. signature. 2. testimony, attestation.

3. a mark put beside an item or sum to show that it has been checked, tic.

सही-सलामत adj. not harmed or injured, unscathed, safe.

सही-सही adv. correctly.

सहूलियत f. 1. facility. 2. amenity.

सहृदय adj. 1. warm-hearted, good hearted, gentle, affectionate. 2. having a (literary) taste.

सहेजना vt. to check/collate/tally; सहेजकर रखना to keep (something) securely.

सहेली f. female companion.

सहोदर adj. sibling. m. (one's) own brother.

सह्य adj. bearable, endurable, tolerable.

साँई m. lord, master.

साँकल f. chain-like hasp for fastening the door.

सांकेतिक adj. relating to a symbol, symbolic.

सांख्य adj. numerical. m. knowledge.

सांख्ययोग m. one of the six schools of Hindu Philosophy propagated by the sage Kapil.

सांख्यिकी f. Statistics.

सांख्यिकीय adj. statistical.

सांग m. = स्वाँग।

सांगोपांग adv. wholly, together with parts, all entire.

सांघातिक adj. deadly, mortal, lethal.

साँच adj. = सच्चा। f. = सचाई।

साँचा adj. = सच्चा। m. mould.

साँझ f. evening.

साँझी m. = साझी।

साँट f. mark of abrasion left on the body caused by a lash.

साँटा m. whip/lash made of twisted cloth. [Fem. साँटी]

साँठ-गाँठ f. complicity, unholy alliance, intrigue.

साँठी f. capital (पूँजी)।

साँड़ m. bull.

साँड़नी f. 1. fast-going she-camel. 2. dromedary.

सांत adj. ending, finite, limited.

सांत्वना f. solace, consolation.

सांध्य adj. of or pertaining to the evening.

सांध्यगोष्ठी f. evening meet.

साँप m. serpent, snake; ~ का ज़हर venom; ~ की केंचुली slough (of a snake); आस्तीन का ~ an enemy masquerading as a friend; कलेजे पर ~ लोटना to feel pangs of envy/jealousy or the like.

सांपत्तिक adj. pertaining to wealth.

साँपिन f. female snake.

सांप्रदायिक adj. communal.

सांप्रदायिकता f. communalism.

साँबर m. South-Indian spiced curry.

साँभर m. 1. a lake in Rajasthan. 2. salt prepared from this lake. 3. a type of Indian antelope.

साँवला adj. having a dark complexion, swarthy.

साँवलापन m. swarthiness.

साँवलिया m. (swarthy complexioned) lover.

साँवाँ m. a variety of rice.

साँस f. breath.

साँसत f. agony (as in suffocation).

सांसद adj. & m. member of the Parliament.

साँसा m. 1. breath. 2. life.

सांसारिक adj. 1. worldly, mundane. 2. materialistic.

सांस्कृतिक adj. cultural.

सांस्थानिक adj. institutional.

सा adj. (suffix) denoting (i) likeness, (ii) alikeness, (iii) distinctness.

सा m. first note of the musical septet.

साइकिल f. cycle, bike.

साइत f. 1. moment. 2. auspicious moment.

साइनबोर्ड m. sign-board.

साई f. advance, earnest money.

साईस m. groom, syce.

साईसी f. work or post of a groom.

साएदार adj. shady.

साका m. Saka era.

साकार adj. shaped, having a shape or form; स्वप्न ~ करना to realise (one's) dream.

साकारोपासना f. idol worship.

साकिन adj. resident/inhabitant of.

साक़ी m. server of wine.

साक्षर adj. able to read and write, literate.

साक्षरता f. literacy.

साक्षात् adj. personified, in flesh and blood. m. before (one's) eyes, face to face.

साक्षात्कार m. 1. being face to face. 2. interview.

साक्षात्कारी adj. & m. (one) who seeks interview.

साक्षी m. 1. witness, eye-witness, deponent. 2. evidence.

साक्षीकरण m. attestation.

साक्ष्य m. evidence, testimony.

साक्ष्यांकन m. = साक्षीकरण।

साक्ष्यांकित adj. attested.

साख f. 1. credit. 2. goodwill, faith, trust, reputation.

साखी m. 1. witness. 2. arbiter, arbitrator.

साखू m. sal tree and its wood.

साख्य f. friendship, friendliness.

साग m. 1. green leaves used as vegetables. 2. cooked vegetable preparation.

साग-पात m. herbs and vegetables; ~ समझना to treat contemptuously/disdainfully.

साग-भाजी f. vegetables.

सागर m. sea.

साग़र m. cup (of wine).

सागौन f. teak-wood.

साज m. equipage, articles of decoration.

साज़ m. 1. accoutrements. 2. set of musical instruments.

साज-सज्जा f. 1. decoration and grandeur. 2. equipment.

साज-सामान m. 1. equipment. 2. furniture. 3. luggage.

साजन m. 1. husband. 2. lover.

साज़िंदा m. one who plays on a

musical instrument, spl. in the company of a dancer, accompanyist.

साज़िश f. conspiracy, plot, intrigue.

साझा m. 1. partnership. 2. co-ownership.

साझी adj. common. m. = साझेदार।

साझेदार m. co-partner, co-owner, co-sharer.

साझेदारी f. = साझा।

साटन f. satin.

साठ adj. & m. sixty, 60.

साठा adj. (person) sixty years old, of sixty years.

साठी m. a kind of paddy which ripens in sixty days.

साड़ी f. saree, sari; the principal outer garment of an Indian woman, especially one of artistic work.

साढ़ी f. = मलाई।

साढ़ू m. husband of wife's sister, brother-in-law.

साढ़े adj. plus half; ~ तीन three and a half.

साढ़ेसाती f. evil influence of pla- net Saturn which lasts for 7½ yrs., 7½ months or 7½ days.

सात adj. & m. seven, 7.

सातत्य m. continuity.

सात फेरे m. (plu.) seven bridal rounds of the sacred fire.

सात्विक adj. 1. purified. 2. pure and pious, honest. 3. virtuous.

सात्विकता f. purity and piety.

साथ m. 1. company; के ~ with. 2. association, cooperation; ~ का खेला playmate; ~ चलना to accompany; ~ छोड़ना/छोड़ देना to finish a relationship; ~ ही (i) besides, in addition to this; (ii) together; (iii) along with.

साथ, के postposition. with.

साथवाला adj. next to, close to. m. someone near to one.

साथ-साथ adv. 1. together. 2. concurrently.

साथिन f. she-companion/ associate.

साथी m. companion, comrade, buddy. adj. of the same group, team, institution, country etc.

सादगी f. simplicity.

सादर adv. with respect, respectfully.

सादा adj. simple, plain.

सादापन m. = सादगी।

सादृश्य m. resemblance, likeness, similarity, analogy.

साध f. long-cherished desire.

साधक adj. 1. religiously persevering. 2. acco-mplishing, effecting, com-pleting. 3. instrumental. m. 1. one who perseveres. 2. one who helps in accomplishing (something); pra-ctitioner.

साधन m. 1. means. 2. resources; प्राकृतिक ~ natural resources. 3. act of accomplishment, completion.

साधना f. 1. great perseverance. 2. act performed with great

स

perseverance. 3. aim, practice. vt. 1. to accomplish. 2. to bring (someone) round.

साधनीय adj. worth being accomplished.

साधर्मिक adj. of or having the same religion.

साधर्म्य m. state or quality of being साधर्मिक।

साधार adj. based, having a basis/prop.

साधारण adj. 1. ordinary. 2. common; ~ कारावास/क़ैद simple imprisonment. 3. normal.

साधारणतः adv. ordinarily.

साधारणीकरण m. generalisation.

साधिका f. fem. of साधक।

साधिकार adj. authoritative. adv. authoritatively.

साधित adj. accomplished, attained.

साधु adj. saintly; ~ - साधु magnificent! superb! sublime! m. 1. saint. 2. mendicant.

साधुता f. saintliness, goodness, nobility, virtue, righteousness.

साधुवृत्ति f. 1. saintly disposition. 2. saintly way of life.

साधू m. hermit, saint.

साध्य adj. attainable, practicable, which can be accomplished.

साध्वी f. chaste and faithful (woman).

सानंद adj. happy. adv. happily.

सान m. 1. whetstone. 2. grindstone.

सानना m. 1. to knead. 2. to mix, to smear. 3. to implicate.

सानी adj. matching. f. prepared fodder for cattle.

सानुनय adv. humbly, modestly.

सानुप्रास adj. with alliteration.

सान्निध्य m. proximity, closeness, neighbourhood.

सापेक्ष adj. relative.

सापेक्षता f. relativity.

सापेक्षिक adj. = सापेक्ष।

साप्ताहिक adj. weekly. m. weekly magazine/journal.

साफ़ adj. 1. clear. 2. clean, neat. 3. frank, guileless. 4. clear-cut.

साफल्य m. success.

साफ़ा m. a turban-like head-dress.

साबका m. dealing.

साबित adj. proved, testified.

साबुत adj. entire, whole.

साबुन m. soap.

साबुनदानी f. soap-case.

साबूत adj. = साबुत।

साबूदाना m. sago.

साभार adv. gratefully, thankfully.

सामंजस्य m. coordination.

सामंत m. feudal chieftain.

सामंतवाद m. feudalism.

सामंतिक adj. feudalistic.

सामंती adj. = सामंतिक।

साम m. one of the four expedients, i.e. a friendly approach.

सामग्री f. collection of articles/requisites.

सामना m. 1. the part or side of something that faces forward, the main side of something. 2. meeting. 3. confrontation.

सामने adv. before.

सामने, के postposition. 1. in front of. 2. before. 3. in someone's presence or life time.

सामनेवाला adj. of or at the front, frontal. m. 1. one who faces someone. 2. other party. 3. opposite party.

सामयिक adj. 1. current. 2. relating to current affairs, topical.

सामरिक adj. pertaining to war, martial, strategic.

सामर्थ्य f. 1. strength, power. 2. capacity.

सामवेद m. one of the four Vedas.

सामाजिक adj. social.

सामाजिकता f. sociality, sociability.

सामाजीकरण m. socialization.

सामान m. 1. goods. 2. luggage.

सामान-घर m. luggage-room.

सामान्य adj. 1. general, common. 2. average.

सामान्यतः adv. generally, commonly.

सामान्या f. harlot, prostitute.

सामान्यीकरण m. generalisation.

सामिष adj. non-vegetarian (dish or food).

सामी adj. semitic.

सामीप्य m. nearness, closeness, proximity.

सामुदायिक adj. pertaining to a community.

सामुदायिक केंद्र m. community centre.

सामुद्र adj. marine, maritime.

सामुद्रिक adj. marine, maritime. m. palmistry, chiromancy.

सामूहिक adj. collective.

साम्य m. similarity, likeness, resemblance.

साम्यवाद m. communism.

साम्यवादी adj. communist, communistic. m. communist.

साम्यावस्था f. equilibrium.

साम्राज्य m. empire.

साम्राज्यवाद m. imperialism.

साम्राज्यवादी adj. imperialistic. m. imperialist.

सायं adj. pertaining to evening. m. evening.

सायंकाल m. evening, evening time.

सायंकालीन adj. vesperal, evening.

सायक m. arrow.

सायत f. auspicious moment (for marriage ceremony and the like).

सायबान m. shed, usually of tin.

साया m. 1. shadow. 2. shade. ~ न पड़ने देना to keep scrupulously aloof (from someone); ~ पड़ना to come under the evil influence (of someone); 3. petticoat.

सायुध adj. armed.

सारंग m. 1. a variety of deer. 2. cloud. 3. swan. 4. conch.

सारंगी f. an Indian stringed musical instrument.

सार m. 1. essence, quintessence, epitome. 2. gist, substance. 3. abstract, purport.

सारगर्भित adj. pregnant with meaning, pithy.

सारग्राही adj. competent to draw

स

out the essence of things, connoisseur.

सारजंट m. sergeant.

सारण m. 1. purging. 2. purification.

सारणी f. table (systematic arrangement in rows and columns).

सारथी m. charioteer.

सारना vt. to accomplish.

सारभाग m. substance, pith, essential portion, epitome.

सारभूत adj. substantial, essential.

सारवान, सारवान् adj. substantial, pithy, sententious.

सारसंग्रह m. digest.

सारस m. crane (bird).

सारांश m. the substance of some passage, speech etc., gist, summary.

सारा adj. whole, entire, all.

सारिका f. cuckoo.

सारी f. 1. = सारिका। 2. dice.

सारूप्य m. similarity of form, likeness, resemblance.

सारोपा m. set of clothes from head to foot.

सार्थक adj. meaningful, significant, fruitful.

सार्थकता f. meaningfulness, significance, fruitfulness.

सार्व adj. pertaining to all, general.

सार्वकालिक adj. pertaining to all times, eternal, perennial.

सार्वजनिक adj. 1. public. 2. common; ~ भूमि common land.

सार्वजनीकरण m. universalisation.

सार्वजनीन adj. सार्वजनिक।

सार्वत्रिक adj. existing every-where and under all circumstances, universal.

सार्वदेशिक adj. pertaining to all countries; cosmopolitan.

सार्वनामिक adj. pronominal; ~ विशेषण pronominal adjective.

सार्वभौम adj. = सार्वभौमिक।

सार्वभौमिक adj. universal, cosmopolitan.

साल m. 1. year. 2. a kind of tree and its timber. f. stiffening of nerves.

सालगिरह f. birthday.

सालन m. soupy preparation.

सालना vt. to cause piercing pain, to cause ceaseless pain.

सालस m. arbiter, arbitrator.

सालसी adj. arrived at through arbitration.

साला m. wife's brother, brother-in-law.

सालाना adj. yearly, annual.

सालिम adj. whole, entire.

साली f. wife's sister, sister-in-law.

सालू m. a kind of cloth of deep, red colour usually worn by women on auspicious occasions.

साव m. = साहू (शाह)।

सावधान adj. 1. careful, cautious. m. attention!

सावधानता f. = सावधानी।

सावधानी f. carefulness, cautiousness.

सावधि adj. having a time-limit, timed, periodic.

सावन m. fifth month of Hindu calendar, the main month of the rainy season.

सावन-भादों m. the two main months of the rainy season.

सावनी adj. of or pertaining to सावन।

सावरण adj. covered, provided with cover.

साश्चर्य adv. with surprise/wonder.

साष्टांग adj. & adv. ~ दंडवत/प्रणाम salutation by lying prostrate with all the eight organs of the body touching the ground.

सास f. mother-in-law.

साह m. = शाह।

साहचर्य m. association, companionship, comradeship.

साहब m. 1. Lord, master, God. 2.officer, boss. 3. a vocable or response of address denoting respect as in डाक्टर साहब। 3. a polite term of address for a man, Sir.

साहबी adj. aristocratic, royal, lordly. f. 1. state or quality of being a साहब। 2. lordliness, officiousness.

साहस m. courage, nerve.

साहसिक adj. courageous, daring, adventurous.

साहसी adj. 1. courageous, brave. 2. enterprising, adventurous, valiant.

साहा m. auspicious time, usually pertaining to marriage.

साहित्य m. literature.

साहित्यकार m. 1. literary person, litterateur. 2. writer.

साहित्यशास्त्र m. Rhetorics.

साहित्यिक adj. of or pertaining to literature, literary; ~ चोरी plagiarism.

साहिल m. 1. coast, shore. 2.bank.

साहिली adj. coastal. f. a small bird of the heron family.

साही m. porcupine.

साहु m. = साहू (शाह)।

साहुल m. plumb.

साहुल-सूत्र m. plumb line.

साहू m. 1. wealthy person. 2. banker.

साहूकार m. 1. wealthy person. 2. banker, money-lender.

साहूकारी f. occupation or status of साहूकार।

साहेब m. = साहब।

सिंगार m. = श्रृंगार।

सिंगारदान m. make-up box/case.

सिंगारना vt. to make-up.

सिंगारहाट m. red-light district, colony of brothels.

सिंगी f. 1. blow-pipe made of a horn; ~ लगाना to draw out impure blood through a सिंगी। 2. horn used as a flute (archaic).

सिंगौटी f. 1. receptacle made of horn. 2. an ornament fitted on the tips of the horn.

सिंघाड़ा m. water chestnut.

सिंघेला m. cub of a lion.

सिंचन m. 1. irrigation, watering. 2. sprinkling.

स

सिंचवाना vt. to cause to be irrigated or watered.

सिंचाई f. 1. irrigation, watering. 2. charges paid for irrigation.

सिंचित adj. irrigated, watered.

सिंदूर m. vermilion, cinnabar; ~ चढ़ना (virgin) to attain bridal status.

सिंदूरदानी f. small receptacle for keeping vermilion.

सिंदूरिया adj. = सिंदूरी।

सिंदूरी adj. 1. of or pertaining to vermilion. 2. of vermilion colour, vermilion.

सिंध m. 1. river Indus. 2. Sindh, a province in Pakistan.

सिंधु m. 1. sea. 2. river Indus. 3. Sindh province.

सिंधु घाटी f. Indus Valley; ~ की सभ्यता Indus Valley Culture.

सिंह m. 1. lion (Fem. सिंही, सिंहनी); ~ पुरुष lion among men. 2. appellation of Rajputs, Sikhs and other warrior classes.

सिंहद्वार m. main gate.

सिंहनाद m. 1. roar of a lion. 2. war cry.

सिंहनी f. fem. of सिंह।

सिंह राशि f. fifth sign of the Zodiac, Leo costellation.

सिंहल m. old name of श्रीलंका।

सिंहवत् adj. lion-like.

सिंहवाहिनी f. goddess Durga, riding a lion.

सिंहावलोकन m. 1. looking all round, circumspection. 2. retrospection.

सिंहासन m. throne.

सिंहोदरी adj. & f. (woman) having a slim waist like that of a lion.

सिकंदर m. Alexander the Great; तक़दीर/मुक़द्दर का ~ extremely lucky person.

सिकड़ी f. 1. chain (ornament). 2. chain (bolt).

सिगड़ी f. small charcoal oven for keeping one's body warm.

सिकता m. sand.

सिकतामय adj. full of sand, sandy.

सिकली m. act of polishing metallic objects, burnishing.

सिकहर m. = छीका।

सिकुड़न f. crumple, wrinkle, crease.

सिकुड़ना vi. 1. to shrink/shrivel. 2. to contract.

सिकोड़ना vt. 1. to contract. 2. to cause to shrink/shrivel.

सिक्का m. coin; ~ मानना to accept (someone's) sway.

सिक्केबंद adj. having original seal, genuine.

सिक्ख m. = सिख।

सिक्त adj. irrigated, watered.

सिख m. follower of Sikhism.

सिखाना vt. 1. to train/instruct. 2. to teach.

सिखावन f. counsel, advice.

सिगनल m. signal.

सिजदा m. obeissance, bowing down in veneration.

सिजल adj. 1. in good shape, tidy, seemly. 2. nice, decent, of better quality.

सिझना vi. to be cooked (said of vegetables, lentils etc.).

सिझाना vt. to cook (vegetables, lentils etc.).

सिटकिनी f. bolt, latch.

सिटपिटाना vi. to be completely nonplussed/stupified.

सिट्टी f. ~ गुम हो जाना/भूल जाना to be dumbfounded.

सिठनी f. caricaturing couplets sung (by women) on ceremonial occasions.

सिड़ f. crankishness.

सिड़-बिल्ला m. simpleton.

सिड़ी adj. cranky. m. crank.

सितंबर m. September.

सित adj. white.

सितम m. oppression, tyranny, cruelty; ~ करना to commit an act of cruelty.

सितमगर adj. cruel, oppressive. m. tyrant.

सितली f. cold sweat/perspiration.

सितार m. sitar, an Indian type of guitar.

सितारा m. 1. star. 2. सलमा-सितारा spangle.

सितारिया m. a professional who plays on sitar.

सिद्ध adj. 1. decided, proved, established. 2. fulfilled, attained. m. saint. [Fem. सिद्धा]

सिद्धकाम adj. & m. 1. having conquered (one's) desires. 2. having fulfilled (one's) object or mission.

सिद्धहस्त adj. adept, deft, dexterous.

सिद्धांजन m. magic collyrium bestowing power of clairvoyance.

सिद्धांत m. 1. principle, canon. 2. theory, doctrine.

सिद्धांततः adv. on principle, theoretically.

सिद्धांतवादी adj. upholder of principles, theoretician. m. high-principled man.

सिद्धांती adj. & m. 1. man of principles. 2. logician.

सिद्धान्न m. cooked grain.

सिद्धार्थ adj. whose mission has been fulfilled. m. Gautam Buddha.

सिद्धि f. 1. achievement, attainment, realisation, accomplishment. 2. success. 3. mastery.

सिद्धेश्वर m. 1. great among siddhas [Fem. सिद्धेश्वरी]. 2. Lord Shiv.

सिधाई f. simplicity.

सिधारना vi. to proceed, to get going; स्वर्ग ~ to leave for the heavenly abode.

सिन m. age.

सिनकना vi. to snot; नाक ~ to blow the nose for expelling mucus.

सिनेमा m. cinema.

सिपाहियाना adj. befitting a sepoy, soldierly.

सिपाही m. 1. policeman, constable, cop. 2. soldier.

सिप्पा m. device, artifice; ~ भिड़ाना/लड़ाना to manipulate.

सिफ़त f. characteristic, speciality.

स

सिफ़र m. zero, cypher.
सिफ़ारिश f. recommendation, commendation.
सिफ़ारिशी adj. recommendatory.
सिमटना vi. 1. to constrict/contract. 2. to near completion.
सियार m. jackal.
सियासी adj. political.
सिर m. head.
सिर-कटा adj. headless, beheaded.
सिरका m. vinegar.
सिरकी f. screen made of reeds.
सिर-खपाऊ adj. brain-racking.
सिरताज m. 1. crown. 2. Lord; मेरे ~ My lord.
सिरदर्द m. 1. headache. 2. botheration, worry.
सिरनामा m. 1. form of address in a letter etc. 2. full address of a recipient. 3. caption of an article.
सिरपच्ची f. ~ करना to rack (one's) brain.
सिर-फिरा adj. & m. crank, crankish.
सिरमौर m. diadem, crown of the head.
सिरहाना m. 1. side of a bedstead where the head rests. 2. pillow.
सिरा m. 1. the extremity of the length of something long as a thread, line, road etc., end. 2. top.
सिरी f. head of an animal slaughtered for meat.
सिरोही f. 1. a variety of sword. 2. a kind of bird.
सिर्फ़ adj. 1. only. 2. very few in number.
सिल f. flat stone used for grinding purposes.
सिलना vt. to stitch/sew. vi. to be stitched/sewn.
सिलपट adj. rendered plane by constant use.
सिल-बट्टा m. stone pestle and flat stone.
सिलवट f. crease, crumple.
सिलवाई f. act of sewing/stitch-ing or charges paid therefor.
सिलवाना vt. to get (clothes etc.) stitched/sewn.
सिलसिला m. 1. sequence, order, arrangement. 2. connection, context. 3. continuity, recurrence.
सिलसिलेवार adv. in orderly manner, in due order.
सिला m. = सिल्ला।
सिलाई f. = सिलवाई।
सिलाना vt. = सिलवाना।
सिला-सिलाया adj. made to wear, ready-made (garment).
सिल्क m. silk.
सिल्ला m. remnants of grains left over after harvesting; gleanings.
सिल्ली f. 1. a large solid rectangular piece of metal, ice etc. 2. whetstone for sharpening metallic tools.
सिवँई f. vermicelli.
सिवा prep. 1. besides. 2. except.
सिविल adj. civil.
सिसकन m. sob, sobbing.
सिसकना vi. to sob.
सिसकारना vi. to make a hissing sound.

सिसकारी f. hiss, hissing sound.

सिसकी f. sob.

सिहरन f. a slight shaking, tremor, thrill.

सिहरना vi. to shake because one feels cold, shyness or fright, to shiver.

सींक f. slender twig-like stick.

सींक-सलाई adj. lean and thin (person).

सींका m. = छींका।

सींकिया adj. lean and thin.

सींग m. horn.

सींगड़ा m. horned animal.

सींगी f. 1. musical pipe made of horn. 2. = सिंगी।

सींचना vt. to irrigate.

सी f. hissing sound.

सीकचा m. = सीखचा।

सीकाकाई f. a vegetable cleansing agent.

सीख f. (n. from सिखाना) advice, instruction.

सीख़ f. broach, skewer, spit.

सीखचा m. iron bar.

सीखना vt. to learn, to receive lessons.

सीखा-सिखाया adj. well-tutored, well-versed.

सीझना vi. to boil.

सीट f. 1. seat. 2. boast, brag.

सीटना vt. to brag, to indulge in bravado.

सीट-पटांग f. bravado, gasconade.

सीटी f. whistle.

सीठना m. = सिठनी।

सीठा adj. tasteless, insipid.

सीठी f. fibrous residual matter, dregs, refuse.

सीड़ f. dampness, damp, moisture.

सीढ़ी f. ladder, staircase, flight of stairs; ~ का डंडा any rung of a ladder.

सीढ़ीनुमा adj. like a flight of stairs.

सीता f. 1. furrow made by a plough. 2. Seeta, wife of Ram Chandra, God-incarnate.

सीताफल m. 1. = शरीफ़ा। 2. pumpkin.

सीत्कार m. sibilance; ~ करना to sibilate.

सीध f. straightness.

सीधा adj. [Fem. सीधी] 1. straight. 2. straightforward, simple. 3. direct. 4. clear. 5. upright; ~ आदमी simple soul.

सीधापन m. 1. simplicity. 2. quality of being too simple.

सीधा-सादा adj. plain and simple, innocent.

सीधे adv. straight-away, directly.

सीन m. scene.

सीना vt. to stitch/sew. m. chest/breast.

सीनाज़ोर adj. high-handed.

सीनाज़ोरी f. high-handedness.

सीनेट m. 1. The main governing body of certain universities, senate. 2. The upper house of legislative body in some countries.

सीप m. shell of an oyster.

सीपी f. small shell of an oyster, often used as a gadget.

स

सीमंत m. one of the sixteen Sanskars of Hindus, performed during the seventh or eighth month of pregnancy.

सीमांकन m. demarcation.

सीमांकित adj. demarcated.

सीमांत m. frontier, border.

सीमा f. 1. border, boundary. 2. furthest extent, limit.

सीमा-चौकी f. terminal post.

सीमातिक्रमण m. 1. crossing the boundary. 2. aggression.

सीमाबद्ध adj. bounded.

सीमा-रेखा f. border-line.

सीमाविहीन adj. having no limit, limitless.

सीमा-शुल्क m. duty paid on import, customs.

सीमित adj. limited.

सीमेंट m. cement.

सीमोल्लंघन m. transgression of territorial limit, violation of territory.

सीयन f. line of stiches, seam.

सीर f. land cultivated by the land-owner himself.

सीरा m. = शीरा।

सील f. 1. सीलन। 2. seal. 3. seal, a kind of sea-animal.

सीलन m. dampness, damp.

सीलना vi. to get damp. vt. to affix a seal to.

सीलबंद adj. sealed.

सीसा m. lead.

सुँघनी f. snuff.

सुँघाना vt. to cause to smell.

सुंडा m. an insect which infests vegetables.

सुंदर adj. beautiful, handsome, comely, pretty, lovey, charming.

सुंदरता f. beauty, comeliness, prettiness.

सुंदरी f. beautiful woman.

सुंबा m. boring gadget. [Fem. सुंबी]

सु prefix. denoting goodness, auspiciousness.

सुअर m. pig, boar.

सुअवसर m. good/favourable opportunity.

सुआ m. big needle.

सुई f. 1. needle; ~ का नाका eye of a needle. 2. a syringe to insert a drug in the body. 3. hand of a watch/clock.

सुईकारी f. needlework.

सुकंठ adj. having a good voice, melodious.

सुकर adj. easy to accomplish, practicable.

सुकर्म m. good deed.

सुकीर्ति f. renown, repute.

सुकुमार adj. delicate, tender, gentle. m. pretty lad. [Fem. सुकुमारी]

सुकुमारता f. delicacy, tenderness, softness.

सुकुल adj. virtuous.

सुकृत्य m. good deed, virtuous act.

सुखंडी f. rickets, rachitics. adj. rickety.

सुख m. happiness, pleasure, comfort.

सुखकर adj. giving pleasure or comfort, pleasing, delightful.

सुखद adj. = सुखकर।

सुखदायक adj. = सुखकर।

सुख-दुःख m. weal and woe, happiness and sorrow, pleasure and pain.

सुखपूर्वक adv. happily, comfortably.

सुखभोग m. enjoyment.

सुखांत adj. with a happy ending. m. comedy.

सुखाना vt. to make dry, to dry up.

सुखाभास m. euphoria.

सुखिया adj. = सुखी।

सुखी adj. happy.

सुख्यात adj. famous, reputed.

सुख्याति f. fame, reputation.

सुगंध f. fragrance, aroma, pleasing odour.

सुगंधि f. = सुगंध।

सुगंधित adj. fragrant, aromatic.

सुगठित adj. 1. well-built. 2. compact, well-knit.

सुगति f. well-being after death, beatitude, salvation.

सुगबुगाहट m. whisper.

सुगम adj. 1. easy, simple, plain. 2. easy to reach, accessible, passable.

सुगमता f. easiness.

सुगम्य adj. easily accessible.

सुग्गा m. parrot.

सुग्राही adj. sensitive.

सुग्रीव adj. having a well-formed neck. m. Sugriva, an ally of Ram in Ramayan.

सुघड़ adj. 1. well-built, shapely. 2. accomplished.

सुघड़पन m. accomplishment, proficiency.

सुघड़ी f. auspicious moment.

सुचारु adj. pretty, charming.

सुचाल f. 1. right move. 2. good ways.

सुचालक m. 1. good conductor (of electricity). 2. good driver.

सुचित adj. serene, tranquil, at leisure.

सुजन m. good man, gentleman.

सुजनी f. a variety of thick bed-sheet.

सुजात adj. = सुजाति।

सुजाति adj. of high caste. f. high caste.

सुजान adj. sagacious, sensible, wise, intelligent, clever.

सुझाखा adj. having (good) eye-sight.

सुझाना vt. to suggest, to indicate.

सुझाव m suggestion.

सुड़कना vi. 1. to take liquid through the nose. 2. to quaff (something liquid or semi-liquid).

सुडौल adj. shapely, well-formed, well-proportioned, beautiful.

सुत m. son.

सुतरां adv. hence, therefore, as such.

सुतली f. hemp or jute string.

सुतीक्ष्ण adj. very sharp.

सुथनी f. a variety of loose pyj- ama worn by women and girls.

सुथरा adj. neat, clean, tidy.

स

सुथरापन m. tidiness.

सुदर्शन adj. beautiful to look at, pleasing to the eye, good-looking.

सुदिन m. happy times.

सुदी f. bright fortnight of the lunar month.

सुदीर्घ adj. (very) long.

सुदूर adj. far off, very far, far away.

सुदूरपूर्व m. Far East.

सुदृढ़ adj. very firm, strong, rigid.

सुदेश m. good country.

सुद्दा m. piece of dry stool/faeces.

सुद्ध adj. = शुद्ध।

सुध f. 1. awareness, consciousness. 2. recollection, remembrance.

सुधरना vi. 1. to be reformed. 2. to improve.

सुधर्मा adj. = सुधर्मी।

सुधर्मी adj. religious, pious.

सुधा f. nectar, ambrosial beverage.

सुधाकर m. moon.

सुधामय adj. full of nectar/ambrosia.

सुधार m. 1. reform. 2. reformation. 3. improvement.

सुधारक m. reformer.

सुधारना vt. 1. to reform. 2. to correct/improve.

सुधारालय m. reformatory.

सुधि f. 1. awareness. 2. consciousness.

सुधी adj. having clear intellect, intellectual.

सुनगुन f. whispering rumour.

सुनना vt. to hear, to listen.

सुनना-गुनना vt. to listen and assimilate.

सुनम्य adj. flexible.

सुनयन adj. having a pair of lovely eyes. [Fem. सुनयना]

सुनवाई f. hearing.

सुनवैया m. listener, especially attentive listener.

सुनसान adj. lonely, desolately, quiet.

सुनहरा adj. = सुनहला।

सुनहला adj. golden, auburn.

सुनाई f. 1. the ability to hear, the capacity to hear. 2. hearing of the law case.

सुनाना vt. to tell/narrate/recite.

सुनाम m. good name.

सुनार m. goldsmith. [Fem. सुनारिन]

सुनारी f. 1. occupation of a goldsmith, goldsmithery. 2. good woman.

सुनिश्चय m. firm determination.

सुनिश्चित adj. frimly determined, ensured.

सुनीति f. equity, wholesome policy.

सुन्न adj. void of all sensation, benumbed, insensible.

सुन्नत f. circumcision.

सुन्ना m. zero, cypher.

सुन्नी m. one of the two main sects of Muslims.

सुपंथ m. good/right path.

सुपत्नी f. good wife.

सुपथ m. good/right path.

सुपथ्य m. wholesome diet.

सुपाच्य adj. easily digestible.

सुपात्र adj. & m. well-deserving.

सुपारी f. 1. betel nut, areca nut. 2. killing contract.

सुपुत्र m. dutiful son.

सुपुर्द adj. entrusted (to).

सुपुर्दगी f. charge, custody.

सुप्त adj. asleep, dormant, latent.

सुप्तावस्था f. state of being asleep, dormancy.

सुप्ति f. sleepiness.

सुप्रतिष्ठित adj. renowned, well-reputed.

सुप्रभात m. good morning, a harbinger of a good day.

सुप्रसिद्ध adj. renowned, reputed, well-known.

सुफल adj. fruitful. m. good result, better result.

सुबकना vi. = सुबुकना।

सुबह f. morning.

सुबह-सवेरे adv. in the early morning, at dawn.

सुबाहु adj. having shapely arms.

सुबुक adj. soft, light.

सुबुकना vi. to sob faintly.

सुबुद्धि f. good sense, better sense.

सुबोध adj. easily intelligible, comprehensible.

सुबोधता f. intelligibility.

सुभग adj. lovely, charming.

सुभगा adj. (woman) comely, beautiful.

सुभाषिणी f. sweet-tongued (woman).

सुभाषित adj. well-said, finely expressed. m. maxim.

सुभाषी adj. 1. sweet-tongued. 2. having the gift of the gab.

सुभिक्ष m. (when alms are easily available) time of plenty, days of affluence.

सुभीता m. convenience.

सुमंत्रित adj. well-advised, well-counselled.

सुम m. hoof.

सुमति f. 1. right way of thinking. 2. concord, harmony.

सुमन adj. nice-hearted. m. flower.

सुमरना vt. = सुमिरना।

सुमिरना vt. to repeat devotedly (God's) name etc.

सुमिरनी f. rosary.

सुमुखी adj. of handsome appearance, pretty-faced, having good/unique features.

सुमेरु m. mythological moun- tain (of gold).

सुयश m. renown, repute.

सुयोग m. happy coincidence/ occasion.

सुयोग्य adj. worthy, very comp-etent.

सुरंग adj. 1. of good colour. 2. of chestnut colour, reddish-brown. f. 1. tunnel. 2. mine (of dynamite).

सुर m. 1. god. 2. tone, note, tune; ~ निकालना to bring out a tune.

सुरकना vt. = सुड़कना।

सुरक्षण vt. act of protecting well.

सुरक्षा f. 1. protection, good protection. 2. security.

स

सुरक्षात्मक adj. defensive.

सुरक्षा-परिषद f. Security Council.

सुरक्षा-बल m. security forces.

सुरक्षित adj. 1. well-protected. 2. defended, well-defended. 3. reserved.

सुरक्षोपाय m. safeguard.

सुरख़ाब m. a bird of the heron family; ~ के पर लगना to be blessed with some unusual feature.

सुरख़ी f. = सुर्ख़ी।

सुरगाय f. = कामधेनु।

सुरत f. recollection, memory.

सुरतरंगिणी f. Milky Way.

सुरति f. pleasant love-play.

सुरती f. tobacco leaves turned into small flakes.

सुरदार adj. = सुरीला।

सुरपति m. Lord Indra, king of the gods.

सुरपुर m. the city where the gods dwell, Indrapuri.

सुरभि f. fragrance, perfume.

सुरभित adj. fragrant, perfumed.

सुरमई adj. of the colour of collyrium, of slatish hue.

सुरमा m. collyrium.

सुरमेदानी f. small collyrium container.

सुरम्य adj. exquisitely charming.

सुरस adj. juicy.

सुरसुराना vt. 1. to itch slightly. 2. to make a sound like that of a creeping/crawling insect/animal or such like.

सुरसुराहट m. state of सुरसुराना।

सुरसुरी f. 1. an insect which eats into grains. 2. = सुरसुराहट।

सुरही f. a game played with 16 cowries.

सुरांगना f. celestial damsel.

सुरा f. wine/liquor.

सुरागाय f. yak.

सुराज्य m. good government.

सुरापान m. drinking of wine.

सुरासव m. 1. methylated spirit. 2. celestial drink.

सुरासार m. alcohol.

सुरासुर m. gods and demons.

सुराही f. ewer; long-necked jar, usually earthen, meant for cooling water.

सुराहीदार adj. of the shape of सुराही, long-necked.

सुराहीनुमा adj = सुराहीदार।

सुरीला adj. melodious, tuneful, sweet, harmonious.

सुरुचि f. good taste.

सुरुचिपूर्ण adj. 1. full of good taste. 2. decorous.

सुरेंद्र m. Lord Indra, chief of the gods.

सुरैत f. concubine, kept mistress.

सुरैतिन f. = सुरैत।

सुर्ख़ adj. red, blood-red, scarlet.

सुर्ख़रू adj. glorified/honoured.

सुर्ख़ी f. 1. redness. 2. powder of bricks used in making brick walls. 3. banner line in a newspaper, headline.

सुलक्षण adj. having traits characteristically auspicious.

[Fem. सुलक्षणा] m. auspicious sign, good omen.

सुलगना vi. to smoulder.

सुलगाना vt. 1. to ignite/kindle. 2. to light.

सुलझना vi. to be disentangled.

सुलझाना vt. 1. to disentangle. 2. to resolve.

सुलटा adj. direct, straight.

सुलतान m. sultan.

सुलफ़ा m. an intoxicant made from tobacco leaves for smoking.

सुलभ adj. easily available/obtainable; ~ मुद्रा soft currency.

सुलभता f. easy availability.

सुलह f. 1. compromise. 2. truce, treaty.

सुलहनामा m. deed of compro- mise.

सुलाना vt. to cause to sleep, to make (someone) sleep.

सुलूक m. = सलूक।

सुलेख m. beautiful handwriting, calligraphy.

सुलोचना f. (woman) having lovely eyes.

सुवर्ण adj. 1. of good colour. 2. of the colour of gold, golden. m. gold.

सुवास m. fragrance.

सुवासित adj. scented.

सुविचार m. good/excellent idea.

सुविज्ञ adj. having special knowledge, well-versed, expert.

सुविज्ञता f. special knowledge, expertise.

सुविदित adj. well-known.

सुविधा f. 1. convenience. 2. facility, concession.

सुविधाजनक adj. convenient.

सुविधानुसार adv. at convenience.

सुव्यवस्थित adj. well-arranged, well-managed, well systema-tised.

सुशील adj. of good disposition, courteous, well-behaved, good-natured, affable, polite.

सुशीलता f. innate quality of good disposition, courteousness.

सुशीला f. fem. of सुशील।

सुशोभित adj. graceful.

सुश्री f. honorofic used for women.

सुश्रुत adj. well-known (object).

सुषमा f. natural/exquisite beauty.

सुषुप्त adj. 1. asleep, in slumber. 2. latent, dormant.

सुषुम्ना f. one of the fourteen main nerves of the body.

सुष्ठु adj. graceful, beautiful.

सुसंगत adj. cogent, relevant.

सुसंस्कृत adj. well-cultured, refined.

सुसंहत adj. compact.

सुसज्जित adj. well-decorated, well-adorned.

सुसमय m. good days, favou- rable times, time of prosperity.

सुस्त adj. 1. lazy, idle, indolent. 2. slow.

सुस्ताना m. to take rest, to relax.

सुस्ती f. laziness, idleness, indolence.

सुस्थिति f. good situation.

सुस्थिर adj. 1. well-poised, calm and balanced, steady. 2. firmly settled, stable.

स

सुस्वादु adj. very tasty, delici- ous.
सुहाग m. a woman's blessed state of life when her spouse is alive.
सुहाग-रात f. night of ceremonious consummation (of marriage).
सुहागवती f. = सुहागिन।
सुहागा m. borax.
सुहागिन f. woman whose husb- and is alive.
सुहाना vi. to be pleasing/agree-able. adj. = सुहावना।
सुहाल m. a dainty, salty preparation.
सुहावना adj. eye-catching, pleasant, delightful, plea-sing.
सुहृदय adj. having a good heart.
सूँघना vt. to smell.
सूँड f. trunk (of an elephant).
सूँडी f. an insect which eats into vegetables.
सूँस f. porpoise.
सूअर m. pig.
सूई f. = सुई।
सूकर m. = शूकर [Fem. सूकरी]
सूक्ति f. quotable quote, good saying.
सूक्ष्म adj. 1. minute, very small. 2. subtle, tenuous.
सूक्ष्मता f. minuteness, subtlety.
सूक्ष्मदर्शी adj. having a keen insight. m. microscope.
सूखना vi. to dry, to get dry.
सूखा adj. 1. dry. 2. without warmness or feeling; सूखी सहानुभूति dry sympathy (without emotion). m. draught.
सूखी तनख़्वाह f. only cash pay (no perquisites).
सूचक adj. indicative, sugges-tive. m. informer, indicator.
सूचकांक m. index number.
सूचन m. act of informing.
सूचना f. 1. information, communication. 2. notice.
सूचनापट्ट m. notice board.
सूचनाप्रद adj. giving (useful) in-formation, informative.
सूचना प्रौद्योगिकी f. Information Technology.
सूचनालय m. information centre.
सूचिका f. needle.
सूचित adj. informed.
सूची f. 1. needle. 2. inventory, list.
सूचीपत्र m. catalogue.
सूचीभेद्य adj. very dense.
सूजन f. swelling, inflammation.
सूजना vi. to swell.
सूजा m. a kind of long and thick stitching needle, distaff, awl, bodkin.
सूज़ाक m. gonorrhoea.
सूजी f. granulated wheat, semolina.
सूझ f. 1. insight, perception, penetrating insight. 2. striking idea.
सूझना vi. 1. to be visible. 2. to occur, to come to mind, to strike.
सूझ-बूझ f. imagination and wisdom.
सूटकेस m. suitcase.
सूटा m. puff.
सूत m. cotton yarn, thread.
सूतक m. state of temporary un-touchability due to some birth or death in the family.

सूता m. thread.

सूतिका f. lying-in woman.

सूतिका-गृह m. lying-in home.

सूती adj. made from cotton.

सूत्र m. 1. formula, aphorism. 2. clue. 3. source. 4. = सूत।

सूत्रधार m. stage-manager (in old Sanskrit dramas).

सूत्रपात m. commencement, beginning.

सूत्री adj. pertaining to सूत्र; त्रिसूत्री योजना three-fold plan.

सूथन f. a type of trousers worn by women, especially in Punjab.

सूद m. interest (on principal); ~ दर ~ compound interest.

सूदख़ोर m. a person who lends money at an exorbitant rate of interest, usurer.

सूदन adj. 1. destroyer. 2. dear, endearing.

सूदी adj. 1. pertaining to interest. 2. (sum) earned as interest. 3. (principal) yielding interest.

सूना adj. lonely, unfrequented.

सूनापन m. loneliness.

सूप m. a handy gadget/appliance used for winnowing grain and the like.

सूफ़ी m. believer of the cult of mysticism among Muslims.

सूबा m. province.

सूबेदार m. 1. governor of a province. 2. a non-commissioned officer in the Indian army.

सूम adj. miserly, penurious. m. miser.

सूमो m. Japanese wrestling.

सूर adj. blind.

सूरज m. sun.

सूरज-घड़ी f. sun-dial.

सूरजमुखी m. sunflower.

सूरत f. 1. appearance, countenance, face. 2. situation, form.

सूरत-शक्ल f. face and looks, general appearance.

सूरत-हराम adj. of deceptive looks.

सूरन m. an edible root.

सूरमा m. warrior, brave fighter, hero.

सूराख़ m. hole, aperture.

सूर्य m. Sun.

सूर्यग्रहण m. solar eclipse.

सूर्यवंश m. a renowned ancient Indian dynasty, solar dynasty.

सूर्यास्त m. sunset, sundown.

सूर्योदय m. sunrise.

सूर्योपासना f. sun-worship.

सूल m. = शूल।

सूली f. an ancient form of capital punishment.

सूहा adj. & m. bright red.

सृजन m. the Creation.

सृजनहार m. the Creator (of the world).

सृष्ट adj. Created, preduced.

सृष्टि f. the Creation.

सृष्टिकर्ता m. Creator.

सृष्टि-विज्ञान m. cosmology.

सेंक m. 1. fomentation. 2. war-mth.

सेंकना vt. 1. to foment. 2. to bake, roast.

सेंकाई f. fomentation.

स

सेंटा m. lower end of a reed (often used as a pen).

सेंतमेंत में adv. gratis, free of cost/charge.

सेंद्रिय adj. organic.

सेंध f. hole made in a house for burglary.

सेंधा नमक m. common salt as a solid mineral, rock-salt.

सेंधिया m. house-breaker, burglar.

सेंसर m. censor.

से postposition. 1. from. 2. to. 3. with. 4. through. 5. by. 6. since, for. 7. than.

सेकंड m. second, one-sixtieth part of a minute.

सेक्रेटरी m. secretary.

सेचन m. irrigation, watering.

सेचित adj. irrigated.

सेज f. luxurious bed.

सेट m. set (of articles).

सेठ m. wealthy/moneyed person [Fem. सेठानी]

सेतु m. bridge.

सेतुबंध m. 1. dam, serving as a bridge. 2. construction of a bridge.

सेना f. army. vt. to serve, to attend upon, to dance attendance on; अंडे ~ to hatch eggs.

सेनाध्यक्ष m. chief of the army.

सेनानायक m. general.

सेनापति m. commander.

सेब m. apple.

सेम f. bean.

सेमई f. = सेवईं।

सेमल m. silk cotton tree.

सेर m. seer (an Indian unit of weight, a little over two pounds).

सेरा m. smaller arm of bedstead.

सेल f. special sale/clearance of goods at reduced rates.

सेलखड़ी f. soap-stone, talc.

सेला m. rice produced from boiled paddy.

सेव m. a salty preparation (gram flour, shredded and fried).

सेवईं f. vermicelli.

सेवक m. 1. servant. 2. worker.

सेवकाई f. service attendance.

सेवड़ा m. salty preparation (long rectangular fried solids of wheat flour).

सेवन m. use.

सेवन-विधि f. method of use.

सेवा f. service.

सेवाकाल m. period of service.

सेवादार m. one who serves as a religious duty (among Sikhs).

सेवाधर्म m. service as duty.

सेवानिवृत्त adj. having retired from work.

सेवानिवृत्ति f. retirement.

सेवापंजी f. service-book.

सेवाभाव m. spirit of service.

सेवा-शुश्रूषा f. attendance (on a patient) and nursing.

सेविका f. 1. a female servant. 2. voluntary female worker.

सेवित adj. 1. attended upon (person). 2. used (object).

सेवी adj. & m. server.

सेव्य adj. fit to be served, worth being served.

सेहरा m. 1. bridegroom's chaplet. 2. eulogical verse composed for a wedding.

सेहरी f. a variety of small fish.

सैंतालीस adj. & m. forty-seven, 47.

सैंतीस adj. & m. thirty-seven, 37.

सैंधव adj. of or pertaining to Sindh. m. 1. inhabitant of Sindh. 2. = सेंधा नमक।

सैकड़ा m. hundred.

सैकड़े adv. in units of hundred.

सैकड़ों adj. & m. hundreds (of).

सैकत adj. sandy.

सैद्धांतिक adj. 1. pertaining to principle. 2. theoretical. m. theorist, theoretician.

सैनिक m. soldier.

सैनिकीकरण m. militarisation.

सैन्य adj. pertaining to an army. m. 1. soldier. 2. army.

सैन्यवाद m. militarism.

सैयाँ m. 1. husband. 2. lover.

सैयाद m. fowler.

सैर f. 1. the act of walking, roving. 2. outing, pleasure trip. 3. picnic.

सैर-सपाटा m. excursion, roving for joy.

सैल f. = सैर।

सैला m. wedge.

सैलानी m. 1. tourist. 2. excursionist, rover.

सैलाब m. flood.

सैलून m. 1. saloon, barber's shop. 2. special carriage, meant for some high dignitary.

सोंटा m. stout walking stick.

सोंठ f. dried ginger.

सोंधा adj. having a light, pleasing (particularly earthen) smell.

सोंधापन m. light, pleasing smell.

सो adj. & conj. so, that.

सोआ m. a variety of leafy vegetable.

सोख़ना vt. to suck/absorb/soak.

सोग m. mourning.

सोगवारी f. period of mourning.

सोच f. 1. consideration, pondering. 2. concern, anxiety.

सोचना vt. 1. to think. 2. to suppose or consider.

सोचना-समझना vt. to weigh the pros and cons.

सोच-विचार m. deliberation, due thought.

सोज f. = सूजन।

सोडा m. soda.

सोता m. spring (of water).

सोद्देश्य adj. purposeful, tendentious.

सोधना vt. = शोधना।

सोनचिरैया f. 1. a bird with gold-coloured plumage. 2. golden goose.

सोनल adj. golden.

सोना m. 1. gold. 2. precious thing or quality. 3. sleeping. vi. to sleep.

सोपाधि adj. conditional, with a condition.

सोपान m. staircase, flight of stairs.

सोपानित adj. stepped; ~ तिपाई stepped stool.

स

सोफ़ा m. sofa.

सोम m. 1. an ancient creeper. 2. moon. 3. elixir.

सोमरस m. 1. celestial beverage from the creeper सोम। 2. elixir.

सोमवार m. Monday.

सोयाबीन f. soyabean.

सोलह adj. & m. sixteen.

सोलह सिंगार m. an Indian style of make-up in all its sixteen traditional forms.

सोल्लास adv. with enthusiasm tinged with joy.

सोहन adj. comely.

सोहना adj. beautiful. vi. to appear comely.

सोहबत f. company, association, society.

सोहर m. a variety of songs sung on auspicious occasions, spl. child-birth.

सौंदर्य m. beauty, loveliness.

सौंदर्यशास्त्र m. aesthetics.

सौंपना vt. to entrust.

सौंफ़ f. fennel.

सौ adj. & m. hundred, century.

सौकर्य m. convenience.

सौकुमार्य m. young age.

सौख्य m. comfortability, plea-sure.

सौग़ात f. some special present for someone brought from outside.

सौग़ाती adj. pertaining to सौग़ात।

सौजन्य m. 1. gentlemanliness, kindness. 2. courtesy, affability.

सौत f. second wife, co-wife.

सौतिया adj. pertaining to a सौत; ~ डाह extreme jealousy as between co-wives.

सौतेला adj. step; सौतेली माँ step-mother.

सौदा m. 1. transaction, bargain, deal. 2. marketing, sundry household articles of day-to-day consumption.

सौदाई m. maniac (usually in love).

सौदागर m. businessman, merchant, tradesman (usually from outside).

सौदामिनी f. lightning.

सौदा-सुल्फ़ m. = सौदा।

सौदेबाज़ m. bargainer, higgler, haggler.

सौदेबाज़ी f. bargaining, horse-trading.

सौध m. mansion, palace.

सौभागिनी f. = सौभाग्यवती।

सौभाग्य m. good fortune.

सौभाग्यवती adj. & f. (woman) whose husband is alive.

सौभाग्यशाली adj. fortunate, of good fortune. [Fem. सौभाग्यशालिनी]

सौभाग्याकांक्षिणी adj. & f. maid (betrothed) seeking the happy state of married womanhood.

सौम्य adj. amiable, serene, pla-cid, tranquil.

सौम्यता f. amiability, serenity, placidity, tranquility.

सौर adj. solar.

सौरभ m. 1. fragrance, sweet smell. 2. mango.

सौर मंडल m. solar system.

सौराष्ट्र m. a region in the western part of India.

सौरी f. lying-in chamber.

सौष्ठव m. grace, elegance, charm.

सौहार्द m. warm and cordial relations, amity.

सौहार्दपूर्ण adj. pleasant and friendly, cordial.

स्कंध m. shoulder.

स्कूल m. school.

स्खलन m. 1. falling down. 2. deviation from the right path. 3. discharge, emission.

स्टांप m. stamp.

स्टेशनरी f. stationery.

स्टोव m. stove.

स्तंभ m. column, pillar.

स्तंभन vi. retention of one's semen.

स्तंभ-लेखक m. columnist.

स्तंभित adj. dazed/astounded/stunned/bewildered.

स्तन m. breast, udder.

स्तनपान m. breast feeding

स्तनपायी adj. & m. breast feeding (animal), mammal.

स्तनी adj. mammalian.

स्तबक m. bunch of flowers, bouquet.

स्तब्ध adj. stunned, stupefied, dumbfounded.

स्तब्धता f. stupefaction, dumb-foundedness, hush.

स्तर m. 1. level, standard. 2. stature. 3. fold, layer.

स्तरण m. stratification.

स्तरी, स्तरीय adj. pertaining to level/stature.

स्तुति f. reverential praise, eulogy.

स्तुत्य adj. praiseworthy, laudable.

स्तूप m. 1. mound. 2. stupa.

स्तोत्र m. hymn, eulogy of a god/goddess.

स्त्री f. 1. woman, female. 2. wife.

स्त्रीत्व m. womanhood.

स्त्री-धन m. property bestowed to a woman (principally on the occasion of her wedding).

स्त्री-राज्य m. gynarchy.

स्त्रीलिंग m. feminine gender.

स्त्रीसुलभ adj. which comes ea-sily to woman.

स्त्रैण adj. effeminate.

स्थगन m. 1. adjournment; ~प्रस्ताव adjournment motion. 2. postponement.

स्थगित adj. adjourned, postponed.

स्थल m. 1. place, site, venue. 2. land.

स्थलचर adj. living on land, terrestrial.

स्थलडमरूमध्य m. isthmus.

स्थल-सेना f. army, land force.

स्थली f. (picturesque) spot; वन ~ woodland.

स्थलीय adj. pertaining to land.

स्थविर adj. 1. steady. 2. venerable.

स्थान m. 1. place. 2. locality. 3. spot.

स्थानांतर m. transfer.

स्थानांतरण m. act of transferring, transference.

स्थानापन्न m. substitute.

स्थानिक adj. = स्थानीय।

स

स्थानीय adj. local.

स्थापक adj. & m. = संस्थापक।

स्थापत्य m. 1. architecture (art). 2. design and style of building.

स्थापन m. act of founding, establishment, installation.

स्थापना f. founding, establishment, installation.

स्थापना-दिवस m. foundation day, installation day.

स्थापित adj. founded, established, installed.

स्थायित्व m. 1. stability. 2. permanence.

स्थायी adj. 1. stable, durable, lasting, permanent.

स्थायीकरण m. confirmation, fixation.

स्थायी कोष m. reserve fund.

स्थायी समिति f. standing committee.

स्थावर adj. immovable, fixed.

स्थित adj. situated, located.

स्थितप्रज्ञ adj. of unperturbed disposition.

स्थिति f. 1. position. 2. situation, state. 3. phase. 4. an attitude towards something, stand.

स्थिर adj. 1. fixed, stable. 2. stationary, immovable, motionless. 3. firm. 4. stabilized.

स्थिरता f. stability.

स्थिरीकरण m. stabilization.

स्थूल adj. bulky, fat; ~ रूप से roughly.

स्थूलकाय adj. bulky, having a bulky body.

स्थूलता f. fatness, bulkiness.

स्थूलबुद्धि adj. dull-headed.

स्थैतिक adj. static.

स्थैतिकी f. statics, the branch of physics.

स्नात adj. bathed.

स्नातक m. graduate.

स्नातकोत्तर adj. postgraduate.

स्नान m. bath.

स्नानागार m. bathroom.

स्नायु f. nerve, tendon, sinew.

स्नायु-तंत्र m. nervous system.

स्निग्ध adj. 1. oily. 2. lubricative. 3. smooth, glossy.

स्निग्धता f. 1. oiliness. 2. smoothness.

स्नेह m. 1. affection, love. 2. oi-ly substance.

स्नेहक m. lubricant.

स्नेहपाश m. bond of love, tie of love.

स्नेही adj. affectionate, loving.

स्पंज m. sponge.

स्पंदन m. vibration, pulsation, throbbing.

स्पर्धा f. emulation, rivalry.

स्पर्धी m. rival, competitor.

स्पर्श m. 1. touch, contact. 2. (Gram.) stop.

स्पर्शजन्य adj. 1. arising from touch. 2. contagious.

स्पर्शनीय adj. tangible.

स्पर्श-रेखा f. tangent line. (Maths.)

स्पर्शी adj. touching.

स्पर्शेंद्रिय f. sense organ of touch, skin.

स्पष्ट adj. 1. clear, obvious, evident. 2. free from doubt or confusion, explicit. 3. frank, honest.

स्पष्टतः adv. clearly, evidently, plainly, explicitly.

स्पष्टतया adv. = स्पष्टतः ।

स्पष्टता f. the state or quality of being clear, clarity.

स्पष्टवादिता f. frankness in speaking, outspokenness.

स्पष्टवादी m. one who talks straight, outspoken, strai-ghtforward.

स्पष्टीकरण m. 1. clarification, elucidation. 2. something offered as a clarification, explanation.

स्पष्टीकृत adj. clarified, explai- ned.

स्पिरिट f. spirit (methylated or rectified).

स्पीकर m. speaker.

स्पृश्य adj. worthy of being touched.

स्पृहणीय adj. 1. desirable. 2. commendable.

स्पृहा f. ardent desire, longing.

स्पृही adj. desirous, covetous.

स्प्रिंगदार adj. provided with spring.

स्फटिक m. crystal.

स्फीत adj. expanded, enlarged.

स्फीति f. expansion; मुद्रा ~ infla-tion of currency.

स्फुट adj. miscellaneous.

स्फुटन m. 1. blowing out. 2. spr-outing.

स्फुरण m. 1. spurt. 2. flashing on the mind. 3. pulsating.

स्फुरना vi. 1. to issue forth. 2. to flash on the mind, to come suddenly to mind.

स्फुलिंग m. spark.

स्फूर्ति f. agility, liveliness, quic-kness.

स्फोट m. eruption, bursting out, explosion.

स्फोटक adj. 1. causing eruption, explosive. 2. detonating. 3. boil.

स्फोटन m. 1. eruption, explo- sion. 2. detonation.

स्मरण m. 1. recalling to mind, recollection, remembrance. 2. memorization.

स्मरण-पत्र m. 1. memorandum. 2. reminder.

स्मरण-शक्ति f. memory, power of memorising.

स्मरणीय adj. memorable, worth remembering.

स्मारक m. memorial, monument, relic.

स्मारिका f. 1. souvenir. 2. me-morandum.

स्मित adj. smiling. m. smile.

स्मृत adj. recollected, brought to memory, remembered.

स्मृति f. 1. memory, recollection, remembrance. 2. any of the 18 books of traditional Hindu law.

स्मृतिकार m. author of the Smritis.

स्मृति-चिह्न m. memento.

स्यंदन m. war chariot.

स्यात adv. perhaps, possibly.

स्यानप f. = सयानापन ।

स्यापा m. 1. traditional, collective mourning. 2. situation that evokes grief.

स्यामल adj. blackish, tawny.

स्यार m. jackal.

स्याह adj. black.

स्याही f. 1. blackness. 2. black ink. 3. ink.

स्रवण m. oozing.

स्रष्टा m. creator, the God.

स्राव m. discharge.

स्रोत m. 1. source, origin. 2. spring of water.

स्लिप f. slip.

स्लीपर m. 1. slippers. 2. sleeper (rail).

स्व prefix. denoting one's own or self. pron. self.

स्वकर्म m. one's deed (s).

स्वकीय adj. one's own.

स्वकीया f. wedded woman devoted to her husband.

स्वगत-कथन m. soliloquy.

स्वचल adj. automatic.

स्वचालक m. self-starter.

स्वच्छंद adj. 1. at liberty, free, unfettered. 2. self-willed.

स्वच्छंदता f. the right to do as one chooses, freedom, liberty.

स्वच्छ adj. 1. clean. 2. limpid, clear, pure.

स्वच्छता f. cleanliness, limpidness.

स्वजन m. kith and kin, near and dear relatives.

स्वजातीय adj. of one's own race/ caste.

स्वतंत्र adj. independent, free, self-governed.

स्वतंत्रता f. independence, freedom.

स्वतंत्रता-सेनानी m. freedom fighter.

स्वतः adv. 1. involuntarily. 2. automatically.

स्वतः निर्मित adj. 1. of one's own making, self-created. 2. self-made; ~ व्यक्ति self-made person.

स्वतः सिद्ध adj. that requires no proof, prima facie.

स्वतः स्पष्ट adj. obvious, self-evident.

स्वत्त्व m. 1. right. 2. ownership.

स्वत्त्वाधिकार m. ownership.

स्वदेश m. native land, mother-land.

स्वदेशी adj. indigenous.

स्वधर्म m. innate quality.

स्वन m. 1. sound. 2. noise. 3. phoneme.

स्वनामधन्य adj. renowned through one's own name, self magnanimous.

स्वनिम m. phoneme.

स्वनिम-विज्ञान m. Phonemics.

स्वनियोजित adj. self-employed.

स्वनिर्मित adj. 1. made by oneself 2. self-made.

स्वप्न m. dream.

स्वप्नदोष m. spermatorrhoea, nocturnal emission, night pollution.

स्वप्नद्रष्टा m. dreamer.

स्वप्नलोक m. dreamland.

स्वप्निल adj. dream-like.

स्वभाव m. 1. nature, tempera-ment, innate disposition. 2. habit.

स्वभावगत adj. habitual, wonted.

स्वभावतः adv. by nature, naturally, by disposition.

स्वयं pron. myself, yourself, himself or herself, one's own self. adv. automatically.

स्वयंपाकी m. one who cooks his own food.

स्वयंप्रमाण adj. self-proved, which needs no testimony.

स्वयंभू adj. self-born. m. God.

स्वयंवर m. ceremony prevalent in ancient India in which the bride chose her husband herself.

स्वयंवरा f. maiden who selects her husband herself.

स्वयंसिद्ध adj. axiomatic.

स्वयंसेवक m. volunteer, one who serves others voluntarily, scout. [Fem. स्वयंसेविका]

स्वयंसेवी adj. serving one's own self.

स्वर m. 1. vowel. 2. voice. 3. tone, tune. 4. intonation.

स्वर-यंत्र m. larynx.

स्वर-संधि f. union of adjacent vowels.

स्वरांत adj. (word) ending in a vowel.

स्वराजी m. votary of Swaraj movement.

स्वराज्य m. self-government, Swaraj.

स्वराष्ट्र m. one's own nation.

स्वरित m. one of the three ways of pronouncing vowels in the Vedas.

स्वरूप m. 1. shape, form, appearance. 2. mask. 3. identity.

स्वर्ग m. paradise, celestial abode in Heaven.

स्वर्गगमन m. departing for Heaven.

स्वर्गवास m. departure for Hea- ven, death.

स्वर्गवासी adj. the late.

स्वर्गारोहण m. ascendance into Heaven, passing away.

स्वर्गीय adj. 1. heavenly, paradisiacal. 2. late.

स्वर्ण m. gold.

स्वर्णकार m. goldsmith.

स्वर्णकाल m. golden period, glory days.

स्वर्ण-जयंती f. golden jubilee.

स्वर्णमान m. gold standard.

स्वर्ण-मुद्रा f. 1. golden coin. 2. gold-currency.

स्वर्ण-युग m. golden age.

स्वर्णाक्षर m. golden letter.

स्वर्णिम adj. golden.

स्वल्प adj. very little (in quantity).

स्वल्पाहार m. small quantity of food, light refreshment.

स्वशासन m. self-government, self-rule.

स्वस्तिक m. Swastik a sign, fylfot.

स्वस्तिमान m. auspicious self. [Fem. स्वस्तिमती]

स्वस्तिवाचन m. chanting of benedictory words/mantras.

स्वस्थ adj. healthy.

स्वस्थचित्त adj. composed and mentally sound, sane.

स्वहित m. concerm for one's own

interests, self-interest.

स्वाँग m. guise of another, in disguise.

स्वांतःसुखाय adv. for one's own happiness.

स्वाँस m. 1. = साँस। 2. asthma.

स्वाक्षर m. autograph.

स्वागत m. 1. welcome. 2. reception.

स्वागत-कक्ष m. reception-room.

स्वातंत्र्य m. = स्वतंत्रता।

स्वाति m. fifteenth of the twenty-seven constellations.

स्वाद m. taste, flavour.

स्वादिष्ट adj. tasty, delicious, relishable, savoury.

स्वादु adj. = स्वादिष्ट।

स्वाधिकार m. one's own right.

स्वाधीन adj. self-sufficient, independent.

स्वाधीनता f. self-dependence, independence.

स्वाध्याय m. 1. self-recitation. 2. self-study.

स्वाध्यायी adj. & m. studious.

स्वानुभूति f. personal experience.

स्वाभाविक adj. natural, spontaneous.

स्वाभाविकता f. naturalness, spontaneity.

स्वाभिमान m. self-respect.

स्वामित्व m. 1. ownership, proprietorship. 2. right.

स्वामिनी f. mistress, proprietress; गृह - ~ housewife, lady of the house.

स्वामी m. 1. master, lord. 2. owner, proprietor. 3. husband. 4. hermit. 5. The Reverend.

स्वायत्त adj. autonomous.

स्वायत्तता f. autonomy.

स्वार्थ m. one's own good, self-interest, selfishness.

स्वार्थ-त्याग m. self-denial, self-sacrifice.

स्वार्थ-परायण adj. self-seeking, selfish.

स्वार्थ-साधक m. self-seeker.

स्वार्थांध adj. blinded by self-interest, selfish to the extreme.

स्वार्थी adj. & m. selfish, self-seeker.

स्वावलंबन m. self-reliance.

स्वावलंबी adj. & m. self-reliant, self-dependent.

स्वास्थ्य m. health.

स्वास्थ्यकर adj. conducive to (good) health, wholesome, salubrious.

स्वास्थ्य-विज्ञान m. Hygiene, science of health.

स्वाहा interj. exclamation made while offering oblation (to Agnidev, the firegod).

स्विच f. switch.

स्वीकार m. act of acceptance; ~ कर लेना to accept/admit/confess.

स्वीकारना vt. to accept, to acknowledge.

स्वीकारोक्ति f. 1. admission, acceptance. 2. avowal, confession.

स्वीकार्य adj. acceptable.

स्वीकृत adj. accepted, admitted, acknowledged.

स्वीकृति f. assent, acceptance, admission.

स्वेच्छया adv. of one's own volition, according to one's own wish.

स्वेच्छा f. one's own volition/wish.

स्वेच्छाचारी adj. self-willed.

स्वेटर m. sweater.

स्वेद m. perspiration, sweat.

स्वेदित adj. perspired.

स्वैच्छिक adj. following one's own volition/wish.

स्वैर adj. uncontrolled, unrestrained.

स्वैराचार m. unrestrained con- duct.

स्वैराचारी adj. 1. self-willed. 2. libertine. [Fem. स्वैराचारिणी]

ह

ह (ha) m. fourth of the sibilants and the last letter of the Nagari alphabet; its sound resembles that of h in hill.

हँकवाना vt. 1. to cause to drive. 2. to scare away (cattle etc.), to halloo.

हँकवैया m. one who directs the course (of cattle etc.).

हँकुआ m. one who partakes in a हाँका।

हंगामा m. tumult, uproar, furore.

हंटर m. whip, lash.

हंडा m. metallic container (usually of brass) for storing water etc.

हंडिया f. small earthen pot used for cooking purposes.

हंडी f. same as हंडिया।

हंतव्य adj. who deserves being killed.

हंता m. killer, murderer.

हंस m. 1. swan, goose. 2. soul.

हंसगामिनी f. (woman) possessing the graceful gait of a swan.

हँसना vi. 1. to laugh. 2. to laugh at, to deride/ridicule.

हँसमुख adj. good-humoured, jolly, facetious, cheerful.

हँसली f. = हँसुली।

हंसवाहिनी f. Saraswati, goddess of Learning whose mount is a swan.

हँसाई f. ridicule, derision.

हँसाना vt. to make (others) laugh, to amuse, to tickle.

हंसिनी f. female swan/goose.

हँसिया f. sickle.

हँसी f. 1. laughter, laugh. 2. joke, fun; ~ उड़ना to be ridiculed, to be made fun of.

हँसीला adj. = हँसोड़।

हँसुआ m. large sickle.

हँसुली f. 1. collar-bone. 2. an ornament worn round the neck.

हँसोड़ adj. & m. jocular, jocose.

हक़ m. 1. right, privilege. 2. claim, title.

हक़दार adj. & m. rightful claimant.

हकबकाना vi. to be startled/ bewildered/confused.

हक़-मालिकाना m. proprietory right.

हक़-मौरूसी m. ancestral right.

हकला adj. & m. stutterer, stammerer.

हकलाना vi. to stutter/stammer.

हकलापन m. state or quality of stuttering/stammering.

हकार m. letter ह or its sound.

हक़ीक़त f. reality, truth, fact.

हकीम m. Hakeem, physician follwing the Greek system of medical treatment; नीम ~ quack.

हक्का-बक्का adj. taken aback, confused, bewildered.

हगना vi. to pass stools, to defecate, to evacuate.

हगाना vt. causative of हगना।

हगास f. urge to defecate.

हचक f. loss of the joint-grip, jerk, shock.

हचकना vi. to lose the joint-grip.

हचका m. mild jolt/shock.

हचकोला m. jolt.

हज f. pilgrimage to Mecca.

हज़म adj. 1. digested. 2. misappropriated.

हज़रत ind. a reverential form of address, Sire.

हजामत f. shave and/or hair-cut.

हज़ार adj. & m. thousand.

हज़ारों adj. thousands, many a thousand.

हज्ज m. = हज।

हज्जाम m. barber.

हटक f. forbiddance.

हटकना vt. to forbid.

हटना vi. to move away/aside.

हटरी f. toy-temple meant for lighting lamps in, during the Diwali festival.

हटवाना vt. to cause to move away.

हटाना vi. 1. to displace/remove. 2. to oust/dismiss.

हटिया f. market.

हटौती f. build of the body.

हट्टा-कट्टा adj. strong in constitution, stout and sturdy.

हट्टी f. shop.

हठ m. stubbornness, obstinacy; ~ करना to show obstinacy.

हठधर्मी f. sheer obstinacy/stubbornness.

हठ-योग m. one of the six kinds of Yoga.

हठात् adv. 1. forcibly. 2. through sheer obstinacy.

हठी adj. stubborn, obstinate.

हठीला adj. = हठी।

हड़कंप m. furore, great commotion.

हड़क f. 1. intense craving. 2. irresistible craving, maddening desire.

हड़कना vi. to be instigated.

हड़काना vt. to instigate.

हड़ताल f. strike.

हड़ताली m. a worker who is on strike, striker.

हड़पना vt. 1. to swallow, to devour in big mouthfuls. 2. to grab.

हड़बड़ f. = हड़बड़ी।

हड़बड़ाना vi. to make undue haste, to act precipitously.

हड़बड़िया adj. & m. hasty, (one) who habitually acts precipitously, rash.

हड़बड़ी f. undue haste, precipitation, hurry-scurry.

हड़हड़ाना vi. to make a loud sound (as in a crash down).

हड़हा adj. = हड़ीला।

हड़ावल f. wreath of bones.

हड़ीला adj. reduced to a skel- eton.

हड्डी f. bone; हड्डियों का ढाँचा a mere skeleton; ~ उतरना dislocation of a bone; ~ टूटना fracture of a bone.

हत adj. 1. killed. 2. murdered.

हतक f. insult, disgrace, dishonour, disrespect.

हतप्रभ adj. 1. deprived of lustre. 2. bewildered, stunned.

हतबुद्धि adj. 1. at one's wit's end, confounded, utterly perplexed.

हतभाग्य adj. hapless, unfortu- nate, unlucky.

हतवीर्य adj. bereft of one's prowess/ masculinity.

हताश adj. despairing, hopeless, disappointed.

हताशा f. despair, despondency.

हताहत adj. killed and wounded, casualties.

हतोत्साह adj. disheartened, dejected.

हत्था m. 1. handle, holder. 2. impression of hand.

हत्थी f. small handle.

हत्थे adv. in hand.

हत्या f. murder, homicide.

हत्यारा m. murderer, assassin.

हत्यारिन f. murderess.

हथ m. allomorph of हाथ used as a prefix in compound words.

हथकंडा m. (lit.) sleight of hand, tactics, stratagem.

हथकड़ी f. handcuff, manacle, shackle.

हथकरघा m. handloom.

हथकल f. hand-operated machine.

हथगोला m. hand-grenade.

हथछुट adj. who slaps even on trifles.

हथनी f. she-elephant.

हथफेर m. given to pinching (things) at odd places.

हथ-मिलाव m. handshake.

हथलपक m. swindler.

हथियाना vt. to grab, wrest.

हथियार m. 1. an object used in fighting, weapon (spl. of offence), arms. 2. tool. 3. any object or procedure that serves to win an opponent.

हथियार-घर m. armoury, arsenal.

हथियारबंद adj. armed, equipped with arms.

हथेली f. palm (of hand).

हथौड़ा m. hammer.

हथौड़ी f. small hammer.

हद f. limit, boundary, bound.

हदबंदी f. act of demarcating.

हदस f. scare.

हदीस f. collection of traditional sayings of Prophet Mohammed.

हनन vt. slaughtering, slaying, murdering.

हनना vt. to slaughter/slay/mur-der/ kill.

हनु f. the jawbone, jaw.

हनुमंत m. = हनुमान।

हनुमान m. monkey-god who helped Ram. (Ramayan)

हफ़्ता m. week.

हफ़्तेवार adv. weekly.

हबर हबर adv. hurriedhy, fastly, quickly, hastily.

हब्बा-डब्बा m. breathing trouble (among children), pneumonia.

हब्शिन f. a female Negro.

हब्शी m. any dark-skinned person of Africa, America etc., Negro.

हम pron. 1. we. 2. also replaces I generally. pref. denoting equality, similarity etc.

हम-उम्र adj. of the same age.

हमजोली m. chum, pal, close associate.

हमदम adj. & m. very intimate friend, chum.

हमदर्द m. sympathiser.

हमदर्दी f. sympathy.

हमनाम m. name-sake.

हमबिस्तर m. 1. one who enjoys the same bed, bedfellow. 2. companion.

हमराह adj. going together. m. = हमराही।

हमराही m. one who accom-panies, co-traveller.

हमल m. pregnancy, conception; ~ गिरना miscarriage; ~ गिराना abortion.

हमला m. attack, assault.

हमलावर adj. & m. assailant, invader.

हमवतन adj. compatriot, fellow countryman.

हमवार adj. even, level.

हमशक्ल adj. resembling in appearance, similar in looks.

हमसफ़र adj. fellow-traveller, fellow-passenger.

हमसाया m. neighbour.

हमाम-दस्ता m. mortar and pestle.

हमारा pron. & adj. 1. our, ours. 2. my, mine.

हमाहमी f. egoism, egotism.

हमें pron. 1. to us. 2. we.

हमेल f. a type of necklace made of coins.

हमेव m. egotism.

हमेशा adv. always, evermore.

हम्माम m. 1. bath-room. 2. large container, provided with a tap, for keeping water hot.

हय m. horse.

हयशाला f. stable.

हया f. innate modesty.

हर adj. every; ~ एक each and every. m. 1. Lord Shiv. 2. denominator of a fraction. (Arith.)

हरकत f. 1. movement, motion. 2. unbecoming/ undesirable behaviour/conduct.

हरकारा m. 1. messenger (usually a postal employee), courier. 2. forerunner, harbinger, envoy.

हरखना vt. to be delighted.

हरगिज़ ind. ~ नहीं under no circumstances, in no case.

हरज m. = हर्ज।

हरजाई m. a spouse who carries on with various persons, promiscuous spouse.

हरण m. stealing/carrying away.

हरता-धरता m. = कर्ता-धर्ता।

हरताल f. an arsenic, used as a pigment, orpiment; ~ लगाना (i) to write off, to cancel; (ii) to undo.

हरना vt. to steal/carry away. vi. to be defeated.

हरफ़ m. letter (alphabet).

हरबोंग m. turmoil, hubbub, furore, tumult.

ह

हरम m. harem, seraglio, female apartment in a palace.

हरमज़दगी f. villainy, rascality.

हरवाहा m. = हलवाहा।

हरहा m. wolf.

हरा adj. green; मन ~ हो जाना to be overjoyed.

हराना vt. to defeat/beat.

हरापन m. greenness.

हरा-भरा adj. 1. lush with greenery. 2. gay and flourishing.

हराम adj. ill-gotten, improper. m. immorality; ~ की कमाई immoral earnings.

हरामख़ोर adj. & m. one who is given to evil earning by shirking work.

हरामज़ादा adj. & m. bastard, illegitimate offspring (used as an invective).

हरामी adj. & m. illegitimate, bastard.

हरारत f. 1. heat, warmth. 2. temperature, feverishness.

हरावल m. vanguard.

हरि m. Lord Vishnu.

हरिआना vi. = हरियाना।

हरिजन m. 1. (lit.) God's own being. 2. (now, in common parlance) one belonging to the scheduled class.

हरिण m. = हिरन।

हरित adj. green.

हरिताभ adj. having a green shade, of a greenish hue.

हरिद्रा f. = हल्दी।

हरिन m. = हिरन।

हरिपद m. abode of Lord Vishnu.

हरियानवी adj. of हरियाना।

हरियाना vi. to turn/become green. m. a Hindi-speaking state of Northern India.

हरियाली f. greenery.

हरिस m. beam of a plough.

हरीरा m. a sweet preparation of pulverised almond and milk.

हरे m. vocative of हरि।

हरेक adj. everybody, everyone.

हर्ज m. 1. loss. 2. harm.

हर्जाना m. something given to compensate, damages, compensation.

हर्र f. myrobalan.

हर्ष m. joy, delight, cheer, happiness.

हर्षध्वनि f. cry of joy/jubilation.

हर्षित adj. delighted, pleased.

हर्षोन्माद m. ecstasy.

हलंत adj. (word) ending with the हल् (्) mark.

हल् m. 1. a stroke (्) placed at the end of a consonant to denote the absence of the अ vowel sound after it, as क्, ख्, ग्। 2. a consonant down below which the aforesaid mark is appended.

हल m. 1. plough. 2. solution (of a problem).

हलक़ m. gullet, throat.

हलका adj. 1. light, not heavy. 2. less than average weight. 3. not fast (said of a colour), light. 4. easy to bear. 5. easy to digest.

हलक़ा m. circle, beat, area, zone.

हलकान adj. = हलाकान।

हलकापन m. 1. lightness. 2. shallowness.

हलचल f. stir, commotion.

हलदी f. turmeric.

हलधर m. 1. ploughman. 2. Balram, elder brother of Lord Krishna.

हलफ़ m. oath.

हलफ़नामा m. affidavit, written statement on oath.

हलराना vt. to rock/cradle.

हलवा m. a dainty Indian dish.

हलवाई m. confectioner. [Fem. हलवाइन]

हलवाहा m. ploughman.

हलाक adj. killed, murdered.

हलाकान adj. harassed.

हलाकू m. killer, murderer.

हलायुध m. Balram, elder brother of Lord Krishna.

हलाल adj. 1. slaughtered as per Muslim convention. 2. hard-earned, well-begotten.

हलालख़ोर adj. & m. 1. (one) who lives on well-begotten earnings. 2. scavenger.

हलाहल m. deadly poison.

हलुआ m. = हलवा।

हल्का adj. = हलका।

हल्ला m. 1. noise. 2. attack.

हल्ला-गुल्ला m. hullaballoo, commotion, tumult, uproar, clamour.

हवन m. ceremony in which oblations are offered to the fire-god.

हवनकुंड m. prismshaped dugout vessel (with square ends) used for performing हवन।

हवन-सामग्री f. the group of articles offered to fire-god.

हवलदार m. sergeant.

हवस f. 1. insatible lust. 2. persistent and excessive desire.

हवा f. air, wind, atmosphere.

हवाई adj. of or pertaining to air, aerial; ~ फ़ायर fire in the air. f. a kind of cracker.

हवाई अड्डा m. aerodrome.

हवाई छतरी f. air-umbrella, parachute.

हवाई जहाज़ m. an aeroplane.

हवाई डाक f. airmail.

हवाई यात्रा f. journey by air.

हवादार adj. airy, well-ventilated.

हवा-पानी m. climate.

हवाबाज़ m. air pilot.

हवामार adj. anti-aircraft.

हवाल m. turn of events.

हवाला m. reference; हवाले करना to hand over.

हवालात f. lock-up.

हवास m. knowledge through sense organs.

हवि m. 1. oblation. 2. sacrificial goat.

हवेली f. 1. mansion, palatial building. 2. temple.

हशीश f. hashish, a kind of intoxicant prepared from dried hemp.

हश्र m. 1. day of judgment. 2. destiny. 3. final outcome, resultant effect.

हसरत f. innate desire, longing.

हसीन adj. handsome, comely, pretty, beautiful.

हसीना f. pretty young girl, belle.

हस्त m. 1. hand. 2. tenth constellation of the stars.

हस्तकला f. handicraft.

हस्तकौशल m. manual skill.

हस्तक्षेप m. interference, meddling.

हस्तगत adj. obtained, come into one's possession, received.

हस्तमैथुन m. masturbation.

हस्तरेखा f. line on the palm.

हस्तलाघव m. 1. skill of hand. 2. sleight of hand.

हस्तलिखित adj. hand-written.

हस्तलिपि f. handwriting.

हस्तशिल्प m. handicraft.

हस्तांतरण m. handing over, transference.

हस्तांतरित adj. transferred.

हस्ताक्षर m. signature.

हस्ताक्षरित adj. signed.

हस्तामलक adj. crystal clear.

हस्तिनी f. 1. female elephant. 2. fourth class of women. (Hindu Sexology)

हस्ती m. elephant. f. being, individuality, personality, figure.

हस्ते, के postposition. through the agency of.

हाँ adv. yes.

हाँक f. calling aloud.

हाँकना vt. 1. to drive. 2. to goad.

हाँडी f. earthen pot meant mainly for cooking purposes.

हाँफना vi. to pant.

हा inter. denoting sorrow or grief.

हाइफ़न m. hyphen.

हाकिम m. 1. ruler. 2. officer.

हाकिमी f. = हुकूमत।

हाकी f. Hockey.

हाजत f. 1. call of nature. 2. custody.

हाजती adj. (person) under duress or custody.

हाज़मा m. power of digestion.

हाज़िर adj. present.

हाज़िरजवाब adj. ready-witted.

हाज़िरजवाबी f. ready wit.

हाज़िरी f. 1. attendance. 2. roll-call.

हाजी m. 1. one who has been to Mecca on pilgrimage. 2. appellation attached to the name of such a person.

हाट f. 1. market. 2. periodical market.

हाड़ m. bone; ~ पेलना to put in extremely hard labour.

हाता m. compound, enclosure.

हातिम adj. generous, liberal.

हाथ m. 1. hand. 2. one round of a card game. 3. a person who does something.

हाथा m. 1. impression of the hand with turmeric etc. 2. = हत्था।

हाथापाई f. scuffle.

हाथाबाँही f. = हाथापाई।

हाथी m. elephant.

हाथीख़ाना m. elephant-shed.
हाथी-दाँत m. ivory.
हाथी-पाँव m. = फ़ील पाँव।
हाथीवान m. an elephant driver.
हादसा m. mishap, accident, tragedy.
हानि f. 1. loss. 2. harm.
हानिकर adj. 1. causing loss. 2. harmful.
हानिकारक adj. = हानिकर।
हामिला adj. pregnant.
हामी f. assent. m. supporter.
हाय inter. alas! f. 1. sigh/cry of a lacerated heart. 2. insatiable hunger.
हाय-तोबा f. uproar, tumult, hullaballoo.
हार f. defeat. m. 1. garland, wreath. 2. necklace.
हार-जीत f. 1. defeat and victory. 2. victory or defeat.
हारना vi. to be defeated. m. act of losing.
हारमोनियम m. harmonium.
हारा suffix. denoting 'doer'; सृ ~ God, the Creator. adj. defeated [Fem. हारी]
हारिल m. a. greenish Indian bird.
हार्दिक adj. 1. hearty, cordial.
हार्दिकता f. heartiness, cordiality.
हाल m. 1. condition, state. 2. time that is passing, recent past. m. hall.
हाल-चाल m. state of affairs.
हालत f. condition.
हालाँकि conj. though, although.
हाला f. liquor, wine. m. = हाला-चाला।
हाला-चाला m. earthquake.
हालात m. plu. of हाल, circumstances.
हाली m. = हलवाहा।
हाव-भाव m. gestures and postures (especially amorous), coquetry.
हावी adj. domineering.
हाशिया m. margin, border.
हास m. laugh, laughter.
हासिल adj. gained, got, acquired, obtained.
हास्य m. laugh, laughter, humour.
हास्यकर adj. humorous, provoking laughter.
हास्यास्पद adj. preposterous, ludicrous, ridiculous, funny.
हाहंत ind. O, the tragedy!
हाहाकार m. cry of distress.
हाहा-हूहू m. joyous hilarity.
हिंकरना vi. to neigh/whinny.
हिंडोला m. 1. swing adorned with a seat. 2. merry-go-round.
हिंद m. India.
हिंदवी f. a rather contemptuous name for Hindi.
हिंदी f. Hindi, the national language of India.
हिंदुत्व m. Hinduism.
हिंदुस्तान m. Hindustan, India.
हिंदुस्तानी adj. Indian. m. an Indian. f. spoken language of Hindus and Muslims in the major part of Northern India.

हिंदू adj. & m. Hindu.

हिंदोस्तान m. = हिंदुस्तान.

हिंसक adj. 1. violent (person). 2. carnivorous (animal).

हिंसा f. violence.

हिंसाचार m. violence.

हिंसात्मक adj. violent.

हिंस्र adj. violent, ferocious.

हिकमत f. 1. Unani i.e. Greek system of Medicine. 2. skill, tact.

हिकमती adj. tactful, skilful.

हिक्का m. = हिचकी।

हिचक f. hitch, hesitation.

हिचकना vi. to hitch/hesitate.

हिचकिचाना vi. = हिचकना।

हिचकिचाहट f. hitch, hesitation.

हिचकी f. hiccup.

हिचकोला m. = हचकोला।

हिचर-मिचर f. undue hesitation, shilly-shally.

हिजड़ा adj. impotent. m. 1. a eunuch. 2. an ineffective man.

हिजरी f. Muslim era.

हिज्जे m. spelling.

हित m. 1. benefit, gain, welfare. 2. interest.

हितकर adj. beneficial, salutary, useful, profitable.

हितकारक adj. = हितकर।

हितचिंतक adj. & m. well-wisher, benefactor.

हितचिंतन m. well-wishing.

हिताहित m. good and evil.

हितू adj. & m. = हितैषी।

हितेच्छु adj. & m. = हितैषी।

हितैषी adj. & m. well-wishing, benevolent, well-wisher.

हितोपदेश m. teaching for (one's) good.

हिदायत f. instruction.

हिनक f. = हिनहिनाहट।

हिनहिनाना vi. to neigh/whinny.

हिनहिनाहट f. neighing.

हिना f. myrtle.

हिनाई adj. of the colour of (grounded) myrtle.

हिफ़ाज़त f. safety, protection, safeguard.

हिम m. 1. snow. 2. frost.

हिमनदी f. glacier.

हिमपात m. snowfall.

हिमशैल m. iceberg.

हिमांक m. freezing point.

हिमाक़त f. folly, stupidity.

हिमाच्छादित adj. snow-covered.

हिमाद्रि m. Himalayas.

हिमानी f. glacier, avalanche.

हिमायत f. support, help, bac- king.

हिमायती adj. & m. supporter.

हिमालय m. Himalayas.

हिमावृत adj. snow-capped.

हिमियानी f. knitted purse used as a belt.

हिम्मत f. courage, boldness.

हिम्मती adj. courageous, bold, adventurous.

हिय m. = हृदय।

हियरा m. = हृदय।

हिया m. = हृदय।

हियाव m. 1. shyness. 2. hitch.

हिरण m. = हिरन।

हिरण्य m. gold.

हिरन m. deer.

हिरनौटा m. young of a deer.

हिराना vi. = हेराना।

हिरासत f. duress, legal detention/custody.

हिरासती adj. pertaining to हिरासत; ~ कोठरी detention cell.

हिर्स f. 1. unfulfilled longing. 2. envy or emulation.

हिलकोरा m. billow, wave.

हिलगना vi. to be attached/entangled/joined/clung (to).

हिलना vi. 1. to move/shake. 2. to quiver. 3. to be chummy (with).

हिलना-मिलना vi. to hobnob.

हिलाना vt. 1. to move/shake; दुम ~ to wag tail. 2. to put (something) in motion. 3. to try being chummy.

हिलोर f. 1. wave, surge. 2. undulation.

हिलोरना vt. to gather.

हिसाब m. 1. account. 2. sum (in Arithmetic). 3. calculation. 4. estimate.

हिसाब-किताब m. accounts.

हिसाबिया adj. calculating.

हिस्सा m. 1. part, portion. 2. share.

हिस्सेदार m. 1. co-sharer. 2. shareholder. 3. partner.

हिस्सेदारी f. co-sharing, partnership.

हींग f. asafoetida.

हीं-हीं f. grinning, subdued laugh.

ही adv. 1. only, solely. 2. none but. 3. indeed, exactly.

हीक f. smell, rather dislikable/unpleasant.

हीन adj. 1. low. 2. destitute. suffix. denoting 'devoid of'; बलहीन devoid of prowess.

हीनता m. 1. lowliness, inferiority. 2. deficiency.

हीनभावना f. 1. inferiority complex. 2. low mentality.

हीया m. = हृदय।

हीर f. pith, quintessence.

हीरक m. diamond.

हीरक जयंती f. diamond jubilee.

हीरा m. diamond.

हीला m. pretext, pretence.

हीला-हवाला m. false excuse.

हीलेबाज़ adj. & m. pretender, one who pretends.

ही ही f. titter.

हुँ m. denoting assent.

हुंकार f. belligerent cry, war cry.

हुंकारना vi. to make a belligerent cry, to chide, to rebuke.

हुँकारा m. = हुंकारी।

हुँकारी f. sound indicating that one is listening.

हुंडी f. bill of exchange.

हुआ vt. pp. of होना।

हुक m. hook. f. crick.

हुकर-पुकर f. = धुकर-पुकर।

हुकुम m. = हुक्म।

हुकूमत f. 1. government, rule. 2. suzerainty.

हुक़्क़ा m. hubble-bubble.

हुक़्क़ा-पानी m. social dealings/relations; ~ बंद करना to boycott socially.

हुक्म sm. order, command.

हुक्मनामा m. written order.

हुक्मबरदार m. obedient servant.

हुजूम m. crowd.

हुजूर m. Your Honour, Sir.

हुजूरी f. = जी हुजूरी, sycophancy.

हुज्जत f. (needless) wrangling.

हुज्जती adj. given to wrangling.

हुड़क f. pang/heartache due to separation (said of a child).

हुड़कना vt. to suffer the pangs of separation (usually said of a child).

हुड़का m. = हुड़क।

हुड़दंग m. uproar, disturbance, noisy confusion, bedlam, commotion, tumult.

हुड़दंगी adj. playful and restive.

हुताग्नि f. sacrificial fire.

हुताशन m. fire.

हुन m. gold coin.

हुनर m. 1. art. 2. skill.

हुनरमंद adj. skilful. m. artist.

हुनरा adj. trained (said of a monkey).

हुमकना vi. to dance/frisk about.

हुमेल f. a variety of necklace, especially of gold coins.

हुलसना vi. to express an exuberance of joy/delight.

हुलास m. jubilation. f. snuff.

हुलिया m. physical features, form, shape; ~ तंग कर देना to harass beyond measure.

हुल्लड़ m. 1. noise, uproar. 2. furore, tumult, ballyhoo.

हुश ind. hush! shut up!

हुस्न m. comeliness, handsomeness, prettiness, beauty.

हुस्नपरस्त adj. & m. worshipper of beauty.

हूँ vi. & aux. v. am. m. 1. assent. 2. attention (to what is being said).

हूँक f. cry (denoting pangs of separation) usually of a cow.

हूँकना vi. to make a हूँक।

हूँठा m. 1. number which is three and a half times a given integer. 2. multiplication table giving such numbers.

हूँस f. appreciation which hurts someone.

हूँसना vi. to appreciate in an objectionable manner.

हूक f. stabbing pain born of some intense longing.

हूबहू adj. exactly alike, resembling on all fours.

हूर f. 1. fairy. 2. beauty celestial, lovely damsel.

हूरना vt. to box, to give blows with the fist.

हूल f. piercing thrust.

हूश adj. vulgar, savage-like, rustic.

हृतकंप m. throbbing of heart, palpitation.

हृदयंगम adj. ~ करना to assimilate mentally.

हृदय m. heart.

हृदयग्राही adj. captivating, fascinating.

हृदय-वल्लभ m. darling of the heart.

हृदयविदारक adj. poignant, heart-rending.

हृदयवेधी adj. heart-piercing.

हृदयस्पर्शी adj. touching the heart, pathetic.

हृदयेश m. lord of one's heart.

हृदयेश्वर m. = हृदयेश।

हृदयेश्वरी f. mistress of the heart, beloved.

हृद्रोग m. heart-disease.

हृष्ट-पुष्ट adj. stout and robust.

हें-हें f. imploring like a syco- phant.

हे ind. particle of address.

हेकड़ adj. arrogant, rude.

हेकड़ी f. bravado and gasconade.

हेठी f. humiliation, especially lowering in the estimation of others.

हेडमास्टर m. headmaster.

हेतु m. purpose.

हेत्वाभास m. fallacy (logic).

हेमंत m. winter.

हेम m. gold.

हेय adj. inferior, bad, deficient, worthless.

हेरना vt. 1. to search, investigate. 2. to gaze.

हेर-फेर m. interchange of articles, manipulation, exchange, alteration.

हेरा-फेरी f. 1. moving about to and fro with some (ulterior) motive. 2. interchange of articles with some (ulterior) motive.

हेल-मेल m. hob-nobbing.

हैं vi. & aux. v. are. interj. denoting an exclamation, what!

है vi. & aux. v. 1. is. 2. art.

हैगा vi. = है।

हैज़ा m. cholera.

हैरत f. wonderment, astonishment.

हैरान adj. suprised and perplexed.

हैरानी f. perplexity, botheration, anxiety.

हैवान m. beast.

हैसियत f. 1. status. 2. capacity.

होंठ m. lip.

होटल m. hotel.

होठ m. = होंठ।

होड़ f. competition, rivalry.

होड़ा-होड़ी f. competition.

होतव्य adj. predestined, desti- ned to happen.

होतव्यता f. destiny, fate.

होता m. 1. offerer of oblation (to the fire-god). 2. one who offers sacrificial oblations in the sacred fire.

होतृ m. = होता।

होनहार adj. 1. predestined, inevitable. 2. promising, full of promise.

होना vi. & aux. v. 1. to be, to become, to take place, to happen. 2. to possess, to have; हो चुकना to be finished.

होनी f. fate, destiny.

होनेवाला adj. would-be, future.

होम m. 1. sacrifice; ~ करते हाथ जलना to suffer while doing a good deed. 2. = हवन।

होमियोपैथी f. homeopathy.

ह

होरहा m. green gram.

होलिका f. = होली।

होलिका-दहन m. lighting the fire of होली ceremonially.

होली f. a Hindu festival of merry-making in which people throw coloured powder/water on one another.

होल्डाल m. hold-all.

होश m. 1. consciousness. 2. sense.

होशियार adj. 1. clever, cute, alert, smart, quickwittted. 2. vigilant.

होशियारी f. cleverness, alertness, smartness.

होस्टल m. hostel.

हो-हल्ला m. commotion, bedlam, tumult.

हौंस f. = हवस।

हौआ m. bugbear.

हौज़ m. reservoir.

हौदा m. contrivance for seating placed on an elephant.

हौल m. nervousness due to fear and the like.

हौली f. 1. smallish distillery. 2. liquor shop.

हौले-हौले adv. 1. with steps, slow and easy. 2. slowly and gently, gradually.

हौवा m. = हौआ।

हौसला m. 1. courage. 2. courageous ambition.

ह्रस्व adj. short; ~ स्वर short vowel.

ह्रास m. 1. decrease, decrement. 2. decay.

ह्रासमान adj. 1. decreasing, diminishing. 2. decaying.

ह्रासोन्मुख adj. 1. decreasing. 2. decaying.

ह्विस्की f. whisky.

ह्वेल f. whale.

वर्गीकृत शब्दावलियाँ
Classified Vocabularies

फल Fruits

अंगूर Grapes
अंजीर Fig
अखरोट Walnut
अनन्नास Pineapple
अनार Pomegranate
अमरूद Guava
आड़ू Peach
आम Mango
आलू बुखारा Plum
किशमिश Raisin

केला Banana
खरबूजा Musk Melon
खूबानी Apricot
चकोतरा Pompelmoose
जामुन Rose-apple
तरबूज Water Melon
नारियल Coconut
नाशपाती Pear
नीबू Lime
पपीता Papaya

पिस्ता Pistachio-nut
फालसा Gromia
बादाम Almond
बेर Jujube
मूँगफली Ground-nut
मौसमी Mozambique
शरीफा Custard apple
शहतूत Mulberry
संतरा Orange
सेब Apple

सब्जियाँ Vegetables

अरबी Colocasia
आलू Potato
ककड़ी Long Cucumber
कटहल Jack fruit
कद्दू, लौकी, घिया Pumpkin
करेला Bitter Gourd
कुंदरू Ivy Gourd
कोंहड़ा Squash Gourd
खीरा Cucumber
गाजर Carrot
फूलगोभी, गोभी Cauliflower

ग्वारफली Cluster Beans
चिंचिड़ा Snake Gourd
चुकंदर Beet Root
टिंडा Round Gourd
तुरई Ribbed Gourd
धनिया Coriander
पालक Potherb, Spinach
पुदीना Mint
पेठा Ash Pumpkin
प्याज Onion
बंदगोभी Cabbage
बैंगन/भाटा Brinjal

भिंडी Lady's Finger
मिर्च Chillies
मूली Radish
मेथी Fenugreek
रतालू Potato Yam
लहसुन Garlic
शकरकंद Sweet Potato
शलजम Turnip
सहजन की फली Drumstick
साग Greens
सूरन Yam
सेम Beans

फूल Flower

कमल Lotus
कमलिनी Lily
कलगा Coxcomb
केवड़ा Pandanus

गुल खैरा Gilly Flower
गुल चाँदनी Moon Flower
गुल दाऊदी Small Chrysantheum

गुलमेंहदी Balsam
गुल लाला Tulip
गेंदा Marigold
चंपा Yellow Jasmine

चमेली Jasmine	नरगिस Narcissus	मोतिया Round Jasmine
जुही Sweet Jasmine	पोस्ता Poppy	सूरजमुखी Sun Flower
डेहलिया Dehlia	फूल दुपहरी Peru Flower	हजारा Double Poppy
तुलसी Basel	मोगरा Daisy	हालीहक Hollyhock

अनाज और दालें Grains and Pulse

अरहर Yellow Gram	चावल Rice	मटर Pea
उड़द Black Gram	जौ Barley	मूँग Green Gram
काबुली चना White Gram	धान Paddy	मोठ Red Gram
कुलथी Horse Gram	बाजरा Millet	रागी Finger Millet
गेहूँ Wheat	मक्का Maize	लोबिया Cow Pea
चना Gram		

विविध खाद्य पदार्थ Miscellaneous Eatables

अंडा Egg	टॉफी Toffee	मिठाई Sweetmeat
इमली Tamarind	दलिया Porridge	मुलैठी Liquorice
इलायची Cardamom	दही Curd	मुरब्बा Jam
काली मिर्च Pepper	दूध Milk	राब Molasses
केक Cake	नमक Salt	रोटी Bread
केसर Saffron	नमकीन Salty Dish	लस्सी Butter Milk
खीर Rice Milk	पनीर Cheese	लौंग Clover
गुड़ Jaggery	पान Betel Leaf	सरसों Mustard
घी Ghee, Clarified butter	पेस्ट्री Pastry	सुपारी Betel Nut
चॉकलेट Chocolate	बिस्कुट Biscuit	सोंठ Ginger
शक्कर/चीनी Sugar	मक्खन Butter	हलदी Turmeric
छेना Light Cheese	मलाई Cream	हलवा Sweet Pudding
	मांस Meat	

कपड़े-लत्ते Clothes, etc.

अँगिया, ब्लाउज Blouse	गद्दा, गद्दी Cushion	जूता Shoe
अग्रवस्त्र Apron	गाउन Gown	जैकिट Jacket
ओवरकोट Overcoat	गिलाफ, गॉव तकिया Cover	टाई Neck Tie
कंबल Blanket	गुलूबंद, मफलर Muffler	टोपी, टोप Cap, Hat
कुरता, कमीज Kurta (Shirt)	चद्दर/चादर Sheet	तकिया Pillow
कॉलर Collar	चोगा Cloak	तौलिया Towel
कोट Coat	जाँघिया Underwear	दस्ताने Gloves

धोती Dhoti
निकर Half Pant
नैपकिन Napkin
पगड़ी Turban
पतलून Trousers
परदा Curtain
पलंगपोश Bed Cover
पहरावा Garment
पाजामा Pyjama
पेटी, पट्टा Belt
पेटीकोट Petticoat
पोशाक Dress
फ्रॉक Frock
बनियान Vest
बिरजस Breeches
बिस्तरा Bedding
बुरका Mantle Veil
बुशर्ट Bushshirt
बूट Boot
मसनद Bolster
मेजपोश Table Cloth
मोजा, जुराब Socks
बड़े मोजे Stockings
रजाई Quilt
रूमाल Handkerchief
वर्दी Uniform
वास्कट Waistcoat
शमीज Chemise
शॉल Shawl
सलवार Salwar, Trousers
साड़ी Saree
स्लीपर, चप्पल Slipper
स्वेटर Sweater
होल्डाल Hold-All

घरेलू सामान Household Goods

अगरबत्ती Agarbatti
अलमारी Almirah, Shelf
आईना Mirror
इस्तरी Iron
ओखली Mortar
कंघी Comb
कटोरा Bowl
कटोरी Small Bowl
कढ़ाई Frying Pan
कागज Paper
किताबें Books
कुल्हाड़ी Axe
केतली Kettle
क्रीम Cream
खाट, चारपाई Cot
गिलास Glass
घड़ा Pitcher
घड़ी Watch, Clock
चरखा Spinning Wheel
चाबी Key
चायदानी Tea Pot
चिमटा Tongs
चूड़ी Bangle
चूल्हा Fire-Place, Stove
झाड़ू Broom
टब Tub
टेलीविजन Television
टेलीफोन Telephone
डिबिया Small Box
डोल, बाल्टी Bucket
तराजू Scale, Balance
पतीला, तवा Pan
ताला Lock
तेल Oil
थाली Platter
दिवान Dewan
दिवाना Earthen Lamp
दूधदानी Milk Pot
पत्र Letter
पलंग Bed
पाउडर Powder
पालना Cradle
तश्तरी Saucer
प्याला Cup
प्लेट Plate
बटुआ Purse
बरतन Utensil, Pot
बल्ब Bulb
बेंच Bench
बेलन Rolling Pin, Roller
बोतल Bottle
मूसल Pestle
मेज Table
मूढ़ामूढ़ा Reed Stool
मोमबत्ती Candle
रस्सी Rope
रेडियो Radio
लालटेन Lantern
लैंप Lamp
शीशा Glass Pane
शीशी Phial
साबुन Soap
सोफा Sofa
स्टूल Stool
स्टोव Stove
हँसिया Scythe
हुक्का Hubble Bubble

शरीर के अंग Parts of the Body

अंग Limb
अँगूठा Thumb
आँख Eye
आँत/अँतड़ी Intestine
उंगली Finger
एड़ी Heel
ओंठ Lip
कंधा Shoulder
कनपटी Temple
कमर Waist, Loin
कलाई Wrist
कान Ear
काँख, बगल Armpit
कोहनी Elbow
खोपड़ी Skull
गट्टा Ankle Bone
गरदन Neck
गला Throat
गाल Cheek
गुदा Anus
गुद्दी Nape of Neck
गोद Lap/Bosom
ग्रंथि Gland
घुटना Knee
चमड़ी, खाल Skin
चूचुक Teat/Breast
चूतड़ Buttocks
चेहरा Face
छाती Chest
जबड़ा Jaw
जाँघ Thigh
जिगर Liver
जीभ Tongue
जोड़ Joint
टखना Ankle
टाँग Leg
ठुड्डी Chin
तलवा Sole
तालु Palate
तिल्ली Spleen
दाँत Tooth
दाढ़ Grinder
दिमाग Brain
दिल/हृदय Heart
धड़ Trunk
नथुने Nostrils
नस Vein
नाक Nose
नाखून Nail
नाड़ी Pulse
नाभि Naval
पलक Eyelash
पसली Rib
पाँव, पैर Foot
पिंडली Calf of Leg
पीठ Back
पुतली Pupil
पेट Belly, Stomach
पेशी Muscle
फेफड़ा Lung
बगल Arm-Pit
बाँह Arm
बाल Hair
भौंह Eyebrow
मसूढ़ा Gum
माथा Forehead
मुँह/मुख Mouth, Face
मुट्ठी Fist
रीढ़ Backbone
लहू, खून Blood
श्वासनली Thorax, Wind Pipe
सिर Head
हड्डी Bone
हथेली Palm
हाथ Hand

पदनाम Designations

अधिकारी Officer
अधिवक्ता Advocate
अधीक्षक Superintendent
अध्यक्ष Head
अपर Additional
अभिलेखपाल Record keeper
आचार्य Professor
आयुक्त Commissioner
आशुलिपिक Stenographer
उप Deputy
कार्यकारी, कार्यवाहक, स्थानापन्न Officiating
कुलपति Vice-Chancellor
कुलसचिव Registrar (University)
कुलाधिपति Chancellor
कोषाध्यक्ष Treasurer
जज, न्यायाधीश Judge
जिलाधीश District Magistrate
तहसीलदार Tehsildar

थानेदार Station-in-Charge Police
दरोगा Sub-Inspector (Police)
निरीक्षक Inspector
न्यायमूर्ति Justice
न्यायवादी Attorney
पंजीयक Registrar
परामर्शदाता Consultant
व्याख्याता, प्राध्यापक, प्रवक्ता Lecturer
प्रशासक Administrator
प्राचार्य Principal
प्रेक्षक Observer
मंत्री Minister
मजिस्ट्रेट Magistrate
महानिदेशक Director General
महापौर Mayor
मुख्य Chief
राजदूत Ambassador
राज्यपाल Governor
राष्ट्रपति President
लिपिक Clerk
लेखपाल Village Accountant, Patwari
लेखा परीक्षक Auditor
लेखापाल Accountant
वकील Lawyer
सदस्य Member
सभापति Chairman
समाहर्ता Collector
सलाहकार Adviser
सहायक Assistant

पशु Animals

ऊँट Camel
कंगारू Kangaroo
कस्तूरी मृग Musk Deer
कुत्ता Dog
खच्चर Mule
खरगोश Rabbit
खरहा Hare
गदहा Ass, Donkey
गाय Cow
गिलहरी Squirrel
गेंडा Rhino
गोरिल्ला Gorilla
घड़ियाल Alligator
घोड़ा Horse
चीता Panther
चूहा, मूस Mouse
छछूंदर Mole, Musk Rat
जिराफ Giraffe
जेबरा Zebra
टट्टू Pony
मेमना Leopard
दरियाई घोड़ा Hippopotamus
नीलगाय Antelope
नेवला Mongoose
पिल्ला Puppy
बंदर Monkey
बकरी Goat
बछेड़ा/बछड़ा Colt, Calf
बनमानुस Chimpanzee
बाघ Tiger
बारहसिंहा Stag
बिल्ली Cat
बैल Ox, Bullock
भेड़ Sheep
भेड़िया Wolf
भैंस Buffalo
भैंसा He-Buffalo
मगरमच्छ Crocodile
मृग, हिरन Deer
मेढ़ा, भेड़ा Ram
मेमना Kid, Lamb
याक Yak
लंगूर Baboon
लकड़ बग्घा Hyena
लोमड़ी Fox
शिकारी कुत्ता Hound
साँड Bull
साँडनी Dromedary
साही Porcupine
सिंह Lion
सियार Jackal
सुअर Pig
हाथी Elephant

कीड़े Insects/Reptiles

अजगर Boa
कछुआ Tortoise
किलनी Tick
केकड़ा Crob
केंचुआ Snail
कोया Cocoon
खटमल Bug
गिरगिट Chameleon
गुबरैला Dung Beetle

गोजर Centipede
घुन Grain Moth
घोंघा Lobster
चींटा Blank Ant
चींटी Ant
छिपकली Lizard
जुगनू Glow Worm
जूँ Louse
जोंक Leech
झींगा Prawn
झींगी Shrimp
झींगुर Cricket
टिड्डा Grass hopper
टिड्डी Locust
तितली Butterfly
दीमक White Ant
नाग Cobra
पतंगा Moth
पिस्सू Flea
बर्रे Wasp
बिच्छू Scorpion
मकड़ी Spider
मक्खी Fly
मच्छर Mosquito
मछली Fish
मधुमक्खी Beet
मेंढक Frog
लीख Egg of Louse
साँप Snake
सीप Mother of Pearls

पक्षी Birds

अबाबील Swallow
उल्लू Owl
हुदहुद, कठपोड़ा Wood Pecker
कबूतर Pigeon
काकातुआ Cockatoo
कूंज Heron
कोयल Indian Cuckoo
कोआ Crow
गरुड़ Garud
गिद्ध, गीध Vulture
गौरैया Sparrow
चकवा Ruddy Goose
चकोर Red-Legged Partridge
चमगादड़ Bat
चील Kite
चूजा Chicken
टिटहरी Pewit
तीतर Partridge
तोता Parrot
नीलकंठ Blue-Necked Jay
पपीहा Cuckoo
पिद्दा Brown-Becked Robin
बगुला Stork
बटेर Quail
बत्तख Duck
बहरी, बाज Falcon, Hawk
बुलबुल Nightingale
मुर्गा Cock
मुर्गी Hen
मुनिया Thrash
मैना, सारिका Canary
मोर Peacock
शुतुरमुर्ग Ostrich
सारस Crane
हंस Goose, Swan

खनिज पदार्थ Minerals

अभरक Mica
इस्पात Steel
कोयला Coal
खड़िया Chalk
गंधक Sulphur
गेरू Ochre
चकमक Flint
चाँदी Silver
जस्त Zinc
डामर Asphalt
ताँबा Copper
तारकोल Coal-tar
तूतिया Vitriol
तेल Oil
नग, मणि Gem
नीलम Sapphire
पन्ना Emeraald
पारस Philosopher's Stone
पारा Mercury
पीतल Bronze
पुखराज Topaz
फीरोजा Turquoise
माणिक्य Ruby
राँगा Tin
रूपा Base Silver
लहसुनिया Cat's Eye
लोहा Iron
सँखिया Arsenic
संगमरमर Marble